Routledge Revivals

Edgar C. Polomé and C.P. Hill

Originally published in 1980, Language in Tanzania presents a comprehensive overview of the Survey of Language Use and Language Teaching in Eastern Africa. Using extensive research carried out by an interdisciplinary group of international and local scholars, the survey also covers Ethiopia, Kenya, Uganda and Zambia. The book represents one of the most in-depth sociolinguistic studies carried out on this region at this time. It provides basic linguistic data necessary to policy-makers, administrators, and educators, and will be of interest to those researching the formulation and execution of language policy.

Language in Tanzania
Routledge Revivals

Edgar C. Polomé and C.P. Hill

First published in 1980
by Oxford University Press

This edition first published in 2017 by Routledge
2 Park Square, Milton Park, Abingdon, Oxon, OX14 4RN
and by Routledge
711 Third Avenue, New York, NY 10017

Routledge is an imprint of the Taylor & Francis Group, an informa business

© 1980 International African Institute

The right of International African Institute to be identified as the author of this work has been asserted by them in accordance with sections 77 and 78 of the Copyright, Designs and Patents Act 1988.

All rights reserved. No part of this book may be reprinted or reproduced or utilised in any form or by any electronic, mechanical, or other means, now known or hereafter invented, including photocopying and recording, or in any information storage or retrieval system, without permission in writing from the publishers.

Publisher's Note
The publisher has gone to great lengths to ensure the quality of this reprint but points out that some imperfections in the original copies may be apparent.

Disclaimer
The publisher has made every effort to trace copyright holders and welcomes correspondence from those they have been unable to contact.
A Library of Congress record exists under LC control number: 81147648

ISBN 13: 978-1-138-30751-3 (hbk)
ISBN 13: 978-1-315-14238-8 (ebk)
ISBN 13: 978-1-138-30758-2 (pbk)

Printed in the United Kingdom
by Henry Ling Limited

LANGUAGE IN TANZANIA

Editors

Edgar C. Polomé
C. P. Hill

Foreword by N. A. Kuhanga, Vice-Chancellor,
University of Dar es Salaam

*This study was partly subsidized by funds from
the Ford Foundation who also financed the Survey of
Language Use and Language Teaching in Eastern Africa.*

Published for the
INTERNATIONAL AFRICAN INSTITUTE
by
OXFORD UNIVERSITY PRESS
1980

Oxford University Press, Walton Street, Oxford OX2 6DP
OXFORD LONDON GLASGOW
NEW YORK TORONTO MELBOURNE WELLINGTON
KUALA LUMPUR SINGAPORE JAKARTA HONG KONG TOKYO
DELHI BOMBAY CALCUTTA MADRAS KARACHI
NAIROBI DAR ES SALAAM CAPE TOWN

ISBN 0 19 724205 7

© International African Institute 1980

Text set in 9/10 pt VIP Times

DEDICATION

To the memory of Julia J. Polomé, who gave so much of herself to the survey.

FOR A DISK

CONTENTS

Foreword, by N. A. Kuhanga, Vice-Chancellor,
University of Dar es Salaam ... ix

Acknowledgements ... xi
Introduction ... xii

PART 1: LANGUAGES OF TANZANIA

1 The Languages of Tanzania, by Edgar C. Polomé ... 3
2 The Bantu Languages of East Africa: a Lexicostatistical Survey, by Derek Nurse and Gerard Philippson ... 26
3 The Nilotic Languages of Tanzania, by Christopher Ehret ... 68
4 Swahili in Tanzania, by Edgar C. Polomé ... 79

PART 2: LANGUAGE USE IN TANZANIA

5 Tanzania: A Socio-Linguistic Perspective, by Edgar C. Polomé ... 103
6 The Ecology of Tanzanian National Language Policy, by Mohamed H. Abdulaziz ... 139
7 Language Use among Ilala Residents, by H. D. Barton ... 176
8 Library Users and their Reading Preferences, by C. P. Hill ... 206
9 The Use of Language in the Law Courts in Tanzania, by Douglas Kavugha and Donald Bobb ... 229

PART 3: LANGUAGE IN EDUCATION

10 The Historical Background to National Education in Tanzania, by John White ... 261
11 Language Teaching in Primary Schools, by Fulgens Mbunda and David Brown ... 283
12 Language Teaching in Secondary Schools, by Fulgens Mbunda, C. J. Brumfit, D. Constable and C. P. Hill ... 306
13 Language Teaching in Higher Education, by C. P. Hill, J. S. W. Whitley, D. Constable and G. Mhina ... 341
14 Some Developments in Language and Education in Tanzania since 1969, by C. P. Hill ... 362

References to Part 3: Language in Education ... 410

Index ... 421

MAPS

1 Tanzania   xiv
2 Major Languages of Tanzania   2
3 Bantu Languages of East Africa   30
4 Possible Extent of Nilotes, c. A.D. 1   69
5 Probable Nilotic Societies, c. A.D. 500–1000   70
6 Nilotes in the Sixteenth Century   73
7 Education in Tanzania   260

FOREWORD

The Survey of Language Use and Language Teaching in Eastern Africa took place during the years 1969–1971. Looked at from 1980, it seems like a long time ago. Fortunately the contributors to the present Volume did not tie themselves strictly to the findings of that survey, but have taken advantage of the developments on the language scene in Tanzania since that time. This makes the articles current and full of relevant information.

The division of the articles into three parts makes the volume very appropriate for the different categories of readers who will definitely study its many pages. Thus for those scholars interested in the history and classification of Tanzanian languages, they will find Part One very useful, with its detailed bibliography on what has been written about these languages and about Swahili in particular. For those who are not so technically minded, Part Two is specifically for them since it is written in non-technical language and deals with subjects which are at the heart of the problems which language planners frequently face.

Sometimes it is assumed that Swahili is so widespread in Tanzania, that almost everyone can freely operate in it. The facts presented in Part Two, although supporting this view in general, sound a note of warning to language planners that they should expect some operational problems for some time to come. This is particularly true in connection with both the use of the vernaculars, especially in family circles, and English in certain areas such as the law courts and institutions of higher learning.

Part Three deals with language in education. This question is more important now than it was when the Survey was being carried out, especially in view of the subsequent literacy campaign, the Declaration of the Universal Primary Education, and the Government Plan of introducing Swahili as the medium of instruction in all post primary institutions in the near future and ultimately as a medium of instruction in higher education.

The papers in this Third Part pinpoint certain problems in the development of Swahili as a medium of instruction which are worth noting by planners. Among them are the standard of teaching materials, preparation of teachers, development of adequate terminologies, etc. The consequent effects of change of policy on other languages such as English and French has to be taken into consideration as well.

Language engineering has always been a very laborious business. It can become especially strenuous when it is done in a hurry. In Tanzania to-day out language experts and educationists are engaged in such an exercise, and any help that they can get in any form is always welcome. That is why I want to particularly recommend this Volume of *Language in Tanzania* to all serious scholars and language planners interested in the question of language development as they will find a great deal that is of help and interest in their work. It supplements the various efforts now being undertaken by the different institutions in Tanzania which are currently grappling with the problems of developing Swahili into a "modern" language, able to cope with the intricacies of a "technological" age.

N. A. Kuhanga
Vice-chancellor
University of Dar es Salaam

5th May, 1980.

ACKNOWLEDGEMENTS

Having assumed the responsibility of the over-all editing of this volume, I have the pleasant task of conveying to all those contributing to the various aspects of the Survey of Language Use and Language Teaching in Tanzania, the warmest thanks and sincerest appreciation of the Tanzania team.

We wish to express our deepest gratitude especially to all the Tanzanian officials without whose help and support none of this would ever have been possible. We could never stress enough the importance of the active encouragement we received from the very beginning from the highest authorities in the Ministry of Education, the University of Dar es Salaam, the National Swahili Council, TANU, and so many others, all over the country, everyone, from the Regional Commissioner to the local information or Rural Development or Social Welfare Officer, was most helpful, and in all the schools, principals, teachers, and students always welcomed us and were more than cooperative. It was really a great moment in our lives to work with all of them, and we keep the fondest memories of our stay in Tanzania and hope that the volume that resulted from it will not disappoint our Tanzanian friends: there was so much to be done, and there was so little time, but maybe this will be the incentive for them to continue the work in their country, so rich in prospects for sociolinguistic research and so important as a model for Africa in the implementation of its national language policy.

The Survey Team also wishes to extend special thanks to the Ford Foundation for financing the research and showing a continued strong interest in its completion. They owe a special debt of gratitude to the Field Directors, especially Dr. J. Donald Bowen, who was in charge at the time the team was in Tanzania.

With my co-editor, C. P. Hill, I would like to extend our deepest appreciation to all the scholars, Tanzanians and expatriates, who have contributed to this volume and have enabled us to profit from their expertise. Our thanks also to the International African Institute for their outstanding job in preparing the present volume for publication.

Edgar C. Polomé
University of Texas at Austin

INTRODUCTION

Habent sua fata libelli ... This often quoted aphorism of Terentius Maurus can hardly apply better to any book than the present volume, which had a long and complex history.

The words of the dedication of the Uganda volume to Clifford Prater would also be most fitting: "It is not the book we wanted but it is the best that we could do."

Though the Tanzania team was not the last in the field in the history of the East Africa Language Surveys, its report comes out last for a number of reasons, the main being that the two editors of this volume have both been engaged, as soon as they returned home, in unexpected heavier academic and administrative tasks which prevented them from devoting to the planned chapters all the time and effort required to complete this work without considerable delay. A comparison of the contents of this book with the outline of the data gathering process given by Edgar C. Polomé in his paper: 'Problems and Techniques of Sociolinguistically-Oriented Survey: The Case of the Tanzania Survey,'[1] will show that only part of the material could be extensively reviewed and analyzed in this book. In some cases, important documents apparently went astray and never became available to the survey team for further processing; in other cases, facilities were not available locally to process the data adequately, as with the Secondary School questionaires, which were left behind in the Institute for Swahili Research, while limited coded data taken from them were processed in London and Austin for reference.

Furthermore, economic imperatives made it necessary to cut the original manuscript of this volume approximately by half, but most of the materials scheduled to appear in it will be or have been published elsewhere. They include:

(1). Derek Nurse, 'Description of 14 Bantu Languages of Tanzania.' This formed a complete issue of *African Languages/Langues Africaines* (London: International African Institute, 1979, vol. 5, no. 1).

(2). Anne Brumfit, 'The Development of a Language Policy in Tanzania.' – To appear in *Sprache und Geschichte in Afrika*, vol. 3 (Cologne, 1981).

(3). Edgar C. Polomé, André R. Polomé, and Ali Abdullah, 'Language and Religion in Tanzania.' — To appear in *Orbis,* vol. 30 (Louvain, 1981). Moreover, Bernd Heine's paper 'Knowledge and Use of Second Language in Musoma Region – A Quantitative Survey,' originally planned for the Tanzania volume, appeared in *Kiswahili*, vol. 46: 1 (1976).

Other sections omitted include a study on the Chaga dialects by Derek Nurse and a brief introduction to Luo by Ben Blount. Further longer contributions, e.g. on Asians in Tanzania and on the mass media have been summarized in Edgar C. Polomé's introduction to chapter 5 of this volume. Shortening has also affected the inclusion of some data, e.g. diagrams of language proficiency based on responses to the secondary school questionnaires; lists of the most popular books (illustrating Tanzanian reading habits); etc.

On the other hand, the entire section on *Language in Education* has been carefully updated by C. P. Hill, and an effort has been made to reflect recent developments elsewhere also, whenever possible.

As it stands, this book tries to provide a delicate balance between linguistic and sociolinguistic information, and a broad study of the role of language in the whole educational system of Tanzania, in a form that is accessible to non-specialists, but with fairly reliable data, and a solid theoretical background.

Edgar C. Polomé

NOTE

[1] In: Ohannessian, Sirarpi, Ferguson, Charles A., and Polomé, Edgar C., (eds.), 1975, *Language Surveys in Developing Nations.* Papers and reports on Sociolinguistic Surveys. Arlington, Va.: Center for Applied Linguistics, 31–50, esp. 39–45.

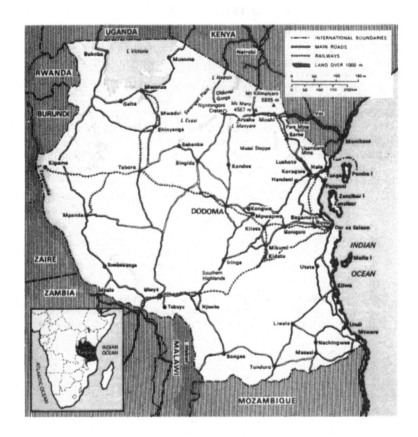

Map 1 Tanzania

PART ONE
LANGUAGES OF TANZANIA

Map 2 Major Languages of Tanzania

1 THE LANGUAGES OF TANZANIA

Edgar C. Polomé

1.0 *Introduction*

For a number of reasons, listing the languages of Tanzania is a rather difficult task.

1.1 *Languages and Dialects*

The criterion that "technically ... mutually intelligible forms of speech are known as **dialects,** and [that] the term **language** is used for mutually unintelligible forms of speech" (Lehmann, 1973: 33), does not apply satisfactorily to such situations as the Chaga continuum from Siha to Usseri. According to native speakers, most of the Vunjo (i.e. central) dialects are mutually intelligible with the Kibosho and Machame dialects of Hai (western Chaga). No typical pattern is found for comparing the Vunjo (central) and Rombo (eastern) dialects, but the Hai (western) and Rombo (eastern) dialects mostly appear not to be mutually intelligible. The statistical data compiled by Nurse (see chap. 2) and their linguistic analysis, as well as the findings of S. Polomé (1971) substantiate the informants' views. Nevertheless, Chaga will have to be considered as one language. Actually, it is culturally and ethnically defined rather than strictly linguistically. In African societies "language and dialect are relative concepts without necessarily clear boundaries, but they are psychologically and socially real concepts, acknowledged by laymen in various ways" (Anttila, 1972: 289). Within the Bantu-speaking area, groups of more closely related tongues can be identified, which all seem to belong to a complex dialect continuum, as in the Musoma area (Heine, 1976). Sometimes clearly distinct groups are linguistically close enough to make intercommunication possible. For example, in the border area between Burundi and Tanzania, the local variants of Ha and Rundi appear to be mutually intelligible.

1.2 *Information available*

Language lists with numbers of speakers based on census figures go back to the 1957 census, since the 1967 census did not collect direct information on languages. The table for continental Tanzania, as given by Angela Molnos (1969: 48) contained the 102 Bantu languages given in Table 1:1, ordered by number of speakers. As regards the non-Bantu languages, the 1957 census lists (Molnos, 1969: 49) those languages given in Table 1:2.

The comparison of the tribal map of P. H. Gulliver (Berry, 1971: 113) with the language distribution gives a more accurate picture. All the peoples can indeed be identified with recognized linguistic units. For continental Tanzania, the list enumerates 108 groups (without counting

LANGUAGES OF TANZANIA

Table 1:1 Bantu Languages[1]

Sukuma	1,093,767	Safwa	63,027	Iambi	20,075
Nyamwezi	363,258	Shubi	61,384	Mavia	19,906
Makonde	333,897	Hangaza	59,916	Kutu	18,085
Haya	325,539	Ndali	59,650	Lambya	15,803
Chaga	318,167	Matengo	59,647	Wungu	14,926
Gogo	299,417	Zinza	55,187	Machinga	14,224
Ha	289,792	Nyika	54,384	Rungu	13,751
Hehe	251,624	Ngulu	52,877	Ndonde	13,165
Nyakyusa	219,678	Rongo	52,721	Ngurimi	12,988
Lugulu	202,297	Matumbi	44,717	Isanzu	12,964
Bena	195,802	Ndengeleko	43,443	Vidunda	12,771
Nyaturu	195,709	Kerewe	41,601	Mbunga	11,682
Shambala	193,802	Kwaya	40,824	Swahili	11,590
Zalamo	183,260	Kwere	39,199	Segeju	11,575
Nilyamba	156,498	Meru	35,814	Pimbwe	11,479
Yao	144,198	Ruanda	35,175	Bemba	11,438
Mwera	138,210	Digo	35,134	Ikizu	11,229
Zigua	134,406	Nyika	34,760	Congo	11,153
Pare	126,048	Nyamwanga	34,706	Kamba	10,865
Makua	123,316	Regi	34,417	Doe	9,734
Nyika	122,233	Bondei	32,118	Wanda	9,477
Langi	110,292	Ndendeule	31,713	Ganda	9,459
Ngindo	88,397	Saghala	31,609	Tongwe	8,746
Kagulu	86,936	Kimbu	31,149	Bende	7,792
Jita	86,712	Sango	29,889	Shirazi	7,176
Fipa	86,462	Tusi	28,138	Rungwa	7,158
Kuria	85,090	Manyema	26,878	Shashi	7,100
Rufiji	79,498	Shashi	25,691	Mbugwe	6,463
Sumbwa	76,435	Mambwe	25,115	Ikoma	6,131
Pogolu	74,047	Zanaki	24,864	Matumbi	6,092
Pangwa	70,721	Wanji	24,283	Kisi	5,291
Ngoni	68,223	Ndamba	21,951	Jiji	4,653
Nyasa	65,514	Malila	20,745	Sonjo	4,593
Kinga	65,467	Konongo	20,479	Vinza	4,135

Total Bantu 8,130,586

Table 1:2 Non-Bantu Languages

Iraqw	135,142	Sandawe	28,309	Taturu	11,372
Luo	82,876	Wasi	13,996	Kwavi	7,378
Arusha	68,370	Mbugu	12,604	Dorobo	1,868
Maasai	62,180	Burungi	12,408	Total	
Barabaig	30,599	Gorowa	11,973	Non-Bantu	479,075

the coastal Swahilis): 96 are Bantu, 5 Nilotic, 5 Cushitic,[2] and 2 Khoisan. Some of the southern Tanzania Bantu languages appearing in this list are not mentioned in Bryan's nomenclature of Bantu languages (1959), nor in Whiteley's linguistic bibliography (1958), namely Machinga, along the coast, above the 10th parallel south, close to the Mwera and the Ngindo areas; Matumbi, on the banks of the Ruvuma on the Mozambique border, next to the Makonde[3] and Makua; Ndendeuli, inland, east of the main Ngoni territory south of the 10th parallel.[4]

Discrepancies of this type are numerous and essentially due to our lack of information. Whiteley's revised bibliography of 1958 lists 107 languages, but for 34 of them, all that is given is their name and zone and number in Guthrie's classification; Margaret Bryan's listings often rely on secondary material or personal communications and, consequently, may contain rather subjective assessments of the linguistic situation, like Whiteley's doubts about the existence of Isenyi and Ikizu (Bryan, 1959: 114): Bernd Heine interviewed mother tongue speakers of Issenyi, a subdialect of the Ikoma group of Zanaki, for his research, and I taped a set of sentences from an informant who described himself as a mother tongue speaker of Ikizu. A number of well-documented languages and dialects are thus left out, for example, in Bryan's Gusii group (1959: 113): Kabwa, close to Kiroba, but nevertheless a separate entity; Ruri, not a dialect of Jita (as Whiteley [1958] thought), but a subgroup of Kwaya; Sizaki, also called Shashi, an important dialect of the Zanaki group; Suba, a major subgroup of the Kuria group.[5]

2.0 *Sources*

In recent years our knowledge of Tanzanian languages has improved somewhat through the publication of linguistic studies. The government of Tanzania has, naturally, with limited resources to hand, been anxious to pursue its policy of focussing effort on promoting Swahili.[6] Tanzanian officials do not, therefore, actively encourage research on the vernaculars in Tanzania. Nevertheless, Bantu and non-Bantu studies will doubtless continue to develop within the framework of the Department of Linguistics at Dar es Salaam. And it is to be hoped that the Library of the University will continue to collect and preserve innumerable documents that are still available in various parts of the country relating to the Bantu languages of Tanzania.[7] The linguistic material presently extant is of three types:
  (a) printed works, either books or articles by linguists or grammars and dictionaries compiled locally by missionaries, beside Bible translations,[8] liturgical texts and teaching materials;
  (b) language study and religious materials duplicated for local use;
  (c) manuscript notes.

2.1 *German Period*

In many cases, some of the most reliable information we have is still what was published by German linguists and missionaries, in particular Carl Meinhof's 'Linguistische Studien in Ostafrika' in the *Mitteilungen des Seminars für orientalische Sprachen* between 1904 and 1908, and O. Dempwolff's 'Beiträge zur Kenntnis der Sprachen in Deutsch-Ostafrika' in the *Zeitschrift für Kolonialsprachen*, vols. 2, 5 and 6 (1911–1916). For languages like Kami, Matengo, Matumbi, Pangwa, Zinza and others, all we have are the pre-World War I publications of A. Seidel, C. Velten, J. Haflinger, B. Krumm, M. Klamroth, H. Rehse in the *Mitteilungen des Seminars für orientalische Sprachen* (Berlin), the *Zeitschrift für afrikanische und ozeanische Sprachen* (Berlin), and the *Zeitschrift für Kolonialsprachen* (Hamburg/Berlin). Some of the best German material has recently been reprinted, e.g.

J. Raum, *Versuch einer Grammatik der Dschaggasprache (Moschi-Dialekt)* [Berlin, 1909 – republished by Gregg Press, Ridgewood, N. J., 1964];

Julius Augustiny, *Kurzer Abriss des Madschame Dialekts* [Berlin, 1914 – republished by Gregg Press, Ridgewood, N. J., 1964];

Ernst Kotz, *Grammatik des Chasu in Deutsch-Ostafrika (Pare-Gebirge)* [Berlin, 1919 – republished by Gregg Press, Ridgewood, N. J., 1964].

2.2 *British Period*

In the British period, very little linguistic work was done: a few papers were published in the South African journal *Bantu Studies*, in which A. Sillery provided the only available outline of *Kwaya* (1932), besides notes on *Kuria* grammar (1936). Alice Werner had supplied 'Specimens of East African Bantu Dialects' to the same journal in 1927, some of which constituted the only linguistic material in print on such languages as Ikoma, Jita, and Zanaki. More substantial work was done in the south by Lyndon Harries, whose 'Outline of Mawiha Grammar,' published in 1940 in *Bantu Studies*, appears to be structured according to Doke's model. An excellent critical survey of these early publications was given by Clement M. Doke (1945: 42–73). The following bibliography attempts to list the major works and papers published[9] since 1945 (arranged by languages and language families).

2.3   Publications Since 1945
(1) Southern Cushitic:
   Iraqw
      Whiteley, W. H., *Studies in Iraqw. An Introduction.* (East African Linguistic Studies. 1) Kampala: East African Institute of Social Research, 1953.
      Whiteley, W. H., *A Short Description of Item Categories in Iraqw.* Kampala: East African Institute of Social Research, 1958.
      Whiteley, W. H., 'The Verbal Radical in Iraqw.' *African Languages Studies* 1 (1960), 79–95.
      Yoneyama, Toshinao, 'Some Basic Notions Among the Iraqw of Northern Tanzania.' *Kyoto University African Studies* 5 (1971), 81–100.
   Mbugu
      Whiteley, W. H., 'Linguistic Hybrids.' *African Studies* 19 (1960), 95–97.
      Green, E. C., 'The WaMbugu of Usambara.' *Tanganyika Notes and Records* 61 (Sept. 1963), 175–189 (Notes on language, 178–185; comparative word lists, 186–8).
      Goodman, Morris, 'The Strange Case of Mbugu' in Dell Hymes, ed., *Pidginization and Creolization of Languages*, 243–254. London: Cambridge University Press, 1971.

(2) Eastern Nilotic:
Maasai
- Tucker, A. N., and J. Tompo Ole Mpaayei, *A Maasai Grammar*. London: Longmans, Green and Co., 1955.
- Hohenberger, Johannes, 'Comparative Masai Word-List.' (Nilotic, Nilo-Hamitic, Masai, Hamitic-Semitic) *Africa* 26 (1956), 281-87.
- Hohenberger, Johannes, *Semitisches und hamitisches Sprachgut im Masai*. Mit vergleichendem Wörterbuch. Eine sprachvergleichende Untersuchung unter Berücksichtigung von rund 50 semitischen, hamitischen, nilo-hamitischen und anderen afrikanischen Sprachen. Sachsenmühle, Switzerland (Im Selbstverlag des Verfassers), 1958.

Ongamo
- Heine, Bernd, and Vossen, Rainer, 'Zur Stellung der Ongamo-Sprache (Kilimandscharo).' *Afrika und Übersee* 59 (1975/6), 81-105.

(3) Western Nilotic:
Luo[10]
- Gregersen, Edgar Alstrup, *Luo: a Grammar*. Ph.D. Dissertation, Yale University, 1962. *Dissertation Abstracts* 31/11, May 1971, 6033-A.
- Stafford, R. L. *An Elementary Luo Grammar, with Vocabularies*. Nairobi/London: Oxford University Press, 1967.
- Blount, Ben, and Curley, Richard T., 'The Southern Luo Languages: a Glottochronological Reconstruction.' *Journal of African Linguistics* 9 (1970), 1-18.
- Blount, Ben G., 'An outline of Luo Grammar.' (= Appendix A to *Acquisition of Language by Luo Children*. Working Paper No. 19. Language-Behavior Research Laboratory, University of California, Berkeley, 181-208). Berkeley, 1969.
- Blount, Ben G., and Padgug-Blount, Elise, (with the assistance of J. H. Obare, E. O. Oluoch, P. O. Olil, Z. A. Lago) *Luo-English Dictionary, with Notes on Luo Grammar*. Nairobi: Institute of African Studies, n. d.

(4) Khoisan:
Sandawe
- Van de Kimmenade, M., *Essai de grammaire et vocabulaire de la langue Sandawe*. Posieux (Switzerland), 1954.
- Ten Raa, Eric, 'Sanye and Sandawe: A Common Substratum?' *African Language Review* 8 (1969), 148-155. [focuses on clickforms in Sanye lexicon]
- Ten Raa, Eric, 'The Couth and the Uncouth: Ethnic, Social and Linguistic Divisions Among the Sandawe of Central Tanzania.' *Anthropos* 65 (1970), 127-153.

(5) Bantu:
Bena
- Swartz, Marc J., 'The Bilingual Kin Terminology of the Bena.' *Journal of African Languages* 7 (1968), 41-57.

Chaga
- Müller, Emil, *Wörterbuch der Djaga-Sprache (Madjame-Mundart)*. Hamburg: Eckardt und Messtorff, 1947.
- Sharp, A. D., 'A Tonal Analysis of the Disyllabic Noun in the Machame Dialect of Chaga.' *Bulletin of the School of Oriental and African Studies* 16 (1954), 157-169. Reprinted in W. E. Jones and J. Laver, eds., *Phonetics in Linguistics: A Book of Readings* (Longmans Linguistic Library, Vol. 12), London: Longman, 1973, 305-319.
- Nurse, D., and Philippson, G., 'Tones in Old Moshi (Chaga).' *Studies in African Linguistics* 8 (1977) 49-80.

Chasu (Pare)
   Kähler-Meyer, Emmi, 'Studien zur tonalen Struktur der Bantusprachen, II. Chasu im und am Fusse des Pare-Gebirges, Tanganyika.' *Afrika und Übersee* 46 (1962), 250–295.
   Kähler-Meyer, Emmi, 'Töne und Akzente in der Formenlehre der Chasu (Tanganyika).' *Afrika und Übersee* 47 (1963), 89–133.
Fipa
   Eléments de Dictionnaire Français-KiFipa. N. p., n. d. (duplicated, 233 pp.).
Gogo
   Cordell, O. T., *CiGogo Grammar*. (a revised edition of the 1941 printed text) N. p., n. d. (duplicated).
Haya
   Rascher, Anna, *Leitfaden zum Erlernen des Ruhaya*. Bethel bei Bielefeld: Bethel-Mission, 1955 (duplicated, 143 pp.).
   Rascher, Anna, *Guide for Learning the Ruhaya Language*. English translation by Prof. Vilh. Pedersen. Bethel (near Bielefeld): Bethel Mission, 1958.
   Betbeder, Paul, and Jones, John, *A Handbook of the Haya Language*. Bukoba: White Fathers Printing Press, 1949.
   Bona-Baisi, Father Ignace J., *Ikani-Ngambo. Oruhaya*. (Haya Dictionary) Rwamishenye-Bukoba, 1960 (Printed by the Pallottine Fathers in Limburg/Lahn, Germany).
   Byarushengo, Ernest Rugwa, 'Strategies in Loan Phonology.' *Proceedings of the Second Annual Meeting of the Berkeley Linguistic Society*, 78–89. Berkeley: Berkeley Linguistics Society, 1976.
   Byarushengo, Ernest Rugwa, Hyman, Larry M., and Tenenbaum, Sarah, 'Tone, Accent, and Assertion in Haya' in: Hyman, Larry M., ed., *Studies in Bantu Tonology* (Southern California Occasional Papers in Linguistics, No. 3), 183–205. Los Angeles: Department of Linguistics, University of Southern California, 1976.
   Byarushengo, Ernest Rugwa, Duranti, Alessandro, and Hyman, Larry M., eds. *Haya Grammatical Structure* (Southern California Occasional Papers in Linguistics, Vol. 6). Los Angeles: Department of Linguistics, University of Southern California, 1977.
Holoholo
   Coupez, André, *Esquisse de la Langue Holoholo*. (Annales du Musée Royal du Congo Belge. Série in-8°. Sciences de l'Homme. Linguistique, vol. 12). Tervuren: Commission de Linguistique Africaine, 1955.
Kinga
   Kähler-Meyer, Emmi, 'Gibt es sprachhistorische Beziehungen der Töne im Kinga (Tanzania)?' *Ethnological and Linguistic Studies in Honor of N. J. van Warmelo*, 1–12. Republic of South Africa, Department of Bantu Administration and Development, Ethnological Publications, vol. 52. Pretoria: Government Printer, 1969.
   Schadeberg, Thilo C., *Zur Lautstruktur des Kinga (Tanzania)*. Inaugural-Dissertation. Marburg/Lahn: E. Symon, 1971.
   Schadeberg, Thilo C., 'Kinga: A Restricted Tone System.' *Studies in African Linguistics* 4 (1973), 23–47.
Makonde
   Guerreiro, M. Viegas, *Rudimentos de lingua Maconde*. Lourenço Marques: Instituto de Investigação Científica de Moçambique, 1963.
   Guerreiro, M. Viegas, *Os Macondes de Moçambique. IV. Sabedoria, língua, literature e jogos*. (II. A língua, 33–37). Lisboa: Junta de Investigações do Ultramar, Centro de estudos de anthropologia cultural, 1966.

Makua

Peixe, Júlio dos Santos, 'Sobre a língua É-Makua.' *Boletim do Museu de Nampula (Moçambique)* 1 (1960), 15–29.

Peixe, Júlio dos Santos, 'A língua É-Makwa e suas afinidades com o I-Maíndo e Xi-Sena.' *Boletim do Museu de Nampula* 2 (1961), 67–82.

Mambwe

Rupya, J. Fr., *KiMambwe Grammar. An Outline.* Pito, 1958 (duplicated, 134 pp.; also contains exercises, 24 pp., and a short dictionary, 24 pp.)

The London Missionary Society, Kawimbe. *CiMambwe Grammar.* Lusaka: Northern Rhodesia and Nyasaland Publications Bureau, 1962.

Matengo

Ebner, Elzear P., *Grammatik der kiMatengo-Sprache.* Liparamba, 1957 (duplicated, 125 pp.).

Mwera

Harris, Lyndon., *A Grammar of Mwera.* Johannesburg: Witwatersrand University Press, 1960.

Ngoni

Ebner, Elzear P., *Grammatik des Neu-Kingoni.* Mission Magagura, Tanzania, 1951 (duplicated, 87 pp.).

Ebner, Elzear P., *Wörterbuch der Sprache des Neu-Kingoni.* 1. Neu-Kingoni-Deutsch (1–153); 2. Deutsch-Neu-Kingoni (155–309). Peramiho, 1953 (duplicated).

Nyakyusa

Marangoka, Ngapona, and Voorhoeve, Jan, *Cursus kiNyakyusa.* Leiden: Rijksuniversiteit, Afrika Studiecentrum, n. d. (duplicated). (4 parts: 1. Basic course [53 pp.], 2. Text [13 pp], 3. *Outline of Nyakyusa Grammar* [in English, 21 pp.], 4. Nyakyusa Wordlist [translated into English; 22 pp.].)

von Essen, O., and Kähler-Meyer, E., 'Prosodische Wortmerkmale im Nyakyusa' in: Greschat, Hans-Jürgen, and Jungraithmayr, Hermann, eds., *Wort und Religion. Kalima na Dini. Studien zur Afrikanistik, Missionswissenschaft, Religionswissenschaft. Ernst Dammann zum 65. Geburtstag,* 34–56. Stuttgart: Evangelischer Missionsverlag, 1969.

Nyanja

Price, Thomas, *The Elements of Nyanja.* Blantyre, Nyasaland: Church of Scotland Mission, 1953.

Sanderson, Meredith, and Bithrey, W. B., *An Introduction to Chinyanja.* Edinburgh: The African Lakes Corporation Ltd. of Glasgow and Blantyre, Nyasaland, 1953.

Thomson, T. D., *A Practical Approach to Chinyanja.* Zomba, Nyasaland: Government Printer, 1955.

Missionários da Companhia de Jesus, *Dicionário Cinyanja-Português.* Lisboa: Junta de Investigações do Ultramar, 1963.

Missionários da Companhia de Jesus, *Dicionário Português-Cinyanja.* Lisboa: Junta de Investigações do Ultramar, 1964.

Missionários da Companhia de Jesus, *Elementos de gramática cinyanja.* Lisboa: Junta de Investigações do Ultramar, 1964.

Stevick, Earl W., and Hollander, Linda, *Chinyanja Basic Course.* Based on Chinyanja texts, exercises and tapes provided by D. Bandawe, A. Boutcha, et. al. Washington, D.C.: Foreign Service Institute (U.S. Government Printing Office), 1965.

Harding, Deborah Ann, *The Phonology and Morphology of Chinyanja.* (University of California dissertation, 1966). *Dissertation Abstracts* 27/6, December 1966, 1803-A.

Nyamwezi
  Turgeon, L., *Dictionnaire français-kinyamwézi*. N. p., n. d. (stenciled, 491 pp.).
Nyaŋwezi (= Nyamwezi)
  Cottino, P. Giovanni, *Grammaire kiNyanwezi*. Langue bantu parlée dans l'Afrique Orientale-Territoire du Tanganyika. Tabora, 1914/Rome, 1957. (duplicated)
Nyiha
  Busse, Joseph, *Die Sprache der Nyiha in Ostafrika*. (Deutsche Akademie der Wissenschaften zu Berlin, Institut für Orientforschung, Veröffentlichung No. 41) Berlin: Akademie-Verlag, 1960.
Rimi (= Nyaturu)
  Olson, Howard S., *The Phonology and Morphology of Rimi*. (Hartford Studies in Linguistics) Hartford, Conn.: Hartford Seminary Foundation Bookstore, 1954.
Rundi
  Bonneau, Henri, *Dictionnaire Français-Kirundi/Kirundi-Français*. Usumbura: Presses Lavigerie, 1950.
  Rodegem, F. M., *Initiation au KiRundi: le KiRundi de base*. (Textbook, with detailed grammatical notes and tone rules [accompanying tapes were available]). Usumbura: Presses Lavigerie, 1958.
  Meeussen, A. E., *Essai de grammaire Rundi*. (Annales du Musée Royal du Congo Belge. Série in-8°. Sciences de l'Homme. Linguistique, vol. 24). Tervuren: Commission de Linguistique Africaine, 1959.
  Stevick, Earl W., *Kirundi Basic Course*. Based on KiRundi texts and exercises provided by Raymond Setukuru, Terrence Nsanze, Daniel Nicimpaye. Washington, D. C.: Foreign Service Institute (U.S. Government Printing Office), 1965.
  Rodegem, F. M., *Dictionnaire rundi-français*. Annales du Musée de l'Afrique Centrale. Série in-8°. Sciences Humaines, vol. 69. Tervuren (Belgium), 1970.
  Rodegem, F. M., 'Syntagmes complétifs spéciaux en rundi.' *Africana Linguistica* 4 (1970), 181–207 (= Annales du Musée de l'Afrique Centrale. Sciences Humaines, vol. 68).
  Mioni, Alberto M., 'Analisi binaria del sistema fonematico di una lingua bantu: il rundi.' *Lingua e Stile*. Quaderni dell' Isstituto di Glottologia dell' Università degli Studi di Bologna. 6 (1971), 67–96.
  Bastin, René, 'Observations sur le rôle phonologique de la hauteur du rundi.' *Revue de Phonétique appliquée* 20 (1971), 3–32.
  Bouquiaux, Luc, 'Quelques réflexions sur le système phonologique du rundi.' *Problèmes de phonologie*, 113–119. (Société d' Etudes Linguistiques et Anthropologiques de France, Vol. 38). Paris: SELAF, 1973.
Rwanda
  Hurel, Eugène, *Grammaire kinyarwanda*. Rwanda: Imprimerie de Kabgayi, 1951.
  Schumacher, Pierre, *Dictionnaire phonétique français-runyarwanda, runyarwanda-français*. Kabgayi: Vicariat apostolique, 1954.
  Coupez, A., Kamanzi, Th., and Rodegem, P. B., *Grammaire rwanda simplifiée. Méthode rwanda à l'usage des Européens*. Vol. 2. Usumbura, Burundi: Edition du Service de l'Information, 1961.
  Givón, Talmy, and Kimenyi, Alexandre, 'Truth, Belief, and Doubt in kinyaRwanda.' *Studies in African Linguistics*, Supplement 5 (October 1974), 95–113.

THE LANGUAGES OF TANZANIA

Overdulve, C. M., Gooday, M., Peck, D., Coupez, A., and Kamanzi, Th., *Apprendre la langue Rwanda*. (*Janua Linguarum*. Series didactica. Vol. 12). The Hague: Mouton, 1975.

Wilkins, Wendy, and Kimenyi, Alexandre, 'Strategies in Constructing a Definite Description: Some Evidence from kinyaRwanda.' *Studies in African Linguistics* 6 (1975), 151-169.

Kimenyi, Alexandre, 'Subjectivization Rules in kinyaRwanda.' *Proceedings of the Second Annual Meeting of the Berkeley Linguistics Society*, 258-268. Berkeley: Berkeley Linguistics Society, 1976.

Kimenyi, Alexandre, 'Tone Anticipation in kinyaRwanda' in: Hyman, Larry M., ed., *Studies in Bantu Tonology* (Southern California Occasional Papers in Linguistics, Vol. 3), 167-181. Los Angeles: Department of Linguistics, University of Southern California, 1976.

Safwa

Voorhoeve, Jan, *A Grammar of Safwa*. Preliminary draft based on previous research by J. van Sambeek, checked by C. K. Mwachusa. Leiden: Afrika Instituut, Universiteit, n. d. (duplicated).

Voorhoeve, Jan, 'Safwa as a Restricted Tone System.' *Studies in African Linguistics* 4 (1973), 1-21.

Shambala

Meeussen, A. E., 'Tonunterschiede als Reflexe von Quantitätsunterschieden im Shambala' in: J. Lukas, ed., *Afrikanistische Studien*, Deutsche Akademie der Wissenschaften zu Berlin, Institut für Orientforschung, 154-156. Berlin: Akademie-Verlag, 1955.

Kähler-Meyer, Emmi, 'Studien zur tonalen Struktur der Bantusprachen. I. Shambala.' *Afrika und Übersee* 46 (1962), 1-42.

Sukuma

Richardson, Irvine, *The Role of Tone in the Structure of Sykyma*. London: School of Oriental and African Studies, 1959.

Richardson, Irvine, and Mann, W. M., 'A Vocabulary of Sykyma.' *African Language Studies* 7 (1966), 1-79.

Richardson, Irvine, ' "Displaced Tones" in Sukuma' in: Kim, Chin-Wu, and Stahlke, Herbert, eds., *Papers in African Linguistics*, 219-227. Edmonton/Champaign: Linguistic Research, Inc., 1971.

Batibo, Hermann, 'A New Approach to Sukuma Tone' in: Hyman, Larry M., ed., *Studies in Bantu Tonology* (Southern California Occasional Papers in Linguistics, vol. 3), 241-257. Los Angeles: Department of Linguistics, University of Southern California, 1976.

The Maryknoll Fathers. *KiSukuma Language Course*, 2 volumes. (1. Lessons 1-15; 2. Lessons 16-33). Musoma: The Maryknoll Language School, n.d. [1969]. (duplicated).

Koenen, Rev. M., *New KiSukuma Grammar*. Mwanza, n. d. (duplicated).

[Rev. M. Loenen] *KiSukuma-English Dictionary*. Mwanza, n. d. (duplicated).

English-kiSukuma Dictionary. (approximately 6,000 words) Mwanza, Tanganyika: Africa Inland Mission, Literature Department, n. d. (duplicated).

A kiSukuma-English Dictionary. Mwanza, n. d. (typescript, duplicated, 185 pp.).

Dictionnaire Sukuma-Français/Français-Sukuma. N. p., n. d. (251 + 271 typewritten pages; duplicated).

Tumbuka

Vail, Hazen L., *Aspects of the Tumbuka Verb*. Ph.D. Dissertation, University of Wisconsin at Milwaukee. In: *Dissertation Abstracts*, 33 (1972), 6896-A.

Yao
    Sanderson, George Meredith, *A Dictionary of the Yao Language*. Zomba (Nyasaland): The Government Printer, 1954.
    Whiteley, W. H., 'Shape and Meaning in Yao Nominal Classes.' *African Language Studies* 2 (1961), 1-24.
    Whiteley, W. H., *A Study of Yao Sentences*. Oxford: Clarendon Press, 1966.
    Meeussen, A. E., 'Notes on Conjugation and Tone in Yao.' *Africana Linguistica* 5 (1971), 197-203 (= Annales du Musée de l'Afrique Centrale, Sciences de l'Homme, vol. 72).

Zalamo
    Dammann, Ernst, 'Der sogenannten Artikel im Zaramo.' *Ethnological and Linguistic Studies in Honour of N. J. van Warmelo*, 47-53. Republic of South Africa, Department of Bantu Administration and Development, Ethnological Publications, vol. 52. Pretoria: Government Printer, 1969.

In addition, the major linguistic features of most non-Bantu Tanzanian languages were reviewed and described by A. N. Tucker and M. A. Bryan in their 1966 volume of *Linguistic Analyses*: Southern Luo, in chapter 30 ('Nilotic Languages', 402-42); Maasai, in chapter 31 ('Paranilotic Languages', 443-94), and the Iraqw group, in chapter 34 (570-91), whereas they provided more limited information on the Bantu languages of northern Tanzania in the fourth volume of the *Survey of the Northern Bantu Borderland* (1957), covering Kuria and Nata (29-32); Sukuma (33-4); Nilyamba, Rimi, and Langi (35-9); Gogo and Kagulu (40-3); Zigulu and Ngulu (44-7); Shambala and Bondei (48-51); Chaga (only the Machame and Moshi dialects, 52-4); but also included Mbugu (72-4), as well as comparative wordlists of Luo and other Nilotic languages (78), Maasai and Barabaig and other 'Nilo-Hamitic' languages (78-83); a short Iraqw vocabulary, in which a number of items seem to correspond to Mbugu (86-7); a set of 35 Sandawe nouns with 9 parallel entries in Hadza (88). These data complement the linguistic data of E. O. J. Westphal in his appendix to Tucker and Bryan's *Non-Bantu Languages of North-Eastern Africa* (1956: 166-73).[11] Recent work in Bantu, including articles on specific rules like Meeussen's paper on 'Meinhof's Rule' (1962) or Bennett's study of Dahl's Law in correlation with the *Thagicū* group (1967), as well as her own comparative examination of tone languages in Tanganyika (1963), is surveyed by Emmi Kähler-Meyer in her contribution to the Subsaharan Africa volume of *Current Trends in Linguistics* (1971). In the same volume, Morris Goodman reviews the problem of Mbugu (1971: 673-5).

2.4 *Manuscript Material*

Among the manuscript material which we found in Tanzania, the following items are relevant to language study and language description.[12] Most of the works are not identified as regards date and place of composition, and they are often anonymous. When information was indirectly available about the author, his name is mentioned in paren-

THE LANGUAGES OF TANZANIA 13

theses. Older materials, not mentioned by Whiteley in his *Bibliography* (1958), are also included:

(a) Nilotic:
  Luo
   Luo Basic Course. Grammar and Exercises.
    [Sister Anita] Musoma: Maryknoll Language School (276 pp.).
  Maasai
   Masai Grammar and Vocabulary.
    Based on *12 Lessons in Masai*, by Ruth Shaffer. N. p., n. d. (13 typewritten pages) [appended to Ruth Shaffer's book (22 pp., duplicated; Nairobi: Eagle Press, 1955)]

(b) Bantu:
  Gogo
   Fragment of a Dictionary of Chigogo. (starting with *Mu-* and following the alphabetic order of root-initials to *Z-*). Dodoma: Diocese of Central Tanganyika, n. d. (290 pp., typescript).
   An Outline Dictionary of ChiGogo.
    [W. W. Preston] Dodoma: Diocese of Central Tanganyika, 1946. (432 pp. of handwritten notes following the model of A. C. Madan, *An Outline Dictionary ... of the Languages of the Bantu*, London: Henry Frowde, 1905, and including a considerable number of inserted pages with additional material, all bound together).
   A Dictionary of Chigogo.
    Dodoma: Diocese of Central Tanganyika, n. d. (145 handwritten pages).
  Ha
   Petite grammaire Kiha.
    N. p., n. d. I (1–123); II (1–235); (Handwritten manuscript in two parts).
   Dictionnaire français-kiHa.
    Ujiji, 1939. (221 pages typewritten manuscript, including a map and grammatical introduction; a 4-page appendix on kinship terms is added).
   Grammaire Abrégée KiHa.
    van Sambeek, J. Ujiji (Tanganyika Territory), 1941. (479 handwritten pages, including index).
   Dictionnaire Kiha-français.
    van Sambeek, J. Ujiji, 1945. (741 handwritten pages).
  Haya
   Dictionnaire Haya-Français.
    Kuipers and Samson. (manuscript copied and revised in 1940 by Father Leo Thijssen and authentified in 1970 by Father Paul Betbeder). N. p., n. d. (522 typewritten pages, with handwritten additions).
  Hehe
   Abriss der kiHehe Grammatik.
    N. p., n. d. (no title page; 55 pages in German 'Fraktur' handwriting).
   Deutsch-kiHehe Wörterbuch.
    N. p., n. d. (no title page; 259 pp. handwritten manuscript).
   KiHehe-Deutsches Wörterbuch.
    N. p., n. d. (no title page, 146 pp. handwritten manuscript).
  Jita
   Some Notes on Kijita.
    Beverly. Mwanza, A. I. M., n. d. (32 pages, mostly typewritten, but also handwritten notes on the verbal system, the noun classes, with basic vocabulary lists).

LANGUAGES OF TANZANIA

Kwaya
KiKwaya Vocabulary.
[Sister Anita] N. p. (Musoma, Maryknoll Language School); n. d.; (no title page; 31 typewritten pages).
Notes on KiKwaya Grammar.
[Sister Anita] N. p. (Musoma, Maryknoll Language School), n. d. (19 pp. typescript).

Lugulu
KiLuguru Grammar.
[Father Vermunt] N. p., n. d. (typescript, 35 + 29 pp.) [Some of the grammatical notes are in Dutch].
KiLuguru Vocabulary.
[Father Vermunt] N. p., n. d. (typescript, 25 pp.). [Some translations are in Dutch; there are parallel lists of Lugulu and Kagulu; Lugulu and Gogo; Lugulu and Nyamwezi words].

Meru
Kiro-Meru Vocabulary and Grammatical Constructions.
Seitar, Joseph (Rev.). N. P., n. d. (79 typewritten pages).

Mwera
Chibeleketo cha Bandu Bamwera. Die Sprache der Mwera. I. Teil.
Amman, Joachim. Ndanda, n. d. (66 pages, typescript, duplicated; covers the essentials of the grammar of the language).

Ngurimi
Notes on kiNgereme. Grammar and Sentences. Exercises. Vocabulary.
[Sister Anita] Musoma: Maryknoll Language School, n. d. (21 + 35 + 20 pages, typewritten manuscript).

Simbiti
KiSimbita Grammar.
[Sister Anita] Musoma: Maryknoll Language School, n. d. (66 typewritten pages).

Sukuma
KiSukuma Grammar (with a suggested seven-vowel orthography for kiSukuma)
[Miss Downey] N. p., n. d. (43 pages, typescript).
Fragment of kiSukuma-English Dictionary (A- to ga-)
[Hess, Charles] Mwanza, A. I. M., n. d. (37 pages, typescript).
Fragments of Kisukuma-English Dictionary. [pp. 11–82 (*bu-* to *n-*) and 127–132 (*ng-*)]
[Hess, Charles] Mwanza, A. I. M., n. d. (79 pages of typewritten manuscript).
Notes on Sukuma.
Hess, Charles. Mwanza, A. I. M., n. d. (27 typewritten pages, with handwritten inserts). [In a separate set containing mainly proverbs, notes on the Sukuma customs, etc., 7 pages on Sukuma verbal forms are inserted].

Sukuma (Kigwe)
Note on Kigwe Grammar.
Bukumbi (Mwanza), n. d. (67 pages of dittoed type-written manuscript).

Zigula
Notes on the Zigula Language.
Zanzibar: Diocesan Library, n. d. (5 pages of 'Summary of the Zigula Verba'; typescript).

THE LANGUAGES OF TANZANIA

A Short Grammar of the Zigula Language, together with a few proverbs and riddles.
    N. p., n. d. (41 typewritten pages) [a 7-page list of verbal stems with Proto-Bantu prototypes is added].
Zigua-English Dictionary.
    N. p., n. d. (254 typewritten pages). Copy preserved in Zanzibar Diocesan Library.
(Zigua-English Dictionary).
    N. p., n. d. (no title page; 486 pp. of handwritten notes).

2.5 Survey Material

In the course of the Survey, samples of 86 Tanzanian languages were collected: except for one case (Ngonde), the text of 75 sentences compiled by Dorothy Lehmann was translated into the relevant language; tapes of the same text read by the native speaker are available for 83 languages. In the case of Chaga, moreover, materials from the three main dialectal areas was collected, and samples are available for (ki)Siha, Masama, Machame, and Kibosho in Hai or western Chaga, for Uru, Old Moshi, Vunjo, Kilema Vunjo, Marangu, and Mwika for Vunjo or central Chaga, and (ki)Mashati and Usseri for Rombo or eastern Chaga. The phonology of the dialects was analyzed on the basis of these materials by Susan Polomé in her Master's thesis (1971). Unfortunately, as the sentences of Dr. Lehmann were geared to collect lexical and grammatical data on Bantu Languages, 82 out of 86 languages documented are Bantu. They are to be found (in alphabetic order) in Table 1: 3.

Table 1:3 Bantu Languages studied in the Survey

Bena	Ikoma	Kuria	Mbugwe	Nyakyusa	Rufiji	Suba
Bondei	Isanzu	Kutu	Mbunga	Nyambo	Ruri	Shubi
Chaga	Jita	Kwaya	Meru	(Karagwe)	Rungu	Sukuma
Digo	Kabwa	Kwere	Mwera	Nyamwezi	Rungwa	Sumbwa
Fipa	Kagulu	Lambya	Ndali	Nyanja	Safwa	Wanji
Gogo	Kami	Lugulu	Ndamba	Nyasa	Saghala	Yao
Gweno	Kinga	Makonde	Ndengereko	(Mpoto)	Sango	Zanaki
Ha	Kimbu	Makua	Ngindo	Nyaturu	Segeju	Zalamo
Hangaza	Kiroba	Malila	Ngoni	(Rimi)	Shambala	Zigula
Haya	Konde	Manda	(Sutu)	Nyiha	Simbiti	Zinza
Hehe	(Ngonde)	Matengo	Ngurimi	Pangwa	Sizaki	
Ikizu	Konongo	Matumbi	Ngulu	Pare	Sonjo	
	Kerewe		Nilyamba	Pimbwe		
				Pogolu		
				Rangi		

The non-Bantu languages documented are Iraqw (Mbulu), Luo, Maasai, Mbugu. For many of these languages, other materials, for example, additional sentences, wordlists (cf. Polomé, 1975b: 35) have also been collected.[13]

16 LANGUAGES OF TANZANIA

To illustrate the structure of Tanzanian languages, outlines of 14 of them are given in four subgroupings:
  (a) Haya and Ha;
  (b) Nilyamba, Nyaturu, Sukuma, and Nyamwezi;
  (c) Gogo, Lugulu, Zaramo, and Shambala;
  (d) Bena, Nyakyusa, Makonde and Yao. (See Nurse: 1979)

A more detailed analysis of Chaga and its dialects completes the set of linguistic data compiled by Dr. Derek Nurse and G. Philippson, with the collaboration of students in linguistics at the University of Dar es Salaam. These last and a linguistic description of Luo by E. Padgug-Blount and Ben Blount have not been included here for reasons of space. An outline of the features of the Nilotic languages of Tanzania by C. Ehret is included in this volume.

3.0 *Classification of the Bantu Languages of Tanzania.*

3.1 *Guthrie's Classification*

The Bantu languages of Tanzania belong to Guthrie's zones D, E, F, G, M, N, P. They can be listed as in Table 1:4. Guthrie's classification (1948) is based on phonological, grammatical and lexical criteria. In recent years, attention has been focused on linguistic geography in correlation with the problem of language classification: a tentative mapping of the data of Johnston (1919–1922) led L.-B. De Boeck (1942) to a number of conclusions concerning the major areas of the Bantu territory and the migrations from which they resulted. Similar techniques are involved in Guthrie's topograms (1967: 64–80, 129–43), which are also essential to him to display the index of relationship between Bantu languages and to show the coefficients of generalness or commonness of definite features or their respective regional coefficients (Guthrie, 1967: 98–110).

3.2 *Word-Geography*

Confining himself to word-geography, André Polomé has recently (1975) examined 105 nouns, adjectives and verbs in 93 continental Tanzanian Bantu languages and dialects (with the exclusion of Swahili). The results of his analysis of isogloss patterns can be summarized as follows:
  (1) Shubi, Hangaza, and Kiha are closely related (shared items: more than 56%);
  (2) Sukuma usually shares lexical items with Nyamwezi (except in 22% of the cases);
  (3) Ngulu, Kagulu, Lugulu, Kami, Kutu, and Saguru share lexical items (29 examples); Saghala is not part of this group in 24 cases; Ngulu associates with Zigula instead in 21 cases;
  (4) Segeju (Daiso) is highly differentiated from the surrounding dialects; in 34 cases its forms correspond to those of Digo.

THE LANGUAGES OF TANZANIA

Table 1:4 The Bantu Languages of Tanzania classified by Guthrie's Zones

D	28 Holoholo	E	21 Nyambo	E	44 Zanaki			
			22 Haya		44a Zanaki			
	(61 Ruanda)		22a Ziba		44b Isenyi			
	(62 Rundi)		22b Hamba		44c Ndali			
	64 Shubi		22c Hangire		44d Siora			
	65 Hangaza		22d Nyakisaka		44e Sweta			
	66 Ha		22e Yoza		44f Kiroba			
	67 Vinza		22f Endangabo		44g Ikizu			
			22g Bumbira		44h Girango			
			22h Mwani		44k Simbiti			
			23 Zinza		45 Nata			
			24 Kerewe		46 Sonjo			
			25 Jita					
E	61 Rwo	F	11 Tongwe	G	11 Gogo			
	62 Chaga		12 Bende		12 Kagulu			
	66a Hai							
	66b Wanji		21 Sukuma		21 Taveta			
	66c Rombo		22 Nyamwezi		22 Asu			
	63 Rusha		22a Nyanyembe		23 Shambala			
	64 Kahe		22b Takama		24 Bondei			
	65 Gweno		22c Kiya					
			22d Mwera		31 Zigula			
	73 Digo		23 Sumbwa		32 Nhwele			
	74 Taita		24 Kimbu		33 Zalamo			
			25 Bungu		34 Ngulu			
					35 Lugulu			
			31 Nilyamba		36 Kami			
			32 Rimi		37 Kutu			
			33 Langi		38 Vidunda			
			34 Mbugwe		39 Saghala			
G	42 Swahili	M	11 Pimbwe	N	11 Manda	P	11 Ndengereko	
	42c Mrima		12 Rungwa		12 Ngoni		12 Ruihi	
	42d Unguja		13 Fipa		13 Matengo		13 Matumbi	
	43 Pemba		14 Rungu		14 Mpoto (Nyasa)		14 Ngindo	
	43a Phemba		15 Mambwe		15 Tonga		15 Mbunga	
	43b Tumbatu							
	43c Hadimu		21 Wanda		21h Lambya		21 Yao	
			22 Mwanga				22 Mwera	
	51 Pogolu		23 Nyiha		(31 Nyanja)		23 Makonde	
	52 Ndamba						24 Ndonde	
			24 Malila				25 Mavia	
	61 Sango		25 Safwa					
	62 Hehe						31 Makua	
	63 Bene		31 Nyakyusa					
	64 Pangwa							
	65 Kinga							
	66 Wanji							
	67 Kisi							

(5) Bondei shows 18 examples of characteristic correspondences with Digo, versus 16 with Shambala and Zigula;
(6) The Chaga group is isolated in 51.4% of the cases, but 58% of the Gweno forms correspond with those of the Chaga dialects;
(7) Jita, Ruri, Kwaya, Ngurimi, Sweta, Kuria, Suba, Kabwa, Zanaki, Sizaki, Simbiti, Ikizu, and Kiroba form a close group for 38 isoglosses, but in 64.7% of the cases, this group splits into a western and an eastern subgroup of dialects;
(8) Pimbwe, Rungwa, Fipa, and Rungu form a single group in 32.2% of the cases;
(9) Manda, Ngoni (Sutu), Matengo, and Mpoto form a single group in 46.6% of the cases.

Except for the Bondei-Digo correspondences, these groupings correspond to and confirm Guthrie's classification, for example for the southern dialects, (8) = Guthrie M 11–14; (9) = N 11–14.

3.3 *Genetic Classification*

Using Swadesh's hundred word list, Bernd Heine (1972) attempted to reclassify the Bantu languages thoroughly from a genetic point of view. All Tanzanian languages belong to his 'Eastern Highland Group' (11.9)[14] (see Table 1:5). A more detailed study of the classification of the Bantu

Table 1:5   Genetic Classification

11.906 Interlacustrine Group	11.913 Irangi (F 33)
11.9062 Ruanda–Rundi	11.914 Gogo–Hehe
11.90623 Ha (D 66)	11.9141 Gogo (G 11)
11.9064 Haya (E 22)	11.9142 Hehe (G 62)
11.907 Sukuma–Nyamwezi	11.9143 Kinga (G 65)
11.9071 Sukuma (F 21)	11.915 Pogolu (G 51)
11.9072 Nyamwezi (F 22)	11.916 Matumbi (P 13)
11.909 Chaga (E 62)	11.917 Makonde–Yao
11.910 Taita (E 74)	11.9171 Makonde (P 23)
11.911 Taveta (G 21)	11.9172 Yao (P 21)
11.912 East Coast Group	11.918 Makua
11.9121 Swahili (G 40)	11.919 Fipa–Konde
11.9122 Shambala–Zalamo	11.9191 Fipa (M 13)
11.91221 Shambala–Zigula	11.9192 Nyiha (M 23)
11.912211 Shambala (G 23)	11.9193 Nyekyosa (Nyakyusa) (M 31)
11.912212 Zigula (G 31)	11.920 Nyanja Group
11.91222 Zalamo (G 33)	11.9202 Tonga

languages of Tanzania by Dr. Derek Nurse is included in this volume (see Chap. 2).

4.0 *Nilotic Languages*

As regards the Nilotic languages, J. Greenberg (1971) has reviewed the recent work on classification, discussing the views of Tucker and Bryan, in particular on 'Nilo-Hamitic' (1956: 106–117) or 'Para-Nilotic' (1966:

443–494).[15] Greenberg had, indeed, adopted the views of O. Köhler (1955) in the 1963 edition of his classification of the languages of Africa (Chapter V. 'Chari-Nile,' 85–129). As Bernd Heine (1970: 8) pointed out, the position of scholars versus the 'Nilo-Hamitic' hypothesis depends largely on the model they choose for describing genetic relationship. Using typological criteria for language comparison, Tucker and Bryan considered the Nilo-Hamitic group as a result of language mixture. Greenberg, on the contrary, strictly applies the method of resemblances (cf. Fodor, 1966: 83–92), to which he added the principle of 'mass comparison' (1963: 1), and relies only on the genealogical model to assess genetic relationship. Using the 200 word list of Swadesh, Heine studied the percentages of correspondences in group internal and external comparisons for Southern Nilotic (especially Kalenjin) and Eastern Nilotic and used the Blount and Curley figures (1971) for Western Nilotic. The genealogical tree of Nilotic emerging from this comparison provides data for the Tanzanian languages (circled), as given in Table 1:6. However, in the present state of our knowledge, this classification of the Nilotic languages – like any other (Heine, 1970: 9) – must be considered as tentative.

5.0 *The Spread of the Bantu Languages over Continental Tanzania*

5.1 *Dalby's Analysis*

The problem of the Bantu expansion has been abundantly discussed in recent years, in particular since the publication of Malcolm Guthrie's four-volume *Comparative Bantu* (1967–1971). Assessing the outcome of the debate, David Dalby (1975: 489–95) indicates that the numerical classification of Guthrie's test languages by Henrici (1973) and Heine's genealogical classification of about 140 languages (1972) are actually compatible with Guthrie's views provided some northwestern languages are traced back to a protolanguage in the Cameroun area. He would recognize three Proto-Bantu nuclei:
  (a) Northern PB 1 (Guthrie's 'Pre-Bantu'), possibly expanding along the coast and the riverways through the forest, as well as along the northern margin of the forest;
  (b) Western PB 2 (Guthrie's 'P.B. *X*' and 'P.B. *A*'), probably expanding northward into the forest (overlapping with PB 1) and southward;
  (c) Eastern PB 3 (Guthrie's 'P.B. *B*'), probably expanding northward and southward with an overlap area with western PB 2 and a major north-central divide at the eastern and southeastern margins of the forest (498).

5.2 *Coordination of Two Views*

Coordinating and mapping out the views of Heine and Dalby, D. W. Phillipson (1977) attempts to correlate the linguistic data with the most recent archeological findings: he suggests an early eastward spread of Bantu from the northern margin of the equatorial forest to the vicinity of

Table 1:6 Nilotic Languages

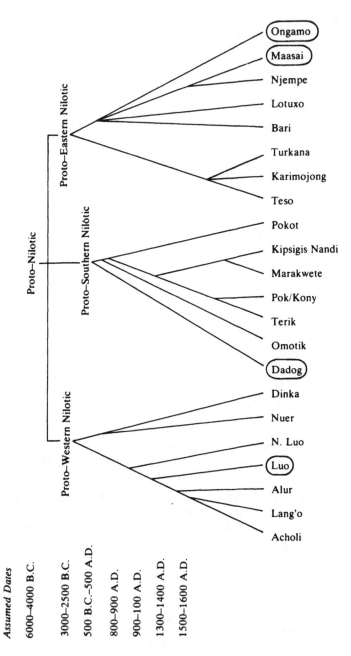

Lake Albert. This group whose language survives in Nyali in northeastern Zaïre, produced the Urewe pottery in the Early Iron Age and, in contact with Central Sudanic people, acquired domestic cattle and sheep, as well as the names for them, as C. Ehret suggests.[18] Another Bantu stream must have spread independently southward in the west where these pre-metallurgical people reached the southern fringe of the equatorial forest belt along the lower reaches of the Congo. Phillipson assumes (1977: 114) that, in the meantime, the Early Iron Age herdsmen and grain growers following the Great Lakes route and bringing with them the Urewe pottery had reached the Angolan grasslands. About 500 A.D. the western and eastern streams apparently met in central Zambia. If, however, the languages of the eastern half of the Bantu linguistic area have to derive from an eastern nucleus (Dalby's PB 3) resulting from an expansion from the lower Congo (Heine, 1972: 182–3), this constitutes a late development according to Phillipson (1977: 114): the distribution of the languages of Heine's Eastern Highland group coincides, to a remarkable degree, with the distribution of the later Iron Age industries, which appear in the archeological record of eastern Africa in the eleventh century A.D. and show connection with the same western origin as Heine considers as the source of his Eastern Highland group.

It stands to reason that this new approach would call for a revision of a number of assumptions concerning the spread of Bantu in Tanzania, but it is obviously premature and beyond the scope of this volume to do so.

NOTES

[1] This list, however, contains a number of entries that are not valid as representative of Tanzanian languages, namely Manyema (region in Zaïre), Congo, Tu(t)si (immigrants from Burundi), Kamba (from Kenya), Ganda, Wemba (=Bemba, the main tribe in the Zambian copperbelt). The term Shirazi designates a subgroup of the Swahili-speaking population of the Mrima coast (Prins, 1967: 13–4). Similarly, Konongo is a subgroup of Nyamwezi, south-west of Tabora (Abrahams, 1967: 13–6). Wungu is a less common name for Bungu, a language closely related to Kimbu and Sumbwa (Willis, 1966: 70). As for the three Nyika entries, two of them refer to two separate groups of Nyiha – those in Ufipa, south of Lake Rukwa, and those in the Mbozi district, Mbeya region (Willis, 1966: 68; Brook, 1968: 59–61). Moreover, Regi does not designate a language, but a small tribe on Ukerewe. On the other hand Nyika could also designate a subgroup of Tumbuka, closely linked with Fungwe, Wenya and Tambo, whose home is in Malawi (Bryan, 1959: 137–8) or apply to the coastal tribes of southern Kenya, including Digo astride the Kenya-Tanzania border (Bryan, 1959: 125, 126, 129).

The two Shashi entries must refer to the same language, also known as Sizaki, a member of the Zanaki group (Heine, 1976:51).

[2] Including Mbugu in Usambara, according to Greenberg (1963: 168), whose view is supported by Sutton (1968: 78, 81, 85; 1971: 110–11). On the complex problem of Mbugu, cf. however, Goodman, 1971: 673–5.

[3] Several parish priests of the Masasi district report their using this language with village people in their area, one of them specifying that different catechists serve as interpreters for Makua and Matambwe.

[4] Machinga and Ndendeuli are listed by Sutton (1968: 80) among the southern

Tanzania Bantu languages. Some of my informants, however, considered Machinga merely as a part of Mwera.

[5] For all of these, see Heine (1976:50-1). His data are also confirmed by the materials I collected in the field (recordings of sets of sentences and interviews of native speakers on the position of their mother tongue and its degree of mutual intelligibility with neighboring languages and dialects).

[6] On recent developments, cf. Legère, 1975.

[7] Very valuable material may be discarded by unaware newcomers, as the old grammars and textbooks removed in 1970 from the Magila library. In checking the holdings in Dar es Salaam we also found that many items listed by Whiteley in his *Bibliography* were no longer in the Museum, nor the Swahili Institute, and could not be traced in the East Africana collection of the University Library to which they were supposed to have been transferred.

[8] At the Saba Saba (July 7th) Fair in 1970, the Bible was available in the following Tanzanian languages: Swahili, Gogo, Haya, Nyiha, Nyaturu, Sukuma, Yao, Maasai, Luo, as well as KinyaRwanda and Rundi, and Gujrati, Urdu and Hindi.

[9] Included in this list are stenciled duplicated works which were found to be widely available in Tanzania or elsewhere. Ph.D. dissertations referred to in *Dissertation Abstracts* and easily obtainable through University Microfilms or Xerox are also listed. Peripheral languages like Nyanja, Rundi, Ruanda, etc. have also been included. Only those articles that deal with important features of the language, e.g., its tone structure or its syntactic structure, have been mentioned. Therefore, short papers on specific subjects like a definite lexical item, e.g. Paul Schönenberger, 'Names for "God" known and used by the Wanyamwezi,' in *Anthropos* 56 (1961), 947-9, have been left out. Not included either are editions of texts, e.g. T. O. Beidelman, 'Some Ngulu texts,' *Tanganyika Notes and Records* 63 (1964), 165-195. Papers on onomastics, e.g. Eric Ten Raa, 'Geographic names in south-eastern Sandawe,' *Journal of African Languages* 5 (1966), 175-207, are omitted as well.

[10] According to Bernd Heine's classification of Nilotic based on lexicostatistic analysis and the studies of Köhler (1955), Blount and Curley (1970), Ehret (1971), as well as his own research (Heine, 1975/6).

[11] In his contribution to the Subsaharan Africa volume of *Trends in Linguistics* (1971), in which he thoroughly reviews the classification of the Khoisan languages and their linguistic features, E. O. J. Westphal removes Sandawe from the Hottentot languages and Hadza from Bushman (382), especially since independent sample checking by Dr. J. Woodburn failed to show any correspondence between Hadza and !xû (378).

[12] Volumes of 'Readings' are excluded, though some of them seem to have been produced until the middle sixties for pedagogical purposes, for example the forty-page *ChiFipa Reader* compiled by Father John Rupya in 1965.

[13] The only languages for which no information could be obtained are:

(a) the 'Khoisan' group: Sandawe and Hadza;

(b) the dialects of the Iraqw group: Burungi, Chasi, Goro(w)a (Tucker and Bryan, 1956: 137);

(c) the smaller Nilotic languages, e.g. Ongamo (Ngasa) in the Kilimanjaro, the Tatoga dialects, especially Barabaig (Tucker and Bryan, 1956: 116);

(d) the following Bantu languages:

Bende	Holoholo	Kisi	Mwamba	Nata
Digo	Issenyi	Mambwe	(Lungulu)	Ndonda
Do(h)e	Kahe		Mwanga	Rusha

Selya	Taita	Vidunda
Siora	Tongwe	Vinza
Sweta	Taveta	Wanda

In most cases, these are, however, subdialects (e.g. of Nyakyusa in the case of Mwamba and Selya), or small languages spoken by less than 10,000 people (e.g. Bende, Doe, Kisi, Tongwe, Vinza, Wanda), or border languages like Digo and Taita, mainly spoken in Kenya, or Holoholo, spread mainly on the Zaïre side of Lake Tanganyika.

[14] Guthrie's zones and numbers are given between parentheses.

[15] The term "Nilo-Hamitic" was coined to designate the Kalenjin (with the Tatoga), the Maasai, the Karamajong-Teso cluster and the Bari cluster on the basis of the Cushitic components of their culture, illustrated by lexical borrowing (Sutton, 1968: 87–8).

On the problem of 'Nilo-Hamitic,' cf. especially the following articles:

G. W. Huntingford, 'The "Nilo-Hamitic" Languages,' *Southwestern Journal of Anthropology* 12 (1956), 200–222.

J. Hohenberger, 'Comparative Masai Word-list: Nilotic-Nilo-Hamitic–Masai–Hamitic–Semitic,' *Africa* 26 (1956), 281–287.

J. H. Greenberg, 'Nilotic, "Nilo-Hamitic," and Hamito-Semitic: A Reply,' *Africa* 27 (1957), 364–378.

J. Hohenberger, 'Some Notes on Nilotic, "Nilo-Hamitic," and Hamito-Semitic, by Joseph Greenberg,' *Africa* 28 (1958), 37–42.

[16] A change in designation partly motivated by the study of the t/k-substrate according to some features shared by 'Nilo-Hamitic' and Cushitic languages (cf. Margaret A. Bryan, 'The T/K Languages: a New Substratum,' *Africa* 29 [1959], 1–21).

[17] For a brief review of the problems involved, cf. Polomé, 1975: 168–71.

[18] Cf. especially, his articles:

'Cattle-keeping and Milking in Eastern and Southern African History: The Linguistic Evidence,' *Journal of African History* 8 (1967), 1–17.

'Sheep and Central Sudanic Peoples in Southern Africa,' *Journal of African History* 9 (1968), 213–221.

'Patterns of Bantu and Central Sudanic Settlement in Central and Southern Africa (ca. 1000 B.C.–500 A.D.),' *Transafrican Journal of History* 3 (1973), 1–71.

REFERENCES

Abrahams, R. G., 1967, *The Peoples of Greater Unyamwezi, Tanzania (Nyamwezi, Sukuma, Sumbwa, Kimbu, Konongo)*. (Ethnographic Survey of Africa: East Central Africa, Part XVII), London: International African Institute.

Anttilla, Raimo, 1972, *An Introduction to Historical and Comparative Linguistics*. New York: The Macmillan Co.

Bennett, Patrick R., 1967, 'Dahl's Law and Thagicũ' *African Language Studies* 8, 127–159. (*Thagicũ* includes *Segeju*).

Berry, L., 1971, *Tanzania in Maps*. London: University of London Press.

Blount, Ben, and Curley, Richard T., 1970, 'The Southern Luo Languages: A Glottochronological Reconstruction' *Journal of African Languages* 9, 1–18.

Brock, Beverley, 1968, 'The Nyiha' in Roberts, A., ed., *Tanzania before 1900*. Dar es Salaam: East African Publishing House (for the Historical Association of Tanzania) 59–81.

Bryan, M. A., 1959, *The Bantu Languages of Africa*. London/New York: International African Institute/Oxford University Press.

Dalby, David, 1975, 'The Prehistorical Implications of Guthrie's Comparative Bantu. Part 1: Problems of Internal Relationship' *Journal of African History* 16, 481–501.

De Boeck, L.-B., 1942, *Premières applications de la géographie linguistique aux langues bantoues*. (Institut Royal Colonial Belge – Section des Sciences Morales et Politiques – Mémories – Vol. X: 5) Brussels: Georges Van Campenhout.

Doke, Clement M, 1945, *Bantu. Modern Grammatical, Phonetical and Lexicographical Studies Since 1860*. London: International African Institute [1967, reprint].

Ehret, Christopher, 1971, *Southern Nilotic History: Linguistic Approaches to the Studies of the Past*. Evanston, Ill.: Northwestern University Press.

Fodor, István, 1966, *The Problems in the Classification of African Languages*. (Studies on Developing Countries, No. 5) Budapest: Hungarian Academy of Sciences, Center for Afro-Asian Research.

Goodman, Morris, 1971, 'Languages in Contact' In Sebeok, Thomas A., ed., *Current Trends in Linguistics*, Vol. 7: *Linguistics in Sub-Saharan Africa*. 664–679. The Hague: Mouton.

Greenberg, Joseph H., 1963, *The Languages of Africa*. (*International Journal of American Linguistics* 29: 1. Part 2 = Publication 25 of the Indiana University Research Center in Anthropology, Folklore, and Linguistics). Bloomington: Indiana University.

1971, 'Nilo-Saharan and Merotic' Sebeok, Thomas A., ed., *Current Trends in Linguistics*. Vol. 7. *Linguistics in Sub-Saharan Africa*. The Hague: Mouton. 421–442.

Guthrie, Malcolm, 1948, *The Classification of the Bantu Languages*. London/New York: International African Institute/Oxford University Press.

1967–1971, *Comparative Bantu*. An introduction to the comparative linguistics and prehistory of the Bantu languages. 4 volumes. Farnborough: Gregg Press.

Heine, Bernd, 1970, *Nilotic and Nilo-Hamitic: A Linguistic Review*. (Institute for Development Studies, University College, Nairobi, Cultural Division, Discussion Paper No. 6). Nairobi. (typescript)

1972, 'Zur genetischen Gliederung der Bantu-Sprachen' *Afrika und Übersee* 56, 164–185.

1976, 'Knowledge and Use of Second Language in Musoma Region – A Quantitative Survey' **Kiswahili** 46, 1, 49–59.

Henrici, Alick, 1973, 'Numerical Classification of Bantu Languages' *African Language Studies* 14, 82–104.

Johnston, (Sir) Harry H., 1919–1922, *A Comparative Study of the Bantu and Semi-Bantu Languages*. 2 volumes. Oxford: Clarendon Press.

Kähler-Meyer, Emmi, 1963, 'Bantu-Tonsprachen und -Nichttonsprachen in Tanganyika' *Zeitschrift für Phonetik, Sprachwissenschaft und Kommunikationsforschung* 16, 101–112.

1971, 'Niger-Congo, Eastern Bantu' in Sebeok, Thomas A., ed., *Current Trends in Linguistics*. Vol. 7. *Linguistics in Sub-Saharan Africa*. The Hague: Mouton. 307–356.

Köhler, Oswin, 1955, *Geschichte der Erforschung der nilotischen Sprachen*. (*Afrika und Übersee*. Beiheft 28). Berlin: Dietrich Reimer.

Legère, Karsten, 1975, 'Zum Verhältnis zwischen dem Swahili und anderen tanzanischen Sprachen' *Zeitschrift für Phonetik, Sprachwissenschaft und Kommunikationsforschung* 28, 343–8.

Lehmann, Winfred P, 1973, *Historical Linguistics. An Introduction.* Second edition. New York: Holt, Rinehart and Winston, Inc.
Meeussen, A. E., 1962, 'Meinhof's Rule in Bantu' *African Language Studies* 3, 25-29.
Molnos, Angela, 1969, *Language Problems in Africa.* A bibliographical summary (1946–67) of the present situation, with special reference to Kenya, Tanzania and Uganda. Nairobi: East African Research Information Centre.
Nurse, D., 1979, 'Description of Sample Bantu Languages of Tanzania' *African Languages/Langues Africaines* 5(1).
Nurse, D. and Philippson, G., 1974, *The North-Eastern Bantu Languages of Tanzania and Kenya: A Classification.* Dar es Salaam: Institute for Swahili Research. (duplicated)
Phillipson, D. W., 1977, 'The Spread of the Bantu Languages' *Scientific American* 236: 4 (April 1977), 106–114.
Polomé, André Robert, 1975, *The Classification of the Bantu Languages of Tanzania.* (Ph.D. Dissertation). Austin: University of Texas.
Polomé, Edgar C., 1975a, 'Problems and Techniques of a Sociolinguistically Oriented Language Survey: The Case of the Tanzania Survey' in Ohannessian, Sirarpi, Ferguson, Charles A., and Polomé, Edgar C., *Language Surveys in Developing Nations.* Papers and Reports on Sociolinguistic Surveys. 31–50. Arlington, Va.: Center for Applied Linguistics.

1975b, 'The Reconstruction of Proto-Bantu Culture from the Lexicon' in Herbert, Robert K., ed. *Patterns in Language, Culture, and Society: Sub-Saharan Africa.* (Working Papers in Linguistics, No. 19), 164–173. Columbus, Ohio: Ohio State University, Department of Linguistics.
Polomé, Susan Elisabeth, 1971, *A Phonological Survey of the Chagga Dialects of Tanzania.* (M. A. Thesis). Austin: University of Texas.
Prins, A. H. J., 1967, *The Swahili-speaking Peoples of Zanzibar and The East African Coast.* (Arabs, Shirazi and Swahili) (Ethnographic Survey of Africa: East Central Africa Part XII) London: International African Institute.
Sutton, J. E. G. 1958, The Settlement of East Africa' in Ogot, B. A., and Kieran, J. A., eds., *Zamani. A Survey of East African History.* 69–99. Nairobi: East African Publishing House/Longmans of Kenya.
Tucker, A. N., and Bryan, M. A., 1956, *The Non-Bantu Languages of North-Eastern Africa.* (with a supplement on the Non-Bantu Languages of Southern Africa, by E. O. J. Westphal). London/New York: International African Institute/Oxford University Press.

1957, *Linguistic Survey of the Northern Bantu Borderland.* Volume 4. *Languages of the Eastern Section: Great Lakes to Indian Ocean.* London/New York: International African Institute/Oxford University Press.

1966, *Linguistic Analyses. The Non-Bantu Languages of North-Eastern Africa.* London/New York: International African Institute/Oxford University Press.
Whiteley, W. H., and Gutkind, A. E., 1958, *A Linguistic Bibliography of East Africa.* Revised edition. Kampala: East African Swahili Committee/East African Institute of Social Research, Makerere College.
Willis, Roy G., 1966, *The Fipa and Related Peoples of South-West Tanzania and North-East Zambia*, (Ethnographic Survey of Africa: East Central Africa Part XV) London: International African Institute.

2 THE BANTU LANGUAGES OF EAST AFRICA: A LEXICOSTATISTICAL SURVEY

Derek Nurse and Gerard Philippson

1.0 *Methodology*

The aim of the survey was to evaluate quantitatively the degree of similarity between the Bantu languages of East Africa by comparing a set body of vocabulary, with the view of putting the languages into immediate groups, and then, where possible, into ever larger groups. Our hope is that historians, archaeologists, and others would be able to combine these results with their own work and form a more meaningful whole than presently exists. For a description of sample languages in the groups identified, see Nurse 1979b.

The method followed involved comparing 400 vocabulary items from 76 languages/dialects. The items were selected from a list of more than 1000 words which were filled out by first speakers of the languages concerned (recruited from University of Dar es Salaam students), who checked their work with other speakers at home. The items were chosen for their unambiguity and reliability, as far as possible, and mainly consisted of parts of the body, names of common animals, household implements (pot, hoe, axe, etc.), natural phenomena (wind, sun, river, etc.), verbs referring to clear functions, and a few adjectives. We should point out that the original list was intended basically for comparison with Proto-Bantu (PB), as set out in Guthrie (1971: vol. 2, 118–45), which explains certain inadequacies from the point of view of this survey. The list is too long to present here, but we found that some items, such as 'shiver' or 'heel' (see Coupez, 1975), although present in PB, were not suitable for comparison due to the extreme diversity of the stems represented; whereas, others, such as 'meat' or 'to drink' were practically identical for all languages.

Because we wished to base the degree of lexical similarity on words inherited from the vocabulary assumed for PB, and to give as little weight as possible to loans, coincidence, etc., we relied not on 'similarity' but on 'cognation,' defining as 'cognate' two or more items deriving from the same single item in a hypothetical common ancestor language by direct oral transmission. To ensure this, we worked out the sound correspondences between PB and each of the languages concerned, and thus between the languages themselves. Two items were considered cognate if each segment in an item in one language corresponded regularly to the equivalent segment of the same item in the other language. Although it is never possible to obviate all non-cognate items, in this way many loans are excluded. For instance, if PB *p and *t give respectively /p/ and /t/ in Swahili, and zero and /d/ in the Old Moshi (OM) dialect of Chaga, then Swahili *-pita* and OM *-ida* 'pass' can be considered cognate, i.e. fully

THE BANTU LANGUAGES OF EAST AFRICA 27

identical. On the other hand, Sw. *kitanda* and OM *kitaRa* 'bed' are not cognate, not fully identical. Three possible ways of rating degrees of similarity present themselves: either apply the yes/no criterion strictly and decide that since the two items are not cognate (e.g. *kitanda: kitaRa*), they should be counted zero; or consider that since they are obviously related in some way, they should be counted as 1; or try to adopt a graded scale which was what we did, although we may have tried to be too sophisticated. Rather than settle for a three point scale (2=cognate; 1=similar in some undefined way, but not cognate; 0=different), we adopted a six way contrast:

5 = complete cognation of stem and affixes;
4 = stems cognate, but nominal affixes or verbal extension different;
3 = minor phonological differences (we counted as minor differences, for instance, permutation of final *-o* and *-u* or *-i* and *-e* – both fairly common in a number of PB items; initial PB *c for *t, e.g. *-catu and *-tatu 'three' – also frequent in PB – and a few other such cases);
2 = a major skewing, but the items still assumed to be cognate (including permutation of *i̯ and *i, *u̯ and *u, with attendant consonant differences, or permutation of consonants in an apparently irregular way, for instance, in West Ruvu, several cases of /h/ where /s/ would be expected from PB *c);
1 = a skewing, normally indicating a loan, involving a completely extraneous sound (e.g. Sw. *kitanda* and OM *kitaRa*, where /t/ in OM is not regularly derived from a PB sound);
0 = totally unrelated items.

This scale gave a total possible maximum of 5 × 400 = 2000, and the figures were then divided by 20 to give a percentage.

We now feel this scale is unnecessarily complicated, and in certain cases it proved difficult to decide on a particular figure, especially between 2 and 3. It is also not clear, for example, that a phonological difference (rating only 3) should be more heavily penalized than a morphological one (rating 4). Nevertheless the scale was consistently applied, and we do not feel that another scale would show greatly different results in terms of groupings (except in points of detail; for instance the exact position of Lugulu vis-à-vis East Ruvu), even though a simpler scale would probably have produced actual figures which were higher.

Having thus obtained the raw figures, we adopted, for grouping, the Group Average method (see Bender, 1971, and Henrici, 1973). This involves placing all the figures in a table. We did not place them all in a single table, which would have been far too unwieldy, and, in any case, it had become obvious that certain languages fell into immediate groups, while others did not. We first inspected the tables for the highest single figure between any two languages, then broke down the columns for these two, and recalculated their relationship to the others by adding their respective figures to each of the other languages and then dividing by two.

E.g. (simplified):

Sumbwa	Nyamwezi	Sukuma	Nilyamba	
x	61.5	59	45	Sumbwa
	x	84.5	55.75	Nyamwezi
		x	55.5	Sukuma
			x	Nilyamba

The highest single figure here is Sukuma-Nyamwezi, 84.5; therefore, these two are combined first by collapsing their figures vis-à-vis Sumbwa and Nilyamba (Sumbwa now 61.5 + 59 divided by two = 60.25: Nilyamba now 55.5 + 55.75 divided by two = 55.75 to nearest .25 percent), which then gives:

Sumbwa	Nyamwezi/Sukuma	Nilyamba	
x	60.25	45	Sumbwa
	x	55.75	Nyamwezi/Sukuma
		x	Nilyamba

The highest figure is now Sukuma/Nyamwezi to Sumbwa, so their columns are combined in the same way, giving:

Sumbwa/Nyamwezi/Sukuma	
50.5	Nilyamba

In this way, most immediate groupings became clear (see Appendix 2: A). In many groups, statistically, there turned out to be a core group of languages and others which were more peripheral. We then took sample languages from all the groups, calculated their percentage to sample languages from other groups, and worked out average figures for intergroup relationships (see Table 2: 1 below). Then we re-applied the procedure just outlined. In the case of distant groups and groups obviously not closely related, we compared just a few of the 'core' languages from each, whereas for geographically closer groups we compared more than just the core languages, often the whole group. In the intergroup comparisons, the figures often spoke for themselves, and minimal human intervention was necessary. Where decisions had to be taken, they were discussed in the proper context. Thus, the number of groups got smaller as they fell together, while membership of the groups got larger, until we were left with a small number of very large groups.

2.0 *Application of Method to East African Bantu Languages*

We do not intend to deal at length with immediate groups, as they do not show any marked differences from previous classifications, except in points of detail. If we try to relate them to Guthrie's classification, we get

THE BANTU LANGUAGES OF EAST AFRICA 29

the following (the names assigned are either the commonly accepted ones or derive from geographical features, except where noted):

Luhya	is basically Guthrie's E30, plus E41 (Logooli).
Rutara	is E11 to E14, and E21 to E24 (name derives from a historical kingdom on the west side of Lake Victoria and was suggested first by Mr. Mosha of Kampala).
North Nyanza	is E15 to E17.
Suguti	is E25, and others unmentioned by Guthrie.
East Nyanza	is E42 to E45.
Western Highlands	is G61 to G67, with the exception to Fuliiro, which we know nothing about.
West Tanzania	is F20 and F30, with the exception of Bungu, which we have not yet investigated.
West Ruvu	is G10, plus G39.
East Ruvu	is G32, G33, G36, G37, and Doe, not mentioned by Guthrie.
Seuta	is G23, G24, G31, and G34 (name of a mythical common ancestor).
Thagicu	is E50, plus E46, which is not dealt with here (name of a historical dispersal area, first used by P. R. Bennett).
Chaga	is E60, with or without E74a.
Kilombero	is G50.
Southern Highlands	is G60.

A few words need to be said about the internal consistency of the immediate groups (see Appendix 2: A), as they range from very homogenous groups, as high as 81.5 in the case of Suguti (which may as well be called one language, with four dialects – Jita, Kwaya, Ruri, and Regi), down to much looser groupings with 47 (Langi to the rest of West Tanzania, if that is considered an immediate grouping) or even 44.5 (Chaga to Dauida). A justification for the latter has to be given here.

Map 3   Bantu Languages of East Africa

Davida's highest figure by far is 62.5 with the other dialect of 'Taita', Saghala, which is higher than its 44.5 figure to Chaga; also its 43 figure to Pare is almost as high as the Chaga figure. On this basis, Davida and Saghala ought to go together to form an immediate group designed as 'Taita', but there is a very good non-lexicostatistical reason to assume that Davida, the largest dialect of 'Taita', is historically a dialect of Chaga[1] and that Saghala, the other 'Taita' dialect, is part of the big North East group.

THE BANTU LANGUAGES OF EAST AFRICA

In the case of Langi and the rest of West Tanzania, it is appropriate to mention Bender's notion of "strong" and "weak" unity (see Bender, 1971): a group is "strong" if all the internal figures for any group are higher than all the external figures; a group is "weak" if some external figures are higher than some internal figures; and a group is not a group at all if some external figures are higher than the internal group average. Using these definitions, some of our groups are weak, and a few (Luhya, West Tanzania/Langi, West Ruvu, East Ruvu, and Chaga/Davida) cease to be groups. But Bender's criteria were meant for rather distantly related languages, using a different scale, rather than for a large number of relatively closely related languages packed on top of each other; if we adopted his criteria, some of our groups, immediate and non-immediate, would fall apart. Therefore, we would prefer to use "very strong" to refer to groups, immediate or otherwise, all of whose internal figures exceed all external figures (Suguti, West Highlands, North Nyanza, Sabaki, Thagicu, Chaga without Davida, Kilombero, and then, at a secondary level, West Ruvu–East Ruvu–Lugulu–Seuta, West Tanzania–Langi, East Nyanza–Suguti); "strong" to groups whose internal average exceeds all external figures (East Nyanza, Rutara, Seuta, West Tanzania without Langi, South Highlands, and at a secondary level, Sabaki–Pare–Saghala, Lacustrine); and "weak" to refer to those groups which do not meet either of these two conditions (Luhya, West Tanzania/Langi at an immediate level; East Ruvu, West Ruvu, Chaga/Davida as an immediate group, and at a secondary level, East Ruvu–Lugulu–Seuta, Interlacustrine, the North East of Table 2:5a, but not 2:5c). By these criteria Langi/West Tanzania is "weak" as an immediate group, and, apart from Chaga/Davida which, as explained, is a special case, has the lowest internal average of all the immediate groups. Against that, as just pointed out, other groups also are "weak", and the exclusion of Langi does not appreciably raise the internal average (47 to 52, a "very strong" group).

The main difference between applying Bender's criteria and ours would be the level at which certain languages fall together. The four large final groups would still appear, but some of the "immediate" groups, those labelled "weak", would disappear, only to reappear at the second or subsequent stages of uniting.

There are three single language immediate groups: Lugulu, Saghala ('Taita' no longer exists since Davida was hived off to Chaga), and Pare (which really belongs with Taveta, but we do not have 400 words to show that here).

The second stage consists of arranging the "immediate" groups in larger units. Table 2:1 gives all the intergroup figures. It can be seen from Table 2:1 that the two highest figures inside the diagonal line are Seuta–East Ruvu, and Lugulu–East Ruvu; since it makes no difference in the final outcome whether they are collapsed in order or simultaneously, we do the latter for reasons of economy, so Lugulu–East Ruvu–Seuta are combined, leading to Table 2:2. Lugulu–East Ruvu–Seuta is a "weak" group, since its internal average is 50.75, but the external high is 51.25 (East Ruvu to West Ruvu).

Table 2:1 Degree of Lexical Cognation

North Nyanza	Luhya	East Nyanza	Suguti	Rutara	West Highlands	West Tanzania	Langi	West Ruvu	East Ruvu	Lugulu
(66)	42.0	35.25	40.0	49.0	39.75	35.5	31.75	26.75	24.25	
	(51.5)	40.0	38.75	37.0	34.25	34.5	28.25	25.0		24.5
		(51.5)	45.0	37.75	38.5	43.0	36.5	27.25	23.25	24.0
			(81.5)	45.75	43.5	40.25	34.25	31.5	27.75	31.5
				(66.5)	47.75	39.5	32.0	29.25	25.75	25.25
					(73)	41.75	32.25	26.25	25.0	27.5
						(52)	47.0	43.0	41.25	36.5
							–	41.75	41.25	35.0
								(58.25)	51.25	47.0
									(65.5)	53.75
										–

In Table 2:2 the new group, East Ruvu–Lugulu–Seuta can unite with West Ruvu (48.5). At the same time, if Langi–West Tanzania is not considered an immediate group, then they may be combined at this point, since they do not conflict with East Ruvu–Lugulu–Seuta. And, at the same

Table 2:2 Collapsed

North Nyanza	Luhya	East Nyanza	Suguti	Rutara	West Highlands	West Tanzania	Langi	West Ruvu	East Ruvu–Lugulu–Seuta
(66)	42.0	35.25	40.0	49.0	39.75	35.5	41.75	26.75	26.5
	(51.5)	40.0	38.75	37.0	34.25	34.5	28.25	25.0	25.5
		(51.5)	45.0	37.75	38.5	43.0	36.5	27.25	26.5
			(81.5)	45.75	43.5	40.25	34.75	31.5	29.5
				(66.5)	47.75	39.5	32.0	29.25	26.75
					(73)	41.75	32.25	26.25	26.75
						(52)	47.0	43.0	39.25
							–	41.75	40.25
								(58.25)	48.5
									(50.75)

THE BANTU LANGUAGES OF EAST AFRICA

between Languages (19 Groups)

Seuta	Sabaki	Pare	Saghala	South Highlands	Kilombero	Chaga /Davida	Thagicu	
28.5	28.5	26.25	27.25	22.0	22.5	27.0	26.25	North Nyanza
26.25	28.0	24.5	25.25	24.25	23.75	25.0	26.5	Luhya
32.25	31.0	30.5	27.5	28.75	27.5	30.0	35.25	East Nyanza
29.75	36.0	33.5	33.5	26.5	26.5	29.25	33.0	Suguti
29.25	29.25	27.75	25.5	24.5	25.0	28.25	31.0	Rutara
28.0	29.75	29.0	28.75	24.0	24.5	28.0	28.75	West Highlands
40.25	41.75	41.5	36.5	34.25	31.25	34.5	36.25	West Tanzania
44.75	43.25	45.25	38.5	36.5	32.75	37.0	34.5	Langi
47.5	42.25	38.5	33.25	42.75	38.5	33.0	30.5	West Ruvu
<u>55.25</u>	46.25	41.5	36.75	37.75	41.5	32.0	28.0	East Ruvu
43.25	39.25	37.25	33.25	38.25	39.0	31.25	30.25	Lugulu
71.25)	49.75	49.0	41.75	35.25	38.25	38.25	34.25	Seuta
	(59.5)	45.25	43.25	32.25	36.25	38.75	36.5	Sabaki
		–	46.0	32.75	30.5	42.0	38.0	Pare
			–	25.5	29.25	–	39.0	Saghala
				(53.25)	40.0	25.75	23.5	South Highlands
					(51.5)	28.0	25.75	Kilombero
						(44.5)	37.75	Chaga/Davida
							(62.75)	Thagicu

time with less justification, North Nyanza–Rutara–West Highlands may be combined, the latter to form Lacustrine. Another solution for the latter would be to unite only Rutara and North Nyanza (49), which would not modify the final picture, but only delay it by one step, since it still would

to 17 Groups

Sabaki	Pare	Saghala	South Highlands	Kilombero	Chaga –Davida	Thagicu	
28.5	26.25	27.75	22.0	22.5	27.0	26.25	North Nyanza
28.0	24.5	25.25	24.25	23.75	25.0	26.5	Luhya
31.0	30.5	27.5	28.75	27.5	30.0	35.25	East Nyanza
36.0	33.5	33.5	26.5	26.5	29.25	33.0	Suguti
29.25	27.75	25.5	24.5	25.0	28.25	31.0	Rutara
29.75	29.0	28.25	24.0	24.5	28.0	28.75	West Highlands
41.75	41.5	36.5	34.25	31.25	34.5	36.25	West Tanzania
43.25	45.25	38.5	36.5	32.75	37.0	34.5	Langi
42.25	38.5	33.25	42.75	38.5	33.0	30.5	West Ruvu
44.5	42.5	37.25	39.25	37.25	39.5	40.25	East Ruvu–Lugulu–Seuta
(59.5)	45.25	43.25	32.25	36.25	38.75	36.5	Sabaki
	–	46.0	32.75	30.5	42.0	38.0	Pare
		–	25.5	29.25	–	39.0	Saghala
			(53.25)	40.0	25.75	23.5	South Highlands
				(51.5)	28.0	25.75	Kilombero
					(44.5)	37.75	Chaga–Davida
						(62.75)	Thagicu

Table 2:3 Collapsed

Interlacustrine	Luhya	North Nyanza	Suguti	Langi–West Tanzania	West Ruvu–East Ruvu–Lugula–Seuta	Sabaki
(43.75)	37	37.25	43	36	24.5	29.25
	(51.5)	40	38.75	31.5	25.75	28
		(51.5)	45	39.75	27	
			(81.5)	37.5	30.5	36
				(47)	41	42.5
					(48.5)	43.5
						(59.5)

lead to Suguti–East Nyanza (45), and then Rutara–North Nyanza and West Highlands (43). Interlacustrine as a group is weak (internal average 43.75; external high 45.75), but there is no alternative except to leave West Highlands as an independent unit until final grouping of the whole area into Lacustrine (39.75, see Table 2:5a). We preferred to collapse North Nyanza–Rutara–West Highlands at this point. West Ruvu–Lugulu–Seuta is very strong (internal low 48.5; external high 44.5), as is Langi–West Tanzania at this stage (internal low 47; external high 45.25). Collapsing these three groups leads to Table 2:3.

In Table 2:3 we see that the three non-conflicting highs are Pare–Saghala (46), Suguti–East Nyanza (45) and Pare–Sabaki (45.25). Suguti-East Nyanza is "very strong" (internal low 45; external high 43), and the combination is strong (internal average 44.75; external high 43.5). Pare–Sabaki–Saghala is "strong". Collapsing these leads to Table 2:4.

Table 2:4 Collapsed

Interlacustrine	Luhya	East Nyanza–Suguti	Langi–West Tanzania	West Ruvu–East Ruvu–Lugulu–Seuta	Sabaki–Pare–Saghala
(43.75)	37	40.25	36	24.5	28
	(51.5)	39.5	31.5	25.75	26
		(45)	38.75	28.75	32
			(47)	41	41.25
				(48.25)	39.75
					(44.75)

THE BANTU LANGUAGES OF EAST AFRICA

to 13 Groups

Pare	Saghala	South Highlands	Kilombero	Chaga/ Davida	Thagicu	
27.75	27.25	23.5	24	27.75	28.75	Interlacustrine
24.5	25.5	24.25	23.75	25	26.5	Luhya
30.5	27.5	28.75	27.5	30	35.25	East Nyanza
33.5	33.5	26.5	26.5	29.25	33	Suguti
43.5	37.5	35.5	32	35.75	35.5	Langi-West Tanzania
40.5	35.25	41	38	36.25	35.5	West Ruvu-East Ruvu-Lugulu-Seuta
45.25	43.25	32.75	36.25	38.75	36.5	Sabaki
–	46	32.75	30.5	42	38	Pare
	–	25.5	29.25	–	39	Saghala
		(53.25)	40	25.75	23.5	South Highlands
			(51.5)	28	25.75	Kilombero
				(44.5)	37.75	Chaga/Davida
					(62.75)	Thagicu

In Table 2:4 a tendency which developed previously becomes very clear: the difference between the higher figures is becoming minimal, and some discussion is necessary of the figures around 40 in Table 2:4.

Around the Lake, East Nyanza/Suguti shows 40.25 to Interlacustrine and 39.5 to Luhya, while the figure uniting Interlacustrine and Luhya is somewhat lower (37). The only other possible candidate for inclusion here is Langi/West Tanzania, but it is high only with East Nyanza/Suguti (38.75) and considerably lower with Interlacustrine (36) and Luhya (31.5). On this basis, therefore, we collapse Interlacustrine/Luhya/East Nyanza-Suguti at the same time: if only Interlacustrine/East Nyanza-Suguti (40.25) were collapsed and then the situation re-examined, the next candidate for inclusion still would be Luhya and not Langi/West Tanzania. So the move is justified: the new super-group, Lacustrine, is strong at this stage (internal average 39.25; external high 38.75).

to 10 Groups

South Highlands	Kilombero	Chaga/ Davida	Thagicu	
23.5	24	27.75	28.75	Interlacustrine
24.25	23.75	25	26.5	Luhya
27.75	27	29.75	34.25	East Nyanza-Suguti
35.5	32	35.75	35.5	Langi-West Tanzania
41	38	36.25	35.5	West Ruvu-East Ruvu-Lugulu-Seuta
30.25	32	40.5	37.75	Sabaki-Pare-Saghala
(53.25)	40	25.75	23.5	South Highlands
	(51.5)	28	25.75	Kilombero
		(44.5)	37.75	Chaga-Davida
			(62.75)	Thagicu

Langi/West Tanzania is, in any case, in an intermediate position, for, although it would be the next candidate after Luhya for inclusion into Lacustrine, this is prevented by other developments in Table 2:4 where there are several other figures around 40; the same question arises: should they be collapsed in strict order or can simultaneous collapsing take place? In the case of West Ruvu–East Ruvu–Lugulu–Seuta/Langi–West Tanzania/Sabaki–Pare–Saghala it does not matter again, for if one takes the single highest figure (41.25) for Langi–West Tanzania/Sabaki–Pare–Saghala and combines them, the next candidate is still West Ruvu–East Ruvu–Lugulu–Seuta, so we collapse all at the same time. At this point this super-group, the North East (NE) is weak – external high 41; internal average 40.75.

All this leads to Table 2:5. The highest single figure in Table 2:5(a) is South Highlands–Kilombero and collapsing them would lead to (b). But (b) is not justified, for to be able to clearly state the position of any group it is necessary to have compared it to all surrounding groups, and this we have not done for Kilombero–South Highlands. To the south and especially the southwest of them, we have done no in-depth investigation: our only figures show that the internal average for Kilombero–Southern Highlands is lower than the external high for Nyakyusa–Southern Highlands (43.5). Therefore, at this point, we drop Kilombero–Southern Highlands, to give (c).

However, Table 2:5(a) makes it clear that all the figures for Lacustrine are significantly lower than those between the North East, Chaga–Davida, and Thagicu, so it would seem natural to combine the latter, giving (d). That is, we are left with two enormous groups, which are justified on the basis of the figures that we have.

But we do not have all possible figures. Lacustrine probably is open to the west: the North East, on the basis of phonology and the few figures that we have, may well go further south, through Kilombero and Southern Highlands, into Zambia. If we had all the figures available, the membership of Lacustrine might be expanded, but it seems to us unlikely that its unity would be destroyed. On the other hand, the inclusion of further material from the south may well affect the uniting of the North East with Chaga/Davida and Thagicu, since Chaga–Davida and Thagicu probably would show low figures to material from the south. So we would prefer to leave the North East, Chaga–Davida, and Thagicu uncombined, even though the present figures justify their combinations.

In that case the four groups of Table 2:5(c) are the best representation of what can be said in the present state of knowledge.

3.0 *Interpretation of Results*

Proponents of lexicostatistics would say that the figures principally reflect underlying genetic/historical relatedness. The classical tree model assumes a proto-community gradually developing dialects, either through one section of the community moving away, or for a variety of internal reasons. At this first point one would expect to find some diversity in the lexicon. The process of dissolution continues, and dialects become lan-

Table 2:5 Lexical Cognation between Languages (Final Stages)

(a)
	Lacustrine	North–East	South Highlands	Kilombero	Chaga/Davida	Thagicu	
Lacustrine	(39.25)	29.75 (40.75)	25.25 35.5 (53.25)	25.0 34.0 40.0 (51.5)	27.75 37.75 25.75 28.0 (44.5)	29.75 34.5 23.5 25.75 37.75 (62.75)	Lacustrine North–East South Highlands Kilombero Chaga/Davida Thagicu

(b)
	Lacustrine	North–East	South Highlands/ Kilombero	Chaga/Davida	Thagicu	
Lacustrine	(39.25)	29.75 (40.75)	25.25 34.75 (40)	27.75 37.75 27.0 (44.5)	29.75 34.5 24.75 37.75 (62.75)	Lacustrine North–East South Highlands Chaga/Davida Thagicu

(c)
	Lacustrine	North–East	Chaga–Davida	Thagicu
Lacustrine	(39.25)	29.75 (40.75)	27.75 37.75 (44.5)	29.75 34.5 37.75 (62.75)
				Lacustrine North–East Chaga–Davida Thagicu

(d)
	Lacustrine	Chaga/Davida– Thagicu–North East
Lacustrine	(39.75)	29.0 (36.75)
		Lacustrine Chaga/Davida– Thagicu–North East

guages. Exactly where the line between dialect and language comes is not clear, especially in an area such as Africa, where the classical definitions do not work. There, mutual intelligibility is relative in dozens, or even hundreds of tongues within five hundred miles; as all of them are, or were until recently, unwritten, the notion of dialect as an unwritten form does not work; also the association with a national state does not obtain. At the language stage the lexical diversity is greater, and as languages progress through time and space, the diversity increases. Lexicostatistics provides a means of quantifying this diversity. By taking 'standard' vocabulary in well-known languages whose ancestor was also well-known and could be placed in time, Swadesh and his followers could work out an average rate of loss through the centuries. This was amenable to cross-checking with other known families, so that the average rate could be assumed to have universal validity and be applied to groups or families whose ancestry could not be timed by other methods. All this is well-known but not always widely accepted. One of the reservations lies in the notion of "average rate of loss", any average presupposing highs and lows. While accepting the general validity of lexicostatistics as reflecting loss of common vocabulary through the centuries – indeed that is the assumption underlying our survey – we are interested in the facts which affect the rate of loss, and disturb the figures. We are particularly interested in the kinds of borrowing that take place, as evidenced in our survey. Ideally, we ought to take all the specific situations where disturbance has obviously occurred, go through the 400 words and isolate what exactly is causing the disturbance. Although this would be worthwhile, we will limit ourselves to more general observations within the framework of this chapter. Based on this survey it is possible to isolate four types of disturbance, all having to do in some way with influencing and borrowing. It is not suggested that these take place independently of each other, but we separate them for analytical purposes.

3.1 *Long Range Influence*

Ignoring the degree of similarity due to genetic factors, it can be seen to be almost universally true that any language or group in our survey bears a relationship to its neighbours proportional to distance: regardless of genetic origins, near neighbours tend to show a slightly higher figure than more distant groups. It follows that any group entirely surrounded by Bantu speaking neighbours will have slightly higher overall figures than languages/groups such as Pokomo, Luhya, or Thagicu, which partly abut on non-Bantu speaking groups. The most obvious example of this is West Tanzania as a group, almost completely surrounded at present by other Bantu groups; all its figures are over 30 (on our scale). Chaga shows a similar phenomenon – the figures for distant groups, such as the Southern Highlands, Kilombero, and Lacustrine, are all below 30, rising over 30 as distance decreases, up to around 40 for neighbours such as Pare. Why? It must be assumed the languages in question have been in position for at least several centuries, more in some cases, and that these slightly higher figures reflect factors associated with this distribution: constant absorption of numbers of population from other Bantu speaking groups, intermarriage, mutual trading contact, domination of one group by another at some point in the past, common exposure to non-Bantu speaking groups, etc. Even though we tried to ensure that our figures reflected only cognation (by having carefully worked out sound correspondences) and therefore genetic relationship, it is evident that some words may slip through, and it is difficult to see how to prevent this. Using our scale, distortions of up to 10% result from this kind of contact – 10%, that is, from the figure in the high twenties which is assumed to be the figure obtaining between any two languages having nothing other than East "Bantuness" in common.

3.2 Short Range Intensive Influence

Particular members of groups, or small groups in their entirety, can be leaned on heavily by often adjacent, though not always larger, groups. Many such cases can be identified from the appendices. The most obvious are:

3.2.1 Davida—Saghala

This is popularly known as 'Taita,' although we identify Davida as an outside member of Chaga, and Saghala as a distant relative of Sabaki, Pare, etc. Davida's figure with Saghala is 62.25, whereas Chaga's figures with Saghala range between 36 and 43, the average being 38.5. Similarly, the figures for the other languages to which Saghala is connected genetically never exceed 43 with Davida. Although the numbers of contemporary Davida speakers far exceed those of Saghala, with the expectation that therefore Davida would have influenced Saghala (which is indeed borne out by the phonology), the figures indicate that the influence has been mutual, presumably because the two groups have been intermingling for centuries, with a resultant distortion of over 20% more than the average of their two groups.

3.2.2 Suguti—Kerewe

Although Suguti is a very small group itself (totalling a little over 200,000 speakers according to the 1967 census), and has been much influenced by the three big groups around it – Rutara, East Nyanza, and West Tanzania – it has influenced Kerewe (population 50,000 +) heavily. Kerewe's figure to Suguti is 62.5; whereas, the average for the group to which Kerewe belongs, Rutara, is only 45.75 (excluding Kerewe itself) to Suguti, a distortion of more than 15% from the group average.

3.2.3 Doe/Kwere—Zigula/Bondei

North and east of Dar es Salaam a strange situation obtains. The Zigula (nearly 200,000) and the Bondei (nearly 50,000) have had much interaction with the Doe (nearly 15,000) and the Kwere (nearly 50,000). On the surface one could tend to judge from present population figures and assume that bigger groups (Zigula, Bondei) would tend to influence smaller (Kwere, Doe), but this does not seem to be the case. Doe (see

Krapf, 1968: 392), and, to a lesser extent, Kwere, have heavily influenced Seuta, especially Zigula, and, to a lesser extent, Bondei. Likewise Zigula, and to a lesser degree, Bondei, have heavily influenced East Ruvu, especially Doe, and to a lesser extent, Kwere. The Doe and the Kwere must have been more influenctial in the past than their present numbers indicate.

3.2.4 *Sumbwa–Southern Rutara*

Sumbwa shows an anomalous pattern of relationships. Not only are its own figures to its group neighbours, Nyamwezi and Sukuma, much lower than they are to each other, but also its figures to Southern Rutara are too high, indicating pressure by Southern Rutara on Sumbwa. Sumbwa's figure to Haya is 49.5, but the groups to which they belong average 37 (excluding Haya/Sumbwa), individual figures going as low as 30.5, a distortion of more than 12% above the group average.

3.2.5 *Sumbwa*

Sumbwa has also been distorted by the Western Highlands: the average figure for West Tanzania to the Western Highlands is 37.75 (excluding Sumbwa figures), but Sumbwa to Shubi, for example, is 48.75. Comparison of the other individual figures suggests that it is the Western Highlands which has influenced Sumbwa, not vice versa. Our figures would therefore suggest that Sumbwa has suffered from both Haya (and probably Zinza as well) and Western Highlands, but the distortion is proportionally greater from Haya.

3.2.6 *Gwere/Soga–Saamia (Luhya)*

The average for North Nyanza – Luhya is 42, individual figures going as low as 33, but Soga – Saamia is 52.5 (and Gwere – Saamia 51.5), a distortion of over 10% from the average. Again, comparison of the individual figures would indicate that it is Soga and Gwere which have influenced Saamia, and, to a lesser extent, Masaaba.

3.2.7 *Gogo–Sangu/Hehe*

The average for West Ruvu to the Southern Highlands is 42.75, individual figures going down to 38, but Gogo–Sango/Hehe is 50.5, 8% over the average. Comparison of the other group figures indicates that it is principally the Gogo who have influenced the Hehe and Sango; to a lesser extent the Hehe have influenced the Gogo.

The factors at work in type B are doubtless the same as those in type A, but with a higher rate of intermingling and intermarriage and considerable bilingualism. The result is a further distortion over the possible distortion already brought about by type A: more than 20% in the first example above, down to 8% over group averages in the last example, but also much lower, as can be seen in many cases by examining the tables. As a rough standard of comparison with well-known events, the celebrated Ngoni invasions in Southern Tanzania in the nineteenth century have left almost no trace in the present day vocabulary of the groups affected by it.

THE BANTU LANGUAGES OF EAST AFRICA

3.3 *Mutual Support by Adjoining Dialects*

It can be seen in many dialect situations that dialects are mutually supporting, be they linear, like Swahili or Chaga, or otherwise. Adjacent dialects tend to be slightly more similar to each other than to more distant ones. When a language protocommunity splits up into dialects, the rate of change presumably is slowed down by the constant proximity of, and interchange with, neighbouring dialects (although this seems self-evident, there is very little objective measurement to support it). Speakers of such dialects are very aware of the differences between them, but at the same time, vocabulary, both new and old, passes easily from one dialect to another.

3.4 *Moving Away*

When a group moves away from the main community, it not only loses the day to day support of the surrounding dialects, but it also comes in contact with new groups and new vocabulary. At the same time, of course, the main community is subject to influences different from the émigrés. The result is a considerable drop in the figures between the émigrés and their old community, and often a compensatory rise in the figures for the émigrés and their new neighbours. A case of drop alone is the Swahili dialect of Ngazija; examples of drop and compensatory rise are Taveta, both 'Taita' dialects, Gweno, Daiso, and Kerewe. In the case of Sonjo, Gusii, Langi, and the Swahili dialect of Mwiini, one sees the drop but not the rise in our figures, since the new neighbours were not Bantu speaking.

4.0 *Some Historical Implications*

The application of the methodology to the figures in Appendix 2:A implies the existence of four large groups of Bantu speaking peoples in East Africa. They are what we have called Lacustrine, the North East, Thagicu, and Chaga.

4.1 *The Lacustrine Group*

A *Lacustrine*, with upwards of 16,000,000 speakers (depending on the exact population figures for Rwanda and Burundi) and an internal average (IA) 39.25, has three subdivisions:

A1 *Luhya*, IA 51.5, has a figure which is low in view of the rather trivial fact that the group is implicitly considered a unity by the assigning of the name Luhya. Our figures would indicate a northern Luhya (Masaaba and Saamia, IA 61.5), and a southern Luhya (Logooli and Isuxa, IA 69.75). But both the low internal consistency and the north/south split may be the result of our having compared only two rather northern and two southern dialects. The inclusion of information from central dialects might have produced a three way division, but would probably not have raised the internal average appreciably. The low overall internal average probably is the result of lexical interference from Luo and Teso, but this assumption would need to be verified by in-depth examination of specific vocabulary.

Without providing an explicit basis for their divisions, Guthrie (1971: 45) and Whiteley (1974:21) both see a two way split between Logooli, which is considered a part of East Nyanza (an error in our opinion), and all the other dialects, which are felt to be coordinate. Ladefoged (1971), using a number of explicit criteria, does not consider any of the Kenya dialects, but finds that Saamia/Gwe, Masaaba, and Nyole are coordinate branches of a group called Eastern Uganda (as opposed to Western Uganda); he then states "that it is actually not altogether clear that there are two distinct groups within Uganda" (Ladefoged et al, 1971:72).'

The most thorough examination is that of Bennett (1972), who uses phonological isoglosses and comes to a tripartite division – Northern (Gisu, Masaaba, and Bukusu), Southern (Isuxa, Idaxo, and Logooli), and Central – which comprises all the intervening dialects. This is argued at some length and would not necessarily contradict our findings, since we examined dialects mainly from his Northern and Southern divisions.

As Appendix 2:B shows, the northern dialects, especially Saamia, historically have come under some pressure from Soga and Gwere.

A2 *East Nyanza/Suguti*, IA 45, consists of the following:

A2.1 *East Nyanza*, IA 51.5, is split into Gusii on the one hand and all the other languages on the other – Kuria, Ngurimi, Zanaki, Shashi, Ikizu Nata, and one or two other smaller groups. The internal average of the non-Gusii set is 74.75, obviously much higher than the figure including Gusii. The latter has one of the most interfered with vocabularies in East Africa – we were struck time and again by the fact that Gusii had lexical items which appeared in no other Bantu language in East Africa; an in-depth comparison with Luo, Nandi, Kipsigis, etc. to determine patterns of influence would be worthwhile. Ehret (1974:24ff and 82ff) also suggests Cushitic influence. Inclusion of Gusii in comparisons with other groups invariably lowered the overall figure for East Nyanza.

A2.2 *Suguti*, IA 81.5, comprising Jita, Kwaya, Ruri, and Regi, is a very homogenous set.

Examination of comparative material for East Nyanza/Suguti with surrounding groups reveals some surprising facts. Both show high figures with Sukuma/Nyamwezi, but the figures would indicate that the influencing has been mutual; consider the figures:

	NN	Luhya	Rutara (excl. Sumbwa)	EN	Suguti
West Tanzania	33.5	34.5	37	43	40.25

where the West Tanzania figures to East Nyanza/Suguti are significantly higher (6 percent average) than to the other figures for Lacustrine, indicating pressure from West Tanzania on East Nyanza/Suguti. But when the opposite is considered, e.g.

	Sukuma/Nyamwezi	Kimbu/Nyaturu/Nilyamba
East Nyanza	46.5	39.5 (difference 7%)
	45.75	37.5 (difference 8%)

THE BANTU LANGUAGES OF EAST AFRICA   43

it can be seen that the East Nyanza/Suguti figures are higher to Sukuma/Nyamwezi than to Kimbu/Nyaturu/Nilyamba, and of much the same order as the influence of Sukuma/Nyamwezi on East Nyanza/Suguti. This mutual raising would imply a period of prolonged and intense contact, reasonable given that the Sukuma adjoin both East Nyanza and Suguti. But in view of the fact that at present Sukuma/Nyamwezi is an enormous group, with a present population of around 2,000,000, whereas Suguti is only about 200,000, and East Nyanza in Tanzania and Kenya between 750,000 and 1,000,000, it would seem that formerly East Nyanza/Suguti were larger and more influential than they are now, since it is usually the larger and more prestigious groups that do the influencing (see section 3:2 above). This would imply that East Nyanza/Suguti have declined in size and influence, whereas Sukuma/Nyamwezi have increased, which would be supported both by what is known of recent history and by the fact that Sukuma/Nyamwezi as a block is relatively homogenous, which is one of the linguistic signs of recent expansion. Both East Nyanza and Suguti show a high degree of correlation, probably the result of a mixture of genetic factors and influence, with other neighbours – East Nyanza slightly with Luhya, Suguti with Rutara (Kerewe of course excessively high, 62.5) and the Western Highlands, which are geographically quite distant. Additionally, both exhibit the results of a degree of interaction with Thagicu, which, although of a much lower order than the foregoing, is significantly higher than that of the other lake groups (Luhya, North Nyanza, Rutara) to Thagicu.

This complicated pattern of interaction has led other linguists to various conclusions. Guthrie and, following him, Whiteley, and others, saw a picture which embraced Rutara, North Nyanza, Suguti, East Nyanza, Luhya, Thagicu, Chaga, Taita, and the Miji Kenda as coordinate members of one enormous block, Guthrie's Zone E, which has little basis other than geographical.

Ehret links East Nyanza/Suguti with Luhya to form what he calls East Victoria, separate from other lake groups on the one side, from Thagicu to the east, and from West Tanzania in the south.

While recognising the complexity of this whole area, our view would be that Suguti/East Nyanza form part of the Lacustrine block which extends west into Rwanda and Burundi, the whole picture being later complicated by the influence of non-Bantu speaking groups, Bantu speaking immediate neighbours, general waves of interaction which lapped around the lake, and also pressure from the south.

A3 *Interlacustrine*, IA 43.75, is formed of three subgroups which also have been held by others in the past to form a unity – Rutara, North Nyanza, and the Western Highlands.

A3.1 *Rutara*, IA 66.5, is much closer to North Nyanza (49), Western Highlands (47.75), and Suguma (45.75), than to East Nyanza (37.75) or Luhya (37.5). The internal average would be 71.5 were it not for Kerewe, which has much lower intragroup figures due to pressure from Suguti. Virtually all other previous commentators have felt these languages (Nyoro, Tooro, Nyankore, Ciga, Nyambo, Zinza, Haya, and Kerewe) to form a unity, but there has not always been agreement about external allegiance; Guthrie (1971:44–5), for example, puts the Western Highlands in his Zone D, but lumps Rutara, North Nyanza, Suguti, etc. in Zone E.

Judging by Ladefoged's (1971:74) figures, Sese, Nabuddu, Kooki, and Naziba, would also form part of this group.

A3.2 *North Nyanza*, IA 66, included, for our figures, Ganda, Soga, and Gwere, but Ladefoged's (1971:71) figures would indicate that Lamogi, Siki, Diope, Vuma, and Kenyi, also belong here. All previous works have felt these languages to have an internal unity, but disagree about their external connections. Guthrie (1971:44) by putting them at the beginning of Zone E, implies a connection with Rutara, Suguti, Luhya, etc., and, for Ladefoged (1971: 69ff) they combine with Luhya to form part of "Eastern Uganda". Our figures indicate that North Nyanza's highest allegiance, by a considerable margin, is with Rutara, which, in turn, is linked clearly with the Western Highlands.

A3.3 *Western Highlands*, IA 73. Considering the number of speakers involved probably is upwards of 8,000,000, this internal average is high and presumably implies historically a recent and rapid expansion. This is a homogenous group, and its unity has not been denied by previous writers. Its allegiance, for us, is with Rutara, followed by Suguti, which is surprising given the distance separating them. Guthrie (1971:44–5) separates Western Highlands from Rutara, etc. – thus implicitly rejecting the notion of a lacustrine group including them – and puts them with other languages spoken mainly in Zaire. We cannot deny or support this idea, for we did not deal with data from any of these languages; it is possible that this whole group, which we have called Lacustrine, is open-ended and may in fact extend further west and south. When new languages or groups are added in this method, it frequently upsets the internal ordering, but less often does it destroy the unity of a whole group.

4.2 *The North East Group*

The North East, IA 40.75, has approximately 6,000,000 speakers, using the 1967 Tanzanian census. As the previous group, its shape implies historically a body of people moving north and east from a point in the west or southwest. It falls into three subgroups: Western Tanzania (WT – including Langi), Greater Ruvu (Seuta, West Ruvu, Lugulu, and East Ruvu), and the Coast (Sabaki, Pare, and Saghala), but this division needs some comment. There is little disagreement about the unity of Greater Ruvu, as the figures speak for themselves (IA 47.25). Recent writers, for example, Hinnebusch (1976:99) see its unity; it is implied by Guthrie (1971:49) and speakers of the languages involved agree there is much similarity. But there is disagreement about the relationship of Greater Ruvu to what we have called the Coast. Both Ehret and Hinnebusch (1976:100) feel that Greater Ruvu and Sabaki form a close unity, and Hinnebusch includes Saghala. Ehret bases his opinion on the evidence of loanwords, whereas Hinnebusch uses phonological isoglosses. Undoubtedly phonological isoglosses in the shape of the way Proto-

Bantu consonants are treated would indicate an underlying unity between Greater Ruvu, Sabaki, Saghala, Pare – and quite possibly Kilombero and the Southern Highlands as well. However, the exigencies of our method dictate that the unity is not so close, mainly because of the presence of Pare and Saghala. Saghala's highest figure by far is with the other so-called 'dialect' of 'Taita' (62.5). For a combination of reasons having to do with phonology and verbal morphology (cf. Hinnebusch, 1976:108 and Nurse, 1978a: chaps 3 and 4), it is likely that Taita as a historical unity cannot be maintained, and that Davida is an offshoot of Chaga, whereas the allegiance of Saghala is to be sought elsewhere. We therefore ignored the Davida-Saghala figure and treated Davida as part of Chaga, leaving Saghala isolated. It might have been preferable to ignore Saghala altogether at this point, but we wanted to include it so as to arrive at some classification for it. The result of this decision is that Sabaki has a higher statistical relationship to Pare and Saghala than to Greater Ruvu. When Sabaki, Pare, and Saghala are combined as the Coast, then it is found that the Coast, Greater Ruvu (GR), and West Tanzania/Langi (WTL) are roughly equidistant statistically: WTL–GR 41, WTL–Coast 41.25, GR–Coast 39.75. It would be possible either to treat these three figures serially – WTL–Coast, then WTL/Coast–GR – or simultaneously, and we chose the latter on grounds that the difference in the three figures was small. Either way, the Coast would not combine primarily with Greater Ruvu. This three-way division would not accord with divisions made on the basis of, for example, historical phonology, which would indicate that Pare–Saghala–Sabaki–Greater Ruvu are very similar, but West Tanzania/Langi are more peripheral. It also should be pointed out that, as for the Lacustrine group, this whole block is open-ended in the southwest. Whereas, from preliminary investigations using a 100 word list and an examination of historical phonology, the languages to the south and southeast, south of the Ruaha/Rufiji Rivers (Rufiji, Matumbi, Ngindo, Makonde, Yao, Mpoto, Matengo, etc. – Guthrie's N10, M20, P20, P30) seem to be quite distant from the groups under discussion, this is not necessarily true of groups in Southwestern Tanzania, and presumably into Zambia (Guthrie's M10, M20, M30). Until we have examined all these languages, it is impossible to pronounce on the position of the Southern Highlands and Kilombero, and to say whether the North East extends into Zambia. The lexicostatistical figures connecting Kilombero and the Southern Highlands to the North East are not very impressive, which is reasonable in view of the distances involved, but these languages have dealt with Proto–Bantu consonants in a way very similar to the North East. It is therefore possible that the North-East might extend to the Southern Highlands and Kilombero, and that this massive block might stretch further into the southwest. The inclusion of the Southern Highlands and Kilombero would fit with what Ehret has called Pela, in which he also includes languages to the southeast, a decision with which we would not agree. We wish to emphasize that this possible southward extension is at the moment hypothetical from our point of view.

B1 *The Coast*, IA 44.75, consists of Sabaki, Saghala, and Pare.

B1.1 *Sabaki*, IA 59.5, consists of Pokomo, the Miji Kenda, and Swahili, for which the data came from four Swahili dialects: Southern Pokomo, Giryama/Chonyi, and Digo/Segeju. The Swahili dialects (IA 79.25) and the Miji Kenda (IA 71.25) are homogenous and fall together first (IA 64.75), Pokomo being more peripheral, doubtless due to interference from Galla. We examined, but did not include, data from Northern Pokomo, and this has suffered even more than the southern dialect from Galla. The figures for Pokomo and the northern Swahili dialects (Amu, Bajun) are not higher than those for Pokomo and the southern Swahili dialects, indicating a lack of historical contacts between northern Swahili and Pokomo. The figures between Giryama/Chonyi and Saghala, and to a lesser extent between the southern Miji Kenda (Digo and Segeju) and Saghala, are higher than those for Saghala and the rest of Sabaki, indicating historical contacts and reinforcing the ancestral unity. This is true to a lesser extent for Pare and the Miji Kenda. There also has been heavy contact between Seuta and southern Swahili/Miji Kenda.

B1.2 Apart from the misleading Davida figure, *Saghala's* highest figures are with the northern Miji Kenda (49.25).

B1.3 *Pare*. There is very little difference between north and south Pare, and between Pare and Taveta. Considerations of phonology, especially nasal clusters, would indicate that ki–Taveta originated from North Pare. Aside from its underlying unity with other Coastal languages, Pare has had significant historical contact with Gweno (49), Seuta (49), Langi (45.25), Davida (43), Chaga (42.25), and Thagicu (38).

B2 *Greater Ruvu* (IA 47.25) falls into West Ruvu (IA 58.25) on the one hand, and Seuta, East Ruvu, and Lugulu (IA 50.75) on the other.

B2.1 *West Ruvu* is rather disparate, for it comprises only three languages (possibly Vidunda, for which we had no data). The figures indicate above average contact between Gogo and Sangu (50.5), Gogo and Hehe (50.5), Gego and Kimbu (47.75), Gogo and Nilyamba (45.5), and between Kagulu and East Ruvu/Seuta, though it is also possible to interpret the latter as the result of underlying genetic unity.

B2.2.1 *Lugulu*, although falling in with East Ruvu, then East Ruvu/Seuta, and then with West Ruvu as well, stands out by the uniqueness of its vocabulary.

B2.2.2 *East Ruvu* (IA 65.5). Doe is very similar to Kwere, and Kutu to Kami. Above average figures indicate historical contacts between East Ruvu and Kagulu (56, but see B2.2.1), Southern Swahili (52), between Kwere and Zigula (62), and especially between Doe and Zigula (69.75), the latter to the point where it is almost a toss up, on lexicostatistical grounds, whether to include Doe with East Ruvu or Seuta. But apart from its connection with Kwere, which validates its inclusion in East Ruvu, there also are structural reasons for this inclusion.

B2.2.3 *Seuta* (IA 71.25), falls into Shambala/Bondei and Zigula/Ngulu, the latter being, by any criterion, dialects. Bondei (as Doe) has undergone very heavy interference from Swahili. Figures for Shambala are slightly higher than the rest of the group for Saghala, Davida, Pare, but the rest of the group is considerably higher than Shambala in their figures to Langi,

THE BANTU LANGUAGES OF EAST AFRICA   47

West Ruvu, Lugulu, and East Ruvu. Apart from the normal tendency of adjacent languages to show somewhat higher figures due to contact, Shambala seems to have been subject, at some point in the past, to more deviation from its inherited lexicon than other members of the group and from a source other than Ma'a. The whole group shows an above average relationship with the Miji Kenda and southern Swahili (53.5) and with Kagulu (53.25); it is not clear whether the latter is the result of a special relationship with Kagulu or depression of the Gogo and Sagala figures due to interference from other languages. Zigula and Bondei have particularly high figures with Doe (average 66.75).

B.3 *West Tanzania/Langi* (WTL), IA 47, is a disparate group indicating either considerable antiquity as a group, or considerable distortion from non-members of the group. Sukuma/Nyamwezi, on the other hand, given their huge numbers but great similarity, could either be explained by recent very rapid expansion or by having maintained remarkable cohesion as a group: what is known of their recent history would seem to favour the former. It also should be noticed from the tables that this group is unique in that, with one minor exception, all the figures for this group are over 30 to members of other groups. Other groups tend to distinguish between their relatives and neighbours, on one side, and remaining groups, usually in the twenties, on the other. Why should this group alone lessen the differentiation? Without detailed analysis of the particular vocabulary involved, one can only speculate. Guthrie (1971:48) probably would attribute it to the fact that this group contains languages (Sukuma) which are part of his nuclear group and so manifest a high rate of retention; since, in *Comparative Bantu*, he puts Kimbu, Nilyamba, Nyaturu, in an immediate relationship with Sukuma/Nyamwezi, they presumably could also be expected to show this high rate of retention. We share Greenberg's view of this idea of a nuclear area, namely, that if one wishes to posit the origins of the Bantu speaking people in the area where the languages are spoken showing the highest rate of retention, it is tantamount to seeing Iceland as the center of the Proto-Germanic area. A modified, but more acceptable, version of Guthrie's view would be to say that this area has been less subject to lexical contamination than other areas in East Africa, but this would need examination. Another possibility would be quite the opposite: because of its central position, this group has maintained constant contact with its neighbours, and this usually results in higher figures. Many of the other groups in East Africa are not subject to compatible influences from all sides, because they adjoin stretches of water or non-Bantu speaking groups or, as in the south, Bantu speaking groups which are more remote linguistically.

B3.1 *Langi* consists of Langi and Mbugwe. We did not have a chance to examine the latter, but from the few bits of information available, from what local people say, and from the little that previous linguists have said, there seems little doubt that Langi and Mbugwe are very closely related. Langi has been interfered with heavily by non-Bantu groups surrounding it, demonstrably by Cushites, possibly by Khoisan, not tangibly by Nilotes. It is anomalous in that its vocabulary, regarded through lexicostatistics, is peripherally more similar to West Tanzania, but its verbal system resembles the Ruvu languages much more.

B3.2 *West Tanzania* (IA 52), falls into two: Sumbwa/Sukuma/Nyamwezi (IA 60.25) and Nilyamba/Nyaturu/Kimbu (IA 57.25).

B3.2.1 *Sukuma/Nyamwezi* (IA 84.5) are dialects, having the same relationship to each other as, for example, the two Meru dialects in Kenya (84.75). We could doubtless have chosen two less similar dialects of each for comparison, but also perhaps two more similar. Figures for Sukuma/Nyamwezi/Sumbwa are significantly higher than Nilyamba/Nyaturu/Kimbu with members of North Nyanza, East Nyanza, Suguti, Rutara, and Western Highlands; Kimbu's position is less clear as we do not have enough figures for it. As this group's ancestral allegiance is with languages to the east, the higher figures with Lacustrine languages must be the result of much contact with them during preceding centuries.

Sumbwa, as mentioned before, is a disturbed language. Not only is it considerably less similar to Sukuma/Nyamwezi than they are to each other, but also its figures to both Rutara and Western Highlands are high, indicating massive interference from them at some point in the past.

B3.2.2 Although *Nilyamba/Nyaturu* (IA 63.5) show lower figures than Sukuma/Nyamwezi/Sumbwa to Lacustrine languages, they do not show higher figures to any other single group in our survey, nor are they very similar to each other. This would indicate the possibility of little contact with other Bantu speaking groups and distortion deriving from interference from non-Bantu speaking groups.

Kimbu figures indicate interference from West Ruvu.

The whole of West Tanzania seems to have exerted some pressure on Gogo.

It should be borne in mind that this group is possibly open-ended in the west.

4.3 *The Thagicu*

Thagicu (IA 67.75) has a present population of approximately 5,000,000. We did not include Sonjo or Daiso in this comparison for lack of sufficient data – their inclusion certainly would have lowered the overall internal average (nor was Tharaka included). Our figures indicate a three-way split: Kikuyu/Embu/Cuka (IA 72.25), Meru (Tigania to Imenti 84.75), and Kamba, for which we had data for Machakos and Kitwi, but did not work out an internal average on the assumption that they would clearly be more similar to each other than to anyone else. For Daiso, phonological considerations would indicate its particular relatedness to Kamba, but this is not borne out by use of a 100 word list, where it shows a fairly constant relation to all the main Thagicu languages. Sonjo is somewhat clearer in that both phonological and lexicostatistical considerations would indicate its affinity to Kikuyu/Embu/Cuka. The figures also indicate that Sonjo split off some time before Daiso.

Bennett (1967:131) also sees a three-way split of Thagicu (using different criteria), but with Chuka/Mwimbi belonging with Meru rather than Kikuyu/Embu.

THE BANTU LANGUAGES OF EAST AFRICA

Table 2:6

(a) A *LACUSTRINE (IA 39.75)*

A1 *LUHYA (51.5)*

N. LUHYA (61.5)	S. LUHYA (69.75)
Saamia	Isuxa
Masaaba	Logooli
etc.	etc.

A2 *E. NYANZA/SUGUTI (45)*

A2.1 *E. NYANZA (51.5)*		A2.2 *SUGUTI (81.5)*
		Jita
(74.75)	Gusii	Kwaya
Kuria		Ruri
Ngurimi		Regi
Suba		
Ikizu		
Shashi		
Zanaki		
Nata		
etc.		

A3 *INTERLACUSTRINE (43.75)*

A3.2 *N. NYANZA* (66)	A3.1 *RUTARA* (66.5)	A3.3 *W. HIGHLANDS* (73)
Ganda	Nyoro	Rwanda
Gwere	Tooro	Rundi
Soga	Nyankore	Shubi
etc.	Ciga	Hangaza
	Nyambo	Ha
	Haya	Vinza
	Zinza	
	Kerewe	
	etc.	

LANGUAGES OF TANZANIA

(b) B. NORTH EAST (IA 40.75)

```
       B3  W. TANZANIA/LANGI              B1  COAST (44.75)
           (47)


                    B3.1            B1.3        B1.2
                    LANGI           PARE        SAGHALA
                    Langi
                    Mbugwe
                                                    B1.1  SABAKI
                                                          (59.5)
           B3.2  W. TANZANIA (52)


B3.2.1 S/S/N    N/N/K                               POKOMO
      (60.25)   (57.25)                             S. Pokomo
                                                    N. Pokomo
                Kimbu
                      B3.2.2 Nyaturu-
                             Nilyamba (63.5)   MIJI KENDA/
Sumbwa (84.5)         Nyaturu                  SWAHILI (64.75)
       Sukuma         Nilyamba
       Nyamwezi       Isanzu
                      Nyambi
                                   MIJI KENDA        SWAHILI
                                   (71.25)           (79.25)

                                   NMK      SMK      (Mwiini)
                                   Giryama  Digo     (Ngazija)
                                   Conyi    Segeju   Tikuu = Bajuni
                    B2  GREATER RUVU   Rabai         Mvita
                        (47.25)        etc.          Mrima
                                                     Unguja
                                                     etc.

   B2.1 West RUVU       (50.75)
        (58.25)
        Gogo
        Kagulu
        Sagulu
        (Vidunda ?)   B2.2.1   B2.2.2
                      Lugulu   EAST RUVU (65.5)
                                                  B2.2.3 SEUTA (71.25)
                               Kutu
                               Kami               Shambala
                               Zalamo             Bondei
                               Kwere              Zigula
                               Doe                Ngulu
```

THE BANTU LANGUAGES OF EAST AFRICA 51

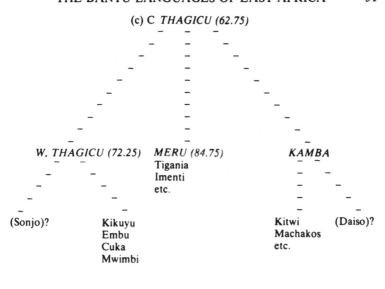

(c) C *THAGICU (62.75)*

W. *THAGICU (72.25)* *MERU (84.75)* KAMBA
                       Tigania
                       Imenti
                       etc.

(Sonjo)?   Kikuyu   Kitwi   (Daiso)?
           Embu   Machakos
           Cuka   etc.
           Mwimbi

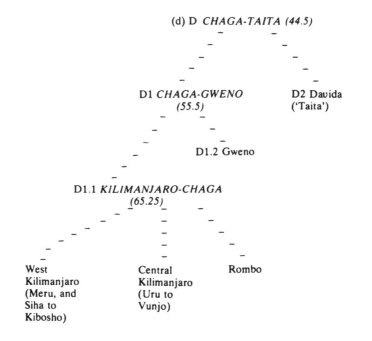

(d) D *CHAGA-TAITA (44.5)*

D1 *CHAGA-GWENO*   D2 Davida
     (55.5)   ('Taita')

              D1.2 Gweno

D1.1 *KILIMANJARO-CHAGA*
        (65.25)

West   Central   Rombo
Kilimanjaro   Kilimanjaro
(Meru, and   (Uru to
Siha to   Vunjo)
Kibosho)

No observer ever doubted the internal unity of the Thagicu block but opinions have varied about its external allegiances, with some observers having suggested a connection to interlacustrine languages, particularly East Nyanza and Suguti, and others talking of connections to Sabaki, etc. Our figures do not support the ancestral connection of Thagicu to any other East African group, but suggest some historical contact with Saghala (39), Pare (38), Chaga and Davida (average 37.75), Sabaki (36), West Tanzania/Langi (35.5), East Nyanza (35.25, but higher without Gusii – 37.5), Seuta (36), and particular contact between Kamba and Rombo, Davida, Saghala, Pare, and the Miji Kenda.

4.4 The Chaga–Davida Group

Chaga–Davida (IA 43.5), has a population of 700,000 plus. We did not have any information for Arusha Chini, which is said to be a Chaga dialect, and only enough vocabulary for use of the 100 word list on Kahe, which indicates its belonging to Central Kilimanjaro. There are good phonological and structural reasons for considering Davida as historically related to Chaga (cf. Nurse, 1979a: chaps 3 and 4). On the basis of loan material, Ehret also posits a Davida–Chaga connection. But the statistics indicate that Davida's primary connection is with the other so-called "Taita" dialect, Saghala: this must be the result of longstanding mutual influence and is the best single example we have of how far lexicostatistical figures can be influenced by contact. The whole group divides into Davida (IA 55.5), the rest then·splitting into Gweno and the other three major dialects (IA 65.25), which are coordinate.

NOTES

[1] "Taita" has three dialects – Davida, Saghala and Kasigau – but as the speakers of Davida outnumber those of the other two combined by a ratio of roughly 10:1, it is clear that when we talk of 'Taita', we are basically talking about Davida. The arguments for positing a historical connection between Chaga and Davida are mainly phonological, only to a minor extent morphological and lexical.

The main phonological data to be considered are:

(1) the reflex of Proto–Bantu *t in Davida is /d/, e.g. *mdi* 'tree'. All Chaga dialects have /d/ or /r/ as reflexes of PB *t, and both can be seen as part of a voicing process which occurs nowhere else in the North East or Thagicu, and only to a minor extent in Lacustrine (in some Luhya dialects);

(2) Proto–Bantu sequences of non-syllabic nasal plus voiceless stop (e.g. in classes 9/10) are realised in Chaga and 'Taita' as nasal plus voiced stop. This occurs nowhere in the North East (except one Swahili dialect in the Comores), spottily in Thagicu, where it must be a recent development, and only to a minor extent in Lacustrine (some Luhya dialects), e.g. *mundu* 'person' *nguku* 'chicken'.

(3) Proto–Bantu *d is consistently reflected in Chaga and Davida by /r/ before the high tense vowels, but by /l/ or Ø before the other five vowels, e.g. Davida *mburi* 'goat' *nguru* 'tortoise' but *lulimi* 'tongue' -*la(l)a* 'sleep' etc. This dichotomy occurs in no other 5-vowel language in East Africa, except Langi. This can also be seen in the class 5 noun prefix before vowel stems, e.g. Swahili *jina* 'name' Davida *rina*, Chaga (*i*)*rina*.

(4) When class 10 is the plural of class 11, it can have a different prefix from class 10 as the plural of class 9. This prefix can be derived (with minor

difficulties) from *nj(i)-; it only occurs with certain nouns, which tend to be virtually the same in Chaga and Davida. The prefix in question is affixed to the entire class 11 form, and this phenomenon occurs nowhere else in East Africa, except Langi, e.g. Vunjo *ulumi* 'tongue' (sg.);
                njulumi 'tongues' (pl.);
                Davida *cwembe* 'horns' (pl);
                [PB*nj → c- in Davida]

(5) The sequence w + e is realized in Davida and certain Chaga dialects as o, e.g. Vunjo and Davida *mori* 'moon'. This form of assimilation occurs elsewhere in East Africa only in one or two languages around Lake Victoria.

When evaluating these sound shifts, it should be borne in mind that Moshi and Udawida are only 60 miles apart as the crow flies; so the correspondences are unlikely to be coincidences given the size of East Africa. They could be borrowings, but that would presuppose a lengthy period of physical contiguity, of which there are no historical traditions.

REFERENCES

Bender, M. L., 1971, 'The Languages of Ethiopia' *Anthropological Linguistics.* 13:5, 165–288.

Bennett, P. R., 1967, 'Dahl's Law in Thagicũ' *African Language Studies.* 8, 127–159

    1972, *A phonologic history of NE Victoria Bantu.* unpublished paper, (cyclostyled)

Bryan, M. A., 1959, *The Bantu Languages of Africa.* Handbook of African Languages, 4. London: Oxford University Press.

Coupez, A., 1975, 'La variabilité lexicale en bantou' *African Languages/Langues Africaines* (London: International African Institute). 1, 164–203

Ehret, C., 1970, *Southern Nilotic History.* Evanston: Northwestern University Press.

    1974, *Ethiopians and East Africans.* Nairobi: East Africa Publishing House

    1977, 'East Africa' chapter 19 in D. T. Niane (ed.), *The General History of Africa* (forthcoming).

Greenberg, J. H., 1963, *The Languages of Africa.* Mouton: The Hague.

Guthrie, M., 1971, *Comparative Bantu*, vol. 2. London: Gregg International Publishers Ltd.

Heine, B., 1974, 'Historical Linguistics and Lexicostatistics' *Journal of African Languages.* 11:3, 7–20.

Henrici, A., 1973, 'Numerical Classification of the Bantu Languages' *African Language Studies.* 14.

Hinnebusch, T. J., 1973, *Prefixes, sound change, and subgrouping in the coastal Kenyan Bantu languages.* University of California Ph. D. dissertation.

    1976, 'Swahili: Genetic affiliations and evidence' *Studies in African Linguistics*, supplement 6, 95–108.

Krapf, L., 1968, *Travels and Missionary Labours in East Africa.* London: Frank Cass and Co. (first pub. 1860).

Ladefoged, P. et al. (eds.) 1971, *Language in Uganda.* Nairobi: Oxford University Press.

Nurse, D., 1979a, *Chaga — dialects.* Hamburg: Buske.

    1979b, 'Description of Sample Bantu Languages of Tanzania' *African Languages/Langues Africaines.* 5(1).

Whiteley, W. H. (ed.), 1974, *Language in Kenya.* Nairobi: Oxford University Press.

APPENDIX 2:A INTRA-GROUP FIGURES FOR IMMEDIATE GROUPS

LUHYA

Masaaba	Isuxa	Logooli	
61.5	52.25		Saamia
	51.75	50	Masaaba
		69.75	Isuxa

Logooli–Isuxa = S. Luhya 69.75
Masaaba–Saamia = N. Luhya 61.5
N. Luhya–S. Luhya = Luhya IA 51.5

SUGUTI

Jita	Kwaya	
81.25	80	Regi
	83	Jita

Regi–Jita–Kwaya = Suguti IA 81.5

EAST NYANZA (EN)

Kuria	Zanaki	Nata	Ngurimi	
61	50	44.5	48.75	Gusii
	77.75	68.25	83.75	Kuria
		81.5	79.75	Zanaki
			73.5	Nata

Kuria–Ngurimi 83.75
Nata–Zanaki 81.5
Kuria/Ngurimi–Nata/Zanaki 74.75
Gusii–Kuria/Ngurimi/Nata/Zanaki = E. Nyanza IA 51.5

RUTARA

Tooro	Nyankore	Ciga	Nyambo	Haya	Zinza	Kerewe	
78	77.5	77.5	67.25	66.25	67.25	62.25	Nyoro
	74.75	68.5	68.25	69.5	67.5	62.75	Tooro
		83.75	78	74	80.75	68.25	Nyankore
			71.75	70	74.75	63.25	Ciga
				83.75	81	68.75	Nyambo
					78.5	75.5	Haya
						76	Zinza

Ciga–Nyankore 83.75
Haya–Nyambo 83.75
Zinza–Haya/Nyambo 80
Nyoro–Tooro 78
Nyoro/Tooro–Ciga/Nyankore/Haya/Zinza/Nyambo 71.5
Kerewe-the rest = Rutara IA 66.5

THE BANTU LANGUAGES OF EAST AFRICA 55

NORTH NYANZA (NN)

Soga	Gwere	
71.5	68.25	Ganda
	63.75	Soga

Ganda–Soga 71.5
Gwere–Ganda/Soga = N. Nyanza IA 66

WESTERN HIGHLANDS (WH)

Rundi	Shubi	Hangaza	Ha	
77	71.25	72	72	Rwanda
	77.5	83.5	78.25	Rundi
		85.25	77	Shubi
			77.5	Hangaza

Rundi–Shubi–Hangaza 82
Ha–Rundi/Shubi/Hangaza 77
Rwanda–Ha/Rundi/Shubi/Hangaza = Western Highlands IA 73

SABAKI

Giryama	Digo	Bajun	Amu	Mvita	Mrima/Unguja	
59	57.75	57.5	60.75	62.75	60.5	Pokomo (Southern)
	71.75	59	61	62.25	63	Giryama/Conyi
		61.75	67.5	70.75	70.75	Digo (=Southern MK)
			85.25	78.25	72.5	Bajun
				86	79.25	Amu
					79.25	Mvita

Bajun–Amu–Mvita–Mrima/Unguja = Swahili 79.25
Giryama/Conyi–Digo = Miji Kenda (MK) 71.25
Swahili–Miji Kenda 64.75
Swahili/Miji Kenda–Pokomo = Sabaki IA 59.5

WEST RUVU (WR)

Sagala	Kagulu	
60.5	56	Gogo
	63.5	Sagala

Gogo–Sagala–Kagulu = WR IA 58.25

SEUTA

Bondei	Zigula	Ngulu	
75.5	68	68.5	Shambala
	75	73	Bondei
		83.25	Zigula

Zigula–Ngulu 83.25
Shambala–Bondei 75.5
Zigula/Ngulu–Shambala/Bondei = Seuta IA 71.25

EAST RUVU (ER)

Kutu	Zalamo	Kwere	Doe	
69.25	65.25	69.25	64.25	Kami
	68.5	63.75	60.75	Kutu
		61.5	61	Zalamo
			73.75	Kwere

Kwere–Doe 73.75
Kutu–Kami 69.25
Zalamo–Kutu/Kami–Doe/Kwere = East Ruvu IA 65.5

WEST TANZANIA/LANGI

Sukuma	Nyamwezi	Kimbu	Nilyamba	Nyaturu	Langi	
59	61.5	48.5	45	43.75	40.5	Sumbwa
	84.5	57.5	55.5	59	49.25	Sukuma
			56.75	58	48	Nyamwezi
			61	53.25	47.25	Kimbu
				63.5	47	Nilyamba
					49.5	Nyaturu

Sukuma–Nyamwezi 84.5
Nilyamba–Nyaturu 63.5
Sumbwa–Sukuma/Nyamwezi (S/S/N) 60.25
Kimbu–Nilyamba/Nyaturu (K/N/N) 57.25
S/S/N-K/N/N 52
Langi-the rest 47

As is stated in the text, it is possible that Langi ought to be united with the rest at a non-immediate level.

THAGICU

Meru (I)	Kikuyu	Embu	Cuka	Kamba	
84.75	62.75	63.5	67	56.75	Meru (Tigania)
	62.75	65.5	67.5	58.75	Meru (Imenti)
		73.5	70.5	67.5	Kikuyu (Southern)
			73	65.75	Embu
				63	Cuka

Meru (T)–Meru (I) 84.75
Kikuyu–Embu–Cuka 72.25
Kamba–Meru–Kikuyu/Embu/Cuka = Thagicu IA 62.75

CHAGA

Central Kilimanjaro Rombo Gweno Davida

Central Kilimanjaro	Rombo	Gweno	Davida	
66.75	62.25	54.5	41.5	West Kilimanjaro (Machame) (WK)
	66.5	56.25	41.5	Central Kilimanjaro (Vunjo) (CK)
		55.75	44	Rombo (Usseri) (R)
			46.5	Gweno (G)

WK–CK–Rombo 65.25
Gweno–WK/CK/R 55.5

Davida–G/WK/CK/Rombo = Chaga IA 44.5
It is possible that Davida ought to be united to the rest at a non-immediate level.

KILOMBERO

Pogolu   *Ndamba*

56.75   69.5   Mbunga
           56   Pogolu

Ndamba–Mbunga 69.5
Pogolu–Mbunga/Ndamba = Kilombero IA 51.5

SOUTHERN HIGHLANDS (SH)

Hehe	*Bena*	*Pangwa*	*Kinga*	*Wanji*	*Kisi*	
56.25	55	58	53.75	59	52.5	Sangu
	65.5	59.25	50.25	48.5		Hehe
		70.75	53.25	51.5	47.25	Bena
			61.25	55.5	61.75	Pangwa
				55.25	54.75	Kinga
					51.5	Wanji

Bena–Pangwa 70.75
Hehe–Bena/Pangwa 62.5
Wanji–Sango 59
Hehe/Pangwa/Bena–Wanji/Sango–Kinga–Kisi = SH IA 53.25

APPENDIX 2:B INTERGROUP RAW FIGURES

This appendix only shows raw figures for intergroup comparisons where more than one comparison is involved, i.e. comparisons where the figures above are the result of an average.

It is organized as follows:

(a) each specific language of the relevant group is paired with specific languages of the target group for comparison, e.g.:

Rutara (Nyoro, Tooro, Nyankore, Ciga, Nyambo, Haya, Zinza, Kerewe) + Western Highlands

The data will be presented as follows:

(Rutara languages)	(Western Highlands languages)	(Relevant percentages)
Nyoro:	+ Rwanda	48.5
	+ Shubi	45
	+ Ha	40.5
Haya:	+ Rwanda	49.75
	+ Shubi	50
	+ Ha	45.5

(b) if only isolated languages are considered, the presentation is slightly different, e.g. Rutara + East Ruvu

(East Ruvu isolated language)   (Rutara languages, with corresponding
                                                percentages)
          Zalamo   + Nyoro 27.25
                                    + Haya 24

(c) if a subgroup as a whole is compared to isolated languages, we have e.g. (Rutara) + Langi: Haya 32 – indicating that the Rutara language Haya shows 32% lexical correspondences with Langi.

NORTH NYANZA = Ganda, Soga, Gwere

+ Luhya:	Soga+ Masaaba 44.75	Gwere+ Masaaba 46.5
Ganda+ Saamia 47.25	+ Saamia 52.5	+ Saamia 51.4
+ Isuxa 33	+ Isuxa 36	+ Isuxa 36.5
+ Logooli 38.25	+ Logooli 35.75	+ Logooli 39
11 figures, average 42		

+ East Nyanza: Ganda+ Gusii 32
                      + Kuria 40.5   Soga+ Kuria 35.5
                      + Ngurimi 35.75   + Ngurimi 32.5
   5 figures, average 35.25

+ Suguti: Suguti + Ganda 40.75, + Soga 39
   2 figures, average 40

In comparisons, Kwaya, Jita, and Regi are used indiscriminately, as they are so similar.

+ Rutara:

Ganda+ Nyoro	53	Soga+ Nyoro	46.75	Gwere+ Nyoro	46.25
+ Nyankore	53.25	+ Nyankore	48		
+ Haya	54.5	+ Haya	46.75	+ Haya	46.75
+ Kerewe	49.75	+ Kerewe	44.5		
10 figures, average 49					

EAST NYANZA
+ Langi: Kuria + Langi 38.25, Ngurimi + Langi 34.5
   2 figures, average 36.5

+ Thagicu: Embu + Gusii 30.75, + Kuria 38.5, + Ngurimi 36.5
   3 figures, average 35.25

W. H. Whiteley suggested a possible connection between Thagicu and Gusii on the basis of similarities in the verbal system; these figures render that connection unlikely.

+ Chaga: CK + Gusii 28.5, + Kuria 30.25, + Ngurimi 28.5
   3 figures, average 29

+ Dauida: + Gusii 29.5, + Ngurimi 31.5
   2 figures, average 30.5

+ West Ruvu: Kagulu + Gusii 23.5 + Ngurimi 28.75, + Zanaki 31.25
   3 figures, average 27.75

THE BANTU LANGUAGES OF EAST AFRICA 59

+ Sabaki: Gusii + Giryama 28.75 + Amu 27.5, Ngurimi + Giryama 36.75
  3 figures, average 31

+ Pare: Gusii 27.5, Ngurimi 33.5
  2 figures, average 30.5

SUGUTI = Jita, Kwaya, Regi – used indiscriminately
+ Rutara: Nyoro 46.25, Nyankore 46.25, Haya 45, Kerewe 62.5
  3 figures (excluding Kerewe) 45.75, 4 figures (including Kerewe) 50

+ Western Highlands: Rwanda 47, Shubi 39.75
  2 figures, average 43.5

+ West Tanzania: Nyamwezi 45.75, Nyaturu 38.75, Nilyamba 36
  3 figures, average 40.25

+ Langi: 34.75

+ Chaga/Davida: CK 29.25, Davida 33
  2 figures, average 31

+ Sabaki: Giryama 37, Amu 35
  2 figures, average 36

RUTARA = Nyoro, Tooro, Nyankore, Ciga, Nyambo, Haya, Zinza, Kerewe
+ Western Highlands:
  Nyoro + Rwanda 48.5   Nyankore + Rwanda 54   Haya + Rwanda 49.75
        + Shubi   45   + Shubi   50
        + Ha   40.75   + Ha   48.25   + Ha   45.5
  Kerewe + Rwanda 47
  9 figures, average 47.75

+ West Tanzania:
  Nyoro + Sumbwa   41.5   Haya + Sumbwa 49.5
        + Nyamwezi 35.75 Nyankore + Nyamwezi 40.75,   + Nyamwezi
                                            41.25
        + Nyaturu 40.75   + Kimbu   36.75
  7 figures, average 39.5, 5 figures (excl. Sumbwa) 37

+ Langi: Haya 32

+ Thagicu: Embu + Nyoro 28, + Haya 33.75
  2 figures, average 31

+ Chaga/Davida: Nyoro + CK 26.75, + Davida 27.25, Haya + Davida 31
  3 figures, average 28.25

+ East Ruvu: Zalamo + Nyoro 27.25, + Haya 24

+ Seuta: Zigula + Nyoro 26.5, + Haya 32
  2 figures, average 29.25

+ Sabaki: Nyoro + Amu 27.5, + Giryama 28.75, Haya + Amu 31.75
  3 figures, average 29.25

+ Pare: Nyoro 24.75, Haya 29.75
2 figures, average 27.25

WESTERN HIGHLANDS + Rwanda, Rundi, Shubi, Vinza, Hangaza, Ha
+ West Tanzania:
    Rwanda+ Sumbwa 46.5   Shubi+ Sumbwa 48.75
          + Nyamwezi 38.5   + Nyamwezi 39.75
                                              + Nyaturu   35
    5 figures (including Sumbwa) 41.75, 3 figures (excluding Sumbwa) 37.75

+ Langi: Rwanda 32.25

+ East Ruvu: Zalamo + Rwanda 25, + Shubi 25
    2 figures, average 25

+ Sabaki: Amu + Rwanda 30, + Shubi 30.25, Rwanda + Giryama 29
    3 figures, average 29.75

+ Pare: Rwanda 29.25, Shubi 28.75
    2 figures, average 29

WESTERN TANZANIA = Sukuma, Nyamwezi, Sumbwa, Kimbu, Nyaturu, Nilyamba
+ Southern Highlands: Hehe + Nyamwezi 34.75, + Nyaturu 33.75
    3 figures, average 34.25

+ Thagicu:
    Embu + Nyamwezi 36.75, + Nyaturu 35.5
    2 figures, average 36.25

+ Chaga:
    CK + Nyamwezi 34.75, + Nyaturu 31.25
    2 figures, average 33

+ Davida: Nyamwezi 37.5, Nyaturu 34.5
    2 figures, average 36

+ West Ruvu:
    Gogo + Nyamwezi 43.25   Kagulu+ Nyamwezi 40
         + Nyaturu   41.5   + Nyaturu   40.25
         + Nilyamba 45.5   + Nilyamba 41.5
         + Kimbu   47.75   + Kimbu   44
    8 figures, average 43

+ Lugulu: Nyamwezi 35.75, Nyaturu 35.75, Nilyamba 36, Kimbu 38.25
    4 figures, average 36.5

WESTERN TANZANIA
+ East Ruvu: Kwere + Nyamwezi 40.75, + Nyaturu 41.5, Nilyamba 40.5, Kimbu
        42.55
    4 figures, average 41.25

+ Seuta: Shambala + Nyamwezi 40.75, Nilyamba 39, Kimbu 40.75
    3 figures, average 40.25

THE BANTU LANGUAGES OF EAST AFRICA

+ Sabaki: Nyamwezi + Giryama 44.5, + Bajun 40.25, Nyaturu + Giryama 42.25, Nilyamba + Mvita 43, Kimbu + Mvita 42.5, + Pokomo 37.75
    6 figures, average 41.75

+ Pare: Nyamwezi 43, Nyaturu 42, Nilyamba 41, Kimbu 40
    4 figures, average 41.5

+ Saghala: Nyamwezi 37.75, Nyaturu 36, Nilyamba 34.75
    3 figures, average 36.25

LANGI = Langi (Mbugwe)
+ Southern Highlands: Sangu 37, Hehe 35.75
    2 figures, average 36.5

+ Chaga: WK 36.25, Rombo 35.75
    2 figures, average 36

+ West Ruvu: Gogo 41.25, Kagulu 44.25, Sagala 39.5
    3 figures, average 41.75

+ East Ruvu: Doe 46.75, Kwere 44, Kami 39.5, Kutu 38.5, Zalamo 37.5
    5 figures, average 41.25

+ Seuta: Shambala 41.75, Bondei 45.5, Zigula 46.75
    3 figures, average 44.75

+ Sabaki: (Standard) Swahili 46, Giryama 46.5, Bajun 39.5, Pokomo 40.5
    4 figures, average 43.25

KILOMBERO = Pogolu, Ndamba, Mbunga
+ Southern Highlands: Pogolu + Bena 36, Ndamba + Bena 41, + Sango 42.75
    3 figures, average 40

+ Lugulu: Pogolu 39, Mbunga 39
    2 figures, average 39

+ Sabaki: Ndamba + Amu 33.75, + Giryama 38.75
    2 figures, average 36.25

+ Chaga/Davida: WK + Ndamba 27.25, Davida + Pogolu 28.5
    2 figures, average 28

SOUTHERN HIGHLANDS = Sangu, Hehe, Bena, Pangwa, Kinga, Wanji, Kisi
+ Chaga/Davida: Bena + WK 24, + Davida 27.25
    2 figures, average 25.75

+ West Ruvu:

	Gogo + Sango	50.5	Kagulu + Sango	45.25
	+ Hehe	50.5	+ Hehe	41.5
	+ Bena	43	+ Bena	39.75
	+ Pangwa	44.75	+ Pangwa	40.5
	+ Kinga	39.5	+ Kinga	40.5
	+ Wanji	42.75	+ Wanji	38
	+ Kisi	40.75		

    13 figures, average 42.75

+ Lugulu: Sango 40, Hehe 40.75, Bena 35.75, Kinga 37.75, Kisi 37.75
   5 figures, average 38.25

+ East Ruvu: Zalamo + Sango 41   Kwere + Wanji   34.75
                    + Bena   36   + Pangwa 40
                    + Kisi   40.75   + Hehe   38.5
                    + Kinga 33.75
   7 figures, average 37.75

+ Seuta: Zigula + Sango 38, + Bena 30, + Kinga 34.75, + Kisi 37.75
   4 figures, average 35.25

+ Sabaki: Giryama + Hehe 34, + Pangwa 35.25, + Wanji 31.75,
       Pokomo + Bena 26.5, + Kisi 31.75, Amu + Sango 34.25, + Kinga 31.5
   7 figures, average 32.25

+ Nyakyusa: Sango 40.5, Pangwa 41, + Wanji 45.25, Kinga 44, Kisi 46.5
   5 figures, average 43.5

THAGICU = S. Kikuyu, Embu, Chuka, Meru (Tigania), Meru (Imenti), Kamba
(also Tharaka, Sonjo, Daiso, etc.)

+ Chaga/Dauida: Kikuyu + Dauida 36, + WK 35.75, + Rombo 36.75,
             Kamba + Dauida 39.25, + WK 37.25, + Rombo 40.75
   6 figures, average 37.75
+ West Ruvu: Kagulu + Kikuyu 30.5, + Kamba 30.5
   2 figures, average 30.5

+ East Ruvu: Zalamo + Kikuyu 29.5, + Kamba 28.5
   2 figures, average 29

+ Seuta: Zigula + Kikuyu 35.25, Kamba 33.75
   2 figures, average 34.25

+ Sabaki:
   Kikuyu + Amu 35.5, + Pokomo 34.75, Kamba + Amu 36.75, + Giryama 39
   4 figures, average 36.5

Had we balanced the three figures for Amu and Pokomo with three from Southern
Swahili and the Miji Kenda, the average doubtless would have been higher.

+ Pare: Kikuyu 36.75, Kamba 39
   2 figures, average 38

+ Saghala: Kikuyu 33.75, Kamba 38.25
   2 figures, average 36

CHAGA = West Kilimanjaro (WK: Meru, Siha to Kibosho), Central Kilimanjaro
(CK: Uru to Mamba), Rombo, Gweno, and, in a wider sense, Dauida)
+ West Ruvu: Kagulu + WK 32, Rombo 31
   2 figures, average 31.5

+ Lugulu: WK 29.25, Rombo 31.25
   2 figures, average 30.25

THE BANTU LANGUAGES OF EAST AFRICA 63

+ Seuta: WK + Zigula 35.5, + Bondei 36.5, Rombo + Zigula 36.75
  3 figures, average 36.25

+ Sabaki: WK + Amu 34.75, Giryama 37.5, Rombo + Amu 37.75, + Pokomo 34.5
  4 figures, average 36.25

+ Pare: WK 36.25, CK 39.75, Rombo 43.5, Gweno 49
  4 figures (including Gweno) 43, 3 figures (excluding Gweno) 40.75

+ Saghala: WK 36.75, CK 37, Rombo 36.75, Gweno 43.25
  4 figures (including Gweno) 38.5, 3 figures (excluding Gweno) 36.75

DAWIDA [-υ-]
+ Seuta: Shambala 41, Zigula 39
  2 figures, average 40

+ Sabaki: Pokomo 40.5, Giryama 46, Digo 43, Amu 39.25, Bajun 38.75,
       (Standard) Swahili 40.25
  6 figures, average 41.25

+ Pare: 43

WEST RUVU = Gogo, Kagulu, Sagala
+ Lugulu: Gogo 43, Kagulu 48.75, Saghala 49.5
  3 figures, average 47

+ East Ruvu:
Gogo + Kwere 46.25   Kagulu + Kwere 59   Saghala + Kwere 54
     + Doe   44.75   + Doe   58.5   + Doe   53
     + Kami   43.75   + Kami   56.5   + Kami   55
     + Kutu   43.75   + Kutu   54.75   + Kutu   52.75
     + Zalamo 42.5   + Zalamo 51   + Zalamo 51.25
  15 figures, average 51.25

+ Seuta:
Gogo + Shambala 42.25 Kagulu + Shambala 50.25 Saghala + Shambala 43.25
     + Bondei   43   + Bondei   55.25
     + Zigula   45.5   + Zigula   54.5   + Zigula   45.75

+ Sabaki:
Kagulu + Bajun 38, + Pokomo 40.75, + Giryama 43, + (Standard) Swahili 46.75
  4 figures, average 42.25

+ Pare: Kagulu 40.75, Gogo 36
  2 figures, average 38.5

LUGULU
+ East Ruvu: Kami 57.5, Kutu 54, Zalamo 53, Kwere 54.25, Doe 49.25
  5 figures, average 53.75

+ Seuta: Zigula 45.5, Bondei 44.5, Shambala 40
  3 figures, average 43.25

+ Sabaki: Giryama 42.25, (Standard) Swahili 41.25, Bajun 37, Pokomo 36.5
   4 figures, average 39.25

EAST RUVU (ER) = Kwere, Doe, Zalamo, Kami, Kutu
+ Seuta: Doe + Shambala 58.25, Kwere + Shambala 51.75, Kami + Shambala 46.5, Zalamo + Shambala 45.5, Doe + Bondei 63.75, Kwere + Bondei 58.5, Zalamo + Bondei 51.5, Doe + Zigula 69.75, Kwere + Zigula 62, Kami + Zigula 54.75, Zaramo + Zigula 48.75, Kutu + Zigula 53.25
   12 figures, average 55.25

+ Sabaki: Kwere + Pokomo 43.25, + Bajun 45.5, + Giryama 50.5, (Standard) Swahili 53.75, Zalamo + Pokomo 41.5, + Bajun 40, + Giryama 46, + (Standard) Swahili 50.25
   8 figures, average 46.25

+ Pare: Kwere 44.75, Zalamo 38.25
   2 figures, average 41.5

+ Saghala:
   Kwere 38.5, Zalamo 35
   2 figures, average 36.75

SEUTA = Shambala, Bondei, Zigula, Ngulu
+ Sabaki: Shambala + Pokomo 45.5, + Bajun 46.25, + Giryama 53, + (Standard) Swahili 53.75, Zigula + Pokomo 46.25, + Bajun 46.75, + Giryama 50.75, + (Standard) Swahili 55.75
   8 figures, average 49.75

+ Pare: Shambala 50.25, Zigula 47.5
   2 figures, average 49

+ Saghala: Shambala 42.75, Zigula 40.75
   3 figures, average 41.75

SABAKI = S. Pokomo, Giryama, Digo, Bajun, Amu, Mvita, Mrima/Unguja
+ Pare: Bajun 41.75, Amu 42.75, Pokomo 43.25, (Standard) Swahili 46, Digo 48.75, Giryama 48.75
   6 figures, average 45.25
+ Saghala: Bajun 39.5, Pokomo 40.75, Amu 41.5, (Standard) Swahili 42.5, Mvita 43.75, Digo 45.75, Giryama 49.25
   7 figures, average 43.25

APPENDIX 2:C 100-WORD LIST LANGUAGES

Results of applying the 100-word list to languages for which we did not have 400 words. The figures are higher than those which would result from application of the 400-word list, but the relative groupings are likely to be the same.

Vinza (Guthrie's D67)
   Ha   90
   Shubi   84

THE BANTU LANGUAGES OF EAST AFRICA

Bende (Guthrie's F12)
Sumbwa	74
Nyamwezi	72
Sukuma Hu	70
Ha	67
Rundi	71
Hangaza	60
Nyankore	58
Holoholo	65

West Tanzania average 72
Western Highlands average 66

Taveta/Tuveta (G21)
S. Pare	93
Saghala	66
Shambala	60
Gweno	59
Davida	54

Daiso (E56)
(=Segeju at Bwiti)
Kikuyu	67
Meru (I)	66
Meru (T)	66
Kamba (K)	65
Kamba (M)	64
Digo	49
Bondei	44
Shambala	40

Thagicu average 65
Seuta average 42

Sonjo (E46)
Kikuyu	59
Embu	57
Kamba (M)	55
Kamba (K)	53
Meru (I)	53
Kuria	50
Ngurimi	50
Gusii	48
Jita	49
Kwaya	51
Regi	50

Thagicu average 55.5
E. Nyanza average 49.25
Suguti average 50

Conclusions

Vinza forms part of West Highlands, particularly similar to Ha. This fits with Guthrie's conclusions: Ha D66, Vinza D67.

Bende is part of W. Tanzania (but lacking data from further west), and apparently closest to Sumbwa, but the division is not so clear as, e.g. with Vinza. Figures for groups other than W. Tanzania are also high, probably indicating a degree of interference; Sumbwa is very interfered with. For Tongwe (F11) we have no information.

Taveta is clearly a dialect of Pare: the phonology would indicate particular connection with N. Pare.

Daiso forms part of Thagicu (Guthrie and Bennett agree). The phonology would point to it being an offshoot of Kamba, but this is not supported by the figures above.

Sonjo is part of Thagicu, especially similar to Gikuyu, Embu. This contradicts Guthrie, but is supported by Bennett and the phonology. Sonjo has either been influenced by E. Nyanza and Suguti or has been subject to the same non-Bantu lexical influence. The Sonjo prefer the name *ba-temi*.

APPENDIX 2:D   RELATIVE HOMOGENEITY

Summary of Appendices 2:A, B and C and Section 2.0.

MERU	Meru (Tigania)–Meru (Imenti)	84.75
	Sukuma–Nyamwezi	84.5
	Haya–Nyambo	83.75
	Chiga–Nyaŋkore	83.75
	Kuria–Ngurimi	83.75
	Zigula–Ngulu	83.75
	Rundi–Shubi–Hangaza	82
	Nata–Zanaki	81.5
SUGUTI	Regi–Jita–Kwaya	81.5
	Haya/Nyambo–Zinza	80
SWAHILI	Bajun–Amu–Mvita–Mrima/Unguja	79.25
	Nyoro–Tooro	78
	Rundi/Shubi/Hangaza–Ha/Vinza	77
	Nyankore/Chiga–Haya/Nyambo/Zinza	75.75
	Shambala–Bondei	75.5
	Kuria/Ngurimi–Nata/Zanaki	74.75
	Kwere–Doe	73.75
WEST	Rundi/Shubi/Hangaza/Ha/Vinza–Rwanda	73
HIGHLANDS	Kikuyu–Embu–Chuka	72.25
	Ganda–Soga	71.5
	Nyankore/Chiga/Haya/Nyambo/Zinza–Nyoro/Tooro	71.5
MIJI KENDA	Giryama–Digo	
SEUTA	Shambala/Bondei–Zigula/Ngulu	71.25
	Bena–Pangwa	70.75
SOUTH LUHYA	Logooli–Isuxa	69.75
	Ndamba–Mbunga	69.5
	Kami–Kutu	69.25
RUTARA	Kerewe–Nyankore/Chiga/Nyoro/Tooro/Haya/Nyambo/Zinza	66.5
NORTH NYANZA	Ganda/Soga–Gwere	66
EAST RUVU	Zalamo–Kami/Kutu–Kwere/Doe	65.5

THE BANTU LANGUAGES OF EAST AFRICA

CHAGA (I)	WK–CK–Rombo	65.25
	Swahili–Miji Kenda	64.75
	Nilyamba–Nyaturu	63.5
KILOMBERO	Pogolu–Ndamba/Mbunga	63
THAGICU	Kamba–Kikuyu/Embu/Chuka–Meru	62.75
	Hehe–Bena/Pangwa	62.5
NORTH LUHYA	Masaaba–Saamia	61.5
	Sumbwa–Sukuma/Nyamwezi	60.25
SABAKI	Pokomo–Swahili/Miji Kenda	59.5
	Wanji–Sangu	59
WEST RUVU	Gogo–Kagulu–Sagala	58.25
	Kimbu–Nilyamba/Nyaturu	57.25
CHAGA (II)	Gweno–WK/CK/Rombo	55.5
SOUTH HIGHLANDS	Kisi–Kinga–Wanji/Sangu–Hehe/Bena/Pangwa	53.25
WEST TANZANIA II	Nilyamba/Nyaturu/Kimbu–Sukuma/Nyamwezi/ Sumbwa	52
LUHYA	N. Luhya–S. Luhya	51.5
EAST NYANZA	Gusii–Kuria/Ngurimi/Nata/Zanaki	51.5
	E. Ruvu–Lugulu–Seuta	50.75
RUVU	W. Ruvu–E. Ruvu/Lugulu/Seuta	47.25
WEST TANZANIA II	Langi–Nilyamba/Nyaturu/Kimbu/Sukuma/ Nyamwezi/Sumbwa	47
EAST VICTORIA	E. Nyanza–Suguti	45
COAST	Sabaki–Pare–Saghala	44.75
CHAGA (III)	Davida–Gweno/WK/CK/Rombo	44.5
INTERLACUSTRINE	N. Nyanza–Rutara–W. Highlands	43.75
EASTERN	W. Tanzania II–Ruvu–Coast	40.75
LACUSTRINE	Interlacustrine–East Victoria	39.25

3 THE NILOTIC LANGUAGES OF TANZANIA

Christopher Ehret

1.0 Introduction

Five Nilotic languages are today spoken by indigenous Tanzanian communities. Two of them, Maasai and Ongamo, are Eastern Nilotic in their affiliations, and two others, Dadog[1] and Akie,[2] belong to the Southern Nilotic branch of the family. These four languages each have a lengthy history of use in Tanzania, and their background and derivations will form the focus of discussion here. The fifth language, Luo of the Western Nilotic branch, has come to be spoken in Tanzania only during approximately the last 100 years and is not dealt with in this volume.[3] In addition to the modern Nilotic languages, one or more extinct Southern Nilotic languages were once spoken in parts of northern Tanzania, the most prominent of which may be called Victoria pre-Southern Nilotic.

2.0 Southern Nilotic

Victoria pre-Southern Nilotic appears to have been one of a set of early Southern Nilotic dialects spoken at the end of the last millennium B.C. by communities spread across the plains straddling the Kenya-Tanzania borders, from Lake Victoria on the west to Mt. Kilimanjaro on the east. They formed the southern fringe of a wider continuum of Southern Nilotic dialects which extended back northward through central and probably west-central Kenya; and their expansion southward, probably in the last centuries B.C., represented the first penetration of Nilotic languages into Tanzania. (Ehret, 1971, esp. chap. 5) (Map 4)

At that point in time, all of them can probably be understood to have been mutually intelligible dialects of a single Pre-Southern Nilotic language (PreSN). The name proto-Southern Nilotic (proto-SN) must be reserved for the particular dialect, or set of dialects within pre-Southern Nilotic from which the extant Southern Nilotic languages descend. The dialects of PreSN formed several collateral lines of descent; of those several lines only that which developed into proto-SN has left modern descendant languages.

2.1 Pre-Southern Nilotic

PreSN can be distinguished from earlier proto-Nilotic by two major consonantal rules: (1) collapsing of the proto-Nilotic dental series (*ṭ, *ḍ, *ṇ) with the equivalent alveolars, and (2) deletion of the voiced/voiceless distinctions in stops.[4] The effect of the two rules was to change proto-Nilotic

	b	ḍ	d		g
	p	ṭ	t	c	ķ
	m	ṇ	n	nʸ	ŋ

to PreSN

p t c k ḳ
m n nʸ ŋ

The Southern Nilotic consonant system also retained unchanged proto-Nilotic *r, *l, and *lʸ. Another notable consonantal development in PreSN was the addition of the fricative *s. It should be noted that no fricatives whatsoever can be reconstructed for proto-Nilotic. Wherever the earlier history of words in Southern Nilotic languages with PreSN *s can be traced, the words turn out to be loanwords from non-Nilotic languages.[4] PreSN may also have differed from proto-Nilotic by equally

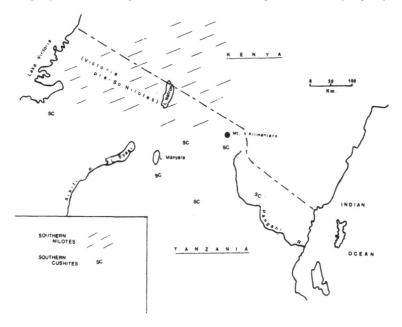

Map 4 Possible Extent of Nilotes, c. A.D. 1

distinctive vowel and tonal rules, but these aspects of Nilotic phonological history have not yet been given sufficient study.

A third major consonantal sound shift, the deletion of *r in last and next-to-the-last consonant positions before *u and *i,[5] subsequently began to develop in some but not all of the PreSN dialects during probably the first two or three centuries A.D. It is this particular sound shift which is the distinguishing mark of the emergence of proto-SN as separate from the rest of PreSN. Proto-SN also differentiated from PreSN by the creation of new affix morphemes. In PreSN, nouns in the singular consisted either of the simple stem or of the stem plus a suffix of the forms

*-ia/*ua or *-Vn (normally *-an, but sometimes *-en). The proto-SN set of dialects formed the additional suffixes *-ia:n and, rarely, *-ua:n, apparently by chaining the two forms of noun suffixes. The presence of vowel length argues strongly for the correctness of the postulation of an underlying *-ia + *-an → *-ia:n.

2.2 Proto-Southern Nilotic

During the first millennium A.D. speakers of the set of Southern Nilotic dialects with the r-deletion rule, that is to say proto-SN, rapidly emerged as the pre-eminent Southern Nilotic communities. In Tanzania this course of events manifested itself in the establishment of the Tato group through the central grasslands of the far north, areas previously occupied by the

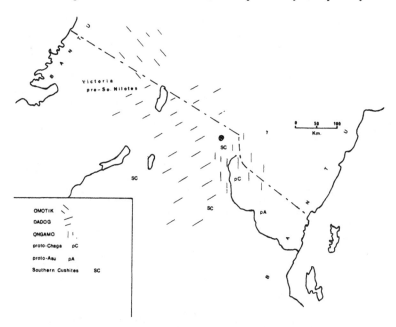

Map 5   Probable Nilotic Societies, c. A.D. 500–1000

closely related pre-Southern Nilotic societies. (Map 5) Two Tato languages remain today. Omotik, spoken by one of the Mau Forest hunter-gatherer bands of Kenya, descends from the form of Tato speech as it apparently developed in the grazing lands around, in, and perhaps south of the Mau Range.[6] The Omotik can be understood as a food-collecting population which adopted a Tato language from their food-producing neighbors during the eras of Tato dominance a thousand or more years ago, then held onto that language, by reason of their isolation in the forest, during the many succeeding centuries of Kalenjin and Maasai dominance. The second extant Tato language, Dadog, evolved to the south of Omotik. By around 1,000 A.D. a very early form of Dadog was spoken from the plains west of the Ngorongoro highlands, eastward to central Maasailand, and probably as far northward from Ngorongoro as the Loita highlands in southern Kenya (Ehret, 1971: chap. 7) It is Dadog which, for its predominantly Tanzanian distribution throughout its separate history, is of particular concern here.

2.3 *Dadog*

Dadog differs from its proto-Southern Nilotic ancestry by a variety of consonantal rules. A preliminary investigation suggests the tentative depiction and ordering of the most important of these rules as given in Tables 3:1.[7]

Table 3:1 Rules for Dadog

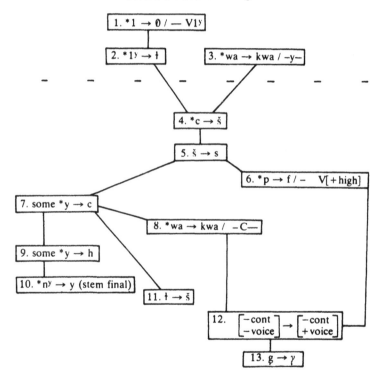

The three rules above the dotted line occur in Omotik also and therefore define its common proto-Tato ancestry with Dadog.

The resulting Dadog-consonant system has replaced the PreSN and proto-SN imbalance of five stop positions and a single fricative with a balanced pattern, thus:

```
b    d    j    g
f    s    š         γ̣
m    n    nʸ   ŋ
```

Dadog retained as well proto-SN/preSN *r and *l, and added /h/.

The PreSN and proto-SN vowel system probably consisted of ten vowels, occurring each long and short,[8] and ordered according to an open*close (lax/tense) dichotomy:

```
i        u        i:       u:
ɪ        ʊ        ɪ:       ʊ:
e        o        e:       o:
ε        ɔ        ε:       ɔ:
     a                a:
     ɑ                ɑ:
```

In proto-Tato, *e and *o fell together with *a by vowel rule #1 --

1. $\begin{bmatrix} -\text{high} \\ -\text{long} \\ +\text{tense} \end{bmatrix} \rightarrow a$

Subsequent rules limited to Dadog appear to be

2. $\begin{bmatrix} +\text{high} \\ -\text{tense} \end{bmatrix} \rightarrow \begin{bmatrix} +\text{high} \\ +\text{tense} \end{bmatrix}$

3. $\begin{bmatrix} +\text{high} \\ -\text{long} \end{bmatrix} \rightarrow ɨ$ 4. $[-\text{tense}] \rightarrow æ\ (:)$

producing the following Dadog vowels (Barabaig dialect):

```
    i    ɨ    u
    e         o
    æ    a
```

of which only the two low vowels occur phonemically both short and long.

2.4 South Kalenjin

The Dadog dominance of the grazing lands of central northern Tanzania began to decline during the first half of the present millennium under the pressure of another Southern Nilotic people, the South Kalenjin. This society expanded its territories southward out of Kenya, along the east of the Rift escarpment in northern Tanzania, and by the sixteenth century could have been found through a continuous belt of territory coinciding closely with present-day Maasailand. The Dadog continued, however, to command the Ngorongoro, Loita, and Serengeti areas to the west, above the escarpment. (Ehret, forthcoming) (Map 6)

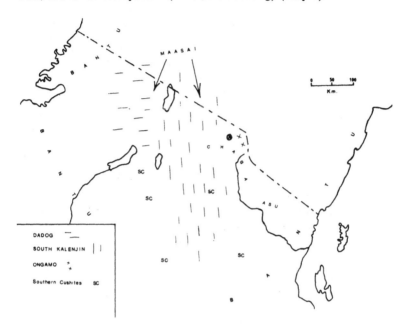

Map 6   Nilotes in the Sixteenth Century

South Kalenjin speech, because it belonged to the Kalenjin branch of Southern Nilotic, shares in the major phonological rules by which Kalenjin diverged out of proto-SN:

(1) *k → /k/;
(2) *1ʸ → /1y/, /V—V,
    → /1/ elsewhere;
and (3) disappearance of the open/close distinction in the low central vowel position.

Kalenjin, as a branch of Southern Nilotic coordinate with the Tato branch, of course shares with Tato languages the prior rule of *r*-deletion. South Kalenjin further diverged from the rest of Kalenjin in its shift of many proto-Kalenjin *ɔ: to /a:/. The full determinants of this shift have not yet been worked out, though.

Nor did the language develop the *ce:p-/kip-* noun-forming prefixes so common in the Kalenjin dialects of Kenya, although Akie, the only remaining South Kalenjin dialect, does attest both the formative elements, *tie:-* and *ki-* which underlie the *ce:p-* and *kip-* innovations respectively. The former derives from a once independent morpheme *tie:* "daughter" plus *ap* "of"; the latter, from *ki-* "thing" plus again *ap.* Exactly parallel constructions occur in Dadog. Like those in Akie they lack the insertion of the connective morpheme *ap*, but in Dadog the pre-fixed elements are *uda-* and *gida-*, the former being a Dadog stem for "daughter" and the latter being the direct Dadog cognate of Kalenjin *ki-*. Dadog *gidayud* "door" is literally "thing (of) mouth," in reference to the common East African metaphor of the door as the mouth of the house; Dadog *udafojæ:nd*, "daughter (of) blood," as the name for red-water fever, refers to the symptoms of that cattle disease. A comparable construction in Akie is *tie:re:mpe:* "hoe," where *tie:-* is the prefixed element and *-re:mpe:* is a stem of unidentified meaning. Thus whatever the specific morphemes applied, a proto-SN process of noun-formation – without the insertion of *ap* which most Kalenjin dialects innovated in much later times – can be reconstructed.

2.5 Historical Background

Each of the Tanzanian Southern Nilotic languages in time began to retreat before the advance of other languages. The Victoria pre-Southern Nilotes were progressively absorbed into East Victoria Bantu populations. They still existed probably as late as 1500 along the southeastern shores of the lake, where we can see late PreSN loanwords in Jita, and Southern Nilotic cultural influences in the age-set institutions of the Kuria, Zanaki, and their neighbors (Ehret, 1971: chap. 5 and App. D4). The possible pre-Southern Nilotic communities of West Kilimanjaro were similarly absorbed into Ongamo and eventually Chaga societies. The Dadog language, which had lost its territories east of the escarpment to South Kalenjin in the first half of this millennium, re-expanded into new territories in the seventeenth and eighteenth centuries, but did so in response to Maasai intrusion into and conquest of the Ngorongoro and Loita highlands.[9] Some of the Dadog moved into eastern Usukuma, where they were eventually assimilated by the Sukuma.[10] Others expanded a previous beachhead in Mbulu, scattering out across modern Hanang and most of Singida.[11] Since 1800 the relative number of Dadog speakers has declined there in relation to respective expansions of Nyaturu, Iraqw, Gorowa, and Mbugwe communities; but they remain a significant factor, particularly in Hanang. A detached smaller grouping of Dadog communities remain also in the Musoma area. The South Kalenjin populations, so important at mid-millennium throughout Maasailand, were mostly absorbed into Maasai speaking society during the seventeenth and eighteenth centuries; and today only one hunter-gatherer people of South Maasai District still maintain the Akie version of the South Kalenjin language.

3.0 Eastern Nilotic

Of the two Eastern Nilotic languages spoken in Tanzania, it is Ongamo which has the longer history in the country. In its earliest form, the language was brought by immigrants from Kenya into the region around

Mt. Kilimanjaro, probably during the second half of the first millennium. Ongamo vocabulary suggests a mixed grain-cultivating and herding economy for its speakers. There is also loanword evidence to indicate that the first Ongamo settlers wrested their lands around Kilimanjaro from Southern Cushites and pre-Southern Nilotes and had significant contacts as well with their early Dadog neighbors to the west (See Nurse, 1976). (Map 5)

In the centuries since 1,000 the Ongamo language has given way progressively before the expansion of the Chaga around the mountain, and the stages of Chaga assimilation of Ongamo communities are recorded clearly in the linguistic data. Ongamo loans in proto-Chaga remain from this process as it took place in the first few centuries of the present millennium, while additional sets of Ongamo loanwords restricted to various of the three primary subgroups of Kilimanjaro Chaga dialects – Rombo, Central, and Western Chaga spoken respectively on the eastern, southeastern, and southern slopes of the mountain – reflect the continuation of the process through mid-millennium.[12] By the beginning of the present century, Ongamo had ceased to be spoken everywhere but in Rombo district; and, with only a few older people still currently speaking it, Ongamo is nearing extinction.

3.1 *Ongamo*

Modern Ongamo differs phonologically from Maasai, its closest related language, in only a few respects. The major rules unique to Ongamo include

(1) *p → /β/;
(2) *k → /h/, before most *o, *ɔ, and *a;
(3) *k → /c/, in most contexts before close front vowels unless the next following segment was a liquid;
(4) *c → /š/;
and (5) * 1 → (Ø, except before close vowels and in the proximity of another liquid.

The ordering of these rules is not intrinsically apparent, with the exception that rule (3) preceded rule (4). But from Ongamo loanword sets in Chaga it can be seen that rules (1) and (2) had already occurred as early as the proto-Chaga period about 800–1,000 years ago, whereas rule (5) had not come into being yet. External evidence is lacking for the placing of rule (3) and indeterminate in the case of rule (4). Ongamo has continued to pronounce the voiced stops implosively as in proto-Maa-Ongamo, but has dropped implosion after a preceding nasal. In vowels and tones Ongamo, on the other hand, retains almost completely unchanged the patterns and system of proto-Maa-Ongamo, as has also Maasai.

3.2 *Maasai*

Maasai, the other Eastern Nilotic language of Tanzania, continues to be spoken by a considerable body of population. Of course, it is also the most recent of the Eastern and Southern Nilotic languages to have become established in the country. (Map 6) The first settlement of Maasai speakers came from central Kenya and intruded into far northern Tanzania only during the seventeenth century, but the use of Maasai in north and north-central Tanzania thereafter expanded rapidly to its present limits. West of the Rift escarpment, in the Ngorongoro and Loita highlands and in Serengeti, the Maasai language displaced Dadog, as previously noted; while through the rest of Maasailand, Maasai replaced the earlier South Kalenjin language among all but the hunter-gatherer Akie of South Maasai District by the end of the eighteenth century.

Maasai has undoubtedly changed considerably since its original divergence from its common proto-Maa-Ongamo ancestry with Ongamo, but these changes have generally been in other spheres than in phonology. Maasai shares with Ongamo the sound shift of proto-Eastern Nilotic *y → *c, which distinguishes the Maasaian group from its next nearest related languages, Lotuko and its neighbors in the far southeast Republic of Sudan. But Maasai preserves the full proto-Maa-Ongamo phonology: a nine-vowel system:

```
    i        u
    ɪ        ʊ
    e        o
    ɛ        ɔ
         a
```

also unchanged in Ongamo, and the consonant system, just as it was in proto-Maa-Ongamo, with the possible exception that *g may not originally have been implosive:

```
ɓ    ɗ    ʄ    ɠ
p    t    c    k
     s
m    n    nʸ   ŋ
     l,r,rr
```

which has yielded in Ongamo, on the other hand, the following pattern, with a partial balance between fricative and stop positions:

```
ɓ    ɗ    ʄ    g
     t    c    k
β    s    š         h
m    n    nʸ   ŋ
     l,r,rr
```

As in Southern Nilotic, so in Maasai and Ongamo all examples of words containing *s are probably ultimately of non-Nilotic provenance.

The diagram in Appendix 3:A summarizes much of the discussion presented in this chapter.

THE NILOTIC LANGUAGES OF TANZANIA

NOTES

[1] Other forms of this name in published sources are Tatoga, Tatog, and Datog. Since Dadog phonology does not make voiced/voiceless distinctions, the form used here must be preferred.

[2] Another name for this language is Mosiro, but the people's own name for themselves and their language is Akie.

[3] See W. Whiteley, 1974: chap. 1.

[4] Cf. examples in appendices to Ehret's *Southern Nilotic History*.

[5] Note that this revises the statement of the rule in Ehret's *Southern Nilotic History*, chapter 3.

[6] Data on Omotik was kindly provided by Professor Bernd Heine, Institut für Afrikanistik der Universität zu Köln.

[7] Letters marked with asterisks represent reconstructed phonemes of earlier Nilotic languages from which the modern ones derive. The sound change rules tentatively proposed here offer a possible ordering of the stages by which the reconstructed phonemes developed into the phonemes of the present-day languages.

[8] The problem of whether there might be three phonemic vowel lengths in Southern Nilotic has been ignored here, since vowel phonological history seems entirely explainable on the basis of a two-length distinction.

[9] Personal communication from Alan Jacobs, formerly of the Institute of African Studies, University of Nairobi.

[10] Personal communication from Bajuda Itandala, University of Dar es Salaam.

[11] This conclusion is based on a re-evaluation of the traditions noted by G. Wilson: 1952 and 1953.

[12] Unpublished research by writer from his own data and from data and criticism kindly provided by Derek Nurse.

REFERENCES

Ehret, C., 1968, 'Linguistics as a tool for historians' *Hadith*. 1.
—— 1971, *Southern Nilotic History: Linguistic Approaches to the Study of the Past.* Evanston: Northwestern University Press.
(forthcoming) 'East Africa: The Interior' in Niané, D., ed., *Africa from the Twelfth to the Sixteenth Century.* Vol. 4. in *The General History of Africa.* UNESCO.
Heine, B., and Vossen, Rainer, 1976, 'Zur Stellung der Ongamo-Sprache (Kilimandscharo)' *Afrika und Übersee*, 59:2.
Nurse, D., 1976, *Language and History on Kilimanjaro, the Pare Mountains and the Taita Hills.* [Ph.D. thesis]. University of Dar es Salaam.
Whiteley, W. H., 1974, ed., *Language in Kenya.* Nairobi: Oxford University Press.
Wilson, G., 1952 and 1953, 'The Tatoga of Tanganyika' *Tanganyika Notes and Records*. 33, 34–7, 34, 35–6.

Table 3:1 Rules for Consonants of Proto-Southern Nilotic to Dadog

APPENDIX 3:A IMMEDIATE RELATIONSHIPS AMONG THE NILOTIC LANGUAGES OF TANZANIA

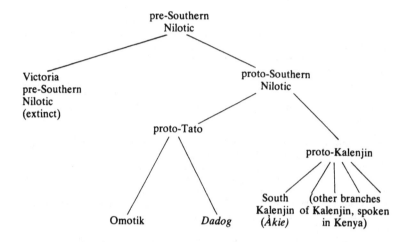

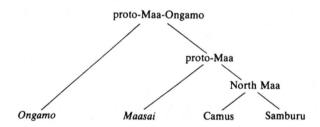

Languages spoken in Tanzania are italicized. The Southern Nilotic and Maa-Ongamo groups are related at a much deeper level to each other through their common descent from proto-Nilotic. For diagrams of overall relationships among Nilotic languages, too complicated to be presented here, see C. Ehret (1968 and 1971:107).

4 SWAHILI IN TANZANIA

Edgar C. Polomé

1.0 *The Earliest Attestations of Swahili*[1]

1.1 *Origin of Swahili*

The term 'Swahili' is derived from the plural form *sawāḥil* of Arabic *sāḥil* 'coast' and accordingly refers to the language used in the coastal trade between the Arabs and local population. The question of the origin of Swahili has given rise to a number of hypotheses: F. Johnson (1930) considered it as "mixed language" resulting from intermarriage between Arab immigrants and Bantu women in Lamu; G. W. Broomfield (1931) expanded this view to include the various Bantu languages with which the Arabs came into contact, considering Swahili rather as a diasystem to which both these Bantu languages and Arabic contributed. Since a careful perusal of the grammatical structure of Swahili indicates that the influence of Arabic on its morphology and syntax has at best been minimal, and that the impact of Arabic phonology on its phonemic system has not affected the regularity of the correspondences of the terms of Bantu origin with their cognates in other Bantu languages, it is obvious that Swahili does not result from a language mixture. As B. Krumm (1932:19) recognized, the Arab traders adopted the Bantu language of the coastal population and introduced a number of loanwords relevant to their commercial activity into it: the main linguistic consequence of this extensive borrowing from Arabic was presumably the establishment of a sub-system covering the unfamiliar phones of the borrowed terms. The problem of the location of the area where Swahili was originally spoken remained to be solved: F. Johnson and B. Krumm thought it must have been Lamu and the neighboring islands. R. Reusch (1953:24) preferred to assume it developed at various places along the coast between Mombasa and Mogadishu in the 8th century. Recently B. Heine (1970:81–83), reviewing all the previous hypotheses, considered the view of B. Struck (1921:178) that Swahili originated around the Tana River estuary as the most plausible. This location would put it closer to the Pokomo area than to the Nyika dialects, in particular Giriyama, with which Swahili is assumed to have "marked affinities" (Bryan 1959:129). T. Hinnebusch (1976) has, however, confirmed, after careful study of the linguistic evidence, that Swahili is clearly connected with Pokomo and Mijikenda (i.e. the Sabaki subgroup of Northeast Coastal Bantu). Not only do they share phonological innovations, but lexicostatistical comparisons confirm their relationship.[2]

2.0 History of the Spread of Swahili

2.1 Spread to the South

If Swahili has originated on the coast of the Indian Ocean near the mouth of the Tana River, its spread to the South is undoubtedly a result of the trading activity of the Arabs and Persians along the coast. Unfortunately, there is little documentation available on this process of expansion: both João de Barros (1552) and the Arabic *History of Kilwa Kisimani* (ca. 1520) date the penetration of Islam southward and the opening of the gold trade with Sofala (in Southern Mozambique) back to the middle of the 10th century; this is traditionally assumed to have led to the foundation of Kilwa by 'Alī ibn al-Ḥusain ibn 'Alī, about 957 (Freeman-Grenville 1962a:66; Mathew 1963:103). The situation there at his arrival appeared to be rather complex: on the one hand, the island was ruled by an African chief; on the other hand, it had already been partly islamized since a mosque had already been erected and the newcomers called upon a local Muslim, *Muriri wa Bari* (obviously a Bantu name), to serve as "interpreter." No indication is given about the language used in the negotiations with the African chief, from whom the island was purchased under the bizarre condition that the newcomer should encircle it with colored clothing – hence the nickname *nguo nyingi* 'many clothes' given to 'Alī. One obviously wonders how apocryphal this story may be, though it is often quoted as evidence for the early presence of Swahili in the area: de Barros merely mentions 'Alī bought the island for some pieces of cloth! The other alleged Swahili nicknames of the early rulers of Kilwa according to Freeman-Grenville (1962a:83, 117): *mkoma watu* for 'Alī's son, Muhammad, and *hasha hazifiki* for Tālūt ibn al-Ḥusain (second half of 14th century) are disputable (Whiteley, 1969:34–35). The former can hardly mean 'Borassus Palm of the People' as Freeman-Grenville claimed: *mkoma watu* must be a compound of the type *mvunja mawe* 'stone cutter' from the verb *-koma*, presumably in the meaning 'kill', with *watu* as direct object, the meaning being 'the killer of men', a nickname for which the text of the *History of Kilwa Kisimani*, unfortunately, does not provide any factual justification. As for Freeman-Grenville's reading (*h*)*asha* (*h*)*azifiki* it is only one among several possibilities of vocalization of the Arabic consonant sequence $sh - z - f - k$. Anyhow, it refers to a much later period, about thirty years after Ibn Baṭṭūṭa visited Kilwa. Though the latter specifically mentions the 'land of the Swahili', the location remains vague: Mombasa is at least two day's journey from there. It is however obvious that, in spite of Freeman-Grenville's suggestion (1962a:105), this 'land of the Swahili' cannot be the dominions of Kilwa: Ibn Baṭṭūṭa quite explicitly states that Kilwa is 'in the land of Zanj'; the people of the town, mostly 'Zanj of very black complexion' are, 'engaged in a holy war, for their country lies beside that of pagan Zanj' (Freeman-Grenville, 1962b:31). Accordingly, his testimony does not supply any information as to the linguistic situation in his time.[3]

Moreover, the alleged 10th century Swahili nickname may also be spurious since it now appears from the research of H. N. Chittick (1965) that it was not until the end of the 12th century that Kilwa became an important trading center, and that Alī ibn al-Hasan, the founder of the local dynasty, may have ruled from Kisimani Mafia (Cf. also Sutton, 1966:10 Chittick, 1968:111; Kimambo, 1969:36).

There is, however, evidence of permanent settlement and trading in Kilwa since the 9th century, but in those early days *Unguja Ukuu* on Zanzibar was flourishing: about 915 al-Mas'udi visited the area and in his description of the "land of Zanj" he quoted three terms in the local language: (a) *flīmī*, plural *waklīmī*, designating the local "kings"; (b) *maliknajlu* 'god'; (c) *kalari*, 'an edible plant' (Freeman-Grenville 1959:11–12; 1962a:40). The first word has been identified with the current Swahili word for 'king': *mfalme*, plural *wafalme*, and the second has been considered a modification of *mkulu-ngulu*, akin to the Zulu name of 'god' *U-nkulu-nkulu:* in both cases, the phonetic changes implied make the interpretations most disputable, though no satisfactory substitute solution has been offered.[4] As for the third word – *kalārī* – Freeman-Grenville's identification of the plant with "the tough leathery sheath of the coconut-flower stem (Swahili *karana*) is unconvincing, since it is supposed to be pulled out of the earth like truffles." However, Jan Knappert's suggestion that it designates the 'sweet potato' (Swahili *ki[l]azi*) is not phonetically plausible, though Whiteley's doubts about the cultivation of yams in East Africa at that time (1969:33) are unjustified (cf. Wrigley, 1970:68–69).[5]

al-Mas'udi also mentions *Kanbalū* as the main island center of Muslim trade in the land of Zanj in his day: this has been equated with Madagascar (Freeman-Grenville, 1962a:40, n.43) but can be more plausibly identified with Pemba (Freeman-Grenville, 1962b:14) or Zanzibar (Mathew 1963:106).[6] This island was mentioned as a major trading center by al-Idrisi in the *Kitab Rujar*, the first Western notice of East Africa (12th century): he indicates that "the principal town is called Unguja in the language of Zanzibar" and that the people of the coastal islands of Zanj go there to trade their goods "for they understand each other's language." He also quotes the local names of 5 types of bananas, namely *kundi, fīlī* (weighing up to 12 oz.), *'omānī, muriyāni* and *sukarī*. These terms do not provide very valuable clues; only *kundi* and *sukarī* correspond to two Swahili varieties of bananas: *kikonde* (round, rather thick, sometimes granulose) and *kisukari* (very sweet); the former is related with Swahili *ukonde* 'small kernel;[7] the latter is obviously an Arabic loan, as are the other three which do not occur in present-day Swahili. However, *fīlī*, from Arabic *fīl* 'elephant', corresponds to Swahili *mkono wa tembo* (literally 'elephant trunk'), applying to large size cooking bananas.

The unreliability of the alleged Swahili material in the early documents does not, however, preclude the use of Swahili as a lingua franca in the trade centers along the coast down to Sofala,[8] but it has to be remembered that until the end of the 13th century, the Arabic settlements are essentially limited to the islands; the East African coast, according to contemporary Arab geographers, is "inhabited by black people who were idolaters" (Ingham, 1962:2). The majority of the inhabitants of the towns were also black as well as most of their rulers, undoubtedly as a result of intermarriage with African women.[9] Piously devout Muslims, they must have maintained Arabic at least as a language of prestige, since ibn Baṭṭuṭa does not seem to have had problems in communicating with the sultan and the high court officials at Kilwa. However, they must have used a language of Bantu origin when dealing with their African subjects: the question is whether, at this early date, the town language was already Swahili?[10]

The only original text that has come down to us from this time is the Kufic inscription in the mosque on Kizimakazi on the east side of Zanzibar stating that Shaikh al-Sayyid Abi Amran al-Ḥasan ibn Muḥammad ordered its building on the first day of the month Khul-Qada in the year 500 A.H. (27 July 1107). Apart from confirming the presence of Muslim rulers on the island at that time, it does not throw any light on our problem.

2.2 *Middle Period*

More important seems the fact that a series of smaller settlements were established along the Tanzanian coast between the 13th century and the 15th century: *Tongoni*, in the Mtang'ata chiefdom south of Tanga; *Utondwe,* south of the Wami River; *Kaole*, south of Bagamoyo; *Kunduchi*, north of Dar es Salaam; *Ras Malibe*, close to Mbwamaji, and *Kisiju*, halfway between Dar es Salaam and the Rufiji River (Kimambo, 1969:39). Increased contact down the coast and closer links with major centers like Zanzibar and Kilwa must have promoted the use of a lingua franca in this period.

The first Portuguese who visited the area in the late 15th and early 16th centuries do not provide any positive clue on the linguistic situation at that time: Vasco de Gama (1498) who mistakes the vegetarian Indians in Mombasa and Malindi for Christians, is aware of their using a different language, but points out their ability to communicate with the Arabs, because they picked up some of their language in years of mutual contact (Freeman-Grenville, 1962b:55). Similarly, Cabral (1500) uses an interpreter who speaks *Arabic* to negotiate with the "king" of Malindi, as he probably also did in Kilwa though it is not indicated specifically there (Freeman-Grenville 1962b:60–62). During his second trip, Vasco de Gama (1502) has an interpreter address the "king" of Kilwa, his court and even the women of the city in the "language of the country", so that they might understand his command (Freeman-Grenville, 1962b:69). Wherever the language of the "Moors", as the Portuguese call the Muslims of the East-African towns, is specified, it is Arabic: describing Sofala, Duarte Barbosa (1517–18) states (Freeman-Grenville, 1962b:127): "The Moors of this place speak Arabic" and he contrasts these Muslim merchants with the "Heathen of the kingdom of Benametapa" (Monomotapa), indicating that "some of them speak Arabic, but the more part use the language of the country", Similarly, the "Moors" of Kilwa "speak Arabic and follow the creed of the African" being very pious (Freeman-Grenville, 1962b:131) – another reason for them to maintain Arabic, besides their continued commercial links with the Arabic peninsula.

Perhaps N. Chittick (1968:117) may have best summarized the sociolinguistic profile of the cities along the Tanzanian coast:

> Their society was primarily Islamic, and their way of life mercantile. This does not mean to say it was Arab; the immigrants were few in number, and intermarrying with African women and those already of mixed blood, their stock was rapidly integrated with the local people. Probably by the second or third generation they would have abandoned their spoken language for Swahili or the local language, though retaining Arabic for writing.

However, his statement about Arabic might be somewhat qualified in view of its use with foreign visitors and, undoubtedly, also in prayer and other religious activities.

At the time of the first Portuguese intervention in the 16th century, the coastal towns constituted a string of largely independent city-states under the control of often feuding "Shirazi" ruling families. Kilwa was the only major settlement in the south, but at the time of its sack in 1505, the island and the town had a population of only 4,000 people according to an eye-witness account (Freeman-Grenville, 1962b:106); the central Tanzanian coast was more sparsely settled; there were a series of small sultanates in the north, e.g. in Mtang'ata (Tongoni) and Vumba. The disruptive impact of the Portuguese on the coastal settlements was increased by migrations of small Bantu clans and tribes starting around the middle of the 16th century and moving mostly from north to south along the hill ranges fringing the coast of Kenya and northern Tanzania. The situation was only stabilized about 1700, at a time when the Portuguese had practically established their supremacy over the Shirazi city-states for more than a century (Berg, 1968:120–122).

Particularly important in this context is the migration and resettlement of inhabitants of Swahili settlements on the north coast of Kenya: some of the refugees went to Pemba, and "most of the Twelve Tribes, which comprise the present Swahili population of Mombasa occupied the island in this period." Further southward, many of the small Swahili towns along the Mrima coast in Tanzania may have been founded as a result of this movement of population (Berg, 1968:129). One wonders how much of an impact this migration from the north may have had on the old southern settlements like Kilwa, if the comment made by M. H. Abdulaziz about the language of the fourteen letters from Kilwa dating back to 1711–1728 found in the Goan archives – " that the Swahili in which they were written is not too dissimilar from his own kiMvita" (Whiteley 1968:38) – proves correct.

Anyhow, by the 17th century, we seem to have some direct evidence of a dialect related to Swahili spoken in the Comoro Islands: the short list of local terms compiled by Walter Payton who visited Johanna *Anjuani* includes five types of words (Gray, 1950:96):

(a) unidentifiable words, like *seivoya* 'cocker nuts' or *quename* 'pine';
(b) Portuguese loanwords, like *surra* (kind of drink) and *figo* 'plantains,' reflecting Port. *sura* 'first juice of palm tree' and *figo* 'fig', presumably applying to what Sacleux (1949:314) calls 'figue banane' and renders by Swahili *ndizi*;
(c) Arabic loanwords, like *soutan* (Swahili *sultani* < Arabic *sulṭan*) and *cartassa* (Swahili *karatasi* < Arabic *qarṭas*);
(d) Bantu terms shared by a number of East coast languages, namely *gombey* 'bullock' < Bantu [C.S. 849] **gòmbè* 'cattle' (Guthrie 3.225); *coquo* 'hen' < Bantu [C.S. 1203] **kúku* (Guthrie 1.123-4§ [74.11-14; topogram 24]; 3.310); *buze* 'goat' < Bantu [C.S. 185] **búdị̂* (Guthrie 3.61) – as regards coastal Bantu languages the change d→z/–i occurs essentially in southern Kenya and northern Tanzania, whereas devoicing to *s* takes place in southern Tanzania; in the Comoro form (Ngazija dialect) *dz* would be expected.
(e) terms with close Swahili correspondents, namely *sinzano* 'needle' = Swahili *sindano*;
arembo 'bracelet' = Swahili *urembo* 'ornaments' (from *-remba* 'adorn, decorate');
tundah 'oranges' = Swahili *tunda* (plural *matunda*) 'fruit' (<*-tunda* 'pluck') with a rather surprising specialization of the meaning, since oranges are definitely *not* the characteristic fruit crop of the Comoro Islands;
mage 'water' = Swahili *maji* – a very valuable sample if the grapheme <g> has the phonetic value [dʒ] of English *-g-* in *image*, since this would be the normal reflex of Bantu **j* in the Ngazija dialect of the Comoro Islands (as the display of the forms under C.S. 937 **ji* and C.S.943 **jí* [Guthrie 3.248,250] shows, the reflexes are also affricates – *dz* or *ts* – in Kenya, but fricatives in Tanzanian coastal dialects: *z* in the north and *s* [occasionally ð] in the south).

2.3 *18th–19th Century*

From the 18th century on, evidence for the use of Swahili becomes abundant: the oldest preserved manuscript is dated 1728 and contains an epic poem *Utendi wa Tambuka* written in Pate (Harries, 1972:5; Knappert, 1967:3, 143–4) the oldest known poet Aidarusi bin Athumani seems to have been active in the same town at the end of the 17th century though the oldest manuscript of his *al-Hamziyah*, an interlinear version of the Arabic poem *Umm al-Qura* is dated 1749 (Knappert, 1968:55). The Northern Kenya coast is indeed the center of Swahili literary activity and Swahili poetry will only start flourishing further south in Mombasa with Muyaka bin Haji in the first decades of the 19th century, though earlier poems from this town already found their way as far south as Anjuani in the Comoro Islands in the last quarter of the 18th century (Knappert, 1969:1–2).

As to Tanzania, literature began in Zanzibar towards the middle of the 19th century and the Mrima coast produced religious poetry like the

Kiyama in the second half of the 19th century. Anyhow, written Swahili literature was essentially didactic and embedded in an entirely Islamic sphere of life until the advent of the German administration in 1884 (Knappert, 1971:4–5, 13).

3.0 The Present Situation

3.1 Swahili Dialects along the Tanzanian Coast

The linguistic situation along the Tanzanian coast is characterized by much less dialectal differentiation than in Kenya: from Vanga to the Rufiji River, facing Mafia Island, *Mrima* is used, especially in towns like Tanga, Bagamoyo and Dar es Salaam; it is very similar to the main Zanzibar dialect – *kiUnguja*; south of the Rufiji a subdialect known as *Mgao* has its main center in Kilwa (Sacleux, 1909:IX). As characteristic features of *Mrima*, Stigand (1915:16–25) mentions:

(1) *l* for *r*, e.g. *balua* for *barua* 'letter';
(2) *s* for *sh*, e.g. *sauri* for *shauri* 'plan, council';
(3) occasional devoicing of *g*, e.g. *kiza* for *giza* 'darkness';
(4) occasional palatalization of *k* to *ch* [tʃ] before front vowels [i], [e], e.g. *kucheti* for *kuketi* 'stay, sit';
(5) trend to realize [m̩] as [mu] and insertion of *u* after *m* before consonants, e.g. *mutu* for *mtu* 'person', *amuri* for *amri* 'order';
(6) insertion of *l* or *r* in various sequences of two vowels, e.g. *njara* for *njaa* 'hunger';
(7) use of *ya* instead of *la*-concords with the 5th class, e.g. *soka ya kuni* 'axe for firewood'; *jiko yake* 'his kitchen'.

Many of these features are shared by Mgao, where they usually appear on a larger scale, in particular:

(1) confusion between *r* and *l*, e.g. *asari* for *asali* 'honey', *kuludi* for *kurudi* 'return';
(4) palatalization of *k* to *ch* before *i*, e.g. *chichwa* for *kichwa* 'head';
(5) *mu* for [m̩] and insertion of *u* between *m* and consonant, e.g. *muti* for *mti* 'tree', *kuamuka* for *kuamka* 'awake';
(6) insertion of *l* or *r* in sequences of two vowels (also in *ia* and *ea* where it does not occur in Mrima), e.g. *kugwira* for (kiMrima) *kugwia* 'seize', *kumera* for *kumea* 'grow'.

Both Mrima and Mgao also show specific grammatical and lexical peculiarities. Typical Mrima words are *kugwia (kugwira)* for *kukamata* 'seize'; *kitumba* for *kanda* 'fisherman's basket'; *machufuko* for *fitina* 'disorders'; a typical archaism in an outlying territory is the old Swahili verb *kuima* for *kisimama* 'stand' preserved in Mgao.[11]

The Mrima coast dialects have close links with the island dialects; there are, for example, noticeable lexical correspondences between Mtang'ata (south of Tanga)[12] and Pemba (Whiteley, 1956:4). A closer relation between Vumba, Mtang'ata, Hadimu, Tumbatu and the northeastern and southeastern Pemba dialects, including further connections with the Comoro dialects, has been assumed (Whiteley, 1959:42).

In the islands, Pemba, spoken on Pemba island, shows four local varieties: (1) *kiPemba cha kusini*; (2) *kiPemba cha kivintongoji (Mvumoni)*; (3) *kiChake-Chake (Chake-Chake)*, and (4) *kiMsuka (Chaleni)*, according to Sacleux (1909:IX). In the late fifties, when W. H. Whiteley visited the islands, Zanzibar Swahili had apparently replaced the local dialects in the Western half of the island due to the influx of migrant workers from Zanzibar and the mainland in the above plantations. Distinctive Pemba dialects still survived in the Micheweni-Wingwi peninsula of the north east, on Kojani island in the east, and the Matela-Kiuyu area south of Kojani (Whiteley, 1958:8). No detailed description of these dialects is available, which Whiteley[13] divides roughly into three groups, with a set of local variations:

(1) northern: Konde, Tumbe, Micheweni;
(2) central: Kowani, Matele, Ndagoni, Ngwachani, Kiuyu, Kambini;
(3) southern: Chokocho.

The differences are essentially lexical, though there is also some variation in the demonstratives and the affixes in the verbal complex. Pemba in general, has two sets of subject prefixes in the singular of the affirmative forms – a feature it shares with Vumba (on the Kenya–Tanzania border), Hadimu (in southern Zanzibar) and Mtang'ata (on the Mrima coast); one of them, is, however, as a rule, restricted to the *-li-* and *-me-* tenses (Whiteley, 1958:12–15).

3.2 Zanzibar and the Coast

On Zanzibar, three distinct dialects coexist: (a) *Unguja*, which has become the basis of standard Swahili, and is originally the language of Zanzibar town and the central part of the island; (b) *Hadimu*, also called *Kae*, is the dialect of the east and south of the island; (c) *Tumbatu* is a sub-dialect spoken on the small Tumbatu island and in Mkokotoni Bay in the northwest of Zanzibar island.

Both Hadimu and Tumbatu share a number of features with Pemba; some of them point to the preservation of older forms where Unguja innovates, e.g. in the case of the development of *fy* (from Bantu *p_i*- before back vowel [u,o] to *s*) as illustrated by Bantu *$p_i^\prime u$* 'knife' (C.S. 1544) > Pemba, Tumbatu, Hadimu *kifyu*, Zanzibar *kisu* (Ingrams, 1924:542).[14] Similarly, the three dialects maintain *vy-* as the reflex of Bantu *b_i-* before vowel, where the cluster developed into *z-* in Unguja, e.g. Bantu *$b_iád$-* 'bear (a child)' (C.S. 136) > Pemba, Tumbatu, Hadimu *vyaa*: Zanzibar *zaa* (Ingrams, 1924:536; Lambert, 1962:66). Also characteristic is Pemba, Tumbatu, Hadimus *s* versus Zanzibar *sh* [ʃ] as reflex of Bantu *k_i*, e.g. Bantu *$k_i\eta g\grave{o}$* 'neck' (C.S. 1086) > *singo* in the three dialects, but *shingo* in Standard Swahili; Bantu *$yók_i$* 'smoke' (C.S. 2114) > *mosi* in the three dialects, but *moshi* in Standard Swahili.

In other cases, however, Pemba goes its own way as opposed to the dialects of Zanzibar island, e.g. in the treatment of Bantu *c* which is reflected by [ʃ] < sh > in Pemba versus [tʃ] < ch > in the Zanzibar dialects, e.g. Bantu *càŋgà 'sand' (C.S. 288) > Pemba mshanga: Unguja mchanga; Bantu *cúpà '(calabash) bottle; jar' (C.S. 425/6) > Pemba shupa: Tumbatu, Unguja chupa; Bantu *cí 'country' (C.S. 331) > Pemba shi: Tumbatu muchi, Hadimu chi, Unguja nchi. An important morphophonemic distinction is the preservation of the prefix ki- before vowel-initial stems, e.g. Pemba kiuma 'iron', kielezo 'float (of fishnet)', kiakwe 'his', kiangu 'my': Unguja chuma, chelezo, chake (Tumbatu chakwe), changu.

As for the Zanzibar island dialects, Tumbatu appears to have preserved the Bantu prefix *di- of class 5 in a number of cases, e.g. dyipu 'abscess' (versus Pemba and Hadimu ipu with zero prefix and Standard Swahili jipu), dicho 'eye' (: Standard Swahili jicho).[15] Prevocalic root-initial and intervocalic -l- (from Bantu *d) appears as -y-, e.g. in yaya 'sleep' (: Standard Swahili lala < Bantu *dáád- [C.S. 456]), vuya 'rain' (:Standard Swahili mvua, in which l → Ø in /V–V/; Bantu *búdà [C.S. 225]).

Characteristic features of Hadimu are:

(a) the "lenition" of /p/ to the voiced bilabial fricative [β] represented by <υ> (Lambert, 1962:51; Polomé, 1967:24), e.g. mυisi 'cook' (:Sw. mpishi); -υita 'pass' (:Sw. -pata); yaυo 'there' (:Sw. hapo);

(b) Future: kachakufwa = Sw. atakufa 'he will die'; akaga kucha muwapa = Sw. akipotea utamtafula 'if he is lost, you will look for him'.

In Hadimu, loss of initial l- occurs in class 3/4 nouns like mwango, plural miango 'door(s)' (: Standard Swahili mlango); mwomo 'mouth', plural miyomo 'lip(s)' (: Standard Swahili mdomo, with [ɖ]!). While Ingrams (1924:540) recorded Tumbatu and Pemba mliango, he also found mwango in Comoran (Ngazija); as for mwomo, this is also the form occurring in the northern Tikuu dialect (cf. Guthrie, 1970:177, s.v. P.B. *-dòmò [C.S. 652]).[16] Similarly, Hadimu shares the shift of l to u in the environment /a–m/ in the reflexes of Swahili mfalme 'chief' with Ngazija, but it also occurs in Tumbatu with the development of a glide between a and u: Hadimu/Ngazija mfaume:[17] Tumbatu mfayume (Ingrams, 1924:538).

3.3 Regional Variation inside Tanzania

The dialects briefly described represent the primary regional differentiation within the Swahili linguistic area. As the language spreads through education, administrative and political use, economic and cultural activities, and especially through the media which now reach even the remotest corners of the country, new varieties are likely to develop. These will be characterized by specific phonological and grammatical features, by semantic shifts and by particular lexical items. Thus, F. Madoshi noted a number of changes in meaning in Swahili words in the Mwanza area (1971:88), e.g. kalua (sect of Indian fishermen) applying to a big boat,[18] mseto (literally: 'mash, mixture', applying in politics to a 'coalition' [Goldklang, 1967:198; Temu, 1971:12] or a 'multi-racial government' [serikali ya mseto; Whiteley, 1961:13]) referring specifically to the 'opposition'. In some cases, however, rather than a semantic shift, direct borrowing seems to have taken place: thus, *mtumba* 'container for snuff or powdered medicine', which Madoshi equates with coastal Swahili *mtumba* 'bale, load' (also meaning 'book-casing' in Mvita and Amu according to Sacleux [1941:617]), is presumably a loan from Sukuma *tumba* (class 3/4) 'snuff-box'. So are a number of local Swahili terms listed by Madoshi (1971:85–88), for example:

Mwanza Swahili	*Sukuma*
palika 'be polygamous'	*palika* 'take a second wife'
udaga 'dried cassava' (= Swahili *makopa*)	*budaga* 'dried or powdered manioc'
sesa 'cut the grass before the real cultivation'	*sesa* 'hoe on the surface, remove the grass before cultivating a field'
sato (a general name for *tilapia*)	*sato* (fish of the carp family)
soga (rather small type of fish)	*soga* (fish variety)
gunguli 'village' (usually with natural boundaries in form of a valley, hills and streams)	*gunguli* 'village' (with locative prefix, also 'on the hill')
mlamji 'sub-chief'	*lamuji* (class 1/2) 'judge'
nsumba ntare 'assistant headmaster'	*nsumba* 'junior' (literally 'young man') + *ntale* 'superior, notable, elder, authority'

It stands to reason that as Swahili takes firmer hold as first language of a large section of the population in many parts of Tanzania, it will expand its lexicon in this way, especially to denote local features and ecological realities, like the typical fish of Lake Victoria, the traditional dances of the area or the plants and trees that are essentially found in the Lake region.

Studies on lexical distribution in the primary dialects of Swahili are few: Ingrams (1924) merely provides a comparative word-list; the model analysis of a set of verbal stems and their extensions by Carol Eastman (1969) covers essentially the dialects of the Kenya coast with Vumba in the south reaching into Tanzania (139); my own outline of the problem in 1968 remains sketchy, but cases like the term for 'refrigerator' indicate how new regional differentiations tend to develop; as I concluded on the basis of field-notes collected in 1963:

> a pure Swahilization *rifrijeratani* in the locative is not uncommon, though the abbreviated form *friji* is more currently used in Zanzibar; more conservative people on the Mrima coast and in rural Zanzibar will resort to phrases like *mashini ya barafu*,[19] *joko la barafu* (literally 'oven of ice'), *sanduku la barafu*, or the vaguer *mtambo wa barafu, dude la barafu*; nevertheless, a typical insular word *rifu* has emerged and is spreading all over Zanzibar and Pemba (Polomé, 1968:610).

Another field of incipient dialectal differentiation is revealed by the repeatedly reported "mispronunciations" of Swahili which local teachers point out. They reflect the well-known phonic interferences characteristic of bilinguals (Weinreich, 1953: 14–28). A few examples based on the observations of Mr. Mhaiki, an experienced Tanzanian teacher, are given in Table 4:1.

4.0 Language and National Development

As a society grows in complexity, the lexicon which expresses the various aspects of its activities expands, using various devices provided by the language to create new lexical items.

4.1 Semantic Development

The use of terms in a new context entails an expansion of their semantic field, and as cultural changes affected the Swahili-speaking community, numerous examples of such expanded semantic content appeared, e.g. in the vocabulary of law:

	Original meaning	New specialized meaning
kura	lot(s)	ballot
utoto	childhood	minority
majaribio	(Plural of jaribio 'test')	probation
-thibitisha	secure, prove	probate
msamaha	pardon	amnesty

Similarly, in the field of mechanical engineering, *kombo* 'crank' applied originally to anything crooked, hook-shaped, for instance, a small curved tool; *chemua* 'exhaust' meant originally 'sneeze'; etc. – but often the extended meaning is also linked with a new set of derivations, e.g. *sharabu* 'absorb' – literally: 'suck up' – and the related nominals *kisharabio* 'absorbent', *usharabu* 'absorption'; *chapuza* 'accelerate' – causative of *chapua* 'speed up' – and the nominals *kichapushio* 'accelerator', *mchapuko* 'acceleration', etc.

The use of the prefix of class 14–Swahili *u-* (< Proto-Bantu *bu-*) – creates new 'abstracts', e.g. in the political terminology:

ubwanyenye	'exploitation'	(:*bwanyenye* 'bourgeoisie');
ubeberu	'imperialism'	(:*beberu* 'strong man', also used for 'colonialist');
ukabila	'tribalism'	(:*kabila* 'tribe')
utaifa	'nationalism'	(:*taifa* 'nation'); etc.

4.2 Derivation and Composition

As in the majority of the Bantu languages, the flexibility of the derivational processes of Swahili greatly simplifies the task of creating a technical terminology: with a semantically adequate combination of suffixes and the assignment of the nominals to the proper classes the same

Table 4:1 Examples of Variation in Pronunciation of Swahili[20]

		Sampling	Language Area
(a)	*devoicing*: [+voice] → [−voice]		
	(1) b → p	*parua* 'letter', *paraparani* 'on the road'	Makua
	(2) v → f	*fiatu* 'shoes', *ufumbuzi* 'discovery', *fyofyote* 'whatever'	Matengo, Nyakyusa, Bena, Ndendeule
(b)	*strengthening*:[21]		
	(1) fricative → stop [+continuant] → [−continuant] f→p	*piga kopi* 'slap', *kopia* 'cap', *nina kipu* 'I am scared'	Makua, Ndendeule, Matengo, Mavia
	(2) fricative → affricate (introduction of the feature [delayed release])		
	(I) s → ch[tʃ]	*chacha* 'now', *chokoni* 'at the market', *chamaki* 'fish'	Mavia
	(II) z → j [dʒ] *after nasal*	*njima* 'alive, sound', *njungu* 'European'	Mavia
	(III) z → ch[tʃ] *with devoicing*	*checha* 'play', *chamani* '(ancient) time(s)', *chawadi* 'present'	Mavia
(c)	*'weakening'*:		
	(1) affricate → fricative [dʒ] <j> → [z]/C$_{[+\ nasal]}$ —	*nzaa* 'hunger', *nzia* 'path', *kunzua* 'spread open', *mzane* 'widow', *mzinga* 'simpleton, idiot'	Sukuma, Kerewe, Kinga
	(2) d → l	*leni* 'debt', *lobi* 'washerman', *lukani* 'in the shop'	Matengo, Haya
	(3) j → y	*kuya* 'come', *yana* 'yesterday', *yumapili* 'Sunday'	Matumbi

root can produce a set of relevant specific terms, e.g. from the verbal root *tum-* 'send' the following nouns can be derived:

- (cl. 3/4) *mtume* 'prophet' (applying to Mohammed),
  mtumo 'employment',
- (cl. 5/6) *tumo* 'paid servant',
- (cl. 9/10) *tume* 'messenger',
- (cl. 14)   *utumo/utumi* 'employment',
  utume 'status of one sent.'

The passive form – *tumwa* 'be sent' – serves as a basis for the nouns *mtumwa* 'slave' (literally: 'one sent'), *utumwa* 'slavery'; *mtumwaji* 'one regularly employed', *kitumwa* '(diminutive) 'one who is employed or sent.' Further derivations are based on *tumisha/tumiza* 'send off, dispatch', e.g. *mtumishi* 'paid servant', *matumishi* 'service', *matumizi* 'employment', *utumishi/utumizi* 'act of service, employment' (Trager, 1973: 45).[22]

There are some very striking examples of new terms coined by such procedures, e.g. *kutoingiliana* 'non intervention', a negative infinitive of the reciprocal of the applicative – *ingilia* ('enter with a purpose, pry into') of *-ingia* 'go into' (Goldklang, 1967: 203) – or President J. Nyerere's *kujitegemea* 'self-reliance', the reflexive infinitive of *-tegemea* 'rely upon' (Besha, 1972: 34).

Composition serves similar purposes, e.g. on the pattern of terms like *mwanafunzi* 'pupil', a large number of new compounds with *mwana* as first element were introduced: *mwanamaji* 'sailor', *mwana sheria* 'lawyer', *mwananchi* 'citizen',[23] etc. Some compounds are particularly descriptive, especially in engineering and the sciences, e.g. *kibadilimwendo* 'cam', containing *badili* 'change' and *mwendo* 'course'; *nusukipenyo* 'radius', consisting of *nusu* 'half' and *kipenyo* 'axis'. Puristic efforts to avoid loanwords will lead to such formations as, e.g. *gendameme*, instead of *dainamo* 'dynamo' – literally 'fastening up electricity' from (*-ganda* 'coagulate' + (*u)meme* 'lightning') – or *kizaameme*, instead of *jenereta* 'generator' – literally '[thing] engendering electricity' (from *-zaa* 'give birth'). Some elements like *da-* from *dawa* 'drug' function as affixes, e.g. in the biological terms:

dakuvu	'fungicide' (:*kuvu* 'mold'),
dabuibui	'arachnicide (:*buibui* 'spider'),
dadudu	'insecticide' (:*dudu* '[large] insect'),
danyungu	'nematicide; (:*nyungunyungu* '[kind of] worm'),
dakono	'moluscidide' (:*konokono* 'snail'),
dagugu	'herbicide' (:*gugu* 'weed').

Similarly, *-mea* (the root of the verb 'grow', applying to plant and animal life) has practically become a suffix in *nyungumea* 'nematode', *kungumea* 'bugs', *kupemea* 'scale insects' (Gurnah, 1974:43).

Often, however, phrases are used to render foreign concepts, e.g. *kuandika kwa ufupi* 'stenography' (lit. 'writing with brevity'); *njia ya ugunduzikwa lijulikanalo* 'deductive method' (lit. 'way to cause what is knowable to be discovered'); *usomaji wa mchanganyiko* 'co-education' (lit. 'education of mixing together').

Compounds and periphrastic expressions are quite common in the case of loan-translations – a device frequently resorted to in order to expand the specialized vocabulary, e.g. in the religious terminology:

habari njema 'good news' for 'gospel' (instead of the loan *injili*);
chuo cha sala 'prayer book'; *jamii ya utawa* 'religious community'; etc.

Similarly, in other fields, 'horse power' is rendered by *nguvu farasi*, 'hexagon' by *pembesita* ('six angles'), 'television' by *kionambali* (lit. 'see far off'), etc.

4.3 Borrowing

As regards loans, previously hardly ever occurring Arabic terms like *thaura* 'revolution' have become more commonly used, also entering in compounds like *mpingathaura* 'counter-revolutionary' (the first element belonging to the verbal root *ping-* 'oppose' [Temu, 1971:4]). New fields of application have been found for terms like *gharadhi* ('aim, intention, wish' → 'everyday goods') or *irabu* (vowel sign in Arabic script → 'vowel'). However, the main source of loans is English, not only in the field of technical development, but also in all aspects of social and cultural life, though a conscious effort appears to have been made in recent years to limit the borrowing of lexical items as much as possible and to encourage Swahilization. In fact, the number of English loans in the legal terminology compiled by A. B. Weston and Sheik Mohamed Ali (1968) is remarkably small: practically, only the so-called 'stabilized anglicizations' (Weston, 1965:9), like *kesi* 'case', *ripoti* 'report', *korti* 'court', have been maintained, but just as the Tanzanian administration replaced *rejinoo kamishna* 'regional commissioner' by *mkuu wa mkoa*, *siti konseli* 'city council' by *baraza la jiji*, or *direkta* 'director' by *mkurugenzi*, the older Swahili *mahakama* 'place of judgement' (related with the Arabic loan *hukumu* 'pass sentence') may eventually replace *korti*.

Efforts to Swahilize the religious terminology are also illustrated by the successive publication of revised lists[24] containing increased number of Swahili equivalents, e.g. *papa* 'pope' → *baba mtakatifu* 'holy father';

retriti 'retreat' → *mafungo* (:*funga* 'shut in');
konsekrasyo 'consecration' → *mageuzo* (:*geuza* 'cause to change');
epistola 'epistle' → *waraka* 'letter';
epifania 'Epiphany' → *tokeo la Bwana* 'apparition of the Lord'; etc.

This includes the use of specific Islamic terminology with a new Christian content, e.g. *tabishi* for the 'rosary', *haji* for a pilgrimage to Rome or Jerusalem, *nabii* 'prophet' (versus *mtume* 'apostle'), etc. Swahilization efforts also include the technical terminology of mechanics, for instance, as the following samples may show:

breki 'brake' → *zuio*, from *-zuia* 'cause to stop';
klachi 'clutch' → *mfumbato*, from *-fumbata* 'make come into contact'.

Sometimes, there even seems to be a choice between an English loan, a Hindi loan, and a Swahili term, as in the case of the constellation of the Charioteer (*Auriga*) for which the names *derava* (< E. *driver*) *gariwala* (Hindi derivation with -*wala*, indicating the operator of a vehicle – *gari*) and *mwendashaji* (Swahili for 'driver') are in competition (Rupper, 1965:75).

Nevertheless the number of English loans in general remains large. Mostly they have been adapted to the phonological structure of Swahili by elimination of the phonemes not occurring in Swahili and reshaping the pattern of syllabification in compliance with Swahili restrictions as regards consonant clustering. Thus, an epenthetic vowel has been added to English words ending in consonants, e.g. *cheki* 'check', *kuponi* 'coupon', *chati* 'chart', *magrovu* 'gloves', *lokapu* 'look-up', etc.[25] Final -*er* is rendered by -*a*, e.g., *silinda* 'cylinder', *poda* 'powder', *jampa* 'jumper', *pasenja* 'passenger', *supa* 'super', etc. Reshaping English words according to the Bantu syllable pattern accounts for (*li*)*kurutu* 'recruit', *landirova* 'Land Rover' (type of car), *sarakasi* 'circus', *sitoo* 'store', etc. Sometimes, this may entail syllable loss as in (*mu*)*enjilisti* 'evangelist', but usually the Swahili rendering is fairly close to the actual phonetic realization of the English loan by local Bantu speakers, e.g. in *fenicha* 'furniture', *spea pati* 'spare parts', *injinia* 'engineer', etc.

Whatever device is resorted to, it is obvious that a language that can coin from its own resources such terms as *kichungi* 'filter tip (of cigarette)' (from *changa* 'sift' [i.e. separate fine from coarse particles]), *papasio* 'antenna (of insect)' (from -*papasa* 'grope about' [i.e. feel one's way in the dark with the hands stretched out]), or *kigongaufizi* 'flap (in descriptive phonetics)' (from -*gonga* 'knock' and *ufizi* 'gum'), is undoubtedly well-equipped to meet the needs of the modern technological world.

NOTES

[1] A first version of sections 1 and 2 appears under the title: *The earliest attestations of Swahili* in a volume in memoriam of Professor P. Pandit (Delhi) published by the Linguistic Society of India. (Polomé: 1978)

[2] In Hinnebusch's subgrouping (1976:99), Swahili would be placed as follows: Sabaki-Seuta subgroup (connecting itself further up with Ruvu)

   A. Sabaki
      1. Pokomo-Mijikenda
         a. Pokomo
         b. Mijikenda (Giryama . . . Digo)
   B. Seuta
      1. Zigula-Ngulu
      2. Bondei-Shambala

A typical Sabaki feature is the treatment of the class 5 prefix */di/ as *dzi*- (Giryama *dzino* 'tooth') or *ji* (Swahili *jino* 'tooth'). Seuta has *zi*- (103). Swahili appears, consequently, as 'coastal Sabaki' (104).

[3] Tolmacheva (1975:21–22), however, points to the use of the term *jammun* for a fruit in Mombasa – apparently *Eugenia jambos* 'rose-apple' ("It has a nut like an olive, but its taste is very sweet." – Freeman-Grenville, 1962b:31). Known as

mpera wa kizungu, the plant actually originated in the South Asian subcontinent, where it is known as *jambú-* (Sanskrit > Punjabi *jammū*, Hindi *jām*, Gujrati *jām*, *jăbu*, etc.). The term *jammun*, mentioned by Ibn Baṭṭuṭa, however, is an Indic loanword reflecting the derived form **jambūna-* (Turner, 1966:283) appearing with *-mb-* > *-mm-* (*-m-*) in a number of Indo-Aryan languages, e.g. Punjabi *jammūn* 'Syzygium jambolanum', Maithili *jāmun* (a tree with a bitter purple fruit), Bhojpuri *jāmun(i)* 'edible blackberry', Hindi *jāmun* 'Eugenia jambolena, Syzygium jambolanum'. Swahili *mzambarao*, designating the Java plumtree ('Syzygium jambolanum') reflects Indic *jambula-* which appears in Konkani as *zāmbaḷ* 'Eugenia jambola' and may have been introduced by the Portuguese from Goa.

⁴ Whiteley (1969:33) quotes Knappert's alternate suggestions: (a) *flīmī/waklīmī* would reflect *iqlimi* 'district head', but this term can hardly be considered as Swahili. Sacleux (1941) does not even list it under the sporadically attested Arabic loans; moreover, as Tolmacheva (1975:21) indicates, the term is derived from the Greek loan *iqlim* 'area, district' in Arabic (< Gk. *kluma* – originally 'slope'), which does not apply to administrative divisions and would hardly be applied to themselves by the Bantu inhabitants of Zanj. (b) *maklandjalou* instead of *maliknajlu*, (in the French translation of al-Mas'udi) is to be read *mukulu ijulu* 'the great one above.'

Whiteley himself wonders whether *wa* in *waklīmī* is not the 'possessive' and the *kl-*cluster related with Swahili *kulu* 'great', since the Arab geographer claims the term means 'son *of the great* Lord'. As for the second term, Whiteley suggests a connection with the Arabic root *m-l-k* 'dominion'.

Ohly (1973:17) compares Mas'udi's *flīmī* (to be read [falimi]) with Shela *mfaulume* 'king' (= Amu, Pate, Mrima *mfaume*) and points to the derived meaning 'one who is violent, oppressive' in Nyika.

In the absence of a properly documented modern edition of al-Mas'udi, with a critical examination of the variant readings of the manuscripts, all this remains highly speculative.

⁵ Tolmacheva (1975:20) assumes a basic meaning 'edible ground-plant', referring to the use of the same term in various Bantu languages, respectively for 'sweet potatoes', 'cassava' and 'ground-nuts'.

⁶ Tolmacheva (1975:22) identifies *Qanbalo* in Al-Jahiz with *Mkumbuu*, an ancient port in Pemba, and wants to recognize a distorted form of *Unguja* in *Lanjuya* in the same author.

⁷ Not derived from *konde* 'cultivated field', as Whiteley (1969:29) assumes: cf. Sacleux 1939:371; 1941:945.

⁸ Additional material was adduced by the Leningrad scholars V. V. Malveyev and L. E. Kubbel, who examined the early Arabic sources. Thus, al-Biruni provides the name of the 'tamarind' under the plural form *makuaju*–Swahili *mkwaju* (:Nyika *mukuaju*; Ohly, 1973:17) – and the name of the 'rhinoceros': *impila*, which Tolmacheva (1975:20) compares with Nyamwezi *mpala/pera*, without taking into account the Swahili dialectal form *pe(r)a* (with initial [pʰ]) found in Mvita and Amu account to Sacleux (1941:738–739).

⁹ According to tradition, the first ruler of Kilwa, 'Alī ibn al-Ḥusain, was the son of a Shirazi sultan and an "Ethiopian" (Freeman–Grenville, 1962a:66, 75). Actually, the term *Shirazi* need not point to direct Persian origin: as Freeman–Grenville indicates, (1962a:78–79), it may apply to some African group along the coast in whom a few original traders from Persia (Shiraz) would have completely merged. More specifically, this seems to have been the case with the "Shirazi" merchant-rulers of Kilwa and Kisimani Mafia who set out from the Banadir coast in the Bantu-speaking area of Southern Somalia to control the sea

route to Sofala and the gold supplies from Monomotapa (Chittick, 1968: 110–112).

[10] After surveying the sociological, linguistic, historical, archaeological and literary data, R. Ohly (1973:23) came to the conclusion that the Swahili language originated before the 10th century, but his position was questioned by M. Tolmacheva (1975:24), who rightly points out:

> "... the available information ... proves that the basic ... phonetics and grammar had been established in the Zanj language by the 9th century and that native literacy was probably being shaped into a literary culture. The question remains whether we may call the language Swahili: ... the dialects of which Kiswahili is composed are still in the process of convergence into a united linguistic entity ..."

[11] Also occurring in Hadimu (Kae); see Lambert, (1962/3:56.)

[12] The study of Mtang'ata – rapidly disappearing dialect of the Mrima coast south of Tanga by Whiteley (1956) does not provide much material: his description of the phonology shows very little difference with the Zanzibar dialect (one feature it shares with Pemba is the absence of palatalization of *ky* to *ch* in terms like *kyumba* versus [Unguja] *chumba*). The main characteristic of Mtang'ata is a special set of singular subject prefixes for the perfect and past affirmative tenses (22, 28–32), i.e. *si* for the 1st person, *ku* for the 2nd person, and *ka* for the 3rd person, which also occur in Vumba (Lambert, 1957:40, 43–46). Pemba and Hadimu also show the forms *ka-* and *ku-* in the 2nd and 3rd person, respectively, but the 1st person form is *n(i)-* (Whiteley, 1958:12). As in these dialects the negative verbal pre-prefix is *k'(a)-* is currently used where standard Swahili has *h(a)-*. As for Mrima, in general it is now "almost identical with Kiunguja" according to a leading Swahili writer (Whiteley, 1956:3).

[13] Whiteley's study (1958) does not provide any data on the phonological peculiarities of the dialects, except for the absence of palatalization of *k* before *i*;* the analysis of the morphology is limited to pointing out the main discrepancies versus standard Swahili, i.e. Unguja. A full listing of noun-classes is provided, as well as a table of the tense markers with dialectal variation within Pemba; the latter is accompanied by a rather extensive illustrative sampling (14–17). The lexical material collected is limited, but reflects the vocabulary of daily usage; the place where the terms were recorded is indicated, but no attempt is made to determine the geographical area over which they are used, though it is pointed out that, while absent in Standard Swahili, they "occur in other dialects of this cluster, notably Hadimu, Vumba and Mtang'ata" (55).

[14] Forms like *fyoma* for *soma* 'read' (Bantu *pjóm-* [C.S. 1543]) were considered as "archaic" in Mrima and Mvita at the time Sacleux (1939:241) collected the data for his dictionary (from the end of the XIXth century until the early twenties); *fyoma* is still used in Pemba (Guthrie 1970:IV.64). Occasionally *fy-* has been maintained in Unguja, e.g. in *fyonza* 'suck'.

[15] Reflexes of Bantu *di-* are also found in Pemba *z(i)-*, e.g. *zicho* 'eye', *ziko* 'kitchen' (:Standard Swahili *jicho, jiko*), parallel with Comoran (Ngazija) *dz(i)-*, in *dzitzo, dziho* (Ingrams, 1924:540, 542).

[16] This confirms the findings of Sacleux (1941:538), who also mentions *mwomo* for Tumbatu and Pemba, with the alternate form *muyomo* in Hadimu and Pemba.

[17] According to Sacleux (1941:544), *mfaume* also occurred in the coastal dialects, namely in Mgao (in the Kilwa area), in Mrima and in Amu (cf. also fn. 3).

[18] The compilers of the Swahili Dictionary (in *Swahili* 36.2 [1966]:181) point to the use of *karua* with the meaning 'boat' in the area of the Kavirondo Gulf.

Patel (1967:63) considers the term as a borrowing from Gujrati *kharvo* 'sailor' with a restricted meaning in Swahili. Etymologically, the Gujrati term appears to have meant 'carrier of salt' (< Skt. *kṣār(a)-* 'alkali' + √*vah-* 'transport').

[19] In Zaïre, the phrase *mashini ya baridi* seems to prevail according to Kajiga (1975:192).

[20] On the processes of consonant strengthening and weakening, cf. in particular, Hyman, 1975:164–69.

[21] Here again, comparing the local Swahili forms with the area Bantu languages provides the clue to the phonological changes. Thus, *nzaa* 'hunger', *nzia* 'path' corresponds to Sukuma *nzala, nzila* respectively. (For a parallel development in Lubumbashi Swahili, cf Polomé, 1968b:18). Similarly, where the local vernacular fails to show a voiced counterpart to the sibilant /s/,* voiceless realizations of Swahili /z/ are likely to occur. Some changes cut widely across the country, especially those affecting Swahili phonemes appearing characteristically in Arabic loans, e.g. the fricatives /θ/, /ð/, and /γ/, spelled respectively < th>, < dh>, and <gh>: the interdental fricatives are shifted to the corresponding alveolar /s/ and /z/ by changing the feature [-strident] to [+ strident], e.g. in *thamani* 'value', *kithiri* 'increase', *theluthi* '1/3', etc; *dhambi* 'sin', *kadhalika* 'likewise', *idhini* 'sanction, permission', etc.

(1) the voiced velar fricative /γ/ is strengthened to the corresponding stop /g/ by changing the feature [+ continuant] to [-continuant], e.g. in *ghali* 'expensive, scarce', *bughudha* 'ill feeling, slander', *ghasia* 'confusion, disturbance', etc.

Also widespread is the weakening of /h/ to Ø, e.g. *(h)asara* 'damage', *(h)uruma* 'compassion', *kwa (h)eri* 'goodbye', *(h)ajui* 'he doesn't know', etc. – entailing the use of hypercorrect forms with *h-*, e.g. *hasali* 'honey', *maharufu* 'well-known', etc.

A typical regional feature on the morphological level is the occurrence of such prefixes as the diminutive *ka-*, e.g. *katu* (instead of *kijitu* 'little man'), *kameza* 'small table', *kapaka* 'kitten', in the Ngoni-speaking area, where the augmentative *gu-* is also found, e.g. *gumtu* (instead of *jitu* 'very big man'), *gumeza* 'large table', *gusimba* 'big lion'.

It may be worth noticing that some of these features also occur in Kenya Swahili Pidgin, characterized by (a) devoicing of *v* to *f* (e.g. *ngufu* 'force, strength', *kufaa* 'put on (clothes)', etc.); (b) weakening of *h* to Ø (e.g. *apana* 'no', *roo* 'heart', etc.); (c) diminutives in *ka-* (e.g. *kamtu* 'dwarf', *kamto* 'brook', *kalevi* 'little drunkard', etc.) (Heine, 1973:75, 84–5).

[22] For a comprehensive survey of the Swahili derivational patterns, see Polomé, 1967: 77–94. The "virtually unlimited" productivity of a pattern of derivation – the nouns of action in *-o* – is described by Knappert (1962/3); the extent to which extensions can be added to verbal roots and the complex structure of the derivations is surveyed by Whiteley (1968:56–68 & tables II–IV), with a sample based on *fung-* 'fasten' (107–110).

[23] On compounds with *mwana-*, cf. Temu. 1971:4, 12. The connotations of *mwananchi* are discussed by Scotton, 1965:528–534; Philippson, 1970:531; Besha, 1972:30–31.

[24] The list submitted by the Tanzania Episcopal Conference and based on the Catholic Swahili catechism (*Swahili* 35.1 [1965], 77–91), was revised and republished with Swahili explanations a few years later (*Kiswahili* 42.2/43.1

---

* This is currently the case in the Chaga dialects, where Machame *fyaa* corresponds to Swahili *-zaa* (dialectal *-vyaa*) 'give birth to', both reflecting Proto-Bantu *bíád-* 'bear(child)' (Guthrie, 1970. III:48), and Machame *nrye* to Swahili *nzige* 'locust', both reflecting Proto-Bantu *-gigè* (Guthrie, 1970, III:219), while the loanword *-suri* from Swahili appears with initial *s-*.

[1973]:86-96; 43.2 [1973]:98-112). In the meantime. Omari (1969) had pointed out some of the problems connected with the creation of a Christian theological terminology (Knappert's papers on 'The Divine Names' [*Swahili* 31 (1960), 180-198] and 'Swahili Theological Terms' [*African Language Studies* 8 (1967), 82-92] deal exclusively with Islamic concepts).

[25] On the rules governing the phonological adaptation of loans, cf. Polomé, 1967:175-76. It should however be observed that 'irregularities' occur, e.g. *jemi* 'jam', *midila* 'medal', *likurutu* 'recruit' (the last case, with final -*u* presumably due to vowel harmony).

REFERENCES

1. *Origin of Swahili*

Berg, F. J., 1968, 'The Coast from the Portuguese Invasion to the Rise of the Zanzibar Sultanate' in Ogot, B. A. and Kieran, J. A., eds. *Zamani. A Survey of East African History*, 119-141. Nairobi: East African Publishing House.
Broomfield, G. W., 1931, 'The Re-Bantuization of the Swahili Language' *Africa*, 4, 77-85.
Chittick, Neville, 1965, 'The 'Shirazi' Colonization of East Africa' *Journal of African History*, 7:3, 275-294.
    1968, 'The Coast before the Arrival of the Portuguese' in Ogot, B. A., and Kieran, J. A., eds. *Zamani. A Survey of East African History*, 100-118. Nairobi: East African Publishing House.
Freeman-Grenville, G. S. P., 1962a, *The Medieval History of the Coast of Tanganyika, with Special Reference to Recent Archaeological Discoveries*. London: Oxford University Press.
    1962b, *The East African Coast. Selected Documents from the First to the Earlier Nineteenth Century* Oxford: Clarendon Press.
Gray, John (Sir), 1950, 'Portuguese Records Relating to the Wasegeju' *Tanganyika Notes and Records*, 29, 95-96. (See Whiteley, 1968: 37, 113.)
Guthrie, Malcolm, 1967-1971, *Comparative Bantu. An Introduction to the Comparative Linguistics and Prehistory of the Bantu Languages*.
    1. The Comparative Linguistics of the Bantu Languages.
    2. Bantu Prehistory, Inventory and Indexes.
    3-4. A Catalogue of Common Bantu with Commentary. Farnborough: Gregg Press.
Harries, Lyndon, 1962, *Swahili Poetry*. Oxford: Clarendon Press.
Heine, Bernd, 1970, *Status and Use of African Lingua Francas*. (IFO-Institut für Wirtschaftsforschung München – Afrika Studien, vol. 49) München: Weltforum Verlag.
Hinnebusch, Thomas J, 1976, 'Swahili: Genetic Affiliations and Evidence' *Studies in African Linguistics*. Supplement 6, 96-108 (*Papers in African Linguistics in Honor of Wm. E. Welmers*).
Ingham, Kenneth, 1962, *A History of East Africa*. London: Longmans, Green & Co.
Johnson, F., 1930, *Zamani mpaka siku hizi*. London (quoted in Reusch, 1953: 22).
Kimambo, Izaria N., 1969, 'The Interior before 1800' in Kimambo, I. N. and Temu, A. J., eds., *History of Tanzania*, 14-33. Nairobi: East African Publishing House.
Knappert, Jan, 1968, 'The Hamziya Deciphered' *African Language Studies*, 9, 52-81.

1969, 'The Discovery of a Lost Swahili Manuscript from the Eighteenth Century' *African Language Studies*, 10, 1–30.

1971, *Swahili Islamic Poetry*.
1. Introduction. The Celebration of Mohammed's Birthday. Swahili Islamic Cosmology. 2. The Two Burdas. 3. Mi'rāj and Maulid. Leiden: E. J. Brill.

Krumm, B., 1932, *Wörter und Wortformen orientalischen Ursprungs im Swaheli*. Hamburg: Friederichsen, de Gruyter & Co.

Mathew, Gervase, 1963, 'The East African Coast until the Coming of the Portuguese' in Oliver, Roland and Mathew, Gervase, eds. *History of East Africa*. Vol. 1, 94–127. Oxford: The Clarendon Press.

Ohly, Rajmund, 1973, 'The Dating of Swahili Language' *Kiswahili* 42.2/43.1, 15–23.

Reusch, R., 1953, 'How the Swahili People and Language Came into Existence' *Tanganyika Notes and Records*, 34, 20–27.

Sacleux, C., 1939–49, *Dictionnaire Swahili–Français*. Part I. A–L (1939), Part II. M–Z (1941), (Travaux et Mémoires de l'Institut d'Ethnologie. Université de Paris. Vols. 36–37.) Paris: Musée de l'Homme. *Dictionnaire Français–Swahili*, 2^d edition. (1949) (Travaux et Mémoires de l'Institut d'Ethnologie. Université de Paris. Vol. 44). Paris: Musée de l'Homme.

Struck, B., 1921, 'Die Einheitssprache Deutsch-Ost-Afrikas' *Koloniale Rundschau*, 1921, 164–196.

Sutton, J. E. G., 1966, *The East African Coast. An Historical and Archaeological Review*. (Historical Association of Tanzania. Paper, No. 1) Nairobi: East African Publishing House.

Tolmacheva, Marina, 1975, 'The Zanj Language' *Kiswahili*, 45.1, 16–24.

Turner, R. L., 1966, *A Comparative Dictionary of the Indo-Aryan Languages*. London: Oxford University Press.

Whiteley, Wilfred, 1969, *Swahili. The Rise of a National Language*. (Studies in African History. Vol. 3) London: Methuen & Co.

Wrigley, Christopher, 1970, 'Speculations on the Economic Prehistory of Africa' in Fage, J. D., and Oliver, R. A. eds., *Papers in African Prehistory*, 59–73. Cambridge (U.K.): University Press.

2. *The Present Situation*

This bibliography makes no claim to exhaustiveness, but covers the materials used for the discussion of the development of Swahili.

Akida, Hamisi M., 1971–1975, 'Msamiati wa Muda wa Sayansi (Elimuviumbe)' *Kiswahili* 41.1 (1971) 8–45; 42.2 (1971) 95–102; 42.2/43.1 (1973) 97–101; 43.2 (1973) 116–120; 45.1 (1975) 57–63.

Alidina, M. M. R., 1975, 'The Switch-over to Swahili' *Kiswahili* 45.1: 51–54.

Baldi, Sergio, 1976, *A Contribution to the Swahili Maritime Terminology*. (Collana di Studi Africani, Vol. 2) Rome: Istituto Italo-Africano.

Besha, R., 1972, 'Lugha ya Kiswahili hivi leo: hasa katika siasa' *Kiswahili* 42.1, 22–38.

Eastman, Carol M., 1969, 'Some Lexical Differences among Verbs in Kenya Coastal Swahili Dialects' *African Language Review* 8, 126–147.

Frankl, P. J. L. et al., 1970, 'Maneno ya Utaalamu wa Sayansi ya Lugha' *Kiswahili* 40.2, 1–5.

Goldklang, Harold A., 1967/1968, 'Current Swahili Newspaper Terminology' *Swahili* 37.2, 194–208; 38.1, 42–53.

Gurnah, Abdulla M., 1974, 'Agricultural Terms in kiSwahili' in *Kiswahili* 44.2, 32–44.
Guthrie, Malcolm, 1967–1971, Comparative Bantu. (4 volumes) Farnborough: Gregg Press.
Heine, Bernd, 1973, *Pidgin—Sprachen im Bantu-Bereich.* (Kölner Beiträge zur Afrikanistik, vol. 3). Berlin: Dietrich Reimer.
Hyman, Larry M., 1975, *Phonology. Theory and Analysis.* New York: Holt, Rinehart and Winston.
Ingrams, W. H., 1924, 'The Dialects of the Zanzibar Sultanate' *Bulletin of the School of Oriental Studies* 3, 533–550.
Kajiga, Balihuta, 1975, *Dictionnaire de la langue Swahili.* Goma: Librairie Les Volcans.
Knappert, Jan, 1962/3, 'Derivation of Nouns of Action in -o in Swahili' *Swahili* 33.1, 74–106.
Lambert, H. E., 1957, *Ki-Vumba. A Dialect of Southern Kenya Coast.* (Studies in Swahili Dialect - II) Kampala: East African Swahili Committee.
  1962/3, (ed. H. E. Lambert) 'Haji Chum: A Vocabulary of the Kikae Dialect' *Swahili* 33, 1:51–68.
Madalla, Amos, 1972, 'Mechanical Engineering Terminology' *Kiswahili* 42.1, 75–86.
Madoshi, F. F., 1971, F. F., 1971, 'KiSwahili Words peculiar to Mwanza' *Kiswahili* 41.1, 85–88.
Mkelle, M. B., 1971, 'Change in Content and Meaning of Words' *Kiswahili* 41.1, 100–105.
Ohly, Rajmund, 1973, 'Word and Civilization' *Kiswahili* 43.2, 52–57.
  1975, 'The Conception of *State* through Swahili' *Kiswahili*, 45.1, 25–33.
  1976, 'Lexicography and National Language' *Tanzania Notes and Records* 79/80, 23–30.
Omari, C. K., 1969, 'Towards the Development of Swahili Theological Terms' *Swahili* 39.1/2, 119–124.
Ostrovsky, V. and Tejani, J., 1967–1968. 'Second Tentative Word List' *Swahili* 37.2, 209–224 (A-I); 38.1, 54–99 (J-T); 38.2, 164–168 (T-Z).
Patel, R. B., 1967, 'Etymological and Phonetic Changes among Foreign Words Kiwahili' in *Swahili* 37.1, 57–64.
Philippson, Gérard, 1970, 'Etude de quelques concepts politiques swahili dans les oeuvres de J. K. Nyerere' *Cahiers d'Études Africaines* 10, 530–545.
Polomé, Edgar C., 1967, *Swahili Language Handbook.* Washington, D.C.: Center for Applied Linguistics.
  1968a, 'Geographical Differences in Lexical Usage in Swahili'. *Verhandlungen des zweiten internationalen Dialektologenkongresses* II (= Zeitschrift für Mundartforschung. Beihefte. N.F., vol. 4), 664–672.
  1968b, 'Lubumbashi Swahili'. *Journal of African Languages* 7, 14–25.
  1978, 'The Earliest Attestation of Swahili' *Indian Linguistics,* 39, 165–173.
Prins, A. H. J., 1970, *A Swahili Nautical Dictionary.* Dar es Salaam: Chuo cha Uchunguzi wa Lugha ya Kiswahili.
Rupper, G., 1965, 'Suggested List of Terms for Stars and Constellations' *Swahili* 35.1, 75–76.
Sacleux, C., 1909, *Grammaire des dialectes swahilis.* Paris: Procure des PP. du St. Esprit.
  1939–1941, *Dictionnaire Swahili-Français* (2 volumes). Paris: Institut d'Ethnologie. Musée de l'Homme.
Scotton, Carol M. M., 1965, 'Some Swahili Political Words' *The Journal of Modern African Studies.* 3, 525–542.

Stigand, C. H., 1915, *A Grammar of Dialectic Changes in the KiSwahili Language*. Cambridge: University Press.

Tejani, J./Ostrovsky, V./Kondo, Ali, 1966–1967, 'Tentative list of new words' *Swahili* 36.2, 169–185 (A–K) 37.1, 103–123 (L–Z).

Temu, Canute W., 1971, 'The Development of Political Vocabulary in Swahili' *Kiswahili* 41.2, 3–17.

Trager, Lillian, 1973, 'The Formation of Nouns from Verbs in Swahili' *Kiswahili* 42.2/43.1, 29–50.

Weinreich, Uriel, 1953, *Languages in Contact. Findings and Problems*. New York: Linguistic Circle of New York.

Weston, A. B., 1965, 'Law in Swahili – Problems in Developing the National Language' *Swahili* 35.2, 2–13.

Weston, A. B. and Sheikh Mohamed Ali, 1968, *Swahili Legal Terms*. Dar es Salaam: The Legal Research Centre Faculty of Law, University College.

Whiteley, W. H., 1956, *Ki-Mtang'ata. A Dialect of the Mrima Coast – Tanganyika*. (Studies in Swahili Dialect – I) Kampala: East African Swahili Committee.

1958, *The Dialects and Verse of Pemba. An Introduction*. (Studies in Swahili Dialect – IV) Kampala: East African Swahili Committee.

1959, 'An Introduction to Local Dialects of Zanzibar. Part I' *Swahili* 30, 41–69.

1961, 'Political Concepts and Connotations. Observations on the use of some political terms in Swahili' *St. Antony's Papers* 10. *African Affairs I* (edited by K. Kirkwood), 7–21.

1964, 'Problems of a Lingua Franca: Swahili and the Trade-Unions' *Journal of African Languages* 3, 215–225.

1968, *Some Problems of Transitivity in Swahili*. London: School of Oriental and African Studies, University of London.

1972, 'Msamiati wa muda wa Masomo ya Maendeleo (Development Studies)' *Kiswahili* 42.1, 70–74.

1974, 'Msamiati wa Muda wa Chuo cha T.A.N.U. Kivukoni' *Kiswahili* 44.1, 67–70.

1974, 'Msamiati wa Muda wa Saikolojia' *Kiswahili* 44.2, 75–81.

PART TWO

LANGUAGE USE IN TANZANIA

5 TANZANIA: A SOCIO-LINGUISTIC PERSPECTIVE

Edgar C. Polomé

1.0 *Society in Transition*

Tanzania in the late sixties and early seventies was a society in transition. Step by step, the old social order inherited from the colonial period was being replaced by the new socio-economic framework defined in the Arusha Declaration (19 January, 1967). On this programmatic statement, President Nyerere had pointed out that one of the major policies of his socialist government was to place the instruments of production and exchange under the control and ownership of the people of Tanzania. The list included:

> land; forests; minerals; water; oil and electricity; news media; communications; banks, insurance, import and export trade, wholesale trade; iron and steel, machine tool, arms, motor-car, cement, fertilizer, and textile industries; and any big factory on which a large section of the people depend for their living, or which provide essential components of other industries; large plantations, and especially those which provide raw materials essential to important industry. (Nyerere, 1968b: 234)

Implementation followed very quickly, though a private sector remained operative under specific provisions (Nyerere, 1968b: 251–6). As early as February 6, 1967, all banks in Tanzania had been nationalized, and the Bank of Tanzania notes became the only legal tender in the country after September 1967. The National Development Corporation, created in 1962, became the agent through which the Government acquired controlling interest in the major enterprises. Since February 1968, the National Insurance Corporation controls practically all insurance business. The State Trading Corporation, after taking over control of all the external trade, was progressively completing the nationalization of the wholesale trade in 1969–1970. These decisions entailed important socio-economic consequences for the Asian community in Tanzania, as it had played a leading role in the wholesale trade and the distribution network for import products; moreover, Africanization which followed nationalization had a serious impact on job opportunities for Asians in the banking and insurance business (Ghai, 1969: 95–100).

Sweeping changes were also taking place in rural development with the application of socialist principles: in a policy statement issued in September 1967, President Nyerere (1968b: 337–366) outlined the objectives of the new policy of *ujamaa* agriculture based on economic and social communities where rural people would live together and work together for the good of all.

As a result of the step-by-step transformation advocated by the President, *ujamaa*-villages were established in various parts of the country, partly in order to mobilize under-utilized labor for agricultural development, but in spite of sustained government and political pressure, the socialist agricultural communities were only partly successful, depending on the commitment of the participants and their experience in farming and related activities, and on the competence and the sense of organization and leadership of the officials in charge.

1.1 *Education*

In the field of education, Tanzania, following the lead of President Nyerere (1968a: 267-290), had embarked upon a reorganization of the school system and curriculum to inculcate socialist values and "encourage the development of a proud, independent, and free citizenry which relies upon itself for its own development". New courses in Civics were instituted, and new examinations syllabi drafted; schools started schemes intended to emphasize service to the community and self-reliance, students helping towards the upkeep of their school. As enrollment increased (in 1968, there were five times as many students taking the Higher School Certificate exam as in 1961), the need for teachers became more acute. In 1963, there were only 12 African teachers holding University degrees out of a total of 677 in Tanganyika. For this reason the supply of secondary school teachers was largely dependent on recruitment from outside the country. In the years following Independence, the main source of teachers was a cooperative venture of the Agency for International Development (A.I.D.) and the British Department of Technical Corporation with the governments of East Africa – the Teachers for East Africa Scheme. In 1964, 120 of them worked in Tanzania, and additional help was provided by the Peace Corps. In the late sixties, Anglo-American assistance was being phased out. There was a dire need, therefore, to produce local teachers in large numbers in the teachers training colleges and at the University of Dar es Salaam. The Government planned to increase the total number of secondary school places (forms I to IV) to 43,000 by 1973, and to bring the enrollment in forms V and VI up to 4,000. To achieve this a total of 1,900 teachers were needed, most of them Tanzanian, since the recruitment of expatriates, (e.g. Dutch, Scandinavian, Canadian) able to teach in English was limited. Simultaneously, the replacement of English by Swahili as the medium of instruction was being completed in primary education and planned for secondary education (in the first two forms to start with, where Swahilization was expected to be achieved by 1973). The target year for total self-sufficiency in manpower in Tanzania education was 1980 (Resnick, 1968: 124). The training of graduate secondary school teachers was entrusted to the University College of Dar es Salaam, where academic study was combined in a three year degree course from which about 280 were to graduate in 1970 (Cameron–Dodd, 1970: 215).

1.2 *Society*

Tanzania society in 1970 was also deeply affected by the changes in its foreign policy: as a result of the economic agreement with China and of the building of the Tanzania–Zambia railway, a considerable amount of Chinese technical and professional aid was being provided. However, the Chinese socialized very little outside their professional activities, so that they had little impact on social life as such. As for the internal relationship within the Tanzanian federation, there were considerable restrictions to the circulation of persons and goods between continental Tanzania (former Tanganyika) and the islands of Zanzibar and Pemba, whose administration (including the police) remained distinct and separate from that of the mainland under the direct control of the first Vice-President A. A. Karume and his Revolutionary Committee.

1.3 *Language*

1.3.1 *Language in Government*

As regards the use of language, the Tanzanian government promoted the total Swahilization of the administration. At all levels, Swahili was being used internally for oral communication and as far as possible for all written messages and outside activities. Similarly, inside the ruling party, Swahili was the language of political life at all levels. The National Swahili Council played an important role in the promotion of language in official and public life. Nevertheless, there were still a large number of inscriptions and official papers in English, and mixed usage prevailed in many cases.[1] Apparently, a large number of forms printed under the colonial regime had merely been reproduced with a new heading for lack of available Swahili translation.[2] Mostly English were, however, the documents likely to be used by foreigners or Tanzanians involved in relations with foreign countries, such as import and export licenses, customs and currency control, declarations, etc. In other cases, old painted boards or other public notices had just not yet been replaced, e.g. notices on public transportation and in government-controlled buildings, road-signs, etc.[3]

1.3.2 *Language in the Law*

In the field of justice beyond the level of the primary courts, Swahilization was hampered or slowed down by various factors: though legal terminology had been developed, the transfer into Swahili of the complex body of laws including Bantu customary law, Islamic law, and English common law was progressing at a slower pace than expected; a number of resident magistrates and judges in the High Court were still non-Tanzanian legal experts who had no sufficient command of Swahili. Moreover, in a large number of cases, interpreters had to be used to help older citizens from rural areas who spoke only tribal languages and were unable to present their argument in Swahili.[4]

1.3.3 *Language in the Media*

As for the press, in 1970 there were only four daily newspapers, two in

English – *The Nationalist* and *The Standard* – and two in Swahili – *Uhuru* and *Ngurumo* – their total circulation averaging less than 68,000 copies. There were a considerable number of weeklies, fortnightlies, and monthlies, some published by governmental services, some by religious institutions, some by private groups. Most important were *Nchi Yetu* ('Our Country') published by the Ministry of Information and Broadcasting, and *Ukulima wa Kisasa* ('Present-day Agriculture'), a joint endeavor of the Ministry of Agriculture and Cooperatives and the Lint and Seed Marketing Board, with a circulation of 32,000. These, as well as a number of other publications in Swahili, such as *Mfanya Kazi* ('Worker') the trade unions official weekly, or *Ushirika* ('Common Interest'), the monthly of the bulletin of the Cooperative Union (34,000 copies circulated), were directly aimed at definite sections of the Tanzania population and were widely read, even at the village level. The Catholic presses at Peramiho published a number of Swahili periodicals: *Mwenge* (12,500 copies), *Mtima* (4,000 copies), *Mlezi* (2,600 copies). The circulation of the fortnightly *Kiongozi* ('Guide') owned by the Tanzania Episcopal Conference was also rather wide (23,000 copies), as was that of the Pentecostal Church publication *Habari Maalum – ya Uzima Tele* ('Famous News – of Abundant Life') with 20,000 copies. The Evangelical Lutheran Church put out a couple of monthlies, including *Uhuru na Amani* ('Freedom and Peace' – 12,000 copies). The relative small number of copies available in comparison with the population of the country (estimated at 13,273,000 in 1970) is, however, misleading in judging the number of readers: papers were passed on from person to person to a rather considerable extent; numerous readers would come and read them in the facilities provided by the Ministry of Information all over the country for this purpose, so that, ultimately, the impact of the press was much wider than actual circulation figures would tend to suggest.[5]

As for the radio, it appeared to play a growing role in Tanzanian socio-cultural life as radio-ownership increased dramatically among the Tanzanian population in the late sixties.[6] Between 1964 and 1969, 253,399 radio-sets were imported for sale in Tanzania, and in 1967, the Philips factory in Arusha started production, so that by the end of 1969, 24,751 locally manufactured radios were also available for sale. With a total of 288,150 new radios in five years, it is easy to understand the shift that was taking place in the relative importance of the sources of news information: among persons with middle grade position in Tanzania society, 54% relied on radio for daily news, whereas 37% still considered the newspapers in Swahili and English as their best source of information.[7] The news was indeed on top of the preference list of a sampling of listeners taken in September 1969 (Dodds, 1970: 3), immediately before "music".[8] Programs focusing on political information were also highly favored by male repondents, but figures were significantly lower for female listeners, who would tune in to such programs 37.5% of the time only (as against 65.2% for the men). Similar results were obtained for farming information and religious programs: respectively, 26.1 and 30.4 frequency of listening for male respondents, and 18.7 in both cases for female respondents. As a source of entertainment, women enjoyed music, but seemed to favor "stories" much more than men (31.2 frequency of listening, versus 17.4 for male respondents). The educational programs of high quality which the Tanzania Broadcasting Corporation was producing, were also highly appreciated: male respondents would listen to them 36.4% of the time, and female respondents 31.2%, but here a considerable difference appeared according to the age-group: people over 40 would tune in 50% of the time, whereas people between 30–39 would do so only 33.3% of the time. Differences connected with age-groups were even more conspicuous for other programs, e.g.

	People between 20–29	Between 30 and 39	Over 40
Farming information	12.5%	33.3%	50.0%
Religious programs	16.4%	37.0%	33.3%
Stories	33.3%	10.8%	16.7%

With two regular Swahili programs, the Tanzania radio stations tried to meet the wishes of their listeners, while serving the national interest in providing educative programs for adults, valuable information on farming and related activities, special programs for the schools. These school broadcasts begun in 1954 are of a particularly high standard and cover almost all subjects of the upper primary and secondary schools. For the primary schools (Monday through Friday, from 2:30 till 3:55 p.m.), the medium is Swahili; for the secondary schools (Monday through Friday, from 4:00 till 5:55 p.m.), it is mostly English, but there are 'Beginning French' and 'Advanced Swahili' lessons, and Civics (*Uraia*) is taught in Swahili. As for the other programs, in the late sixties there were (a) the *National Program* in Swahili, broadcasting 13 hours a day and including news, commentaries, music, magazine and children's programs; (b) the *Second Program* in English, transmitting 5 hours a day and relying mainly on taped material and outside sources such as the B.B.C. but with an emphasis in the news on Tanzania from a national point of view; (c) the *Third Program* only broadcast for one and a half hours from Monday to Friday on such subjects as advanced language courses in French and Swahili, music from various countries, cultural material (e.g. art and drama critiques, classical music). Swahili feature programs produced over the National Program are sent out again, e.g. *Ulimwengu Siku Hizi* ('The World Today'); (d) and the *Commercial Service,* using predominantly Swahili, and started in October, 1965, was devoted essentially to light music, news and advertising for about 10 hours a day (Widstrand, 1966:2–5; *Tanzania Today,* 1968: 108–9). Nevertheless, the majority of respondents did not seem totally satisfied with their own broadcasting system and many of them, mainly the older ones, often tuned in to foreign stations.[9] However, one of the major reasons was also the poor reception of the National Program in certain areas distant from Dar es Salaam.

1.3.4 *Entertainment and Sport*

Besides the radio, the main source of entertainment was the cinema, but here, on the contrary, Swahili material hardly ever appeared on the screens, which were shared by the slightly outdated British and American productions and the current products of the Indian film industry, with occasional Russian and East European or Japanese films in their English version. There was little theatrical activity, except for the experimental group in the Faculty of Arts at the University, who staged a few plays in Swahili and started Ebrahim N. Hussein on his dramatic career with *Kinjeketile* (1969), and for the non-professional group at the Little Theatre, which performed such musicals as *South Pacific* or modern English plays.

Swahili pop-music was very popular, especially the type produced in the Congo at that time, but records were hard to come by. Juke-boxes often contained mostly Indian film music which African teenagers would sing along in Hindi or whatever without understanding the words.

The greatest form of entertainment was soccer, and the big games would draw capacity crowds to the stadiums. The language there was definitely Swahili to encourage one's favorite player or to blast him if he fumbled . . .

1.3.5 *Language in Advertising*

All round Dar es Salaam, advertising showed the transitional stage in which the society was: expensive sky-signs or neon-signs were almost all in English, as were the older big boards on the roadside, but in the shops, on the buses, in the gas stations, on the side of vehicles more and more advertisements appeared in Swahili. Churches had notice boards in both languages, but big construction enterprises still listed all their contractors in English, and sales were announced in the same language. Packaged goods, electricity bills and other everyday things were increasingly labelled in the two languages.[10]

1.3.6 *Reading*

Another interesting clue to the actual use of Swahili in some aspects of Tanzanian socio-cultural life was supplied by the survey of the reading habits of the more educated part of the population. A study of the use of public libraries and of their visitors is included in chapter 8; it also provides a list of the books most frequently read as well as a list of some of the books taken out by the sampling used in the survey; these lists are particularly indicative of the use made of literacy, of the concerns and interests of the readership and of the limitation of the choice of materials available in Swahili.

2.0 *Multilingualism*

2.1 *Patterns of Multilingualism*

If we turn our attention to Tanzanians themselves and their use of languages, various patterns emerge, reflecting various degrees of multilingualism. The studies of Henry Barton on Ilala and selected locations outside Dar es Salaam illustrate the situation in a number of African households in urban and semi-rural communities. But they do not show the linguistic behavior of individuals in the day-to-day running of their active life. An effort to document this was made through the keeping of diaries by about 25 persons, whose linguistic activity was recorded on a full workday and a holiday. The sampling represented people of both sexes with various professional, religious and ethnic backgrounds; one third of them had received no formal education; another third had gone to primary school (at most up to standard 8 of upper primary); the rest had attended secondary school and some had gone to university. For all of them Swahili was used more frequently than their own language in proportions that varied from a high of 15:1 to a low of 3:2.[11] With highly educated people, English only appeared once with a higher frequency than Swahili, namely 42% versus 34% (with 20% Chaga and 4% Meru). Usually, however, the proportion of use of English versus Swahili varies between 7:1 and 3:2. Non-Africans would, of course, show completely different patterns of usage, e.g. an Asian would use English 26% of the time versus Kachi 52% and Gujrati 14.5%, with Swahili only 7.3%. Hezekiah Mlay and David Mkindi who conducted this investigation in August 1970, also examined the amount of switching done by the respondents, noticing that switching from English or a vernacular into Swahili was far more frequent than the reverse, and trying to determine the circumstances that triggered the change of language: in 44% of the cases, it seemed to result from an arbitrary personal choice; 23% were ascribed to a desire by the speaker to express himself in a more effective way; 11% were due to the need to resort to a language understood by a third party entering the conversation. Furthermore, in 10% of the cases, the switching was initiated by the other party, forcing as it were the speaker to use the same language for the listener's convenience. Switching to vernaculars was connected with kinship, relationship and familiarity of the parties, recognition of belonging to the same area, etc. and accounted for 8% of the cases.

All this tended to show that Tanzanians in all aspects of their social activities played various roles for which various linguistic codes were being used with a definite amount of discrimination. But Tanzanian society, though less diversified than that of a developed industrial country, presents typical features in the complexity of its multilingual sociolinguistic patterning. Let us illustrate this by briefly examining some of the most characteristic types of Tanzanians and their linguistic behavior:

2.1.1 *The Farmer*

"Farming is the way of life to most people in Tanzania, either on the large estates or small holdings run by a single family" (*Tanzania Today,* 1968: 111). Traditional agriculture is based on a system of land tenure regulated by customary law; it is characterized by subsistence farming and shifting cultivation as a result of soil deterioration. With the activity of the Department of Agriculture, the social and political changes of recent years were having an impact on land use, and semi-permanent and permanent cropping with smallholder farming became the dominant pattern in some areas more favored by nature and with better access to markets (Ruthenberg, 1968). Cooperatives, encouraged at an early date by the British administration, have also helped the smallholders market their cash crops, e.g. of cotton around Lake Victoria, or of coffee in the foothills of Mount Kilimanjaro. A new pattern has developed with the establishment of the *ujamaa* village and its experiments in collectivization, with far-reaching social implications.[12]

Traditionally, farmers would live in essentially monolingual areas and most of their activities would be confined to their village environment where they would speak their own language constantly. Language continuity would be insured by the family pattern, which practically excluded marriage outside the local community. At the market-place, the vernacular would be commonly used by local people, but Swahili would be resorted to with outsiders. Thus, farmers might be expected to have a fair to poor command of Swahili, depending on the area. Swahili would also be the language of the radio-programs beamed to rural areas and specially designed for farmers. In the field of politics, larger meetings would be conducted in Swahili, but smaller village meetings would be more frequently run in the local vernacular (e.g. Sukuma or Nyamwezi).[13]

In church, the local language is also likely to prevail, but if a Sukuma cotton farmer goes and sells his crop in the cooperative he may have to use Swahili depending on the official he deals with; similarly, when a cattle-buyer comes around, though the latter may know Sukuma (or Maasai, as the case may be) and tend to bargain in the local language. When a Chaga coffee-grower delivers his beans to the cooperative, the transaction usually occurs in Chaga, as it will be when he goes shopping in the *dukas* run by Africans in his area. In Sukumaland, though, the shopkeeper is more likely to be an Asian, who will use Swahili, possibly pidginized, but some Asians may have a sufficient command of the vernacular to conduct their business in it as well.

Farmers' children have access to rural primary education, but barely 50% of the younger generation takes advantage of this opportunity. There they receive at least four years instruction in Swahili and are taught some amount of English, which, however, rapidly deteriorates if they neither go beyond standard IV, nor have an opportunity for practice of the language. Few children from rural areas enter secondary education and the lack of job opportunities as *karani* ('clerk') in the towns has reduced the attraction of the cities as a motivation factor.

In certain areas, farmers also have contact with the neighboring languages, which accounts for partial bilingualism, e.g. along the outskirts of Sukumaland, where the Jita often also speak Sukuma. Nomadic pastoral tribes like the Maasai, will also pick up the dominant languages on their regular migration route: thus, those who serve as cattle drivers for the Tanganyika Meat Packers Corporation through the Uluguru mountains have acquired a sufficient knowledge of Luguru beside Swahili to conduct their trade in it.

2.1.2 *The Shopkeeper*

Many shopkeepers in Tanzania are of Asian descent and accordingly speak Kachi (a Sindhi dialect), Gujrati or some other Indo-Aryan language. They are to a large extent trilingual, having a reasonable command of English and being fluent in *duka*-Swahili, i.e. a substandard upcountry pidginized form of the language. In many cases, they may also be quadrilingual, if they have acquired a working knowledge of the vernacular.

In the market-place, the vendors are more likely to be Africans who will use either Swahili or the vernacular, and since Independence there has been a growing number of African shopkeepers as well, who are actively bilingual, using the dominant language of the area with local people besides Swahili, and knowing some English as well.

2.1.3 *The Craftsman (Fundi)*

The majority of the craftsmen were Indians, especially Sikhs, but the number of skilled African craftsmen having gone through technical colleges was increasing steadily. Both groups were trilingual, and at work, Swahili seemed to be the dominant language, while at home, Punjabi would prevail for the Sikhs, and their own vernacular for the Africans; the third language, resulting from their education, was English, but upcountry, it would be of little use, e.g. to a *duka* tailor, who would more likely be trilingual in Swahili and more than one vernacular.

2.1.4 *The Unskilled Laborer*

Wage-earners tend to show a limited bilingualism: beside their own vernacular, they have acquired Swahili as a result of their migrant status. Actually, some may even have picked up other vernaculars on the way, e.g. while working on sisal plantations or tea estates, where some of them married women from the surrounding area, thus becoming trilingual: Swahili + their own vernacular + their wife's language.

2.1.5 *The Clerk (Karani)*

Clerks are basically trilingual – Swahili, English and their own vernacular – but often actually quadrilingual (or even more multilingual) as a result of their migration from one urban center to another. They mostly work outside their own area and pick up the vernacular of their new location, e.g. non-Sukuma in the Mwanza area learn enough Sukuma for greetings and bargaining when handling *shamba* cotton at the market-place.

2.1.6 *The Professional*

Professionals are as a rule trilingual, with English prevailing mostly over Swahili; depending on their ethnic background, they will also speak an African language or an Asian language. Even expatriates will show enough knowledge of Swahili to meet their professional as well as practical needs; in the case of doctors, thorough command of a lot of medically oriented Swahili vocabulary will be necessary, but lawyers can operate at certain levels of the judicial system without any Swahili at all.[14]

2.1.7 *The Manager/Administrator*

Africans in positions of responsibility are at least trilingual, with a ready command of their own vernacular, Swahili and English. They frequently switch languages, even within one sentence.[15] In the course of their career, they are often moved from one part of the country to another and while in residence there, they usually learn at least a smattering of the local vernaculars with which their profession brings them in contact. This situation has direct consequences on the education of their children, whom it loosens even more from the traditional influences and encourages to use Swahili in most of their verbal communication.

2.1.8 *The Teacher*

Tanzanian teachers are trilingual and often quadrilingual. Primary teachers use Swahili as the medium and teach English as a subject, and are trained accordingly (with Radio Tanzania offering help with its school programs). Beside their own vernacular, as they are often appointed to schools outside their original home area, they have to acquire a sufficient working knowledge of the local vernacular to teach in Standard I, where the children coming in from rural areas often have only a rather limited knowledge of Swahili.[16]

Secondary school teachers would be fluent in Swahili, English and their own vernacular. The dominant language at school in the early seventies was still English, except for the Swahili teacher and the teacher of Civics. In the course of his training and of his career, the teacher had had the opportunity to acquire a limited knowledge of vernaculars other than his own, e.g. a Zalamo teacher could reach a certain degree of competence in Sukuma or Chaga, for example, depending on his contact with his fellow students in College or with the local population if stationed, for example, in the Mwanza or Marangu area. In the staffroom, with his colleagues, he would presumably speak English, as several of them would be expatriates, but with fellow Tanzanians a lot of switching to and fro with Swahili was to be expected.

2.2 *Urban v. Rural Patterns of Multilingualism*

In a different perspective, if we examine the use of languages in a situational dimension in a rural versus an urban context, the following picture obtains:

	URBAN	RURAL
I.	At work:	
	Swahili	Vernacular
	Special Situations:	
	(1) an industrial worker will use the vernacular with fellow laborers if they belong to the same area but this is usually *not* the case.	(1) If agricultural advisors or government officers visit the fields, Swahili is likely to be used. Farmers and rural laborers will try to deal with all officials

A SOCIO-LINGUISTIC PERSPECTIVE

	in Swahili unless they are from the same area.
(2) White and/or blue collar workers will resort to English with their superiors and with the public, e.g. in a bank, but with equals Swahili will prevail, as well as with such part of the public which they identify as 'lower class'. If they recognize people from the same area, they will switch to the vernacular. Asians will similarly address fellow Asians in the relevant Indian language, e.g. Gujrati.	(2) If farmers go to market, they will use either Swahili or vernacular depending on circumstances and their own competence.

II. Shopping:

(1) *Market*: Swahili and local vernacular. In Dar es Salaam, Kariako merchants also use English as a number of expatriates shop there.	(1) *Market*: Swahili and local vernacular.
(2) *Shops*: Swahili, especially if kept by Asians. In some cases, multilingual notices, e.g. prices chalked on board in Arabic, English, Gujrati and Swahili in Dar es Salaam *duka*.	(2) *Shops*: Swahili and local vernacular.

III. Recreation:

(1) *Bar*: discussions carried on in Swahili and vernacular.	(1) *Bar*: discussions carried on in local vernacular; Swahili used sometimes when outsiders received as visitors.
(2) *Sports Events*: comments in Swahili, but the local team may be encouraged in the local language during soccer games.	(2) *Sports*: the language of the prevailing sport – soccer – is Swahili, with typical English loans, e.g. (*piga*) *goli* '(shoot) a goal'; shouting is in Swahili as in town, though vernacular is also used.
(3) *Playing cards*: always done in Swahili, as well as the accompanying gossip, except for the Asians who use mostly Gujrati.	(3) *Playing cards*: done in the vernacular, but with the Swahili technical terminology (the gossip is exclusively in the vernacular)
(4) *Radio*: listening to Swahili programs.	(4) *Radio*: listening to Swahili programs
(5) *Dances:* (a) *Ngoma*: traditional dancing, organized on an area basis and therefore strongly emphasizing local songs.	(5) *Dances*: more of the traditional type and with prevailing use of the vernacular. If mixed groups are formed, as is often the case, even in the smallest trading centers, which are usually mul-

(b) *Western style*: taking place in regular dance halls, they give the 'clerk-playboys' the opportunity to show off their English, but, for the major part, Swahili pop music prevails.	tiracial, Swahili tends to be used. However, in conservative areas, like Uhaya, only the local vernacular would be used; this would also apply to Ha in remote rural areas.
(6) *Cinema*: all films are either in English or in Indian languages, except for a few Russian films with English subtitles.	(6) *Cinema*: Only rarely does a mobile cinema unit of the Ministry of Information come through to show documentary/propaganda films in Swahili.
IV. Health: Hospital and dispensary services are available in town, and the language of communication between patient and doctor is Swahili as a rule, except for the rare cases when they are from the same community and will converse in their own vernacular.	Where medical care is available in mission hospitals and dispensaries, like Dr. Taylor's at Mvumi, the local vernacular prevails (in the case in question, Gogo).

2.3 The Church and Multilingualism

As for other dimensions of social life, the situation of the churches will be examined elsewhere (Polomé, 1980): the shift to Swahili is practically complete in African urban communities and taking place progressively in rural areas, even in conservative territories like Uhaya: there is obviously a generation gap, some parish priests and ministers preaching in vernacular for the older people, and the old hymn-books dating back to pre-World War I German missionary action are still being used in the Pare Mountain for speakers of Chasu or Pare. However, decline in the sale of vernacular bibles indicates the change that has taken place (Polomé, 1975: 45).

2.4 Politics and Multilingualism

In political life, as already mentioned, the Tanganyika African National Union (TANU), the party controlling the country since Independence, has promoted the use of Swahili at every level of its organization and activities, but even at the village level, extensive use of vernaculars may often still be required to achieve adequate communication in some parts of the country. The Union of Women of Tanzania – *Umoja wa Wanawake wa Tanzania* – an affiliate of TANU, is predominantly urban; its language is officially Swahili, and though Swahili mostly prevails, the local vernacular may often be used in some regions like Uhaya. But in the small villages all women still meet going to the well, and their conversation is entirely in vernacular. The National Union of Tanganyika Workers (NUTW), constituted in 1964, encompasses all types of labor force activities and trade union functions, and its members accordingly constitute a quite heterogenous set of people, for whom the use of Swahili necessarily follows. Occasionally, shop stewards and definite members may use vernaculars, but all operations at the level of union and employers as well as with Labor Ministry officers are conducted in Swahili.

2.5 Labor and Management

With growing Africanization, the language barrier between labor and management tends to disappear, as Swahili prevails as language of communication, for example, in the nationalized hotel industry between menial and managing personnel; in state-run factories between workers and managers. However, in 1969–1970, this Africanization had not eliminated the contrast in language use (English versus Swahili) between the lower echelons and the upper level officials in parastatal enterprises where the people in authority would often be Asians as well as Africans or even expatriates and had constant contacts with foreign technicians. Similarly, in the nationalized banks, most positions of higher responsibility were still occupied by Asians, especially Goans, whereas the common clerks were usually Africans: here again, the role of the banks in the transitional economic life explains the continued prevalence of English in the higher echelons.

2.6 The Army and Police

The language of command in the army was Swahili, and the Government was having the basic British training manuals translated into Swahili by experts from Zanzibar like S. Farsi.

The police wrote its reports in Swahili, but used English in cases when expatriates were involved. In dealing with the public, the usual language of communication was Swahili, but when necessary, the local vernacular was used.

2.7 Multilingualism and Language Skills

This short survey of socio-cultural situations in Tanzania illustrates the multilingual pattern of the society. If multilingualism is defined as a speaker's competence and performance in a number of languages in multiple social settings, it is obviously necessary to determine which language or languages are actually used in each specific context and what degree of proficiency the user demonstrates in any particular context. A distinction also needs to be made between the various language skills: understanding, speaking, reading and writing – keeping in mind that though there are no detailed national statistics on literacy. In the late sixties, hardly 45% of the children went to school. With wastage and dropouts, the percentage of those becoming actually literate was even lower. 80% of the adult male and 89% of the female population was illiterate; however, illiteracy was spread unevenly, reaching up to 95% in some areas, and being as low as 40–50% in others.

2.7.1 Oral Competence

In the case of oral performance, the competence of a person in a language can be measured on the basis of his or her ability to understand

and respond in the following situations:

(1) exchanging greetings;
(2) understanding and/or giving directions;
(3) selling and/or buying things at the market and bargaining about the price of goods;
(4) carrying on a simple conversation;
(5) talking about health, farming, the weather, etc.;
(6) talking about mechanical things, e.g. repairing a bicycle;
(7) talking about one's work (in non-technical terms);
(8) listening to a political speech and discussing it;
(9) making a speech on a specific occasion;
(10) understanding jokes or telling funny stories (e.g. with puns);
(11) understanding baby-talk;
(12) discussing complex technical problems (including, e.g. mathematical calculations);
(13) understanding songs and rapid speech on the radio; etc.

Though such a sampling of situations may not be adequately graded for certain linguistic contexts, it definitely implies different levels of competence in the relevant language.[17] The "first" language of an individual could be defined as the language he resorts to automatically in the absence of outside pressure to use any specific language: asking the respondent to count aloud, for example, usually provides an efficient means of identification.

2.7.2 *Literate Competence*

As far as literate people are concerned, the use of literacy is an important clue to their linguistic competence: for many Tanzanians, lack of practice leads to loss through regression of the limited amount of English learned in primary school, though some of it may still be known passively.[18] Literacy in the vernaculars would be expected to be largely on the wane, since all adult literacy programs had switched to Swahili and the religious publications in other languages had become fewer after Independence. However, literacy in Swahili seemed to enable most Bantu language speakers to write their own vernacular, using the orthographical conventions of Swahili and disregarding phonemic differences for which Swahili did not provide graphemic representation.[19] As regards Swahili and English, the degree of competence of respondents in these languages could be partly measured on the basis of their ability to read road and shop signs; magazines or newspapers; religious, educational or technical books; materials for pastime or pleasure; or more serious materials requiring a higher intellectual acumen. Similarly, involvement in writing could range from personal or business letters to the composition of essays, prose fiction and poetry, or the redaction of legal documents.

2.8 *Choice of Language*

An equally important factor in determining the degree of multilingualism of an individual is the choice of language he makes in definite social settings. As in other societies, home work, social and cultural activities, and official functions are determining factors in this evaluation in Tanzania. Verbal communication at home is generally monolingual, except in the case of mixed marriages, which are more common these days, even in the rural areas.[20] A bilingual home will be characterized by constant switching between two vernaculars, but in the coastal area and among the literate population, bilingualism is also common with spouses with the same mother tongue, the languages used being their common mother tongue and Swahili. Also reflecting the process of change in the country is the generation gap in language use: parents with the same mother tongue use it when talking to each other, but resort to Swahili when addressing their children.[21] As regards the use of languages in the various aspects of socio-economic life, the subject has already been discussed at some length, so that we can summarize it as follows:

(a) though English is on the wane as a result of nationalization and Africanization of a considerable number of enterprises (banks, import and export trade, wholesale distribution to retail dealers, etc.) it is still used on a wide scale in the upper levels of economic life;

(b) in industry, Swahili prevails as the labor force is recruited from various parts of the country, and it is indispensable as a lingua franca;

(c) in government, Swahili is strongly promoted officially and except for certain specific cases, all transactions are in this language; public services are assumed to run in Swahili, but as many forms are still in English, local people have to rely on friendly bilingual employees to help them or take along a child who has studied Swahili and some English at school.[22]

On the basis of such situations, a set of questions is asked to respondents to evaluate their use of a language in correlation with their competence in it, namely: 'What language do you use when

(1) conversing with your father?
(2) conversing with your mother?
(3) conversing with your father's parents?
(4) conversing with your mother's parents?
(5) conversing with your brothers and sisters?
(6) conversing with close friends?
(7) conversing with strangers (of your home area; of Tanzanian origin; from other African countries; of non-African origin)?
(8) conversing with an inferior at work?
(9) conversing with a superior at work?
(10) discussing technical matters at work?
(11) at the post-office (and other public services, e.g. the bank, the town hall, etc.)?
(12) describing an accident at the place where it occurred?
(13) reporting something that happened at a police station?' – etc.'[23]

Using the informants' ability to operate in different languages in a number of situations as a basis, tentative ratings can be established for his degree of proficiency in each language under consideration. Thus, on the basis of the Tanzania adult survey questionnaires (Polomé, 1975: 40), the following scales were used for respondents from rural areas:

(a) understanding: 0–13;
(b) speaking: 0–12;
(c) reading: 0–6;
(d) writing: 0–6.[24]

Similarly, their actual use of the language in definite social contexts were rated as follows:

(a) at home: 0–13;
(b) in social life 0–14;
(c) in professional life: 0–12 for men; 0–5 for women.

In such an analysis of the data, the first language will always reach high or even maximal scores, but only *real* bilinguals will score high on the "second" language, whether it be Swahili or any vernacular. The scores in English tend to be lower, except for people whose professional and related social activities entail the extensive use of that language. In the case of vernaculars, the third language very seldom scores high, whereas the fourth and following ones will seldom rise above 10 as regards the level of proficiency (maximum: 37) and will also be very low in occurrence in definite social contexts (0–5 out of maximum of 39 or 32, depending on the sex of the respondent). Swahili is vigorously expanding in all aspects of Tanzanian life. The history of Swahili in Tanzania has been described in detail from its very beginnings (Polomé) to its prominent role in nation-building since the foundation of TANU and the independence of Tanganyika (Abdulaziz). Its use in education, in the mass media and in government, the establishment of a regulating body (the National Swahili Council) to insure its promotion, the development of adequate technical terminology in all fields are so many assets that have contributed to its spread. Other important social factors are geographical mobility and upward mobility: the former is a result of a deliberate policy of the Tanzanian government to assign officers outside their area of origin and to increase their experience by acquainting them with various parts of the country; to insure that a large percentage of the student population in secondary schools and teachers training colleges comes from other regions of the country and to increase the "melting pot" effect of education by enlisting students in the National Service, where all activities are conducted in Swahili, during their vacation period; to transfer people of various regional backgrounds to resettlement schemes (*ujamaa* villages) in government estates, e.g. sisal plantations, or semi-industrial projects, e.g. the Kilombero sugar estate, in various parts of Tanzania. As for upward mobility, children of farmers and low level employees like messengers obtain better positions through better education and identify themselves

A SOCIO-LINGUISTIC PERSPECTIVE

with their new social status by shifting to Swahili as the language of their socio-cultural life as well as of their professional activity.

Nevertheless, the Swahilization of Tanzanian society is slowed down by two major factors:

(a) the still very strong linguistic loyalty to the vernaculars, especially in those areas where the people have preserved strong traditional cultures, since the language remains one of the basic means to identify with the tradition;

(b) the insufficient development of the educational system, which in 1970 was still unable to provide basic primary education to about half the children of school-age in rural areas, and whose secondary schools are too few[25] and remain concentrated in a few urban areas.

2.9 Typology of Multilingualism

It is possible to establish a tentative typology of multilingualism in Tanzania on the basis of the considerations made in connection with the Tanzania Survey. If we use the signs 'S' for Swahili, 'E' for English, 'V' for vernacular and 'A' for Arabic, the tabulation in Table 5:1 can be made (leaving out the Asian minority).

Table 5:1 Typology of Multilingualism

1. *Monolingual*	2. *Bilingual*	3. *Trilingual*
(a) V	(a) VS or SV	(a) VSE
(b) S	(b) SE	(b) VSA
	(c) SA	(c) VVS
	(d) VV	(d) VVV

4. *Quadrilingual*	5. *Plurilingual*	Key
(a) VSEA	(a) VV(V..)SEA	V vernacular
(b) VVSA	(b) VVV(V....)SE	S Swahili
(c) VVSE	(c) VVV(V...)SA	E English
(d) VVVS	(d) VVVV(V...)S	A Arabic

By providing each symbol with indices indicating the scores of a respondent in both scales – degree of proficiency (maximum: 37) and amount of use in specific social environments (maximum: 39 [for men] or 32 [for women]), it is possible to evaluate his or her command of the languages he or she claims to know and the extent to which he or she uses them, e.g. a 26 year old Muslim clerk, whose "first" language is Swahili and mother tongue Rufiji, but who also claims to know English and Arabic, scores: $V9/20\ S37/28\ E21/3\ A1/0$, which means that he has total command of Swahili, though he may not use it in some social contexts, like talking to an expatriate or a relative of his wife, in which case he uses, respectively, English or Rufiji. His knowledge of English is more limited; he uses it more for reading than for talking; he never speaks it at home, and practically never uses it at work. His use of Arabic is strictly limited to prayer. His knowledge and use of Rufiji is limited to domestic matters and he does not claim any literacy in this language, which he does not use in his social activities outside the family circle, since he is living in a Zigula-speaking area.

2.9.1 *Rural Areas*

An examination of the Tanzanian evidence shows the following patterns prevail in the rural areas:

(a) V (mainly inland)
(b) S (mainly in the coastal area)
(c) VS (mainly in the coastal area; sometimes the vernacular will be the mother tongue, sometimes Swahili)
(d) VV (only inland)
(e) VVS
(f) VSA (Muslims)

Though knowledge of English is found among educated people in rural areas, these will be essentially government agents, teachers, medical assistants, etc. – not farmers. The trifocal type VSE, described by Abdulaziz (1972), prevails in towns; the other plurilingual types show considerable discrepancies in their level of command of the respective languages they claim to know, and which usually reflect the mobility of the speaker.[26]

Using the responses to the secondary school survey (Polomé, 1975:41) and analyzing a random sampling of about 1,550 respondents, statistical data were compiled to illustrate the degree of proficiency of the informants in a selected set of languages and to determine the relative frequency with which these languages were used by them in various contexts. The languages chosen were:

(a) Swahili and English;
(b) Hindi, Gujrati, Kachi (for Asians)
(c) the 15 Tanzanian vernaculars with the highest number of speakers, namely Sukuma, Nyamwezi, Makonde, Haya, Chaga, Gogo, Ha, Hehe, Nyakyusa, Lugulu, Bena, Nyatura, Shambala, Zalamo, Nilyamba.
(d) a selection of non-Bantu languages, namely Sandawe, Maasai, Iraqw, Luo;
(e) a set of smaller Tanzanian Bantu linguistic-ethnic units, Zanaki, Tongwe, Pogolu, Matumbi, Makua, Matengo, Fipa, Safwa, Kerewe.[27]

C. P. Hill did a graphic analysis of the data which illustrates a number of interesting facts: proficiency profiles dip as the type of linguistic accomplishment gets more complex, and for the vernaculars they sink particularly low as far as question 14 (Do you ever think out what to say in this language before you speak in another?) is concerned, indicating that none of the respondents apparently tries to think out what he is going to say in English, for instance, in his mother tongue first. The frequent recourse to vernacular in greetings is also illustrated by the peaks in questions 1 (Do you understand greetings in this language?) and 6 (Can you greet people in this language?). Profile analyses of language use in various situations yield quantitative data for frequent, occasional and rare use of the same set of languages by the informants and illustrate a number of interesting facts: the prevalence of English and Swahili for writing and reading; apart from Hindi and Gujrati, only very few vernaculars score significantly as regards the written language or the printed word; Haya shows the highest figures, which is in keeping with the strong language loyalty of the area and the continued use of the language in some publications, for example, *Rumuli*, published twice a month by the Diocese of Bukoba in Haya and Swahili (3,000 copies in 1970–71). Languages of people with strong ethnic traditions, like the Sukuma, the Nyamwezi, the Chaga, and the Nyakyusa, also seem to have maintained a relatively high level of literacy in the vernacular, presumably also under the influence of the availability and still fairly widespread use of a rather extensive religious literature in the language. Such is no longer the case with other important people like the Gogo or with those living closer to the coast like the Sambaa or Zalamo. Remarkable also is the scarcity of the use of the vernacular in oral communication in a large number of situations, for example, in shops, at home, or when selling produce at the market. It is more understandable that Swahili should be used in places like the railway station or the post office where the officials may not be local people. More complex are situations with political implications like "self-help schemes": evidently, the deliberate use of Swahili is expected to be high, but the incidence of the vernaculars can be quite significant, as in Haya, or even in Chaga, whereas in other cases, languages like Sukuma or Nyamwezi are only used occasionally or just rarely. Striking are the low scores of the vernaculars in the case of playing games like football or bao: again the Haya and the Chaga are the only ones who use their language frequently in this context; the scores in Sukuma definitely point to a scarcer use of the vernacular, and in Gogo or Hehe, the language seems to be resorted to even less frequently. Thus the statistical data confirm the growing importance of Swahili in every field of social life.

If we try to determine regional differences in the degree to which the impact of Swahili on socio-cultural activities can be felt, it is obvious that a number of factors are going to affect the results of any inquiries, such as (a) historical factors, like the degree of Swahilization due to pre-colonial contacts along the caravan routes and the lines of penetration of Islam;[28] (b) change in attitude due to political motivations, in particular in the period leading up to the Arusha Declaration (1967).[29]

Two inquiries done in the second part of the sixties illustrate this shift in attitude: one, conducted by Anders Andersson, of the Institute of Education of the University of Uppsala (Sweden), revealed that the main factors determining students' attitudes towards Swahili were their 'home language', i.e. whether they spoke a vernacular or Swahili at home, and their family background, i.e. their father's occupation and their coming from a rural or an urban area. The inquiry showed that students from more "educated" homes display a less favorable attitude towards Swahili. Sex and religion, according to Andersson's corpus of data, played no specific role (Andersson, 1967:17, 39). However, his aim was to measure how secondary school students in Tanzania responded to English versus Swahili as a language and as a medium, and therefore, his results were definitely lopsided and inadequate to reflect upon the major problem of the position of Swahili versus the vernaculars.[30] The other study was a more modest project directed by J. Mittelmeyer with the students of the Morogoro Teachers' College from 1965 to 1967. Dividing continental Tanzania (former Tanganyika) in five major areas, it tried to establish whether the vernaculars were losing ground or not in these territories, what the feelings of the speakers were towards their own language and toward Swahili, and whether aesthetic connotations in the vernacular were partly responsible for those feelings.

The results of the enquiry were rather complex to interpret, as can be seen from Table 5:2. The reason why these figures cannot be interpreted at face-value is that between 1965 and 1967, the regional spread in the recruitment of students in Morogoro college changed considerably as the following figures may show:

	South	Lake area	Center	Kilimanjaro	Coast/Tanga Morogoro
1965	38.5%	27.3%	16.1%	9.8%	8.3%
1967	16%	22.1%	20.9%	20.5%	20.5%

This shift in distribution may partly account for the fluctuation in the responses about the situation of the vernacular: while the number of students from the more conservative areas in the west and the center (Uhaya, Usukuma, Uha, etc.) has not changed dramatically, the doubling of the enrollment from the Chaga-speaking area and the even sharper increase from the coastal regions, including Tanga (and, further inland, Morogoro), with the concomitant drastic cut of the flow of students from the south must necessarily have influenced the results of the survey, since it accounts for 38.7% of the parents speaking *only* vernacular to their children. But this strong hold of the vernacular on the family circle is not the main reason for the change in percentages of those who think "dialects are losing ground to Swahili": in the middle sixties there was a strong action to promote Swahili, and the younger generation was also motivated by patriotic feelings to prefer the national language over the vernacular, which appeared as a feature of the divisions which the vigorous efforts to build a new nation wanted to eliminate. Hence, the shift in preference: in 1965, 53% of the students preferred their vernacular over Swahili; in 1967, 62.4% gave Swahili the preference over the vernacular. In the meantime, the aims of the Tanzanian national policy had become well-defined after the Arusha declaration; Swahili and the traditional languages had their respective places and functions in the new society, and a better balanced judgement on the aesthetic values of the vernacular was given, as it was no longer felt it was threatened with disappearance, and as growing awareness of Swahili literary achievements

Table 5:2 Language Attitudes

Area	Dialect 1965	Dialect losing 1967	Dialect 1965	'nicer' 1967	Prefer 1965	vernacular 1967	Prefer 1965	Swahili 1967
West (West Lake, Mwanza, Kigoma)	67	35	90	65	64	42.5	36	57.5
North Kilimanjaro	93	58	86	58	36	39	64	61
East (Coast Region, Tanga, Morogoro)	75	58	100	52.6	33	42.1	67	57.9
South[31] (Ruvuma, Mtwara, Iringa, Mbeya)	79	34.2	80	41	50.9	31	49.1	62
Center (Tabora, Singida, Dodoma, Shinyanga, Mara)	83	42.1	96	57.9	61	26.3	39	73.7

and rich modes of expression changed the views on the assumed limitations of this language.³²

A project directed by J. Mittelmeyer and his students at the Morogoro Teachers Training College (1965–67) considered the question of the language spoken at home: percentages are provided for the five major areas considered for two sets of situations:

(a) parents speaking with each other;
(b) parents speaking with children,

as well as for the use by the respondent of Swahili or the vernacular – or – exclusively of the local tribal language in a town or village. The results (i.e. percentages) can be tabulated as found in Table 5:3. The table provides clear evidence of the generation gap in the use of Swahili in certain parts of Tanzania: in the large areas of the west, the north and (partly) the center, the Haya, the Ha, the Sukuma, the Chaga and others continue to use their own languages at home, but as their children are educated in Swahili in primary school, they try to use this language as well when talking to them, though, usually, much less frequently when speaking to each other. For many, indeed, Swahili presents a number of problems, even on the phonological level, and sound substitutions like the Chaga use of [s] for the dental fricatives [θ] and [ð] are not uncommon. Being exposed to a considerable amount of Swahili through the mass media, the governmental services, the political action of TANU and, recently, also the Church (though vernaculars were still widely in use in the late sixties, including the Bible and religious literature), the older generation gradually improves its knowledge of Swahili and uses it more with the younger people. The differences between the 1965 and 1967 figures are quite impressive in this regard and dramatize the success of the campaign for the shift to Swahili among the upcoming generation of Tanzanians. In talk with peers, young Chagas who, two years before, would still be 50% dialect-users only in their familiar surroundings use Swahili as well in a proportion of 4 to 1 in 1967.

The most dramatic change is presumably to be found in the data from the eastern part of the country, but they are rather misleading: the 1965 students come mostly from rural backgrounds, hence the high percentage of use of their own language by their parents at home (92%). Actually, Swahili had a very high frequency of use beside the vernaculars in this area, as shown by the percentages in the village (1965: 92%; 1967: 97.4%). This is due to a number of reasons:

(a) the majority of the population is Muslim:

	Muslims	Christians	Other
Tanga	71.9%	19.8%	7.3%
Dar es Salaam	75.0%	16.1%	8.4%

(b) there is considerable influence from Zanzibar (the coast used to be controlled by the Sultan who still appointed *liwalis* in the colonial period);

Table 5:3 Language in the Home

| | | Parents Speaking | | | | | Students Speaking in town/village | |
| | | with each other | | with children | | | | |
		vernacular only	vernacular + Swahili	vernacular only	vernacular + Swahili		vernacular only	vernacular + Swahili
West (West Lake, Mwanza, Kigoma)	1965	90	10	87	13		72	28
	1967	92.5	7.5	60	40		17.5	82.5
North (Kilimanjaro)	1965	(no data)		86	14		50	50
	1967	80	20	47	53		19	81
East (Coast Region Tanga, Morogoro)	1965	92	8	25	75		8	92
	1967	21	79	10.5	89.5		2.6	97.4
South (Ruvuma, Mtwara, Iringa Mbeya)	1965	94.2	5.8	58.2	41.8		30.9	69.1
	1967	48.2	50	27	73		13.7	86.3
Center (Tabora, Singida, Shinyanga, Mara, Dodoma)	1965	91	9	87	13		48	52
	1967	65.8	34.2	44.7	55.3		13.2	86.8

(c) the missionaries mostly neglected the vernaculars in recent years and shifted to Swahili;
(d) there are numerous marriages between people of different language background.

Even so, there is a considerable difference between the coast and the inland territories, e.g. the percentages for preference of vernaculars in 1966 are:

0 for the Coastal Region;
10 for Tanga;
but 42.9 for Morogoro.

In non-Bantu areas like the territory of the Iraqw in the north, there is little interest in speaking Swahili, except in the semi-urban center, Babati, where there are a hospital, a bus station, dukas, etc. When children enter school, no knowledge of Swahili can be assumed for any practical purposes, but Swahili becomes more effective from Standard II on.

Studies such as these provide more depth and perspective to our knowledge of the language situation of which we tried to capture one phase of change at the turn of the sixties. In 1974 new decisive steps were taken to speed up the process of Swahilization: 'From August 1, all correspondence, forms and sign posts in all parastatal and public organizations must be in Swahili' (Legère, 1975:346).[33] Thus, the implementation of the program of making Swahili the national language of Tanzania at all levels of public and socio-cultural life moves ahead, and future research will be able to measure Tanzania's progress to the achievement of its goals in the field of language use and nation-building.[34]

NOTES

[1] An Examination of documents in public buildings in Dar es Salaam in the Spring of 1970 yielded the following results:

Town Council
At City Hall, of 26 notices on a board, twelve were in English and 14 in Swahili (they involved advertisements for the sale of a vehicle, announcements about vacant posts, etc). On the wall, such indications as 'City Engineer's Office'/'Fundi Mkuu wa Jiji' were bilingual, but the main listing of offices was in Swahili.

As regards licenses issued by the town council like the 'license to hawk', the application was in Swahili, but the license in English; for retail trading, the applications were available both in Swahili and English, but the licenses were in English, whereas the Internal Revenue Office had bilingual Swahili/English retail licenses. For a number of other licenses (liquor licenses, auctioneer's licenses, petrol installation permits, etc.) both applications and licenses were in English. At the Accounts Department, the ledgers, the notations on payments and receipts, estimates, schedules of payments, final accounts, etc. were all in English (for the Councilors' benefit, authorizations for payments were in Swahili). However, the minutes of the Town Council meetings were in Swahili and English, and the language used in correspondence depended on the addressee: letters to all ministries were usually in Swahili, except when they dealt with very technical matters; letters of appointment of staff, promotion and transfer were in English –

mainly because the relevant rules and regulations had not yet been officially translated into Swahili; letters to traders and various enterprises were consistently in English or Swahili. Written communication between the heads of Departments was in English, except with the Town Clerk (because of the mixed origin of the staff including Asians and non-Tanzanians). Verbal contact with the public was mostly in Swahili; verbal instructions to the staff were nearly always in Swahili.

Department of Health
Most of the correspondence was conducted in Swahili, since most of the complaints recorded, e.g. came from Africans and were transacted in Swahili, but when appropriate, English was used. Reports for and from Health Officers were in Swahili. Interstaff communication was also in Swahili, at least at the junior staff level; if the senior staff consisted of expatriates, English would be used. 70% of the verbal contacts took place in Swahili, but with foreigners, e.g. embassy staff, English was used – also in all correspondence. Vaccination forms, Infant Welfare Clinic forms and such documents were still in English; health reports, licenses, etc. were in both English and Swahili.

[2] This was particularly obvious in public places like the post office or the banks. Thus, in 1970, practically all the forms of the East African Posts and Telecommunications in Dar es Salaam, such as a list of registered postal packets, a dispatch note, a requisition for a money order, a telegram, were still monolingual in English. The only exception was the Postal Savings Service, whose forms were also in Swahili.

[3] To illustrate this the situation on the ships on Lake Victoria could be mentioned: on the M.V. "Victoria", all public notices were bilingual, with the Swahili text first, e.g. *Hakuna ruhusa y kupita hapa/No Admittance*; only the bulletin board was in English only, except for navigation notices – but on the S.S. "Usoga", all notices were still in English only, except for the obviously later addition of *Hakuna ruhusa ya kupita hapa* in one case. Similarly, on the train from Dar es Salaam to Tabora and Kigoma all notices were in English, and all tickets, vouchers, receipts, etc. as well. In the Tanzania Railway hotels, the situation varied: in Tabora, all notices, except on the staff notice board, were only in English; in Dodoma, they were in Swahili and English, e.g. *Chumba cha chakula/Dining-room*; *Msalani/Toilets*, etc. Elsewhere, e.g. in Mwanza, one hotel had all its notices in Swahili, and another all in English, except for the indication in Swahili of the time at which the room should be vacated.

[4] For examples, see chapter 9 on 'The use of Language in the Law-Courts' by D. Kavugha and D. Bobb.

[5] Nevertheless, transportation problems are responsible for the fact that more than half of the newspapers are sold in Dar es Salaam and that the news is stale by the time it reaches places like Songea which have only limited air service, so that the papers have to go by bus. A table for the main distribution centers for the four dailies is given below with the respective percentages:

	Uhuru	Ngurumo	Nationalist	Standard
Arusha	250(1.4%)	1,800(15.0%)	139(1.6%)	900(4.7%)
Coast (less Dar es Salaam)	130(0.7%)	50(0.41%)	34(0.39%)	500(2.6%)
Dodoma	285(1.5%)	300(2.5%)	134(1.5%)	390(2%)
Iringa	304(1.6%)	280(2.3%)	136(1.5%)	493(2.6%)
Kigoma	120(0.65%)	500(4.1%)	75(0.87%)	125(0.6%)
Kilimanjaro	200(1.1%)	400(3.3%)	190(2.2%)	795(4.2%)
Mara	133(0.73%)	—	59(0.78%)	190(1.0%)

	Uhuru	Ngurumo	Nationalist	Standard
Mbeya	216(1.2%)	100(0.82%)	140(1.6%)	315(1.6%)
Morogoro	495(2.7%)	750(6.2%)	155(1.8%)	685(3.6%)
Mtwara	437(2.4%)	100(0.82%)	189(2.2%)	210(1.1%)
Mwanza	750(4.1%)	200(1.6%)	180(2.1%)	845(4.4%)
Ruvuma	79(0.43%)	50(0.41%)	60(0.69%)	130(0.68%)
Shinyanga	580(3.1%)	50(0.41%)	20(0.23%)	185(0.97%)
Singida	15(0.08%)	—	5(0.06%)	130(0.68%)
Tabora	240(1.3%)	250(2.1%)	100(1.2%)	339(1.8%)
Tanga	1,781(9.7%)	1,300(11.0%)	290(3.4%)	1,345(7%)
West Lake	190(1.0%)	20(0.16%)	90(1.0%)	240(1.3%)
Dar es Salaam	11,573(63.0%)	6,000(49.0%)	4,327(50.0%)	10,365(54.0%)
outside Tanzania	163(0.88%)	—	755(8.7%)	125(0.65%)

The consequences of this distribution pattern are obvious when one looks at the frequency of reading in some locations assessed e.g. by the survey conducted by Graham L. Mytton, of the University of Manchester (U.K.), in 1967–68: in Dar es Salaam 44.2% of the newspaper readers would read them every day; another 11.6% 4 to 5 times a week and 26.3% more than 2 to 3 times a week; in the Kilimanjaro urban centers – Arusha and Moshi – reached by air every day, the corresponding percentages are 33.3, 3.7 and 33.3, but here 29.6% of the readers read the newspapers only *once* a week, whereas in Dar es Salaam only 11.1 did so, and in the rural area of the Kilimanjaro this percentage climbs up steeply to 60%. Kigoma which gets the newspapers with 2 or 3 days delay by train from Tabora, to where they are flown in from Dar es Salaam, shows the following percentages: 8.3% read the papers every day; 41.7% 2 or 3 times per week; 25% once a week, but in the neighboring rural areas these percentages drop to 7.7, 15.4 and 15.4 respectively, 53.8% of readers getting to see a newspaper less than once every two weeks. This time lapse is particularly evident when respondents are asked when they last read a newspaper: in Dar es Salaam 59.5% answer 'today' or 'yesterday'; in Kigoma, the majority (66.7%) says 'within the last week'; in the Kilimanjaro area, 37% reply 'today' or 'yesterday', but 55.6% 'within the last week'. And the gap in communication between the urban and rural areas is even greater (e.g. in Kigoma rural area, 23.1% 'within the last week', but 38.5% 'more than a week ago') ...

[6] In 1960, there were only 72,232 radio-sets in Tanganyika, of which 41,144 were owned by Africans: 31,195 in rural communities; 7,449 in urban areas; 2,500 in schools, clubs and other institutions (TBC Survey, 1960:3).

[7] Widstrand (1966:7) points out that only 13% buy their own paper daily; 23% read the paper daily, 42% about once a week. On the other hand, the Tanzania National Radio news program – *Taarifa ya Habari* – is preferred by 87% of the respondents, though 32% also listened to the Voice of Kenya and 20% to the B.B.C.

[8] The sampling discussed in Tony Dodds' report covered a wide geographical area in Northern Tanzania, including the districts of Bukoba, Arusha, Kilimanjaro, Pare, Tanga, Lushoto, Chunya, Morogoro and Dar es Salaam. As it was conducted by University students during their home vacation time, it was strongly biased towards the environment of the students' family: it included 36% of professional people (teachers, magistrates, government officers), 17% of clerical or secretarial staff, 14% of skilled workers and craftsmen, 12% of unskilled labor, 12% of farmers and 9% of businessmen, and there was a strong imbalance between urban and rural participants as well as between both sexes (only 28% of the sampling

were female). 82% of the respondents were between the ages of 20 and 39; 78% had a higher than Standard V educational background, and 35% actually attended secondary school (6% continuing their education beyond Form IV).

[9] Only 60% of the people under 20 listen to foreign broadcasts, compared to 87% for the 20–29 age-group, 96.4% for the 30–39 age-group and 100% for those over 40 (Dodds, 1970:5).

Among the foreign stations most listened to were the following, with the assumed percentage of those listening according to two surveys in the late sixties:

	According to Mytton (1968:12)	According to Dodds (1970:15)
The Voice of Kenya	63.0%	61%
B.B.C.	17.3%	32%
Voice of America	3.9%	23%
Deutsche Welle (West Germany)	4.3%	23%
Radio Uganda	7.5%	21%
Radio Voice of the Gospel (Ethiopia)	7.1%	18%
Radiodiffusion Congo (Lubumbashi mainly)	9.1%	13%
Radio Burundi	10.6%	13%
Radio Rwanda	7.5%	11%

Though the coverage of the two surveys was not the same (Mytton interviewed 838 persons in 1967–8 in the districts of Mzizima, Kisarawe, Kigoma, Mwanza and Kilimanjaro, beside the Dar es Salaam area, choosing representatives of every age-group, social and professional status, and educational background, in urban as well as rural contexts as far as possible), the data are significantly indicating a trend to the increased listening to broadcasting stations; particularly dramatic is the increase in the case of the Voice of America and the Deutsche Welle, especially since the latter had installed its powerful relay station in Kigali. On the other hand, the sharp drop registered by the All India Radio (Mytton: 10.2%; Dodds: 2%) and Radio Pakistan (Mytton: 6.7%; not even mentioned by Dodds) is also indicative of a shift of interest among the Asian population. Interest for such stations as Radio Moscow or Peking remains rather limited (together with East Germany, less than 4% in Mytton; 3% for Moscow and 2% for China Radio in Dodds). Radio Zanzibar (*Sauti ya Unguja*) which continued its independent programming and operation after the establishment of the United Republic in 1964, remained a favorite among continental listeners (it drew 11.8% of them in 1967–8 according to Mytton).

[10] On Dar es Salaam buses, e.g. Philips (radios) and Suzuki (motor-bikes) advertised in Swahili, but Shell/Afrigas in English. All the National Milling Corporation products, e.g. *Nguvu* flour, were labelled in Swahili and English. As regards posters, English and Swahili were found: the Saba Saba advertisements and the National Lottery posters were in Swahili, but a Ngoma (dance) of TANU Womens Union and a Yugoslavia exhibition were announced in English. The inscriptions on all official vehicles were in Swahili, as were those on the vans of the power company (*Tanesco*), including *Kwa maisha bora tumia umeme* 'Use electricity for better living'. Breweries (Chituku, Tusker, Kilimanjaro) would also use Swahili, but other industries (Leyland paints, Tasini fabrics, etc.) would prefer English; even the TANU Youth League would have its name in English painted on

its vehicles. Coca-Cola had its truck with Swahili inscriptions, but its billboards (for Coca-Cola, Sprite and Fanta) were in English only. Tanzania cigarette brands like *Sportsman* advertised mostly in Swahili, as did Embassy Shirts, and Cafenol.

In this context, it might be worth mentioning that English language advertising would often appear in Swahili language papers and periodicals like *Uhuru* and *Mfanya Kazi*, covering respectively up to 8% and 14% of an issue in July/August 1970.

[11] The usual pattern of difference in frequency of use is however less aberrant:

(a) for people who use Swahili and *one* vernacular, it may rise to 5:1 in favor of Swahili, but is usually around 4:1 or even much less (e.g. Swahili 72%: Yao 28%; Swahili 66%: Bondei 34%);

(b) for people who use Swahili plus *more than one* vernacular, we find percentages like 59.6% Swahili: 35% Chaga: 5.2% Zalamo;

(c) for people who speak English as well as Swahili besides vernacular, the vernacular often shows the lowest level of use, e.g. Swahili 59.4%: English 28.8%: Chaga 11.7%; but the reverse occurs almost as frequently, English being less used than the vernacular (this may depend very much on the contacts and context of conversation on the days of the survey), e.g. Swahili 56.8%: Nyakyusa 23.5%: English 19.6% – sometimes even on a par with the *second* vernacular, e.g. English 8.3% = Nyakyusa 8.3% versus Kinga 33.3% and Swahili 50%.

[12] Two major traditional structural components of village life – the patrilinear extended family and the hierarchical organization of the community as a 'chiefdom' are done away with. In two important papers, C. R. Hatfield (1972a and b) has given a penetrating analysis of the strains that result from this reorganization of socio-economic life in the village and shown how these stresses affects a major livestock development project in Sukumaland.

[13] Cf. Hatfield (1972a:20), who points out that "at local meetings initial discussion always centered around whether Kiswahili or the local language was to be used. Arguments for the former were strong; it is progressive to use Kiswahili, primitive to use the local dialect; do you want our government to think we are not conscious of our responsibilities. The problem is that few local individuals understand Kiswahili well enough to be effective listeners, and even fewer have facility in using the language to make their opinion known (for rhetoric and metaphor are extremely important in public speaking and the Sukuma and Nyamwezi pride themselves on their abilities in speaking elegantly) ... Meetings conducted ... in Kisukuma or Nyamwezi involved greater discussion, greater local rhetoric, but I think greater mutual information flow."

[14] Thus, in 1970, the Resident Magistrate in Moshi was a non-Tanzanian who did not know any Swahili at all.

[15] Abdulaziz, 1972: 207–210. Personal observation in the offices of high officials in Tanzanian ministries confirmed Abdulaziz' results: in the course of a Swahili telephone conversation with a Regional Director, the Principal Secretary of the Education Ministry, for instance, switched several times to English phrases and back to Swahili, using expressions like 'claim per diem' in a Swahili context.

[16] As has been demonstrated by W. M. Shedu Chamungwa (1971), when showing school entering children a set of culturally adequate, easily identifiable pictures, for which a correct interpretation in their own vernacular does not appear to create any major problem, the response in Swahili, on the contrary, varies considerably, depending on the part of the country: thus, in rural areas in the south, where Nyakyusa prevails, the correct answers in Swahili amount to 44–56% and the response in vernacular *instead of Swahili* to 32–25% (the rest of the answers being invalid); similarly, in Muganza, near Lake Tanganyika, the scores are respectively 33.3% and 31.9%, and in Bukandwe, near Lake Victoria, 40.2% and

37.3%. As soon as an area shows a strong Muslim influence, is urbanized and has lost a marked identity (e.g. Kipampa and Uvinza, near Lake Tanganyika) or gathers many different groups in an urban centre or rural community (e.g. Magomeni Nursery, in Dar es Salaam; Bunda, near Lake Victoria), the percentages change dramatically:

Kipampa	Swahili 95.6%	Vernacular 0%
Uvinza	Swahili 88.8%	Vernacular 0.4%
Magomeni Nursery	Swahili 88.5%	Vernacular 0%
Bunda	Swahili 87.7%	Vernacular 3.3%

Distance from the coast is also an important factor as is demonstrated by the scores of Mwakidila (suburb of Tanga), Lusanga (22 miles from Tanga), Mgombezi (further inland), and Lushoto (in the Usambara mountains, 100 miles from the coast):

Mwakidila	Swahili 97.9%	Vernacular 0%
Lusanga	Swahili 91.0%	Vernacular 1.0%
Mgombezi	Swahili 86.4%	Vernacular 1.9%
Lushoto	Swahili 67.9%	Vernacular 17.7%

[17] Further indices of command of a language would be "spontaneously thinking or dreaming" in this language, but this criterion can be contextually restricted, e.g. a Chaga informant indicated that he dreamt about his girl-friend in his mother-tongue, but his nightly concerns about his job came up in Swahili. Other forms of oral performance, such as singing and praying, can point to a different type of familiarity with the language, e.g. a Muslim will pray in Arabic, even if his knowledge of that language is minimal, because he memorized the text of the relevant prayer in Quranic school.

[18] A medical assistant in the Gogo-speaking area near Dodoma, who *never* used English either in his professional or in his social activities, indicated that, in his dreams, English sentences would occasionally flash through his mind.

[19] Seven vowel languages would, for example blur the contrast between /ɛ/ and /e/, and /ɔ/ and /o/; such sounds as [ʋ] would be reproduced either as <b> or <v>. For the mother tongue speaker, these orthographic approximations or loss of phonemes in the transliteration never seemed to constitute a serious obstacle to comprehension.

[20] This will occur particularly where smaller, not necessarily related groups come in contact. More complex links can even develop along these lines, e.g. a Sandawe farmer married a Maasai woman and, later, gave in turn his daughter in marriage to a Maasai, both families, his own and his daughter's, being perfectly bilingual in Sandawe and Maasai and using both languages at home.

[21] There are actually considerable differences in attitude: beside this progressive attitude geared to serve the national purpose in making Swahili the first language of the upcoming generation, there is a whole gamut of diverging positions. About 4/5 of the last-year students in the teachers training colleges interviewed on a person-to-person basis in 1970 declared that they would make their children learn their mother tongue as well as Swahili, though they would give the national language priority. The motivation was most often self-identification, the vernacular being the genuine bearer of traditions; important also was the need for the child to be able to communicate adequately with his/her grandparents, whose knowledge of Swahili may have been limited. One high government official actually complained about his teenage children's practical ignorance of their vernacular and traditions and felt that a very important part of their heritage was getting lost.

²² This situation also occurs frequently in dispensaries, where a young boy will accompany his grandfather to the medical assistant's office to explain the older man's ailments in Swahili.

²³ A complete study of language use would also imply the examination of linguistic behavior under emotional stress, e.g. what language does the respondent use when involved in a heated argument; when insulting or cursing someone; when teasing a girl or flirting with her. But coping with such situations within the framework of a survey would be a rather complex and delicate matter.

²⁴ Standard ratings on lexical and grammatical levels, like those of the Foreign Service Institute in Washington, could not be readily used in surveying Tanzanian multilingualism, but a five-point scale was used to measure the degree of inter-communication between two languages or dialects from a mother tongue speaker's point of view. The method used was to ask a speaker of language A: "If a story is told to you in language B, can you:

(a) understand every single word and meaning?" (positive answer = rated 5)
(b) understand almost everything, though you might miss the meaning of a few words here and there?" (positive answer = rated 4)
(c) understand the general meaning of the story, though you miss quite a few words and phrases?" (positive answer = rated 3)
(d) understand only a few phrases here and there, without being able to follow the whole story properly?" (positive answer = rated 2)
(e) catch only a few isolated words, without being able to make any sense out of the text?" (positive answer = rated 1).

²⁵ Less than 5% of the children entering primary schools will make it into secondary schools. Regional distribution of the students is not too much affected by the location of the latter, since most of them are boarding schools.

²⁶ A sampling of cases may illustrate the situations described:

(a) farmers: – Respondent A: scores $V^1 24/25$ $V^2 11/4$; 21 year old Protestant woman, whose first language is Nyambo (the language of Karagwe where she has lived all her life), but who also knows Haya, the neighboring, closely related language. She was illiterate and unmarried, and she occasionally switched to Haya when talking to her parents; otherwise her use of Haya was restricted to church and socialization at the market.

Respondent B: scores V27/23 S37/19; young Catholic woman, whose first language is Sabi, though she has a thorough command of Swahili and has acquired literacy in it through 4 years in primary school. The pattern indicates a shift to almost exclusive use of Swahili outside the family circle (she read a lot, including the Swahili language daily paper *Uhuru*).

Respondent C: scores $V^1 13/10$ $V^2 10/2$ $V^3 10/0$ S32/31; 38 year old Muslim man, from a bilingual family, using Hehe (V^1), which he still speaks with his father and father-in-law, and Swahili, which was the language of his mother's family. His wife is a mother tongue speaker of Gogo (V^2), but at home she speaks only Swahili with her husband and children. Since they live in a Kaguru (V^3)-speaking area, this language is also used by him at the market and with the people in his neighborhood.

(b) shopkeeper: Respondent's scores: $V^1 26/12$ $V^2 27/11$ ($V^3 7/5$ $V^4 6/3$ $V^5 5/1$) S33/13; 38 year old Protestant man, from the Gogo speaking area; his father was, however, a Hehe. He has moved around quite a bit in the area and picked up some knowledge of the languages, of which he takes advantage for his trade, though he is essentially trilingual: Swahili, Hehe (V^1) and Gogo (V^2); the other languages are Kinga (V^3) Maasai (V^4), and Nyakyusa (V^5).

(c) village executive officer: Respondent's scores: $V^1 37/27$ $V^2 37/6$ $V^3 37/7$ $V^4 37/6$ $S 37/24$; 34 year old Protestant man from a mixed marriage (father: Gogo; mother: Hehe). Involved in village matters with Gogo (V^1), Hehe (V^2), Kaguru (V^3) and Nyambwa (V^4), he has acquired a very thorough command of these languages, enabling him to translate from Swahili into these vernaculars. He has only a limited reading knowledge of English (E2).

[27] The data were computerized at the University of London, and C. P. Hill took care of the graphic representation of the results. It was planned to include Hadza and Mbugu in the limited analysis, but the data on these languages proved to be insufficient for this purpose.

[28] Struck (1921) has given a comprehensive survey of the language situation found by the Germans in Tanganyika, with a very useful map of the extent to which Swahili was used, known or understood in those days.

[29] Cf. for example, the comments of Lyndon Harris (1969).

[30] The study of Andersson was essentially a group factor statistical analysis based on questionnaires listing a set of statements whose 'truth' was investigated. These questionnaires contained 'negative' statements such as: 'I think that it takes so long to learn Swahili that the attempt is not worth while' – or – 'I wish that we had very little Swahili in school' – or – 'I wish that no schoolbooks were written in Swahili'. Though the same questions were asked about English and 'positive statements like: 'I think that everyone should be taught Swahili' – or – 'I try to do something everyday to improve my Swahili vocabulary' – or – 'When I think of Swahili I become happy,' it appears that the Tanzanian authorities were rather displeased with the enquiry and its focus on the confrontation of English and Swahili at a time when they were trying their utmost to upgrade Swahili teaching and to give the language additional prestige and value as a tool of nation-building, while planning to substitute it gradually for English in secondary education. As a result of their discontent, the team of the Tanzanian Survey was specifically advised not to conduct research in attitudes versus languages in the country, especially in the schools.

[31] In 1967, 7% of the respondents showed *no* language preference.

[32] There is a considerable amount of diversity in the motivation that the younger generation was given for its linguistic behavior in the late sixties.

In the western part of the country where the Sukuma, Ha and Haya continued to find their vernacular 'nicer' than Swahili, they emphasized the national role of Swahili, its role as means of intergroups communication, the possibility to use it in a wider field (e.g. for writing letters) thanks to education; some even claimed an insufficient knowledge of their own language in 1967 to explain their preference of Swahili.

In the north, the Chaga, after feeling their language was losing out as a result of the strong action in favor of the national language in 1966, realized that, ultimately, things were evening out: Swahili and Chaga each has their area of wider use for communication – the former, e.g. in the public services; the latter, especially, at home, in tribal functions, etc. Compulsory education was a decisive factor for the spread of Swahili, and many youngsters did no longer understand a number of vernacular words used by the older generation. Some of the younger people remained very attached to their home language, as they were fluent in it and could talk to older people and understand their interesting tales about traditions.

In the non-Bantu Mbulu speaking section, Swahili was promoted by education, politics, religion and the medical service, the younger people encouraging the older to participate in the Swahili adult literacy program, but both generations would lapse again into the vernacular at home.

In the east, the older people in Usambara and Uluguru would use practically only their vernacular, but Muslims would use Swahili. There again the spread of Swahili depended essentially on education, with compulsory primary schooling for the younger generation and literacy programs for the older people. The Christian churches still used the vernaculars to a large extent, whereas Islam used Swahili (beside Arabic). The language of politics was basically Swahili. In 1965, when most of the students from this part of the country in Morogoro came from rural areas, they considered their vernacular as the 'nicest' language, but felt it was threatened. In 1967, with a shift to more urban representatives, a better balanced view of the situation is reflected by the data: there is still a high level of language loyalty to the vernacular in Usambara and Uluguru, and even the younger generation feels more at ease with friends and older people speaking its own language, like the majority of the villagers; they will only shift to Swahili when they feel quite confident in their command of the language, but may still use the vernacular as a kind of 'secret language' with kinsmen versus outsiders.

In the south, the younger generation is motivated by the following factors in its choice of languages:

Vernacular	Swahili
Ethnic pride: loyalty to vernacular as means of ethnic identification	*Nationalism*: avoidance of vernacular to prevent identification with specific ethnic group
Village language: familiar, more homely	*Wider communiaation*: used with people from all parts of the country

After completing primary school, where Swahili is the medium, students tend to use Swahili among themselves, as the population of secondary schools and teacher colleges is linguistically very mixed; this accounts for their vernacular being largely forgotten by the younger educated generation.

In the central regions, education, politics, and religion are major factors in the attitudes versus Swahili and the vernaculars – the churches shifting rapidly to Swahili. Important also is the rise of the ethnic group, since members of small groups are usually able to speak the language of the neighboring larger group or Swahili beside their own vernacular, even if it is non-Bantu, e.g. Sandawe. Nevertheless, a strong feeling for the place of the ethnic language remains obvious, though the 1967 figures presumably provide a more realistic picture of the situation: many feel they can express themselves better in their vernacular (up to 61% in 1965), but the role of Swahili as a uniting factor stressed by TANU slogans and the influence of multiethnic urban situations strongly favor Swahili. With a majority of students from rural areas, vernaculars prevail in 1965 (61%), but with shift in recruitment to the urban areas and a change of attitude in 1967, Swahili is preferred by 73.7%

This assessment based on the work of S. Kamatta (West), S. Shayo and F. Tlemu (North), M. Sempombe (East), G. Haule (South), and P. Warrantse (Central), valuable as it is, has to be judged in the right perspective: it elaborates on the personal statements of teachers' college students and does not result from field work covering a random sampling of the Tanzania population. The data reflect the personal background of these students, but provide hardly any information on the status of their family and the level of education of their parents, which are major factors conditioning their language use. Within these constraints, they are, however, quite useful, as an illustration of the crisis of linguistic identity that gripped younger Tanzanians in the late sixties.

[33] On the implementation of this measure at the University of Dar es Salaam, cf. Brauner, 1975: 332–338.

[34] A complete examination of the linguistic situation should include a special chapter on the Asian minority. For lack of space, only a short note can be devoted to this important subject (the information recorded here being based mainly on A. O. Kassam's report on the Asian community in Tanzania (1971), sponsored by the Tanzania Survey). According to the 1967 census, there were 85,000 Asians living in Tanzania. They speak five different Indian languages or dialects, all of them Indo-Aryan:

(1) Kachi (a dialect of Sindhi)
(2) Konkani
(3) Gujrati
(4) Punjabi
(5) Urdu

The subgroups of the Asian community are not based on linguistic, but on religious differences: (1) The largest group are the *Ismailis* – followers of the Aga Khan – who use mainly Kachi, but many of whom also speak Gujrati and some Hindi (a number of them migrated in 1964 from Zanzibar and are mainly using Swahili; otherwise, Swahili, in which they are mostly fluent, is not used at home); they used to have an excellent education system and their command of English is usually excellent.

(2) Among the Muslims, four subgroups are further to be distinguished:
   (a) the *Ithnaasheries* (Sunni Muslims) who are mostly bilingual – Gujrati and Swahili (30% of them migrated from Zanzibar) – and use Kachi and read Quranic Arabic, beside having some Persian, Hindi and Urdu and often a fair reading knowledge of English;
   (b) the *Bohoras*, native speakers of Gujrati, with a fair knowledge of English and a lesser command of Swahili;
   (c) the *Kachi-speaking Sunnis*, 40% of whom are literate in Gujrati, whereas all can read Quranic Arabic and their level of competence in English depends on education;
   (d) the *Urdu-speaking Sunnis*, showing the same proficiency in reading Quranic Arabic and command of English determined by educational background, and mostly able to read and write Urdu.

(3) Gujrati is also the language of the Parsees and the Hindus:
   (a) the *Parsees* are Indian Zoroastrians, whose sacred writings are still in Avestan, but in Gujrati or English script; their command of English is usually excellent, but they have hardly any knowledge of Swahili;
   (b) the *Hindus* are essentially Vaishnavite, whose community association – the *Arya Samaj* – runs classes in Hindi, Gujrati and Sanskrit so that some of them can read the Bhagavadgita in the original text and many speak Hindi beside Gujrati; a subgroup – the Bhattias (Lohanas) – speaks Kachi. The Hindus are usually able to speak English fluently, but they hardly read; Swahili is neglected.

(4) The *Sikhs* constitute a separate group with their own beliefs; their mother tongue is Punjabi, but they have an excellent command of Swahili, an many have become fluent and literate in English as well. Those more recently arrived from India also know Urdu, which they studied at school there.

(5) The *Goans* are Roman Catholic; though they still speak the Konkanese of their original homeland, English is their mother tongue for all practical purposes. Many also know Portuguese.

Until 1961, Asian education was separate from African education (Cameron and

Dodd, 1970: 125), and social contacts between Africans and Asians were minimal: the various closely-knit Asian groups were very community-minded and intermarriage did not occur. In their professional activities, the level and depth of contact with Africans was the greatest for the Ithnaasheries, the Sunnis and the Sikhs; it was lesser with the Ismailis and the Bohoras, and even more with the Hindus. The Goans kept quite aloof from the Africans, and the Parsees had practically no relation with them.

In the new Tanzanian society many forces are at work to break the barriers to inter-racial social mingling, but will this lead in the long run to genuine social integration of the Asians? (Ghai, 1969: 103–106) A first consequence would certainly be an improved knowledge of Swahili, which in many cases now appears as a mixed language of Kuchi verbal stems with Swahili morphemes, as in the following examples:

'we will meet'	*tutamale*	(Kuchi *male* 'meet')
'to understand'	*kusamje*	(Kuchi *samje* 'understand')
'you will come'	*utaache*	(Kuchi *ache* 'come')
'it will do'	*itahale*	(Kuchi *hale* 'do').

REFERENCES

Andersson, Anders, 1967, *Multilingualism and Attitudes*. An explorative-descriptive study among secondary school students in Ethiopia and Tanzania. Uppsala: Institute of Education, University of Uppsala. [mimeo].

Angogo, Rachel, 1978, 'Issues in the Use of Standard Swahili'. Paper presented at the 9th Annual Conference on African Linguistics at East Lansing, Michigan.

Berry, L., 1971, *Tanzania in Maps*. London: University of London Press.

Brauner, Siegmund, 1975, 'Swahili an der Universität Dar es Salaam' *Zeitschrift für Phonetik, Sprachwissenschaft und Kommunikationsforschung*, 28: 3/4, 331–342.

Cameron, J. and Dodd, W. A., 1970, *Society, Schools and Progress in Tanzania*. Oxford: Pergamon Press.

Chamungwana, W. M. Shedu, 1971, 'Primary School Entrants' Knowledge and Use of Swahili'. Research paper submitted to the Tanzania Survey at University of Dar es Salaam. Stenciled [with pictograms].

Cliffe, Lionel (ed.), 1967, *One Party Democracy*. The 1965 Tanzania General Elections. Nairobi: East African Publishing House.

Dodds, Tony, 1970, 'Report of a Survey of Radio Ownership and Listening Habits in Tanzania.' Report submitted to the Institute of Adult Education, University of Dar es Salaam. Manuscript (typewritten).

Dryden, Stanley, 1968, *Local Administration in Tanzania*. Nairobi: East African Publishing House.

Ghai, D. P. (ed.), 1965, *Portrait of a Minority. The Asians in East Africa*. Nairobi: Oxford University Press.

Ghai, Dharam and Ghai, Yash, 1969, 'Asians in Tanzania: Problems and Prospects' in Svendsen, Knud Erik, and Teisen, Merete (eds.), *Self-Reliant Tanzania* (Dar es Salaam: Tanzania Publishing House), 91–110. Published previously in *Journal of Modern African Studies* 3:1 (1965), 35–51.

Harries, Lyndon, 1969, 'Language Policy in Tanzania' *Africa* 39, 275–279.

Hatfield, C. R., 1972a, 'The Agent of Change. The Agent of Conflict.' Paper presented at the Third World Congress for Rural Sociology, Louisiana State University, Baton Rouge, La.

   1972b, 'Livestock Development in Sukumaland: The Constituents of Communication'. I. Interface Structuring and the Development Process. Paper presented at the Third World Congress for Rural Sociology, Louisiana State University, Baton Rouge, La.

Herrick, Allison Butler et al., 1968, *Area Handbook for Tanzania*. Washington, D.C., U.S. Government Printing Office.

Hyden, Göran, 1969, *Political Development in Rural Tanzania. TANU yajenga nchi.* Nairobi: East African Publishing House [focuses on Uhaya].

Ingle, Clyde R., 1972, *From Village to State in Tanzania. The Politics of Rural Development.* Ithaca: Cornell University Press.

Ishige, Naomichi, 1969, 'On Swahilization' *Kyoto University African Studies* 3, 93-108.

Kassam, A. O., 1971, 'The Linguistic System within the Asian Community in Tanzania (with particular reference to Dar es Salaam).' Report submitted to the Tanzania Survey. Manuscript [mimeo].

Kurtz, Laura S., 1972, *An African Education. The Social Revolution in Tanzania.* Brooklyn, N.Y. Poseidon Ltd.

Legère, Karsten, 1975, 'Zum Verhältnis zwischen dem Swahili und anderen tanzanischen Sprachen' *Zeitschrift für Phonetik, Sprachwissenschaft und Kommunikationsforschung* 28: 3/4, 343-348.

Liebenow, J. Gus, 1971. *Colonial Rule and Political Development in Tanzania. The case of the Makonde.* Nairobi: East African Publishing House.

MacDonald, Alexander, 1966, *Tanzania: Young Nation in a Hurry.* New York: Hawthorn Books.

Maguire, G. Andrew, 1969, *Toward 'Uhuru' in Tanzania. The Politics of Participation.* Cambridge: University Press [focuses on Sukumaland].

Mbilinyi, Marjorie J., 1969. *The Education of Girls in Tanzania. A Study of Attitudes of Tanzanian Girls and Their Fathers towards Education.* Dar es Salaam: Institute of Education, University College.

Mittelmeyer, J. et al., 1967, 'Growth of Swahili. Language Situation and Attitudes towards Dialects and Swahili, 1965-1967'. Morogoro: Teachers' College, Linguistics Department [unpublished typewritten manuscript].

Mlay, Hezekiah, and Mkindi, David, 1970, 'An Investigation into the Pattern of Language Use of a number of Multilinguals in Tanzania through keeping of Linguistic Diaries.' Report submitted to the Tanzania Survey. Manuscript [stenciled].

Molnos, Angela, 1969, *Language Problems in Africa.* A bibliography (1946-1967) and summary of the present situation with special reference to Kenya, Tanzania, and Uganda (EARIC Information Circular No. 2) Nairobi: East African Research Information Centre, The East African Academy.

Mytton, Graham L., 1969, 'Tanzania: A Mass Media Audience Survey. Some preliminary Results and Observations.' Manuscript (typewritten).

1970, 'Tanzania: The Problems of Mass Media Development.' pp. 89-100 [xerox].

Ntemo, Finehas D., 1964, 'The Language Situation in Tanganyika.' Report submitted to the Institute of Education, University of Exeter (Great Britain). Manuscript [stenciled].

Nyerere, Julius K., 1967, *Freedom and Unity. Uhuru na Umoja.* A selection from writings and speeches. 1952-1965. Dar es Salaam: Oxford University Press.

1968a, *Ujamaa. Essays on Socialism.* Dar es Salaam: Oxford University Press.

1968b, *Freedom and Socialism. Uhuru na Ujamaa.* A selection from writings and speeches. 1965-1967. Dar es Salaam: Oxford University Press.

1974, *Man and Development. Binadamu na Maendeleo.* London/New York: Oxford University Press.

O'Barr, William M., and Jean F., 1976, *Language and Politics*. (Contributions to the Sociology of Language, vol. 10) The Hague: Mouton.

Polomé, Edgar C., 1973, 'Sociolinguistic Problems in Tanzania and Zaire' *The Conch*, vol. IV, No. 2 (September, 1972) 64–83 (edited as separate volume by Sunday O. Anozie under the title *Language Systems in Africa*).

—— 1975, 'Problems and Techniques of a Sociolinguistically Oriented Language Survey: The Case of the Tanzania Survey' in Ohannessian (S.), Ferguson (C.) and Polomé (E.), eds. *Language Surveys in Developing Nations*. Arlington, Va.: Center for Applied Linguistics, 31–50.

—— (forthcoming) 'Rural versus Urban Multilingualism in Tanzania. An Outline.'

Polomé, Edgar C., Polomé, André R. and Abdullah, Ali, 1980, 'Language and Religion in Tanzania' *Orbis* 30 (forthcoming).

Resnick, Idrian N., 1968, 'Educational Barriers to Tanzania's Development' in Resnick, Idrian N. (ed.) *Tanzania: Revolution by Education*, Arusha: Longmans of Tanzania, 1968, 123–134.

Rigby, Peter, 1969, *Cattle and Kinship among the Gogo. A Semi-pastoral Society of Central Tanzania*. Ithaca: Cornell University Press.

Ruthenberg, Hans (ed.), 1968, *Smallholder Farming and Smallholder Development in Tanzania. Ten Case Studies*. (IFO-Institut für Wirtschaftsforschung München – Afrika Studien, vol. 24). Munich: Weltforum Verlag.

Rweyamamu, E. (ed.), 1970, *Nation-Building in Tanzania*. Nairobi: East African Publishing House.

Struck, B., 1921, 'Die Einheitssprache Deutsch-Ostafrikas' *Koloniale Rundschau* 1921:4, 164–196 [with map].

Svendsen, Knud Eric, and Teisen, Merete (eds.), 1969, *Self-reliant Tanzania*. Dar es Salaam: Tanzania Publishing House.

Tordoff, William, 1967, *Government and Politics in Tanzania*. Nairobi: East African Publishing House.

Widstrand, C. G., 1966a, 'Radio and Adult Education in Tanzania: Some Considerations'. (*Adult Education Studies*, No. 1) Dar es Salaam: Institute of Adult Education, University College.

—— 1966b, *Development by Exhortation*. A study of nation-building over the radio in Tanzania. Paper given at the Social Science Council Conference organized by the University of East Africa in Nairobi. Typescript draft.

Yoneyama, Toshinao, 1969, 'The Life and Society of the Iraqw – Introductory Remarks' *Kyoto University African Studies*, 77–114.

1960, *Listener Research Survey – Tanganyika Broadcasting Corporation*. Dar es Salaam: Market Research Company (MARCO) of East Africa.

1968, *Tanzania Today*. Nairobi: University Press of Africa (for the Ministry and Tourism, United Republic of Tanzania).

1969, *1967 Population Census*. Volume 1: *Statistics for Enumeration Areas*. Dar es Salaam: Central Statistical Bureau, Ministry of Economic Affairs and Development Planning.

1969, *Quotations from President Julius K. Nyerere*. Morogoro: Teachers' College.

1970, *The Economic Survey and Annual Plan 1970–71. The United Republic of Tanzania*. Dar es Salaam: The Government Printer.

1970/71, *Press Directory*. United Republic of Tanzania. Dar es Salaam: Information Services Division.

1971, *Ostafrika: Sprachraum des Suaheli*. (Special number of the *Zeitschrift für Kulturaustausch*, with contributions of E. Dammann, [language and religion], W. Küper [on education], H. Helmschrott [on economic development], etc.) Stuttgart: Institut für Auslandsbeziehungen.

6 THE ECOLOGY OF TANZANIAN NATIONAL LANGUAGE POLICY[1]

Mohamed H. Abdulaziz

1.0 Introduction

The concept of ecology appears to have been borrowed from a branch of biology that deals with the interaction between animals and plants and their environments. Einar Haugen, among sociologists who applied ecology in the description of language situations, defines the term as follows: 'Language ecology may be defined as the study of interactions between any given language and its environment . . . the referential world to which language provides index. . . . The analysis of ecology requires not only that one describe the social and psychological situations of each language, but also the effect of this situation on the language itself.' (Haugen, 1971:325)

My own view of ecology of language to a large extent tallies with that of scholars like Haugen. It attempts to study the growth of a fast-developing African language (in this case, but could equally be applicable in the case of declining or 'dead' languages) in terms of the dynamics of the socio-political, socio-cultural bases on which a given language is functioning. Whiteley asks: 'What are the factors which at different historical periods have led people to use one language rather than another, or within a particular language in one set of circumstances and another one in a different set?' (Whiteley, 1969:vii)

There is no doubt that a clear explanation of the fortunes of a language can be sought by a careful look into the historical, political, social, and psychological factors that have operated in the relevant atmosphere in which that language existed. This chapter intends to analyze these factors in the case of the development of Swahili, a modern national/official language of Tanzania. It is hoped that this example will provide another case study of the development of a small minority language (cf. English, Latin, Arabic, French . . .) into the great lingua franca of a large portion of Eastern and Central Africa, and a national language of three East African countries. In this chapter, the author will concentrate on factors that have contributed to making it possible for Swahili to be so readily acceptable in Tanganyika (later Tanzania) and to develop as a workable language in a developing modern state. I shall deal mainly with the British colonial administration up to the present day, since the earlier times are dealt with in chapter 4 of this volume.

2.0 The Background

2.1 Demography

Tanzania is a large country covering approximately 362,688 square miles with a population of about 16,000,000 people. The country is on the whole sparsely populated, with only a few pockets, such as the areas inhabited mostly by the Chaga, Haya, Sukuma, Nyamwezi, and Nyakusa, having relatively heavy densities of population. In addition, there are only a few natural barriers to movement of people. These geographical conditions facilitated the opening of the interior by the appearance of great caravan and trade routes since the early 19th century, running from the coast to the north, west, and south. The caravans in most cases were organized and led by Swahili-speaking people from the coast, a fact which laid the foundation of the growth of Swahili as a lingua franca along the trade routes. The fact that over 90% of the people were (and still are) mother tongue speakers of Bantu languages (as is Swahili) facilitated the rapid acquisition of this language by speakers of other languages.

The population of Tanzania comprises over 100 ethno-linguistic groups with no group predominant enough in numbers to assert itself politically. The biggest group is the Sukuma, who comprise less than 2,000,000 people. Most of the other groups are under a million strong. Furthermore, there is a good balance between Muslims and Christians. It is said that the Muslims number slightly more than the Christians, but I have found no reliable census data to prove or disprove this. These demographic facts have gone a long way towards making all territory-wide organizations essentially nationalistic in attitude, and compellingly supra-tribal in composition, a situation that paved the way for the healthy growth of a strong national base in all socio-political and socio-cultural movements.

2.2 *The German Period*

As is mentioned elsewhere in this volume (see also Abdulaziz, 1971:62), by the last decades of the 19th century, Swahili had already emerged as a strong lingua franca, a fact which made the Germans entrench it even more by using it in schools and in the administration, giving the language prestige and helping it to spread. In the 20 years preceding World War I, the Germans had already created three types of schools: village primary schools (Nebenschulen), of which there were sixty giving three years of education in Swahili, nine middle schools (Hauptschulen) giving a two year course in reading, writing, and arithmetic, and one high school (Oberschule) in Tanga, which offered clerical, industrial and teacher training education (J. Cameron and W. A. Dodd, 1970:56). By 1914, the administration in Tanganyika carried on its correspondence in Swahili. "On the mission side no less than 11,000 copies of a Swahili series of booklets on religious and general knowledge had been sold by 1910." (Cameron and Dodd, 1970:57).

2.3 *The British Period*

Tanzania became a British mandate territory in 1920, after the defeat of the Germans in World War I. The British found almost a fait accompli situation with respect to the status of Swahili. The language had already established itself as an important medium in administration, especially at those levels dealing with the masses of the people, and also as an important language in the educational system, especially at the primary school level. This was true in spite of the fact that certain missionary groups insisted on the use of the local vernacular languages. It is characteristic of the German period that very little German was to be taught in schools.

Perhaps the most significant step towards further consolidating the position of Swahili during this period was the passing of the "Education Ordinance and Regulations" in 1927 (See Eggert, 1970:203). This regulation came into force in 1928, stating the conditions to be fulfilled by schools in order to receive grants from the government. British government policy, contrary to the widespread approach of the missions, favored the promotion of Swahili and English in schools. The idea was to train potential staff to man the administrative machinery. The British also seemed to favor greater academic achievement than the mission schools intended. For example, in teaching, emphasis was put on language and communication skills. Mission schools thus rarely qualified for grants (Eggert, 1970:200-203). Of course, the missions themselves, since the German times, were opposed to any supervisory attitude on the part of the government. They wanted to run the schools so that their own purposes could be achieved adequately.

Moreover, the government did not build enough schools, partly because of the fear of overproducing educated people without jobs; the government's main purpose was to produce a sufficient number of lower administrative officers to man the 'native administration'.

The economic crisis of the late twenties and the thirties forced the missions to pay more attention to the government educational language policy. They also saw the need to concentrate on the development of suitably designed so-called higher levels of education (including middle schools and teacher training colleges). With the cut-down on the government budget in the early thirties, Swahili began again to play a leading role in the education system, as the British administration required. While the German administration and their missions discouraged the imposition of the German language, British government policy was to encourage the use of both Swahili and English in schools and in the administration. By the early thirties, Swahili and English had established themselves as the only languages of instruction, as well as subjects, in the middle or junior secondary schools. The same was true of Teacher Training Colleges. For example, grade 2 teachers for elementary schools had a two-year teacher training course with Swahili as the language of instruction. Grade 1 teachers for middle school and teacher training colleges trained four years with English as the medium of teaching (Eggert, 1970:204). The missionaries gradually complied with government language ordinances, although this went against their original approach which favored a broad-based, intellectually less demanding education given in the mother tongue and aimed at reading, writing, and religious instruction. It would seem that everyone realized Swahili was a stepping-stone to acquiring education in English, the final objective. This gave English an important element of prestige. Apart from the material benefits derived from knowledge of English, this language, it was realized, opened many opportunities, such as the ability to read newspapers and books, that might have contributed to the formation of a small but influential English-speaking 'elite' group, who were getting suspicious of the authenticity of even Swahili sources of information.

According to Eggert (1970:201–4), Rivers–Smith, who became the Director of Education in 1926, did not seem to favor the wide use of Swahili in Tanganyika schools, although Cameron and Dodd (1970:59) picture him as a man who had a love of the Swahili language. A delegation of missionaries only succeeded in persuading him to concede the use of Swahili in primary schools, but he still insisted that this language need not be the medium of instruction in elementary schools, although the language continued to function as the medium of examination. According to the missionaries, this hindered the children's progress in acquiring language skills necessary for doing their examinations well.

In 1931 a new Director of Education, Isherwood (see Cameron and Dodd:59), was much more accommodating from the point of view of missionaries concerned with education. The world economic crisis was adversely affecting availability of subsidies. This necessitated a reduction in the number of government central (middle) schools. Isherwood agreed with the missionary view that it was better to use the scarce funds to raise the standards of the bulk of school population than to spend large sums on giving "good education" to a few pupils. German mission schools which were still operating were badly hit by stringent foreign currency regulations, and although teachers accepted pay cuts, the mission schools could hardly make full use of the opportunity for introducing education to a wider section of the community. Some mission schools, such as the one at Rungwe, took advantage of the new policy by attempting to completely cancel English classes. Africans interpreted this as a deliberate move to bar them from English-based education, which was then considered superior. The situation was sometimes contradictory; for example, when Isherwood offered extra funds for an English teacher to be employed in 1937, the Nyasa Synod rejected the offer. However, not all mission schools were fanatical about language policy, and many saw the importance of maintaining both English and Swahili.

From the 1920s, and especially during the Governorship of Sir Donald Cameron, the British Government attitude was "to develop the people, as far as possible, on their own values and customs, purified where necessary." (Cameron and Dodd, 1970:40). This attitude further facilitated the growth of Swahili in all educational and administrative spheres concerning the people of Tanganyika as a whole. The Colonial Office Memorandum on Educational Policy in British Tropical Africa, which was inspired by the Phelps–Stokes Commission Reports, further helped to bring about cooperation between the government and the missions. Cameron and Dodd (1970:61) note that between 1939 and 1945 there was an increase of 43% on the total enrollment of all government and government aided schools. Government expenditure was more than doubled.

An interesting aspect of the development of the education system in Tanzania was the emergence of the so-called Native Authority schools in 1926. The initiative for opening these schools came from the people of

Tanganyika themselves, who presumably thought that their children would not get the sort of education considered suitable by their parents as long as they did not have a full say in the matter. The governor, Sir Donald Cameron, was of the opinion that the Native Authority schools should be regarded as government schools. It is not clear what the educational language policy was in these schools with regard to the vernacular languages, Swahili, and English, but the impression one gets was that Swahili had a prominent place. Cameron and Dodd (1970:71) observe that the question of the medium of instruction often cropped up in the 1930s and early 1940s: "The Africans themselves were ambivalent about the problem, recognizing, on the one hand, cultural values inherent in the local language of the home and, on the other, the need to communicate with outside people over a much wider area." Swahili, during this period, continued to gain ground as the medium of instruction in the primary schools, as did English in the secondary. By 1945 the vernaculars had all but disappeared from the education system – both government and non-government. Thanks to educational policy, the future national language then was firmly established (Cameron and Dodd, 1970:71).

However, Swahili in some ways suffered in prestige. It is true that it was the language of the colonial administration. As Whiteley put it: "It was thus a mark, if only secondarily, of social distance – a means of reaching down to people rather than of enabling them to reach up to the administration." (Whiteley, 1969:61).

In the 1940s, Swahili was used as a medium of instruction in primary schools and as a subject up to Cambridge School Certificate standard. But in secondary schools and institutions of higher learning, English remained the medium of instruction. The fact that English teaching materials were far better organized and in much greater supply and variety added to the prestige of English. English also functioned as the language of the higher courts, of commercial and banking transactions, and of the more interesting magazines, newspapers, and British and American films.

The above survey of the educational and administrative language policy in the first half of the twentieth century could provide an explanation of the fact that in post-World War II years Swahili had established itself already as a sociolinguistic base on which all future mass organizations depended. By the middle decades of this century, all educated Tanganyikans, as well as a very large proportion of those who had never gone to school, had become bilinguals with great facility in the use of Swahili. Those Tanganyikans who also managed to acquire post-primary school education added English to their language repertoire. By 1950, therefore, Tanganyika had emerged as a territory unique among all the multilingual territories of Africa, in having an African language widely spoken as a lingua franca and extensively used in the administrative and educational systems of the country. It was also remarkable that Swahili encountered little, if any, real competition or resentment from the over one hundred vernacular communities.

Up to the present time, I cannot think of one multilingual African country that has succeeded in developing a single indigenous African language to a level of making it fully acceptable as a national/official language, although a number of countries are in the process of initiating a situation in which the concept of one nation/one language can be accepted.

3.0 *Swahili in Modern Tanzania*

The existence of a widely-used local language has greatly facilitated the formation of movements that transcended ethnolinguistic affiliations in Tanzania (Abdulaziz, 1971:165). The first of such movements was the Maji Maji War of 1905-7 when Tanzanians of several ethno-linguistic communities fought together against German colonial rule. Other movements of national appeal which took advantage of the existence of a common Tanzanian language were the Tanganyika Territory Civil Servant Association (T.T.C.S.A.) founded in Tanga in 1922; the African Welfare and Commercial Association (A.W.C.A.), founded in Dar es Salaam in 1934, aimed at looking after the interests of African traders; the Tanganyika African Association (T.A.A.) and Tanganyika African National Union (TANU). The T.T.C.S.A. had a Swahili newspaper called *Kwetu*, which circulated between 1932 and 1952. The T.A.A., a territory-wide political movement which many people would consider as the fore-runner of TANU, did most of its organizing in Swahili and had its constitution in Swahili (Abdulaziz, 1971:165). It would seem that most of the nationalist or popular movements started in the coastal towns, especially Dar es Salaam and Tanga, both strong Swahili speaking areas of the country. The fact that the capital city has always been situated on the Swahili speaking coast has contributed a great deal towards entrenching Swahili as the national language. The dialect of Dar es Salaam, the center of government administration, commerce, and the mass media, is probably emerging as the most influential form in formal "standard" usages.

3.1 *Role of TANU in promoting Swahili*

TANU, from the time of its inception in July, 1954 to the present day, has been one of the most effective and integrated parties in African politics. There were a number of characteristic factors of TANU that later were to play an important role in making it a truly nationalist movement, a fact (as will be shown) which contributed greatly to the strong position of Swahili in particular and to the national language policy in general. TANU was born in Dar es Salaam (the coastal capital) on 7th July 1954 during the annual conference of the Tanganyika African Association. The delegates of this annual conference became the founder members of TANU. It was significant that membership included people from all tribal and religious groups represented among the Tanzanian populace. It was also significant that the President of the party, Julius Nyerere, came from one of the smallest tribal groups in the country, the Wazanaki, who live in a village near Musoma on the shores of Lake Victoria.

T.A.A. and TANU differed in one major aspect. The former was a semi-political, semi-cultural association that had no clearcut basic ideology or guidance relating to national matters. So the first task that the TANU executive committee undertook was to inject the Party with clear objectives. Among the relevant objectives for our purpose were (Kaniki, 1974:1-2):

(a) to prepare the territory for self-rule and to fight for national freedom
(b) to fight tribalism and any other factors which would hinder the development of unity among Africans
(c) to abolish all sorts of segregation
(d) to encourage and help workers establish trade unions
(e) to cooperate with other organizations whose aims and objectives were not contradictory to those of TANU.

Thus right from the outset TANU emerged as a nationalist party seeking support from the masses, making Swahili the only possible vehicle for the achievement of its objects.

TANU condemned the policy of limiting African primary education to four years, "because it did not prepare the recipients to be productive members of that community." They recommended that the government fundamentally modify the "extremely hopeless" middle school education by introducing vocation-based education. It was resolved further that Kiswahili be promoted in elementary as well as higher schools (Kaniki, 1974:3). A special fund, collected from all the provinces of Tanganyika, was set up by TANU to help promote national education.

TANU succeeded in opening branches in all urban areas and district centers by the middle fifties, with Swahili serving as the language of party organization, debates, meetings, and of written minutes. Thus Swahili became an instrument of national political organization. "Kiswahili as a lingua franca of Tanganyika played a substantial role in uniting the activities of TANU. The language was understood almost everywhere in the country, and, in most cases, TANU leaders, especially those at provincial and national levels, addressed public meetings in Kiswahili. Most leaders were (and are) fluent in the language, and, therefore, there was direct and undiluted communication between the leaders and the masses. Kiswahili made TANU leaders easily acceptable as leaders of Tanganyika rather than of this or that ethnic group." (Kaniki, 1974:13). Tanganyika attained self rule on December 1, 1960, and at once the new government embarked on activities intended to develop national institutions. Nyerere delivered the Republic Day Speech in Swahili for the first time on December 10, 1962, in Parliament. He said that he had set up a new Ministry of National Culture and Youth: "I have done this because I believe that its culture is the spirit and essence of any nation. A country which lacks its own culture is no more than a collection of people without spirit which makes them a nation . . ."

In 1964 the post of Promoter for Swahili was created with the duty of coordinating various groups engaged in the promotion of the language. Active public groups already were engaged in developing literary Swahili. Among these were the Swahili Poets' Association which later developed into the nationwide organization called *Usanifa wa Kiswahili na Ushairi Tanzania* (UKUTA), and the *Jumuiya ya Kustawisha Kiswahili*. Matters relating to the development of a Swahili curriculum and the production of Swahili teachers and syllabuses were handled by a special Ministry of Education Committee.

The Ministry of Culture was charged with promoting the expanding indigenous culture of the masses of the people of Tanzania, the vast majority of whom were peasants and workers. Therefore, indigenous dances and other cultural activities such as oral literature were encouraged. In many cases the "tribal" dances, songs, and folklore were interpreted into Swahili making them understandable to everybody in the country. Promotion of culture was emphasized particularly in the schools, within the TANU youth league, and among youth in general. (For policy on culture see Mbuguni, and Ruhumbika, 1974.)

In 1967 Vice-President Kawawa declared that, henceforth, as much Swahili as possible was to be used in all government and para-governmental bodies. Other languages such as English were to continue to function only in those areas in which Swahili was not yet fully developed.

Right from the start, therefore, the Tanzanian ruling party has closely associated language with national identity, integration, and development. Fishman notes this aspect of nationalism which has been repeated again and again in the history of nations: "Nationalism as an integrative movement seeks to go beyond the primordialities to family and locality (which defined the affiliative horizon of the common man in predominantly pre-industrialized and pre-urban times) and to forge wider bonds that can draw the rural, the urban, and the regional into a broader unity: *the nationality*. In its birth this nationalism stresses the inherent unity of populations that have never been aware of such unity before." (Fishman, 1971b:3).

Fishman then lists three factors as essential for nationalism: unification, authentification, and modernization. In the African context of new nations, the triangular need for unification, authentification, and modernization is everpressing. Tanzania is making full use of Swahili as one of the instrumental factors to achieve these ends. It will be noted that in present-day Africa most of the problems facing these new countries are those concerned with reconciling primordial ethnic loyalties with those of the nation as a whole. Since ethnic groups in Africa sharply coincide with linguistic and cultural ones, the question of national language and culture as a basis of nation-building is one of the most crucial.

3.2 *The Arusha Declaration and its Influence on the Language Situation*

The Arusha Declaration, which was to be the blueprint of the ideological base for Tanzanian nationalism, emphasized among others the following factors:

(a) equality of all human beings;
(b) dignity of the individual;
(c) an opportunity for every Tanzanian to participate fully in the affairs

of his government from the ten-cell system to the highest legislative body, the Parliament;
(d) that the natural resources of the country belong to everyone, and therefore, to ensure this, the government must control the means of production and distribution;
(e) to ensure that Tanzania is ruled by a government of the people in the ideals of democracy and socialism;
(f) that there will be no exploitation of man by man of any kind: economic, cultural, educational, tribal, or racial.

Within the Arusha Declaration also emerged the ideology of self-reliance, a belief that Tanzania should be developed by Tanzanians themselves and on the bases of their own socio-political and socio-cultural systems. This did not mean not accepting outside help or ignoring the vital total human contribution in the field of sciences, technology, and the arts, but that any such incorporation must suit the needs of the country and its ethos of socialism and self-reliance.

The above socio-political "ecology" was to create great repercussions on the development of Tanzanian national language policy. The resultant policies affected particularly the following areas.

3.2.1 *Education*

In 1967 a pamphlet entitled 'Education for Self-reliance' was issued. The basic ethos of the policy was that education must be relevant to the needs of Tanzania, a country which for many decades to come will continue to be mainly agricultural. It must be realistic in the sense of producing young people who could be absorbed into the economy of the country. These objectives are now the focal points of debate in all African countries. The pre-independent colonial education had a number of inherent drawbacks looked at from the point of view of an independent country. It has been an education that has succeeded in producing a small minority of Western-educated, culturally Western-oriented elites, who until now provided the leadership core in African countries. These have been labelled the "self-appointed" natural rulers. They have tended to approach matters of economic, social, and cultural development from their minority standpoint. Economic development, for example, has meant aspiring to develop urban areas to the economic and cultural standards of the former colonial metropolitan capitals. This has meant that in the same country one has a pocket or a couple of pockets of highly urbanized centers with the trimmings of modernity, existing side by side with the vast rural areas comprising 90% or more of the population, which maintain more or less the same subsistence level of life as in colonial times.

Education as it is presently given in many countries of Africa seems to be based on the assumption that children will continue to the university level. But the hard fact is that only 10 to 15% of the primary school children in fact do well enough to go on to the secondary school. Hence the explosive problem of a huge and increasing mass of frustrated young "failures" loitering in the bright streets of the urban centers with poor or no prospects of employment, and with little training to do anything they consider, with inflated hopes, worthwhile, since education has been considered a passport to white collar jobs in the city. Again, only a small proportion of those who do get into secondary schools succeed in entering high school, which is basically a preparation for university education. Of those who do go on to high school, again only a fraction succeed in finding a place in the university. For example, Eric Ofoe Apronti notes: "What of the notion that the free-educational system of Ghana is a guarantee that everyone will be given a fair chance for social advancement through the acquisition of an English-based and English medium educational background? The statistics show that only as few as five percent of the children who enter class one (at the age of 6) are able to get placement in secondary schools.... Indeed, many people would agree that even those five percent or so of those class one entrants who manage to go through the five-year secondary school program are, at the end, hardly effective users of English." (1974, 2–3).

Another African scholar, Adekunle (1972: 193), argues strongly for the entrenchment of local languages: "It is during this period that the attitudes and aptitudes are developed. It is during this period also that the child requires intelligent care of his physical needs and trained guidance in his mental, emotional, and social potentialities. It is our thesis that if the Nigerian child is to be encouraged from the start to develop curiosity, manipulative ability, originality, initiative, industry, manual dexterity, and mechanical comprehension, he should acquire these skills and attitudes through his mother-tongue which is the most natural way to learn. This is the way children in Europe and America learn. The European, American, Japanese, Russian, French, Scandinavian, German, and other children particularly at the elementary level, explore their own natural environment in their own native tongue...."

In *Education for Self-reliance*, Nyerere argues: "But even if this suggestion was based on favorable fact, it could not be allowed to override the need for change in the direction of educational integration with our national life. For the majority of our people the thing which matters is that they should be able to read and write fluently in Swahili, that they should have an ability to do arithmetic, and that they should learn something of the history, values, and working of their country and government, and that they should acquire the skills necessary to earn their living. (It is important to stress that in Tanzania most people will earn their living by working on their own or on a communal *shamba*, and only a few will do so by working for wages which they have to spend on buying things the farmer produces for himself.)" (Nyerere, 1967b:24). It is through education that children must be inculcated with values compatible with the building of a common sense of cultural identity and a commitment to Tanzanian socialist principles. Such education, especially in the early years of a child's life and for the vast majority of the people, could only succeed if it were based on the national language.

3.2.1 *Primary Schools*

To implement this basic educational principle, Swahili was made the sole medium of instruction in primary schools. Other educational levels have to take this fact into consideration. In the secondary schools up to the university level, although many "technical" subjects are still taught in English, political education is taught in Swahili. The teacher training colleges, especially those that deal with primary schools, also take Swahili very seriously. English, however, is taught as a subject from standard I in the primary school, the argument being that if this language is taught properly the children should have acquired enough competence in it relative to their needs, by the time they reach standard VII or above.

The policy of leaving Swahili as the sole medium of instruction has kept very busy those preparing curriculum and teaching materials especially in the fields of mathematics, science, geography, and nature study. A huge primary school vocabulary covering the various subjects is building up. I have had numerous opportunities to visit Tanzanian schools and to see the system working smoothly. The children, not knowing any other alternative medium of learning, such as English children, learn happily and naturally through a language which for most is the second mother tongue or at worst a strong second language. Lexical elaboration of school "language" would need a chapter of its own, but we may indicate a few areas which may serve as an example and a credit to those whose duty was to implement the Swahili educational policy.

The work of preparing teaching materials in Swahili has always been centered in the Institute of Education of the University of Dar es Salaam. It was in this institute in the late sixties that a great deal was done to implement the call for the use of Swahili as the medium of teaching. Here wordlists pertaining to the various primary school subjects were elaborated. The approach was to give charge of preparation of materials to educational researchers with specialization in the various subjects. Thus materials in mathematics, biology, geography, chemistry, and elementary physics would be given to specialists in these areas. They would be people with excellent competence in the Swahili language, with a knowledge of the subjects and therefore its interrelated system of concepts, and educators with experience in curriculum development. These curriculum developers would be in constant touch with heads of subjects, especially in the teacher training colleges but also in primary schools. They would keep in touch with one another through correspondence, continual visits, and more important regular annual or bi-annual subject meetings usually held at the University of Dar es Salaam, where problems of terminologies and concepts and approach to teaching in general would be discussed. Curriculum experts at Changombe Teacher Training College also played a great role especially in the early years of the implementation of the Swahili-medium policy in primary schools. A fundamental approach was the understanding that it was not the technical terminologies that were a real problem since these could be somehow translated from English into Swahili; the problem was really one of making sure that the children understood the concepts. So the idea of the emphasis on a practical approach to learning was followed. For example, in the teaching of concepts related to the circle, the children would be involved in the practical construction of local circular huts. In doing so they would need to peg into the ground a piece of wood or other material, tie a rope round it, and, by using this rope, draw the circle. While doing this the concept of center of the circle, radius, diameter, and circumference would be practically introduced; the subsequent naming of these concepts then would follow quite easily. The same in the sciences; children would be made to handle test tubes, funnels, and relevant science equipment, see what was happening, and record the events, before facts were introduced in words. This was a striking departure from the old methods where the emphasis was verbal teaching with little concrete reference. I visited schools in almost all the regions of Tanzania between 1967 and 1970 and was amazed at the smooth working of this approach. The children were active and interested since their curiosity was aroused through learning by self-discovery. Also since all the children had excellent command of Swahili they did not only participate with confidence but often even innovated words for learning activities in which they were engaged; some of these words were found to be so useful that they were incorporated into the school "jargon".

Word lists then were prepared. To give a few examples of mathematical words that start with the letter R in English:

radius	= *nusu kipenyo*
ratio	= *uwiano*
rational number	= *namba ya uwiano*
ray(s)	= *mwale*
reciprocal	= *kinyume katika kuzidisha*
rectangle	= *mstatili*
rectangular prism	= *mche mstatili*
reflection	= *pindu*
reflex angle	= *pembe kuu*
region	= *chenezo*
rhombus	= *msambamba sawa*
right angle	= *pembe mraba*
right angled triangle	= *pembe tatu mraba*
root(s)	= *kipeo(vi)*
rotational movement	= *uhamisho wa mviringo*

A few words in an agricultural word list follow:

meiosis	= *ungawachembe*
metamorphic rock	= *mwambo uliogenzwa namna*
micropyle	= *tunduke*
molecule	= *kichembelele*
monocotyledon	= *mmeuwauzazi*
osmosis	= *osimasi*
ovule	= *chembegeuke*
oxidation	= *chasilihewa*

photosynthesis = *ugungo*
pistil = *kidakanzao*
pith = *chanaummea*

A series of primary school books has been produced in Swahili both for pupils and teachers. Most of these are very well illustrated by pictures, figures, and diagrams making it easy for the pupils to follow the lessons. A very interesting and very colorful series of books, each naming specific objects, is a good illustration of lexical elaboration and its wide circulation.[2]

The idea is that if primary school children in Tanzania are to develop their experience of the immediate and wider world to the degree that children in the so-called developed countries do, then there must be an adequate and continued process of planning to produce good and interesting reading materials in their national language so that they in fact do learn what is expected of them by the time they complete their primary education, and get an education that will benefit them in their economic, social, and cultural pursuits as well as the country in its endeavor to build a new society based on its national aspirations. This statement cannot be taken for granted, because failure to achieve this will, in time, not only bring about frustrations and lack of confidence in the educational system, but also might give ammunition to those many people in Africa who still believe that the only way to education is through a metropolitan language and that African institutions, including languages, are inherently inferior and incapable of meeting the demands of a modern society. Personally I believe through practical observation of the situation that it can be done successfully in Tanzania, but I would like to urge that there will be enormous demand for highly-trained manpower to produce the relevant teaching materials and of course adequately trained and qualified teachers. The policy will no doubt entail a need for a relatively large national budget, but any amount of money spent for the success of the objectives outlined will have been worth sacrificing.

3.2.1.2. *Secondary Education*

In the secondary school the medium of instruction is mainly English except in the teaching of Swahili language and literature and political education. There is no reason why such "factual" subjects as history could not likewise be taught in Swahili. I believe some schools already do this, and it may be the long term policy to develop enough materials and produce adequately qualified teachers to teach most subjects in Swahili at this level.

3.2.1.3 *Swahili at the University*

At the university level major progress has been made with the establishment of the Department of Swahili five or six years ago. This department, which is wholly staffed by Tanzanians who are remarkably enthusiastic about developing this language as an academic media, has achieved what certainly would be considered impossible if it had not been attempted. In the last three years I have had the opportunity of acting as external examiner for the university examinations in this department. The progress in the teaching of Swahili structure and literature within the framework of modern linguistic and literary theories is significant. The syllabuses, teaching, and examination questions are all in Swahili. Complex phonetic, phonological, and grammatical terms have been coined in Swahili. From the answers to examination questions one gets a positive feeling that these concepts are understood and that an academic register in the field of language is fast developing.

3.2.1.4 *Adult Literacy*

Another factor which is playing a major role in the spread of the knowledge of Swahili is the countrywide adult literacy program conducted in this language. The program has been supported by UNESCO; its aim is the promotion of Functional Literacy. Functional Literacy is seen as a program that can play a vital role in the socio-economic development of member countries (Bhola, 1970). The program, according to figures and press statements, is proving very successful, so much so that it is the target of the Tanzanian government to eliminate illiteracy totally before 1980. So we have on the one hand children being socialized into Tanzanian nationality and ideology in schools and youth camps, and on the other a similar practice undertaken in respect of adults. If this two-pronged promotion of Swahili continues with the present tempo, it is conceivable that within a very short time almost all Tanzanians will have been exposed to the Swahili language and will have developed competence in it, though of course to varying degrees. Figures are not yet available as to how successful this program has been in eliminating illiteracy.

3.3 *Language and Political Organization*

TANU as indicated above is one of the most closely organized political parties in Africa. TANU has been actively promoting Swahili as a basis of identity of Tanzanian nationalism and as an instrument in its ideological struggle, and the very way in which the party is organized has meant extensive use of this language. There is copious literature in the sociopolitical organization of TANU, some of which will be included in the bibliography. In short the party is led at the top by the TANU National Executive Committee. Each region has a regional committee, each area, an area committee, each district, a district committee until we reach the bottom of the pyramid, the ten-cell units, which comprise units of ten houses, with a local TANU cell leader. This sort of organization is bound to involve almost everybody in the affairs and policies of the party. Decisions and recommendations go upward to the National Executive Committee. Meetings are supposed to be conducted in Swahili, even in a vernacular speaking rural area. How often this happens in practice is not clear, but at least minutes of meetings which are supposed to be channelled upwards must be written in Swahili.

Party ideology and political and economic statements are expounded by the National Executive Committee. Political education of the "leaders", i.e. civil servants and members of para-governmental bodies, is undertaken at the Party's ideological institute, Kivukoni College, Dar es Salaam. The idea is that those in responsible positions in the service of the people must receive training in the ideological tenets of the Party so that they may fully appreciate the ideological stand of the country. As a result of this close party organization a large socio-political, socio-economic vocabulary has emerged. This large vocabulary has made possible the translation into Swahili of such complex sociopolitical and economic works as Dumont's *False Start in Africa* and Kwame Nkrumah's work on class struggle in Africa. I also believe Fanon's *The Wretched of the Earth* is about to be translated into Swahili, if it has not already been done. In addition there are numerous original political works in Swahili. Actually a provisional politico-economic vocabulary was prepared at Kivukoni College and published for general circulation as well as in *Swahili*, a journal of the Institute of Swahili Research. As Lionel Cliffe indicates (Cliffe and Saul, 1973:197):

"At the national level Tanzania has built up a tradition of "consensus politics" and a set of tactics aimed at associating all key national institutions with the single national movement."

3.4 *Ujamaa Villages*

In his work *Socialism and Rural Development* President Nyerere calls upon the nation to base a more satisfactory form of socialist living on the traditional village way of life. This led to a great urge for people all over the country to live in socialist communal villages working together and sharing the fruits of their labor. There has been a remarkable response to this policy. By March 1973, for example, about 2,000,000 people lived in 5,556 Ujamaa villages. For statistical data see Kaniki (1974:26-27).

The close social, economic, cultural, and political intercourse among peoples, many of whom may be from different ethno-linguistic background, should give rise to further linguistic innovations in the form of new words and concepts and even subdialects. It has been noted that these villages are some of the most productive innovative areas for colloquialisms and slang in Swahili. The process of working and participating together in recreational activities should generate oral folk literature and dance songs in Swahili.

The areas along the TANZAM Railway from Dar es Salaam to Zambia should provide interesting ground for researchers into the expansion of language in a railway traffic area. This railway is being built by Tanzanian and Chinese workers whose main language of interaction is Swahili. It would be interesting, for example, if it so happens that some of the new words related to the railway system are Chinese borrowings. Swahili, like English, has always borrowed freely from other languages with which it has come into contact, for example, Arabic, Portuguese, English, Persian, Indian, and now perhaps Chinese at least in this limited domain. It should be regarded as a sign of a healthy growing language.

3.5 *The Mass Media*

The mass media have proved second to none in the spread and

dissemination of Swahili, especially of the standard form, not only in Tanzania but also throughout the Swahili-speaking world.

A great number of people own a radio or have access to one belonging either to a town or village center or a friend. On a weekday the Voice of Tanzania broadcasts almost continuously from 6 a.m. to about 11:15 p.m. The programs include news items, religious instructions, news commentaries, music and songs, cultural programs, discussions relating to the Swahili-language, news from the various regions of Tanzania, miscellaneous programs covering such social matters as health, family planning, good animal husbandry, etc. The radio has been one of the most effective instruments of standardization. Radios all over the world, broadcasting in Swahili, seem to use more or less the same jargon and terminology. Broadcasters are among the most important innovators of words. They are often called upon to translate into Swahili news items originally received in English. In some cases there are competent bilinguals in English and Swahili (I am now thinking of radio stations all over the world transmitting in Swahili), and one gets fairly accurate translations. Difficulties arise with completely new concepts, which sometimes are rendered inadequately or even incorrectly in Swahili. For example the word 'missile' was once translated *Mizinga yakupeleka makombora mbali,* literally 'guns for sending bullets far'; the phrase "The Arabs and the Jews exchanged fire at the border" was once translated: *Waarabu na Mayahudi walibadilishana risasi mipakani,* the Swahili version, through literal translation of 'exchange' meaning 'bartered bullets at the border'. I heard 'board meeting' called *mkutano wa mbao,* lit. 'meeting of timber boards'.

Often when a new word is coined the broadcasters introduce the Swahili word with an explanation of the type *kizazi bora* (family planning) *yaani* ... (that is), until people get used to the concept.

Some of the Swahili coined terms show great skill, e.g. 'outer-space' *anga la juu,* 'astronauts' *wanaanga* as opposed to *wanahewa* ('flyers of airplanes') and render the original English ideas well.

Due to the nature of the urgency of delivering the news there often are usages that people complain about as being incomprehensible or totally wrong. I think until such time that the translators are perfect bilinguals with a gift for translation and interpretation, or until news items are originally conceived in Swahili, we shall continue to get some words and phrases that seem peculiar or wrong to listeners. However having visited a number of stations in East Africa, Europe, and the United States where Swahili is broadcast, and having listened to others from other parts of the world there is no doubt that broadcasters ought to be congratulated on a very difficult task quite well done! One wonders if the so-called experts could do better given the same time and sense of urgency.

3.5.1 *Newspapers*

Without dealing with this topic in detail I would like to make a few remarks. Since Swahili newspapers are recognized as good media for disseminating news to the masses of the people, great care is taken to provide the news in as interesting a manner as possible. Already, thanks to a relatively long tradition of news reporting in Swahili, a style of news reporting has emerged. It is doubtless copied from English from the point of view of headline presentation and sentence structures of the news items. In some cases the structures used are so alien to indigenous Swahili that old men not exposed to English or standard forms often ask to be told what the news is about.

Another interesting feature of Swahili newspapers in Tanzania is that they are succeeding in developing newspaper registers including sports news, caricatures, commercial and job advertisements, legal notices, letters from the readers, crossword puzzles, and sometimes even "Your Stars".' I was interested the other day to notice that there are now Swahili words for stars like Scorpio, Aquarius, Leo, Virgo, and the rest of them. Also every Swahili newspaper has a literary page, usually poems on current matters. These seem particularly interesting to readers. Swahili papers in the past have been considered dry and would be read only by non-speakers of English, but today in Tanzania it is not unusual to see English-speaking urbanites buying Swahili dailies and weeklies. The mass media therefore are helping the development of various forms, styles, and registers of usage, an important language developmental factor, since African languages have been rather lacking in varieties that cover modern contexts of usage.

3.6 *Use of Swahili in the Civil Service and Elsewhere*

The policy of the Tanzanian government, briefly, has been to use Swahili wherever possible without loss of communicative efficiency. The initial steps taken to make this policy work were to prepare comprehensive Swahili glossaries and their English equivalents of names of ministries and parastatal bodies, together with the names of the various departments and the hierarchy of officials. This work was done by the National Swahili Council, the permanent government-sponsored body charged with the promotion of Swahili. (See also below, section 5.0 on *Language Planning*.)[3]

Together with such glossaries there was standardization of the formats of civil service and para-governmental correspondence.

Today most official correspondence between Tanzanians is in Swahili.

Another important area of Swahili usage is in meetings. Meetings normally are conducted in Swahili. There also have developed formats for the preparation of agendas as well as for preparing minutes along the lines of the English forms.

3.7 *Swahili in Parliament*

Since December 1962 when President Nyerere made history by delivering his Republic Day Speech in Swahili, there has been a gradual shift from the use of English to the use of Swahili. In the beginning there was some sort of understanding of such shifts; for example, Budget Day speeches would be in English, and generally the policy has been the same – to use Swahili wherever this can be done without loss of communicative efficiency. Use of Swahili in Parliament has had a tremendous influence in the socio-political affairs of the country. In many sub-Saharan African countries the official languages of National Parliaments are the former colonial languages: English, French, Portuguese. Actually in many African countries an aspiring candidate for membership of the national assembly has to pass a proficiency test in the relevant European official language of Parliament. This has tended to restrict the leadership recruiting ground to the Western-educated elites. However popular with his constituency a prospective candidate may be, and however great his natural abilities as a politician and his desire to serve his country, the candidate would have this linguistic hurdle to jump, and many a potentially effective popular leader has been barred on these linguistic grounds. Another result of the policy of using Swahili in Parliament has been further to open the doors to leaders elected by people from among "themselves", i.e. leaders who share the socio-economic status with the people they represent. The Tanzanian Parliament has been labelled by some outside skeptics as an assembly of workers, peasants, and fishermen, an observation that would make many Tanzanians, committed as they are to their present ideology of socialism, view the state of affairs as further proof of the consolidation of democracy and socialism.

The use of Swahili in Parliament sparked off a situation that required new expansions in language. Clerks had to be especially trained. A Select Committee was appointed in 1962 to look into the problem of using Swahili in Parliament. It included among other well-known names in the field of Swahili, the late Sheikh Mathias Mnyampala and Sheikh Amri Abedi, both writers and poets, Sheikh Salim Kombo, a well-known Swahili expert, and the clerk of the assembly, Mr. Yasin Osman, (to whom I am indebted for this information on the use of Swahili in Parliament). Due to the stereotype phrases of parliamentary jargon it was not difficult to build a glossary of the popular terms that contributed to the development of parliamentary language. So, from 1962, Swahili and English were both used as the official languages of debating. For Swahili especially, audio-typists were employed since Swahili shorthand had not been adequately developed, nor had adequate personnel been trained to a level to enable them to take proceedings in shorthand. Since then a Pitman's Swahili Shorthand has been developed, and there are comprehensive secretarial courses run by the Secretarial College in Tabora aimed at training people in Swahili shorthand and typing. There are still too few secretaries with adequate speeds, but they gradually are coming out. The other day I met one with speeds of 60/100 respectively for typing and shorthand in Swahili. The point is that it can be done, and it is being done.

With the Union between Tanganyika and Zanzibar the process of using Swahili in Parliament accelerated. Many of the Zanzibari delegates either did not know English or already were used to debating in Swahili in the Zanzibar Revolutionary Council. They thus brought with them a large vocabulary relating to debating government matters. Up to today the Standing Orders allow for the use of both Swahili and English. The process is taking a gradual evolutionary course. Decisions on what language can be used for any item would depend on the Speaker, but one of the standing orders is that if a speaker uses one language then he must not mix or shift to the other unless he is quoting. The Speaker has final say on language use in Parliament. Bills, however, due to their very precise legal terminology, are still drafted in English. There was an attempt to have them presented in Swahili, but this proved difficult. Also Acts are in English. In 1968 a glossary of Swahili legal terms was produced by a panel of lawyers and Swahili experts working every day for a couple of years. But this is still not adequate to enable important legal enactments to be done in this language. Further research to develop the legal register would need to be done in a comprehensive manner.

3.8 Development of Literature[4]

Swahili has had a literate tradition going back many centuries. Up to the time of European colonial rule, most of this tradition was based along the Muslim Swahili coast in the various urban areas. The script used was an adapted form of the Arabic script. Most of the materials preserved are in the form of poetry belonging to the 18th and 19th centuries, but the presence of a well developed literary poetic tradition of the eighteenth century is evidence of a much older tradition. Much of this old literature is preserved in the archives of the Institute of Swahili Research and the University of Dar es Salaam Library. There have been numerous publications of these by scholars such as W. E. Taylor, Alice Werner, W. Hichens, Lyndon Harries, John Allen, and Jan Knappert.

There are numerous works, mostly grammars and dictionaries by European scholars like Edward Steere (*Handbook of Swahili Grammar*, 1870), Madan (1894), R. W. Taylor (*Swahili Aphorisms*) and an unpublished chart indicating main features of Swahili Grammar by Alice Werner (1927).

It was, however, in the twentieth century, with the introduction of the Roman script, that modern Swahili writing of various genres was born.

We have, for example, Velten's *Safari za Waswahili*, the various recorded accounts of Tippu-Tipp's caravan trade adventures, Mohamed Abdulla's *Tenzi* writings like *Utenzi wa Uhudi, Vita vya Wadachi* – Mrima, *Kassim bin Jaafar*. These tended to continue the old tradition although the writings originally were in Roman script.

The spread of Swahili among the masses really began with the publications of the various newspapers. The first newsletter ever printed in Swahili in Roman script would seem to be *Habari ya Mwezi*, which was published in 1895 at Magila by the U.M.C.A. missionary group. It contained articles of secular and religious interest. Another newspaper that did a lot to popularize the language was *Mamboleo* which started appearing in 1923. *Mamboleo* had great influence in the spread of Swahili and its emerging standard forms; it also had always had a literary page which contained poems from readers on topical matters. The paper proved so popular that it had circulation all over East Africa, and it may have had influence in interesting later poets and writers such as Shaaban Robert, Amri Abedi, Mdanzi, Anasa, Mzee Waziri, and Mnyampala, to develop interest in literary writing. Other newspapers that had similar influence were *Mwangaza* which was a daily paper by 1957 (Whiteley, 1969:63) and *Baraza*. Lately, the newspapers include *Uhuru, Ngurumo* which are dailies and *Mzalendo,* a weekly paper. All of these papers contain literary columns, mostly in the form of popular poetry.

In 1934 Mbotela published his *Uhuru wa Watumwa* which was to contribute to modern prose writing. Then came Shaaban Robert, who might be considered the pioneer of modern prose and poetic writing in published forms. He published relatively copiously on numerous themes. Another Tanzanian who had a great influence in the spread of Swahili in the late forties and in the fifties was Amri Abedi. His book on the art of writing Swahili poetry still is considered the standard model of the traditional rhymed and measured verses. Writers such as the late Mathias Mnyampala followed. He was an energetic writer and a greater advocate of the development of literary and "correct" Swahili. Among the many contributions he will be remembered for are his pioneering of voluntary private Swahili writers' and poets' associations. Among the most successful of these was UKUTA which is still functioning as a publicly run association of people interested in Swahili. Mnyampala started a form of dramatic presentation in poetic style called Ngonjera which was meant to be performed on the stage especially by young people with a view to inculcate them with Tanzanian policies of socialism and human equality. This now was the post-independence period. In this period numerous modern writers have emerged. These include Mohamed Suleiman, author of *Kiu* (E.A.P.H.), and Mohamed Said Abdulla who has written at least four books, mostly in the modern detective story genre. With these post-independence writers we see the emergence of the modern novel in the Western style. Katalambula, who started film type magazines illustrated by pictures with the characters actually engaged in "verbal" interaction, developed into a writer of detective novels, the most well-known being *Simu ya Kifo*. Another novel writer who may prove most effective is E. Kezilahabi. He is one of the first group of writers with a university education and academic training in theories of literature. His books *Rosa Mistika, Kichwa Maji, Dunia Imewendea*, are fine examples of the development of a truly modern novel in Swahili. Critics of Kezilahabi would say that he is much influenced by Western literary styles, especially in his poetic works (see *Kichomi),* which represent a total departure from rhymed and metered poetry to modern free verse. I find Kezilahabi's writing most interesting from both the linguistic (use of language) and the literary viewpoints.

Playwriting, a new genre in Swahili literature, also is fast developing. Among the most well-known playwrights is Ebrahim Hussein, a young graduate of Dar es Salaam University who studied language, literature, and drama. He then went to East Germany for further studies in drama up to the Ph.D. level. Among his popular plays are *Kinjeketile, Mashetani,* and *Michezo ya Kuigiza*. Other writers of the modern school are Penina Mhando, another graduate in literature and drama, and Uhinga. With active writing by such authors we should see the emergence of a modern literature of various genres, a literature I hope will be of as good a standard as any in other languages in form, style, and content.

We are also witnessing the appearance of school readers in Swahili. Among the contributors are the Tanzanian Ministry of Education curriculum developers, and such Kenyan educationists as the late Shihabuddin Chiraghdin, Mohamed Kamalkhan and Zacharia Zani.

Poets who still continue the old tradition but use modern themes are Abdilatif Abdulla and Ahmed Nassir Bhalo, both of Mombasa.

Publishers would seem to be very active in promoting the publication of Swahili books. We now have numerous titles, and hardly a month passes without the appearance of more new publications.

Translations also are enriching Swahili reading material. These include political, economic and generally sociological works, as well as literary works from other languages. Among the better known of these are Shakesperian translations such as Mwalimu Nyerere's translation of 'Julius Caesar' (*Juliasi Kaizari*) and 'Merchant of Venice' (*Bepari wa Venisi*); Mushi's translations of 'Macbeth' and 'The Tempest' (*Tufani*) and Moliére's work 'Le Tartuffe' (*Mnafiki*).

In the pre-independence period most of the school literature was in fact translations either from Arabic/Persian stories or English novels. Among these the most famous were *Abunwasi, Alfulela-u-lela, Mashimo ya Mfalme Suleimani (King Solomon's Mines), Safari za Gulliver (Gulliver's Travels), Hadithi za Esopo (Aesop's Fables), Snow White, Robinson Crusoe* and other adventure stories.

3.9 *Language Use*

The policy of expanding Swahili has really succeeded. Within its contextual base Swahili seems to serve most of the national institutions well. It is a language of great prestige in Tanzania, because of the opportunities it affords, its wide functions in the socio-economic life of the country, and its status as a symbol of Tanzanian nationality. Herbert C. Kelman, (1971-23) in his article 'Language as an Aid and Barrier to Involvement in the National Systems', distinguishes two aspects for the legitimacy of a national system:

(1) the extent to which it reflects ethnic-cultural identity of the national population:
(2) the extent to which it meets the needs and interests of that population . . .

Kelman then distinguishes sentimental attachment from instrumental attachment to the national system: "An individual is sentimentally attached to the national system if he sees it as representing himself. The system is legitimate and deserving his loyalty. . . . An individual is instrumentally attached to the national system to the extent that he sees it as an effective vehicle for achieving his own ends and the ends of members of other systems. For the instrumentally attached, the system is legitimate and deserving his loyalty because it provides the organization for a smoothly running society, in which individuals can participate to their mutual benefit. . . ." (1971:25). I think the Tanzanian government by promoting a policy of one indigenous language intends to bring such psychological and material attachments to the national system of their country. The leaders see this as the only salvation in their bid to build one unified people with common political, economic, and cultural aspirations. Swahili then is seen as a powerful instrument for achieving this.

4.0 *Language Attitudes*

It is remarkable that in such a multilingual, multi-ethnic society as Tanzania, there has not been organized opposition to the present policy of promoting Swahili, even at the apparent expense of the other indigenous languages, and English. There may be a number of explanations. In a country with over 100 ethno-linguistic communities, the biggest of which has less than two million members, what choices in respect to the national language question are possible? President Nyerere always stresses the tenet "Planning involves decision as to choices", especially in a new developing nation with scarce resources and all the other problems of national development.

One choice would have been to maintain English as the national/official language, as many African countries have done with respect to English and French. Even if we discount the role of Swahili and other Tanzanian languages, the choice of English would have been contradictory to the national ideology of self-reliance and the building of Tanzanian socialism that is led by workers and peasants. The choice of English might have the effect of building a Western-oriented English-based elite whose economic and social interests differ from those of the rest of the people.

Another choice would have been to promote all or a number of local languages as national/official. This policy would have needed enormous manpower and financial resources to implement considering the linguistic implications. Even then some nationalists might argue that it might have gradually defeated the purpose of building one integrated people.

I think the people themselves realize the practical difficulties of a multilingual national language policy, and welcome the existence of one local Bantu lingua franca that politically is not associated with any one significant group. And the very evolution of the linguistic situation in the past 175 years has naturally tended to favor the spread and evolution of Swahili as the most acceptable medium of national communication.

4.1 *The Vernacular Languages*

What of the position of the other Tanzanian languages? While officially recognized as indigenous languages of Tanzania, and considered positively as the present and future sources of the enrichment of the Swahili language in the field of vocabulary, songs, culture, and dances, these languages are not given a definite place in schools or the mass media, for reasons outlined above. However, mother tongue speakers often use their languages when speaking among themselves. Research at university level in these languages is also being encouraged. Oral tradition, songs, and

TANZANIAN NATIONAL LANGUAGE POLICY   161

dances from all ethnic groups are taught in schools (often in Swahili) as part of the total Tanzanian heritage. It also is an explicit policy ruling that new vocabulary should as much as possible come from Swahili or other Bantu languages, before looking at other sources. This has happened, and we have a number of new words, for example 'Ikulu,' (the presidential palace), borrowed from other Tanzanian languages.

In history we have numerous examples of certain languages, or dialects, emerging as the national languages of vast territories, formerly the homes of several languages and dialects. In the case of Swahili what is being developed is a sister Bantu language that is closely related to many other Bantu languages at all linguistic levels, and to all other Tanzanian languages, at least relatively speaking, in the common areal semantic base.

It is, furthermore, becoming increasingly evident that dialects of Tanzanian Swahili are gradually emerging through interference with mother tongues. Educators and policy makers may wish to take this into consideration in their bid to maintain one more or less standard form of the language.

4.2 *The Place of English*

It is clear that policy-makers are aware of the importance of this World Language, as a language in which most human knowledge in the sciences and arts is recorded. It would be folly in my opinion not to give this language an important place in the life of the country, especially in the educational system. The expansion of Swahili usage in various registers is closely influenced by English forms, e.g. journalistic, legal, military, sports, educational, debating, and official correspondence forms tend to develop on the lines of English. English would appear to be one of the most important reference languages for the expansion of Swahili, as it is for the expansion of many other languages in the world. Great attention will need to be paid, therefore, to the teaching of this language in schools so that children will emerge with adequate knowledge of it for the various purposes of acquiring further knowledge and for the pleasure of being introduced to world knowledge and literature.

The attitude of the people towards Swahili is a positive one. At the moment it is the language of prestige and national identity. No Tanzanian can hope to go far in the life of his country without adequate knowledge of this language. The attitude to the mother tongue is one of natural sentimental attachment to the language of the "home", and of one's primordial identity and culture. The mother tongues should not be discouraged, for they represent the total heritage of Tanzania; they are a source of the cultural and linguistic history of the country; they are full of beautiful oral literary tradition and dance songs. In fact they should form the cultural basis on which Swahili will continue to flourish in the future.

4.3 *Bilingualism and Multilingualism*

This is a wide subject and one which needs separate and detailed treatment. In brief, we have on the one hand a bilingual situation affecting the majority of the people and involving Swahili and the various mother tongues. Code-shifting and code-mixing are very common (see Abdulaziz-Mkilifi 1972:197–213). In fact Swahili and the vernaculars often appear in a 'diglossic' relationship. Speakers of a mother tongue (V) may use V for certain topics and Swahili (S) for others, e.g. TANU political meetings. They may mix them freely. Many young Tanzanians when asked when they think they started learning Swahili, seem not to know. Their bilingualism often starts at home, or very early in their lives. Most children pick up this language naturally and achieve high enough competence to innovate colloquialisms and slang expressions. By the time they complete primary school they seem to have very good control of the language.

Another form of bilingualism is that involving Swahili and English. While the former type of bilingualism is more prevalent in the rural areas, the latter type is apparent in urban centers. Again Swahili and English are often in a 'diglossic' situation both in respect to spoken as well as to written language. Educated bilinguals mix English and Swahili freely in their conversation. As indicated, Bills, Acts, and other legal matters are mostly in English; the official gazette itself is bilingual. Some areas like banking and modern commercial transactions are done in English. English is the medium of instruction for many subjects in secondary schools and higher institutions of learning like the university.

For those who command Swahili and English besides the mother tongue, a 'triglossic' use of language is often observed especially in oral inter-action. People mix the three languages freely when speaking to speakers of their mother tongue who also happen to know Swahili and English (see Abdulaziz Mkilifi 1972:207–211). The situation is one of unstable language shift, but there is a conscious tendency to maintain Swahili as much as possible as a mark of competence in this language, and to separate the codes, especially English and Swahili.

4.4 *Other Registers of Usage*

It is interesting to note that official forms for applying for such documents as passports and driving licenses are in Swahili (and also English). So are other application forms. In many public places notices are either in Swahili alone or in Swahili and English.

The armed forces including the police have Swahili as their main language of command, instruction, and reporting. International hotels, too, have taken the initiative of listing their menus in Swahili, with the equivalent English or French translation. A few examples will indicate development of usage in this area:

1. SABOYAN MARSALLA = *Mayai yaliyopigwa na kuchanganywa na divai ya Marsalla*
2. TARTE DE POMMES ET CREME FRACHE = *Andazi la Toffa*
3. DESSERTS DU JOUR = *Uchaguzi wa tamutamu*

4. SPAGHETTI   = *Tambi na nyama ya*
   BOLOGNAISE   *kusaga na jabini*
5. A PRIME SIRLOIN STEAK COOKED TO YOUR PREFERENCE AND SERVED WITH A RED WINE SAUCE, GARNISHED WITH TOMATO AND WATERCRESS = *Nyama iliyochomwa na mchuzi wa mvinyo mwekundu*
6. CHICKEN, CASSEROLED WITH WHITE WINE, BACON AND MUSHROOM = *Kuku aliyepakwa kwenye mchuzi, mvinyo mweupe, nyama ya nguruwe na uyoga.*

Some scholars have described typologies of language development in terms of hierarchical steps for example, Ferguson (1968:27–35); Kloss (1968:69–85). But having watched the growth and use of Swahili I think it is equally important, if not more relevant, to discuss the notion of development also in terms of functional adequacy of a language in a modern state (Haugen, 1966). Swahili would seem to function well in a variety of spheres of national life. Even in the urban setting a Swahili-speaking Tanzanian is not at a loss with respect to achieving his needs through verbal interaction. Swahili therefore covers a large area of the socio-cultural matrices of modern urban life and is functionally more important than English from the point of view of communicative intensity and efficiency.

5.0 *Language Planning*

Under this heading I shall attempt to view the main language planning (LP) agencies and the way they seem to function.

Hypotheses on language planning have made great progress in recent years. "Language planning is deliberate language change." (Rubin and Jerimudd, 1971:introduction, xvi). If for the moment we examine LP processes involving CODIFICATION (choice and definition of standard variety), ELABORATION (actual promotion of the variety), and DISSEMINATION (how the language planners implement their policies) (Fishman 1974:79–102), then we can look at the history of LP in Swahili with reference to policy decisions and agencies of implementation.

Swahili had already become an important lingua franca and medium of education and religious instruction outside its original home ground by the last decades of the nineteenth century. There have consequently always been policy statements, especially regarding which dialect to be chosen as standard and how the spelling problem in Roman script was to be approached. A number of early scholars and missionaries such as W. E. Taylor were advocates of Mvita as a candidate for standard Swahili. But it was in 1930 that a special interterritorial committee was set up to look into the problem of selecting the form that would be recognized officially as standard for the purposes of public writing. The aim of the committee was "to promote the standardization and development of Swahili Language" (Whiteley, 1969). The Unguja dialect was chosen as the basis for the standard form of Swahili. There were recommendations relating to orthography and word formation. An important policy statement was that henceforth all published work in Roman script meant for the general public must be in Unguja, the committee being the authority charged with validating a manuscript before it was accepted for publication. The result is that, from the thirties, a form of Swahili has emerged which most people use in communicating with speakers of other dialects, in writing, in the mass media, and in public speeches.

As we have seen in the pre-independence period the initiative lay on the one hand with the administrators who were interested in the instrumental efficiency of communication within the administrative and legal systems and the need for middle-level manpower, and on the other hand with the missionary groups which controlled the schools.

The objectives of the committee were, in brief:

(1) Standardization of the orthography acceptable to all the East African territories.
(2) Securing uniformity in vocabulary, grammar, and syntax through publishing vetted materials.
(3) Revising books already published, and making sure all published materials are in standard form.
(4) Translating works of interest, especially to schools.
(5) Dealing with all matters relating to the promotion and development of Swahili language and literature (see Whiteley, 1969: 81–93).

Whiteley divides the operations of the committee into four periods: (a) between 1930 and 1947 under the aegis of the Conferences of East African Governors; (b) the period between 1948 and 1952 when the committee came under the jurisdiction of the East African High Commission; (c) the period when the committee was organized at Makerere, which lasted from 1952 to 1962; and (d) from 1962 to the present.

During the first period the main achievements were in the field of Swahili lexicography. Madan's dictionary was revised under the committee's then Secretary, Fredrick Johnson. The dictionaries that came out – Swahili/English and English/Swahili – are still the most authoritative published dictionaries in this language, apart from the new long word lists in various areas that have since appeared. The second important task that was achieved was the standardization of all books. The committee's bulletin started to appear in the early thirties.

In the second period the committee's affairs were directed by C. Richards of the East African Literature Bureau and H. E. Lambert, one of this period's great scholars who contributed enormously to the progress of Swahili. The East African Literature Bureau, supported by the three territories, undertook the literary role of encouraging writers and undertaking publishing materials at subsidized costs.

In 1959, during the secretaryship of J. W. T. Allen, the committee received $9,000 from the Calouste Gulbenkian Foundation and another similar sum from the Colonial Welfare Funds. These grants went a long way towards establishing the committee as a Research Institute. Jan

Knappert was appointed Senior Research Fellow. He supervised the movement of the committee to Mombasa and then to Dar es Salaam, where it finally was transformed into the Institute of Swahili Research of the University of Dar es Salaam. The first director was the late W. H. Whiteley, who contributed enormously to the development of scholarship in the language, and who organized the Institute into a modern language research center during his period of directorship in the middle sixties. Whiteley also played a major role in getting the University to establish a Department of Language and Linguistics of which he was the first Professor and Head.

The fourth period includes the time around 1967 when the present ideologies of self-reliance and socialism came into being. With the expansion in the use of Swahili in all spheres of national life, the Institute grew very fast into an important research center and an implementation area of the national language policy. For the first time the Institute was headed by a Tanzanian director, who was given both adequate physical facilities and a relatively large staff of researchers. Among the most important of the functions of the Institute has been the preparation of the big Swahili/Swahili dictionary, which I am told has over 50,000 entries. The manuscripts are already in galley forms and are now being proofread and corrected. This dictionary is being awaited with great excitement to provide "authority" for Swahili usage. Along with this dictionary is a project to revise and produce new editions of the English/Swahili and Swahili/English dictionaries. The production of these dictionaries will go a long way towards further developing the use of the language. The Institute through its bi-annual journal *Kiswahili* continually produces word lists in various areas of usage: medical, agricultural, religious, mathematical, scientific, and terms of everyday use. The journal also produces articles of linguistic and literary interest on Swahili in English or Swahili. It has world-wide circulation in centers interested in the Swahili language as well as among individual contributors. The journal also produces regularly a supplement called *Mulika*, which deals mostly with literary materials in Swahili. The Institute now has a large staff of highly-trained lexicographers, linguists, and specialists in the Swahili language and its literature.

At the University, as we have mentioned before, there is also an active Department of Swahili, separate from the Department of Foreign Languages and Linguistics. This department is producing the much needed teachers and specialists of Swahili. As I indicated above they are succeeding in approaching the teaching of linguistics and literary aspects of Swahili through the medium of the language itself. They have developed a large vocabulary in the area of modern phonetics, phonology, grammar, and literary theories. There is also a Department of Drama and Theatre which trains young people in the production of Swahili materials for theatrical performance, dance songs, and play materials that may be performed live or over the Voice of Tanzania.

The seriousness with which the Government of Tanzania takes the promotion of Swahili is evidenced by the passing of an Act of Parliament in August, 1967, setting up the National Swahili Council whose functions are clearly spelled out as follows:

(a) to promote the development and usage of the Swahili language throughout the United Republic.
(b) to co-operate with other bodies in the United Republic which are concerned to promote the Swahili language and to endeavor to coordinate their activities.
(c) to encourage the use of the Swahili language in the conduct of official business and public life generally.
(d) to encourage the achievement of high standards in the use of the Swahili language and to discourage its misuse.
(e) to cooperate with the authorities concerned with establishing standard Swahili translations of technical terms.
(f) to publish a Swahili newspaper or magazine concerned with the Swahili language and literature.
(g) to provide services to the Government, public authorities, and individual authors writing in Swahili with respect to the Swahili language.

Membership of the council consisted of 21 representatives, five of whom were from Zanzibar. Members included language scholars from the university, TANU officials, Swahili experts, well-known Tanzanian writers, and representatives from recognized Swahili promotion bodies. When the council started it was within the Ministry that dealt with Regional administration and village development, but was, after 1969, incorporated within the Ministry of National Education. Today, planning of the promotion of Swahili is within the Ministry of Culture and Youth, which has five directorates namely: the Directorate of Art and National Language, Antiquities, Youth and Sport, Planning and Archives.

The Directorate of National Language that concerns us has two branches, Language and Art. The overall Director of Culture and Youth is the Minister himself. Under him is the National Language Promoter (or Director) who is assisted in the work of promotion by 20 Regional promoters, under whom are the District language promoters, Divisional Language promoters and village level language promoters. There are also public committees and private language bodies whose activities are somewhat regulated by the national language directorate.

The structure of language promotion agencies coincides with both the administrative set-up and the ruling Party organizational hierarchy, thus reinforcing the agencies at all administrative and Party hierarchical levels, since all the administrative and party machineries are basically run using the medium of Swahili, making the components of the system mutually supportive and strengthening, as regards language policy making and implementation, the role of the ruling Party[5] and the National Swahili Council. The National Swahili Council has various committees which deal with problems of language standardization, research and publication. In addition day to day research and promotion is undertaken by the Institute of Swahili Research, the Institute of Adult Education and the language

Table 6:1 Policy Making Body: Guidelines

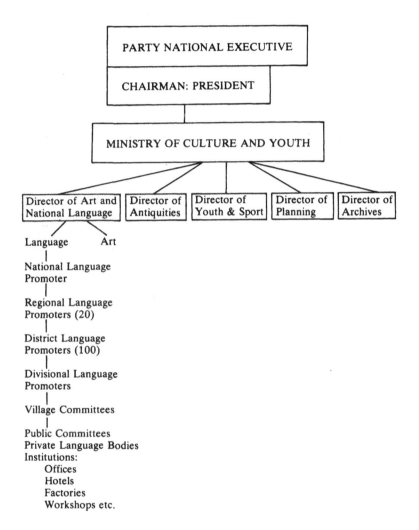

departments of the University of Dar es Salaam. Tables 6:1 and 6:2 summarise language promotion and implementation structures.[6]

The council can then be conceived of as having overall authority on matters of language policy. Another task is that of approving any provisional terminology lists, and generally of guiding the operations of language and cultural bodies. Although there is some understanding that borrowing and coining of words should be based as much as possible on

Table 6:2 National Language Planning and Promotion System

Director

National Swahili Council
(20 + 20 = 40 members)

Standardization Committee			Research Committee				Publication Committee
			University of Dar es Salaam				
Institute of Swahili Research			*Institute of Adult Education*	*Dept. of Foreign Languages*		*Dept. of Swahili*	*Institute of Education*
Language Committee	Library Committee	Publicity Committee	Lexicography Dictionary Word List	Adult Literacy Villages Factories Work places	English teachers linguists	French teachers linguists	Portuguese teachers linguists	Language teachers Applied linguists Linguists	Swahili Curriculum Dev. Section Teaching materials
Grammar Usage Dialects Bantu languages		Journals etc.							

indigenous Bantu sources, it is generally recognized that such languages as Arabic and English will continue to contribute to the development of Swahili vocabulary. In fact a multitude of words of Arabic and English origin are being added all the time.

Up to now the usual pattern of creating new terminologies has been to gather together Swahili language experts and experts in a particular field such as law or mathematics. These people work together to produce terminologies that would be appropriate for the new concepts, either borrowed from other languages or originally conceived. Those charged with the creation of terminologies could learn a great deal from the work of the Swedish Centre of Technical Terminology in Stockholm, one of the most methodical and successful establishments in the world in the area of lexical elaboration. They have produced numerous word glossaries covering various topics such as Rubber terms, Plastics terms, Hydraulic terms, House-painting terms, Corrosion, Hydrobiological terms, and Astronautics to name but a few.

It is difficult to assess how much language planning can be controlled by statutory bodies. In certain areas, like the schools, the forces, civil service, and other institutions where those in charge have the final say, language planning in Tanzania seems to work as envisaged. But in the field of everyday usage, the need for free communication has created a great demand for new words and terms, words that people create themselves in the course of their daily lives. Then there are people in the mass media who, because of the urgency of their work, continually create words that get wide publicity; most of them seem to establish themselves and become standard like:

kutorosha = 'kidnap'
kuteka nyara = 'hijack'

Others disappear after a little while.

Visiting Tanzania one always gets the impression that Swahili is fast developing at the day to day level of usage. Very interesting colloquialisms and slang expressions can be heard. The people seem to be really productive in their command of this language.

6.0 *Conclusion*

I have tried to trace the historical, social, and political ecology on which Swahili grew and developed as a lingua franca and then as a thriving national language. I have outlined the main language policy decisions beginning with the British period to the present day. I am aware that the subject is indeed vast, especially if one intends to discuss it in the framework of modern hypotheses relating to language development and planning, that each topic really needs separate treatment. It is hoped that a reader interested in language policies and language planning will read some of the literature in the references in order to put the statements made in their theoretical context. The exercise being undertaken in Tanzania is unique in sub-Saharan Africa. It should shed further light on the present knowledge of how language works in society.

As for the practical use of the language, it can safely be said that without the presence of this powerful medium the present egalitarian policies of socialism and self-reliance would have been most difficult to implement in such a short time. Conversely the socio-political, socio-cultural ethos of Tanzania has made it possible for Swahili to grow in the way it has, into one of the most dynamic and fast developing languages of Africa.

NOTES

1. I would like to acknowledge with deep gratitude the generous help I received from Tanzanian colleagues, friends, acquaintances, and officials since 1967 when I was lecturer for three years in the University of Dar es Salaam's Department of Language and Linguistics. In 1968 I had the opportunity of touring almost all the regions of the country, visiting schools, TANU headquarters, churches, mosques, and public places. Wherever I went, I found the people generous, charming, and ever ready to help me in my research. I would like to mention particularly my colleagues in the Institute of Swahili Research, from the Director to other staff, who always have been kind and helpful to me, along with colleagues in the Department of Swahili, and the Institute of Education, University of Dar es Salaam, whose first-hand knowledge of the linguistic situation was invaluable to me. My thanks also go to Ministry officials, members of the National Swahili Council (on which I had the honour to serve in 1967 and 1968) for their cooperation. And lastly I must mention the average Tanzanian, who seems to have a great interest in his national language. His statements on language matters show a deep appreciation of what is being done. My thanks also to my colleague in the Department of Linguistics and African Languages, Mr. James McGivney, a sociolinguist who has read my article and made useful suggestions. Finally, I would like to thank Professor Polomé, the Director of the Tanzania Language Survey, for making available to me any research material he and his assistants had collected.

2. These books are published by McGraw–Hill for Eastern Publishers (S) Ltd. – based in Singapore but with branches in many capitals outside Africa. On the list of these beautifully illustrated *Jifunze* books are the following:

Jifunze kwa Herufi A, B, Ch.
Jifunze na Namba
Jifunze Mwili wa Mwanadamu
Jifunze Majina ya Matunda
Jifunze Maarifa ya Wadudu
Jifunze Majina ya Wanyama
Jifunze Majina ya Ndege
Jifunze Majina ya Mashini
Jifunze Ngoma na Vinanda
Jifunze Maarifa ya Viumbe wa Bahari
Jifunze Majina ya mimea na maua
Jifunze Majina ya Samaki

These are the titles of the books so far available. It is hoped more of them will be produced covering other areas. They should provide an interesting introduction to names of objects; the authors may want to concentrate, to begin with, on objects familiar to young children or on those that they can actually see or feel, leaving things like "oil drilling machines, hovercraft, monorail, tramcar" until later. Actually illustrated materials like these could form the basis for a future illustrated children's encyclopedias in Swahili.

3. Lists of such names and titles appear in the various issues of the Council's journal, e.g. Issue 1 of 1974 if I may quote a few examples:

Ofisi ya Baraza la Mawaziri	= Cabinet Secretariat
Idara ya Wendeshaji/Utawala	= Administrative Division
Idara ya Fedha na Utumishi	= Finance and establishment Section
Tume ya Kudumu ya Uchunguzi	= Permanent Commission of Inquiry
Mkurugenzi	= Director
Katibu Mtendaji	= Executive Secretary
Msarifu Msaidizi	= Assistant Bursar
Kaimu Mkurugenzi	= Acting Director
Mchumi Mwandamizi	= Senior Economist
Ofisa wa Utibabu Wanyama Mwandamizi	= Senior Veterinary Officer
Kaimu Mhasibu Mkuu	= Acting Chief Accountant
Idara ya BaraBara na Viwanja vya Ndege	= Roads and Airports Division

Formal correspondence items such as our Ref. No., addressee's and addressor's forms are in Swahili (by the way, everyone in Tanzania must now be addressed *Ndugu*, literally 'brother,' presumably as part of a campaign to eradicate within the civil service, official bodies, party organizations, and general public, the mentality of senior-junior relationship in its negative senses).

One of the official institutions that also may adopt the habit of internal correspondence in Swahili might be the university itself. Earlier this year (1975) while I was at the university I was shown a long list of titles, departments, and faculties in Swahili side by side with their English equivalents, e.g.

Chancellor	= *Mkuu wa Chuo*
Department of Civil Engineering	= *Idara ya Uhandisi Ujenzi*
Students' Sections	= *Sehemu ya Wakurufunzi*
Botany Department	= *Idara ya Elimuviumbe*
Plant dark-room	= *Chumba-giza cha mimea*
Chemistry	= *Kimia*
University Physics Society Bulletin Board	= *Kibao cha Taarifa ya Chama cha Fizikia cha Chuo Kikuu*
Statistics	= *Takwimu*
Faculty	= *Kitivo*
Dean	= *Mkuu wa Kitivo*
Poultry Unit	= *Kitengo cha Kuku*
Lecturer	= *Mhadhiri*
Professor	= *Profesa*
Associate Professor	= *Profesa Mshiriki*
Tutorial Assistant	= *Mkufunzi*
Postgraduate	= *Uzamili*

The above are only a few of a long list of glossaries covering all departments of the University, titles of officials, names of places, and other labels.

As a result it is now possible to write memoranda in the university in Swahili. Although up to the present English predominates as the language of correspondence in this institution, one can foresee a gradual extension of the use of Swahili.

4. Bibliographical details for many of the works mentioned in this section will be found at the end of Part 3 of this book.
5. The new name of the national party, which has amalgamated TANU and the former ruling party in Zanzibar, is *Chama cha Mapinduzi* (lit., 'revolutionary party').
6. This information was given to the author in 1977.

REFERENCES

Abdulaziz, M. H., 1971, 'Tanzania's National Language Policy and the Rise of Swahili Political Culture' in Whiteley, W. H. (ed.) *Language Use and Social Change*. London: Oxford University Press, for International African Institute.

(-Mkilifi) 1972, 'Triglossia and Swahili-English Bilingualism in Tanzania.' *Language in Society*, Vol. 1, 197-213.

1974, 'Patterns of Language Acquisition and Use in Kenya Rural/Urban Differences.' Paper read at the Eighth World Congress of Sociology, Toronto, August 18-24th.

1979, *Muyaka 19th Century Swahili Popular Poetry*. Nairobi: Kenya Literature Bureau.

Abrahams, R. G., 1967, *The Peoples of Greater Unyamwezi, Tanzania*. London: International African Institute.

Adekunle, M. A. 1972, 'Multilingualism and Language Function in Nigeria.' *African Studies Review*, 15:2, 185-207.

Allen, John W. T., 1970, *The Swahili and Arabic Manuscripts and Tapes in the Library of the University College, Dar es Salaam* (a catalogue) Leiden: Brill.

Apronti, E. O., 1974, 'Sociolinguistics and the Question of a National Language: The Case of Ghana.' *Studies in African Linguistics*, Supplement 5, 1-20.

Armstrong, R. G., 1963, 'Vernacular Languages and Cultures in Modern Africa.' in Spencer, J. (ed.). *Language in Africa*, Cambridge, 64-72.

Ashton, E. O. 1944, *Swahili Grammar*, London: Longman.

Bascom, W. R. and Herskovits, M. J., 1959, 'The Problem of Stability and Change in African Culture.' in Bascom and Herskovits (eds.). *Continuity and Change in African Culture*. Chicago: The University of Chicago Press.

Bhola, H. S., 1970, *Literacy Teachers of Adults* – UNDP/Tanzania, Work-Oriented Adult Literacy Pilot Project, 1970.

Bienen, H., 1967, *Tanzania: Party Transformation and Economic Development*. Princeton, N. J.: Princeton University Press.

Bryan, M. A., 1959, *The Bantu Languages of Africa*. London: Oxford University Press for International African Institute.

Cameron, J. and Dodd, W. A., 1970, *Society, School and Progress in Tanzania*. Oxford: Pergamon Press, Oxford University Press.

Cliffe, Lionel and Saul, J. S., (eds.) 1973, *Socialism in Tanzania: An Interdisciplinary Reader. Vol. II: Policies*. Dar es Salaam: East African Publishing House.

Darnell, Regna, 1974, 'Rationalist Aspects of the Whorf Hypothesis,' *Papers in Linguistics*, 7:1-2, 41-50.

Das Gupta, J., 1968, 'Language diversity and national development' in Fishman, J., Ferguson, C. A., and Das Gupta, J., (eds.) *Language Problems of Developing Nations*. New York: Wiley, 17-26.

1970, *Language and National Development*. University of California Press.

Deutch, Karl W., 1953, *Nationalism and Social Communication: An Inquiry into the Foundations of Nationality*. (2nd ed. 1966) Cambridge, Mass: MIT Press.

Dumont, Rene, 1966, *False Start in Africa*. [translated from French by Phyllis Nants Ott] London: Deutch.

Eastman, Carol M., 1977, 'The Emergence of an African Regional Literature: Swahili' *African Studies Review,* 20:2, 53–61.
Eggert, Johanna, 1970, *Missionsschule und sozialer Wandel in Ostafrika.* Bertelsmann Universitätsverlag.
Fanon, F. 1965, *The Wretched of the Earth.* [translated from the French original *Les damné de la terre* by Constance Farrington.] London: McGibbon and Kee.
Fellman, J., 1973, *The Revival of a Classical Tongue.* Mouton: The Hague.
Ferguson, C. A., 1968, 'Language Development' in Fishman, J. A., Ferguson, C. A., Das Gupta, J., (eds.), *Language Problems of Developing Nations.* New York: Wiley, 27–35.
Fishman, J. A., 1968, 'The Language Component of the Problems of Developing Nations.' in Fishman et al., eds, *Language Problems of Developing Nations,* 3–16.
  (ed.), 1970, *Readings in the Sociology of Language.* The Hague: Mouton.
  (ed.), 1971a, *Advances in the Sociology of Language.* Vol. 1. The Hague: Mouton.
  1971b, 'The Impact of Nationalism in Language Planning.' in Rubin, J. and Jernudd, B. (eds.), *Can Language Be Planned?* Honolulu: University of Hawaii Press, 3–20.
  1972. *Language and Nationalism.* Newbury House.
  (ed.), 1974, *Advances in Language Planning.* The Hague: Mouton.
  [forthcoming] 'A Sociology of Bilingual Education.'
Gulliver, P. H., 1959, 'Tribal Map of Tanganyika.' *Tanganyika Notes and Records,* 52: 61–74.
Guthrie, M., 1948, *The Classification of the Bantu Languages.* London: Oxford University Press for International African Institute.
Gumperz, J. J. and Hymes, D. (eds.), 1972, *Directions in Sociolinguistics.* New York: Holt, Rinehart, and Winston.
Halliday, M. A. K., 1972, 'National Language and Planning in a Multilingual Society.' Public Lecture given at the University of Nairobi on 24th May.
Harries, Lyndon, 1962, *Swahili Poetry.* Oxford: Clarendon Press.
  1965, *Swahili Prose Texts.* London: Oxford University Press.
Haugen, Einer, 1966, 'Linguistics and Language Planning'. in Bright, W., (ed.) *Sociolinguistics,* The Hague: Mouton.
  1971, 'The Ecology of Language' *The Ecology of Language,* selected and introduced by Anwar S. Dil. Stanford: Stanford University Press, 1972, 325–39.
Heine, B., 1970, *Status and Use in African Lingua Francas.* Munich: Welt Forum.
Hichens W., 1939, (ed.) *Al-Inkishafi,* London: Sheldon Press.
  1940, *Diwani ya Muyaka,* Johannesburg: University of Witwatersrand Press.
Hyder, M., 1966, 'Swahili in a Technical Age.' *East Africa's Cultural Heritage.* Contemporary African Monographs Series No. 4. Nairobi: East African Institute of Social and Cultural Affairs.
Iliffe, J., 1967, 'The Role of the African Association in the Formation and Realization of Territorial Consciousness in Tanzania.' [Paper for the University of East African Research Conference Dar es Salaam, December, 1967]
Johnson, Fredrick, 1939, *A Standard English–Swahili Dictionary* and *A Standard Swahili–English Dictionary.* Interterritorial Language Committee of the East African Dependencies. Nairobi: Oxford University Press.
Kaniki, M. H. Y., 1974, 'TANU – The Party of Independence and National Consolidation' in Ruhumbika, G. (ed.), *Towards Ujamaa.* Nairobi: East African Literature Bureau.
Khamisi, A. M., 1974, 'Swahili as a National Language' in Ruhumbika, G. (ed.), *Towards Ujamaa.* Nairobi: East African Literature Bureau.

Kiswahili, Journal of the Institute of Swahili Research, University of Dar es Salaam.
Kloss, H., 1968, 'Nation-State and Multinational State' in Fishman et al., (eds), *Language Problems of Developing Nations,* 67–85.
Knappert, Jan, 1971, *Swahili Islamic Poetry.* Leiden: Brill.
Knappert, Jan, 1972, *Anthology Swahili Love Poetry.* Berkeley: University of California Press.
Knappert, Jan, 1967, *Traditional Swahili Poetry.* Leiden: Brill.
Lambert H. E., 1958, *Chi-Jomvu and Ki-Ngare, sub-dialects of the Mombasa Area.* Kampala: E. A. Swahili Committee, Makerere College.
  1958, *Ki-Vumba, a Dialect of the southern Kenya Coast.* Kampala: E. A. Swahili Committee, Makerere College.
  1958, *Chi-Fundi, a Dialect of the southern Kenya Coat.* Kampala: E. A. Swahili Committee, Makerere College.
Lawton, D., 1968, *Social Class, Language and Education.* London: Routledge & Kegan Paul.
Legal Research Centre and Faculty of Law, 1968, *Swahili Legal Terms.* University College, Dar es Salaam.
Lensdale, J. N., 1968, 'Some Origins of Nationalism in East Africa.' *Journal of African History,* 9:1, 119–46.
Mazrui, A. 1967, 'Language and Politics in East Africa.' *Africa Report.* XII, No. 6. 'Kiswahili International: Is it the Only International Language that Africa has Produced?' [Unpublished paper].
Mazrui, A. and Zirimu, P., 1974. 'Church, State and Market-Place in the Spread of Kiswahili: Comparative Educational Implications.' [Paper prepared for the Eighth World Congress of Sociology, Toronto, August, 1974.]
Mbuguni, L. A. and Ruhumbika, G., 1974, 'TANU and National Culture.' in Ruhumbika, G. (ed.) *Towards Ujamaa.* (Twenty years of TANU Leadership). Nairobi: East African Literature Bureau.
MULIKA, Supplement to the journal *Kiswahili.*
Mushi, S. S., 1966. 'The Role of the Ministry of Culture in National Development.' *East African's Cultural Heritage.* Contemporary African Monographs Series No. 4. Nairobi: East African Institute of Social and Cultural Affairs.
Nyerere, J. K., 1966, *Freedom and Unity.* London: Oxford University Press.
  1967a, *Socialism and Rural Development.* Dar es Salaam: Government Printer.
  1967b, *Education and Self-Reliance.* Dar es Salaam: Government Printer.
  1968, *Freedom for Development.* Dar es Salaam: Government Printer.
Nkrumah, Kwame, 1970, *Class Struggle in Africa.* New York: International Publications.
Ogle, R., 1973, 'Aspects of Rationalist and Critique of the Whorf Hypothesis.' *Papers in Linguistics* 6, 3–4: 317–350.
Okot p'Bitek, 1973, *Africa's Cultural Revolution.* Nairobi: Macmillan Books for Africa.
Pride, J. B. and Holmes, J., (eds.), 1972, *Sociolinguistics.* Penguin Books.
Prins, A. H. J., 1961, *The Swahili-Speaking Peoples of Zanzibar and East Africa Coast.* London: International African Institute.
Ranger, T. O., 1968, 'The Movement of Ideas, 1850 to 1939.' [Paper delivered at the Conference on the History of Tanzania, Dar es Salaam, 1968.]
Resnick, I. N. (ed.), 1968, *Tanzania: Revolution by Education.* Dar es Salaam: Longmans of Tanzania Ltd.
Rubin, Joan, 1968, *National Bilingualism in Paraguay.* The Hague: Mouton.
  and Jernudd, Björn, (eds), 1971, *Can Language Be Planned?* Honolulu: University of Hawaii Press.

and Shuy, Roger, 1973, *Language Planning: Current Issues and Research.* Washington, D. C.: Georgetown University Press, 1973.

Steere, Edward, 1928, *Swahili Tales,* London: Society for the Promotion of Christian Knowledge.

1929, *Swahili Exercises.* London: Society for the Promotion of Christian Knowledge.

1943, *A Handbook of Swahili Language* [revised by A. B. Hellier]. London: Sheldon Press.

Tauli, Valter, 1968, *Introduction to a Theory of Language Planning.* Uppsala: Almquist and Wiksells.

Taylor, W. E., 1891, *African Aphorisms,* London: Society for Promoting Christian Knowledge.

Trimingham, J. S. 1964. *Islam in East Africa.* Oxford: Clarendon Press.

Vygotsky, L. S., 1966, *Thought and Language.* [Translated by Eugenia Haufman & Gertrude Vaker] Cambridge, Mass.: MIT Press.

Werner, Alice, 1919, *Introductory Sketch of a Bantu Language.* London: Kegan Paul, French, Trubner & Co. Ltd.

1930, *A First Swahili Book.* London: Sheldon Press.

Whiteley, W. H., 1964, 'Problems of a Lingua Franca: Swahili and the Trade Unions.' *Journal of African Languages* 3:3 215–225.

1969, *Swahili: The Rise of a National Language.* London: Methuen & Co. Ltd.

7 LANGUAGE USE AMONG ILALA RESIDENTS

Henry David Barton

1.0 *Introduction*

A local study of Ilala, a suburb of Dar es Salaam, conducted by the Survey of Language Use and Language Teaching East Africa (SLULTEA) provides a basis for two different kinds of findings. First it gives a general picture of language use among clerical and laboring-class Tanzanians in the national capital, discussing what groups are identifiable by their choice of language, and the situations over which different languages' use predominates. These groups are defined by ethnic identity; sex; urban or rural, coastal or non-coastal upbringing; religion; and other features. The second type of findings considers the same population and social groups but studies language choice and use among the Ilala respondents as a reflection of the general linguistic forces which are working in Tanzania as a whole.

These trends may be generalized as the expansion of Swahili complementing or replacing the use of vernacular languages, English, or other non-African languages, particularly in everyday life situations.

Information on language use among Ilala residents was collected on just under 1% of the population according to the 1967 Census: 221 usable interview schedules. The interviews comprised some 200 substantive questions on personal history, background, and language use plus a series of 82 situations for which the respondent stated which of his languages he used. All data on language use are based on the interviewees' own report. In the description of the sample population which follows, it will become evident that the population may not only be taken as representative of language choice in Ilala, but that the diverse groups which comprise it also represent the direction of the sociolinguistic forces active elsewhere in Tanzania outside the cities and towns or the coast.

1.1 *Characteristics of the Ilala Respondents' Group*

The people who dwell in Ilala are mostly newcomers – probably even many of the Zalamo, whose tribal area it is and who made up 28.1% of the population in the 1967 Census (and 28.5% in the sample) and many of the Lugulu (9.5% in the Census and 8.1% in the sample).[1]

The bulk of the population comprises smaller representations of a large number of tribes, representing a considerable change in the ethnic composition of Ilala since 1957 when the Census showed 60% of the population to be Zaramo. Indeed, only 28.3% of the Census Ilala population claim to have been born locally (whether same division or district, is not defined by the Census question). A mere 8% of the sample population claimed to have been Dar es Salaam born and only one respondent in five had lived there over five years. The other key feature common to 1967 Census data and the sample is religion: 63.1% of the Census heads of household reported themselves Muslim (70.2% in the sample), 33.7% Christian (27.6% in the sample) and 3.2% "other" (2.3% in the sample). Another feature which allows of comparison is occupation, as can be seen in Table 7:1.

Table 7:1 Occupation

Occupation Category	Ilala according to 1967 Census %	Present Sample %
Professional	6.2	5.7
Managerial	3.8	1.9
Clerk	12.6	11.3
Sales	7.6	5.7
Agriculture	4.0	7.5
Transportation	13.1	13.8
Labor	22.3	23.9
Factory	16.2	21.4
Service	14.1	8.8

The similar set of percentages in Table 7:2 for education must be taken carefully. The sources of the Census and sample percentages differ: the Census includes all the population in Ilala, including infants, children in school, and women; the sample includes only heads of households or

Table 7:2 Educational Background

Education	Ilala according to 1967 Census %	Present Sample %
None	48.5	33.3
Lower Primary	23.9	18.3
Upper Primary	20.6	33.8
Secondary	6.3	13.7
Higher	0.70	0.91

spouses of heads of households – those who have completed their schooling. This latter is an important point to remember when considering the sample as a reflection of language use in Ilala: the Survey sample respondents are adults (average age 31 years). Furthermore, as observed above, many are newcomers: the average residence in Dar es Salaam was reported as 4.42 years, which increases only to 6.02 when taking just those who had been in the city a year or more. In sum, while the sample is representative of Ilala in religious and ethnic composition, it comprises a mainly immigrant population better educated than the average for all Tanzania or Ilala as a whole, heads of households rather than of all ages.

In addition to being a population mostly new to the city, Ilala residents show the effects of having a changing way of life. While only 11 of 221 of them said their occupation was farming (and seven were women), 104, or almost half, said their fathers were farmers. No occupational data are available on respondent's mothers, but among the women respondents in the Ilala sample, 41 or 53.9% claimed to be housewife by occupation[2] with another 5.3% claiming no occupation. This is in contrast to rural custom and indeed that of the fringe of Dar es Salaam, where wives have and are expected to cultivate garden plots or proper fields.

The Ilala respondents can be further characterized by two other features of the place the respondent feels is his home: whether his home area is urban or not and whether it is located on the coast or not. The majority of the respondents' home areas do not share the features of Dar es Salaam as a coastal, urban area. Only 18.6% claim homes in urban areas and only 27.6% claim homes in the coastal belt.[3]

Thus, the Ilala respondents may be characterized as largely immigrant from non-coastal, rural areas. They are mostly Muslim, but Christians comprise over one-fourth their numbers. They apparently represent a change in manner of living from their parents, of whom many were farmers, although one out of seven's father held a white-collar job. The majority of the women respondents claimed to be housewives; perhaps residual of rural habits, almost a tenth of the women reported themselves occupied in farming. The population is therefore one in which the habits of life in upcountry or rural areas should still be represented, even while they are being influenced by the social and linguistic pressures of living in an urban, coastal setting.

1.2 *Pattern of Life in Ilala*[4]

Ilala can be termed a dormitory suburb, although provided with the institutions and facilities which could make it self-contained.[5]

Most Ilala residents are tenants; in the typical house in Ilala there are six rooms, three per side opening onto a central hallway.[6] There is a certain amount of moving about from one house to another. Friendships tend to occur among fellow workers rather than on a neighborhood basis; visiting one's friends around town is a very common form of recreation. The compression of people into the houses of Ilala may be mitigated by its systematic, rectangular layout and wide streets, about one third of which were paved at the time of the Survey study. By Western standards, the lack of sanitary facilities, relative absence of piped-in water and varied construction of the houses in Ilala would point towards a lower-class area.

Within Dar es Salaam, however, Ilala is at the least an average place to live for the person of moderate means. It nevertheless has no real stamp of identity to it. Neighbors among the people who live in Ilala may be close friends, or friends may live on the other side of town. There is no onus attached to living in Ilala as there is to living in Buguruni; nor is it a prestigious location. Initially populated by resettlement of city dwellers, it continues to have a mixed ethnic composition, and no real identity of its own.

2.0 *Sociological and Historical Background*

The patterns of language choice and language use in Ilala are in part attributable to two waves of foreign influence, whose impact was felt in rather limited sections of the country. Arabs and Persians came earliest, settling mainly on the coast until the nineteenth century. The nineteenth century also brought Western colonization to East Africa. Missionaries were their not too distant forerunners.

This has led to a mosaic of different Muslim groups living beside and assimilating some indigenous Tanzanians and different Christian or Western groups governing or missionizing and having their effects on others. All this is overlaid on the ethnic mixture of peoples who dwell in Tanzania. These two outside religions have brought their different attitudes to language use along with systems of education, again with differing language emphases. Because the length of influence and the geographic location of these colonialists have varied, environmental features have become important in assessing language choice and use. Education is also important, although in many ways it is an after-effect of religious and cultural influences. The features to be discussed below are religion, education, sex, coming from a rural or urban home area, and coming from a coastal or non-coastal one.

2.1 *Religion and Education*

The religious groups and influences in contemporary Tanzania will be described in terms of the two colonizations in Tanzania of Persians and Arabs on the one hand and Germans and British on the other. Taking this point of view, one can distinguish between the religion, language and culture of the colonizers and the colonized on one level and then between the two colonizers on the other. The ethnic make-up of Tanzania is quite complex, even excluding non-African groups, and this complexity undoubtedly contributed to the Census classification of principal religious groups in Tanzania: Islam, Christianity, and traditional religions.

Unfortunately, these three groups, while encompassing the entire African population for all practical purposes, are neither equivalent terms in popular use, nor is their reference mutually exclusive. Hence, it is necessary to qualify what is meant when one is discussing classification by religion in Tanzania. As is suggested in the distinction between colonizers' religions and those of the colonized, Islam and Christianity have a place among African Tanzanians, who regard Islam and Christianity as different from traditional beliefs and culture. Since education is an instrument of establishing or expanding culture, and yet is used in quite different ways among the three general groups, it will be included in the following discussion.

2.1.1 *Traditional Religion and Education*

The very notion of what traditional religion comprises is problematic. Yet there is a common feeling that an individual must be educated and socialized into his group, that mere birth does not suffice. Further, the language of the group is seen as a keystone to the teaching of beliefs, customs and identity. In discussions with older Tanzanians in various stations of life, the Survey researchers encountered common worries that it was difficult for their children to learn their vernacular adequately. It is the medium of instruction for ethnic history, beliefs and so on, and the language in which many important ceremonies and rites such as weddings were conducted in the home town or village.

This same sense of need was found among teacher training college students when asked how they would like to raise any children they might later have. The general feeling was the necessity for children learning their own language, even if this required sending the child home to live with grandparents for a time. It was said that the child must learn who it is and where it comes from, and this is something which cannot be properly and completely taught except in the vernacular.

The local nature and inexportability of traditional teaching seem to go together with the assumption that such learning is something any African Tanzanian must have in order to understand his own ethnic identity. These and similar characteristics of local religion are mostly likely the basis of the common assumption encountered by Leslie, Castle and the Survey researchers among others that "religion" means a choice of Islam or Christianity to the ordinary Tanzanian. Even though the traditional education and socialization systems education are in some ways analogous to those in Islam and Christianity, they serve only as complements to the common feature of ethnic identity and beliefs or customs. As will be further seen in the discussions of Islam and Christianity, for many Tanzanians the two colonial complexes of religious beliefs, customs, and educational systems can be adopted as means of entry into the more politically and economically powerful groups with which they are identified. A common sign of either group in current times is the knowledge and use of Swahili.

2.1.2 *Islam and Islamic Education*

The Swahili language is a product of the culture which developed along the coast of East Africa with the settlement of Arab or Persian traders as resident middlemen. They created an Afro-Arab culture which developed its own language of coastal and internal trade and communication: Swahili. This commerce between Middle Easterners and East Africans began during the Middle Ages. The Afro-Arab descendants of these early traders, called Swahili, and having no tribe to name as their own, remained settled in their coastal location until the mid-19th century, when the pace of trade was increased and trading routes and posts began to be established inland by Arab organizers with Swahili or coastal agents and henchmen. As the traders expanded and established themselves inland, so did Swahili, a language thus identified with the coast and Islam.

Swahili was also the language of the literate. Until the 20th century Islamic education in East Africa was based on Koranic schools and discipleship to a sheikh or other great teacher. Students were first taught how to sound out the Koran and prayers and how to transcribe them in Arabic script. For many there was no more education. Some continued their education in Islam; and some learned to read and write Swahili in the Arabic script taught in Koranic schooling, creating a source of educated, literate men from whom the German colonizers of the late 19th century were to draw their lower and middle bureaucrats.

The Germans also established a system of Swahili language primary schools, mostly along the coast, mainly to train future government functionaries. There were some Christian mission schools at this time, but they were almost entirely of British origin and so regarded as politically unreliable.

The backing of the German administration gave knowledge of Swahili a new importance outside the coastal area and trade centers where it was either a long standing dominance or was the language of the Koran. The language of the African Muslims was Swahili.

Islam was then, as it is today, quite tolerant of other beliefs within the general profession of Islam. This has permitted a large number of Tanzanians to claim Islam as their organized religion, while still keeping their own traditional beliefs. In this they differ greatly from the Swahili peoples of the coast, who have little or no ethnic identity other than their membership in the coastal culture.

Nevertheless, Swahili has been a sign of their membership and is an essential feature of Islamic education, either as a prerequisite or as something which is learned along with one's study. Until quite recently, the bulk of the literature in Swahili has been written either by Muslims or in the patterns established by the coastal culture.

So, a strong identification remains between the Muslim, Swahili community and the Swahili language, even though from German times it has been more and more used by other groups for their own purposes.

2.1.3 *Christianity and Mission Education*

As mentioned previously, there were Christian missions in East Africa at the time of German colonization. Their greatest impact in terms of successful conversion was away from the coast, with its strong, well-established Islamic traditions. The work of the missionaries, missionary schools, liturgy, and conduct of services has been much more diverse than that of Islam, with its emphasis on an Arabic holy writ and Swahili as its medium of teaching and conduct for most African Tanzanians.

Early Christian endeavors divided themselves roughly on the lines of Roman Catholic, with Swahili as the medium of texts and teaching, versus Protestant, with vernacular texts and teaching. Mission schools, however, from their beginning as bush schools for training catechists, have grown in number, in their financial support by the government, in their common curriculum, and in their use of Swahili as a medium of instruction. Government support has also brought increasing government regulation and control. Now all schools are under government control, and Swahili is the medium of all primary education.

With the advent of a British government for Tanzania came a need for civil servants in the new administration. English was the language of higher administration, and the mission school graduates were an obvious source of personnel. This led to and fed on a tendency of the mission schools to be looked on by some missionaries as a means of attracting

Africans, who could then be proselytized as their appreciation of Western and Christian culture and values grew. That is, the Western education obtainable at mission schools was a means of attracting Africans to a locus of Christian teaching and influence. For many Tanzanians, this was a valid approach; for others, however, the schools were perceived as a necessary step in advancement within the British colonial government and economy. On the other hand, for many Muslims the domination of Western education by missionaries led to fears that their children would be educated but converted from their faith, so that many were kept out of the Western government or mission schools. The lesser chance to attend Western schools also reduced the opportunities for the Muslim to learn English.

The now fading use of vernaculars in Christian services, translations, texts and teaching stands in contrast to the almost sole reliance of Islam for these things on Swahili. Further support for this difference comes from the more vigorous effort to publish written materials in vernaculars or Swahili by Christian groups, versus Muslims.[7]

2.1.4 *Summary: Religion and Education*

The current trend is for the differences between the Christian and Muslim communities to be reduced or disappear as far as Swahili is concerned. Vernacular languages are going in the same general direction. The use of English remains a source of difference which may take a little longer to reduce. With the nationalization of all primary and secondary schools, the fears among Muslims of Christian and Western influence should be allayed.

Also, with the shift of schooling to government control and the exclusion of the Koranic schools, it should be evident to Muslims that advancement within their community is the limit for those who do not obtain government schooling. Government schooling is the key to a much wider range of opportunities. In time, this should also resolve differences between coastal Swahili and non-coastal Swahili by teaching a common form of the language.

2.2 *Sex*

The traditional limitation on what roles or occupations are open to women tend to cut across all three religious groups, although they are probably weakest among Christians. There are two effects of particular interest to this study. One is the restriction of women to work in or close to the home, where it is more likely the first language will be sufficient. The second is the tendency of few women to get education; there are generally more doubts about giving a female child any education and the female is more likely to drop out or be taken out of school once attended (girls just turned pubescent are often removed from public schools). Similarly, there are fewer jobs open to women. Coupled with the tendency of wives to become housewives, this increases the likelihood that women will gradually lose the educational skills which they gained, including non-household languages such as English.

2.3 Home: Coast or Upcountry; Urban or Rural

As is evident from the discussion of religion and education, Islam and the use of Swahili are particularly strong along the coast, where they have been established for centuries. Given that a person's language knowledge is conditioned by where he has lived, and that the use of Swahili (particularly as a language of everyday usage in contrast to use in trade, government, or intertribal communication) is strong and characteristic along the coast, some measure of this factor was necessary. The one chosen was whether the place which the respondent said was his home town or home area fell within one of the coastal divisions (or if the division was not named, a coastal district) or not. Home (the Swahili word was *kwenu*) refers to the place which is home for the respondent's family, and is similar to the notion of one's home town in American usage.

It is obvious that since the coast is a stronghold of Islam, and also, since Christian proselytization has little success there (reflecting Islam's strength), that people from the coast will tend to be Muslim. This holds true for the sample, for 91.6% of the coastal respondents are Muslim.

One can similarly expect that since there are few Christians among the coastal peoples, most of them will be from upcountry, as they are: 92.4% vs. 7.6%.

Only 35.5% of the Muslims, however, were from coastal homes. This is partially attributable to the conversion of many members of tribes near the coastline, but now within the zone defined in this study. It is worth noting that while there is a close relationship between being coastal and being Muslim, the statements that being Muslim always implies being coastal, or being non-coastal implies being Christian are not true.

Urban areas tend to be centers of Swahili use and, to a lesser extent, English use. In part this can be attributed to the origin of many towns as Arab trading settlements along the coast (Dar es Salaam, Tanga, Mtwara, Lindi, Bagamoyo) or along the trade routes upcountry (Ujiji, Tabora). For many Africans Islam is the religion of the towns and a way of identifying one's self as urban. Other influences which have come to have an equal or greater effect are the nature of towns as centers of trade, with Swahili being the trading language in Tanzania; that towns contain a majority of the educated Tanzanians, all of whom know Swahili. Towns contain a diverse mixture of ethnic groups, requiring the use of a language for intertribal communication, again Swahili. Although English will not be in everyday use as is Swahili, the towns are the most likely place to encounter it outside the schools. Thus, a person who makes his home in a town is likely to have daily need to use Swahili. He is also more likely to be educated and to encounter people who will almost certainly know Swahili and may also know English.

2.4 Summary

Taken together, their social and linguistic background lead one to expect Muslims and coastal peoples to be similar in their greater use of Swahili and relatively less frequent use of vernaculars or English. They would also tend to be lower in the education scales. Those claiming to follow traditional beliefs would more likely be rural, less educated, and most loyal to vernaculars. Protestant Christians would be somewhat loyal to their vernacular and Catholics would be better educated and more likely to use Swahili extensively and know English. Both traditional and Christian religious groups would be likely not to be from the coast. Women will tend to be less educated than men, have less interaction with other groups and so probably more vernacular use, less of Swahili and certainly less of English. Men as a group and Christians as a group are likely to be better educated and more likely to obtain positions which require the use of Swahili, and particularly English, thus reinforcing the knowledge of these languages.

3.0 Interrelationships of Social Variables in Ilala Group

In the preceding section it has been pointed out that there are several interrelationships between the social factors underlying differences in language use among the Ilala respondents. One has already been mentioned, namely the fact that of the coastal respondents, 91.6% are Muslim while only 7.6% of the Christian respondents are from the coastal area. Differences between the two religious groups also appear in the amount of Western education: 3.63 years average for Muslims against 7.30 for Christians. As noted above, this is partially attributable to a negative attitude towards Western education among some Muslims; in addition, the Koranic schools do provide Muslims with an alternate source of education. Several additional sociological factors may well contribute to the lower use of vernaculars among the Muslim respondents. Far more Muslim respondents than Christian ones were the children of mixed marriages as is shown in Table 7:3. Also, Christians had generally

Table 7:3 Parents' Ethnic Identity

	Number		Percentage		
	Same	Different	Same	Different	Total
Muslim	113	41	73.4	26.6	100
Christian	62	3	95.4	4.6	100

remained longer in their home area (16.6 years) than Muslims (14.4) and a shorter time in Dar es Salaam (2.61:5.21). As expected, education and consequent occupations differ between Muslims and Christians. The difference in years of Western schooling has already been given; one practical consequence is that on the average, the Muslim respondents received only a lower primary education (4 years) while the Christian ones had nearly completed upper primary school (7–8 years).

Neither level of education carries much weight for employment in Dar es Salaam, but the upper primary graduate has completed the first stage of formal schooling and might qualify for basic clerical work requiring adequate Swahili skills and minimal English (see further on this point in section 6).

The lower primary leaver, although literate in Swahili, has little more attractiveness on the employment market in Dar es Salaam than the man with no education; even among upper primary leavers the market is glutted. The difference remains even when considering just those respondents who had received some Western schooling; Muslims 6.32 years and Christians 8.18; again the critical difference between the early leaver and those who complete primary schooling remains. The partial consequences of this difference can be seen in Table 7:4 giving the percentage of Muslims and Christians in different general occupation groupings.

Table 7:4   Relations between Occupation and Religion

	Occupation						
	Number			Percentage			
	White Collar	Farming	Other	White Collar	Farming	Other	Total
Muslim	17	11	120	11.5	7.4	81.1	100
Christian	22	1	42	33.8	1.5	64.6	100

Education is similarly different between men and women respondents. Men averaged 5.60 years of schooling against only 3.03 for women. Significantly, however, the difference among men and women who have some schooling (7.27 for men, 6.41 for women) was not so great, nor does it lie across a watershed as was the case for Muslims or Christians. There is, of course, the socially predictable difference in occupation, with most of the women being occupied at home in *kazi za nyumbani*. Interestingly, if one excludes housewives, distributions of jobs on a white collar or non-white collar basis is quite similar between men and women.

Certain other relationships were interesting. The greater mobility of the urban-born respondent was corroborated by the lower percentage of urban respondents who claim to have been born in the same location as both their parents (34.1% as against 47.7% for rural respondents) and the higher percentage of those whose birthplace was different from that of either parent (43.9% as opposed to 22.4% for rural). A less easily explained difference occurred when comparing coastal and non-coastal respondents: only 23.7% of the coastal respondents had the same birthplace as both parents and 44.1% different from either as against 53.2% same and 19.8% different for non-coastal.

One reason for this is found in recollecting that intermarriage (with the mother belonging to a group different from that of the respondent) was more frequent among Muslims (26.6%) than among Christians (4.6%).

In substantiation of this, one finds that 52.3% of the coastal respondents' mothers were of a different group while only 20.6% of the non-coastal ones were. The earlier-mentioned difference between rural and urban respondents regarding their birthplace is also paralleled by greater mixed ethnicity percentage among urban respondents (31.8%, but 15.4% for rural). The same characteristics might apply to the Swahili coastal peoples. As a last observation, also concerning parents, Western education was higher among the fathers of Christians; it was also higher among educated respondents' parents when compared to their less-educated peers'. All these factors would tend to reinforce Swahili use and learning among coastal people and Muslims while relatively encouraging vernaculars among the non-coastal, rural ones.

4.0 *General Patterns of Language Use in Ilala*

Swahili is by far the predominant language in use in Ilala. It was the sole language of interviewing in a very mixed population containing 54 different vernaculars, of which only Zalamo and Lugulu were represented by more than 5% of the total African population. (27 vernaculars had only one representative.) In the situational measure of use, where 82 situation items were asked, Swahili was used more than any other language. Swahili also predominated in almost all the 82 individual situations, the best measure given in this study of language use in Ilala.

English and the vernaculars had smaller places. English, the alien language, had a fairly stable position but a very limited one. Although English was the language of secondary and higher education at the time of the Survey, and the language of much national government and business communications, it had little or no place in administration and commerce at the division and local level in Ilala. The place of vernaculars in Ilala was a tenuous one, complementary to the use of Swahili. That is, for Swahili – vernacular bilingual respondents, the general tendency was for those with extensive use of Swahili to have a more restricted use of their vernacular and vice versa (remembering, of course, that in no instance did an African, Tanzania-born respondent claim to use his vernacular more than Swahili).

From Table 7:5 one can see beyond all that respondents, having claimed Swahili, three-fourths claimed to use their own language, over

Table 7:5 Summary of the Responses about Language Choice in 82 Situations

Percentage	*Number*	*Combination*
10.9	24	Swahili only
6.8	15	Swahili and vernaculars or non-African languages
40.0	88	Swahili and the respondent's mother tongue only
5.5	12	Swahili, the respondent's mother tongue and other languages
2.3	5	Swahili and English only
4.5	10	Swahili, English, and languages not the respondent's mother tongue
23.4	52	Swahili, English, and the respondent's mother tongue
6.4	14	Swahili, English, the respondent's mother tongue and other languages
100		

one-third claimed some use of English and almost one in four use of some other language. Only one in nine claimed to use only Swahili. The average number of languages claimed is about 2.5, also indicating somewhat diverse linguistic skills.

This highlights the overall dominance of Swahili, demonstrating that there were other languages in use in the Ilala population, but that this diversity notwithstanding, Swahili still dominated.

There is one area in which other languages were used more than Swahili: when respondents were in conversation with their grandparents. When conversing with their parents, the respondents as a whole showed a small preference for Swahili. The direction of language change and the probable impact of living in a coastal, urban environment were found in the figures for conversation with spouses and children, where the ratio of Swahili use to vernacular use went from about 2:1 for spouses to over 5:1 for children. However, averages for the 17 family situations were higher for vernaculars than in other situations. These averages were indicative of the strength and expansion of Swahili against a still strong tendency to retain vernaculars in family situations. This was corroborated by the figures for women only: although Swahili use was almost constant, use of own vernaculars increased by about 50% from the two most public situations (in the market place) through those which might involve public training (sewing and antenatal care) to the two most private (talking about newborns and about *ngoma* 'ethnic dancing').

The shift of language learning from vernacular to Swahili in the urban environment and in Tanzania as a whole was evidenced by the drop in first language knowledge of respondents' vernaculars when compared to the respondents' children: 76.5% of the respondents claimed Swahili as a first language and 73.3% their own vernacular but only 53.3% of those with speaking children had any who knew their vernacular. Literacy would encourage language retention, and here there was a difference: 71.5% claiming literacy in Swahili but in their vernacular the same level as English (33.9%). The respondents also represented a large decrease from the 97.7% of their fathers and 98.2% of their mothers who knew their own vernacular.

English was found in topics concerning work, machinery, doing mathematics, reading (but interestingly, less so for religious matters) and casual writing, talking with European or Asian doctors, and talking with one's superior at work seemed the high points. The high points of English were at best only one-third as great as the comparable Swahili frequencies, and were limited to what may be together called education or technical matters. Among the respondents who had some knowledge of English, as many as two-thirds claimed to use it in such occasions, but these still comprised only one-fourth of the whole population, one in which everyone used Swahili. The English users were therefore restricted in the situations in which they would use it, but they were a significant minority.

The general situation for Ilala has been described as one in which Swahili was the dominant and pervasive language in the midst of much linguistic diversity and bilingualism. It was the one with the most first language speakers, and there were far more literate in it than in other languages. Vernacular use was strongest in situations with older family members and shows signs of declining from older generations to the younger. A minority knew English: its use was greatest in areas where education or technical matters were of importance.

5.0 *Variations in Swahili Use*

The general patterns of Swahili use have been discussed above; the following discussion looks at Swahili use as it varied among different subgroups of the Ilala respondents. These differences are then related to historical or social factors in order to provide possible explanations for the differences in use. In this respect, the mixed and immigrant nature of the Ilala sample was a great help, as became evident in section 3.0: the respondents represented most of the features important to this study, male versus female, Muslim versus Christian, and geographical differences in the place claimed as home.

5.1 *Sociolinguistic Features of Swahili Use*

As has been already mentioned, religious affiliation and place of upbringing could not be neatly separated. This becomes evident when religious differences among non-coastal respondents were considered. However, Christians showed lower use of Swahili compared to Muslims in the area less favorable to Swahili but more than Muslims among those from urban areas where greater use of Swahili was expected. Differences within the religious groups were in the expected direction for being urban or coastal among Christians, but the differences among Muslims were quite small.

Education presents another stronger set of contrasts, which tends to override the basic Muslim and Christian differences. Swahili was a first language for most of the Muslim respondents (85.8%) but for only about half the Christians (54.5%). The larger proportion of coastal and urban Muslims can explain the difference in part but not in full. The effect of education could be seen cutting across this difference when it was noted that while 61.9% of the Muslims were literate in Swahili, fully 93.9% of the Christians were. It was assumed that literacy was easier in a first language than in a later one. This difference in education was also an important factor in literacy differences between men and women. Differences between the averages for men and women were small, and there was no significant difference in knowledge of Swahili as a first language. The difference in literacy, however, was patent: 83.4% among men but 48.7% among women. The relationship between education and occupation has already been described; this too, would reinforce literacy differences by giving school-acquired literacy a practical, even remunerative use.

Differences across the total sample in Swahili use were rather small, however, and were the reverse of what might have been expected, namely that Swahili use would increase with level of education. Among those with no schooling, the average was 67.11 compared to 66.67 for those with primary schooling, 64.73 for secondary schooling and 63.86 for Koranic schooling.[8] A possible explanation is that these figures reflected a smaller range of linguistic choices among the lesser-schooled respondents. The less educated were likewise more likely to be restricted to unskilled or low skill occupations where the demands for the lingua franca would be higher but for English would be no lower or nil. Literacy was predictably high for Swahili among the Western schooled, about 95%, but under 50% for the Koranic schooled and about 20% for the unschooled. Again, there were fewer options in occupation for the illiterate, unschooled, who had a smaller repertoire of languages and so depended on Swahili all the more.

The two geographic features of coastal origin and rural origin have already been introduced when discussing the influence of religion. Both showed the expected differences when taken by themselves. The average among coastal respondents was 69.0, non-coastal 65.6; among urban respondents it was 68.0, rural 66.1. Knowledge of Swahili as a first language was parallel: 73.3% of the rural respondents but 90.2% among the urban ones; 70.2% among non-coastal respondents and 93.3% among the coastal ones.

Considering them at the same time, it seems likely that the coastal feature was the more important one, for among rural respondents there was a coastal–non-coastal difference (69.33 and 65.85); the same difference appeared among urban respondents (69.00 and 65.86). However, the differences between urban and rural respondents among those from the coast was small (69.00 and 69.33) and nil among the non-coastals ones (65.86 and 65.85). A similar effect was seen when considering rural–urban differences among Muslim respondents, although not among Christian ones.

5.2 *Summary*

The hypothesized effect of religion and location of origin by two features, coastal and rural–urban was borne out both by the overall averages, and for first language knowledge of Swahili. Use of Swahili for the subset of family situations was also in the expected direction, greater with Muslims than Christians, coastals than non-coastals, and urban respondents than rural ones. Education reversed the expected increase in use from the less educated to the more educated; it was hypothesized this might be due to greater number of languages known among the more educated; the lesser education among Muslims could contribute to the reverse in direction as well. Apart from this, however, education was seen to be a strong, obvious factor in determining literacy, which overrode the influence of religion and coastal origin.

Taking the three features of religion, coast, and urban–rural by twos revealed some evidence for ranking them by their relative influence. The coast feature was arguably dominant over the rural–urban one; among Muslims rural–urban differences were likewise negligible. The Christian respondents showed a difference in the expected direction. The same pattern occurred when religion and the coast feature were considered; there was no coast as opposed to non-coast difference among Muslims but the expected one among Christians. It is possible that there is greater pressure on Christians growing up in the coastal belt because they will certainly be a religious minority and may also be of a non-indigenous group. Conversely, among coastal respondents the difference between Muslims' and Christians' averages was not significant[9] while it was among the non-coastal ones, and in the expected direction with the Muslims' average being greater. The failure of differences to appear when examining differences among coastals along religious lines or among Muslims along coastal–non-coastal lines did not permit ranking these two features. The apparent anomaly of the high average among coastal Christians is a question which deserves further study.

Literacy is a language feature which does not allow description in terms of these same three features, as has already been pointed out. Literacy was largely mediated by education for Swahili and almost completely so for English, as will be seen. While there were differences in literacy between Muslim and Christian, they must be explained for the most part in terms of the differences in education between the two groups. The same was true of differences in literacy between male and female respondents. Perhaps more obvious, there is no reason to hypothesize that, all other things being equal, Tanzanian men were more likely to be literate in Swahili than women. The much more limited access to education among women went far to complete the explanation. As will be corroborated in discussing English use, the question was much more one of literacy per se than literacy in a given language.

6.0 Variations in English Use

The place of English among the people of Ilala was relatively small but fairly stable. It was a place dependent largely on national and international business and government, but especially on education. English is, like Arabic, the language of a former colonial rule; unlike Arabic it is the medium of secondary and higher education. Equally unlike Arabic, it had very little role in Western religious services of the people in suburbs like Ilala or in rural areas. Both city council and TANU business in Ilala were conducted in Swahili, however, and the general pressure was to restrict English to higher and higher levels of government.

6.1 Socio-linguistic Features of English Use

As already mentioned, English use was greatest in technical areas, education or international matters. Its close relationship to government or mission schooling would have led one to expect differences in use between Muslim and Christian, also. English almost inevitably indicated complete upper primary education at least. It was thus an indication of contact with western education, and possibly Christianizing influences, until most recent times.[10] This symbolic value may somewhat counterbalance its utilitarian one for Muslims, whose knowledge and interest was marginal.

Taken as a whole, the Christian respondents had averages of 17.8, the Muslims 5.51. The differences remained even when just the English-speaking respondents were considered: 20.4 among Muslims but 26.1 among Christians. A number of probable contributing factors have already been discussed. To them can be added the fact that there was a slightly disproportionate number of Christians in occupations which were likely to require the use of English: clerical, teaching, and professional positions. As was predictable, literacy among Christians was much higher than among Muslims: 54.5% as against 25.2%. The difference in final level of schooling was important here and will be discussed next.

English and schooling went together as Table 7:6 illustrates. A usable knowledge of English occurred only infrequently among those respondents

Table 7:6 Relation between Use of English and Schooling

	Years of Education	Number with this Education	Number that Use English[11]
No schooling	0	73	3
Lower Primary	1-4	40	3
Upper Primary	5-6	25	7
Upper Primary	7	16	8
Upper Primary	8	33	30
Secondary	9-12	30	29
Higher		2	2

who had less than upper primary completion.[12] Even among the upper primary students who were non-leavers or standard VII, only one-third maintained a usable knowledge of English, while just one in ten of those who were primary school leavers failed to retain this knowledge of English. The average years of schooling for the 82 respondents who used English was 8.66, again an average at the level of primary leaver. English use for the 82 situations showed the expected gradations among the whole sample from 0.64 for the unschooled and 2.6 for the Koranic schooled to 8.86 for primary and 29.14 secondary schooled respondents. The same steps occurred when considering just the English-speaking respondents: no schooling – 10.3; Koranic schooling – 10.0; primary schooling – 20.4; and secondary schooling or higher – 31.0. No respondent literate in English was not also literate in Swahili, an indication of the primacy of Swahili and also its position as the medium through which Tanzanian students learned second languages.

Education was also at the heart of the difference between the average number of situations for men, 12.5, and that for women, 2.84. The difference can almost certainly be interpreted to mean that, while men in Ilala had a limited but usable knowledge of English, among women as a whole it was vestigial at best. The difference in education was not so great: 5.60 for men and 3.03 for women, but was significant; taking just those who had had some schooling, the difference for English was much smaller: 7.27 for men and 6.41 for women.[13]

The strong relationship between education and literacy did not fail to maintain difference between the sexes; there was 43.4% literacy among male respondents and only 15.8% among female. Again, this only reflects the smaller access of females to Western schooling and the fact that Western schools were almost the only means of learning English at that time.

The two geographical features showed small differences in the direction one would expect if pressed. The average for urban respondents was 11.0 compared with 8.76; the average for non-coastal was 10.7 versus 5.13. These differences are probably best explained as side-effects of the concentration of Muslims and Swahili use along the coast and to a lesser degree in the towns. Cross-classifying with religion showed the same secondary weight of the rural–urban feature for English as for Swahili. Rural–urban differences among Christians were small as were those among Muslims; in contrast differences among urban respondents along religious lines were fairly strong: Christian 21.0 and Muslim 8.91. The same held true among rural respondents,[14] and for sex differences in use of English. Thus it is not unfair to consider the overall rural–urban difference as the likely by-product of other differences.

The coast feature did not permit such a relegation so easily.

The overall coastal–non coastal difference has already been cited: 5.13 compared with 10.7. The same difference in direction remained when considering just the respondents who claimed use of English: 16.2 among coastal respondents and 25.3 among the others. The difference was continued when literacy was considered. Among Christian respondents 37.2% were literate while only 25% were among the Muslim ones. Taking together both religion and the coastal feature, one found that when the two positive factors of being Christian and non-coastal combine there was a striking difference from the remaining combinations. This group's average was 19.8, while the rest ranged from 5.00 to 5.76. The coastal feature and sex showed a simpler combinatory effect, with the latter feature stronger, for the non-coastal male average of 14.3 and coastal one of 7.43 were much large than the female ones of 3.76 (non-coastal) and 1.22. Within the males or females, differences among coastal and non-coastal were in the expected direction. Here again, the explanation was probably attributable to the educational differences between male and female respondents.

6.2 *Summary*

Education and the use of English are closely linked to one another historically, and the differences in use among the Ilala respondents bore out expectations based both on the past and on present differences in access to education among different segments of the population.

The differences attributed to variation in education or other features of the respondents must be taken in the light of the small place which English occupied among the people of Ilala, even for those with educational and occupational encouragement for its use. The average among English using secondary school leavers was indeed 30 of 82 situations; but they comprised only 32 of 221 respondents.

As seen in the preceding discussion, the two geographical features were operative in themselves but were overridden by the effects of sex and religion. That is, the differences obtained comparing respondents of one sex or one religion along rural–urban or coastal–non coastal lines were much smaller than those obtained using the same figures but comparing for differences among coastals along religious lines, and so on. Yet both religion and sex are features which were matched by differences in education which paralleled the differences they revealed in use of English.

Thus, it is fair to assume that some of the variation in use of English seen in regard to religion and sex was attributable to the general effects of education.

7.0 *Variation in the Use of Vernaculars*

The use of vernaculars among the Ilala respondents tended to be complementary to their use of Swahili. That is to say, for respondents bilingual in Swahili and a vernacular, generally the greater the respondent's range of situations in Swahili, the more restricted his range of situations in the vernacular.

Vernaculars were similarly expected to be strongest among those groups where Swahili was less developed: Christians, non-coastals, rural, and less educated respondents, with there being some reinforcement among Christians through vernacular use in religious literature and services. The stronghold, however, would be in the rural, up-country homelands of the ethnic groups.

7.1 *Sociolinguistic Features of Vernacular Use*

Comparing differences in averages across the five main features considered, the two geographical ones stand out. The average among rural respondents is 23.23 to 17.24 among urban ones; similarly non-coastal respondents showed a high average, 25.41, compared to coastal ones, 13.28.

Religion showed a difference, also, 20.63 among Muslims but 25.60 among Christians.

There is no strong reason to hypothesize a difference along lines of sex or education; the latter averages were quite similar. The average for groups by education ranged from 20.12 for the unschooled to 25.91 for those with secondary schooling or better.[15] The picture changed when just vernacular speakers were considered.

Considering only those respondents who claimed use of their vernacular, all differences became very small except that between coast and non-coast respondents, 18.53 to 27.46. All others fall within the range of 23 to 27. The apparent primacy of geographical features in describing vernacular use was not unexpected. Unlike English, and to a certain extent Swahili, which were taught in the schools, the only learning place for vernaculars was at home. This is also language learning early in life, when the effects of linguistic influences such as these two will be least likely to have been muddied by later factors such as education, religion, and sex-role differences.

The distinction is further reinforced by considering the information obtained on literacy. On this point, education, religion and sex again played their expected roles; as seen by the percentage of literate by each category as given in Table 7:7.

There was some rural–urban difference in literacy as well, 36.1% compared to 29.3%, but the greater difference lay between coastal (23.3%) and non-coastal (39.1%). Literacy pointed up two important notions. The first was that already seen in Swahili literacy, the difference between the socio-linguistic characteristics of the first language and those acquired later. The second was particular to vernacular use: the coastal–non-coastal difference was a statistically significant one, overriding the possible effects of religion, sex and education.[16] The rural–urban one was in the expected direction, but was not statistically significant. There was yet a third notion to be remembered, and that was the contrast between the linguistic characteristics of the population as a whole and those of just the vernacular-speaking subgroup.

It has already been stated that across the whole population of Ilala respondents vernacular use was higher among rural respondents, non-coastal ones, and Christians. By comparison, among the vernacular-speaking respondents only the non-coastal respondents showed a significantly higher average than their counterparts. Obviously, these were two different sets of comparisons. Taken together they indicated that the coastal feature was a much stronger one than the others, in that differences persisted even when knowledge of the vernaculars was controlled.

In practical terms this meant that one could characterize Muslim, coastal, and urban respondents as generally using vernaculars in fewer situations than their counterparts. But only on the coastal feature could one generalize among the vernacular-speaking respondents to say that non-coastal respondents tended to use their vernaculars across a wider range of situations.

As for Swahili, averages were obtained for the 17 situations within the total group which concerned language use with members of the respondent's own household and his parental family. The patterns were exactly parallel to those for the averages as a whole. Among all respondents there was a significantly higher average use of the vernacular for rural and non-coastal respondents and the average for Christians likewise was higher than for Muslims as shown in Table 7:8(a).

Again, all the differences were attenuated when just the vernacular-speaking respondents were considered, but the difference between coastal and non-coastal respondents remained fairly clear.

The difference in averages etween male and female was 0.54 for all respondents and 0.09 for vernacular speakers; the range for the four educational groups was from 8.45 to 9.32 and 10.42 to 11.08, as these features as well showed no impact.

Considering factors together further confirms the above pattern, showing the two geographical features generally predominant over religion, and sex, as Table 7:8(b) illustrates.

The geographical features generally dominated when paired with religion or sex; for instance, the difference along rural–urban lines among

Table 7:7 Factors affecting Literacy

	Religion		Sex		Education			
	Muslim	Christian	Male	Female	None	Primary	Secondary	Koranic
Percentage Literate	27.7	51.5	43.4	18.4	7.8	50.9	44.1	13.3
Non-literate	72.3	48.5	56.4	81.6	92.2	49.1	55.9	86.7
	100	100	100	100	100	100	100	100

Table 7:8 Factors affecting the Use of the Mother Tongue

(a) Family Situations only (total 17)

| | Rural | Region | | | Religion | |
		Urban	Coast	Non-Coast	Muslim	Christian
All Respondents	9.80	6.56	5.40	9.81	7.94	10.19
Vernacular Speakers Only	10.62	9.96	8.52	11.05	10.35	10.85

(b) All Situations (total 82)

| | Religion | | Sex | | Region | |
	Muslim	Christian	Male	Female	Coastal	Non-Coastal
Rural	21.7	27.0	23.3	23.3	14.47	25.35
Urban	17.3	17.6	17.4	16.9	11.7	13.8
Coastal	13.4	13.8	14.4	11.4		
Non-Coastal	24.8	27.1	24.6	26.4		
Male	20.3	26.9				
Female	21.3	24.1				

Numbers denote the average number of situations in which the mother tongue was used by respondents male respondents was quite large compared to male–female differences among rural or urban respondents. Here, too, the coast feature was more consistently dominant than was the urban one. Both were clearly dominant when matched with the feature of sex; when matched with religion, coast was still the defining feature.

Religion and the rural–urban feature presented a more complicated picture, however. There were no religion-related differences among urban respondents and there were clear urban–rural differences within each religious grouping. There remained a fairly large difference in average between rural Muslim and rural Christian respondents, which will be further discussed in section 8.

The same complication occurred when sex and religion were considered together. There were no strong grounds for hypothesizing differences. Those obtained did not permit an easy post hoc explanation. The two geographical features taken together presented a fairly good picture of interaction between two variables. That is, there were favorable and unfavorable environments for both the coast and rural features. Differences were small between the doubly unfavorable subgroup (urban coastal) and those with one unfavorable feature; both favorable features together, however, resulted in a strong difference. It also provided no grounds for arguing that one geographical feature was more powerful than the other in predicting the number of situations for which vernacular use was claimed.

One remaining point of interest requires returning to the averages for vernacular use in the 17 family situations (see Table 7:8(a)). Comparing the differences between subgroups for vernacular use for all respondents in all situations to the differences for the family situations showed that only a part of the differences could be explained as differences in use in the family. This contrasts with Swahili where differences in overall use could almost be attributed entirely to differences in family use.

This must serve as a warning that variation in vernacular use was not restricted to home situations, at least for the Ilala population; hence, however much vernacular use might be restricted, it still retained limited use in alternation with Swahili for some residents of Ilala, beyond use within the family.

7.2 *Summary*

Generally, vernacular use seemed most easily determined on the basis of the location of the respondent's upbringing.

Vernaculars had, for a fairly long time, been excluded from regular use in education or government and since independence had been forbidden as a medium of Christian literature and of services. This left little room for acquisition and reinforcement other than in the individual's family and cultural group. Because the range of use was limited to non-western topics, the effects of education were doubly irrelevant. The restriction of women to the home and traditional roles had no effect.

Furthermore, vernaculars were almost exclusively learned as first languages among the respondents, which also argued for the importance of early sociolinguistic environment.

The crux of these environmental differences was exemplified by the interaction of the non-coastal and rural features. It is in these two environments that the ethnic culture was at home and at its strongest. They were also the locations where Swahili was weakest. It is the aim of the next section to argue that the relationship of Swahili and vernaculars seen in the Ilala respondents in a static form was in fact a cross section example of the spread of Swahili at the expense of the vernacular languages.

8.0 *Interrelations Between Swahili, English and the Vernaculars*

The three language levels considered in this study seemed to vary according to two general, different types of social factors. On the one hand were the geographical features of childhood, most effective during the time of first language learning. On the other were sex and education.

Schooling was an obvious means of second language acquisition; sex role discrimination in education and occupation was indirect in its effect, but the greatest impact would normally fall after first language learning.

Religion was a more complex feature, for it participated in both sorts of influences. During early childhood it was part of the family and local environment. As also seen, religious differences were matched by social differences at later times, in schooling, occupation, and indeed a person's entire milieu. To further complicate matters, of course, the Muslim faith and Islamic culture along the coast are, historically, closely allied.

Thus, the question of variation according to religious persuasion combined the two geographical features, which together will be labelled "early". It also involved education from the other two features, hereafter labelled "late", through the presence of Muslim parochial schooling and Muslim antipathy to western and government schooling.

The language levels in question can themselves be separated into two general groups and their use likewise described on separate bases. English differed from Swahili and the vernaculars in being learned exclusively as a second language among the respondents. In consequence, most of the variation in its use can be described in terms of "late" features, education, and role discrimination according to sex. Moreover, the sex-related variation was mostly attributable to lesser access to public schooling among females. One feature of use was also closely tied to education: literacy.

Hence, a second partition could be made between literacy skills and all other skills or first language knowledge. Religion interacted with sex and coast features so that the Christian–non coastal and Christian male subgroups stood out. The two geographical features showed differences in the direction one would expect on religious grounds.

Swahili and the vernaculars generally presented symmetrical pictures. That is, among groups where Swahili use was high, vernacular use was low and vice versa. The same held true within the family situations, where there were differences. One category was excepted, differences by sex where the total differences were small in any event. First language knowledge of Swahili was similarly symmetrical to the vernaculars. In each instance Swahili use was higher among coastal, urban, and Muslim respondents while the vernaculars were higher among non-coastal, rural, and Christian ones. Literacy cut across this pattern, however, with the only contrast being higher vernacular literacy among rural respondents. Otherwise, literacy was higher among non-coastal, Christian, male respondents with government schooling.

The Swahili and English patterns were exactly parallel. This again illustrated the difference between literacy and other language performance characteristics measured: what may well be termed the difference between a "late" language feature and "early" or general ones.

Religion, sex, and the geographical features taken together as pairs confirmed these findings. As seen in the discussion for English, sex was a more powerful tool for describing variation in average than either geographical variable, and acted in an additive manner when considered together with religion – itself generally stronger than either geographical feature. Just so, the geographical features were generally the better basis for describing Swahili and vernacular averages, with the exception of the apparent overcompensation among coastal and urban Christians in Swahili.

8.1 *Dynamics of the Interrelationships*

English differed from the African Tanzanian languages in its nature as a second language to all its speakers, depending for all practical purposes on the schools for its teaching. In a very real sense its position was the least dynamic, since, in theory, English could be removed from the curriculum of the schools, although this might be far from practicable. Likewise, the use of English in government and party communications could be and was being restricted for social and political reasons, not through any sociolinguistic weakness of the language as a vehicle of communications but because of the symbolic value of Swahili and the desirability of reinforcing its use.

Swahili and the vernaculars were indigenous and had their own constituencies. The expansion of Swahili among the several generations described in the present survey has already been presented. This is quite consistent with the symmetry of Swahili and vernacular use averages just described, for if one assumes that Swahili was expanding for the most part at the expense of the vernaculars, one would expect that the larger the number of situations in which Swahili was used, the smaller the number in which the vernacular was used.

The importance of the schools in Swahili's expansion was revealed by the switchover from use averages among Muslims, coastals and urban respondents to higher literacy rates among urbans, non-coastals, and Christians. Not only did the schools provide an additional use which supported the retention of Swahili, but they overcame the social forces which brought greater use among the coastal, and Muslim respondents. Nevertheless, although education supported increased Swahili use, the basic growth existed apart from education. How far vernaculars will be retained, and for how long remains to be seen. Based on this study, one would expect them to be weakest among the urban, coastal and Muslim groups and strongest among rural, non coastal, and Christian ones.

9.0 *Comparison with Four Local Interview Studies in Other Parts of Tanzania*

In addition to the Ilala study there were four smaller studies carried out by interview. These were conducted in the Bagamoyo former township, Kerege Ujamaa village (both locations being coastal), the Lyamungo area on Mount Kilimanjaro and the Pasua section of Moshi Town, at the foot of Mount Kilimanjaro. The four studies were aimed at obtaining one sample in each of the four cells of an urban/rural, coastal/non coastal matrix. The aim was achieved in part. The studies do at least serve to provide instances of the way in which a sample of persons were characterized, albeit a nonsystematic one.

9.1 *Bagamoyo*

The Bagamoyo sample was the most representative, in the statistical sense. Ten-house groups were selected on an arbitrary basis from all those in the (former) township and three households in each likewise. Thirty such households' heads were interviewed, using a modification of the Ilala interview schedule; the interviewees included three Arabs.

The sample population was entirely Muslim or non-respondent in religion, 23 and 7. Education was low with 1.73 years overall and only 4.3 among the 12 with any western schooling. 21 of 30 respondents were either farmers, herdsmen, or fishermen. Of 30 respondents, 13 were children of tribally mixed parents.

A former principal trans-shipping point for the Arab trade in slaves, Bagamoyo is a thoroughgoing part of the coastal Muslim environment, and a trading settlement of longer standing than Dar es Salaam.

In such an urban, coastal environment, one would expect a high degree of Swahili use and a great disproportion between its use and that of vernaculars. In fact, the average use for Swahili was 66.1 of 82 situations, that for respondents' own vernaculars 9.8. All respondents spoke Swahili but only 17 their own group's vernacular. The sample population was a more settled one than the Ilala one and Bagamoyo more stable as witnessed by the average age: 54 years. If one assumes expansion of Swahili use and contraction of vernacular use across generations, one could argue that vernacular use in Bagamoyo might be even lower among younger adults contemporary to the Ilala population.

The other common measures were also consistent with the characterization hypothesized and confirmed by the Ilala sample. There was negligible English use (only two respondents) and use of other vernaculars (3.5 for 11 respondents). Language use for the 17 family situations was likewise very much dominated by Swahili (13.13 for 26 respondents versus 2.7 for 10 in vernaculars). Literacy was almost entirely in Swahili: two for English, one for a vernacular, but 11 for Swahili. Swahili was also predominant as a first language: 28 of 30, while only nine claimed their vernacular as a mother tongue, a particular contrast with the survey sample and the Lyamungo one. The average number of languages claimed was also quite low at 1.53.

Language shift could be seen in the reduction of vernacular knowledge generation by generation. Of the 24 respondents belonging to closely knit ethnic groups, 19 claimed to know the language of their father, 20 that of their mother, and four of five that of the spouse where the data was obtainable. However, only two of 20 who had at least one talking child had passed on their vernacular to the child.

9.1.1 *Summary*

The Bagamoyo picture obtained is therefore consistent in its details with what one would expect for a coastal, urban sample on the basis of the hypotheses posed and the Ilala findings. Swahili predominated in all aspects. One found an almost total loss of vernacular learning as a mother tongue among the children of the respondents.

9.2 *Kerege Ujamaa Village*

Kerege presented a mixed picture. This was inherent in the nature of the village as a farming cooperative amalgamating an indigenous village, a resettlement from the cities, and another of migrants from the south. Thus it was coastal, but not fully rural. Of the 40 respondents chosen within the ten-house units, 30 were Muslim while eight were Christian and two non-respondents. None were non-Africans. The high number of respondents who were farmers, 36 of 40, was predictable, although they were not engaged in the common subsistence agriculture. Few were the children of ethnically mixed parents, 10 of 40.

Given the odd mixture of populations, a slightly higher level of education (2.4 years overall) and lower age (37.6), it was difficult to predict the extent of residual vernacular use. Among this mixed group, Swahili use remained high at 65.7 and vernacular quite low, 9.8 average and 15.0 among the 26 who claimed use of their vernacular. English and other vernaculars were just as vestigial as in Bagamoyo (1.1 and 1.4). Use in the family situations might point out the restricted locus of vernacular use: all used Swahili, the average 12.5. The vernacular average was 4.9 but 10.77 for the 18 who claimed to use their vernacular in the situations.

There were other indications of a natural restriction of vernacular use, with more knowledge than was apparent. For instance, more respondents claimed their own vernacular as mother tongues than Swahili, 23 to 20. Swahili remained the language of literacy (Swahili 17, English and vernaculars one each). But looking across generations, vernaculars were passed on to a much greater degree. Respondents knew their mothers' languages in 33 of 40 instances, their fathers' in 31. All 18 who were married to ethnically identifiable spouses married speakers of their own vernacular. The greatest contrast with Bagamoyo was among the respondents' speaking children: in 14 of 26 families, vernaculars were passed on as mother tongues.

9.2.1 *Summary*

The picture at Kerege was confused by the mixed nature of the population. Nevertheless, the data point to considerably greater strength of vernacular use and retention among these people, even though there appeared to be little use outside the family environment.

9.3 *Lyamungo*

The Lyamungo sample was the weakest of the lot. Data were obtained by requesting that the students of a Standard VI class use the Bagamoyo interview schedule to interview their fathers. Many confused matters by including data obviously describing themselves rather than their parent. The data were culled through and 14 of 30 found usable, but with reservation. All were local and of the same group, Chaga. Thirteen were Christian and only one Muslim. Seven respondents were engaged in agricultural work. Education was surprisingly high at 5.6 years, and may be a product of confusion, although Lyamungo was a secondary school location, and education was high in the Kilimanjaro area.

The language use picture was very different from that of the two coastal locations, resembling the questionnaire survey more closely. Swahili use overall was reduced to 53.0 and vernacular use greatly increased to 36.7, all respondents being vernacular speakers and all claiming their vernacular as a first language (half also claiming Swahili). The English average was surprisingly high at 11.8 for 11 respondents; no respondent claimed use of a second vernacular. In family situations the previous situation was reversed, for the Swahili average was only 3.1 against 12.6 for the vernacular. In an almost certain point of confusion, the respondents were attributed universal literacy in Swahili and English and half in the vernacular. Given the high level of education in the Kilimanjaro area, this was not inconceivable – but did seem unlikely. There were no reliable data on generational variation in vernacular retention.

9.3.1 *Summary*

However confused the information might be, it did point out salient differences from the coastal samples which were in the direction hypothesized for a rural non-coastal population as compared to a coastal sample. It illustrated the probable strength of vernaculars for family situations while remaining consistent with the spread of Swahili. While Swahili use was surprisingly high, Lyamungo was, as mentioned, a minor commerce center, an education center, and also located in a tribal area where Swahili, not the local tongue, had long been the choice for religious literature.

9.4 *Pasua*

Pasua was a working class section of Moshi, the capital of Kilimanjaro region; it was similar to Ilala in its semi-urban complexion. Eleven of the 20 respondents were engaged in agriculture, the rest in a variety of occupations – more rurally-oriented than in Ilala. Five of the 20 were of the local tribe, Chaga, but the rest were immigrant, the largest contingent being nine from the neighboring Pasua tribe. Data were obtained here in the same manner as at Lyamungo, but with a higher degree of success. The respondents comprised a fairly old (44.8 year) and fairly well educated group (4.4 years). There were four respondents of mixed parentage and 11 Muslims.

Their linguistic characteristics fell somewhere between the Lyamungo and coastal samples. Swahili averaged 58.3 and vernacular 16.72 (20.1 among the 15 who used their vernaculars). English use was higher at 5.8 and other vernaculars the same as the coastal groups' at 3.8. Literacy was again mainly Swahili, 17 of 20, but seven claimed English and four their vernacular. The average number of languages claimed was 3.0, a great difference. In mother tongue languages, they resemble more the Lyamungo and Kerege samples, for 14 of 20 claimed their vernaculars, 12 Swahili, and five other vernaculars. The picture from generation to generation also showed strong vernacular retention with 19 respondents classifiable. All of these were married to a speaker of their vernacular, all but one were children of fathers whose vernacular they knew, and all knew their mother's vernacular. Nine had children who knew their vernacular.[17]

9.4.1 *Summary*

The Pasua sample fell between the Lyamungo one and the coastal ones in its characteristics, being perhaps closer to the coastal ones. It illustrated the possible differences between the coastal city and the non-coastal one, where vernacular use was lower than in rural areas, but higher (and Swahili lower) than in Ilala.

9.5 *Overview*

These four local studies provide a second type of corroboration for the findings on general trends across the country. While not as strong as one might wish, the patterns they show were those to be expected from the basic hypotheses as substantiated, with some extrapolation, by the Ilala data.

10.0 *Conclusion*

The four local studies give added dimension to the findings from the Ilala study and serve to corroborate or substantiate the conclusions of that study. All studies point to linguistic variations along lines of home location, religion, sex, and education. The general picture has been demonstrated to be one in which Swahili was overlaid on an historically vernacular speaking populus for the most part, complementing or replacing vernacular use to a greater or lesser degree depending on the social characteristics of the population. English was almost a veneer laid over parts of the Swahili speaking population, its limits being defined most clearly by education and its social correlates. Although Swahili predominated among the samples drawn except for one local study at Lyamungo, that one points out the likelihood that in the true rural, non-coastal, less schooled population, Swahili and vernacular use were probably much more balanced or favored vernaculars.[18]

Based on comparisons across educational and other lines, it has been argued that the direction of change is from vernaculars to Swahili, vernaculars becoming more and more restricted to family and ethnic identity matters and rural areas. With the linking of Swahili and particularly English to a secular education system with no parochial counterpart, it is quite possible that differences along religious lines will be reduced, perhaps to insignificance in terms of proportion of speakers, Rural–urban differences will almost certainly persist, especially while primary education is not universal and almost all secondary and advanced education and educated jobs are located in the towns.

10.1 *Epilogue*

The matter of education and its role in the expansion of Swahili use must be given with one caution. As has been seen, literacy in English and to some extent Swahili is closely tied to the highest level of education attained. To the extent that government schooling is expected to provide citizens with functional literacy, it is possible an all the loaf or none situation exists. That is, unless these levels of education are obtained, the citizen will have spent his time and the government its funds to teach literacy skills too weak to survive on their own. The point warrants corroboration through further research, but could be of some relevance to educational planning.

NOTES

[1] Census data are based on unofficial tabulations of census areas within Dar es Salaam. All subsequent 1967 Census data come from this same source.

[2] The Swahili term used was *kazi za nyumbani*, 'work (done) at home' in contrast to *kazi za nyumba* 'house work' used to denote domestic service.

[3] The definition used here is that of Prins (1967: 15), taken to be just those divisions which actually lie along the coast.

[4] The best general description of life in Dar es Salaam known to the writer is Leslie's (1963), supplemented by the Marco Surveys data cited in Castle (1968).

[5] The current design of Ilala includes a large market place, Christian church, several mosques, a primary school and Muslim primary school, ward level TANU office and representation on the city council, and a large soccer stadium.

[6] Some houses contain only four rooms, others may have a three room annex standing separately behind the house.

[7] This is also part of the background for the current questioning of which dialect of Swahili should be the model: the traditional language and dialects of the Muslim coast in which all the historic Swahili literature is written, or the language of the government schools and upcountry usage, much influenced by Christian and western participation?

[8] The Koranic group included only those whose Koranic schooling equalled or exceeded the years in western schools; this means that some of both groups, western and Koranic, have had some schooling of the opposite type.

[9] The value of t for coastal Muslim vs. coastal Christian averages is 1.88 with 58 df, not significant at the .05 level of probability, one-tailed test, predicting Muslim to be greater than Christian.

[10] It was instructive to note that the root for English or European, contrasted with the root naming the Swahili language, not only as English language versus Swahili language but was also used to denote the differences between Muslim schools, *shule za kiSwahili*, and government of mission ones, *shule za kiZungu*.

[11] Use here was restricted to those who claimed English in five or more situations, to approximate a minimal functional knowledge of English.

[12] Standards VII and VIII were separated in that Standard VII included primary leavers for the years 1964–1970 but not leavers whose schooling ended before that year.

[13] Using the t-test, the difference among all men and women was significant at the .05 level, t being 4.35; t was 1.32 for educated men as opposed to educated women and did not indicate significant difference.

[14] 18.7 among Christians but 4.47 among Muslims.

[15] Only this extreme difference is statistically significant, $t = 2.308$, p less than .05.

[16] The actual frequencies were coast + literate, 14; non-coast + literate, 63; non-coast + non-literate, 98; and coast + non-literate 46. Chi-square was 4.805, indicating difference at .05 level of significance.

[17] Nine of 16; some of the interviewees were probably relatives with whom the student interviewers had been sent to live.

[18] In 1970 an examination into the relationship between the performance of pupils in the school subjects of Swahili and English and some aspects of the linguistic behaviour of their parents was carried out. The project covered a sample of approximately 6,000 standard VI pupils from all areas of Tanzania where there are Colleges of National Education, the interviewers being student teachers from these Colleges. Parents of 1,500 of the pupils were interviewed using the same schedule as was used for the Ilala Survey. Parents were selected for interview so that there was appropriate representation of parents whose children scored high, low and middling on the language tests. The information provided by the interviews was then digested and the results correlated with the test scores to discover whether any pattern emerged. Copies of all documents relating to this project are available from the Institute of Education, University of Dar es Salaam, PO Box 35094, Dar es Salaam. They bear the reference numbers CRP 70/01 to /04 Form C. C.P. Hill reported that the results of this test were "highly inconclusive", perhaps "a reflection of conflicting tendencies in language use in the Tanzanian community as a whole". (Hill, 1970).

REFERENCES

Castle, E. B., 1968, *Growing Up in East Africa*. London: Oxford University Press.

Hill, C. P., 1970, 'The Combined Research Project 1970'. (unpublished typescript).

Leslie, J. A. K., 1963, *A Survey of Dar es Salaam*. London: Oxford University Press (for the East African Institute of Social Research).

Prins, A. H., 1967, *The Swahili-speaking Peoples of Zanzibar and the East African Coast (Arabs, Shirazi and Swahili)*. Ethnographic Survey of Africa, East Central Africa, XII. London: International African Institute.

8 LIBRARY USERS AND THEIR READING PREFERENCES

C. P. Hill

1.0 *Introduction*

As part of the work of the Survey of Language Use and Language Teaching in Tanzania, it was decided to make a study of the reading preferences of those who used the library services available in Tanzania. With this in view, discussions were held with the Director of Library Services, Mr. Max Broome and with the Senior Librarian at Dar es Salaam, Mr. J. R. Haselgrove. An initial draft questionnaire was prepared. Further discussions with Mr. Broome and members of his staff, drawing on their experience in conducting a survey of library readers in 1967, resulted in a modified questionnaire in exactly parallel Swahili and English versions (Appendices A and B).

Library Services in Tanzania are provided from a number of different sources. The most important of these is the Tanganyika Library Service. The central library for this service is in Dar es Salaam, housed in a most attractive building and having available a stock of some 23,000 non-fiction books suitable for adults and a further substantial number of volumes of fiction, besides the volumes in the children's library. Area libraries are situated in Bukoba, Iringa, Kibaha (as part of the Tanzania Nordic Project), Karagwe, Moshi, Mwanza and Tanga, giving a total of 225,000 volumes available to the people in these towns, whereas the total population of mainland Tanzania numbers almost 12 million.

In addition to the Tanganyika Library Service, the British Council maintains libraries in Dar es Salaam, Moshi and Mwanza. The United States Information Service, the Goethe Institute, and the Service Cultural Français, also maintain libraries in Dar es Salaam.

2.0 *Aims and Method*

The object of the study now being reported was to obtain information from a representative sample of the users of these libraries. Some of the information sought was of what might be called the "vital statistics" kind (See Q1–5, Appendices A & B). Some concerned the languages used (Q. 6, 7, 8), others the pattern of use of the library (Q. 9, 10, 11), and the remainder the actual books read and the books the readers would like to see published in Swahili (Q. 12, 13).

All of the libraries mentioned above agreed to take a 10% sample of the borrowers of books for the purpose of the study. Every tenth borrower's card was flagged and when he came in to change or renew the loan of books he was asked to complete whichever version of the questionnaire he felt was most appropriate. The sampling began on 24th November 1969 and ran for six weeks. Any cards remaining flagged at the

LIBRARY USERS AND THEIR READING PREFERENCES

end of that time were reported as NIL returns. There was some uncertainty about the numbers of NIL returns from several libraries as a full check was not kept and the number of NIL returns had therefore to be estimated. The numbers of questionnaires distributed are given in Table 8:1.

Table 8:1 Distribution of Questionnaires

Library	Distributed		Returns	
Tanzania Library Service	English	Swahili	Completed	Nil
Dar es Salaam	725	60	460	(43)
Bukoba	74	10	–	–
Iringa	125	40	55	12
Kibaha	80	55	37	(4)
Karagwe	25	20	16	(7)
Moshi	145	30	–	–
Mwanza	170	30	93	(9)
Tanga	250	40	267	22
US Information Service	80	20	69	(15)
Goethe Institute	20	5	15	(5)
Service Culturel Français	12	8	10	0
British Council	100	–	56	(23)
Totals	1806	318	1078	140

3.0 Results

It may be observed that while the returns do not represent a full 10% sample, they nevertheless provide a reasonably representative cross section of those who use the libraries in Tanzania. The smallness of the numbers of people using the Goethe Institute and the Service Culturel Français Libraries make those sections of the sample extremely unreliable. However, the information gathered from the other libraries does seem to reflect fairly well the pattern of use, as reported by the librarians themselves.

Of the 1078 questionnaires returned, 18 proved unusable for various reasons. Some of them were clearly completed as pure hoax, others were spoiled in more than 50% of the questions, or only completed for one or two questions. So the final processing was carried out on 1060 questionnaires. The results of the "vital statistics" questions are given in Table 8:2, of the language use questions in Table 8:3, and of the library use questions in Table 8:4. The profile of the typical reader that emerges is discussed further in later sections but first we look at the actual books read (Q. 12 and 13).

3.1 Reading Preferences

Question 12 asked for the four most recently read books and an indication of which one the reader preferred. The classification of the books, not all of which were easily or fully identifiable, may seem at times a little odd even to someone who is not a professional librarian. The

208 LANGUAGE USE IN TANZANIA

Table 8:2 Responses to Questions 1–5: "Vital Statistics"

Total number of questionnaires processed: 1060. The category numbers used here are followed in later tables.

Q.1 *Age*
(1) Under 18   226
(2) 18 to 25   447
(3) 26 to 44   323
(4) 45 and over   62
    Void   2

Q.2 *Sex*
Male   832
Female   219
Void   9

Q.3 *Ethnic background*
African   536
Asian   302
European   151
Void   71

Q.4 *Education*
(1) Primary only   245
(2) Secondary to Form IV   439
(3) Secondary to Form VI   111
(4) University   216
    Void   49

Q.5 *Work*
(1) Farmer   48
(2) Shopkeeper   59
(3) Craftsman   66
(4) Unskilled   16
(5) Clerk   174
(6) Professional 206
(7) Housewife   78
(8) Student   286
(9) Others   52
(10) Unemployed   22
     Void   53

Table 8:3 Responses to Questions 6–8: Language Use

Q.6 *All languages read*

Swahili	856
English	981
Gujrati	205
French	154
German	44
Arabic	82
Others	203

Q.7 *Easiest language to read*

Swahili	181
English	268
Gujrati	18
French	3
German	1
Arabic	0
Others	0
Void	588

Q.8 *Languages used*

(i) At home

	All answers	First or main answer		All answers	First or main answer
Swahili	440	303	Nyakyusa	18	12
English	274	202	Bena	5	5
Gujrati	210	194	Shambala	9	9
Other Asian languages	51	51	Zalamo	6	6
			Luo	14	14
Sukuma	30	25	Zanaki	5	5
Nyamwezi	14	13	Pare	16	15
Haya	37	30	Kerewe	5	5
Chaga	15	12	All others	21	21
Hehe	10	7	Void	14	14

LIBRARY USERS AND THEIR READING PREFERENCES

Table 8:3 (contd.)

(ii) *At work or school*

	All answers	First or main answer			
Swahili	534	327	Sukuma	7	–
English	793	615	Haya	10	6
Gujrati	23	19	Hehe	4	–
All others	14	9	Bena	2	–
Void	90	90	All others	55	–
			Void	80	80

(iii) *With friends not members of the family*

	All answers	First or main answer
Swahili	557	430
English	582	408
Gujrati	130	94
Other Asian languages	13	11

(iv) *With African strangers*

	All answers	First or main answer
Swahili	739	628
English	465	331
All others	21	8
Void	93	93

Table 8:4 Responses to Questions 9-11: Use of the Library

Q.9 *Frequency of use of library*

Once a week	694
Once a month	237
Less often than that	77
Void	52

Q.10 *All uses of library*

To consult books for information	534
To borrow fiction	592
To borrow non-fiction	521
To borrow records	55
As a place to read own books	156

Q.11 *Main use of library*

To consult books	177
To borrow fiction	209
To borrow non-fiction	152
To borrow records	11
To read own books	34
Void	477

classification was attempted with the help of local library assistants none of whom had had any professional training and there are certainly deviations from professional standards. The results are summarised in Tables 8:5 and 8:6.

The information collected by means of the questionnaires was tabulated on code sheets, using a code system specifically devised for this purpose, and corresponding programming instructions were given for computer treatment of the data. The results obtained are given in the tables in this study. The titles of the most popular books were cross-classified against the age, sex, education and occupation of the respondents (Table 8:5). This showed, for example, that the most frequently mentioned title,

Table 8:5 Books in Order of Popularity (Q.12), by Age, Sex, Education and Occupation of Respondents
(See table 8:2 for categories used)

Author Title	Number of times mentioned	Age 1	2	3	4	Sex M	F	Education 1	2	3	4	Occupation 1	2	3	4	5	6	7	8	9	10
1. Achebe: Things Fall Apart	28	8	15	5	0	26	2	4	16	5	3	2	0	1	0	0	6	4	0	14	0
2. Abbott: Ordinary Level Physics	17	7	10	0	0	16	1	0	15	2	0	0	0	0	0	0	1	0	1	14	0
3. Gatheru: A Child of Two Cities	16	6	9	1	0	11	5	5	12	3	0	0	1	0	0	1	0	1	12	1	0
4. McLean: When Eight Bells Toll	15	5	6	4	0	12	3	0	9	2	4	0	1	0	0	1	2	2	8	0	1
5. Fleming: From Russia With Love	14	3	7	4	0	12	2	1	8	1	4	0	0	0	0	2	1	5	0	4	2
6. Nyerere: Ujamaa	13	4	5	3	1	13	0	6	4	0	1	0	1	3	0	1	1	0	5	2	0
7. Fleming: Live and Let Die	13	1	7	5	0	12	1	4	5	0	4	1	1	0	0	2	4	0	2	1	2
8. Shah: Kantak Chayo Panth	13	2	3	5	3	6	7	7	3	0	2	2	3	0	0	3	1	1	1	1	1
9. Kolak: Sowa	12	3	4	4	1	6	6	8	1	1	1	1	2	0	0	2	1	4	0	1	1
10. Fleming: Thunderball	11	3	4	3	1	8	3	2	4	2	3	2	1	6	0	2	1	3	0	1	0
11. Gardner: The Case of the Cow Bell	11	4	4	2	1	8	3	2	7	0	1	0	0	2	0	2	1	1	4	0	1
12. McLean: Ice Station Zebra	11	7	2	1	1	11	0	0	7	0	3	0	0	0	0	0	3	1	6	0	1
13. Canning: The Hidden Face	11	2	3	5	1	7	4	3	6	0	1	0	0	1	0	2	2	2	3	1	0
14. Michener: The Source	11	4	4	4	1	5	5	1	3	2	5	1	2	0	0	1	2	2	2	1	0
15. Desai: Twai Dsehitya	11	2	1	6	2	8	3	2	6	0	2	0	4	0	0	1	1	3	1	1	0
16. Stamp: Commercial Geography	11	2	5	4	0	10	1	2	7	0	1	0	0	2	0	1	5	1	2	0	1
17. Hadley Chase: You Find Him, I'll Fix Him	10	4	5	0	1	10	0	1	4	3	0	1	1	0	0	2	0	0	7	0	0
18. Hess: Chemistry Made Simple	10	6	3	1	0	8	2	1	8	0	0	1	1	0	0	0	1	0	8	0	1
19. Pasternak: Dr. Zhivago	10	1	6	3	0	10	0	4	5	0	1	1	0	2	0	0	2	2	2	0	2
20. Haggard: King Solomon's Mines	10	2	4	4	0	5	5	3	3	0	3	0	2	0	0	0	4	1	2	0	0
21. Desai: Gram Laxmi	10	0	0	8	2	7	3	4	2	1	2	2	0	0	0	2	2	2	1	0	2
22. Carter: Safari for Spies	9	0	7	1	1	8	1	0	6	1	1	1	0	0	0	4	2	0	3	0	0
23. Leech: Practical Bookkeeping	9	1	4	4	0	8	1	2	6	6	0	2	0	0	1	3	2	1	1	1	0
24. Munro: Bookkeeping	9	0	6	3	0	9	0	3	3	0	0	0	0	3	1	2	1	1	1	0	1
25. Carr: Death of an Owl	9	4	3	2	0	6	3	2	6	0	1	0	0	2	1	0	0	0	5	1	0
26. Robert: Insha na Mashairi	9	0	6	2	1	9	0	3	4	1	1	1	1	0	0	0	1	0	3	2	0
27. Anon: Alfu-Lela-Ulela	9	5	1	3	0	8	1	7	1	1	0	0	1	2	0	1	1	0	3	1	1
28. Gallico: Scruffy	9	2	2	3	2	2	7	0	5	1	2	0	0	0	0	1	1	5	2	0	0

LIBRARY USERS AND THEIR READING PREFERENCES 211

Things Fall Apart by Chinua Achebe, was mentioned overwhelmingly by men of the 18 to 25 age group, with secondary education up to Form IV, who are currently students, and virtually the same pattern obtains for the next two most frequently mentioned books. In contrast *Scruffy* by Paul Gallico was mentioned most often by women, spread fairly evenly in age, with secondary education up to Form IV, who were housewives – many probably Europeans. Each title may be looked at in this way. However, the dominant pattern appears to be that of the first title.

Table 8:6 shows how by far the most extensive use of books appears to be for recreation in the reading of fiction, predominantly in English, but

Table 8:6 Subject Areas of Books Mentioned More than 20 Times in Response to Q.12, in Order of Frequency

1.	English Literature	956
2.	Swahili Literature	244
3.	Political Science	178
4.	Indian Literature	145
5.	American Literature	96
6.	Zoology	95
7.	English Language	66
8.	Physics	64
9.	Engineering	62
10.	Accountancy	46
11.	Mathematics	45
12.	Economics	42
13.	Recreation and Sport	42
14.	Chemistry	35
15.	Geography of Modern Africa	32
16.	Social Sciences	29
17.	Biography	27
18.	French Literature	25
19.	Management	24
20.	Sex-information	23

also substantially in Swahili. The enormous popularity of political science as a subject area is also very clear, and the extent to which the libraries are used for study, particularly in the sciences and applied sciences is also very striking. (The interest in recreation and sport – especially football – is one which those responsible for the development of rural library services since 1969 have actively pursued, and there are now several titles for neo-literates in this area.)

The responses to Question 13 on the kind of book readers would like translated into Swahili proved difficult to deal with, but a summary of the results achieved is shown in Tables 8:7. The pattern appears to be consistent with that for the popularity of books; requests for translation into Swahili of books on political science being easily the most frequent of all. Some library users even asked for Swahili translations of some of President Nyerere's writings which in fact had first appeared in Swahili,

Table 8:7 Categories of Book Most Frequently Requested for Translation into Swahili (Q.13), in Order of Frequency

Non-fiction (subject area of kind of book)

Political Science	30	Engineering	2
Biography	6	Logic	2
Zoology	6	Mathematics	2
Business Training	5	Medicine	2
Economics	5	Psychology	2
Physics	5	Pure Science	2
Geography	4	Sport	2
History of Africa	4	Building	1
Sex-information	4	Chemistry	1
Social Science	3	History – General	1
History of N. America	3	Home Economics	1
Printing	3	Law	1
Religion	3	Linguistics	1
Accounting	2	Literature	1
Agriculture	2	Management	1
Astronomy	2	Philosophy	1
Education	2	Photography	1

Fiction (mainly by author)

Achebe	10	Haggard	2
Molière	4	Ekwensi	2
Dickens	3	Milne	2
Ngugi	3	Orwell	2
Maugham	3	Dainam De	2
Shakespeare	3	"Science Fiction"	2
Courlander	2	"Children's Books"	2

seemingly unaware of just what was available. Again the demand for books on the sciences and applied sciences is apparent, as is the need for fiction. Achebe came out as easily the most popular author whose work it was felt should be translated into Swahili. The pattern by age, sex, education and occupation of those who asked for these translations was again similar to that for those who read the most popular books, mostly men, in the 18–25 age range, with Secondary Form IV education, but this time they were clerks rather than students, though overall the students still responded most often to this question. Responses from other occupations, levels of education, and age groups could not really be regarded as significant.

3.2 *Profile of the Library User*

The picture of the typical library user in Tanzania which might appear to emerge from the overall results is of a male African student of political sciences, aged between 18 and 25, with secondary school education, who reads both Swahili and English but who finds English easiest to read. He normally uses Swahili at home with his family, English at work or at school, Swahili or English almost equally with friends who are not

LIBRARY USERS AND THEIR READING PREFERENCES 213

members of his family, and Swahili predominantly with African strangers (see Table 8:3 above). He uses the library about once a week mainly to borrow fiction (see Table 8:4 above). His favourite author is Chinua Achebe and he would like to see the work of this author translated into Swahili.

However, this picture is clearly a gross oversimplification and Tables 8:8–13 show some of the more complex relationships between the various factors. All discrepancies between totals are due to failure on the part of respondents to complete the relevant part of the questionnaire and in each case the gross totals would amount to 1,060 if the "void" questionnaires had all been included. Where cross tabulations of two or more factors are involved a void in any of the relevant returns means that the whole questionnaire has been disregarded and so recorded as void. This accounts for the discrepancies between the primary tabulations and cross tabulations of this kind.

3.2.1 *Ethnic Groups*

From Table 8:8 it may be observed that the largest single indigenous ethnic group to use the libraries are the Haya, with substantial groups of Sukuma, Chaga and Nyakyusa. If we consider these groups as proportions of the total number of library users we find that the Sukuma constitute 4.5%, the Haya 6.2%, the Chaga 4.1%, and the Nyakyusa 3.2% whereas in terms of the population as a whole the Sukuma constitute 12.6%, the Haya only 3.8%, the Chaga 3.7%, and the Nyakyusa 2.5%. In other words the Sukuma make less use of the libraries than might be expected, while the Haya, the Chaga and the Nyakyusa make more use of them than the size of the groups might suggest. Interestingly this matches the stereotypes of these ethnic groups as being those which are enthusiastic about education and literacy. However, the large number of Africans who did not specify any ethnic group (38 out of 536) has to be remembered.

If we consider the age grouping of the different ethnic groups, especially that between 18 and 25, the Haya, the Chaga, and the Nyakyusa again come out as the groups using the libraries more than others at 9.5%, 6.8% and 3.7% respectively, as opposed to the Sukuma at only 5.1%. The age pattern for the Luo is strikingly different from most groups, with the greatest number of Luo library users being in the 26–44 category.

Curiously the proportion of Haya women (8%) is smaller than the proportion of Chaga women (21%) or of Nyakyusa women (11.5%) or even of Sukuma women (13.8%), though actual numbers are too small to make the differences very significant. Male dominance is very clear among Asians too, where only 25% of library users of this ethnic group are women in contrast to the Europeans where 50% of the users are female.

The pattern related to education for each of the major African ethnic groups is very similar. Almost equal proportions of library users, of no matter which ethnic group, have had only primary or secondary to Form IV education, at somewhere around the 48% mark for each. This contrasts sharply with the Europeans where some 78% of the group are University graduates or have had some kind of further education.

Table 8:8 Ethnic Group of Respondents, by Age, Sex and Education
(See table 8:2 for categories)

	Age				Sex		Education				Total
	1	2	3	4	M	F	1	2	3	4	
Africans	96	300	135	5	475	61	185	168	42	41	536
Sukuma	9	15	12	–	31	5	14	18	2	2	36
Nyamwezi	7	13	6	1	25	2	13	110	3	1	27
Haya	10	28	12	–	46	4	19	24	4	3	50
Chaga	7	20	6	–	26	7	14	14	3	2	33
Hehe	3	12	6	–	18	3	6	13	2	–	21
Nyakyusa	4	11	10	1	23	3	10	11	2	3	26
Bena	4	4	3	–	11	–	4	6	1	–	11
Shambala	3	7	5	–	14	1	6	7	1	1	15
Zalamo	3	16	1	–	18	2	8	9	–	3	20
Pare	4	12	4	–	17	3	6	12	–	2	20
Zigula	4	9	–	1	14	–	5	8	–	1	14
Luo	1	7	11	–	18	1	7	9	1	2	19
Europeans	3	28	81	30	71	71	1	7	24	110	142
Anglo–Saxons	2	25	67	27	60	61	1	5	19	96	121
Others	1	3	14	3	11	10	–	2	5	14	21
Asians	112	80	85	25	226	76	50	167	36	49	302

Details are given only where the full information was available for ten or more respondents in the group.

3.3 Language Use

3.3.1 Languages Used at Home

From Table 8:9 it is clear that a very large number of library users use Swahili at home – some 38% of all respondents – and that there are substantial groups that use English, 23%, and Gujrati, 18%. The largest proportions of respondents using Swahili are the 18–25 group, male, with secondary Form IV, full-time students, corresponding with the pattern over the whole sample.

The largest proportion using English come in the 26–44 age group, slightly older than for Swahili; again they are mainly men but in a 2:1 proportion rather than in the 10:1 proportion for Swahili; they tend to be graduates and professional men. (It will be noticed that these peaks reflect the profile of the Anglo-Saxon component of the sample, which is not surprising.) Among the African ethnic groups it is striking to what extent the vernacular is used at home, especially by males; however, Sukuma, Nyakyusa and Haya are proportionately used much more than Chaga in the home. It is interesting to speculate as to why this might be so, and the reasons are clearly a matter for serious investigation by further research. It might be, for example, that the Haya sense of ethnicity is stronger than that among the Chaga, or that the greater linguistic homogeneity of the Haya favours the maintenance of the vernacular – the Chaga speak some thirteen different dialects some of which are mutually unintelligible and so perhaps are more open to linguistic invasion.

LIBRARY USERS AND THEIR READING PREFERENCES 215

Table 8:9 Languages Used at Home (Q.8 (i)), by Age, Sex, Education and Occupation

	Age				Sex		Education				Occupation										Total
	1	2	3	4	M	F	1	2	3	4	1	2	3	4	5	6	7	8	9	10	
Swahili	96	233	107	8	399	41	142	212	31	37	15	13	38	12	84	87	13	128	33	29	440
English	49	79	113	34	179	95	20	83	39	122	12	12	13	—	29	89	38	62	6	15	274
Gujrati	77	65	54	15	153	57	33	110	22	28	11	23	4	—	34	25	22	78	3	11	210
Hindi	3	3	7	—	11	2	—	6	1	6	—	1	—	—	1	3	—	5	1	2	13
Kachi	8	2	1	—	4	7	1	8	—	1	2	1	1	—	—	1	1	7	—	—	11
Sukuma	4	14	12	—	28	2	9	16	3	2	2	1	1	—	7	7	1	8	2	1	30
Nyamwezi	2	9	2	1	13	1	5	6	—	1	1	—	2	—	5	5	1	—	3	—	14
Haya	6	22	9	0	34	3	10	21	3	3	—	2	6	2	5	2	—	12	2	6	37
Chaga	3	10	2	0	12	2	6	7	—	2	—	—	1	0	4	3	0	3	1	1	15
Gogo	0	0	2	0	2	0	1	1	0	0	0	0	—	2	1	1	—	0	—	—	2
Ha	1	1	0	0	2	0	0	1	0	1	—	—	—	0	—	—	—	0	0	2	2
Hehe	1	6	3	0	8	2	3	6	1	0	1	1	0	1	2	1	0	3	0	2	10
Nyakyusa	3	7	7	1	17	1	5	8	2	3	2	1	—	—	5	4	—	3	—	2	18
Lugulu	0	1	1	0	2	0	1	1	0	0	0	0	0	0	0	0	0	2	0	0	2
Bena	2	3	1	0	5	0	2	2	1	0	0	0	0	0	0	0	0	4	0	0	5
Turu	0	1	0	0	1	0	0	0	0	0	0	0	0	0	0	0	0	0	1	0	1
Shambala	1	6	2	0	9	0	3	5	1	0	1	0	1	1	2	1	0	3	0	0	9
Zalamo	1	4	1	0	6	0	2	4	0	0	0	0	0	2	0	1	0	2	1	0	6
Iramba	0	0	1	0	1	0	0	1	1	0	0	0	0	0	1	0	0	0	0	0	1
Maasai	0	2	1	0	3	0	0	1	0	1	0	0	0	0	0	1	0	0	1	0	3
Iraqw	0	1	0	0	1	0	0	0	0	0	0	0	0	1	0	0	0	0	0	0	1
Luo	1	4	9	0	13	1	7	5	1	1	0	0	3	1	4	2	0	0	2	1	14
Zanaki	0	4	1	0	4	0	2	2	1	0	0	0	0	0	1	1	0	2	1	0	5
Pogolu	0	1	0	0	1	0	0	1	0	0	0	0	0	0	0	0	0	1	0	0	1
Maku	0	1	1	0	2	0	0	1	0	1	0	0	0	0	0	0	0	1	0	0	2
Matengo	0	3	0	0	2	1	0	0	1	0	0	0	0	0	0	1	0	3	0	0	3
Fipa	0	2	0	0	1	1	0	0	0	1	0	0	0	0	0	0	0	0	0	0	2
Safwa	0	1	0	0	1	0	1	0	0	0	0	0	0	0	0	1	0	1	0	0	1
Kerewe	0	2	3	0	4	1	0	4	0	1	0	0	0	0	1	2	0	0	0	1	5
Pare	3	10	3	0	13	3	4	9	0	2	0	0	0	0	8	5	1	1	0	1	16

The greatest use of the vernacular appears to be in the 18–25 age group in most cases (apart from the Luo). Similarly those who have education to Form IV are the educational group which most uses the vernacular at home, around 50% of all users being in this group. However, in both cases the profile very much follows the distribution of respondents found in Table 8:8 and no great differences in proportions emerge consistently. Almost no one in professional or other high level occupations seems to use an African vernacular at home – Swahili predominates, with English and Gujrati also widely used; among the occupations it is only the students who appear to use a vernacular to any extent at home and that is most prevalent among the Haya.

3.3.2 *Languages Used at Work or School*

Table 8:10 confirms very strongly the generally held view that the vernacular languages are very little used in such public situations as work or school. Swahili and English dominate all other languages to the point where the use of such other languages is virtually totally insignificant. The differences in the patterns of use of English and Swahili are of some interest, however. English appears to be used in the work/school context rather more by the younger generations than is Swahili, a trend which is less marked among older respondents. 56% of men use English at work, while 73% of the women respondents do so. Those with lower levels of education use English and Swahili approximately equally at work, but those with higher levels of education use English up to 25% more than that. Among the occupations 57% of clerks use English rather than Swahili at work, 61% of students do so, 68% of professionals and 75% of housewives. This last figure can only be accounted for by the high proportion of European women who borrow books from the libraries for light entertainment reading.

3.3.3 *Languages Used with Friends*

The vernacular languages are very little used by library users, even with their friends (see Table 8:11). Here again Swahili and English dominate the pattern of language use. Of the African respondents, it is only the Haya and Sukuma who report using their own language to a significant degree. Even here, among the Haya, for example, use of the vernacular with friends is reported only by one fifth of the total claiming to be Haya (see Table 8:8 above). Only Gujrati comes anywhere near Swahili and English in frequency of use.

Though no more than 536 respondents claim to be of African ethnic origin (see Table 8:2), 557 claim to use Swahili with their friends, so it might appear that Europeans, and probably still more Asians also use Swahili for informal exchanges with those whom they know well. Similarly though only 151 respondents claim to be of European origin, 582 claim to use English among friends, so the evidence for considerable code switching among Asians and Africans is quite convincing. This is just as might be expected among those of these ethnic groups who use the libraries.

The pattern of use related to age, sex, education and occupation

LIBRARY USERS AND THEIR READING PREFERENCES

Table 8:10 Languages Used at Work/School, by Age, Sex, Education and Occupation

	Age				Sex		Education				Occupation										Total
	1	2	3	4	M	F	1	2	3	4	1	2	3	4	5	6	7	8	9	10	
Swahili	117	258	134	27	477	57	159	249	48	61	24	33	49	13	96	84	14	156	35	34	534
English	173	335	243	41	632	161	119	369	88	187	31	32	40	7	136	177	42	245	32	52	793
Gujrati	6	7	6	4	15	8	3	13	4	2	0	3	1	0	6	2	5	3	0	3	23
All other languages	4	5	4	1	9	5	6	3	–	4	1	1	–	–	1	2	3	3	2	1	14

Table 8:11 Languages Used with Friends, by Age, Sex, Education and Occupation

	Age				Sex		Education				Occupation										Total
	1	2	3	4	M	F	1	2	3	4	1	2	3	4	5	6	7	8	9	10	
Swahili	113	289	139	18	497	60	174	266	47	52	24	27	50	11	115	81	11	165	37	39	557
English	122	214	202	44	444	138	59	248	74	176	20	25	25	9	81	156	47	157	19	41	582
Gujrati	41	44	36	9	90	40	19	69	13	20	7	9	1	0	22	18	16	46	3	8	130
Hindi	1	0	6	0	6	1	0	2	0	4	0	0	1	0	0	4	0	1	1	0	7
Kachi	6	0	0	0	4	2	1	5	0	0	0	0	0	0	0	0	0	5	0	1	6
Sukuma	1	3	3	0	6	1	2	2	0	3	1	0	0	0	0	1	1	3	1	1	7
Haya	1	7	2	0	7	3	2	6	2	0	0	0	0	0	1	0	0	6	1	2	10
Hehe	1	2	1	0	3	1	1	3	0	0	0	0	0	0	0	0	0	2	0	1	4
Bena	0	1	1	0	2	0	0	1	1	0	0	0	0	0	0	0	0	1	0	0	2
All others	2	21	25	7	38	17	8	10	15	22	2	4	7	1	5	15	6	11	3	2	55

Table 8:12 Languages Used with African Stranger, by Age, Sex, Education and Occupation

	Age				Sex		Education				Occupation										Total
	1	2	3	4	M	F	1	2	3	4	1	2	3	4	5	6	7	8	9	10	
Swahili	172	313	211	41	587	148	182	324	65	128	33	45	44	7	122	140	52	213	39	44	739
English	63	204	161	36	364	100	65	183	60	140	19	20	27	7	74	117	34	108	24	35	465

Details are given here only of English and Swahili as other answers were insignificant, or aberrant because of a misunderstanding of the question.

appears to match pretty well the pattern of these factors in the responding population, so no conclusion can be drawn other than that this degree of multilingualism is common to all library users. It appears to be very slightly more in evidence in the 18 to 25 age group, and among men, among those with secondary education to Form IV and among clerks and students, and slightly less in evidence among professionals. Among housewives it is very much less in evidence. Again the expatriate on a short term contract who has not learned Swahili would seem to be in evidence. English appears to be used rather less among those with only primary education and rather more among university graduates; more frequently by those in the 18 to 25 age group, and by professional people and rather less by farmers, shopkeepers, craftsmen, and clerks. All of these tendencies are highly predictable given the Tanzanian sociolinguistic situation.

3.3.5 *Languages Used with African Strangers*

The results show an overwhelming dominance of Swahili as the language used with African strangers (Table 8:12). English would appear to be used to some extent, but a much lesser one. The use of Swahili almost exactly matches the distribution of the various features of age, sex, education and occupation, so would appear to be virtually universal among library users for this purpose.

Only the university graduates showed a majority using English and there appeared to be some slight tendency for users in the 26 to 44 age group to prefer it. Again this probably reflects the fair number of expatriates, who formed part of the sample, for whom English would be the preferred lingua franca. Respondents in the professional occupations also tended more to use English to speak to African strangers.

3.3.6 *Different Ethnic Groups' Use of Language*

The responses demonstrated very clearly the extent to which Swahili and English dominate language use among library users even in their own homes (Table 8:13). Virtually every ethnic group represented at all substantially, included at least a minority who used English, as well as the large proportion who used Swahili and the vernacular. Even among the Asians 13% claimed to use Swahili at home; among the Sukuma the proportion was 56%, among the Haya 34%, among the Chaga 57%, and among the Nyakyusa 53%. In contrast no more than 59% of the Sukuma, 46% of the Haya, 30% of the Chaga, and 53% of the Nyakyusa used the vernacular language at home. Clearly in many families both Swahili and the vernacular are commonly used. This kind of proportion seems to hold for most ethnic groups, however among the Bena respondents the proportion who use Swahili at home rises to 91%, and among the Zalamo to 85%; the latter are a coastal people so it is easy to see how Swahili might well become the language of the home, but it appears difficult to account for the case of the Bena whose home area is around Njombe in the central sourthern part of Tanzania near the head of Lake Nyasa, except perhaps by suggesting that it is the very mobility of this

LIBRARY USERS AND THEIR READING PREFERENCES 219

Table 8:13 Relationship between Ethnic Group and Languages Used at Home

Ethnic Group	No. of Respondents	Language Used at Home			Ethnic Group	No. of Respondents	Language Used at Home		
		English	Swahili	Vernacular			English	Swahili	Vernacular
Europeans	142	127	0	27[1]	Zalamo	20	—	17	6
Asians	302	82	41	221[2]	Iramba	2	1	2	1
Sukuma	36	1	20	22[3]	Maasai	2	—	3	2
Nyamwezi	27	2	16	11	Iraqw	1	—	1	1
Haya	50	5	17	23	Luo	19	3	6	12
Chaga	33	4	19	10	Zanaki	6	—	2	4
Gogo	3	2	3	1	Pogolu	3	—	3	1
Ha	3	—	2	1	Matumbi	1	—	1	—
Hehe	21	1	10	3	Makua	3	—	—	1
Nyakyusa	26	2	14	14	Matengo	4	—	1	3
Lugulu	6	—	5	2	Fipa	5	—	3	2
Bena	11	1	10	5	Safwa	1	—	—	1
Turu	1	—	—	1	Kerewe	8	—	4	2
Shambala	15	—	7	8	Pare	20	1	10	12
					Zigula	14	1	10	2

[1] This includes 7 Danes, 4 Dutch, 3 French, 3 Germans, 2 Finns, 2 Italians, and 1 each Greek, Norwegian, Swede, Pole, Yugoslav and Swiss.
[2] This includes 197 Gujrati, 11 Kachi, 13 Hindi.
[3] This includes 1 giving ethnic group as Sukuma and language used as Nyamwezi.

group – there was no library in the Njombe area to be sampled – that has led them to the use of Swahili.

Relating ethnic group to language use reconfirmed the overwhelming use of Swahili and English, at work, with friends and with strangers. Only the Haya and Sukuma among library users seem to use the vernacular to any significant extent even among their friends; in every other case it is Swahili which is used among friends, twice as often as English is used – except of course among the Anglo-Saxons where English is the favoured medium. At work and in school African library users seem to use Swahili and English about equally; the Anglo-Saxons use English predominantly; and the Asians use mainly English, but also use Swahili to a surprisingly large extent, about half as often as they use English. This last fact probably reflects the much greater commitment to Tanzania as a nation and hence to the national language among Asians as opposed to the generally expatriate Anglo-Saxons. Even among their friends Asians claim to use Swahili about 25% of the time. The results confirm that Swahili is the favoured medium for addressing African strangers, no matter what ethnic group is involved, being used about twice as often as English by everyone except the Europeans.

3.4 *Uses Made of the Library*

It is interesting to note the high proportion of users who simply use the library as a place to read, in the youngest age group 13.6% of them (see Table 8:14). If consultation use is added to this, then the proportion rises to 41.1% in this age group, to 39.7% in the next age group, to 33.4% in the next, and to 26.6% in the oldest age group. The falling proportion with age probably reflects the fact that older users probably have a home of their own and hence at least the possibility of a quiet place to read and work at their books. They are also likely to be better able to afford their own dictionaries and other reference books, while younger readers might well not have ready access to such facilities.

3.5 *Languages Read*

Table 8:15 interestingly appears to show a decline in the ability to read in Swahili vis à vis the ability to read in English in relation to the amount of education. Thus primary level respondents are more likely to claim to read in Swahili than in English in the proportion of about 1.1:1; for those of secondary Form IV level exactly this proportion is reversed with more claiming to read in English; for those of secondary Form VI level, the ability to read in English slightly further exceeds Swahili, in the proportion of about 1.4:1; for those at the University level the proportion rises to 1.8:1. However, the high proportion of Europeans at the higher educational levels may be having a disproportionate effect here.

There are many Gujrati speaking parents who wish to ensure the transmission of the cultural values they hold and who require their children to attend out of school classes in the reading and writing of Gujrati as a means to that end, so that, as the table shows, even young Gujrati continue to be able to read their own language.

Table 8:14 Relationship between Uses Made of Library (Q.10) and Age

Uses made of library	Under 18	%	18–25	%	25–44	%	45 and over	%
To consult books for information	103	27.5	235	30.5	169	28.1	26	23.9
To borrow fiction	117	31.3	231	30.0	203	33.7	40	36.7
To borrow non-fiction	93	24.9	213	27.7	178	29.6	36	33.0
To borrow records	10	2.7	20	2.6	20	3.3	4	3.7
As a place to read own books	51	13.6	70	9.1	32	5.3	3	2.7
Totals	374	100	769	100	602	100	109	100

Table 8:15 Relationship between Languages Read and Education

Languages read	Primary only		Secondary to Form IV		Secondary to Form VI		University		Total
		%		%		%		%	
Swahili	219	43.7	401	36.6	79	28.0	117	21.7	816
English	198	39.5	424	38.7	108	38.2	210	39.0	940
Gujrati	29	5.8	103	9.4	26	9.1	30	5.6	188
French	4	.8	46	4.2	26	9.1	77	14.3	153
German	1	.2	8	.7	8	2.8	25	4.7	42
Arabic	20	4.0	39	3.6	8	2.8	14	2.6	81
Others	30	6.0	74	6.8	28	10.0	65	12.1	197
Totals	501	100	1095	100	283	100	538	100	

LIBRARY USERS AND THEIR READING PREFERENCES 223

The increase in the teaching of French at secondary level as a result of the decision to foster linguistic rapprochement between anglophone and francophone Africa shows itself in the table. The very high level of French reading ability among respondents with University education, however, probably arises partly from the presence of a sample from the Service Culturel Français in the survey, and also from the fact that most European graduates are likely to have at least some slight reading knowledge of this language.

The proportion of those who can read Arabic appears to drop slightly with increasing education from 4% at primary level to 2.8% at Secondary Form VI level. Many primary school children have also received instruction at Koranic schools but such schools have not traditionally fostered academic study in the way that Christian Mission schools have.

From Table 8:16 it would seem justifiable to conclude that occupation does not substantially affect the overall pattern in which the ability to

Table 8:16 Relationship between Languages Read and Occupation

Languages read	Occupation									
	1	2	3	4	5	6	7	8	9	10
Swahili	35	42	57	15	155	143	37	266	48	58
English	43	49	58	13	171	198	65	274	43	67
Gujrati	9	22	8	0	39	28	23	60	3	13
French	7	4	2	0	14	56	16	40	3	12
German	2	1	2	1	0	17	7	9	3	2
Arabic	3	4	6	2	16	12	2	28	4	5
Others	9	9	12	1	22	57	11	50	14	18

read English marginally dominates. The only groups where this pattern is reversed are (i) the unskilled labourers, who are likely to be of low educational attainment and therefore predictably mainly Swahili readers, and (ii) the miscellaneous group of occupations where the lack of precision in terms may very well conceal low levels of education. The extent to which the craftsmen seem to read Swahili and English almost equally is also interesting and hopeful for the development of this group of occupations, since many manuals are in English though the greater part of the craftsman's work must be done through the medium of Swahili.

The answers on the "easiest language to read" (Q. 7, see Table 8:3 above) showed a clear tendency to claim English as the easiest language. At the upper age and educational levels this may reflect a disproportionate number of Europeans answering the question and the large number of void questionnaires (588) make it difficult to draw firm conclusions. However, the breakdown by age interestingly shows 68 (59.1%) of the under 18 group finding English easiest and 44 Swahili; and 104 (54.2%) of the 18–25 group English as against 86 Swahili. The breakdown by education showed 65 (67.0%) with primary education finding Swahili easiest as against 27 English, dramatically reversed in the Secondary to Form IV group to 120 (54.3%) English as against 95 Swahili.

The pattern of reading ability among library users is one of a marginal dominance of English but with most library users substantially at home in both English and Swahili.

4.0 *Conclusion*

The final picture that emerges from all this data is of a very complex situation, with a high degree of multilingualism among virtually all library users in Tanzania. Perhaps most encouraging for those who hope for, and work towards a united and well integrated Tanzania is the extent to which the national language dominates the practices of library users, the obvious interest there is in the development of literature, in the widest sense, in Swahili, and the hints that are made about the directions in which this development might take place.

LIBRARY USERS AND THEIR READING PREFERENCES

APPENDIX 8:A SWAHILI QUESTIONNAIRE

UCHUNGUZI WA MATUMIZI NA MAFUNDISHO YA LUGHA ZA TANZANIA

Orodha ya Maswali ya Wanaotumia Maktaba

Uchunguzi wa Matumizi na Mafundisho ya Lugha za Tanzania ni jaribio muhimu kutafuta ni nani anayeitumia lugha gani, kwa ajili gani, katika hali ipi na mahali gani katika Tanzania. Uchunguzi huu unafanywa kwa mafikiano na Chuo Kikuu cha Dar es Salaam, na unategemezwa na Serikali ya Tanzania. Wakati uchunguzi huu umepangwa, mahitaji na matarajio ya Tanzania ndiyo mambo ya kwanza kufikiriwa.

Utumizi mmoja wa lugha katika nchi hii ya Tanzania ni kusoma. Ili habari za utumizi huu muhimu zikusanywe, watu wanaotumia maktaba yoyote mahali popote katika Tanzania wanaombwa kujaza orodha ya maswali ya aina hii hii.

Tutafurahi sana kama utashiriki katika kazi hiyo ambavyo utasaidia maendeleo ya taifa hili.

Tafadhali andika majibu ya maswali katika nafasi zilizotengenezwa katika kurasa zifuatazo.

Ikiwa wakati utakapojibu itakuwa lazima kuchagua, onyesha jibu lako kwa kutia tiki √ katika kisanduku kinachofaa.

Utaona kwamba uchunguzi huu ni wa siri kabisa – hutakiwi kutoa jina lako.

1. Una umri gani?
   Chini ya miaka 18
   Kati ya 18 na 25
   Kati ya 26 na 44
   45 au zaidi

2. Je, wewe u mwanamume au mwanamke?
   Mwanamume
   Mwanamke

3. Wewe wa kabila gani?
   _____

4. Ulisoma katika shule gani?
   Shule ya msingi tu
   Shule ya sekondari mpaka Form IV
   Shule ya sekondari mpaka Form V au VI
   Chuo Kikuu, au masomo yoyote mengine ya juu

5. Unafanya kazi gani?
   Mkulima
   Mfanyi biashara
   Fundi
   Kibarua
   Karani
   Mjuzi (mganga, hakimu, mwalimu, n.k.)
   Mke nyumbani
   Kazi nyingine _____
            (Taja ipi)
   Bila kazi

6. Unaweza kusoma lugha zipi?
   Kiswahili
   Kiingereza
   Kigujerati
   Kifaransa
   Kijeremani
   Kiarabu
   Lugha nyingine _____
            (Taja ipi)

7. Lugha unayoweza kusoma kwa urahisi zaidi ni ipi? (Onyesha jibu lako kwa kutia tiki mbili ✓)

8. Kwa kawaida unazungumza lugha gani wakati
   (i) unapokuwa nyumbani pamoja na jamaa zako? _____

   (ii) unapokuwa kazini au shuleni? _____

   (iii) unapokuwa na marafiki wasiokuwa jamaa zako? _____

   (iv) unapokutana na wageni Waafrika? _____

9. Unatumia maktaba hii mara ngapi kwa kawaida?
   Mara moja kila wiki
   Mara moja kila mwezi
   Chini ya mara moja kila mwezi

10. Je, unatumia maktaba hii kutafuta habari kutoka vitabu visiivyoruhusiwa kutolewa katika maktaba?
    kuazima vitabu vya hadithi?
    kuazima vitabu vya maarifa?
    kuazima sahani za santuri?
    kama mahali pa kusomea vitabu vilivyo mali yako?

11. Utumizi upi ni muhimu mno kwako?
    (Onyesha upi kwa kutia tiki mbili ✓)

12. Tafadahli taja vitabu vinne ulivyosoma hivi karibuni.

Jina la kitabu.	Mwandishi.	Tarehe ulipokisoma.	Kipi ulikipenda zaidi.
1.			
2.			
3.			
4.			

(Onyesha kipi ulikipenda zaidi kwa kutia tiki moja tu katika safu ya mwisho)

13. Ikiwa umesoma vitabu vilivyotungwa katika lugha nyingine isiyo Kiswahili vya aina utakayopenda kuona imetolewa katika lugha ya Kiswahili, tafadhali toa mfano.
    Nitapenda kuona kimetolewa katika lugha ya Kiswahili kitabu kama

    (Jina la kitabu) _____ kilichotungwa na _____
    au (Jina la kitabu) _____ kilichotungwa na _____
    au (Jina la kitabu) _____ kilichotungwa na _____
    Tunakushukuru kwa msaada wako.

Tafadhali weks orodha hii ya maswali uliyokwisha kujaza katika kisanduku kilichowekwa kwa kusudi hilo karibu na mahali pa kuazimia vitabu.

LIBRARY USERS AND THEIR READING PREFERENCES

APPENDIX 8:B ENGLISH QUESTIONNAIRE

SURVEY OF LANGUAGE USE AND LANGUAGE TEACHING IN TANZANIA

Library Users Questionnaire

The Survey of Language Use and Language Teaching in Tanzania is a large scale effort to try to discover who uses what language, for what purpose, under what circumstances, where in Tanzania. This research is being conducted under the auspices of the University College, Dar es Salaam, and has the support of the Government of Tanzania. In planning it the needs and aspirations of Tanzania have been kept foremost.

One of the uses to which language is put by many people in Tanzania is reading. In order to collect information about this important use of language people visiting any of the libraries anywhere in Tanzania are being asked to complete questionnaires like this one.

We would appreciate it very much if you would be kind enough to participate in this, and so contribute in some way to the future development of this nation.

Please write the answers to the questions in the spaces provided in the following pages.

Where the question involves making a choice indicate your answer by putting a tick √ in the appropriate box.

You will observe that this enquiry is entirely confidential – you are not asked to give your name.

1. What is your age?
    Under 18
    18 to 25
    26 to 44
    45 and over

2. Are you male or female?
    Male
    Female

3. What is your tribe or ethnic background? _____

4. What education have you had?
    Primary only
    Secondary to Form IV
    Secondary to Form V
    or Form VI
    University or other further education

5. What work do you do?
    Farmer
    Shopkeeper
    Craftsman
    Unskilled labourer
    Clerk
    Professional man (Doctor, lawyer, teacher, etc.)
    Housewife
    Full-time student
    some other _____
            (Say which kind)
    Unemployed

6. What languages can you read?
    Swahili
    English
    Gujrati
    French
    German
    Arabic
    Some other language _____
            (Say which one)

7. Which language do you find easiest to read? (Indicate your answer by a double tick ✔/)

8. Which language or languages do you usually speak
   (i) when you are at home with your family? ─────────────

   (ii) When you are at work or at school? ─────────────

   (iii) When you are with friends who are not members of your family? ─────────────

   (iv) When you meet Africans who are strangers to you? ─────────────

9. How often do you use this library?
   Once a week
   Once a month
   Less often than once a month

10. Do you use this library?
    to consult books for information?
    to borrow fiction?
    to borrow non-fiction?
    to borrow records?
    as a place to read your own books?

11. Which of these represents the *main* use you make of the library?
    (Indicate your answer by a double tick ✔/)

12. Please list four books you have read recently in any language.

Title.	Author.	Date read.	Liked best.
1.			
2.			
3.			
4.			

(Indicate which one you liked best by putting only one tick in the last column)

13. If you have read books in a language other than Swahili of a kind which you would like to see published in Swahili please give examples.

I would like to see published in Swahili a book like

(Title) ───────────────── by (Author) ─────
or (Title) ───────────────── by (Author) ─────
or (Title) ───────────────── by (Author) ─────

Thank you very much indeed for your helpful cooperation.

Please put the completed questionnaire in the box near the borrowing desk which has been provided for this purpose.

9 THE USE OF LANGUAGE IN THE LAW COURTS IN TANZANIA[1]

Douglas Kavugha and Donald Bobb

1.0 *Introduction*

The purpose of this survey is to determine through percentage analysis the use of Swahili as the national language of Tanzania by comparison with the use of English and the vernaculars. The law courts in Tanzania constitute a characteristic social medium for a language use study, and they are one aspect of social life which definitely provides a strikingly typical pattern for sociolinguistic analysis.[2] As the use of Swahili grows within the nation, this preliminary survey may provide a basis for a more substantial study which will indicate the particular situations and regions in which Swahili has achieved obvious predominance as well as the specific problems yet to be faced if Swahili is to prevail throughout every area of the national life.

The legal system of Tanzania can be illustrated as shown in Table 9:1.

Table 9:1 The Legal System of Tanzania

```
         Civil        Court of Appeal       Criminal
                      for Eastern Africa
                            ↑ ↑
        ┌──────→  High Court of  ←──────┐
        │         Tanzania               │
   ┌─────────┐      ↑    ↑          ┌─────────┐
   │Resident │      │    │          │Resident │
   │Magistrate│                     │Magistrate│
   │Court    │                      │Court    │
   └─────────┘                      └─────────┘
              ┌────────┐  ┌────────┐
              │District│  │District│
              │Court   │  │Court   │
              └────────┘  └────────┘
                  ↑           ↑
              ┌────────┐  ┌────────┐
              │Primary │  │Primary │
              │Court   │  │Court   │
              └────────┘  └────────┘
```

The research information was gathered by Douglas Kavugha from visits to 52 courts:

- 3 High Courts
- 9 Resident Magistrate Courts
- 15 District Courts
- 25 Primary Courts

The visits were of 1–2 days' duration each. The total number of cases examined was 87. The total number of people under language observation was 443. The data originated from the courts as listed in Table 9:2 and arranged by geographical regions.

The persons observed in the court sessions functioned in the following roles:
  magistrate/judge
  state attorney/prosecutor
  advocate
  court assessor/clerk
  interpreter (usually court clerk)
  accused/defendant
  plaintiff/complainant/appellant
  witnesses (for the defense and the prosecution)
  doctor

In the course of the visits to the courts, the national or ethnic background of the individuals involved in the court proceedings was noted, and, when possible, the number of years of education they had received was indicated.

The analysis of the data collected attempts to specify the situation in each court session attended and observed with a view to determine the percentages of use of English, Swahili and the vernaculars by the different individuals, as well as drawing some conclusions regarding language switching and interpreting (see Appendix 9:A).

2.0 *Analysis*

From the data given in Appendix 9:A the number of situations per language can be determined and the results are as shown in Table 9:3.

Thus far, we can draw the following tentative conclusions:
(1) English is not used as extensively in the Northeast and Northwest regions as in the other parts of the country.
(2) The vernaculars are used in the Northeast, Northwest, Southwest and Central regions while the West and the East do not use them.
(3) The West and the Southwest use English quite a lot more than the other regions.
(4) The greatest preponderance of Swahili occurs in the Northwest, where vernaculars are used and in the East where English is used.
(5) The West and Southwest regions have the lowest percentage use of Swahili.
(6) The higher the court the greater the use of English. The lower the court the greater the use of Swahili. No English was used in the primary courts.
(7) No conclusions can yet be drawn with regards to the vernaculars; in the RMC their use is negligible, whereas on the other three levels their usage is considerable.
(8) The percentages for the Northeast regions are probably more accurate, given the greater number of language situations.
(9) The totals for the entire country show Swahili to be used in 78% of the situations, English in 16% and the vernaculars in 6%.

Table 9:2 Courts visited

Court	Regions					
	Northeast	Northwest	West	Southwest	Central	East
High	Arusha			Mbeya	Iringa	
Resident Magistrate	Arusha Tanga Moshi	Mwanza Shinyanga	Tabora		Dodoma	Dar-es-Salaam Morogoro
District	Arusha Mbulu/Arusha Korogwe Muheza Monduli Tanga	Maswa Nzega Ukerewe	Tabora	Tukuyu Rungwe	Iringa Dodoma	Morogoro
Primary	Endarini/Mbulu Pangani/Tanga Amboni/Tanga Tanga Manundu/Korogwe Muheza/Tanga Same/Pare Gonja/Pare Ugweno/Pare Ugweno/Same Marangu Sanya Juu Machame Kahe	Methe Shinyanga	Tabora	Mbeya	Bahi Dodoma Mufindi Kalenga Iringa	Kingalwina Morogoro

LANGUAGE USE IN TANZANIA

Table 9:3 Languages Used in Court

(a) Number of situations in which the different languages are used, by region

	Northeast	Northwest	West	Southwest	Central	East
High Courts						
Swahili	4			2	1	
English	5			6	4	
Vernaculars	1			1	1	
	(Safwa)			(Nyakyusa)	(Bena)	
Resident Magistrate Courts (RMC)						
Swahili	33	9	6		2	5
English	29	1	4		2	6
Vernaculars	1				2	
	(Maasai)				(Gogo)	
District Courts						
Swahili	53	27	11	14	9	6
English	9		9	2	4	
Vernaculars	(Iraqw) 2			1	1	
	(Kuria) 2			(Nyakyusa)	(Gogo)	
	(Maasai) 2					
Primary Courts						
Swahili	94	21	14	7	57	21
English						
Vernaculars	(Iraqw) 3	8			(Gogo) 3	
	(Chaga) 1	(Sukuma)			(Hehe) 3	

(b) Language Use by Region (percent)

	Northeast	Northwest	West	Southwest	Central	East
Swahili	77	86	70	70	78	84
English	18	2	30	24	11	16
Vernaculars	5	12	0	6	11	0
	100	100	100	100	100	100

(c) Language Use by Type of Court (percent)

	High	RMC	District	Primary
Swahili	28	56	79	92
English	60	43	15	0
Vernaculars	12	1	6	8
	100	100	100	100

THE USE OF LANGUAGE IN THE LAW COURTS 233

2.1 *Use of English*
English was used in the following situations:

calling up the case;
reading of the charges;
taking of oath;
prosecution of accused;
defense of accused;
cross-examination of accused, plaintiff and witness;
conversations between judge, attorneys and court clerk;
summary of charges;
medical evidence,

and in a very few cases:

answering of questions by witnesses, plaintiff and accused, pleading by the accused or plaintiff.

From the data given in Appendix 9:A the following points emerge:

(1) English was used by court personnel (judges, advocates, clerks) in 93.5% of the situations and by witnesses, accused and plaintiffs in only 6.5% of the activities.
(2) In 74.5% of the situations the speakers probably knew Swahili as Tanzanians, Kenyans or Asians living in Tanzania. 5.5% of the situations involved known foreigners who probably cannot speak Swahili or are unable to use it in court situations. In 20% of the situations we are lacking information, with the vague mention of "African" or no mention at all.
(3) The educational background is too scant to draw any conclusions.
(4) The regional origin does not provide sufficient clues either.
(5) In 32% of the situations English was used in cross-examinations, while in 68% it was used in court procedures and discussions.

2.2 *Use of the Vernaculars*
The vernaculars were used in the following situations:

pleading in self-defense;
interpreting and explaining of charges;
taking of oath;
answering of questions in cross-examination;
discussions between witness, plaintiffs and/ or accused;
summary of charges and judgment.

Table 9:4 gives the names of the languages and the number of times used.
By comparing Tables 9:3 and 9:4, the following conclusions as to the use of the vernaculars may be drawn:

(1) The western and the eastern regions used no vernaculars. The West has the highest percentage use of English (30%). The east has a high percentage use of Swahili (84%), second only to the Northwest with 86%. It is in 4th place in its use of English (12%).
(2) The Northeast displays more use of vernaculars. This may be due to

Table 9:4 Vernacular Languages Used

Language	Number of Situations
Safwa	1
Nyakyusa	2
Bena	1
Maasai	3
Gogo	8
Iraqw	5
Kuria	2
Chaga	1
Sukuma	8
Hehe	3

a far higher percentage of situations having been recorded there, especially since the use of the vernaculars occurred in only 5% of the situations, the smallest percentage of all the regions.
(3) The Northwest and its high percentage use of Sukuma in 12% of the situations indicates the importance of that language there.
(4) An equally important use of Gogo in the Central region indicates the importance of that language there, though shared with Bena and Hehe.
(5) The fact that there is no record of vernaculars used in the West, while there is a high percentage of English, may indicate that the vernaculars are of less importance in Tabora while Swahili and English have assumed a greater importance there.
(6) The Northwest has the highest percentage use of vernaculars (12%) concentrated in one language (Sukuma). It also has the lowest use of English, meaning that Sukuma will perhaps remain for a long time a dominant language.
(7) The Central region's higher percentage may also be due to a greater number of recorded situations. It is worth noting that even in the Dodoma urban situation Gogo is extensively used.

2.3 Choice of Language

Much of the choice of which language to use may depend on the people leading the proceedings, so it is interesting to look at their background and their use of the different languages. Table 9:5 shows the origin and education of judges presiding over different levels of court and analyzes their language use first as individuals and secondly according to the situation they are involved in. The same data are given for prosecutors in Table 9:6, showing less frequent use of English, more frequent use of Swahili. The presence of advocates in court situations occurred too rarely (in ten cases only) for the figures to be very indicative on the general level. These advocates were mostly Asian and 80% spoke English only. In the lower courts the court clerks play an important part and the predominance of Swahili and even the introduction of some vernaculars (Maasai, Iraqw and Gogo) is manifest in Table 9:7.

Table 9:5 The Judges and their Use of Language

(a) Origin[1]

Tanzanian	50	African	5	Asian	1
Nigerian	1	West Indian	1	Unknown	12

(b) Education

	Years of Education							
Court	17 years or LLB	12 years	10 years	9 years	8 years	6 years	Unknown	Total
High	3	—	—	—	—	—	—	3
RMC	17	—	—	—	—	—	—	17
District	—	5	4	—	1	—	7	17
Primary	—	1	7	2	10	2	11	33
Total	20	6	11	2	11	2	26	70
Percentage	28%	8%	16%	3%	16%	3%	26%	100%

(c) Use of Language

	By Judge				By Situation		
Court	English only	English and Swahili	Swahili only	Total judges	English	Swahili	Total situations
High	3	—	—	3	8	—	8
RMC	10	5	2	17	25	8	33
District	1	8	8	17	11	32	42
Primary	—	—	33	33	—	74	74
Total	14	13	43	70	44	113	157
Percentage	20%	18.5%	61.5%	100%	28%	72%	100%

[1] It can be assumed that 8 of the 12 unknown are Tanzanian. Moreover, probably all of the Africans are likewise Tanzanians. This would give a total percentage of 90% Tanzanian and 10% foreigners. All of this latter group were found in the High and RMC Courts.

2.4 *The Interpreters*

Since there is a good deal of interpretation required from one language to another in Tanzanian courts, a special analysis of this facet of language use is necessary. The interpreters (total 34) can be summarized as follows:

court clerks	19
court attendants messenger interpreter	4
clerical assistant	3
police officer	1
unknown	6
hotelier	1

Thus, 70% were court personnel, and it is conceivable that the percentage is really higher. It is impossible to deduce much from the

LANGUAGE USE IN TANZANIA

Table 9:6 The Prosecutors and their Use of Language

(a) Origin[1]

Tanzanian	34	African	1	Unknown	8

(b) Education

	LLB	12 years	10 years	9 years	8 years	7 years	Unknown	Total
Number	1	4	10	1	8	1	18	43

(c) Use of Language

Court	By Prosecutor				By Situation		
	English only	English and Swahili	Swahili only	Total prosecutors	English	Swahili	Total situations
High	3	—	—	3	4	—	4
RMC	4	4	4	12	13	10	23
District	1	4	10	15	6	22	28
Primary	—	—	13	13	—	20	20
Total	8	8	27	43	23	52	75
Percentage	18.5%	18.5%	63%	100%	30%	70%	100%

[1] It can be assumed from their use of Swahili that 96% of the prosecutors were probably Tanzanian. Even the remaining 4%, 2 prosecutors in the High Courts at Mbeye and Iringa, were quite possibly Tanzanian, even though they used only English.

Table 9:7 Court Clerks and their Use of Language

(a) Origin and Education

All 50 were Tanzanian. However, the education level was only recorded for 8 of them. Of these, one had 12 years' education, five had 8 years, one 7 years and one 4 years.

(b) Use of Language

Court	By Clerk					By Situation		
	English only	English and Swahili	Swahili only	Vernacular	Total clerks	English	Swahili/ Vernacular	Total situations
High	—	—	—	—	—	—	—	—
RMC	—	2	3	—	5	3	5	8
District	—	1	6	1	8	1	10	11
Primary	—	—	35	2[1]	37	—	62	62
Total	—	3	44	3	50	4	77	81
Percentage	—	6%	88%	6%	100%	5%	95%	100%

[1] One also used Swahili

educational level, for 53% of the information is lacking. But of the other 47%:

1 had 15 years
5 had 12 years
1 had 10 years
1 had 9 years
6 had 8 years
2 had 4 years

As to the ratings, only 15 of the 34 were recorded. Of these:

2 were given A   (= excellent);
4 were given B   (= good);
4 were given C   (= mediocre);
3 were given D   (= poor);
1 was given B/C
1 was given C/D

No ratings were given for Swahili/vernacular translation except in the case of Chaga, which was rated B. The level of education seems to have no relationship with the ratings.

2.5 *Language Switching*

We now pass to an analysis of the switching from one language to another through the use of phrases, words or total sentence constructions. Appendix 9:B contains information describing these language switching situations. Language switching seems to have occurred in all types of situations, been used by all types of individuals regardless of rank, origin or level of education. Most of the switching occurred between Swahili and English. That which occurred between the vernaculars and Swahili was for clarification or emphasis, not because of necessity. It was noted that most of those using the vernaculars actually knew Swahili but preferred to plead or answer questions in court in their own language. Hence, the switching that sometimes occurred with the vernaculars under emotional stress.

Many times the aforementioned words could have been found in Swahili but because of the prevalence of the English name, they still come easier to mind than their Swahili counterpart. Other times, however, the Swahili term may not be known or may not even exist. Such is especially the case with legal terms which may be known to the court personnel but not to the general public. Such is also the case with technical and administrative words which are slowly entering the common everyday vocabulary.

3.0 *Conclusions*

It is necessary, in concluding, to point out the difficulties involved in analyzing the use of language in the Tanzanian courts.

First of all, it was not possible to report the activities of all the courts with similar details. Depending on circumstances, such situations as the taking or conducting of the oath, the calling up of the case, the reading of the charges, the discussions between court personnel, the cross-examinations, the summary of charges and judgment could be included or not. This made it difficult to tabulate accurately the total number of language situations observed. Should the oath taking be included in definite cases if not in all? With the judgment mentioned in some cases and not in others, should the reading and the summary of the charges be included?

Secondly, not all individuals involved in the case were represented always in the data, making the total figures inaccurate. Even the judge was sometimes not included. Again, restrictions in the data collection were occasionally responsible for such situations.

Thirdly, the interpretation of language switching poses particular problems: only a few examples could be noted; the overall switching would be far more numerous and complex than is implied by the information on the forms.

Fourthly the person of the court clerk serving as interpreter made it difficult both for the observer and the analyst to distinguish between translation and cross-examination or answering of questions.

As regards ratings for translations, only Swahili and English could be considered by the observer, but since Chaga is the mother tongue of Douglas Kavugha, he also rated the vernacular translation in that specific case.

Finally percentages have to be considered critically in the light of the fore-going remarks. If percentages are based on the number of situations and activities, obviously the tabulations in this paper cannot be more than relatively accurate. If length of time were to be considered, then the observations would have to include the time element. If the importance of the activity were to be included in the rating, then a ranking by level of importance would be required.

All in all, however, in spite of its limitations, this paper provides a fair picture of the use of language in Tanzanian courts. No doubt the situation will remain in this rather fluid state until such time as Swahili does in reality become to the average Tanzanian the language of the street, bar, office, religion and marketplace.

NOTES

[1] This paper is based on the field work done by Douglas Kavugha in 1970 under a grant from the Survey of Language Use and Language Teaching in Tanzania. The data analysis was done by Donald Bobb on the basis of Douglas Kavugha's original material, while they were both working as Swahili instructors at the University of Texas at Austin.

[2] See, for example, the account in Cole and Denison (1964), especially pp. 90–120.

REFERENCE

Cole, J. S. R., and Denison, W. N., 1964, *Tanganyika. The Development of its Laws and Constitution.* London: Stevens and Sons.

Appendix 9:A   DATA COLLECTED ON LANGUAGE USE IN THE LAW COURTS

Locality	Court	Speaker	Origin	Education	Language	Situation	Interpretation
Arusha	High	Judge	W. Indian	18 years	English	(1)[1] discussion with prosecutor	—[2]
					English	(2) talking with prosecutor/advocate	—
					English	cross-examination	Swahili
		prosecutor	Tanzanian	LLB	English	(2) prosecutor	—
		advocate	Hindu	23 years	English	(2) defense of accused	—
		accused	Nkamba	—	Swahili	(1) defense/appeal	English
			Nyamwezi	—	Swahili	defense	English
			Tanzanian	8 years	Swahili	defense	English
		appelant	Tanzanian	—	Swahili	appeal	English
Mbeya	High	Judge	—	—	English	(1) cross-examination, summary, judgement	Swahili/Safwa
			—	—	English	(2) cross-examination, summary, judgement	Swahili/Nyakyusa
		prosecutor	—	—	English	(1) prosecutor	—
			—	—	English	(2) prosecutor	Swahili/Nyakyusa
		advocate	—	—	English	(1) defense of accused	—
			Asian	—	English	(2) defense of accused	—
			—	—	Swahili	talking with accused	—
		accused	Safwa	—	Safwa	(1) pleading	Swahili/English
			—	—	Swahili	talking with advocate	English
			Nyakyusa	—	Nyakyusa	(2) cross-examination	Swahili/English
Iringa	High	Judge	—	—	English	cross-examining witness	Swahili/Bena
		prosecutor	—	—	English	cross-examining witness	Swahili/Bena
		advocate	Indian	LLB	English	cross-examining witness	Swahili/Bena
			—	—	English	cross-examining witness	Swahili
		witness	Bena	—	Bena	answering questions	English
		witness	—	—	Swahili	answering questions	English

[1] Bracketed number refers to particular case observed in court.
[2] Blank normally implies 'not known'. In this column it implies 'not used'.

Locality	Court	Speaker	Origin	Education	Language	Situation	Interpretation
Arusha	RMC	Judge	—	LLB	English	(2) talking to prosecutor	—
					English/Swahili	cross-examining accused	Maasai
		prosecutor	Nyakyusa	12 years	Swahili	(1) cross-examining witness	—
					Swahili	(2) cross-examining witness	—
		clerk	Arusha	10 years	Swahili	(1) calling up case	—
		witness	Nyamwezi		Swahili	(1) taking oath, answering questions	—
			Simbiti	10 years	Swahili	(1) taking oath, answering questions	—
			Mbulu	—	Swahili	(2) answering questions	—
		accused	Maasai	—	Maasai	questioning witness	—
					Swahili	questioning witness, answering questions, taking oaths	—
Tanga	RMC (1)	Judge	African	17 years	English	(1) reading of charges	Swahili
			Tanzanian	—	English/Swahili	(2) cross-examining witness	Swahili
		prosecutor	Tanzanian	10 years	English	cross-examining witness	—
		witness	Bondei	—	Swahili	taking oath	—
					English	answering questions	—
			Zigua	—	Swahili	taking oath, answering questions	—
			Chaga	8 years	Swahili	taking oath, answering questions	—
Moshi	RMC	Judge	—	LLB	Swahili	(1) reading of charges	—
			Tanzanian		English	(2) talking to prosecutor	—
					English	(3) cross-examining witness	Swahili
			Asian	LLB	English	(4) calling up case/talking to prosecutor with advocate	Swahili
					English	(5) questioning witness	—
		Judge	Nigerian	LLB	English	(2) cross-examining witness	Swahili
					English	talking with prosecutor	Swahili
		prosecutor	Tanzanian	10 years	Swahili/English	(2) cross-examining witness	Swahili
					English	(2) talking to judge	—
					Swahili	(3) cross-examining witness	—

240

			Years	Language	Activity	Other
	advocate	African	10 years	English	(5) cross-examining witness	Swahili
		Asian	—	English	talking with judge	—
				English	(4) talking with judge	—
		British		English	questioning witness	Swahili
					talking with judge, advocate, accused	—
	clerk	—	8 years	Swahili	(1) calling up case	—
		Chaga		English	(3) talking to judge	—
				English	(4) talking to judge	—
				Swahili	taking of oath	—
	witness	Chaga		Swahili	(2) answering questions	—
		Pare	4 years	Swahili	answering questions	—
		Pare	2 years	Swahili	(4) answering questions	—
		Kenyan		English	answering questions	—
		Tanzanian		English	answering questions	—
		African		Swahili	answering questions	—
	accused	—		Swahili	(5) pleading, answering questions	—
		Chaga		Swahili	(1) answering questions, questioning witness	—
		Tanzanian		Swahili	(4) answering questions	—
		African		Swahili	(5) answering questions	—
Mwanza RMC	Judge	Chaga	—	English	talking with prosecutor	—
				Swahili	cross-examination, judgement	—
	prosecutor	Bondei	12 years	Swahili	evidence for prosecutor	—
	clerk	Sukuma	—	English	calling up case	—
				Swahili	reading charges	—
	accused	Rungi	—	Swahili	answering questions	—
Shinyanga RMC	Judge	Haya	18 years	Swahili	cross-examining witness/ talking with prosecutor	—
	prosecutor	—	—	Swahili	cross-examining accused	—
	witness	—	—	Swahili	answering questions	—
	accused	—	—	Swahili	cross-examining witness/ taking oath	—

Locality	Court	Speaker	Origin	Education	Language	Situation	Interpretation
Tabora	RMC	Judge	Chaga	17 years	Swahili	(1) cross-examining accused	—
					English	summary of charges	Swahili
					Swahili	(2) questioning accused	—
		prosecutor	Shambala	—	English	cross-examining prosecutor	—
					English	(1) talking with judge	—
					Swahili	(2) talking with judge	—
		clerk	Haya	—	Swahili	calling the accused	—
					Swahili	(2) reading charges	—
		accused	Nyamwezi	—	Swahili	(1) defense, litigation	—
			Asian	—	Swahili	(2) answering questions	—
Dodoma	RMC	Judge	Chaga	17 years	English	talking with prosecutor/clerk	—
						cross-examining accused	Gogo
		prosecutor	Kuria	—	Swahili	cross-examining witness	—
		witness	Gogo	—	Gogo/Swahili	answering questions	Swahili
		accused	Gogo	—	Swahili/Gogo	questioning witness	Swahili
Dar es Salaam	RMC	Judge	Chaga	LLB	English	(1) talking to prosecutor/advocate	—
					English	(2) talking to prosecutor/advocate	—
		prosecutor	Tanzanian	—	English	(1) talking to judge	—
					English/Swahili	(2) cross-examining witness	Swahili
					Swahili	cross-examining witness	—
		adocate	Hindu	—	English	submission	—
					English	(1) cross-examining plaintiff	Swahili
		witness	—	—	Swahili	(2) cross-examining witness	Swahili
			Gogo	—	Swahili	(2) answering questions	—
		plaintiff	Tanzanian	—	Swahili	(1) answering questions	English
Morogoro	RMC	Judge	Tanzanian	17 years	English	(1) talking to prosecutor	—
					Swahili	cross-examining witness	—
			Chaga	17 years	English	(2) reading charges, judgement	Swahili
		prosecutor			English	(1) talking to judge, judgement	—

242

Court	Role	Ethnic group	Years	Language	Activity	Language
Arusha District	advocate	Mwanga	10 years	English	(2) cross-examining plaintiff / giving of evidence	Swahili
				Swahili		—
	witness	Asian	19 years	English	(1) cross-examining witness	Swahili
	accused	Nguru	—	Swahili	(2) answering questions	—
		Tanzanian	—	Swahili	(1) answering questions	—
		Yao	—	Swahili	(2) answering questions, defense	—
	judge	—	10 years	Swahili	cross-examining accused/talking with prosecutor and court clerk	—
	prosecutor	—	8 years	Swahili	cross-examining accused and witnesses, asking for exhibit	—
	witness	Meru	—	Swahili	answering questions	—
	plaintiff	Meru	—	Swahili	answering questions	—
	accused	Arusha	—	Swahili	answering questions	—
Mbulu District	judge	Pare	10 years	Swahili	cross-examining	Iraqw
	prosecutor	Chaga	8 years	Swahili	cross-examining accused talking with judge and clerk	Iraqw
	plaintiff	Iraqw	—	Iraqw	answering questions	Swahili
	accused	Iraqw	—	Iraqw	answering questions	Swahili
Korogwe District	judge	Fipa	—	English	(1) reading charges / explaining charges	Swahili
				Swahili		—
				English	(2) reading charges / explaining charges and cross-examining	Swahili
				Swahili		—
	prosecutor	Chaga	—	Swahili	(1) cross-examining accused and witness	—
	clerk	Shambala	—	Swahili	(2) cross-examining	—
	witness	Zigula	—	Swahili	(2) calling up case, conducting oath	—
		Shambala	—	Swahili	(1) answering questions	—
		Zigula	—	Swahili	(2) answering questions	—
	accused	Shambala	—	Swahili	(1) answering questions, questioning witness	—

Locality	Court	Speaker	Origin	Education	Language	Situation	Interpretation
Muheza/Tanga	District		Ruanda	—	Swahili	(2) answering questions	—
			Haya	—	Swahili	answering questions	—
			Chaga	—	Swahili	answering questions	—
			Nyiha	—	Swahili	answering questions	—
			Shambala	—	Swahili	answering questions	—
			Sukuma	—	Swahili	questioning plaintiff	—
		judge	African	8 years	Swahili/English	(1) talking with prosecutor	—
					Swahili	(2) cross-examining witness	—
					English	talking with prosecutor and court clerk	—
					Swahili	cross-examining accused	—
					English	talking with prosecutor	—
					Swahili	(3) cross-examining accused	—
		prosecutor	Zigula	10 years	Swahili	(1) talking with judge	—
		clerk	Chaga	10 years	English	(3) talking with judge	—
			Pare	8 years	Swahili	(2) reading charges	—
		witness	Bondei	8 years	Swahili	(3) reading charges	—
			Bondei	—	Swahili	(1) answering questions/cross-examining accused	—
					Swahili	(1) testimony/answering questions	—
		accused	Shambala	—	Swahili	(1) questioning witness	—
			Arab	—	Swahili	(2) answering questions	—
			Bondei	—	Swahili	(3) answering questions	—
Moduli	District	judge	Digo	12 years	Swahili	(1) cross-examining accused	Kuria
					Swahili	reading judgement, ordering constable	—
					Swahili	(2) cross-examining	—
					English	talking to prosecutor	—
		prosecutor	Mbunga	10 years	Swahili	(1) cross-examining accused	Kuria
					Swahili	*cross-examining witness*	Maasai

		Role	Ethnicity	Years	Language	Activity	
Tanga	District	clerk	Maasai	8 years	Swahili	talking to judge	—
		witness	Pare	—	Swahili	(2) cross-examining	—
			Kuria	12 years	English	talking to judge	—
		accused	Maasai	—	Maasai	(1) conducting oath	Swahili
					Maasai	answering questions	—
					Kuria	answering questions	Swahili
					Swahili	(2) answering questions	—
Maswa	District	judge	Digo	—	Swahili	cross-examining accused	—
		prosecutor	Chaga	10 years	English	talking to prosecutor	—
					Swahili	cross-examining witness	—
		witness	Shambala	—	English	talking to judge	—
			Bondei	8 years	Swahili	answering questions	—
		accused	Bondei	8 years	Swahili	answering questions	—
					Swahili	questioning plaintiff	—
Nzega	District	judge	Haya	10 years	Swahili	cross-examining witness and accused, talking to prosecutor	—
		prosecutor	Pare	12 years	Swahili	cross-examining witness	—
		clerk	Tanzanian	—	Swahili	calling up case	—
		witness	Nyaturu	—	Swahili	answering questions	—
		accused	Sukuma	—	Swahili	answering questions, questioning plaintiff	—
	District	judge	Nyakyusa	10 years	Swahili	(1) reading charges, cross-examining accused, talking with prosecutor	—
					Swahili	(2) reading charges, cross-examining witness	—
		prosecutor	Ngoni	—	Swahili	(2) cross-examining	—
		witness	Hindu	4 years	Swahili	(1) answering questions	—
			Tanzania	—	Swahili	(2) answering questions	—

Locality	Court	Speaker	Origin	Education	Language	Situation	Interpretation
		accused	Fipa	—	Swahili	(1) answering questions, questioning witness	—
			Nyamwezi	—	Swahili	(2) answering questions, questioning witness	—
Tukuya/ Mbeya	District	judge	—	—	English	talking to prosecutor	—
					Swahili	cross-examining witnesses	—
		prosecutor	—	—	English	talking to judge	—
					Swahili	cross-examining witnesses	—
		witness	Nyakyusa	8 years	Swahili	answering questions	—
			Meru	8 years	Swahili	answering questions	—
		accused	Nyakyusa		Swahili	answering questions/questioning witnesses	—
Rungwe	District	judge	Haya	—	Swahili	cross-examining accused	Nyakyusa
					Swahili	talking to prosecutor/ cross-examining witnesses	—
		prosecutor	Tanzanian	—	Swahili	cross-examining accused and witnesses	Nyakyusa
					Swahili	talking to judge	—
		witness	Nyakyusa	—	Swahili	answering questions	Nyakyusa
			Bena	—	Swahili	answering questions	Nyakyusa
		accused	Nyakyusa	—	Nyakyusa	answering questions	Nyakyusa
Iringa	District	judge	—	—	English	cross-examining witness/ talking to prosecutor	—
					Swahili	cross-examining accused	—
		prosecutor	Sukuma	—	English	talking to judge	—
					Swahili	cross-examining witness	—
		witness	Tanzanian	—	English	answering judge's questions	—
					Swahili	answering prosecutor's questions	—
		accused	Hehe	—	Swahili	answering questions/questioning witnesses	—

Location	Court	Role	Ethnicity	Experience	Language	Activity	
Ukerewe	District	judge	Kuria	12 years	Swahili	cross-examining, talking with prosecutor	—
		witness	Luo	—	Swahili	answering questions/questioning other witness	—
			Kerewe	—	Swahili	answering questions	—
			—	—	Swahili	answering questions	—
		accused	Kerewe	—	Swahili	answering questions	—
Tabora	District	judge	Sukuma	12 years	English	(1) cross-examining witness	—
					English	(2) talking with prosecutor	—
		prosecutor	—	—	English	(1) cross-examining witness/ talking to judge	—
					Swahili	(2) cross-examining accused and witness/reading of charges	—
		advocate	Shambala	12 years	Swahili	(1) cross-examining accused	—
		clerk	Indian	15 years	English	(1) calling up case	—
					English	explanation of charges	—
					Swahili	(1) talking oath/answering questions taking oath	—
		witness	Tanzanian	—	English	(2) answering questions	—
			Chaga	—	Swahili	(1) defense/questioning witness and other accused	—
		accused	Fipa	—	Swahili	answering questions	—
			Arab	—	English	(2) pleading before court/questioning witness	—
					Swahili		—
Dodoma	District	judge	Tanzanian	12 years	Swahili	reading charges	—
		prosecutor	—	—	Swahili	(1) cross-examining witness	Gogo
		witness	—	—	Gogo	answering questions	Swahili
					Swahili	(2) answering questions	—
		accused	—	—	Swahili	questioning witness.	—
Morogoro	District	judge	Nyamwezi	12 years	Swahili	calling up case/cross-examining cross-examining appelant/talking to judge and other clerk	—
		clerk	Lugulu	—	Swahili		—

Locality	Court	Speaker	Origin	Education	Language	Situation	Interpretation
Endarimi/ Mbulu	Primary	appellant	Lugulu	—	Swahili	answering questions	—
		judge	Tanzanian	8 years	Swahili	cross-examinining accused	Iraqw
		clerk	Iraqw	—	Swahili	cross-examining plaintiff/ talking to assessors talking to judge	—
		witness	Iraqw		Swahili Iraqw	cross-examining of witness answering questions	— Swahili
		plaintiff	Iraqw		Iraqw Swahili	answering questions	Swahili —
		accused	Iraqw		Swahili	answering questions	—
Pangani	Primary	judge	African Digo	— —	Swahili Swahili	(1) cross-examining accused (2) cross-examining accused/ calling court messenger (3) cross-examining plaintiff	— —
		clerk	Swahili Arab Bondei	— — —	Swahili Swahili Swahili	(1) explanation of charges questioning plaintiff (2) answering questions	— — —
		witness	Digo Arab	— —	Swahili Swahili	oath and testimony answering questions	— —
		plaintiff	Digo Digo	— —	Swahili Swahili	(1) answering questions (2) answering questions	— —
		accused	Bondei Swahili	— —	Swahili Swahili	(1) answering questions (2) answering questions	— —
Same/Pare	Primary	judge	Nguru	9 years	Swahili	calling up cases/reading charges/ cross-examining accused/witness cross-examining witness/ talking to judge	—
		prosecutor	Makonde	8 years	Swahili		—
		clerk	Pare Zigula	— —	Swahili Swahili	questioning witness questioning witness	— —
		witness	Pare	4 years	Swahili	answering questions	—
		accused	Pare	4 years	Swahili	questioning witness	—

Location	Court	Role	Ethnicity	Years	Language	Activity
Gonja/Pare	Primary	judge	Shambala	8 years	Swahili	calling up case/judgement/cross-examining
		prosecutor	Tanzanian	8 years	Swahili	prosecution/talking with judge
		clerk	Pare	—	Swahili	talking to judge/summary of case
		accused	Pare	—	Swahili	pleading guilty
Ugweno/Same	Primary	judge	Pare	6 years	Swahili	calling up case/talking with clerks
		clerk	Pare	6 years	Swahili	questioning accused/witness/talking to judge/other clerk
		witness	Pare	7 years	Swahili	answering questions
				8 years	Swahili	answering questions
		plaintiff	Chaga	4 years	Swahili	answering questions
		accused	Pare	8 years	Swahili	answering questions
				4 years	Swahili	answering questions
				3 years	Swahili	answering questions
Amboni	Primary	judge	Zigula	—	Swahili	(1) cross-examining accused
			Bondei	—	Swahili	(2) cross-examining
		clerk	—	—	Swahili	reading charges
		witness	Nyasa	—	Swahili	(1) answering questions
			Swahili	—	Swahili	(2) answering questions
			Zigula	—	Swahili	answering questions
		plaintiff	Pare	—	Swahili	(1) answering questions
		accused	Pare	—	Swahili	answering questions
Tanga	Primary	judge	—	10 years	Swahili	cross-examination/summary
		witness	Shambala	—	Swahili	answering questions
		accused	Shambala	—	Swahili	answering questions
			Nyamwezi	—	Swahili	answering questions
Manundu/Korogwe	Primary	judge	—	—	Swahili	(1) cross-examining defendent/talk with clerk
				—	Swahili	(2) reading charges/judgement
			Shambala	—	Swahili	(3) cross-examining accused

Locality	Court	Speaker	Origin	Education	Language	Situation	Interpretation
Muheza	Primary	clerk	Zigna	—	Swahili	cross-examining accused	—
		accused	Shambala	—	Swahili	answering questions	—
			Pare	—	Swahili	(1) pleading	—
			Bondei	—	Swahili	(2) answering questions	—
			Zigula	—	Swahili	(3) answering questions	—
		judge	Bondei	—	Swahili	cross-examining accused/ talking with clerk	—
		clerk	Pare	8 years	Swahili	reading charges/ administering oath	
		witness	Swahili	—	Swahili	answering questions	—
		accused	Zigula	—	Swahili	answering questions	—
Marangu	Primary	judge	Shambala	8 years	Swahili	calling up case/cross-examining accused/witnesses/ talking with clerks	—
		clerk	Chaga	—	Swahili	cross-examining accused/ witnesses/talking with judge	—
		witness	Chaga	5 years	Swahili	answering questions	—
		plaintiff	Chaga	8 years	Swahili	answering questions	—
		accused	Chaga	3 years	Swahili	answering questions	—
Sanya Juu	Primary	judge	Zanaki	10 years	Swahili	(1) cross-examining accused/ witness	—
						(2) cross-examining accused	Chaga
		prosecutor	Mwera	8 years	Swahili	(1) reading charges/cross-examining accused, plaintiff, witnesses	
						(2) talking to judge	—
		clerk	Chaga	7 years	Swahili	(1) calling up case	—
				4 years	Swahili		—
		witness	Chaga	—	Swahili	answering questions	—

Court	Type	Role	Ethnic group	Years	Language	Activity	Other
		plaintiff	Chaga	—	Swahili	(2) answering questions	—
		accused	Kisii	—	Swahili	answering questions	—
			Nilyamba	—	Swahili	(1) answering questions	—
			Chaga	—	Swahili	(2) pleading	—
Machame	Primary	judge	Zalamo	10 years	Swahili	calling up case/talking with clerks/cross-examining	—
		clerk	Chaga	—	Swahili	questioning accused/calling out to attendant/talking with judge/other clerk	—
		accused	—	—	Swahili	pleading/answering questions	—
Kahe	Primary	judge	Chaga	8 years	Swahili	calling up case/cross-examining accused/talking with clerks	—
		clerk	Kahe	—	Swahili	questioning accused/talking to judge	—
		plaintiff	Kahe	—	Swahili	answering questions	—
		accused	Pare	—	Swahili	answering questions/complaining of attendants conduct	—
Methe	Primary	judge	Haya	8 years	Swahili	talking to prosecutor and clerks/calling court attendant	—
		prosecutor	Kuria	8 years	Swahili	cross-examining	Sukuma
					Swahili	cross-examining/talking to judge	Sukuma
		clerk	Sukuma		Sukuma	conducting oath	—
					Swahili	calling up case/reading charges	Sukuma
		witness	Sukuma	—	Swahili	talking with judge	—
					Sukuma	taking oath/answering questions	Swahili
		accused	Sukuma	—	Sukuma	questioning witnesses/answering questions	Swahili

Locality	Court	Speaker	Origin	Education	Language	Situation	Interpretation
Shinyanga	Primary	judge	Zalamo	10 years	Swahili	(1) cross-examining/talking to clerks	—
			Segeju	10 years	Swahili	(2) cross-examining/talking to clerks	Sukuma
			Zalamo	10 years	Swahili	(3) calling up case/reading charges	—
		clerk	Ngoni	—	Swahili	(1) questioning accused and witnesses	—
			Zalamo	—	Swahili	cross-examining/talking to judge	Swahili
		plaintiff	Sukuma		Sukuma	(2) cross-examining	—
			—	3 years	Swahili	(3) questioning accused/plaintiff	Swahili
			Nyamwezi	6 years	Sukuma	(1) answering questions	—
		accused	Sukuma	—	Swahili	(2) answering questions	Swahili
			Sukuma	—	Sukuma	(1) answering questions	—
			Sukuma	—	Swahili	(2) answering questions	Swahili
						(3) pleading	—
Tabora/Urban	Primary	judge	Nyamwezi	8 years	Swahili	(1) reading charges/talking to prosecutor/cross-examining	—
					Swahili	(2) reading charges/talking with clerks/questioning accused	—
		prosecutor	Jita	7 years	Swahili	(2) cross-examining/talking with clerk	—
		clerk	—	8 years	Swahili	cross-examining	—
			—	—	Swahili	talking with judge/questioning accused/plaintiff/witnesses	—
		witness	Nyamwezi	—	Swahili	answering questions	—
			Vinza	—	Swahili	answering questions	—
		plaintiff	Nyamwezi	—	Swahili	(1) answering questions	—
			Nyamwezi	—	Swahili	(2) answering questions	—

Location	Court	Role	Ethnicity	Years	Language	Activities	Other
Mbeya Urban	Primary	accused	Rundi Nyamwezi	— —	Swahili Swahili	(1) answering questions (2) answering questions	— —
		judge	Ngoni	8 years	Swahili	(1) reading charges/cross-examining accused (2) reading charges/talking with prosecutor/cross examining	—
		prosecutor	—	—	Swahili	(1) cross-examining plaintiff	—
		plaintiff	Nyamwezi Nyakyusa	9 years —	Swahili Swahili	(2) talking with judge (1) explanation of charges/answering questions	— —
		accused	Chaga Nyakyusa	— —	Swahili Swahili	(1) pleading/answering questions (2) answering questions	— —
Bana	Primary	judge	Zarawa	12 years	Swahili Swahili	cross-examining talking with clerks	Gogo —
		clerk	Hehe	—	Swahili Gogo	talking with judge questioning accused	— Gogo
		accused	Gogo Maasai	— —	Swahili Gogo	questioning accused talking to judge answering questions	Swahili — Swahili
Dodoma Urban	Primary	judge	—	9 years	Swahili	(1) summary of charges/judgement (2) cross-examining accused talking with clerks/judgement	— Gogo —
		prosecutor	Zigula	10 years	Swahili Swahili	(3) cross-examining witness (2) cross-examining accused talking to judge	Gogo — Gogo
		clerk	Nyamwezi Zalamo	— —	Swahili Swahili	(2) cross-examining accused questioning accused/talking with clerks	— Gogo
		witness plaintiff accused	Gogo — Rangi	— — —	Swahili Swahili Swahili	(2) answering questions answering questions (1) answering questions	— — —

253

Locality	Court	Speaker	Origin	Education	Language	Situation	Interpretation
Mufidi	Primary	judge	Gogo	—	Gogo/Swahili	answering questions/defence	Swahili
			Rangi	—	Swahili	(3) answering questions	—
		judge	Hehe	8 years	Swahili	(1) cross-examining plaintiff	—
		prosecutor	Tanzanian	—	Swahili	(2) talking with clerk	—
		clerk	Hehe	—	Swahili	(1) cross-examining	—
						(2) cross-examining witness/talking with judge	—
		witness	Hehe	—	Swahili	(1) Oath and testimony	—
			Kinga	—	Swahili	(2) answering questions	—
		plaintiff	Hehe	—	Swahili	(1) answering questions	—
			Kinga	—	Swahili	(2) answering questions	—
		accused	—	—	Swahili	(1) answering questions	—
			Hehe	—	Swahili	(2) questioning plaintiff	—
Kalenga	Primary	judge	Nyakyusa	8 years	Swahili	reading charges/cross-examining witness	Hehe
						talking to clerk	—
		prosecutor	Ngoni	8 years	Swahili	cross-examining accused/talking to judge	—
		clerk	Hehe	—	Swahili	cross-examining witness	Hehe
						cross-examining accused and witnesses	—
		witness	Hehe	—	Hehe	answering questions	Swahili
		plaintiff	Hehe	8 years	Swahili/Hehe	answering questions	—
		accused	Hehe	—	Swahili	answering questions	—
Iringa	Primary	judge	Ndali	10 years	Swahili	(1) reading charges/cross-examining/talking with clerks	—
						(2) reading charges	—
		prosecutor	Ngoni	—	Swahili	(1) cross-examining plaintiff	—
		clerk	Hehe	—	Swahili	cross-examining accused/	—

			Subi	—	talking with judge cross-examining talking with judge
				Swahili	(2) cross-examining accused and witnesses
		witness	Hehe	—	answering questions
		plaintiff	Bena	—	(1) answering questions/additional accusations
		accused	Hehe	—	answering questions
				Swahili	(2) answering questions/ questioning witnesses
Kingalwina	Primary	judge	Chaga	8 years Swahili	(1) cross-examining accused and witnesses
				Swahili	(2) cross-examining accused/ talking to meddenger
		clerk	Lugulu	—	(1) cross-examining witnesses/ talking with judge
				Swahili	(2) cross-examining accused
		witness	Lugulu	—	(1) answering questions
		plaintiff	Lugulu	—	(1) questioning accused
			Zalamo	—	(2) answering questions/ questioning accused
		accused	Lugulu	—	(1) answering questions/ questioning plaintiff
			Kwere	—	(2) answering questions and giving statement
Morogoro	Primary	judge	Lugulu	—	reading charges
		prosecutor	Meru	—	cross-examining accused and plaintif/talking to judge
		plaintiff	Lugulu	—	answering questions
		accused	Zulu	—	answering questions giving statements

255

Appendix 9:B LANGUAGE SWITCHING IN COURT

Locality	Court	Person	Origin	Training	Lang(1)	Lang(2)	Activity	Situation
Arusha	RMC	accused	Chaga	—	Swahili	English	pleading	English words only
		judge	—	LLB	English	Swahili	cross-examining	translated into Maasai
		prosecutor	Nyakyusa	12 years	Swahili	English	cross-examining	English words
		court clerk	Arusha	10 years	English	Swahili	talking to prosecutor	entire sentences
Tanga	RMC (2)	judge	African	LLB	English	Swahili	cross-examining	one phrase: *saa sita*
		prosecutor	African	10 years	English	Swahili	cross-examining	entire sentences
	RMC (1)	judge	Tanzanian	—	Swahili	English	talking to prosecutor & police officer prosecutor	entire sentences
Moshi	RMC	prosecutor	Tanzanian	10 years	English	Swahili	cross-examining	word: *askari*
		accused	African	—	Swahili	English	pleading	word: "private road"
		witness	Pare	—	Swahili	English	answering questions	word: "operate"
		prosecutor	Tanzanian	10 years	English	Swahili	cross-examining	Swahili to stress point
		witness	Pare	2 years	Swahili	Pare	answering questions	one word only

Locality	Court	Person	Origin	Training	Lang(1)	Lang(2)	Activity	Situation
Mwanza	RMC	court clerk	Chaga	—	Swahili	English	translation	single words
		witness	African	12 years	Swahili	Arabic	oath taking	Moslem words
		Prosecutor	Bondei	12 years	Swahili	English	prosecution	answering judge
Shinyanga	RMC	prosecutor	Nyanya	—	Swahili	English	cross-examining	English words in Swahili sentence

Tabora	RMC	witness(2) accused judge	— — Chaga	— — 17 years	Swahili Swahili Swahili	English English English	answering answering talking to prosecutor during cross-examining	English words only English words only used English even though Swahili known by both
Dodoma	RMC	witness	Gogo	—	Swahili	Gogo	answering questions	entire portions of speaking entire Swahili sentences
Dar-es-Salaam	RMC	prosecutor advocate	Tanzanian —	— —	English Swahili	Swahili English	cross-examining cross-examining	clarify Swahili question
Morogoro	RMC	advocate prosecutor	Asian Nyamwanga	19 years 10 years	English Swahili	Swahili English	cross-examining prosecution	one English word one English sentence
Korogwe	DC	prosecutor	Chaga	—	Swahili	English	cross-examining	answering question from judge
		judge	Fipa	—	English	Swahili	charges	reading in Swahili explaining in English
Muheza	SC	judge	African	8 years	Swahili	English	cross-examining	questioned prosecutor in English to question accused
		judge	African	—	English	Swahili	cross-examining	answer question from judge
Monduli	DC	prosecutor	Chaga	10 years	Swahili	English	cross-examining	used English to talk with prosecutor
		judge	Digo	12 years	Swahili	English	cross-examining	used English word only
		witness	Pare	12 years	Swahili	English	answering questions	
Tanga	DC	prosecutor	Chaga	10 years	Swahili	English	cross-examining	used English with judge
Maswa	DC	judge witness	Haya Nyakuru	10 years —	Swahili Swahili	English English	cross-examining answering questions	used English words used English word

Locality	Court	Person	Origin	Training	Lang(1)	Lang(2)	Activity	Situation
Tabora	DC	witness	Tanzanian	—	Swahili	English	evidence & questions	used English for technical word
		accused	Fipa	—	Swahili	English	answering questions	used English words
		witness	Chaga	—	Swahili	English	answering questions	used English words
Tukuyu		witness	Bena	—	Swahili	English	answering questions	one English word
Endarini	PC	court clerk	Iraqw	—	Swahili	Iraqw	cross-examining	clarify question
Pangani	PC	judge	African	—	Swahili	English	cross-examining	one word only
		court clerk	Bondei	—	Swahili	English	cross-examining	one word only
Amboni	PC	judge	Bondei	—	Swahili	English	cross-examining	one word only
Manundu	PC	judge	—	—	Swahili	English	charges	one word only
		accused	Pare	—	Swahili	English	pleading	English words only
		judge	Shambala	—	Swahili	English	judgement	quoting the law
Gonja	PC	prosecutor	Tanzanian	8 years	Swahili	English	prosecution	one word only
Kalange	PC	plaintiff	Hehe	8 years	Swahili	Hehe	answering	one sentence

The column "language switching" is probably quite inadequately completed. It no doubt may have been difficult to distinguish between interpretation and switching. Conversations between the court personnel in the midst of cross-examinations can be considered a switching from Swahili to English, although this is rarely mentioned on the forms. Clarification of points in another language, whether English or a vernacular, likewise was no doubt frequently not noted. The following words were mentioned as having been used in the midst of Swahili sentences:

lock up	serious	shortage	application form
mason	cage	executive officer	remark
sick sheet	accused	messenger	entry permit
statement	private road	safe	licence
why	frame	judiciary	appeal
exhibit	operation	cash box	fact
bond	repair	arrest warrant	
		cash book	
		council	
		strong room	
		in charge	
		authorize	
		duplicate	
		telegraphist	

The following Swahili words were used in the midst of English sentences: *saa sita, askari*.

258

PART THREE

LANGUAGE IN EDUCATION

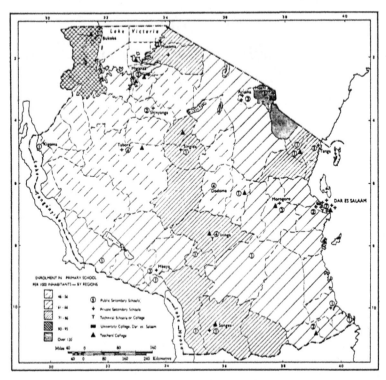

Map 7 Education in Tanzania. Reproduced with kind permission from *Tanzania in Maps*, edited by L. Berry (University of London Press, 1971)

10 THE HISTORICAL BACKGROUND TO NATIONAL EDUCATION IN TANZANIA

John White

> The education provided must therefore encourage the development in each citizen of three things: an enquiring mind; an ability to learn from what others do, and reject or adapt it to his own needs; and a basic confidence in his own position as a free and equal member of the society, who values others and is valued by them for what he does and not for what he obtains.
>
> *Education for Self-Reliance*
> President Julius Nyerere[1]

1.0 Introduction

A necessary preliminary to any real understanding of the modern educational system of Tanzania is the reading of three short works by President Nyerere, namely 'Education for Self-Reliance', 'Socialism and Rural Development' and 'Freedom and Development'. With the publication, in 1967, of the 'Arusha Declaration', and of these three guide lines to development, Tanzania has gone further than any other developing country in defining its political standpoint, its social values and its economic aims (see Nyerere, 1968a). Briefly, the 'Arusha Declaration' calls for the establishment of a socialist democracy, in which the major means of production are under the control of peasants and workers, and the exploitation of man by man is progressively eradicated. The socialist democracy is being built on the firm foundations of the three principles of the traditional African family, namely respect for the individual, sharing of all the basic necessities of life and obligation to work. To these principles are added, in the President's words, "the knowledge and the instruments necessary for the defeat of the poverty which existed in traditional African society" (1968a: 110). The Tanzanian form of socialism known as *Ujamaa* (familyhood), emphasises the concepts of self-reliance and the development of people through democratic decision making. It also emphasises that the only way in which you cause people to undertake their own development is by education and leadership.

The structure of education in Tanzania is in an extreme state of flux, as the Government attempts the transformation of a system for the schooling of a minority that was based upon the assumptions of a colonial and capitalist society into a system that will inculcate a sense of commitment to the total community, and will prepare young people to raise their living standards through socialist organisation. The history of educational endeavour, particularly over the past fifty years is a case study of the achievements and problems of education as an extrusive agent of social change, and is a necessary preliminary to any understanding of the raison d'être of the current structure of education.

2.0 The Colonial Inheritance

In the pre-colonial period, education was carried on by elders and parents. Children would be taught in an informal manner about agriculture and animal husbandry and, in the case of young girls, about housekeeping and child care. Some youths would be taught crafts such as iron-working and pot-making. Others would learn how to treat sickness by the use of herbs and other remedies. They would learn while they were doing. In the evenings they would get to know about the culture, history and beliefs of their community by listening to the stories of the elders. The values of the society would be passed on in actual social situations. In many ways, this form of education was admirably suited to the needs of the people.

Even before the German government announced its colonial intention in 1885, Catholic and Protestant missions had opened up schools in various parts of the country. The aims of these schools were usually two-fold. First, they sought to impart literacy in order that those passing through these institutions would become able to read Christian literature and later help to spread mission teaching. Secondly, technical training was given as a means towards obtaining certain types of craftsmen and skilled manual workers who were required for mission development. In the early years it was difficult to obtain pupils. Usually the wishes of the local chief decided whether or not a school had any scholars. Girls' education was particularly disliked.

Official participation in education began when the colonial regime perceived that more of the indigenous people would have to become proficient in arithmetic and Swahili (using the Latin script) if the new needs for clerks and craftsmen in administration, railways and plantations were to be met without recourse to expensive immigrant labour. The first German government schools were opened in Tanga in 1893 and schooling in the town was made compulsory six years later. By 1903 there were 20 public primary schools in Tanganyika, with some 1,550 pupils. A German commentator, Martin Schlunk, writing in 1914, summarising the aims of education at that time, noted that the German government was in the beginning interested only in educating a sufficient number of Africans to be used as interpreters, clerks, policemen, etc., and that while the mission schools were concerned mainly with moral and character training, the government schools concentrated heavily on vocational instruction. The same author noted his concern at problems which were already apparent at this early stage of development; namely, that there was a tendency for students to leave their respective villages and make their way to the cities to find employment with the government or with private business firms in order to raise their social position and that if they did not find suitable positions, they often ended up as members of an educated proletariat unwilling to do any work that they considered beneath them. This, he considered, not to be the fault of the schools as such, but was the necessary by-product of colonial development.

Formal education in schools, whether it included some practical education or not, was to a very large degree intellectual education. How then could the schools be reformed so that education for work would become an integral part of the education process? The answer to that problem appeared to be that it was necessary to integrate the school into the neighbourhood in which it was situated. Would it not be possible to devote three days a week to agricultural training? Only then would the schools be able to counter the migration to the cities. Only then would they educate useful members of society.

During the first decade of the 20th century, means of communications and, subsequently, cash crop production, developed rapidly. This economic progress led to increased demands for literate labour. To meet these demands the colonial authorities encouraged the missions to expand their educational facilities. Those who did so received government grants. At the same time, the number of government schools was increased. There were in 1913 nearly a hundred of these schools, mostly sited along the coast and in the larger towns. Of more than 6,000 pupils in attendance, about 3,500 were in lower primary schools (Standards I–IV), while the remainder received the equivalent of an upper primary course with a technical bias. Already a government education department was in existence, having an establishment of 16 Europeans and 159 African teachers.

The main role in education at this time was played by the missions. At the outbreak of the 1914–18 war, they claimed to be teaching over 110,000 pupils in more than 1,800 schools, although many of these establishments can hardly have warranted the title. The missions, it would seem, participated in providing vocational education on ethical grounds, believing that regular work developed good character. Pupils were trained for crafts which it was thought the local community might desire, but, as the strength of this demand was difficult to assess, eventually the churches began to educate for mission enterprises as well. One reason for their willingness to prepare clerks for government service was the missionaries' belief that the Muslim civil servant was instrumental in the spread of Islam in the interior. Schools during this era could hardly have presented an attractive image. They lacked books and pens and all the aids nowadays regarded as essential. Their classrooms were exceedingly simple and sometimes non-existent. Yet, in spite of these deficiencies it is estimated that by 1914 perhaps 10% of the school age population was in school. During the First World War, however, schooling virtually disappeared. The German government teachers were engaged in the fighting while the German missionaries were either interned or removed on the arrival of the Allied forces.

As a result of the war, mainland Tanzania's political status changed significantly. The British, who took over the administration of the country, unlike the Germans, were not ruling by right of conquest. They governed Tanganyika by appointment of the League of Nations. One consequence was that they were legally bound to promote the material and moral well-being and social progress of its inhabitants and to help them to, eventually, stand by themselves. Although the League intervened little in the affairs of administration, the "mandate" had some influence upon the government's role in education. Even so, it was taken for granted by the new administration that many years would have to elapse before mainland Tanzanians could be granted independence. Thus the accent in education was still largely in training individuals for the service of a colonial state.

One of the first measures of the governing authority was the appointment in 1920 of a Director of Education. The next three years were mainly spent on planning aims and programmes, and in surveying needs and possibilities. Yet by 1924, 5,000 children were attending some 72 public educational institutions. Most of these were lower primary establishments, but a small number offered a slightly higher education. Another 162,000 pupils studied in schools run by missions. Altogether about 21% of the child population was registered as attending school, although only about 13% did so regularly. During this period, most of the schools were primary schools, offering a four-year course designed to achieve literacy in the vernacular, to inculcate a knowledge of arithmetic, hygiene, simple agricultural improvements, and, in mission schools, to impart an understanding of, and belief in, Christianity. Equipment was scarce and the standard of teaching low. "Wastage" and infrequent attendance were, not surprisingly, major ills.

The Phelps–Stokes missions, which visited mainland Tanzania in 1924, and the Ormsby–Gore Commission, which came to East Africa shortly afterwards, both considered that the administration was not paying sufficient attention to African education and ought to cooperate more closely with the missions in this field. Among the members of the Phelps–Stokes Commission were Thomas Jesse Jones of the Hampton Institute in the United States, with long experience of educational work with rural American Negro communities and James Aggrey the most distinguished of West African educationists. The achievement of the Commission was to crystallise the concept of "adaptation", which remained the foundation of educational policy in Tanganyika until Independence.

The Phelps–Stokes Commission saw language as a major vehicle for adaptation, viewing the vernacular languages as particularly valuable:

> With full appreciation of the European language, the value of the Native tongue is immensely more vital, in that it is one of the chief means of preserving whatever is good in Native customs, ideas and ideals, and thereby preserving what is more important than all else, namely self-respect ... no greater injustice can be committed against a people than to deprive them of their own language. (T. J. Jones, 1925: 8; see also Colonial Office, 1925.)

Following these visits, a special conference was held in Dar es Salaam to draft a bill to provide for a state system of African education, with provision for grants-in-aid to approved voluntary agencies. As a result of this legislation, recurrent expenditure on education, which had been £15,000 or 1.2% of the country's total revenue in 1924/5, rose to more than £80,000 or 3.35% in 1928/9.

The new impetus in education coincided with the arrival of Sir Donald Cameron as Governor in 1925. The reorganisation of the system involved the creation of village schools providing a four year terminal course in the vernacular and Swahili. The curriculum was to be aimed at producing a literate and enlightened farmer, though it is doubtful if either aim was effectively achieved with the majority of pupils.

The period which saw the introduction of "Indirect Rule" by the British Administration through African Chiefs, also witnessed the setting up of Central Schools, with a selection bias towards the sons of chiefs. These institutions gave a further four years of schooling, in which more advanced work in the 3 Rs and practical subjects was undertaken. Agricultural instruction, which had been the keynote of the 1922 programme, was not neglected but the knowledge imparted was more suitable for a local agricultural adviser than for a practical farmer. Doubts were expressed, based upon the Indian experience, of the wisdom of the rapid expansion of academic education in the Central Schools. By 1927 there were 14 of these schools in existence, 4 under government aegis, and 10 run by missions. All were boarding institutions, a necessity in view of the scattered population at that time. It was recognised in the same year that even the Central School could not provide the degree of education required for the increasingly complex occupations in the public and private sectors of the expanding economy and it was proposed that a Commercial Secondary School should be founded. Staff shortages, however, delayed the start of the school until 1929, when it began at Tabora. Here a course in book-keeping, typing and office routine was grafted on to the existing Central School.

In 1930 the steady economic development upon which educational "progress" depended came to a sudden and staggering downturn, with the onset of world-wide economic depression. Between 1929 and 1931 the country's exports dropped from £3.7 million to £1.6 million, while public revenue fell by 25%. "Retrenchment" became the order of the day in all government departments, including Education. Even when the worst of the economic slump was over the revival of German colonial claims to mainland Tanzania tended to discourage planning and development. In 1934 a review of the country's education system was undertaken and it showed clearly the dangerous, regressive effects of the depression. Local authorities, after the damage suffered by the peasant sector, were less active in expanding education than in the provision of better medical services. Throughout this period the main contribution to education came from the missions. The immediate effect of the depression could be seen too, in the fact that the 15 mission and 7 government schools providing technical training were producing more skilled manpower than the economy could absorb.

Yet the subsequent strong official reactions against central and technical schools led to a situation where in the late 1930s there were insufficient young men coming forward with the education necessary for a clerk or a craftsman. Innovations were held back on financial grounds. There was more thought about the future than efforts to build it. At this time, mainland Tanzania had only one public junior secondary school, this school, Tabora, having advanced to this status between 1929 and 1934. It was not until 1938 that a government grant of £100,000 for the enlarging of Makerere College made possible a slight expansion of secondary education opportunities for young Tanzanians.

By 1939, the number of children registered as at school, 85,000, was actually less than in the early 1920s. The total of junior secondary schools, four, (three of which were run by missions) had not changed since the mid-1930s. Only one in a thousand school children passed on to a junior secondary school, and all of these fortunate few were boys. Yet, although fewer children were registered as at school, more public funds were being spent on education. At this time, due to the effects of the 1927 African Education Ordinance, 4.6% of central government funds were devoted to this purpose (Govt. of Tang., 1927).

Education in the primary schools, theoretically of 4 years duration took many children 5 to 8 years to complete, as a result of irregular attendance. At the end of it, pupils possessed a grounding, through the medium of Swahili in the 3 Rs, together with a slight knowledge of geography, history, hygiene and general science, plus certain useful agricultural ideas. The announced aim of these schools was to "make good farmers and good citizens". For the select few, central schools carried on the educational process for a further four years. Instruction during the first two years was in Swahili; for the final period in English. Students who left after two years were qualified to enter upon a Grade 2 primary school teachers training course. Those who lasted the full four years had a choice of a junior civil servant's career, a teaching post (after further training) or a clerical or craft occupation. In the main, this education was calculated to prepare for the lower grades of paid employment or fitted the pupil, if such was his rank, to become a chief in the Indirect Rule system. It was also, for the exceptionally intellectually gifted, the stepping stone to a secondary school. There, Africans were trained to become teachers in central schools, medical and agricultural assistants and for the middle ranks of government service. Such was the pattern and position of the education system in 1939.

The Second World War brought all development to a standstill. Nevertheless, it was the War which was to be the cause of the country's greatly accelerated rate of political and economic advance after 1945. Beliefs and attitudes were changed by it. Africans and Europeans alike began to become "development conscious". The great world-wide shortage which followed in its wake drove up the prices of the country's exports, providing thereby, with the addition of Colonial Development and Welfare Funds, the means to realise new hopes and ambitions.

The need and desire for progress in education were clearly apparent. With the coming into being of the United Nations, mainland Tanzania

HISTORICAL BACKGROUND TO NATIONAL EDUCATION 267

became a Trusteeship Territory. Under Article 6 of the Trusteeship Agreement the administering authority had to assume a new responsibility, namely "to promote the development of free, political institutions suited to Tanganyika, and to that end develop the participation of its inhabitants in advisory and legislatives bodies, and in the government of the Territory, both central and local, as may be appropriate to the particular circumstances of the Territory".

These obligations could not be fulfilled with the education system as it existed in 1945. Then, only 7.5% of the nation's children attended school, and less than 1,500 of these were in secondary institutions. Few were permitted to pass beyond Standard IV, with its uncertain promise of permanent literacy. No school was capable of preparing pupils for the Makerere entrance examination. Yet the local school had become a feature in many villages and there was a widespread ambition to become literate. Indications of the spread of literacy were to be found in the stocking of pencils and writing paper by all small traders and in the 25,000 readership of the journal *Mambo Leo*. The language of the primary school, Swahili, was already making its contribution to the creation of an African, as distinct from an ethnic consciousness. It is symptomatic of the growing African renaissance, however, that indigenous circles were becoming critical of an education which was seen now to be too Euro-centric in its philosophy, and at least one attempt was made to revive a traditional ethnic school, at Malangali, in the Iringa Region.

Education was given major emphasis in the Ten-Year Development Plan introduced in 1946. The overall target was to have 36% of the children of Primary School age in Primary School by 1956. Middle School education was to be greatly expanded. ("Middle School" was the name given in 1950 to the former Central Schools.) Goals were set of 200 such schools for boys and 32 for girls. Secondary Schools were also to be increased in number.

An ambitious target was necessary if the gaps left by the inadequate system of the 1930s were to be filled and the trained manpower provided for the planned economic and social development. Later, in the light of circumstances, these targets had to be revised in an upward direction. More places were then provided for pupils generally and girls in particular, as well as for teacher training and technical education. The original Ten-Year plan estimated for annual capital costs on educational expansion of £$\frac{1}{2}$ million and an increase in annual recurrent expenditure of £$\frac{1}{2}$ million. The revised Plan raised both figures to £1.4 million.

The rapid rise in public expenditure on education is well illustrated in the figures given in Table 10:1. Meanwhile, there was a growing awareness of defects in the Middle School curriculum. Its concentration on fitting pupils to earn their living in urban occupations was not in keeping with the economic realities. In particular it was questioned whether a six year primary course served any useful purpose for that large majority of African children who would receive no formal education at all beyond Std. VI. In 1950, therefore, the Ten-Year Development Plan was recast and a new structure for education was introduced. This was based on three

Table 10:1 Sources of Funds and Total Expenditure

	General Revenue	Development Funds	Non-African Education Authorities	African Treasuries	Total Expenditure
1939	£100,000	–	–	£14,500	£114,500
1948	£379,000	£118,000	–	£98,000	£595,000
1952	£1,175,000	£275,000	£798,000	£274,000	£2,522,000

four-year cycles, the primary school (Standards I–IV), the middle school (Standards V–VIII), and finally the secondary school from Standard IX onwards. It was envisaged that about 20% of those pupils who completed education up to Standard IV would be selected for middle school, and that this percentage would rise gradually.

This phase of educational history is worthy of more detailed study, both because the bulk of today's leadership received a middle school education and because some modern commentators appear to imply that the middle school concept of 1950 in many ways foreshadowed the vocational thesis of 'Education for Self-Reliance' in 1967 (Nyerere, 1968a). It is important to stress that this reorganisation of the primary school system applied to African children only, there being separate educational systems with differently oriented curricula for Asian and European children. This fact, not surprisingly, influenced African attitudes towards the middle school curriculum, which was designed, in the words of the Provisional Syllabus of Instruction for Middle Schools:

> ... to be complete in itself so that those who pass through it, whether they proceed further or not, will have received an education which will assist them to follow in a more intelligent and capable manner whatever pursuits they take up and, generally, to play a more useful part in the development of the locality to which they belong. To this end the form and bias of the course at any particular school will, so far as is possible, be related to the needs and reflect the life of the area in which the school is situated. In an agricultural area, for example, the bias will be agricultural, in a pastoral area the bias will be more towards animal husbandry, while in an urban area the bias may be commercial or industrial. In the girls' middle schools there will also be, in all cases, a bias towards homecraft. These biases will be of a practical nature and will form a special feature of the middle school course ... the practical approach not only makes the knowledge gained more real to the pupil and of more immediate value to him but can also enable a higher standard to be reached if the practical work is intelligently applied ... In the activities and project work of the middle school programme every opportunity will be given for group work and for the demonstration of the need for and practice of cooperation as well as for leadership and initiative.

During the period 1952–1959 a tremendous effort was made by the colonial administration to implement the idea of the middle school. Agricultural Instructors were trained for the schools, but were afforded

HISTORICAL BACKGROUND TO NATIONAL EDUCATION

little status in the school society due to their limited educational background. One could see some schools with excellent farms, significantly in those areas where local cash crop farming had already developed. There were some schools where the pupils, under the guidance of the teachers were able to purchase items for the improvement of the farm or their comfort in the school. Yet only very, very rarely did a few pupils on completing Standard VIII leave school to become farmers rather than clerks, school teachers or civil servants.

The reasons for the basic failure of the middle school concept, which faded from official recognition two years before Independence, are not difficult to assess in retrospect. The syllabus was introduced by Europeans without any serious consultation with African opinion, despite the fact that it was to apply only to African pupils. Not surprisingly it was seen by many nationalists as a deliberate attempt to condemn the African to become forever subservient peasant farmers, whilst the other races eased themselves into the well-paid urban employment. The material rewards to be gained at that time from any urban salaried employment were very obviously so much greater than that which could be earned in almost any agricultural area. There was the major problem of land acquisition by youths graduating from Standard VIII, yet if they were allowed to cultivate part of their parents' land, undesirable land fragmentation could follow. Parents who had invested so much in their son's education, were naturally reluctant to accept as a sole result of their investment the return of their son to their own impoverished soil. Pupil or parental attitudes to farming were not improved by the efforts of many teachers who made extra digging a standard punishment in school, and who acted out the role of supervisor whilst the schoolboy labourers sweated in the sun to cultivate excessive acreages. Finally, despite all the pretensions of the syllabus about the importance of agriculture, the subject was not an examined subject, and its zealous pursuit had no influence upon the pupils chance of secondary school selection, which was the cherished common ambition of all the family. English which was studied as a subject from Standard V, until 1958 when it was first introduced at Standard III level, was the real key to success. The secondary school selection examination was set in English comprising mainly essay-type questions, the medium of instruction in Standards VII and VIII was English, and even interviews and applications for jobs were normally conducted in English. In many schools it was an "offence" to use either the vernacular or Swahili during classroom hours, hence the status afforded by both pupils and teachers to Swahili was superior only to that afforded to agriculture.

Nevertheless, the Ten-Year Plan generally achieved its original quantitative goals. In the Five Year Plan, which followed it, the emphasis was placed on increasing the number of Middle Schools and in removing the necessity for double sessions in Primary Schools. Due to financial difficulties, the duration of this Plan was extended to seven years, and even so it still lagged behind its original schedule.

In comparison with the longer period of the Mandate, much was achieved in education during the Trusteeship Era. Primary school places were available for over 50% of children reaching school age. School Certificate classes had been started in 1947 and by 1961 the number of African pupils sitting for the School Certificate examination was a little short of 700.

However, much more was still left to be done when mainland Tanzania became independent in 1961. On the eve of the country's independence only about one in eight of those entering school received more than four years education. The new nation possessed only a handful of African citizens with university or professional qualifications. As a direct consequence, there was a grave shortage of properly trained local personnel to fill the many top level and medium grade posts in government service, commerce, industry and the professions.

Another prominent feature of the colonial legacy was the separate racial education systems. Asian and European education authorities had been set up by law in 1949, and were thereafter in part financed by the colonial government.

Colonial syllabuses and curricula at both primary and secondary school levels had been based on British prototypes, and were in many ways inappropriate to the Tanzanian situation. Thus, the educational establishment, as it was taken over in 1961, was ill equipped and not really designed to meet the requirements of an independent African country with strong aspirations for economic and social change.

3.0 *The Early Years of Independence, 1961–1967*

Almost the first move of the Tanzanian Government upon independence was to introduce the new Education Ordinance which came into force on 1st January, 1962, and with regular amendments by Regulations, remained in force until March 15th 1970. The Ordinance abolished the former racial divisions of the educational system and substituted a single national school system based on a common syllabus and common organisation. The semi-independent religious school systems were now effectively controlled by the State in respect of conditions of service for their staff, admission policies and syllabus for secular instruction. In return the Church managing agencies received the same share of public funds for the running of their schools as was given to Government or Local Authority schools.

The other major provision of the 1961 Education Ordinance was for the devolution of both financial and administrative reponsibility for primary education to Local Education Authorities. A system of Central Government subventions of financial aid was devised, aimed at progressively leaving Local Authorities financially responsible for all Primary educational activities within the area. (In retrospect it can be seen that this was a premature move. In common with her neighbouring countries, Tanzania has encountered difficulties in ensuring that the administrative manpower, financial machinery, level of social conscience and local wealth were adequate to meet the challenge of local educational administration. Thus from July 1969 the financial responsibility for planned Public Primary Schools reverted to Central Government).

HISTORICAL BACKGROUND TO NATIONAL EDUCATION

Secondary Education, mainly in boarding schools, was free to those who were selected for it, except in a very small number of "private" schools receiving no financial assistance of any kind from the government. Primary education was fee paying. Fees were fixed by the Local Authorities and ranged from as little as Shs. 5.00 per annum to as much as Shs. 30.00 or more in various circumstances with a national average of about Shs. 10.00. For cases of genuine hardship there was a system by which fees might be excused.

Immediately after independence the primary system was changed from a 4:4 (Stds. I–IV Lower Primary, V–VIII Upper Primary) to a 4:2:2 system (Stds. I–IV Lower Primary, V–VI Extended Primary, VII–VIII Upper Primary). With the introduction of the 1st 5 Year Development Plan in 1964 (Un. Rep. of Tanz., 1964), the structure was again reorganised into a 4:4 system (Stds. I–IV Lower Primary, V–VIII Upper Primary), the Standard VI cut-off point being phased out over a period of three years. The Primary school enrolment grew from 486,470 in 1961 to 825,000 pupils in 1967. Efforts were made to reduce the excessive reliance on boarding school education which was expensive and tended to isolate pupils from their rural background. Efforts were also made to improve the quality of education that was offered at this level. One of the major aims of the 1964 5-year plan was to increase the output of Grade A teachers, those with four years of secondary education and two years professional training. Upgrading in-service courses for over a thousand Grade 'C' teachers, those with a Primary Education and two years professional training, were also undertaken at considerable public cost. In each area "model" primary schools were established as local course centres, and as growth points for the improvement of professional standards and the spreading of new ideas. Syllabus revision had been a slow but continuous process since Independence. A new Primary School syllabus had been issued in 1963, but by 1967 there was still very little by way of textbooks written by citizens for the national school system, and shortage of funds in some areas severely restricted the use of those new books that had been published. A significant feature of the 1963 syllabus is that practical agriculture as a core of the curriculum disappears entirely; only gardening as a means of beautifying the school, and a little plant experimental work linked with General Science, survived from the 1952 syllabus. Stresses within the system grew, as academic selection procedures at the Standard IV and VIII level denied further educational opportunity to the large majority of pupils, whereas employment in the modern sector of the economy was available for only a minority. An expanding Primary School system, wholly geared to academic examinations, was effectively stimulating parental and pupil aspirations that the economy of the nation could only partially meet.

Like all newly independent developing countries, Tanzania's greatest educational priority during this period was the supply of trained manpower that could make political and economic independence a reality. Manpower planning began in earnest in 1963, and the enrolments courses offered, and teacher recruitment in Secondary Schools were profoundly influenced by the findings of successive manpower studies. Between 1961 and 1967 the number of pupils in Secondary Schools increased from 11,832 to 25,951 and, much to the credit of all concerned, this was achieved with very little drop in academic standards as indicated by external examination performance. The structure of the system remained similar to that in colonial times, a four year course to Cambridge Overseas School Certificate, followed after a selective examination by a two-year sixth form course to Higher School Certificate and university entrance. In cooperation with the Kenya and Uganda Ministries of Education, there was fairly continuous syllabus revision during this period, the pace of which increased with the setting up of the Institute of Education in 1964. The teaching staff, however, was largely made up of expatriates serving on two-year contracts. Immediately after Independence, most of these teachers were British or American, but subsequently more and more teachers were recruited from Canada, Scandinavia and "Third World" nations. Clearly, any major transformation of the system would be impossible until the majority of the teachers were citizens, hence the vital importance of the teacher training programme centred on the University College at Dar es Salaam.

The University College, Dar es Salaam, was founded in October, 1961, and was significantly housed in a brand new building that had been built as the National Headquarters of the Tanganyika African National Union. The first full time students were all Law undergraduates, fourteen in 1961, thirty-four in 1962 and a further thirty-nine being enrolled in 1963. In 1962 an Institute of Public Administration was established, to assist in the training of civil servants for public service, and an Institute of Adult Education to foster the education of adults throughout the nation. In June 1964 the College moved to the Observation Hill Site, some 13 kilometres from the city of Dar es Salaam. A Faculty of Arts and Social Science was opened in 1964, together with an Institute of Education that was to assist with the improvement of the quality of teacher education and curriculum development. The Institute of Swahili Research, aimed at the preservation and development of Swahili as the national language and as the medium of much of East Africa's culture, was also founded in 1964. The first intake of the Faculty of Science entered the college in July 1965.

From the birth of the University College the government had not only provided the money to cover the costs of education for the large majority of the students, but had also determined the numbers that would enter each faculty by reference to manpower survey reports. Government bursaries were offered to selected students on condition that they accepted direction of employment for five years after graduation. Emphasis was placed upon science-based courses, and particularly for the training of secondary school teachers of Science. Degree courses for a B.A. (Education) and B.Sc. (Education) directly tailored to suit the needs of the secondary schools, began in July. Following the normal cyclical pattern of educational expansion, intakes with the requisite post-Form VI academic qualifications grew rapidly as secondary school output increased from 176 in 1961 to 761 in 1966. Yet, by 1967, the University output of

HISTORICAL BACKGROUND TO NATIONAL EDUCATION 273

graduates was still small and most of the citizen graduates at work had received their education outside the country.

Non-graduate teacher education had been located immediately prior to independence in twenty-two scattered and mostly very small colleges, all except three of them managed by Christian missions. These colleges were training three categories of teacher, offering two years of professional training leading to a Grade "C" certificate for students who had completed 8 years primary education, a Grade "B" certificate for those who had completed 10 years of school education and a Grade "A" certificate for those who had completed 12 years of education. By 1966 the number of colleges had been reduced to 18, and most of these had developed to allow for larger intakes. As part of the 1964 plan for improving the quality of education in the primary school Grade "C" training was being progressively reduced and Grade "A" training rapidly expanded. The output of the latter category of teacher increased from 47 in 1961 (of whom only 9 were women) to 694 in 1967 (of whom 183 were women). A new two-year course of training for Form VI leavers, aimed at producing non-graduate teachers for secondary schools was introduced at Dar es Salaam Teachers College in 1965. The colleges, again, were still largely staffed by expatriate tutors, and increasingly they were short term contract teachers with no experience of African primary schools. Any systematic revision of the curriculum in the colleges foundered as the result of the inexperience and instability of staffing. Considerable progress was made, however, in the in-service upgrading of teachers and useful small-scale research activities were undertaken.

Two other major innovations of the 1961–1967 period are worthy of note. The citizen teachers in the educational system were united for the first time, and as members of the Unified Teaching Service established in 1962 they all enjoyed similar conditions of service. Before this time teachers working for the Voluntary Agencies had worked under conditions of service determined principally by the employing agency and markedly different to those of the Central or Local Government teachers. A second major innovation was the recruitment and training of a whole cadre of citizen District Education Officers. The responsibility for the supervision of the primary school system was now shared by District Education Officers (Administration) and Primary School Inspectors (later called District Education Officers-Inspectorate) all of whom had been specifically trained for their new responsibilities.

Yet, despite all the considerable quantitative achievements of the early years of Independence, by 1966 there were clear signs of dissatisfaction with the status quo both in the schools and in the wider community. One climax came when some three hundred students of the University College of Dar es Salaam openly voiced their opposition to participation in the government's plans for a form of National Service which would have enabled them to make a token repayment to a poor society for the privilege of their own education. To add further to the difficulties much of the overseas aid that was anticipated for educational development was not forthcoming, or could only be obtained on conditions that threatened the independence and political integrity of Tanzania. Thus when President Nyerere published his pamphlet 'Education for Self-Reliance', in March 1967, he had this to say:

> There are four basic elements in the present system which prevent or at least discourage, the integration of the pupils into the society they will enter, and which encourage attitudes of inequality, intellectual arrogance and intense individualism among the young people who go through our schools ... First ... it is basically an elitist education designed to meet the interests and needs of a very small proportion of those who enter the school system ... second ... Tanzania's education is such as to divorce its participants from the society it is supposed to be preparing them for ... third ... our present system encourages school pupils in the idea that all knowledge which is worthwhile is acquired from books or from "educated people" ... Government and Party themselves tend to judge people according to whether they have "passed school certificate", "have a Degree" etc ... our pupils learn to despise even their own parents because they are old fashioned and ignorant ... Finally our young and poor nation is taking out of productive work some of its healthiest and strongest young men and women ... they do not learn as they work, they simply learn. ... The vast majority do not think of their knowledge or their strength as being related to the needs of the village community. (1968a: 54–59)

4.0 *The Post 'Arusha Declaration' Period, 1967–1970*

Certainly no period in Tanzania's history has witnessed such a change in educational practice as that during the years 1967–1970. People are thinking ahead, to a mainly rural society where the 'Ujamaa' village is the norm. It is fully recognised by the leadership that there are only two democratic ways in which you can cause people to undertake their own socialist development. Whatever the time scale, those ways are by providing leadership through education and by encouraging democracy in decision making. Since 1967, therefore, major policy decisions in the educational field have been centred both on the improvement of leadership and upon creating a structure within which the aims of "Education for Self-Reliance" have the best chance of being achieved.

The headships within the public schools and teachers colleges (Colleges of National Education) are now completely Tanzanian, a situation not yet achieved in any other former dependency in Africa. Over 500 graduate citizen teachers have entered the public educational system and the large majority has been trained in the University in Dar es Salaam. Many of these young graduates are being appointed as Second Masters, Careers Masters and Heads of Subject Departments as part of a national policy decision to localise all posts of major responsibility. Thus by mid-1970 some 60% of all secondary school teachers were Tanzanians, and there was a firm expectation of this percentage increasing to 75% by mid-1972. As the conditions of service for all graduate employees in government service and the large nationalised parastatal sector of the economy are very similar, it seems likely that most of these teachers will remain in the educational system. Every teacher, graduate or non-graduate male or female, now completes a full time period of para-military National Service and then works on part pay in National Service uniform for a further period of eighteen months.

Again in the words of President Nyerere, "in Tanzania the only true justification for secondary education is that it is needed by the few for service to the many" (1968a: 62). This "few", nevertheless, is many more than at Independence, there being over 30,000 pupils in Public Secondary Schools in 1970 compared with less than 12,000 in 1961. In the latest 5 Year Development Plan, 1969–1974 therefore, secondary school expansion is restricted to estimated manpower needs, and effort is being concentrated upon making the education more relevant to the sponsorship of committed leadership. To this latter end, TANU Youth League branches have been established in all schools, and political education has been integrated within the curriculum. The East African Examinations Council, established in 1967, inter alia, to progressively take over the setting and marking of Secondary School leaving examinations in Kenya, Uganda and Tanzania, from the Cambridge (England) Syndicate, offers positive encouragement to the much needed curriculum reform. Significantly, all Tanzanian candidates for the East African Certificate of Education must sit for Swahili, a mathematical subject and at least one science subject as part of the normal seven-subject entry. The first Swahili course at Advanced Level was introduced on an experimental basis in 1970, and should help to break the existing bottleneck in well qualified and trained teachers of the national language. A comparable Advanced Level syllabus in English Language has also been prepared for probable introduction into the schools in 1971. By 1974 it is planned to have agricultural, technical and commercial courses in every secondary school, emphasis in the desire to concentrate upon productive learning within a science-based curriculum. As part of a general governmental move to decentralise control from Dar es Salaam, the national Central Inspectorate of secondary schools was disbanded at the end of 1968, and replaced by part-time curriculum coordinators stationed in ten regional headquarter towns. Thus the supervision of and stimulation for progressive teaching methods in the Secondary Schools is now fully in the hands of citizen educators. Discipline problems, which were particularly prevalent in the urban day secondary schools during the early years of Independence, have been lessened both by political education and by placing much greater disciplinary powers with the citizen heads of schools. The hours of work and study have now been standardised for all schools, with self-help schemes for providing midday snacks in schools which closed at 1 p.m. in bygone days. The secondary school is expected both to contribute economically towards the cost of its own upkeep and to provide services to the surrounding community. With such varied climatic and soil conditions the nature of the economic effort naturally varies considerably from school to school. Community service activities that are widespread include assistance with farming in the Ujamaa Villages, adult education, the decoration of public buildings and local road or bridge construction projects.

Tanzania, as becomes a state aspiring to socialism, is anxious to offer universal primary education to its children in the shortest possible time. The 1969–74 Development Plan is aimed at increasing the percentage of children who can enter the first standard from the 1969 figure of 47% to 100% by 1989. Every child who does enter school in the future will receive a minimum of seven years education, a privilege afforded to only 40% of the Standard IV pupils of 1967. Past inequalities of opportunity between districts, whereby some urban areas could send all their pupils to seven years of primary education, whereas other rural districts could offer four years of education to only 30% of their children, are also being progressively redressed. Likewise efforts are being made through TANU to enlist the support of parents to ensure equality of opportunity for education for girls. 1969 enrolment figures show seven boys in Standard VII for every three girls, a situation which can be mainly attributed to parents' reluctance to keep their girls at school.

Very significant structural changes in the system, designed to make the concept of "a people's school" a reality, have come about as the result of the passage into law of the Education Act of 1969. This Act, in its own phraseology, is "to provide for the development of a system of education in conformity with the political, social and cultural ideals of the United Republic". The local administration of all the Primary Schools within a given area, including those formerly managed by church agencies, will now normally be carried out by Local Education Authorities. Central Government, however, has relieved the local authorities of much of the financial burden of education, including that of paying for teachers' salaries and school materials in an attempt to accelerate the development of education in the less economically favoured areas.

The Local Education Authority, with the advice of its own Education Committee, and the professional assistance of a Central Government appointed District Education Officer, has the following major functions in respect of the primary schools in its area:

(a) to submit to the Minister for National Education for his approval plans for the promotion and development of education and to carry out such plans as are approved;
(b) To prepare and submit to the Minister responsible for Local Government, for his approval, estimates of revenue and expenditure;
(c) to administer, in accordance with approved estimates, subventions or grants in aid from the Government or Local Authorities;
(d) to prescribe, subject to a minimum fee fixed by the Minister for National Education, collect and receive school fees;
(e) to make recommendations to the Minister with respect to the ownership, management and registration of new schools;
(f) to manage any school owned by the local authority.

The Minister for National Education, however, has the overriding authority to transfer any or all of the above functions to his Ministry or any other body.

Thus the new Education Act marks the end of that chapter in Tanzania's educational history which divided the responsibility for the Management and administration of schools between Church and State. However, the Act makes clear the responsibility of the school authorities to afford facilities for religious instruction for any pupil whose parents wish it, and conversely to excuse from any form of religious instruction a pupil whose parent has specifically requested this. The Minister for National Education, as the people's representative, is the final arbiter in all matters educational, as by Section 32, Sub-Section 4: "if the Minister is satisfied, by such evidence as he shall deem sufficient, that any school is being conducted in a manner detrimental to the interests of peace, order or good government or the physical, mental or moral welfare of the pupils attending it, or contrary to the national education policy, he may order that the school be closed".

Within this new system of people's community schools, the fundamental aims of primary education in Tanzania are to establish, over a seven year period, permanent and functional literacy in Swahili and to provide a basic education that can make an impact on the quality of life in the rural areas. It is expected that every school will make some contribution to the expenses of its upkeep, and that the school community will come to realise that its life and wellbeing depends to some extent upon the production of wealth by farming or other activities. Policy directives advocate the integration of the school self-reliance activities with those of the local community, and considerable progress has been made in this direction within a relatively short period. The people's school is now in process of becoming an adult education centre, providing for the people not only a training in elementary politics and economics and literacy classes, but also offering a training in the skills that should strengthen economic and social progress in the village. The head-teacher of the village school is provided with funds and given the responsibility for organising the adult education programme.

It is futile to generalise concerning the present stage of progress towards realising the nation's ideals in the most important unit of the school system, the village classroom. Inevitably, with over 800,000 pupils and nearly 20,000 teachers involved, not all the classrooms are at the same stage of reform. Every teacher, however, is likely to have attended at least one seminar on "Education for Self-Reliance", and he will be visited by school inspectors far more regularly than in the past. He has been issued with a new Primary School Syllabus, and for some few years now he will have been receiving newly published textbooks, written locally and centrally distributed by the para-statal Tanzania Elimu Supplies.

One major change in policy at the Primary level came in 1967 with the decision to make Swahili the medium of instruction in all Primary Schools, save for a small number that were to cater for the needs of the children of expatriates working in Tanzania. One effect of this decision has been to intensify the development of the language, through the enforced production of teaching materials in all subjects of the curriculum. Thus recent publications in Swahili for the primary school market include an atlas, texts in new mathematics, science and the social sciences as well as a completely new language course. In the meantime, English has been introduced as a subject into Standard I, whereas previously it had been started in Standard III, and a new set of textbooks is being compiled.

The Tanzanian primary school teacher, regardless of his age or with what employer he started his service, now works as a member of the national Unified Teaching Service, with his salary and other benefits guaranteed by Central Government. He spends most of his classroom time teaching in the national language, and his pupils have the comfort of knowing that their examinations will be set, save for English as a subject, in Swahili. Virtually everybody in authority within the primary school system will be a Swahili speaking citizen. Every school will have its School Committee comprising staff, representative parents and local leaders, and its Agricultural Committee, with staff and pupil participation in democratic decision making. At present the greatest barrier to revolutionary change in the classroom remains the external examination for Secondary School selection, the familiar bogey of parents, pupils and teachers alike. As circumstances allow, in the words of the Minister for National Education addressing the Biennial Conference of TANU in June, 1969:

> The examination will be changed so as to make it a test of performance and attainment related to the work and purpose of the school in its community aspect, rather than just an academic test of potential success in the secondary school ... it will test capabilities of direct relevance to service in the community and become, therefore, a general terminal examination as well as a selective test.

National concern for the in-service training of all teachers in the subject content, methodology and personal behaviour that is appropriate to the people's school, is shown by the massive scale of the recently formulated Tanzania/Unesco/Unicef In-Service Scheme. Within five years every Primary School teacher will have undergone a year's course, involving full time courses at teachers colleges, correspondence and assignments, broadcasts or tapes and visits at the school by itinerant teacher educators. Increasing numbers of teachers have undergone a period of National Service, and school TANU Youth League branches offer good training grounds for the practical commitment of the teacher to socialism.

The long term strategy of primary education is fairly clear. The focus is a group of children, all of them individuals yet interacting as a group must. The group can be influenced through leadership and education: the leadership and example of model figures such as the President, parents, teachers and priests; an education which offers practical experience of, as well as theoretical knowledge of socialist principles. Children and adults share the people's school, and study, though at different times and at different levels, the means for improving the living standards of the community within a socialist framework. The teaching materials that they use, the mass media of newspapers, magazines, films and radio that they

HISTORICAL BACKGROUND TO NATIONAL EDUCATION 279

read, look and listen to, all support the efforts of the leadership and educators to promote socialist development. The most receptive individuals within the classroom group, begin to practise cooperative endeavour, and eventually the norms of this particular peer group change. Each child remains an individual, with certain personality traits, ideas and study habits that are his own, but he tends to internalise the social values of peer group, classroom and school. When the school groups find that the new school norms are also welcomed outside the school, when they find opportunities to be of service to the community and when they find that society supports their efforts to farm communally, then the educational revolution is near to realisation.

Teacher education is a key factor in educational reform, whether it be the short term changes in school administration, the longer term reorientation of the school curriculum or the necessary modifications to pupil attitudes. The teacher has to be persuaded, first of all, of the new political and sociological significance of everything he says and does in school. Above all the preservice and inservice training of the teachers has to contribute to the formation both of professional and political values that are consistent with the national educational aims. Significant changes, therefore, have been introduced in recent years to the pattern and structure of teacher education.

From 1970 there are five major categories of teachers to be trained in Tanzania. Specifically trained for primary schools are:

GRADE "D" – Minimum academic education of Std. VII, plus paramilitary National Service, plus one year of professional training.

GRADE "C" – Minimum academic education of Std. VII (though many candidates have received some secondary education), plus three years of professional training.

GRADE "A" – Minimum academic education of Form IV plus two years of professional training which includes paramilitary National Service.

Teacher education programmes for Secondary School teachers are for:

Education Officer Grade III (Diploma) – Minimum academic education of Form VI, plus two years of professional training which includes para-military National Service.

B.A. or B.Sc. with Education – Minimum academic education of Form VI, or equivalent, plus three-year degree programme with Education component, preceded by National Service.

All categories of teachers attend colleges where all the Principalships and most of the senior appointments are held by Tanzanian citizens. The general aims of teacher education, as listed in the Grade "A" course prospectus, exemplify the new approach to teacher education:

(1) To educate students in the true meaning of the Tanzanian concept of Ujamaa.
(2) To train students to be dedicated and capable teachers with understanding of, and care for, the children placed in their charge.
(3) To deepen the students' own general education.

Students receive financial allowances during their training, in return for which they are obliged to serve as teachers in government prescribed institutions for five years. At graduate level particularly, the modern Tanzanian structure is unique in Africa. Students are offered bursaries only on condition that they accept particular courses and that their employment is prescribed by government for five years, after graduation. As conditions of service have been made fairly similar throughout the governmental and large para-statal section of the economy, it is unlikely that there will be major mobility of personnel after the five year period. Thus with over 500 citizen graduates already employed in the school system, and nearly 600 studying Education as one of their subjects in the East African Universities, Tanzania expects to be largely self-sufficient in secondary school teachers by 1974.

The teachers colleges, now known as Colleges of National Education, are being reduced in number, but expanded in student capacity. Under the terms of the 1969 Education Act, all these colleges and the secondary schools, including those formerly managed by such agencies as the Christian churches and Muslim communities, now are managed on behalf of the government Director of National Education. The Minister is now obliged to appoint an Advisory Board for every public teachers college or secondary school and may delegate to the Board specific responsibilities of management for the school.

One interesting aspect of education in Tanzania in the last decade or so which is worth examining a little further is that which is concerned with curriculum development. In 1950 the African Teachers Examination Board, chaired by what was then known as an Assistant Director of Education, came into being. As its name indicates this body was primarily concerned with the setting and marking of the professional written examinations and with the assessment of practical teaching. It was a representative body in that the major teaching training institutions, government and non-government were members. In 1958, the name was changed to the Teacher Training Advisory Board (T.T.A.B.). In its new guise the board's functions were enlarged to include not only concern for syllabuses directly relevant to teacher education, but also, by virtue of the fact that teachers had to be trained to teach a particular body of material, with what that body of material should be. Subject panels (sub-committees of the board) were set up to deal with all the subjects taught in the primary schools – English, Swahili, Mathematics, Geography, History, Art and Craft, and so on, and thus a period of considerable activity in syllabus revision and text book production began. Membership of the board was widened to include representatives of the teachers union, the

HISTORICAL BACKGROUND TO NATIONAL EDUCATION

East African Literature Bureau and other bodies which were not themselves directly engaged in teacher training but which had a contribution to make to it. The T.T.A.B. dissolved itself and handed over the torch to the Institute of Education in 1964. Here the system of subject panels continued but their vertical responsibilities were extended to include secondary education as well as primary education, and some panels notably the Mathematics, Science, English and Swahili panels have effected major syllabus revisions. In addition to the vertical subject panels, horizontal panels for primary, secondary, and teacher education were also set up within the Institute. For several years these horizontal panels were not particularly active but there are now signs that the important co-ordinating function of these panels is being re-vivified. It is important to recognise however that curriculum reform in independent Tanzania is "not merely a matter of content and method but of national spirit and ethos. As the changes in textbooks and teaching techniques have taken place more attention has been paid to inculcating a feeling of national unity and purpose in the schools, by the introduction of self help schemes, open days and parades. TANU Youth League groups have been started in schools to link the life of the scholar with that of the people." (Cameron and Dodd, 1970).

On July 1st, 1970 the University College of Dar es Salaam, which had been a constitutent college of the University of East Africa, became a national institution and was renamed The University of Dar es Salaam. The objects and functions of the new University, as listed in its legal Act, include:

> to preserve, transmit and enhance knowledge for the benefit of the people of Tanzania in accordance with the principles of socialism accepted by the people of Tanzania;
> to create a sense of public responsibility in the educated and to promote respect for the learning and pursuit of truth;
> to prepare students to work with the people of Tanzania for the benefit of the nation.

The President of the United Republic is the Chancellor of the new national University, and he appoints the three senior officials of the University, namely the Vice-Chancellor, the Chief Administrative Officer and the Chief Academic Officer. It is noteworthy that the first Vice-Chancellor under the new Act was Secretary-General of TANU immediately before his appointment, and the Chief Administrative Officer was Principal Secretary in the Ministry of National Education. The governing Council of the University of Dar es Salaam includes appointees of the Chancellor, the Government Ministers for National Education, Finance Economic Affairs and Development Planning, N.U.T.A., the Cooperative Union of Tanganyika, the National Assembly and the University Students as well as University faculty representatives.

A fitting conclusion to this summary of recent developments in the history of education in Tanzania, is afforded by this quotation from

President Nyerere's inaugural speech as Chancellor of the University of Dar es Salaam on 29th August, 1970:

> Our universities have aimed at understanding Western society, and being understood by Western society, apparently assuming that by this means they were preparing their students to be – and themselves being of service to African society... The Universities of Africa which aim at being 'progressive' will react by trying to understand, and be understood by Russian, East European, or Chinese society. Once again they will be fooling themselves into believing that they are thus preparing themselves to serve African society... The truth is that it is Tanzanian society, and African society, which this University must understand. It is Tanzania, and the Tanzanian people, who must be able to comprehend this University ... We are training for a Socialist, Self-respecting and Self-reliant Tanzania. (Nyerere, 1970b).

NOTE

[1] Nyerere, 1968a: 53. All bibliographical references will be found at the end of this Part of the book.

11 LANGUAGE TEACHING IN PRIMARY SCHOOLS

Fulgens Mbunda and David Brown[1]

1.0 *Swahili*

In considering the teaching of languages in primary schools, the first language to be discussed is Swahili. Within the framework of the policy of Ujamaa and of education for self-reliance it is the aim of Tanzania to teach the child in the primary school in such a way that he will be given a permanent grounding in the national language, that his understanding and curiosity may be enlarged, and that he may be able to live out the principles of African socialism and to contribute to the building of the nation. The work of all subjects in the curriculum then has as its target the preparation of the child to be able to stand on his own feet in the life he will lead with his fellows in the predominantly rural communities of the country.

There are two important policy matters which are likely to affect the teaching of Swahili to a considerable extent in a general way in the next few years. First the attempt to make primary education a self-contained entity will have consequences for the age range for which it caters. Up to the present many of the children entering standard I have been very young, only six years old. At the end of seven years of education they are still little more than children. It would appear then that if school leavers are to be regarded as near adult, ready to take a significant part in the life of the community then the age at which children begin their schooling will have to be raised and indeed this is already happening. For the teacher this means that methods, materials and approaches to the teaching of initial literacy which were appropriate to very young children will have to be modified and developed somewhat.

Secondly the commitment to attempting to achieve universal primary education by the year 1989 means that there will have to be a considerable expansion of support systems for education. Not only will school buildings have to be enlarged or newly erected but there must be a very substantial expansion of teacher training facilities. Tanzania is fortunate in that virtually all its teachers are trained with at least a two year programme behind them. If the high standards that this makes possible are to be sustained, especially in teaching the technically demanding initial literacy skills, then a very great deal of effort and expenditure of resources will be needed. The scale of this problem is very great indeed and anyone who cares about the quality of Swahili teaching must look forward to this prospect with some trepidation and considerable determination.

The languages taught in Tanzanian primary schools are of course Swahili and English. Swahili is the language which is used as the medium of instruction and is the language of initial literacy. There is no formal teaching of any of the local languages, though some teachers in some schools find that they have to use the local language for explanation and the carrying out of various class activities especially right at the beginning of Standard I. However by and large Swahili is genuinely the language of teaching. English is taught simply as a subject (now begun in Standard I instead of Standard III as was the case up to 1970). There are a very few schools operating in rather special circumstances where the medium of instruction is English and where Swahili is taught as a subject.

1.1 *Problems Involved*

The plan for education in Tanzania stresses very strongly that Swahili must be developed and advanced as the national language. For the time being English is to be retained as the language of instruction at the more advanced levels of the secondary schools and beyond. One of the problems in the primary school however is that the child is learning two languages at once. Swahili for a great many children is a second language, and the fact that they are faced not only with that but also with yet another language (and that which is utterly foreign) before they have mastered the first strange symbol system of Swahili is a source of very serious difficulty. These difficulties can only be resolved when the whole of the initial stages of education are given in one language, Swahili, and English is not introduced, even as a subject, until the child has laid a proper foundation in Swahili, let us say not until Standards III or IV. If it so happens that Swahili is the child's first language the difficulties are not quite so serious, though they still remain quite substantial.

A further complication is that many teachers who teach in the lower classes do not themselves have a particularly good grasp of the foreign language and indeed have problems coming to grips with many of the fundamentals of the situation, such as the principles of learning and teaching any second language. To be familiar with a set of techniques which may be used to impart the rudiments of initial literacy is not sufficient in this kind of situation. It would appear that a fairly high degree of sophistication about language learning in general is required. One possible solution to the difficulty might be to require that the lower classes be taught by Grade A (see preceding chapter, p. 279) teachers who are already familiar with the underlying principles and the commonest procedures useful for second language teaching. However there appears to be considerable resistence within the teaching profession to the acceptance of this sort of idea in spite of the fact that many teachers recognise that it would probably benefit the children enormously.

Swahili has been a subject and the medium of instruction in Primary Schools for a long time now and so is well established. The aims of teaching Swahili as a subject are to impart to the child the skills of listening, speaking, reading, and writing in the language so that he may understand and be understood with ease, have full control of the four skills so that he can employ them for a wide range of purposes in a wide range of circumstances, retain these skills permanently and be able to develop them further, and come to love Swahili as the language of his country.

In order that these objectives may be fully achieved the materials that are used must be related to the work which the child will be doing in the future and to the kind of part he will be expected to play in the life of the nation. To these must be linked the kind of language which they will demand. The materials should make the child think, stimulate his curiosity, teach him about and encourage him in the the way of life of African Socialism and Tanzanian citizenship.

As has already been remarked Swahili is a second language for many children – although this state of affairs is changing little by little – and as a result in the teaching of it both teachers and pupils face many problems. The extent to which Swahili is a second language for various pupils differs from one area of the country to another. The kinds of situation which occur may be specified in four ways. Firstly there are those comparatively few children for whom Swahili is a first language. For them the primary difficulty is mastering the basic literacy skills, though they also of course need to have the range and delicacy of the forms of expression which they can use extended. Secondly, there is the very large group of those who use Swahili as a matter of necessity in school, in the market, for trading or to talk to people they meet who do not happen to know the language of their homes. For these children there is a secondary problem of acquiring Swahili more fully but they do use Swahili in their daily lives and so motivation to learn is high. Thirdly, there are those who live in remote rural areas to which Swahili has not fully penetrated, but the language of the home and the out of school environment is a Bantu language. Here the problems are fully those of learning a second language, though they are somewhat alleviated in that Swahili is a related language and the structural patterns are readily recognisable and fundamentally familiar. Fourthly, there are those who have not been touched by Swahili at all and whose first language is one of the small number of non-Bantu languages spoken in Tanzania. Here the problem is a full scale second language learning one with all the difficulties that a totally exotic structure base creates. These four groupings obviously create great differences in the way in which Swahili can be taught and learned. In that Swahili is used to teach other subjects too, the problems are, in the last two instances especially, even further magnified. If we add to these the normal difficulties that arise from differences in the individual children themselves, differences of intelligence, home background, parental status, cultural tradition, or previous school experience then the possible number of obstacles to effective teaching becomes formidable indeed.

1.2 *Syllabus*

To try to deal with some of these difficulties the Syllabus for the teaching of Swahili in Primary Schools has been produced, this is the *Muhtasari ya Kiswahili* (Min. of Nat. Educ., 1969d).[2] This offers the teacher a great deal of help and guidance. It enumerates certain basic principles, for example, that the teaching of Swahili has aims and objectives which are in harmony with the overall objectives of the complete Primary School curriculum, as for instance in the part that Swahili has to play in the creating of a sense of national identity; that there is an ordered sequence and emphasis in the teaching of the various uses and skills of Swahili and that effective teaching follows this sequence; that there is a range of appropriate techniques for the teaching of the language; that there is an appropriately graded and selected series of materials for teaching the language; and so on.

The syllabus suggests that the effective Swahili teacher will have certain essential knowledge. Firstly, he will know something about the structure of language in general and about the structure of Swahili in particular. He should know something about the phonetics of Swahili, how the sounds are articulated, whereabouts in the vocal tract they are made, and what kind of sound each is. He should be aware of the form and function of stress and intonation in the language and of the factors involved not only in the pronunciation of individual words but also of phrases and whole sentences or even paragraphs and longer stretches of discourse. He should also know something of the grammar of Swahili, of the nature, type, classification, and status of its various forms, of its rules of syntax, its derivational processes and its basic sentence types. He should know something of its sematics, of the range and delicacy of its lexical sets, of the patterns of synonymy, antonymy, and class inclusion or exclusion which it makes use of and all of this on the most practical level.

Secondly, he will know something about the nature of the pupils he is teaching in terms of their level of psychological development, their motivation (intrinsic and/or extrinsic), their intellectual ability, the specific local environment (physical and linguistic) in which they have grown up, and of their real needs if they are to leave school personally enriched and prepared to play the fullest possible part in the building up of the nation.

Thirdly, he will know something of efficient language teaching methods. It is clear that if one wants to go on a journey it is necessary to make suitable arrangements, and to choose the most direct, easiest and quickest route to one's destination. It is exactly so with teaching. The extensive range of hints offered in the syllabus and in the books it recommends are based on the best modern practice. They demand careful specification of objectives, overall, and week by week, and lesson by lesson; careful planning of procedures, with a proper balance between the various language skills; a wide variety of activities meaningfully related to the child's present and future experience with the use of simple teaching aids of a number of different kinds; and above all flexibility and extensive pupil participation in all that goes on in the classroom. The whole tendency of the syllabus is away from the traditional pattern of work wherein pupils have tended to be far too passive to one wherein the pupils are active, where they learn by doing.

Fourthly, the teacher will know the syllabus itself and be familiar with the prescribed books and materials – for both teacher and pupil – which it specifies.

It is of some interest to observe what all this means in a little detail and in practice. (The time allocation given to Swahili within the curriculum is shown in Table 11:1.)

Table 11:1 Timetable for Swahili

Standard	I	II	III	IV	V	VI	VII
Number of Periods per week	9	9	13	7	6	5	5

It might at first appear that the time allocation in Standards I and II was disproportionately low, but it should be remembered that these two classes operate only on a half-day basis, so that these nine periods represent almost half of the total time spent in school. The proportion of time spent on Swahili language activities in Standard III remains high in order to ensure that the grounding in basic literacy skills is well sustained, by Standard IV and from that level on the continuous use of Swahili as the means of imparting other knowledge begins to pay dividends in deepening and widening pupils' knowledge of the language so that the proportion of time allocated can be progressively reduced. Further details of the time allocation appear in Appendix 11:B at the end of this chapter.

Next let us consider the teaching of the four basic language skills: listening, reading, talking and writing, in Swahili.

In teaching listening and talking for example it is pointed out that the aim of talk in the classroom is to lead the child to be able to explain himself clearly, correctly, fluently and easily. In Standard I the first aim is to increase the amount of Swahili the child knows before he ever begins to master the literate skills. Talk in the classroom is of two kinds, what the teacher does, i.e. developing the listening skill in the child; and what the children themselves do. In Standards I and II it is suggested that the basis of talk should be "news": telling about happenings or events which have been witnessed by the children or in which they have participated, at home, in the village or town, as they come to school and so on; perhaps at the very beginning this may be too difficult so that talk may centre around real things, for example an oil lamp, what its parts are called, who uses it, when, what for; or around pictures, simple ones in the first instance, more complex ones later, the picture being described, interpreted and used as the base for imaginative extension by telling what happens next and so on. Talk may also centre around the description of the preparation or construction of things, for example how a local-style house is built. In the upper standards it is suggested that talk will be more concerned with the preparatory work for written composition, reading aloud, the production of set speeches, discussing the interpretation of things the children have read, or of proverbs or riddles, and may even manifest itself in formal debates.

The suggestions regarding the teaching of reading are a nice compromise between the "Look-and-Say" and the "Phonic" methods. First of all there should be a series of preparatory steps involving visual perception and discrimination exercises, matching shapes and patterns, learning the left to right eye and hand movements which are part of the Swahili literacy repertoire, and the formalisation of a great many of the skills the children already possess by making use of realia (like leaves and grasses) and of pictures. Details of other suggested activities for this stage are given in the *Kitabu cha Kufundisha Lugha*. The length of time which needs to be spent on these activities and the intensity with which they need to be pursued will vary from child to child and from area to area across the country. Of key importance is that they should be pursued until the children show themselves to be truly "reading ready".

After the preparatory stage there follow a series of reading exercises without a book either from the blackboard or from flash cards using whole word, sentence, and syllable methods. The high degree of regularity in the correspondence between the written and the spoken forms of Swahili make "phonic" approaches to the teaching of reading easier to employ than in English where the patterns of regularity are a little more obscure. The fact that Swahili uses only a five vowel system for speech and that these five vowels conventionally correspond to the five vowel letters, 'a', 'e', 'i', 'o', and 'u' also make a syllable method quite viable either on the 'ba-', 'be-', 'bi-', 'bo-', 'bu-', or the 'ba-', 'pa-', 'ka-', 'ga-', 'nga-', 'na-', 'ma-' etc. pattern. In fact a mixture of all of the above ways of learning to make the right noises with meaning for the right black marks on paper is used.

Then the children come to reading from a book. This is the *Kitabu cha Kwanza cha Kusoma* which is the first of a series developed and still being developed with the special needs of Tanzanian children in mind. A series of teachers' workshops have been held for this purpose, one each year, and it is hoped to have publishable materials ready by the end of 1972, even for Standard VII. Details of the full sequence of books recommended and of some of the supplementary reading suggested will be found in Appendix 11:A to this chapter. By the end of Standard II it is hoped that real literacy has been achieved through the continued development of the methods begun in Standard I. The whole word and syllable methods are supplemented with training in the use of alphabetic strategies explicitly taught and the emphasis gradually shifts to understanding the meaning of the whole sentences which have in the first instance been only recognised at a mechanical level.

In Standard III it is this understanding of the printed or written symbol that is stressed and a deliberate effort is made to show the children that reading can be a source of pleasure so that a love of reading is fostered in them. In Standards IV to VII these basic aims are continued but attention is also given to increasing reading speed and to teaching pupils to read at different speeds for different purposes.

A good deal of the work on reading is supposed to be done in small groups of five or six. Sometimes these groups are mixed ability groups, sometimes their members are of roughly equal ability. A further point that is emphasised in the upper standards is that reading of the close, intensive kind should lead to full understanding of the text. There is to be quite a lot of comprehension work done on texts of significance for furthering the ideals of African socialism. This intensive reading will be the basis for discussion so that the pupils will learn to be critically appreciative and not to accept the printed word as sacred.

There is also a strong emphasis at these later stages on extensive supplementary reading where the children themselves choose books to read which they can enjoy. The teachers are exhorted to encourage the children to read as much as they can. It is a matter of sheer quantity in the first instance. In the past too many children have left school – even secondary school – without having read anything more than what the set textbooks and primers have contained. Now much more than this is required and the importance attached to supplementary reading is reflected in the time allocation given to this activity (see Appendix 11:B to this chapter) and in the thought which has been given to selecting texts for use in the various standards. The numbers of titles given for each class (see Appendix 11:B) may seem small but this is partly a function of the developmental stage that Swahili has reached in its functions as the national language, and partly of the economic pressures which are restricting growth and expansion in many areas of Tanzania's life. The requirement that even this small number of books should be read over and above the basic texts is itself however a major step forward and should help to foster the reading habit and permit the children to develop beyond initial literacy to permanent functional literacy.

When it comes to the teaching of "writing" the syllabus very properly points out that there are two kinds of writing. Firstly there is the largely mechanical manual skill of actually forming the shapes of the letters – "handwriting", and secondly there is the skill of expressing one's thoughts and ideas through the special forms of the language which are appropriate for the visual-kinaesthetic medium – "composition". Both kinds of writing need to develop at the same time with each contributing to the enhancement of the other. This linking of mechanical skill with linguistic, rhetorical and intellectual skills is appropriate not only for the Kiswahili lesson but for all lessons and it continually needs to be re-emphasised that the teacher teaching any subject is also teaching Swahili and in so far as he sets written work he is also a teacher of "writing". Obviously in Standard I there must be greater emphasis on "handwriting", and this will continue in Standard II. By Standard III the emphasis has begun to shift towards "composition" and in the upper standards this becomes the dominant aspect.

It is repeatedly emphasised in the syllabus and the teachers manuals for teaching Swahili that the main purpose of "writing" is to convey meaning. Therefore, it is argued, when children write they should write meaningful things in order to enjoy what they are doing. There is substantial evidence to show that good handwriting depends very much on the extent to which the child is involved with the meaning of what he is writing. If he is interested in it, understands what he is saying, wants to say it and has a sympathetic reader in mind then not only the quality of his "composition" but of his handwriting will be high. The importance of a good relationship between the pupil and his teacher once again shows itself to be of supreme importance.

According to the syllabus all composition work should be introduced by talk. Notice how this requirement helps to make all the work in Swahili coherent, the work in each different kind of language skill supporting and enriching work in each of the others. It is by talking round a topic, discussing it, asking about it, working it over verbally as it were, that the child makes the topic his own, and it is also through this oral preparation that the teacher can exercise a degree of control over his pupils' composition and progressively lead them to more elaborate and more elegant forms of expression. It should also be remembered that any kind of written work is "composition" in this broad sense. The written answers to a series of questions, the making of notes as an *aide mémoire*, the completion of an incomplete paragraph or story, sorting out a jumbled paragraph, summarising information presented diffusely, or the full scale recounting of a story, the elaboration of information presented skeletally, or the filling out and exemplification of an argument, or the writing of different kinds of letters are all composition exercises which may be properly attempted by pupils in the primary school, more especially in the uppermost classes.

Certain points are stressed in the syllabus as being of particular importance. Firstly, the children should be stimulated. The activities carried out and the topics dealt with should be those which provoke them to further thought. The kinds of things which might do this are real objects of various kinds, things they can touch and see and smell and handle and taste.

Secondly, the children should be given the opportunity to express their own ideas. They should not be required to copy everything from the blackboard or the teacher's dictation. The control which the teacher exercises through his talk must not be too rigid.

Thirdly, the exercises in writing should be related to things in the children's own environment. If they are writing a letter to the manager of a shop let it be a shop they know, a man they know, not some hypothetical personage.

Fourthly, the work should be linked to what they read in their extensive reading so that a child who has been reading *Hadithi za Baba zetu wa Tanganyika* ('Tales of our Tanganyikan Forefathers') should be encouraged to write a similar tale which he may have heard in his own home. What they have read can provide them with a pattern for what they write. It does not have to be original or elegant, but simply straightforward telling of a tale.

Fifthly, every effort should be made to avoid mistakes in writing. This means that the control which is exercised by the teacher should be properly gauged. The written work must be suitably prepared, the teacher must ensure that the work is appropriate to the abilities of the children, he must define his objectives and topics clearly and proceed step by step towards those objectives, and he must always himself provide models and examples which are correct, no spelling mistakes, no errors of concord, no incorrectly formed letters in his handwriting. If mistakes do occur their ill effects can be minimised by correcting them as far as possible on the spot.

LANGUAGE TEACHING IN PRIMARY SCHOOLS 291

This means that the teacher's supervision of the pupils' written work must be close and helpful, he must move round the classroom looking over shoulders. He cannot sit at the front and do something different while his pupils are writing. Self correction on the part of pupils should be encouraged to the full. Small groups of pupils working together to produce an agreed accurate version succeed in doing this very well, since each pupil in the group must copy the agreed version correctly and the cooperative spirit generated by this leads to mutual correction giving highly satisfactory and satisfying results. Every piece of written work ought to be inspected by the teacher, and where corrections are necessary they should be done by the children afterwards – as soon as possible afterwards. The teacher's marking should show what the fault is and where necessary indicate how to set the fault right without actually doing so as far as this is possible. A comprehensive system of marking symbols is recommended. It is also suggested that each piece of written work should be allotted a grade mark. In the lower standards this should be out of 100, but in Standard IV and upwards the mark should be out of ten or a letter grade from A to E.

Ability to use the four basic language skills of itself does not constitute a real depth of competence. There is an integrative and aesthetic aspect to learning any language which it is essential to foster if pupils are to come to appreciate the flexibility, beauty and power of their national language. It is this special ability which is a function of all the kinds of ability discussed above that gives a language user a sense of appropriate style. Most children enjoy the element of play in language, they enjoy riddles and jokes, and they love listening to stories. It is very easy to exploit this natural delight in language to lead children to enjoy poetry, plays, and oratory. They very quickly become sensitive to the rhetoric, the balance, the beautiful elaboration of language; they can offer informed critical opinions and perceive beauty and weaknesses in literature. They can also be led to aesthetically satisfying creativity in using language themselves. They can write their own riddles and jokes, their own poetry, stories and plays and it is when they come to this point that they can be said to truly achieved "competence" in the language. This kind of linguistic competence is also a function of the national culture so that the content of what the pupils read should conform to national ideals. What the children read should conform to the ideals of Ujamaa, should depict the realities of the life and customs of the peoples of Tanzania, in their homes and villages, in what they eat, and what they produce. It should reflect the beauty of the country's mountains, lakes, rivers, plains and the great ocean that borders it; the patterns of work and recreation; the traditions of the society as a whole in family, religion and politics. The discussion and listening, the intensive and extensive reading and the writing activities discussed earlier in this chapter should all tend to foster this kind of competence, but it is not only strictly linguistic experience of this kind that contributes to it. Almost any experience can play its part, watching films, listening to the radio, visiting places of interest in the towns or countryside – factories or game parks, acting in plays, participating in hobbies or sport, making music, dancing or any of the myriad activities which lead to an enrichment of children's lives – and it is precisely for this reason that it is suggested in the syllabus that all of these should form part of the curriculum as and when they can. Most important of all, perhaps, is that the teacher should constantly show his admiration for, and try himself to practice clarity and elegance of linguistic expression, he should be aware of the traditions and heritage of the nation and the beauty of the world about him. Thus he may impart to his pupils or help to that 'competence' in Swahili which is the rich treasure of the real speaker of it.

1.3 *Swahili as a Medium of Instruction in the Primary School*

In Tanzania it has been assumed that since the fundamental structure of Swahili is Bantu and that the majority of Tanzanians speak a Bantu language as their mother tongue that they are likely therefore to have only minimal difficulty in using Swahili as the vehicle for learning in the primary school. However the nature of the linguistic, psychological and intellectual difficulties faced by children doing this have never been seriously investigated and the extent or depth of their problems have never been mapped. That they do have such difficulties may be fairly deduced from the experience of all teachers in all parts of the world where a non-native language is used to teach children. It is perhaps sometimes forgotten that Swahili is not only Bantu but also partly Arabic and this undoubtedly introduces certain linguistic difficulties.

For example many Bantu languages – like Sukuma – have no phoneme which corresponds to the Swahili /θ/ or /ð/, and so children whose first language happens to be one of these are likely to have difficulty in saying Swahili words like *thelathini* or *adhabu*. Children may also find it difficult to adjust to finding familiar local language words with a new technically specialised meaning, as for example in the legal vocabulary created by the commission appointed to translate the laws of Tanzania.

What the nature of the psychological and intellectual difficulties children may have is we have virtually no idea. One might suspect difficulties with ideas like SAME, DIFFERENT, BIGGER THAN, BIGGEST, and notions associated with various kinds of taxonomy, class inclusion or exclusion, sequence, ordering and gradience, since the Swahili devices for expressing some of these are a little less explicit than in some other languages. For example comparison in Swahili is stated in absolute terms – *Kitabu hiki ni kubwa kuliko kile* (lit. 'Book this is big in-the-place-where-is that-one') – not in gradient terms as in English. There is also evidence of at least one instance where mistranslation from English into Swahili has caused almost immeasurable difficulty. A widely used textbook for teaching arithmetic presented multiplication as a quick way of doing addition. Thus $2 + 2 + 2 = 6$ in English 'Three times two is six'. If this is translated word by word into Swahili it becomes *Tatu mara mbili ni sita* which means. 'Three two times is six' or $3 + 3 = 6$, so instead of a table of two's $2 + 2 + 2 + 2 \ldots$ etc. we have a table of two times $2 + 2$, $3 + 3, 4 + 4, \ldots$ etc. and the possibility of confusion in the minds of the children becomes very great indeed.

Apart from this kind of conceptual and psychological difficulty there are a number of more practical and mundane difficulties in using Swahili as the medium of instruction. Chief among these must be the scarcity of materials and books prepared and written in Swahili in various subject areas like the sciences and history. In some instances what materials do exist are unsuitable, either because they are extremely old fashioned (as was the case with the arithmetic text-book referred to above, which has indeed since been replaced with a modern, carefully written text) or because the ideas they contain are contrary to the ideals of African socialism. This considerable handicap is in the course of being overcome. Basic textbooks in the three Rs have been prepared or are in active preparation. These books conforming to the requirements of the nation are written in an up-to-date idiom underpinned by modern principles. They have been or are being produced by an energetic series of self-help projects mainly in the form of Teachers Workshops assisted by experts from the Institute of Education in Dar es Salaam and elsewhere. With these basic texts in hand it becomes possible to move forward to producing a wealth of supplementary materials of all kinds, maps, diagrams, games activity materials and books for reference and enrichment not only for the children but also for the teachers of the nation. Provided a minimum allocation of funds and the technically expert manpower can be provided for the printing and production of these materials there are hopeful signs that the enthusiasm of the people will carry Tanzania forward to a fine future when all subjects taught in Primary Schools will have a wealth of Swahili materials available to them. The initial effort we are witnessing is an excellent indication of the kind of fruits that the policy of education for self-reliance may bear.

2.0 *English*

Turning now to the teaching of English, the only other language taught in the primary schools of Tanzania, it may be observed that the policy concerning the teaching of this language contains a certain element of paradox. On the one hand a formal recommendation that English should cease to be used as a medium of instruction in primary schools, which appears to have emanated from the English Panel of the Institute of Education at the University College Dar es Salaam in December 1966, has been accepted by the Ministry of National Education. On the other a recommendation from the same panel at the same time that English should be taught as a subject throughout the primary school has also been accepted. In making the recommendations the Panel observed that using English as the medium of instruction in Standard VI and VII resulted in little more than parrot-like rote learning for the majority of pupils, and that this had little to do with real education. At the same time it was felt that it was important that pupils should still have access to the world of wider communication and knowledge which English opened to them. For those who would go on to courses of instruction where the medium would be English, special provision at the transition point would need to be made.

This solution to the problem of access to a language of wider communication is a novel one among anglophone countries. The usual patterns elsewhere appear to be either, teaching English as a subject in the lower primary classes with a view to using it as a medium as early as possible (normally somewhere about the middle of the primary stage) or, using English as the medium of instruction throughout the entire educational scheme. There appears to be no other country where the language is taught as a subject from the first primary class, with no intention that it should be used as a medium of instruction anywhere in the initial stage of education.

There is of course no guarantee that this situation will persist. It is a feature of Tanzania at the present time that while there is a clearly and ably stated language policy, there is a singular lack of a detailed and comprehensive plan of how that policy is to be implemented in terms of cost, manpower needs, and time-tabling. The role intended for Swahili is stated in the syllabus in global terms such as "to extend the use of the language into all areas of national life", but there appears to be little awareness, outside the small groups of specialists in language, how enormously complex a process this is likely to be. If plans for the extension of the national language have not yet been worked out, it is scarcely to be expected that an official pronouncement on the place and function of English in the national life should have been formulated.

However, so far, the policy of teaching English in the primary school has not been seriously questioned. Because English, in some form has been part of the primary school programme for a long time now, it may be difficult for Tanzanians to think of a primary curriculum with no English at all in it. And there may be other reasons for the continuance of English in the primary school programme. Perhaps it is being retained because of the recognition of the value of access to a world language; perhaps because of a realization that the already widespread knowledge of English in Tanzania is a resource which ought to be husbanded; perhaps because the individualistic and self-interested values of a colonialist education system die slowly, even in a nation dedicated to African socialism, and English is still seen as the key to personal advancement, security, and power. None of these reasons have ever been explicitly acknowledged in any policy statement, but they may be nonetheless operating.

Meanwhile English is assuming a position somewhere half-way between a second and a foreign language. It is no longer the country's major language for all functions above those of a very local nature, but there are still many activities in government as well as in commerce, which are carried out in English. The language retains much of its popularity, whatever the reason for it may be. For example when English was generally introduced in Standard I early in 1970 the Ministry of National Education was faced with a strong demand that it should be introduced in Standard II also. This had not been part of the plan, but many parents and teachers evidently felt that it was somehow unfair that there should be only one class in the primary school which had no English. What appears to be happening is that English is being allowed to find its own new level.

Conscious of the Government's evaluation of Swahili as the national language, schools, training colleges, ministries, mass media, and administrations are all striving to use Swahili as much as possible, each of them finding a point in their particular activities at which the necessity of using English becomes sufficiently strong for English to in fact be used.

In these circumstances the goals for the teaching of English in primary schools have been determined by the way the English language Panel of the Institute of Education has interpreted the Government's generally stated language policy. These goals are stated in the official Syllabus for Primary Schools, thus: "The overall aim of the course will be to give the primary school leaver a *permanent reading knowledge* of English" (author's italics; see Min. of Nat. Educ., 1969a).

The aim has been arrived at from an assessment of the probable uses a primary school leaver in Tanzania will make of his knowledge of English, and from a consideration of the function of the primary school in President Nyerere's "Education for Self-Reliance" (see 1968a). The latter makes it clear that the primary school course must be self-contained. The requirements of the secondary schools and the University, which only a small fraction of the children will reach, will not be allowed to distort the curriculum, which is to be shaped to fit the needs of the masses. A corollary of this principle is that nothing which is unlikely to be of some real value to the citizen living in his Ujamaa village in rural Tanzania should be included in the primary curriculum; whatever is taught in the primary school should be learned permanently.

2.1 *New Syllabus*

The new English syllabus therefore sets out to emphasise those aspects of the knowledge of English likely to be used after the children leave school, and which are therefore likely to be retained. In this it differs from the old syllabus which aimed at an all round development of the four basic language skills, understanding what is said, speaking, reading, and writing. In effect this meant covering the ground work of language learning to the point at which the secondary school teacher took over. It transpired, apparently, that none of the skills was developed to the level of permanence and the children who did not reach the secondary school usually forgot what English they had learned. The new syllabus assumes that the primary leavers' likeliest use of English will be for reading, and that it will be possible to develop to the level of permanence the childrens' ability to read. The goal is thus restricted: English is to be taught in order to add another dimension to literacy.

It will be apparent that this goal includes a subsidiary one not explicitly stated, and that is that the few who go on to stages of education in which English is used as a medium of instruction should have enough preparation in the skills other than reading for their ability to be made active when the need arises. This activation is however likely to be the responsibility of the secondary teacher or of the teacher involved in any special instruction which may be offered at the intermediate stage. The primary English syllabus is thus essentially self-contained, but glances (just as parents undoubtedly do) towards the secondary school.

2.2 *New Course*

With the new syllabus, there has arisen the need for a new course. In planning this new course, which will be called *English for Tanzanian Schools* (Min. of Nat. Educ., 1969–73), certain particular assumptions have had to be made – about the children, about the teachers, and even about the structure and timing of the course itself – apart from those already discussed above.

The first of these particular assumptions, which concern the children is that the language of the children is Swahili. This assumption is of course, difficult to justify. It is quite clear that Swahili is the first language of only a minority of the children, and there is no evidence of the degree of competence in Swahili achieved by children whose first language is not Swahili. However, it would appear to be impractical to try to take account of the immense linguistic diversity of the Tanzanian languages other than Swahili which might affect the structure of a primary school course in English for Tanzania. In planning for the course, Swahili has been taken as representative of all the Tanzanian languages; at least it is a Bantu language and current estimates are that 97% of Tanzanians speak a Bantu language as their first language. The possibilities of interference from Swahili at various points in the course have been considered, but interference from other languages (even from languages like Sukuma spoken by very large minority groups within the nation) has had to be left out of account.

The second assumption about the children is that they will enter school at from 7 to 8 years old. The validity of this assumption may also be questioned. There appears to be little reliable evidence of childrens' real ages on entering Standard I, but it is the Government's present aim to have children entering school at such an age that they will be ready to join the work force of the community when they leave Standard VII, at, presumably, age fifteen or so.

The third assumption is that the motivation of children to learn a foreign language can be sustained even when there appears to be no prospect of the language being effectively used in the immediate future as, for example, the medium of instruction in higher classes.

The fourth assumption about the children is that they will become literate in Swahili by the middle of their second year in primary school. There would appear to be some hope that this assumption might well be justified on the basis of the plans and activities discussed in the earlier part of this chapter.

As for the assumptions which concern the teachers, the first is that they will have studied English themselves at least to the top of the primary school.[3] This is an assumption which seems very likely to be a justifiable one to make.

The second is that the teachers will have received some training in the principles of language teaching. One may be hopeful about this too, since at the present time there are virtually no untrained teachers in the primary schools of Tanzania.

The third assumption about the teachers is that though they may not have sufficient command of English to be able to use it as the medium of instruction they will be capable of handling the limited lexical and structural material of the course in the Primary School.

The fourth assumption about the teachers is that the form of training they have received will have prepared them to teach effectively only by following a detailed programme which is fully explicit.

Most of the assumptions listed above have at least been discussed, commented on, or noted at various official levels, but it is astonishing that the most fundamental assumption of all appears to have been made without discussion and without comment. This assumption is that to compensate for the fact that English is no longer used as a medium of instruction in Standards VI and VII that it is appropriate to introduce a new course in Standard I. Further, it would appear to be assumed that given the teachers and materials currently available that starting to teach English in Standard I will be more effective than starting in Standard III. The project for the development of the new course could have provided the opportunity to match Standard I with Standard III classes both working from new materials, but this possibility does not seem to have been considered.

So with this rather formidable list of assumptions made, work has begun on the development of the new course.

The number of periods allotted to English in the primary school timetable remains much the same as it has in the past (see Table 11:2). It

Table 11:2 Timetable for English

Standards	Time Allocated
I to II	5 periods of 30 minutes
III to V	7 periods of 40 minutes
VI to VII	7 periods of 45 minutes

should be observed that it is necessary to express the allocation in terms of "periods" rather than of minutes or of proportion of time in the day. The primary timetable, even in Standards I and II, is divided into distinct "subjects" in Tanzania and is rigidly adhered to. The justification offered for this is that it gives the the Inspectorate a means of controlling the work of the teacher, but it gives little chance of matching the teaching to the childrens' interest of the moment.

What is new in this allocation as compared to the period in the history of Tanzanian primary schools before 1970 is the appearance of English in the first two standards. There has been some reluctance, mainly on the part of older Standard I teachers to accept English in the Standards I and II timetable, but it is doubtful whether this is any more than the inevitable resistance of a conservative profession to any kind of innovation.

At the present time (May 1970), the texts in general use in the primary schools are shown in Table 11:3. There are in fact three grades, Standards I, II and III all starting English this year. It is expected that this year's Standard III will be the last class to use Book 1 of the *New Oxford English Course* (French 1956–61). The remaining books of *English for Tanzanian*

Table 11:3 Books for English

Standards	Books
I to II	*English for Tanzanian Schools*, Book I
III to V	*New Oxford English Course*, Books I to III
VI to VII	*English for Tanzanian Schools*, Books VI and VII.

Schools (Min. of Nat. Educ., 1969–73) will come into use at the rate of one a year until the course is complete.

There are a very few schools still living with the consequences of earlier trials, official and otherwise, with other text books. One or two schools in Dar es Salaam are using the *New Nation* series, a few more are still listed as *Peak* schools. Throughout the country, a rather larger group has had its Standards I and II working on an experimental Longmans course, the ancestor of the new official course. Mainly because the people concerned in these experiments have either left Tanzania or been transferred to other posts in the country, there is no official record of these trials, and no organisation to keep track of them. It is to be hoped that children who have already had two years of English before entering Standard III this year are not being expected to start again with the *New Oxford English Course* Book 1.

English for Tanzanian Schools, Books VI and VII are something of an anomaly. When the Ministry abandoned English as a medium, the first need was thought to be the provision of a subject course for the two classes which had previously been taught everything in English. This course was conceived as a "consolidation course within the primary hierarchy" (the quotation is from the Minutes of the English Panel), and in effect the course aims at covering in two years the gap between the end of the *New Oxford English Course* Book 3 and "full' English. Its content is thus very dense indeed, and children at present in Standards VI and VII, who have been affected most by the change of medium to Swahili, find it very difficult. Another objection to these two books has arisen. They are based on passages written by students in the Grade A training Colleges of Tanzania and adapted by P.S. Tregidgo to fit a language progression he had devised. Writing these books, and trying them out in a sample of primary schools, took two years. During that time the Government's conception of the role of the primary school changed. The result is that Books VI and VII have been heavily criticised for inappropriateness of content. For example, sections of the books are related to the traditions of specific peoples of Tanzania, and this has been considered as likely to encourage tribalism. Some chapters which deal with urban life have been construed as likely to attract children into the towns. Books VI and VII will clearly have to be remade to match the new concept of primary education.

The stages of the new *English for Tanzanian Schools* which have been produced so far consist of a Teacher's Book, a Pupil's Book entirely in pictures, and Class Pictures, for Standard I. The materials about to be published for Standard II will have the same format. The Pupil's Book is intended to give the children the opportunity for individual practice based on the pictures. The Class Pictures are used for the usual purpose of introducing situations that could not easily be presented with realia in class. The Teacher's Book consists of a set of detailed lesson notes, setting out for each step the teaching point, a procedure for presenting and practising it, an indication of the pronunciation, and notes to the teacher on probable difficulties.

The first year's work is entirely oral; reading is not introduced until the middle of the second term of Standard II. There will be a set of flash-cards for use in the second half of Standard II and the first few weeks of Standard III. In the middle standards, the course is expected to take the form of a Teacher's Book that will contain the essentials of the language progression, plus a large number of pamphlet-size readers, intended to enable the children to work on their own, or in groups, at appropriate language levels, in extended contexts. The traditional pattern of a book of "extracts" preceded and followed by exercises is not likely to be used.

Books I and II of *English for Tanzanian Schools* show signs of the underlying assumptions. Since the children are considered young enough to be able to reconstruct the basic systems of English grammar, provided they are given the evidence without formal rule giving, the content of the first two years is essentially a series of related structures, with the lexis of familiar objects and concepts incorporated to enable the children to practise the structures. Since the teachers are thought to need the guidance of a highly explicit course, the material to be taught is set out in very great detail, even to giving the pupil's expected responses along with the teacher's utterances, although such detail risks having teachers reject other possible utterances that happen not to be given in the Teacher's Book. Since it is thought that while the teachers can handle the English to be taught, they may have difficulty in understanding English statements of methodology, Book II provides the explanatory notes in both English and Swahili.

The methodology expounded in the course is directed to ensuring that the children get practice in the language without needing the support of the teacher. Each lesson is made up of a series of "standard" stages, the order of the series varying slightly to give at most four lesson patterns. The standard stages are *Revision, Presentation, Group Imitation, Group Demonstration* and *Group Practice*. The first two are self-explanatory; the point that has to be made to teachers is that even the clearest presentation relies heavily on the children's perception of, and inferences from, what they can see and hear. *Group Imitation* is a form of limited chorus work, intended to give the children the chance to practice the noises, in the same context as the presentation. The model for the imitation must be repeated by the teacher before any group is asked to speak. This stage provides for the practice of both questions and answers; the inclusion of practice in questions for the children has seemed new to some teachers. Group imitation also gives the teacher the chance to hear any serious mispronunciations, which should be corrected at this stage.

The *Group Demonstration* stage gives the children a model for the group practice that forms the last stage of the lesson. The children for the *Group Demonstration* are chosen one from each practice group, so that each practice group will have a leader who has been through the practice himself. In the *Group Demonstration*, the teacher goes through the practice with the first children in the group, and then hands over the direction of it to the children, who take it in turns to manipulate the situation, and ask the necessary questions, of the other children. Meanwhile, the children in the rest of the class watch and listen; it will be their turn next.

In the *Group Practice* stage the children from the demonstration group return to their groups and lead the other children through the same practice. Each group is supposed to have the necessary "props", generally simple realia, that the teacher used in the presentation. Each child is supposed to have a turn at both questioning and answering making sure that he moves the "props" to fit his questions. At this stage the teacher's role is that of listener and adviser. He is not supposed to be the focus of the practice (neither are the group leaders) but merely the organiser of it.

It is hoped that the "game" element in the practice stage, the fact that they are talking to other children, rather than to the teacher, will provide adequate motivation in the early stages. Further, it is hoped that since the children are obliged to use the new items of language in relation to changes in a situation, however simple, that they will develop "competence" in the language. In the planning, careful attention has been given to "combined revision", the rehearsing in new combinations of structures and vocabulary learned earlier, in order to promote just this competence in the children.

The degree of "tramlining" in the course may appear excessive. The justification offered for the systematised lesson patterns is that they invoke what are for Tanzanian teachers novel techniques, and by following them teachers may be induced to let the children talk to other children; with only minimal professional training behind them teachers need to be given maximum assistance to produce even minimally acceptable standards. In the short orientation courses teachers took before the new books were introduced the emphasis was on this aspect of devising method that would enable the children to work on their own; to be, in the well-known phrase, *self-reliant*, instead of teacher-reliant, and it is this point that must be emphasised over and over again in the future training or retraining of teachers who will be involved in handling this material.

When reading is introduced, there is a similar kind of control. The problem in teaching the reading of English appears to be, to give the pupil confidence that strategies based on a belief in a regular relation between sound and written symbol will serve for English as well as Swahili, while allowing for the fact that the regularities are different. The early reading lessons are confined to those words already taught in oral lessons, where

LANGUAGE TEACHING IN PRIMARY SCHOOLS 301

the relation between symbol and sound in English is parallel to that between symbol and sound in Swahili. Thus the children can read the words as though they were in Swahili, and still get the answer right. (This principle has led to the inclusion of some odd candiates in the vocabulary of Standard I). The pattern of reading lesson advocated is that of an oral revision, followed by a reading presentation, a word/picture matching stage, and a direct reading stage, where the reading will not be supported by a picture to refer to. In most lessons these are followed by a writing stage, a similar practice to that of the primary Swahili course where the teaching of writing follows hard upon that of reading. It will be seen that the English course does not concern itself with teaching reading as a basic skill, but with the modification of an existing approach.

The materials for Standard III onwards are still in embryo, but their features can be discerned. They will rely for their basic sequence on a series of situations likely to be within the children's experience; the language sequences will be subordinated to the situational sequence; more opportunity will be given for games and dramatisations. The writing lessons will probably include a programmed element. However, all these materials are still to be tried out in the primary schools; their final content and format will depend on the results of the trials.

2.3 Conclusions

To summarise then, it is clear that there is no significant future for English as a medium in the primary schools of Tanzania. The Government recognises its current obligation to provide some courses using English as a medium for the children of the various foreigners in its service. There is however no Government primary school which is entirely English medium; a few town schools have been allowed to retain English medium streams but Tanzanian citizens are excluded from them, except in the unlikely event of there being places in the English medium stream concurrently with over-crowding in the Swahili streams.

The future of English as a subject will depend to a great extent on the Government's view of the function of English in the country as a whole. If books in Swahili become as widely and usefully available as they are in English, the case for English as a necessary extension of literacy will decline. If secondary level and university courses are to be entirely in Swahili, the demand for English will again diminish. With the small investment now being made, however, it seems unlikely that books in Swahili will be available in the foreseeable future, on anything like the scale required for the needs of the whole gamut of subjects, much less in the range and variety of general reading now on offer in English. The use and teaching of English in Tanzanian primary schools will be determined very largely by the degree to which the functions of Swahili in the life of the nation are extended.

NOTES

[1] The section on the teaching of Swahili was written by Fulgens Mbunda; that on the teaching of English by David Brown. David Brown was at the time seconded by

the British Council to the Ministry of National Education under the Aid to Commonwealth English Scheme; his section, however, does not necessarily reflect the views either of the British Council or of the Ministry of National Education.

[2] Bibliographical details of all publications referred to in this chapter will be found in the bibliography at the end of this Part of the book.

[3] It may be noted that at the beginning of the project for the development of the materials for Standards I and II of *English for Tanzanian Schools*, it was assumed, on the assurances of the Ministry of National Education, that Grade A teachers would be available to teach English in the lower primary classes. This supply of Grade A teachers never materialised, and the trial teaching was all carried out entirely by Grade C teachers. The actual course may, in the future, be taught by the proposed new Grade D teachers.

It should perhaps be a matter of concern that fewer and fewer Primary Teachers are likely to have been taught or trained by native speakers of English. There seems to be little point in expending large amounts of time, energy and money on teaching children a language of wider communications if in fact they are unable to communicate more widely in it. A special "Tanzingereza" may questionably be useful within the nation, but will be of little use outside it.

APPENDIX 11:A BOOKS RECOMMENDED FOR USE IN EACH STANDARD

(a) Essential – for classroom use
Standard

- I *Kitabu cha Kwanza cha Kusoma*
   Kitabu cha Pili cha Kusoma
- II *Kitabu cha Tatu cha Kusoma*
   Kitabu cha Nne cha Kusoma
   Mazoezi na Mafumbo
   Hadithi na Vitendo

(a) Essential for classroom use
Standard

- *Jozoeze Elimu ya Kiswahili I & II*
- III *Kiswahili–Darasa la Tatu*
- IV *Kiswahili–Darasa la Nne*
- V *Kiswahili–Darasa la Tano*
- VI *Kiswahili–Darasa la Sita*

(b) Possible/Optional –
supplementary reading
Standard

- I *Someni Kwa Furaha I, II*
   Musa na Sara
   Paka Jimi
- II *Someni Kwa Furaha II, IIB*
   Esopo, Chuo I, II, III
   Hadithi za Mzee Kobe
   Kwa nini simba anguruma
   Mwezi katika maji
   Mvulana na Nguruwe
   Hadithi za Wanyama zimeandikwa
   Kwa nini Twiga hana Sauti
- III *Msafiri katika Nyumba ya Sultani*
   Hadithi za Kale za Sungura na Hadithi Nyingine
   Mafiga Yapita Yote
   Sungura Mjanja
   Kisa cha Yohana Mjinga na Utilivu Wake
   Kisanduku cha Dhababu
   Hanahela
   Kichwa Uplande
   Elisi katika Nchi ya Ajabu
   Mamba na Kima
   Tabibu Asiyependa Utabibu
   Mdoe na Mama yake
   Mfalme na Nyoka
   Binti na Mfanyi Biashara

(b) Possible/Optional –
supplementary reading
Standard

- *Hadithi wa Baba zetu wa Tanganyika*
   Mchana na Usiku
   Taabani na Rahani
- IV *Malimwengu, I na II*
   Mchnuzi Mungwana
   Hadithi za Rafiki Saba
   Mashairi Yangu
   Robinson na Kisiwa Chake
   Kambi Kando ya Ziwa Samaki
- V *Mgeni Karibu*
   Afadhali Mchawi
   Kisa cha Mfalme
   Malimwengu III na IV
   Paukwa Pakawa
   Kisima chenye Hazina
   Isa Bin Tajiri
   Majitu Matatu
   Barka na Wanyang' anyi
   Tumbuizo la Jioni
- VI *Safari za Gulliver*
   Hadithi za Maugli
- VII *Alfu Lela Ulela I na II*
   Mashujaa
   Kisa cha Germana, Monica na Shetani
- VII *Malimwengu VI, VII, na VIII*
   Kiboko Hugo
   Hadithi ya Allan Quartermain

APPENDIX 11:B   ALLOCATION OF PERIODS TO SWAHILI ACTIVITIES

Standard I

		Term 1	Term 2	Term 3	Total
Language		43	42	34	119
Reading and Writing		106	–	–	106
Kitabu cha Kusoma I		–	39	–	39
Kitabu cha Kusoma II		–	–	33	33
	Total	149	81	67	297

Standard II
(From this standard upwards all periods are labelled "Kiswahili".)

		Term 1	Term 2	Term 3	Total
Kiongozi kwa Kitabu cha III Sehemu 1 na 2		116	–	–	116
Kitabu cha III cha Kusoma					
Kiongozi kwa Kitabu cha III Sehemu 3					
Kitabu cha III cha Kusoma		–	63	–	63
Kiongozi kwa kitabu cha IV Sehemu 1					
Kitabu cha IV cha Kusoma					
Kiongozi kwa Kitabu cha IV Sehemu 2 na 3		–	–	52	52
Kitabu cha IV cha Kusoma					
	Total	116	63	52	297

Standard III

		Term 1	Term 2	Term 3	Total
Kiongozi kwa Kitabu cha Darasa la III		165	90	75	330
Kiswahili–Darasa la III Supplementary Reading		49	27	23	99
	Total	214	117	98	429

Standard IV

		Term 1	Term 2	Term 3	Total
Kiongozi kwa Kitabu cha Darasa la IV		83	45	37	165
Kiswahili–Darasa la IV Supplementary Reading		33	18	15	66
	Total	116	63	52	231

LANGUAGE TEACHING IN PRIMARY SCHOOLS

Standard V

		Term 1	Term 2	Term 3	Total
Kiongozi kwa Kitabu cha Darasa la V		66	36	30	132
Kiswahili–Darasa la V Supplementary Reading		33	18	15	66
	Total	99	54	45	198

Standards VI and VII

		Term 1	Term 2	Term 3	Total
Viongozi kwa Vitabu vya Madarasa ya VI na VII		66	36	30	132
Kiswahili–Madarasa ya VI na VII Supplementary Reading		16	9	8	33
	Total	82	45	38	165

12 LANGUAGE TEACHING IN SECONDARY SCHOOLS

Fulgens Mbunda, C. J. Brumfit, D. Constable and C. P. Hill[1]

1.0 *Swahili*

Much that has already been said about the teaching of Swahili in the primary schools is also relevant to the teaching of Swahili at the secondary level. Even as there are certain policy matters which affect the teaching of Swahili at the primary level, so also policy matters affect the teaching of Swahili at the secondary level. For example the Five Year Development Plan calls for a moderate expansion, no more than will keep pace with population growth, of secondary schools involving the increasing of the number of classes in existing schools and the building of a small number of new schools (see chapter 10). This expansion will equally call for an increase in the number of adequately qualified Swahili teaching staff: staff who are already in notably short supply. There is also a proposal to make Swahili at some time in the future the medium of instruction in secondary schools as well as in primary schools. The consequences of this for the teaching of Swahili at the secondary level are incalculable. To implement the proposal would demand at least an all-Swahili-speaking teaching force in the secondary schools. This virtually excludes any expatriate staff and could scarcely be seriously considered before 1974. The principle that every teacher is a teacher of the language used as medium of instruction would need to be heavily emphasised and all teachers would need to be given some understanding of the fundamental role of language in education.

1.1 *Problems Involved*

In the same way as policy matters affect the teaching of Swahili at both primary and secondary levels so also do matters relating to the general linguistic situation in the country. For the majority of secondary school pupils Swahili is a second language (as it is for primary school pupils). The range of problems encountered at the secondary level is almost identical with that of the primary level. However there is an additional dimension to that of the pupils' first language to be considered at the upper level, and this is what might be called the dialect variations in Swahili. Pupils entering the secondary school will have learned their Swahili, firstly, perhaps as urban dwellers whose Swahili will be full of slang expressions, it will be town Swahili with usages like *kutega* 'to chase girls', or *Kuchapa gange* 'to work, hold employment', and so on. Secondly pupils may have learned their Swahili in a rural area where their language is heavily influenced by the local vernacular and where pronunciations like those discussed for primary school pupils are widely used, e.g. *selasini* for *thelathini*, or where local tribal forms of Bantu words in Swahili are current – for example, the use of *ntu* for *mtu*, *nke* for *mke*, which is widespread in the Songea/Mtwara area of Tanzania. Thirdly, pupils may come to the secondary school speaking good standard Swahili such as is current on the radio, in government offices, etc., the standard towards which all teaching is directed. Pupils whose Swahili is of either of the first two varieties are likely to have certain difficulties when they are studying the language at the secondary school.

1.1.1 *The Status of Swahili*

It has to be admitted that the current state of Swahili teaching in secondary schools is far from satisfactory. The reasons for this are various. In the first place the slightly ambiguous status of Swahili in the secondary school probably has something to do with it. The situation at the moment is the rather curious one where the national language is not the medium of instruction. It is taught simply as a subject, and indeed the time allocation given to it is remarkably small: three periods a week. There is also the fact that up till 1970 there was no senior school course leading to an examination at the end of the sixth form in Swahili, so that pupils felt that once they had passed the Form Four examination there was no more for them to learn. The absence of that higher level as a goal towards which everyone in the school should strive undoubtedly had a deleterious effect. Even the University in Dar es Salaam did not have a separate Swahili department until 1970 and the influence of this lack too filtered down to the lower levels of the educational structure.

1.1.2 *The Swahili Syllabus*

In the second place, the syllabus for Swahili in the secondary school has left a good deal to be desired. It was couched in general and vague terms: terms which made it possible for teachers to deal with the subject in a great variety of ways, mainly on a kind of ad hoc basis, and for the examiners at Form IV to set papers which bore very little relation to what the pupils might have been doing in class. There has been sometimes a too heavy emphasis on translation out of and into English, and indeed the whole atmosphere and orientation of the examination has been that of the traditional British foreign language examination. What is required obviously is much more an examination with an orientation towards testing the ability of speakers to use their first language – in spite of the fact that Swahili may be a second language for the majority of pupils. Some moves are afoot to revise the examinations and constant revision is now going on (1970). However, it is quite clear that a new, detailed comprehensive syllabus is required with a true Tanzanian orientation, a syllabus which will make it quite clear what kinds of skill in using the language will be expected of the pupils at the end of the course, and which will be formulated in terms which are also academically respectable.

1.1.3 *Swahili Books*

In the third place the state of Swahili teaching is unsatisfactory because of the scarcity of suitable books. Many of the books currently in use in secondary schools were clearly not intended primarily for that purpose. For example, neither the literary not the critical works of Shabaan Robert are really suitable since they demand a degree of sophistication and a sense of literary tradition and perspective which is well beyond most secondary pupils, and yet they are widely used. Furthermore, the fact that books such as those were not specially written for schools means that it is almost impossible to grade them as suitable for one age group or another, and certainly few of the teachers actually engaged in teaching Swahili in the secondary schools are capable of doing this kind of grading of them. Another factor is that a good many of the books have been translated from some other language and deal with events, happenings, customs and values which are so exotic as to present considerable difficulties to pupils reading them – even such perennially popular books as *Alfu-lela-Ulela*[2] in 'The Thousand and One Nights' where the combination of elements of fantasy and Arabic culture often present problems for Tanzanian pupils. Books with a familiar African cultural background would be much more suitable at the earlier levels especially. Yet another difficulty arises over reference books. The dictionaries currently available are on the whole somewhat out of date. They lack a great many words in widespread current use, and almost all the recently developed technical terminology. Moreover the best of them are translation dictionaries, not single language Swahili dictionaries, with definitions, explanations and quotations all in Swahili. As for books on the structure and phonetics of Swahili, any that are available are foreign, written by foreigners in a foreign language for the use of other foreign scholars; and there is simply no book available as a reference work on Swahili usage equivalent to Fowler's *Dictionary of Current English Usage* or the Perrin and Smith *Handbook of Current English Usage* (1955). Finally the sheer smallness of the number of Swahili books available which can be used at all at the secondary level brings its own problems. There is a tendency for the same few books to be read over and over again, and naturally pupils soon lose their enthusiasm for learning more Swahili. There is also a certain amount of difficulty in obtaining copies of Swahili books from printers and publishers, and when this is combined with an attitude on the part of administrators which seems to give Swahili a relatively low status as a school subject, the consequence is that the supply of Swahili books reaching the classrooms is seriously inadequate. There have been cases reported of teachers trying to deal with a set book in a class of 35 pupils with four copies of the book available to them.

1.1.4 *Staffing*

In the fourth place the state of Swahili teaching is unsatisfactory because of staffing difficulties. Until recently Swahili teaching tended to be put into the hands of whichever of the citizen teachers was least well qualified academically. This was all part of the low status syndrome discussed already. "It requires a specialised teacher, a graduate, to teach science, or mathematics, or even English, but anyone who knows a bit of Swahili can teach that" was the attitude. As a result the pupils sometimes found that they knew more than the teacher, and obviously their confidence in his ability to teach them anything about the language or of it declined rapidly. This tendency was exacerbated by the fact that many of these Swahili teachers of relatively low academic standing were from up-country and spoke a variety of Swahili which was already by that very fact suspect. Teachers who came from the coast or even the big towns on the other hand inspired much greater confidence in their pupils. No teachers until relatively recently had been specifically trained to teach Swahili. As a result a tremendous variety of methods were used, many of them on an experimental, trial and mostly error basis. Even where teachers were using the same books and materials, the way they handled them was often radically different, ranging from a simple formal reading with a seasoning of vocabulary explanation, through wholesale translation into English, to detailed and careful comprehension work, or superficial and rather unsophisticated, literary appreciation. Many teachers faced with a low time allocation, inadequate book supplies and unenthusiastic pupils, simply opted out and taught other things during the Swahili periods, or retreated into teaching simply for the Form IV examination, working over past examination papers and practising translation into English, formal précis, and rather sterile grammar and vocabulary exercises. The thought of creative work in Swahili, producing a Swahili play, or a magazine of pupils' writing – poetry and short stories and feature articles – or even examining critically an important government document like 'The Arusha Declaration' (Nyerere, 1968a) would have been quite out of the bounds of what they believed possible in a Swahili class. In the few instances where schools have had well qualified, adequately trained teachers the tendency has been for the one teacher to carry the full burden of Swahili teaching for the whole school – up to twelve classes with three periods each and no other subject. The effect of this is, of course, to ensure that if he is at all conscientious, he is completely overwhelmed by the task, and to force a degree of monotony upon him which becomes almost intolerable.

With all these factors militating against good Swahili teaching it is small wonder that the state of the art is as it is.

1.2 *Future Plans*

The picture for the future, however, is not quite so gloomy. The Swahili subject panel of the Institute of Education has been very active, so have the Promoter for Swahili and other officials of the Ministry of National Education, and a series of recommendations have been produced which, if they are implemented (and some of them are indeed in the course of being implemented) should bring about a dramatic improvement.

1.2.1 *New Syllabus*

Firstly there are recommendations which require action at the upper levels of administration and organisation, within the Ministry of National Education, the University and other agencies which are concerned for the growth and development of the National Language. The first requirement is a new, detailed, up-to-date syllabus whose primary aim would be to extend the kinds of control over the uses of Swahili which the Primary School leaver has, in power, effectiveness and range. The publication of the document *Kiswahili katika Sekondari* by the Institute of Education at the University (Mbunda, 1969) is almost as valuable a contribution towards the development of an adequate syllabus as the corresponding document for the primary school. With this as a basis the signs are most hopeful. A number of important points relevant to the development of the new syllabus emerge. Firstly, the rudimentary kinds of literary appreciation fostered in the primary school should be fully developed so that by the end of the secondary school course pupils would have attained considerable literary sophistication and would be ready to enter on university level studies or at least to read works of literature for themselves with proper appreciation. Secondly, some pupils at least should be introduced to the intricacies of the techniques of translation. This should not simply be a matter of practising translating into Swahili but should include some introduction to the theory of translation, guidance on re-writing material so that the rhetorical structure and pattern of presentation becomes more suitable for transmission in Swahili, and generally preparing pupils for the work of translating whole books, not just short texts, so that they will leave school prepared in some measure to contribute to the fuller flow of Swahili materials in all subjects that is so essential to the growth of the language. Thirdly, some attention would need to be paid to the needs of those Tanzanian citizens whose first language is not a Bantu language, in particular those minorities who speak a language of Nilotic or Asian origin. If secondary schools were to become regional schools fed from particular geographical areas of the country this would become even more important, but indications of the kinds of teaching which might be suitable for such pupils still need to be written into the new syllabus. Despite this special section on teaching Swahili as a second language, the primary orientation of the new syllabus – which ideally should be presented in the form of a comprehensive Teachers' Handbook, complete with schemes of work, descriptions of techniques and procedures, and all essential basic information for the Swahili teacher – should be towards teaching the language as the principal means of communication, as the first language (L_1) rather than as the second language (L_2).

1.2.2 *New Books*

The second kind of action required at Ministry level is a big effort towards book and materials production. A very high priority is the production of a specially written series of Swahili language text books for the secondary school and, fortunately, a beginning has been made on this, using similar techniques to those used for developing the primary school materials. However, a great wealth of additional material is also needed to supplement and enrich the basic course books. It is important that the greatest possible encouragement be given to teachers and others to provide these materials. In the first instance the materials might be reproduced simply in mimeographed form, so that they might be tried out fairly widely before a commitment to producing them in print is made. To encourage the trial and dissemination, area Swahili Teachers associations might be formed, perhaps as sections of the Language Association of Tanzania, or under the aegis of the Regional Swahili Co-ordinators. These associations should be given an allocation of funds to, at least, pay for the duplicating; even better would be a sum of money to help to finance at least one yearly meeting of all the Swahili teachers in a region which might function as a materials production workshop. A more substantial encouragement would be to give teachers copyright so that they could draw royalties on the sales of the books they write and even aspire to becoming full-time professional writers. It is extremely discouraging to a teacher who has given up a great deal of his spare time and expended a great deal of effort in the production of a book, to see a publisher making a considerable amount of money out of it while he receives no reward at all beyond knowing that he has contributed a little more than his share towards the building of the nation. It would seem that if the authorities are going to be serious about encouraging writers, then incentives to write should be provided. There might be something to be said for having an annual writers' competition with really substantial cash prizes, of the order of Shs 6,000.00: enough to allow someone to live for a year and devote himself to further writing. Another substantial form of support might be to release teachers or other workers who have useful ideas for books from their normal employment simply so that they can write. They could perhaps be seconded to a Swahili Book Production Unit where the potential author could be given technical assistance in preparing his manuscript for publication. The unit would require a minimum permanent staff of an experienced editor and a competent designer/book illustrator with at least three skilled, intelligent audio-typists/stenographers. The editor might expect to have four or five authors working under him at any one time, but they would be a constantly changing group. With the kind of technical support envisaged above, authors could be expected to really get on with the job and no author would be likely to be away from his regular employment for more than one school term. However it is not only books that are needed but a whole array of other supportive materials: pictures, diagrams, maps, tape recordings and models. It would seem that the Colleges of National Education might well be encouraged to design and try out materials of this kind, perhaps with groups of five or six students working together on sets of such materials as one of the projects undertaken during training. The best of these materials might be replicated and facilities for this would need to be provided at some central place. Possibly an additional member of the staff of the Swahili Book Production Unit might take responsibility for these supplementary materials. Obviously a unit of this kind would cost money but the long term benefits from it could be enormous. An initial project with a target of say one hundred titles and some fifty sets of supplementary materials within a five year period would seem realistic provided the editor in charge was energetic and enthusiastic and had access to good facilities (including a suitable and efficient printer) besides an adequate budget.

1.2.3 *Reform of Examinations*

A third high level requirement would be that the Swahili examinations should be reformed. First of all it is essential that there should be a Form VI examination as well as one at Form IV. This suggestion is indeed under active consideration and the East African Examinations Council (E.A.E.C.) has produced a syllabus for an 'A' level examination. The examination would consist of three papers. Paper I (2 hours) would include translation from English into Swahili, questions on grammar and usage and either practical criticism or the development of Swahili. Paper II (2 hours) would require the candidate to write a composition, make a summary, and show that he comprehended a Swahili text. Paper III (3 hours) would require candidates to answer four questions on 6 set books. Two of these would be plays, two works of prose, and two books of poems. One question would have to be answered on each of these different kinds of work and the fourth might be chosen from any of them. A typical set of books would be:

Plays:	Ebrahim Hussein – *Kinjeketile*
	Ebrahim Hussein – *Mashetani*
Prose:	M. S. Abdullah – *Mzimu wa Watu wa Kale*
	Shabaan Robert – *Kusadikika*
Poetry:	A. Abdala – *Utenzi wa Nabii-Adamu na Hawaa*
	S. Chiraghdin – *Matenga wa Mvita*

(This selection shows very clearly how severely limited the range of books available for advanced work in Swahili is.)

It would also seem to be sensible that the reformed examinations match the new syllabus and were a logical conclusion to the several stages outlined in it. The E.A.E.C. syllabus might be criticised in this connection in that it appears to give high importance to translation whereas under the new syllabus translation ought to be allotted a less important and optional place in the examination. Those who took the translation option might be required to translate a short story or an article of general interest of a given length, the titles of these to be approved by examiners appointed regionally. Candidates might be given up to a month to work on this, making full use of whatever help they can get. Stories and articles which were found to be well translated could then be collected and published so that the efforts of the sixth form Swahili students would not simply be wasted, locked up in cupboards and eventually destroyed, but would contribute to the fuller development of Swahili.

1.2.4 *Staff Training*

A fourth requirement which it is within the competence of the Ministry of National Education to fulfil is that the training of specialised Swahili teachers should be accelerated. The prognosis for this in the long term is hopeful. The University now has a fully fledged Department of Swahili and the staff of the Institute of Education are enthusiastically involved in promoting modern, interesting and lively methods of teaching the language. The fact that there will be an examination at the end of the sixth form should also help to ensure that many more teachers come forward for training with a substantial competence in the language. In the short term better teaching and proper specialisation can only be fostered by in-service training of existing teachers. More refresher courses are urgently needed. It may be that these could be organised on a semi-snowball principle so that the first to be re-trained would be groups of potential teacher trainers or senior staff in schools, who could themselves subsequently mount retraining exercises in their own areas. Within any particular area retraining ought to be accomplished school by school. All the teachers involved in the teaching of Swahili in any one school being required to attend the refresher course together so that re-organisation and the new approach and techniques could be introduced simultaneously throughout the school with all the conflicts between those who held fixedly to the traditional ways of teaching and those who were open to more modern and up-to-date ways of going about things might be resolved outside the staff-room in an atmosphere of cooperative learning under the guidance of respected advisers and experts.

1.2.5 *Status*

Perhaps the most important requirement of all is that the Ministry and indeed all the other high level agencies involved, would need to step up even further their efforts to raise the status of Swahili teaching. The efforts that are being made are not inconsiderable. The prospect of Swahili becoming the medium of instruction in the secondary school (even partly) will make a big difference, so too will the new high level examinations and courses of study. It is perhaps in the matter of the amount of time allocated to Swahili in the timetable that the greatest immediate practical effect can be achieved. If the minimum allocation were raised to five periods a week that would immediately begin to give some indication of how much the language was really valued. All of the other improvements suggested above for the provision of books, teachers, and more clearly defined objectives will also help to raise the status of Swahili as a school subject and make it possible for teachers to look forward to having enthusiastic and hard working classes all the time.

1.2.6 *Reallocation of Funds and Time-tabling*

Also among the recommendations formulated are some which affect the levels of the educational system below that of the Ministry and the University. In the schools themselves for example it is certainly possible for a rather larger allocation of the funds available for the purchase of books and materials to be made to Swahili. This is not only a matter of books for the classroom but also for the school library. It is particularly important that as many as possible of the Kiswahili newspapers should be regularly taken. It is shameful that there should be any Secondary School in Tanzania which takes no Swahili newspaper. *Uhuru, Kiongozi* and the rest are essential teaching materials as well as sources of information and news and vehicles for the transmission of national policy. These papers should not only be taken regularly but they should be readily available and accessible to the pupils. A good selection of those reference works that are available for Swahili should be bought for the library, and books and magazines which may be read for pure entertainment should be provided too – even to the level of *Film Tanzania*. At the school level too the deployment of available staff can contribute to better Swahili teaching. The best qualified teachers with the highest personal status should teach Swahili and should show that they regard it as important. No teacher should find himself teaching nothing but Swahili for every teacher needs a little variety to spice his life. Whenever possible a teacher should be given the chance to follow through with a class for more than one year. This gives him an opportunity to observe how his pupils develop over the longer period and promotes greater job satisfaction.

The teachers themselves can, indeed must, of course, play their part. The teacher should familiarise himself with the syllabus and should follow it. He should exploit what books and materials are available even now, including the radio, tape-recordings and newspapers. It is often surprising what books are lying in stores or cupboards while the pupils are reading *Alfu-lela-Ulela* (the Thousand and One Nights) for the third time: it is the teachers' responsibility to find out just what is available. The teacher can also make use of human resources to improve his Swahili teaching. For example, in many areas, particularly along the coast, there are many older people whose knowledge of the language is deep and wide, and who have a treasure of knowledge and experience which they can convey with elegance and precision in Swahili. There would seem to be no good reason why such people should not be invited into the Swahili classroom to give the pupils the benefit of their wisdom. Similarly there are all sorts of people who have particular sorts of expertise – in poetry, for example – members of UKUTA, or the National Swahili Council, broadcasters and authors all of whom could be called on.

The teacher must of course also ensure that his own knowledge of the language is as good as possible. His learning of the language must never cease. It is his duty to read widely in Swahili and to keep in touch with linguistic and professional ideas. He should at the very least read the journal *Kiswahili* regularly and try to familiarise himself with the current work of the National Swahili Council and the various committees or commissions which work under it. He also needs to prepare every lesson carefully and thoroughly, and he should take pride in the excellence of his own Swahili. With teachers like this the quality of the teaching of Swahili could not help but improve.

1.3 *Present Syllabus and Examination*

If we look now briefly at the present syllabus we may note that the fundamental objectives seem to be right. The principal aim is said to be to build on the foundations laid in the primary school so as to develop the use of Swahili as the national language as fully as possible. A fuller statement concerning this fundamental aim may be found in the introduction to the syllabus itself. The kinds of activities suggested also seem to be generally of the right kind too, perhaps a little too formal and traditional, but very similar to those suggested for the upper forms of the primary school. They include:

- (i) oral and written composition – stories, discussion, explanation of an object or picture, debates;
- (ii) reading – in class, reading aloud (the importance of being able to read aloud clearly and well for the benefit of others is self-evident in a society where only a minority of the citizens are literate) – improving reading speed, reading for different purposes, reading for thorough understanding; – out of class, reading for pleasure and for information from books, newspapers, articles and pamphlets;
- (iii) language exercises – for vocabulary development, synonyms and antonyms, definitions, inferring meaning from context, derivational processes; – for sentence structure development, expanding, completing, and combining sentences and phrases; – dealing with aphorisms, proverbs and riddles; – for punctuation and graphic layout, as in letters;
- (iv) learning to use a dictionary – alphabetisation, the forms of Swahili words used in dictionary entries, how to read the dictionary – etymologies, definitions and quotations;
- (v) reading poetry and plays simply for pleasure, and later for the purposes of the examination;
- (vi) the beginning of literary criticism;
- (vii) the beginning of grammar, the basic word classes – notions like singular and plural, tense, and word form; derivational processes, extended verb forms, nominalisation, and so on.
- (viii) in the fourth year, translation from English into Swahili (and vice-versa) is introduced, apparently with the examination principally in mind.

The latest version of the terminal examination available consists of one paper of two and a half hours duration. Candidates are required to answer four questions. The first is a composition of between 300 and 500 words in Swahili; the second question presents a choice between either a summary, where the candidate is required to reduce a Swahili text to approximately one third of its original length, or, a translation of a Swahili text into English. The third question is a comprehension test (some of the questions of which may be open-ended and some of the multiple-choice type) and explanations of vocabulary items as well as of longer sections of the text are called for. The fourth question is an "objective test of the candidate's knowledge of the structure and vocabulary of Swahili" [sic]. The examiners do not bind themselves to set any particular type of question in any one year, but concords, extended verb forms and general vocabulary will be tested each year together with other areas of grammar and usage.

The time allocation envisaged by the syllabus is, as has already been mentioned, three periods per week, but the distribution of the various activities and the emphasis placed on each of them is left entirely up to the teacher – hence some of the problems mentioned above.[3]

1.4 *Conclusions*

This then is what things look like in the teaching of Swahili in secondary schools in Tanzania. There are problems, but, following the policy of education for self-reliance, energetic efforts are being made to solve them through meetings and workshops set up mainly through the Institute of Education at the University of Dar es Salaam jointly with the Ministry of National Education. Success will follow so long as those initially concerned succeed in removing the last vestiges of any low esteem for Swahili as a school subject which may yet linger on, and in finally dissipating that lack of self-confidence that still seems to affect some teachers.

2.0 *English*

The teaching of English has been an important issue in Tanzania ever since the British took over the Mandate in 1919. Throughout the Colonial period discussion by individuals and commissions ranged over the whole question of the relative merits of Swahili, the vernaculars and English. Until the 1950s, however, when independence was imminent, the numbers of secondary schools were so small that the discussion of language policy at that educational level was rather academic. Only the attitudes of the last decade of colonial rule have had any significant effect on the post-independence secondary school system.

The few secondary schools in existence before independence tacitly regarded English as one of the most important subjects, and in most of the schools both language and literature carried considerable prestige, as the allocation of periods in the timetable clearly shows (nine or ten periods being not uncommon). This prestige arose partly because of the obvious necessity of a mastery of the language for advancement in Government Service, a fact which was recognised in making a pass in English Language essential to the obtaining of a School Certificate, and a credit essential to being placed in the first class.

The general approach to language teaching was much more literary than is favoured now, and teachers no doubt viewed their role as that of cultural missionaries, introducing students to the great English literary tradition. Part of this attitude still remains, and the history of attitudes to English teaching since independence is, to a considerable extent, the history of an attempt to attain cultural independence without sacrificing international contacts. Since independence the status of Literature as a School Certificate choice (and therefore as a secondary school subject) has declined steadily, but English Language retains a strong position, partly because it has been the medium of instruction. This situation is likely to change however now that English is being superseded as the medium of instruction by Swahili. The most optimistic projections expect that by 1973 all subjects will be taught through the medium of Swahili up to School Certificate level. This seems very unlikely, but certainly by about 1976 nearly all pre-Form IV teaching will be in Swahili, and already, early in 1970, certain subjects: civics, domestic science, sometimes biology, are being taught in Swahili at the lower secondary level. Thus the role of English in the secondary schools is changing from year to year.

2.1 *Examinations*

The effective goal of secondary school English language teaching at the moment is the School Certificate examination, taken after eleven years of education, four of them in the secondary school. This examination is set and marked in England by the Cambridge University Examinations Syndicate. Again, this situation is changing and the examination has already been nominally taken over by the East African Examinations Council. In a few years it will be set and marked in East Africa if not in Tanzania.

Until 1965 the School Certificate English Language examination was designed on the same principles as examinations for native speakers of English in England. The syllabus was not well suited to the needs of speakers of English as a second language. It was concerned more with knowledge about the language than with ability to use it, and competence was assessed very largely on the student's imaginative response and literary ability. It was not sufficiently recognised that most candidates were likely to need English more for the writing of reports than for the creation of short stories, and that the main need of Tanzanian pupils was effective and confident control of an accessible range of structure and lexis. In 1965, however, as a result of discussions by teachers and others interested in this field, led in Tanzania by the senior English Inspector, Mr. P. H. C. Clarke, a new syllabus for this examination was designed for the three East African countries. This syllabus had a much more utilitarian approach than the previous one. It has been found highly successful, and in 1970 is still being used without modifications of any kind.

The syllabus places the teacher of English in Tanzania in the happy, though unfortunately all too rare, position of having the educational goals which he would wish to set himself corresponding closely to the requirements of the terminal examination. The candidate is tested in ability "to use and understand current English". He is asked to "write adequately and relevantly on a subject", to produce a piece of situationalised writing "appropriate to the demands made and implied by the situation", to draw out information from a passage, to show understanding of the "content and argument or narrative sequence" of a passage, and to handle the structure and vocabulary of English.

In the Oral Examination which goes with the written, the candidate has to read a prepared passage out loud, and to carry on a conversation with the examiner for about five minutes.

Thus the aims are very practical. Only two parts of the whole examination – the isolated treatment of structural items, and the reading passage in the oral examination – do not test activities which candidates may be required to engage in after they leave school. Until recently it would have been true to say "will be required to engage in", but the rapid promotion of Swahili makes it less likely that Tanzanian secondary school pupils who do not go on to further education will need much more than a reading knowledge of English. The implications of this have not yet been explored in any policy document, and the official instructions to teachers are simply to continue as before. Indeed the introduction of English as a subject in Standard I (instead of Standard III where it used to be introduced until 1969) means that candidates will eventually finish school at the secondary level with eleven years of English behind them, instead of the nine years which they have at present.

For the moment however we may point out that the task of the various advisers on English teaching has been made much easier by the close identity of aims between the examination syllabus and the actual needs of secondary school pupils. At the same time much of the work of the former inspectors of English, of the present Principal Co-ordinator of English, and of the English Language Advisory Panel of the Institute of Education has been devoted to a re-education programme for teachers who have either been trained to teach English in first language conditions, or who have long experience of teaching the old, pre-1965 syllabus. Simultaneously an extensive programme of training secondary English teachers has been launched at Dar es Salaam College of National Education, and at the University of Dar es Salaam. These new teachers, of course, have received training in techniques appropriate to local conditions. Until recently very few teachers had been trained specifically for the second language situation. Thus, apart from the change in the medium of instruction, the arrival of many local, appropriately trained teachers is likely to be the most significant factor in English teaching in the next few years.

2.2 *Problems*

The problems throughout the 1960s have been very great for two main reasons: first, the lack of training for the specific situation, and second, the rapid turnover of staff. Most contracts for expatriate teachers last two years; volunteers come for one- or two-year spells. Not many teachers have renewed their contracts, and very few permanent and pensionable teachers were left from the (in any case very small) colonial service education personnel. As a result of this situation new English teachers frequently rose rapidly to responsible positions before they had had time to discover the very considerable problems of the new African conditions. Few English teachers would have called themselves competent within the new situation before they had been teaching for over a year, and then most of them went home after only two years in all. Very often the fundamental notions which underlie the teaching of English as a second language had never been encountered by good teachers who would work hard for a year or more before working out, by trial and error, principles which could have been easily and effectively taught in appropriate training courses. Many more teachers of course never really grasped what all the fuss was about and went on happily teaching as they would in England, the

United States or Canada. The situation was further complicated by the tendency to place English native speakers, whatever their training or inclinations, in charge of English teaching. All this is not to deny that training programmes of various kinds (London University, Makerere College, and the Peace Corps orientation courses, being probably the most important) did provide many teachers with a useful background, but it was always a very low proportion of English teachers who had had the benefit of these. Further, after the breaking off of British aid, and the rejection of the Peace Corps, more and more teachers have been volunteers from other countries in Europe and the "Third World" who themselves do not speak English as a mother tongue. Sometimes teachers have found this to be an advantage but on the whole it has only confused the pupils even further.

2.3 *Solutions*

The obvious response to this situation is to increase central control and to concentrate on providing in-service training. This has indeed been the consistent policy of the Ministry of National Education, but the task has been enormous. There are about 120 secondary schools, and the rapid turnover of staff has tended to cancel out the advantages derived from in-service training courses almost as quickly as the course could be mounted. There has only been a limited budget available and the "colonial" language has been sinking steadily down the list of educational priorities, for reasons which are sometimes educationally sound and sometimes necessary responses to political and social pressures. None the less major courses were held at the Dar es Salaam University in September 1967 and in April 1969. At each of these courses at least one teacher attended from every secondary school, preference being given to local teachers or to those who would be staying for some time.

The first course was concerned largely with putting over the ideas underlying the syllabus which the English Language Panel of the Institute of Education had prepared for secondary schools and published in 1967. This syllabus was a series of guidelines on the various aspects of teaching in the second language situation. The then Inspector of English, Mr. P. J. Roe, was instrumental in adapting many of the ideas current in the field of foreign language instruction in England and America to the specific Tanzanian situation, and through this syllabus, the first in-service course mentioned above, and his visits to "inspect", encourage and advise teachers in schools all over the country he sought to achieve a broad measure of agreement on the aims and methods of English teaching. Within two years, the enthusiasm generated by his activities led to the organisation of English Teachers' Associations all over the country as the result of a suggestion put forward at the September 1967 course, and there was a demand for something a bit more specific in the way of guidelines. The Advisory Panel redrafted the syllabus and expanded its schemes of work into a full *Handbook for English Teachers* which was published by the Institute of Education of the University of Dar es Salaam in July 1969 (Eng. Lang. Panel, 1969). This is a printed book of 110 pages together with two mimeographed appendices. The first appendix, of 76 pages, sets out all the necessary syllabuses for the exams taken by Tanzanian pupils, together with specimen papers, lists of recommended textbooks, readers and equipment of various kinds. The second is a listing of the commonest "errors" observed in the written work of Tanzanian secondary school pupils over a number of years together with references to textbooks and course books which provide suitable exercises for the correction and elimination of these errors. Every English teacher in the country is supposed to have these materials and they provide a common frame of reference for all discussion of teaching problems. The *Handbook* itself gives detailed instructions for programmes of work, sets out basic principles, and describes useful and well-tried techniques which have been found to work in Tanzanian secondary schools. It is indeed a goldmine of excellent ideas and sound practice.

To ensure the continued use of these materials and, hopefully, their continued improvement, all student teachers being trained to teach English in secondary schools are trained with reference to the *Handbook*. At the moment this is a satisfactory situation, but as the medium of instruction in the secondary schools changes, and the place of English in the curriculum changes too, a handbook may become a force against necessary adaptation. The compilers of the *Handbook* were aware of this danger. It is for this reason that the statements of principle are often bald and dogmatic, under the belief that they will always hold good, but the actual way in which the principles may be carried out in teaching has been left as open and as flexible as possible. Nonetheless there is an obvious danger to be guarded against. A quotation from the introduction to the *Handbook* should indicate the approach favoured and the level of simplicity it has tried to achieve.

For the time being English is still used as a medium of communication in Tanzania, although on an ever decreasing scale, for a limited number of specific purposes. Although not the only one, the most important of these purposes is the acquisition of new knowledge and new skills. Thus English can be said to supplement the national language, but only to perform a limited and practical function.

Knowledge of a language is not an end in itself. A pupil's command of language is to be assessed only in terms of the tasks he can carry out successfully through the medium of that language. A language is used most effectively when the user is least aware of the mechanics of what he is doing and is conscious only of the job in hand – that is to say of the 'meaning' of what he is trying to express.

The task of the teacher of English is to train the pupil in the highly efficient use of English as a study tool which can be used subconsciously for the acquisition of new knowledge and new skills.

The first important part of this task is to train the pupil to make *effective use of the English he has already been exposed to before entering secondary school.*

Only when the pupil has learned to apply this knowledge of English effectively and with confidence should we attempt to extend it.

The English department therefore organises for the pupil a carefully graded programme of training in study skills through the medium of English. Both the intellectual and the linguistic burden placed on the pupil must be carefully graded. (Eng. Lang. Panel, 1969: 4)

The *Handbook*, then, is the basic guide for the teacher of English in Tanzania. It suggests a possible allocation of periods as given in Table 12:1.

Table 12:1 Timetable for English

	Periods per week			
	Form I	Form II	Form III	Form IV
Composition/Structure	3	3	3 or 4	3 or 4
Intensive Reading	1 or 2	1 or 2	2 or 1	2
Extensive Reading/Library	1 or 2	1 or 2	1 or 2	1
Oral and Remedial Work	1 or 2	2	2	2 or 1

The oral and remedial work would be distributed throughout the week in short sessions of ten minutes or a quarter of an hour. It should, however, be noted that the assumption of 8 periods a week of English language work on which these suggestions are based is almost certainly going to be modified and it seems likely that the number of periods available to English will stabilize at about 6. At the moment some schools still have as many as ten periods a week for English, and some, through staff shortages, are not being taught English at all.

The most important principles which underlie the attitude to second language teaching put forward in the *Handbook* are the principles of pupil activity, integration, and control. In other words the teacher is expected to make the pupils use the language as much as possible, to avoid treating the various aspects of language as isolated phenomena, and to control the language activity of the class in such a way as to prevent any of the pupils making mistakes. This is a counsel of perfection, but a scheme of work is offered which integrates remedial structural work into a system of composition training which takes the pupils through from completely controlled work (little more than copying exercises) to completely free writing. It is hoped to integrate the practice of correct oral patterns into this scheme by linking it to the initial re-presentation of structural items, but this is something which has not yet been fully worked out.

The decision to base the course on a foundation of remedial work deserves some comment. One of the basic problems in the secondary school class is the fact that Form I pupils are already fairly adept at using a language which closely resembles standard English but which is full of interference from their first languages producing deviations from standard English which are constantly reinforced unwittingly by primary school teachers and by the conversation of their peers. Eradication of these deviations is essential if English is to remain a language of wider communication, and thus attention has to be focused upon them since they are very deeply ingrained. For this reason and also because it is a goal that should be within the reach of all secondary school pupils, the prime objective of the secondary school course is to give pupils fluent and complete mastery of the English which they already "know" (somewhat inadequately) from primary school. In fact, full mastery of the primary school material would in itself be a thoroughly satisfactory basis for further advance without a teacher, and this material has indeed been specifically selected with this end in view. The problem is that probably no secondary school leavers have full mastery even of the range of structures dealt with in primary school.

Some idea of how the various language skills should be dealt with, the patterns of integration and activity, may be gathered from the following "Notes for Teachers" provided with the *Handbook*:

Relation of Composition to Structure

Each composition in the first fifteen stages is based on a structure pattern. The composition should not be attempted until most of the class is able to complete the drills and exercises on the structure without making any mistakes. Thus each composition should be based on structure work completed a week or a fortnight beforehand – so revising and consolidating the previous work.

Basic Format

Ideally there will be five or six compositions for each stage, graded in difficulty within the stage, and the class will do as many of them as necessary according to its interests and needs. At first it will be necessary to give fairly detailed oral preparation under the guidance of the teacher. Then with the later compositions in each stage, pupils may be given progressively less help.

Oral Preparation

At first the teacher may ask individual pupils to do all or part of the composition orally to show the method, and he will help until the right answers are produced. Then the composition may again be produced orally in groups or pairs with the pupils correcting each other until they are sure of it. Only after all this oral preparation is the class ready to write, at least for the first composition in each stage.

Writing

The exercise may be written in one of three ways:
  (i) in groups – each member of the group writing the agreed version, sentence by sentence.
  (ii) in pairs, using the same method as in groups.
  (iii) individually, without any consultation.

It is especially important that hardly any mistakes are made in the final version and the oral preparation should be thorough enough to ensure this.

Correction

In most of the early stages the only possible errors (apart from copying mistakes) are those in the structure that has been worked on already. For this reason we can again use:
  (i) groups – here the purpose is for a final version or versions to be agreed upon (depending on the amount of freedom the exercise gives). Pupils may start by exchanging exercise books in pairs within the group and finish by reading accepted answers around the group while the others pounce on mistakes.

(ii) pairs – here the two will examine one book at a time and the writer will defend his answers or adapt them if he is convinced of his mistakes.
(iii) late in the stage individuals may check other people's books separately before the teacher looks at them.

Fairly frequently and especially before going on to a new stage the teacher should take in the books and check them quickly. During the lesson of course he should be generally supervising going from group to group.

Later Stages (Stages 16–35)
The procedure suggested above may still be used for preparation and writing, but it will become increasingly necessary for the teacher to look over the class's work himself after it has been corrected by the pupils.

General
These techniques should be varied with each exercise tried to avoid monotony. As the class becomes confident within each stage exercises may be started without full oral preparation. Writing may start with groups, pairs or even individual work when the teacher is sure that all except a very few of the class will produce completely correct answers. Please note that successful group work may take over a term to develop so do not be discouraged if results are not spectacular at first. Also please note that 'correction' here is not the marking of a finished product but a process of improving the composition. It is part of the training in the correct use of language as much as the actual writing is. A possible time scheme with junior classes would be about half an hour each for preparation, writing and correction; the exercises must be short enough to allow ample time for the preparation and correction. (Eng. Lang. Panel, 1969: 8–35)

The work outlined above is augmented by work on intensive reading, again making use of group discussion techniques, and a large scale programme of extensive reading of readers graded for the appropriate level. Few schools are in fact well organised in their extensive reading programme as it requires a certain amount of careful and detailed planning and organisation and a substantial initial outlay on suitable books. These books are not bought in class sets, but in threes or fours so that, whereas in the past the expenditure of a certain sum of money provided one title in sufficient numbers for all the pupils in a class to read that one book simultaneously, now ten or more titles can be provided for the same outlay, and pupils read at their own rate under appropriately devised supervision. The situation is slowly changing however, and the *Handbook* offers help and guidance of a very direct and useful kind.

The schemes of work are compulsory for all secondary schools. They are also being used as the basis for a projected course book for Tanzanian secondary schools. One of the weaknesses in the overall pattern of English teaching which has revealed itself over the past few years has been the tendency for advisers on the teaching of English to recommend the rejection of existing teaching materials and courses – often for very good reasons – without their being able to provide really satisfactory alternatives. The *Handbook* schemes of work can now be used as a basis on which to write exercises for a course in secondary reading, writing and speaking, which is as far as possible integrated, contextualised and relevant to Tanzanian needs. Work on this has in fact already started. In 1969 the Ministry of National Education divided the country into ten educational "zones" and appointed in each zone a co-ordinator for each subject, including English, with a Principal Co-ordinator based, in the case of English, at the Institute of Education. At the same time Regional English Language Teachers Associations were starting to work on producing their own teaching materials by co-operative effort between teachers in the schools in a particular Region. These two sets of local activity have now combined so that the official Zonal Co-ordinator for English often works through and in the unofficial local association. The material which is produced varies greatly in quality, and in many cases it is perhaps the teacher training aspect of the exercise that is more significant than the actual materials produced, but it is hoped that before the end of 1970 a general supervisor for the course book will have been appointed to co-ordinate and edit the work done by the various zones.

2.4 *Higher School Certificate*

The huge majority of secondary school teachers in Tanzania are deeply involved primarily in work leading to the School Certificate at the end of Form IV. There are however an increasing number who are also involved with work for the Higher School Certificate. At the present time no paper in English Language is set at the Higher level and a great many teachers and others interested in the upper levels of education are concerned and dissatisfied that this should be so. In recent years a number of proposals for the establishment of an appropriate paper for English Language at the Higher School Certificate level have been put forward. A detailed syllabus with specimen papers has been prepared by a working party of the English Language Panel (H.S.C.) of the Institute of Education. It is hoped that these proposals can be implemented in a year or so but in the meantime they are being discussed and scrutinised very carefully.

English Literature has of course long been studied at both School Certificate and Higher School Certificate levels, but since this involves study of how language is used, and matters of aesthetics, personal psychology, and cultural growth and appreciation, and does not directly involve language teaching as such only brief mention will be made of it. The Cambridge Syndicate syllabuses have been used and the 'set book' system which is embodied in them has made cramming particularly easy so that some schools obtained spectacular results in Literature with students who did very badly in the English Language examination. Here again the relevant subject panels of the Institute of Education have been active, and a series of proposals for the re-organisation of the syllabus including some valuable ideas on the choice of the books which students ought to be expected to have read have been forwarded to England, and hopefully may be adopted by the East African Examinations Council.

It should be obvious from everything that has been said that the total situation is far too unstable for anything very certain to be predicted about future developments. All that is possible at the moment is to give some picture of the state of English teaching in Tanzania now, and to point at some of the exciting and worthwhile efforts being made to carry the principles of African socialism even into the teaching of English.[4]

2.5 *English as a Medium of Instruction*

English has been the medium of instruction in Tanzanian secondary schools for the whole of the post-Second World War period, but paradoxically it was only when the announcement of the change to Swahili as a medium of instruction was imminent that the major problems of teaching in a second language were beginning to be faced by curriculum developers. This situation has to be seen against the background of the whole of teaching in African secondary schools. It was not until well after independence – in Tanzania somewhere in the mid 1960s – that the broad assumptions of the colonial educational heritage were effectively questioned. Even three years after independence, in 1964, most schools were still studying British History, learning to add up in pounds, shillings and pence, and concentrating on discovering what the principal products of the industrial Midlands of England were, learning, that is, what their contemporaries in England were expected to learn. The move to re-design the curriculum followed the setting up of the Institute of Education at The University of Dar es Salaam in 1964. The subject panels which were set up in 1966 were asked to evaluate and modify existing syllabuses in every secondary school subject. Before this the problem of language had been much discussed – though more at the primary than at the secondary level.[5] No doubt the complaints that "their English is not good enough," or "they can't even write their notes correctly," and such like were being made in staffrooms all over the country, but the general assumption was that it was all the business of the English department. The English department, anyway, was preparing pupils for a School Certificate Examination which had been designed for English native speaking candidates and was hardly suitable for local Tanzanian conditions.

In 1965, however, School Certificate candidates for the first time sat an examination in English Language which was specially designed for East Africa. At the same time new ideas on the teaching of the sciences, mathematics and the social sciences were being increasingly discussed and publicised, so that the revision of the syllabus by the subject panels of the Institute of Education was carried out while both the content and methodology of the old courses were under serious and radical attack. To some extent this may not have been wholly a good thing, because the enthusiasm for the new methodology which was built into the design of the new mathematics course, for example, or the materials for the Nuffield Science Projects, tended to obscure some of the fundamental problems which had been inherited from the earlier period – including that of the medium of instruction. This is not to say that the members of the panels were unaware of the problems, in fact at least one secretary of a panel reports that the question of the language of instruction was indeed much discussed but no firm proposal on this matter was ever minuted largely because the members of the panel felt themselves to be unqualified to pronounce on so complex a matter. Certainly in the minutes of the panel meetings of the period there is only one explicit reference to language problems: the Biology Panel invited Mr. R. Isaacs to attend one of its meetings in November 1967 and discuss the "language level" of the materials they were engaged in writing, using English as the medium of instruction. The Chemistry Panel also consulted Mr. Isaacs, but unofficially, and other panels made overtures to various other members of the English Language Panel. In general, however, the awareness that things "need to be kept simple" was thought sufficient, even at this late stage. This made for most erratic degrees of structural complexity and lexical control in the materials being written, but even so the kind of improvement effected may be illustrated by the following two extracts – disregarding basic differences in approach to the subject written about:

> The range of living things is set out in the table of plants and animals at the foot of this page. The animals can be divided into groups, in each of which all the members show strong likenesses to one another. These similarities are not always immediately obvious but soon become apparent when the characteristics of the group become known. Bees and butterflies, for example, though differing considerably in appearance, size, colour and habits, belong to the same group because they both have hard outer skeletons, three divisions to their bodies, six legs and two pairs of wings. (D. G. Mackean, *Introduction to Biology* (John Murray), p. 8.)

> As soon as you begin to sort out any group of living things a question arises: 'By what features can the group be divided?' If you had a handful of seeds which contained some bean seeds and some maize seeds, you could easily sort them out. The two kinds of seed would be different, in colour and shape. Animals have differences of colour, shape and many other characteristics. (*Pupils' Book 1* of the *Schools Science Project, East Africa*, p. 15.)

The first of these was published in England in 1962, the second in Dar es Salaam in 1968. The Biology and Chemistry Panels in particular concentrated carefully on the linguistic levels in the material being written, with satisfactory results in making it easier for the pupils to understand what was presented to them through the written form of English.

2.5.1 *Learning Through Language Course*

The easing of their problems in comprehending the spoken form of the language was not so easy to deal with. At least the conventions of print are reasonably uniform when school textbooks are involved, but the variety of accent, dialect and register that pupils had to be prepared to cope with was daunting in the extreme. In fact the only attempt to face this difficulty at all was the *Learning through Language* course (Isaacs, 1968). In 1968 all primary schools became Swahili medium schools. Suddenly, and not necessarily correctly, everyone assumed that the standard of English of secondary school entrants would drop alarmingly. Whether or not this would be so, some sort of adaptation would be necessary when students found themselves under instruction in English in all subjects where they had been accustomed to being taught in Swahili. Mr. R. Isaacs was instructed by the Ministry of National Education to design a course of massive exposure to the kind of English students would need in secondary school. This course was largely written at a workshop of about a dozen teachers in April 1968, tested by the editor/designer and a number of other teachers during 1968, and put into operation as a six week pre-full secondary entrance crash course in December–January 1968–69. The whole process from start to finish had taken about 14 months, a staggering achievement, and in some parts, inevitably, the course (consisting of a *Pupils' Book* and a *Teachers' Book*, both published by Tanzania Publishing House, see Isaacs, 1968) shows signs of its hasty preparation, but in general it proved highly successful. Apart from introducing many new methodological ideas about language teaching to a great many teachers who happened to be in Tanzania at that time, it provided highly concentrated practice in a number of language skills. Very soon after it was first used it was announced that the secondary schools would go over progressively to the medium of Swahili as quickly as possible, so that the future of *Learning through Language* as the basis for a course of the kind for which it was first designed would appear to be somewhat limited, but as a source book for original, locally oriented and intrinsically interesting exercises in comprehension – both aural and written (in composition, and in summary work as opposed to précis), it will long remain extremely valuable. Its quality and the results of its first use have attracted considerable interest outside Tanzania in countries where problems of a similar kind to those set before Mr. Isaacs and his collaborators rear their heads.

The course consisted of seven sections called "Bricks". The first of these dealt with reference finding skills. After some early work on alphabetical order pupils work independently answering a series of questions on a different reference volume each day. Each reference volume has a project sheet designed for it, and this is constructed in such a way that pupils can mark their own answers. The projects are graded in difficulty, the easier ones obviously coming earlier in the course. Later such complex activities as interpretation of timetables, graphs, sketch plans, and diagrams is demanded.

The second "Brick" deals with aural comprehension. There are 50 graded passages in the *Teacher's Book* which are read aloud to the pupils. Each passage consists of three paragraphs each of about 50–70 words, and each paragraph is followed by four spoken questions. The first three are short, requiring only one word answers, and the last is slightly longer and requires a full sentence answer. The content of the passages is largely factual and this Brick is particularly valuable, precisely because it introduces the pupils to the voices of the teachers who will be teaching them with all the variety of voice quality, pronunciation, and rhythmic pattern that they manifest.

Brick three contains 36 written passages each with a set of multiple choice comprehension questions on it. The answers to these are first arrived at individually, then discussed in groups while the teacher moves round the class helping the discussions. Next answers agreed upon by whole class discussion are written on the blackboard. These, written one after the other in sequence, automatically form a summary of the passage, and the pupils finally copy this.

The fourth Brick follows a similar pattern, but each answer, this time, involves a particular area of linguistic structure, usually one known to present difficulty to Tanzanian pupils. When the summary is written on the board the key elements of the structure are rubbed out and the pupils have to supply these themselves as they copy down the summary. This only happens after some time has been spent on oral rehearsal of the complete answers so that the likelihood of error is very slight. The class is thus exposed to the correct use of particular linguistic structures, and required to use them themselves under conditions of control which minimise the making of mistakes.

The fifth Brick is a faster reading course based on the Webster/McGraw Hill Reading Skill cards.

The sixth Brick is a programme of extensive reading. A wide range of mainly non-fiction titles was selected and appropriately graded. Pupils were expected to have read a minimum of three books each week.

These six Bricks constitute the formal course, taught intensively by all the teachers who would teach the new Form I during the rest of the year. The time allocation was as follows:

Brick 1: 1 period each day for six weeks.
Brick 2: 1 period each day for six weeks.
Brick 3: 2 periods – sequential – each day for six weeks.
Brick 4: 2 periods – sequential – each day for six weeks.
Brick 5: 5 periods weekly for six weeks.
Brick 6: 5 periods weekly for six weeks.

To follow this up and to establish a link with the normal English course after the intensive *Learning through Language* course was over, a seventh Brick was added. This consisted of work concentrating on remedying common structural and lexical errors found in the speech and writing of Form I entrants in Tanzania. This Brick was allotted 30 periods too.

The greatest criticism this course encountered was that it was monotonous over a period as long as six weeks, for the routines do not vary from lesson to lesson beyond the differing patterns of the seven bricks, and while the novelty of technique carries and sustains interest in the first few weeks, thereafter the lack of essential variety makes the work routine and interest flags. As a result of this experience in 1970 the course was used for four weeks only, and the remainder of the materials provided by the course was used in English lessons during the first half of the first year. It was widely agreed that this pattern was very effective, making possible rates of progress and degrees of understanding that would have been impossible without the course. In a way, it is sad that an original and effective solution to a problem that faces many countries, once it had been found for Tanzania, should be forgotten and work on it abandoned because of the decision to make Swahili the medium of instruction in secondary schools, though the reasons for this decision are readily acknowledged to be sound and consistent with the objectives of nation building.

2.6 *Conclusions*

The future of English as a medium of instruction in Tanzanian secondary schools is likely to be brief. The optimists hope that all classes in all secondary schools will be taught entirely in Swahili by the mid-1970s. Already a number of subjects in the lower forms are being taught through the medium of Swahili, particulary civics and the geography of Tanzania within East Africa, history and mathematics are likely to follow soon, and it will not be long after the change over is complete that the last expatriates teaching up to School Certificate level will leave Tanzania. The main difficulty will be over the translation of suitable textbooks, but this has begun and if it is pursued vigorously with adequate resources of manpower and money there should be no difficulty in achieving the desired end. It seems to one observer at least, however, that in pursuing the very proper objective of having all teachers in secondary schools citizens there is a danger that a valuable resource may be imperceptibly dissipated. At the moment the variety of English spoken by the majority of Tanzanian secondary school graduates is certainly acceptable as a language of wider communication. If, however, no native speakers of English are to be found teaching in the schools in the future then it may be that 'Tangereza' will develop to such a point that it can no longer be used easily for wider communication. Just as in France or Germany or Japan when a school wants to raise the standard of its English teaching it recruits a native speaker to help to sustain and improve the English of the rest of the English teaching staff as well as to actually teach in the classroom, so also it would seem sensible for Tanzania too to preserve the high standard of English spoken in its schools by recruiting a sufficient number of native speakers with appropriate professional training and genuine sympathy for the aspirations of the country to allow each secondary school to have one such teacher on the staff.

English will probably remain as the medium of instruction in post-School Certificate education for some years to come. In those secondary schools where work to the Higher School Certificate level is done there seems to be little evidence that the problems of the second language situation are considered at all, and virtually all teachers seem to assume that their pupils have very few linguistic difficulties. How justifiable this is still remains to be seen.

Whatever transpires, it is clear that the situation with regard to the teaching of English in Tanzanian secondary schools is extremely fluid. What is true this year may not be true next, and much of what is written here will have little interest except as a historical record, a statement of what things were like in 1970. The fact that there are a growing number of young, enthusiastic, well-trained Tanzanian teachers beginning to take responsibility for English teaching in the country's secondary schools leads one to look forward hopefully to a period of interesting development conforming to the needs of the growing nation.

3.0 French

Despite public pronouncements about the importance of Africa unity and contact with francophone Africa there was no great upsurge in the teaching of French in Tanzanian secondary schools immediately after independence. This was of course a result of the whole process of determining educational priorities and overcoming what might be called the educational inertia generated during the long period of British/ anglophone administration. A few French speaking missionaries (French Canadian Fathers, Swiss Sisters and the like) provided a limited amount of coherent and sequential teaching, but on the whole the picture in the early 1960s was of fragmentary ad hoc teaching. How limited the teaching done at this time was is reflected in the fact that it was not until 1969 that among the students signing on to study French and Linguistics at the University of Dar es Salaam there were any who had "done" some French beforehand. Having "done" French does not necessarily mean having passed an examination such as School Certificate French, or the Local French Test (see below) but includes casual teaching or even a few extra-curricular classes. The overall situation is however improving slightly. In 1969 there were over 40 of the 112 secondary schools in the country offering French to School Certificate level, but the subject is still considered by many Headmasters to be a somewhat peripheral one, with the result that it may be taught for a couple of years, squeezed into odd corners of the timetable or of the school buildings, only to be dropped when the expatriate wife who had been teaching it goes home. An irregular supply of French *Coopérants* (young graduates doing their military service) has provided the only sure continuity.

3.1 Numbers Involved

Some idea of the state of French teaching in Tanzania may be obtained by considering first of all the number of candidates entering for French at School Certificate. In 1968, 82 candidates took School Certificate French of whom 50% were successful. In 1969 150 candidates sat the examination of whom 52% were successful. The likelihood is that this expansion in number will continue, and if we make the assumption that each of the 40 secondary schools now offering French enters one stream for French at School Certificate, then by 1974 or 1975 the numbers of candidates should be around 1200. However, it must be recognised that this projection is purely hypothetical with only the weakest of bases.

3.1.1 1970 Questionnaire

In January of 1970 a questionnaire was sent out to all secondary schools to try to collect reliable data on the teaching of French in Tanzania. From the replies received it would appear that 66% of the teachers teaching French were expatriates, 34% were Tanzanians. The average experience of the teachers was $2\frac{1}{2}$ years. 13% had more than ten years experience, 47% had much less than two years. The vast majority of French teachers had between 10 and 25 periods of subjects other than French on their timetables. The only full time French teachers were four native Frenchmen. Some 80% combined English with French, presumably on the assumption that if you can teach one then you can teach the other. The average number of teachers per school was two and this was necessary if they were to be partly teachers of other subjects and still assure four forms within the school of French.

The books being used were:

Pierre et Seydou (BELC, 1964–72) by 34% of all the classes learning French
Practical French by 36% of classes
Maugier et al. (1964–7) by 18% of classes
Assorted other books by 10% of classes
No textbook by 2% of classes

Comments from teachers about the first two of these books were enthusiastic. Those who used Maugier defended it as a "serious" book on grammar for Forms III and IV. Overall the picture was of an astounding shortage of textbooks. One teacher had three forms learning French and only a single copy of any textbook and that one he had borrowed from the school down the road. Readers for extensive reading or any work beyond that of the course book seemed to be few in number and rarely used. The only ones mentioned to any noticeable degree were those of the *"Mieux Vivre"* series (published by Didier), a number of which had been distributed through the good offices of the Service Culturel Français.

So far as timetabling was concerned most respondents to the questionnaire felt that French was being hard done by, 66% of the schools had one or more double periods of French each week, 27% had less than 4 periods a week and periods were often given in the late afternoon or the late morning at the hottest or most exhausting part of the day.

In all the schools where French was being taught pupils were working towards one of the two public examinations taken in Tanzania. The first of these was the Local French Test. This is an examination set and marked in Tanzania. Originally it was intended that pupils should sit for it at the end of Form II; they now sit for it in Form III. The examination is potentially a useful adjunct, to the Form IV Regional examination and might help in the selection of Form V entrants. It is in form very similar to the East African School Certificate Examination in French except that the range of vocabulary that it tests is rather narrower.

3.2 *Change of Examination Pattern*

The East African School, Certificate Examination in French has in the past been set by the Cambridge Examination Syndicate in England. Control of the Cambridge Examinations is gradually being passed to the East African Examinations Council, and the paper for French is now mainly prepared in East Africa. The changeover of control has allowed the East African French examination to escape from the rigid formal pattern of the British version of the examination and permitted the introduction of techniques of testing parallel to those for English Language, with emphasis on the oral part of the examination, multiple choice or other kinds of objective testing devices, and a reduction in the importance given to translation. In its present form it appears to be a very good examination.

In 1969 Tanzania had had no Higher School Certificate or Advanced Level French examination for secondary schools. However plans were under way to establish courses at this level in one or two schools, and proposals for a syllabus and examination which would do away with translation altogether and greatly reduce the element of literary study based on the classics of the literature of metropolitan France had been formulated and were likely to be submitted to the East African Examinations Council fairly shortly.

The general impression of the attitude of the pupils was of an enthusiastic and involved Form I deteriorating into an unenthusiastic and unresponsive Form IV. This may well be only a temporary situation, but it would seem to arise from the pupils increasing awareness of French as a poor relation among the subjects, as reflected in all the factors discussed above. Form IV pupils are also aware that after School Certificate their French will lead nowhere: there is no Form V or Form VI work available yet. As the supply of textbooks improves along with the quality and degree of continuity of the teaching, and prospects of Form V and VI work open up, we may expect the attitude of Form IV pupils to alter.

3.3 *Staffing Changes*

Improvements in the supply of teachers are already apparent. There is a steady trickle of refugees from the Congo, Ruanda, and elsewhere who speak French more or less fluently and who are capable of teaching the language. There are also a number of Tanzanians returning from France. These teachers were sent to France for periods of up to three years, where they followed standard *cours de langue et civilisation françaises* for foreigners. In a country which is itself having some difficulty in transforming its educational system to suit modern needs it is of course just such courses as these which are likely to be among the last to be affected. The command of French which these teachers have is good, and their knowledge of French life and institutions impressive but they normally have no pedagogical training or knowledge of linguistics. Most importantly, however, there is the increasing supply of graduates from the University of Dar es Salaam. These graduates are only just joining the schools and it must be said that the actual level of their command of French after only three years of effective exposure to it at the University, where it constitutes less than a third of their programme of studies, leaves a good deal to be desired. It would appear that one of the functions that the French section of the University of Dar es Salaam could usefully perform in the future would be to provide refresher up-grading courses, especially for the earlier graduates who have been rather rushed out into the schools. If these teachers advance to positions of seniority without an appropriate improvement in their qualification to teach French it may result in their being placed in a rather invidious position when younger and better qualified teachers whose spoken French is more fluent and accurate come to serve under them in the French department of a school.

If present Manpower Planning figures are to be taken as a guide the University of Dar es Salaam is to produce 15 French graduate teachers each year until 1973 by which time the appropriate quota of teachers to allow French to be taught in 40 schools with two streams in Form I and II and one stream in Forms III and IV. It should be remembered that Tanzanian teachers are bonded for five years after graduation so that figures for the supply of French teachers appear to be quite healthy. What sort of wastage there will be after the first five years is not yet at all clear, but future production of teachers must clearly be a function of this. The teachers are almost all very young too, so that it is likely that there will be a marked slackening of the output of French graduates when replacements will be virtually unnecessary. It is at that point that efforts should be seriously made to establish a useful scheme of continued in-service training.

French teachers can also look forward to a better deal over timetabling arrangements. The participants at an In-service course for French teachers held at the Dar es Salaam University in June 1969 asked for and were granted Ministerial approval for a minimum of four periods of French each week, with no double periods.

This then gives some notion of what the current situation is, with guesses at what the immediate future holds. There remain however a number of more speculative matters which arise from the consideration of certain basic principles in relation to this matter.

3.4 *Motivation for Learning French*

First of all in 'Education for Self Reliance,' President Nyerere has written: "The object of the teaching – at post-primary level – must be the provision of the knowledge skills and attitudes which will serve the student when he or she lives and works in a developing and changing socialist state" (1968a: 72). That is to say: the curriculum of the secondary stage as much as that of the primary stage ought to be self-contained and self-sufficient, and should not be designed simply for the benefit of the small minority of citizens who proceed to university. If this principle is to be applied to the teaching of French, then it would appear that the content of the French courses offered at the secondary level Form I to IV needs to be specified in terms of the needs of Tanzanian society.

Secondly, it is fairly generally recognised among language teaching theorists and practitioners that desultory low-intensity language teaching with poor pupil motivation is likely to produce inferior results. Learning a foreign language is learning a complex mental skill. In two years of not very systematic or intense study a pupil can acquire a certain watertight integrated chunk of knowledge about Greenland or electricity, or even be persuaded to adopt a new attitude to personal advancement and the part he has to play in society. When it comes to the business of mastering the intricacies of the code that is a foreign language, however, two years or more of even moderately well organised study can leave the pupil with nothing whatever.

Thirdly, there is a widespread belief among language experts that the earlier a language is begun the better – whatever that may mean. It would seem, for example that it is because this principle has been accepted (unquestioningly) that English has been introduced as a subject in Standard I of the primary school.

Fourthly, there is another popular opinion among educationists whose primary concern is language, namely that a language course is likely to be most effective if it is based primarily on the spoken form of the language, that is to say if the course leans heavily on the oral and aural skills. It must be said however that the experimental evidence in support of these last two "principles" of language teaching is somewhat conflicting, and their theoretical bases are being seriously challenged.

However, suppose we consider the teaching of French in Tanzanian secondary schools in the light of these principles. First of all, if we try to imagine what the most likely uses for French Form IV leavers are likely to find, we must conclude that the number of pupils who will be able to find any use for it at all must be quite small, unless, of course, there is a sudden and massive interchange of personnel between francophone and anglophone Africa, the reason for which it is difficult at the moment to conceive. Certainly, it is unlikely to be in the region of 1200 pupils a year as estimated above. Form IV leavers are likely to become mainly middle grade officials, civil servants, administrators or financial officers in government or the parastatal organisations: higher level officials, diplomats, scientists, engineers and other professional cadres are likely to be university graduates from whom higher levels of competence might be expected. These classes of people are likely to need French primarily it would seem for reading purposes, they might need some facility in translating from French into Swahili or English, together with the ability to summarise the content of French newspaper or magazine articles, reports or documents issued by Unesco or one of the other United Nations organisations, or indeed by the metropolitan French government or another French-speaking nation. There might be a small number of people working in the tourist industry who would need a sufficient command of the spoken form of the language to be able to deal with visitors from France and other French-speaking countries. Thus it would appear that what French is taught in Tanzanian secondary schools ought to lay special emphasis first on the reading skill (perhaps something on the lines of the *Learning through Language* course (Isaacs, 1968) described in section 2 of this chapter dealing with English as a medium of instruction). And yet spoken skill will be required by a few. Clearly this conclusion conflicts with the fourth principle enumerated above, but the conflict is far from being irreconcilable in that it would be perfectly possible to devise a French course in which the primary contact with the language was oral/aural but where the greatest effort was devoted to mastery of the written forms of it.

Next it is all too apparent that in 1969 the teaching of French in

Tanzania manifests rather too many of the features described above as leading to ineffective instruction. The logical next step then would seem to be to concentrate the small number of French speakers that will be required into a small number of schools where they could be taught using high intensity methods, where, because of the high degree of selectivity involved, French would be regarded very much as a prestige subject, and where objectives and purposes could be clearly seen, and moved towards quite quickly.

And so we come to the consideration of when this programme should begin. To integrate a programme of foreign language teaching like that outlined above into the normal activities of a secondary school would probably prove highly disruptive. The only possible place for it then would seem to be after Form IV, even perhaps after leavers had some idea of their future employment placements. It would be relatively simple to include a language aptitude battery of tests in the programme of terminal examinations, and this would make selection to the specialised language teaching schools that much easier. Clearly this late beginning conflicts with the third principle above, but as has already been suggested there is some question of its validity anyway. The kind of considerations that are being brought to bear here are that secondary pupils are capable of formal operational thinking – unlike the child learning his first language or even the younger child learning a foreign language in the lower forms. Secondary pupils have a much greater experience of the world as a whole and of learning in particular to draw on. In Tanzania this learning experience will probably include learning at least two other languages besides his mother tongue. High motivation and good teaching is likely to more than outweight any advantages that earlier beginning might bring. One of the principal benefits claimed for an early start in foreign language learning is that the child acquires a good accent, but for this to be true his teachers need to approximate closely to native speakers, and he needs to be very young, seven or eight years old at most; by the time he is twelve or thirteen his early linguistic plasticity is already lost.

3.5 *Possible Future Developments*

And so one is tempted to speculate a little on one way in which the teaching of French in Tanzania might develop. There would be a small number of schools, say ten or twelve, not quite one in each region, which would have a special foreign language service unit as part of them. These units would supply the limited language elite that the nation needs for French; it is easy to see these units extended to provide facilities for teaching Tanzanians an appropriate level of competence in other world languages, for example, Russian, Chinese, Spanish or German. The units could be encouraged to take a fresh inventive look at language teaching as they would constitute a break with tradition and would be in a position to experiment. It would be possible to staff them with skilled and well qualified teachers and even perhaps to provide them with electronic classroom facilities.

To make the work of the units really efficient a programme of basic research might be necessary beforehand. Just what sort of competence in French is necessary for a civil servant in the Ministry of Agriculture and Fisheries? How active or how passive does it need to be? What level? What lexicon does he need to know? Answers to questions like these, somewhat beyond the crude guesses that have been made earlier in this paper, would be needed. The range of possibilities is enormous. It is obvious that a Foreign Office Official welcoming French speaking guests and making arrangements for their visit will need a sound oral command of the language with facility in all four of the basic language skills. But a minor official in the Ministry of Cooperative Development, or the manager of a branch of the State Trading Corporation, or any one of a host of others might need no more than the barest passive reading knowledge. A person working in the West Lake Region might need a greater range of skills than one working in Tanga. If the needs were clearer and more precisely defined then the path towards them would be more easily traced. A thorough investigation of just what the nation's needs for French and, indeed, other foreign languages are would be well worth while.

Once these needs were defined, the special language service units could provide specified skills on economic terms. It should prove possible, for example, to have a translators' stream, a readers' stream, a tourist trade stream, and so on even to the extent of providing specialist help for people who might have to deal with speakers of a particular dialectal variety of French. The courses run by the units would perhaps last for about three months at a high level of intensity and there would then be follow-up courses, with pupils attending one or two evenings a week where this was possible, and being recalled for two week refresher courses or skill extension courses. It would be a very small step from there to Adult Education language activities still using the same nucleus of highly qualified personnel and the specialist equipment available. So French would be seen for what it is in Tanzania: a service subject, a means to an end, not a branch of humanitarian study in its own right except for a tiny minority at university level.

4.0 *Technical Colleges*[6]

Language work in Technical Colleges in Tanzania presents certain special problems, though in most ways the programme can be similar to that in other secondary schools. Until 1970 the technical colleges were, indeed, no more than a special kind of secondary school. It is intended, however, that after that date, they should develop so that they produce not only craftsmen but technicians of various grades between simple craftsman and graduate engineer. The language problems remain basically the same.

So far as Swahili teaching is concerned much the same kind of programme as for other secondary schools can be followed. With the increasing use of Swahili as the medium of instruction there may well be problems in the development of appropriate technical vocabularies and forms of expression but until such time as the necessary citizen teachers can be trained (and this is not something that can be done in two or three years since the experience required of a teacher-craftsman or teacher-technician takes at least seven or eight years to acquire) the medium of instruction in the technical college is likely to remain English.

4.1 *Problems Linked to Staffing*

This means that there are a number of basic difficulties in communication that have to be faced. One of these is that the technical instructors in most Tanzanian technical colleges are from a large number of different regions in different countries of the world. Almost all of them speak English with a marked regional if not a foreign accent. Pupils are thus faced with the difficulty of having to "tune in" to each new teacher. Sometimes they find it easier to understand a non-native speaker of English than a native speaker, say a German rather than an American. These difficulties extend beyond mere accent and involve other dialectal features like vocabulary and grammar and usage especially when colloquial, highly context-dependent speech is involved. Consider samples like: "Just grab the hoo-ja with these whats-its and twist her round gently," or the different terms used by British and American speakers for parts of a car, where 'boot' = 'trunk', 'hood' = 'top', 'bonnet' = 'hood', 'mudguard' = 'fender', and so on.

Similarly, there are difficulties in the way of the expatriate teacher understanding his Tanzanian pupils. One of the commonest sources of confusion arises from the Tanzanian way of saying 'yes' with the meaning: It is so/It is as you say! – a direct translation of the Swahili *Ndiyo*. Thus when the teacher says: This work isn't very good,' and the pupil responds: 'Yes,' he is not contradicting but agreeing with the teacher. A variant of this is when negative questions, with tags, are asked. Q: 'You don't have a pencil, do you?' A: 'Yes'. But of course the pupil can't produce a pencil because he is agreeing that he does not in fact have a pencil. Another cause of confusion is the Tanzanian way of pronouncing certain English words: the confusion of vowels in Tanzanian English leads to problems in understanding whether a student thinks he is doing wood-work when he might be 'filling knots,' or motor engineering when he might be 'feeling nuts' (See Perren, 1956). Perhaps even more important is the use of Tanzanian intonation patterns, so that perfectly polite and well-meant responses are interpreted as hostile or rude. For example if a teacher asks a pupil to do something for example, 'Close the door' and the pupil replies 'Yes, sir!' on a low-falling intonation, the native speaker is likely to react unfavourably though the pupil may be totally unaware of what he has done. Much of this kind of difficulty could be got over by proper briefing of expatriate staff. The commonest features of Tanzanian English are easily described and if this information could be written into a suitable expatriate technical teacher's handbook; which might also include details of syllabuses and schemes of work, this would be most useful.

Another kind of difficulty arises when teachers rely too heavily on their textbooks for their teaching. The language of these books is often complex, overelaborate, highly formal and heavy and so difficult enough for the native speaker to understand. The solution here would seem to be to write books specially for the work being done in the colleges. It might be best if these were in the form of rather elaborate schemes of work giving skeletal outlines of what was to be done and taught. These skeletons would then have to be fleshed out by each teacher in his own way and this would hopefully lead to much less formality of language. Compiling these schemes would have the further advantage of making possible clear lines of continuity between one expatriate teacher and the next as contracts end and are taken up.

The way in which publically posted notices are written may also constitute an area of difficulty in communication. The importance of absolute lack of ambiguity in safety instructions posted up in laboratories and workshops is quite apparent. To achieve this it is probably necessary to put up the notices in both English and Swahili. It is in translating the English into Swahili that difficulties sometimes arise. It is probably best if the translator is a technically trained Tanzanian working closely with a native English speaking counterpart who knows some Swahili at least, so that both can be fairly sure that the Swahili version means the same as the English. Full use needs to be made of standard symbols and colour codes to help to make the meaning more clear: for example the red cross on the first aid box, and the black and red flame symbol which is now widely used to mark fire fighting equipment. Care does need to be taken, however, to ensure that the colour codes have the same meaning in both Western European and Tanzanian culture.

4.2 *Requirements*

In all this it is clear that a certain amount of careful teaching of staff as well as of pupils – is needed. The most important point of emphasis in the English teaching given to the pupils, however, must be on English as a "tool"; clear, simple, direct ways of saying things need to be cultivated, and the flowery, polysyllabic, elaborate forms of expression, so beloved of so many Tanzanian schoolboys, should be eschewed.

One extremely interesting programme for English teaching in technical colleges is set out in a working paper written by J. Trevett of Ifunda Technical College in June 1969 and distributed by the Language Association of Tanzania. Read in conjunction with the *Handbook for English Teachers in Secondary Schools* (Eng. Lang. Panel, 1969) this paper makes excellent sense and one would hope to see its proposals widely adopted. The difficulties discussed above are squarely met by the programme Mr. Trevett suggests except perhaps for the matter of familiarising pupils with a number of varieties of spoken English, and the linking of this programme with the more general programme for secondary schools ensures that the fundamental philosophy of education in Tanzania, that education, particularly specialist education, is for service, is properly upheld.

LANGUAGE TEACHING IN SECONDARY SCHOOLS

NOTES

[1] The section on Swahili was written by Fulgens Mbunda; that on English by C. J. Brumfit; that on French by D. Constable; and the last, on language work in technical colleges, by C. P. Hill.

[2] Bibliographical details for this chapter will be found in the bibliography at the end of this Part of the book.

[3] A typical selection of books which might be used in a Tanzanian secondary school for Swahili is the following:

First Year: *Mashimo ya Mfalme Sulemani*
 Uhuru wa Watumwa
 Nakupenda Lakini . . .
 Mashairi ya Mambo Leo I
Second Year: *Kisa cha Hassan-li-Basir*
 Lila na Fila
 Macbeth
 Mashairi ya Mambo Leo II
Third Year: *Adili na Nduguze*
 Simu ya Kifo
 Diwani ya Akilimali
 Masomo yenye Adili
Fourth Year: *Maisha Yangu na Baada ya Miaka Hamsini*
 Kusadikika
 Wasifu wa Siti binti Saad
 Juliasi Kaisari
 Diwani ya Mnyampala
 Pamba la Lugha

The syllabus suggests that books like these should be fully exploited. For example, when the pupils read a certain chapter of *Uhuru wa Watumwa* that chapter should give rise to the following: (a) study of the language and style; (b) questioning and discussion leading to full understanding of the chapter; (c) written work – say in the form of an essay related to some aspect of what is described in the chapter, or a summary of the chapter, or written answers to questions on the text; (d) work on particular points of grammar and usage, on the proverbs, aphorisms and figures of speech which may occur. It is suggested that books like Hollingsworth and Alawi's *Advanced Swahili Exercises* or Ashton's *Swahili Grammar* or Farsi's *Swahili Sayings* should *not* be used as class texts but they may be used by the teacher as source books or for reference. All the work done in class should be contextualised and derive from the book being read.

All of this is, however, soon likely to be superceded. As has already been pointed out a project to produce a specially written series of books for use in the secondary school is already in hand. The plan for this is first to collect suitable manuscripts, stories, articles, extracts from speeches and so on – most of these are now available to the editors. The texts must next be arranged in a suitable sequence according to the age and interests of the pupils and the class they are in. Then within each broad age-group/class chapters must be prepared according to what is manageable within a reasonable amount of class time, and what is likely to be of most benefit to the pupils at whatever stage of language development they have reached. Then each book in the series will have to be written up in full, edited and printed. Once this project is complete and we begin to move forward along the lines suggested earlier the problems related to the teaching of Swahili in secondary schools will be greatly reduced.

⁴ Since this was written two interesting and relevant documents have appeared, published as so many documents mentioned here are by the Institute of Education of the University of Dar es Salaam. These are "Background Notes for Literature in English in Tanzanian Schools," which contains some excellent critical material on the books set for the examination in Literature in 1971, and C. J. Brumfit's *The Report on a Questionnaire on the Teaching of English sent to all Secondary Schools in Tanzania – January 1971* (not now available). This document gives details of the numbers and quality of teachers in the schools, the text-books and equipment available, and a brief summary of comments made by the teachers. It gives a picture of the "average" Tanzanian secondary school in the year 1970 which can be summarized as follows. The average Tanzanian secondary school will have 3.49 streams to School Certificate. It will have 4½ people teaching English of whom 1.96 will be full time. 0.80 of a teacher will be a literature graduate with L_2 training, 0.65 a language graduate, 0.72 a non-graduate with L_2 training 0.31 a non-graduate without L_2 training, 0.33 a graduate in some other subject with L_2 training, 0.72 a graduate in some other subject, and 0.71 has some other qualification. 0.08 of a teacher will be completely unclassifiable for lack of data. 1.68 teachers will be citizens of Tanzania and 1.19 will speak English as a first language. The Head of Department will have taught for ten years and nearly seven months. He will have taught English as a second language for 7 years and 9 months, and in Tanzania for 5 years and about 10 months. Form I will be given 7.56 periods of English a week, Form II will be given 7.68, Form III 7.51, and Form IV 7.62. The school will posses 3 full copies of the *Handbook* and another with about 3½ pages torn out. The school will also have just over a half of a qualified teacher who is not teaching English, and will be the proud possesser of 1.14 tape recorders. The most popular text books are Mackin: *A Course of English Study*; Allen: *Living English Structure*; Wingfield: *Exercises in Situational Composition*; Munby: *Read and Think*; Munby, Thomas and Cooper: *Comprehension for School Certificate*. The most chosen set books for the literature paper were Laye: *The African Child*; Bolt: *A Man for All Seasons*, Soyinka: *The Lion and the Jewel* and *Borther Jero*; Shakespeare: *The Merchant of Venice*, Beti: *Mission to Kala*. Eleven schools do Higher School certificate work. The most chosen set books were Ngugi: *A Grain of Wheat* and Miller: *View from the Bridge*. Overall this provides an interesting and remarkably precise picture.

⁵ See, for example, C. P. Hill, 1965.

⁶ This section is based on information provided by Roger Wilson.

13 LANGUAGE TEACHING IN HIGHER EDUCATION

C. P. Hill, J. S. W. Whitley, D. Constable and G. Mhina[1]

1.0 *Colleges of National Education*
Probably the best short guide to the work of the Colleges of National Education in Tanzania is the *Programme for Grade 'A' Teacher Education* issued by the Ministry of National Education in Dar es Salaam in August 1969 (1969b). The basic philosophy and the pattern of activities set out there is similar for all grades of teacher education in the United Republic, *mutatis mutandis*. The key elements in the two year course are National Service, National Education, Political Education, Languages, Social Studies, Natural Sciences, Domestic/Health Science, National Culture, Religious Education, Teaching Methods and Teaching Practice, Nation Building Projects, and Games, Sports, and Hobbies. The prime aims of the course are:

(1) To educate students in the meaning of the Tanzanian concept of Ujamaa.
(2) To train students to be dedicated and capable teachers with understanding of and care for the children placed in their charge.
(3) To deepen the student's own general education.

These general aims are kept in view in the "Language" element of the course just as much as in any of the others. To quote the *Programme* again:

> The language course aims at enabling the students to think clearly and critically and to express themselves fluently in correct Swahili or English. An important part of the course is propaganda analysis and the study of official Government publications in Swahili and English.
> Students must be able to translate and interpret material accurately from both languages.
> To make full use of a language it is necessary to have mastery of the four basic language skills: listening, speaking, reading and writing. Students learn to apply these principles in the teaching of Swahili and English.

1.1 *Swahili*
In addition to what has been said above, the course in Swahili aims at showing the student the beauty of the language in forms of writing which express typical African feelings and ideas and at enabling students to grasp, translate and Africanise useful foreign concepts. Students are also trained in story telling and reading to audiences.

1.2 *English*

In addition to the general aims stated above, the course in English aims at functional English. The students need English:

(a) for their own studies;
(b) because they will have to teach it in primary schools, and
(c) because of its use as an international language.

The English they already know is consolidated and improved so that they will be efficient and progressive teachers.

The difficulties which Tanzanian children encounter in learning English as a second language and the reasons for these difficulties are an important part of the study of "Teaching Method". A real understanding of these difficulties and the reasons for them also leads to an improvement in the students' own English. (Min. of Nat. Educ., 1969b)

1.3 *Final Examinations*

The importance placed on language is reflected in the place given to it in the final examinations of the teacher education programme. These are centrally set and marked papers in Swahili and English each carrying two fifteenths of the total marks for the examination. In addition one fifteenth of the marks is awarded for a Swahili project devised and carried out under the auspices of the Swahili Department at each College, that is to say that, in all, one third of the total marks is awarded for work directly related to language. Furthermore, one of the papers set internally by colleges is on an optional subject; this carries a further two fifteenths of the total of marks and the option chosen is very often language-related.

1.4 *Programmes of Work*

Full details of the Swahili programme in Colleges of National Education are set out in the book *Kiswahili Vyuoni*, edited by F. L. Mbunda (1970)[2]. Students come to the Colleges of National Education after seven, eleven or thirteen years of education according to the Grade of teaching they are being prepared for (see chapters 11 and 12), and their programme will differ slightly according to this and according to the type of school in which they expect to teach. Only a small number of students in Colleges of National Education are destined to teach in secondary schools, but their training is inspired by the same underlying philosophy, and so what is said below with regard to primary teaching relates similarly to secondary work if the syllabuses described in chapters 11 and 12 are taken as the basis for this work.

From the general drift of the *Programme* quoted above it will be seen that the actual day to day work of students falls into roughly four categories.

Firstly there is work leading to the students becoming familiar with the language programmes for the schools in which they will teach. In particular, this means gaining an understanding of the processes involved in achieving basic literacy so that students are equipped to teach not only young children but also adults how to read and write Swahili. This obviously entails becoming familiar with the instructions and procedures set out in the *Teachers' Books* of the recommended courses – see, for example, chapter 11, Appendix A on Swahili, and section 2.2, chapter 11 on English. The whole methodology of teaching the language skills in the primary school has to be put across. This involves considerable analysis of the nature of the skills, discussion of the merits of "Look and Say" as against "Phonic" approaches to the teaching of initial reading, and a consideration of how the two are used in the prescribed course. It also involves analysis of the hand movements needed for writing, and is likely to lead to the student having to learn to modify his own handwriting to conform to the required model, to draw and write quickly and neatly and effectively on the chalk board, to devise, design and make appropriate teaching aids from a minimum of resources as well as to make use of the wide variety of classroom teaching techniques in the variety of patterns and sequences described in the books. Some details of what is required have already been given in chapter 11. Much of the literature on methodology for language teaching is still available only in English, but the publication of *Kiswahili Vyuoni* has made a good deal of basic information available in Swahili too.

Secondly, the students are led to an elementary understanding of what language is, and to some knowledge of basic facts about the structure of both Swahili and English. These facts include details about their sound systems, segmental and suprasegmental, about spelling conventions, and about the lexical and grammatical patterns of the two languages. For example, they would be expected to understand what is meant by saying that Swahili is a language whose syllable structure is almost entirely of the "open" type – CV–, or by saying that the sentences 'John gave Mary a book' and 'Musa told the teacher a lie' have the same grammatical pattern, at one level of analysis at least. They will also be made familiar with some of the differences between Swahili and English which lead to the occurrence of certain very common errors, and similarly of differences between Swahili and others of the local languages which help to create problems too. For example, most Sukuma children are likely to have difficulty in saying the Swahili word *thelathini* and will pronounce it [selasini] simply because there is no /θ/ phoneme in Sukuma, or, almost all Tanzanian children have difficulty in distinguishing between the two expressions 'at that time' and 'by that time' largely because of the peculiar division of the semantic fields that 'by' is involved in, in contrast to the much less finely differentiated usages of Swahili "prepositions". The students need to know about these and the many other similar difficulties which are familiar to experienced teachers in Tanzania, and many of which are described and listed in *Kiswahili Vyuoni* (Mbunda, 1970), *Kiswahili katika Sekondari*, (Mbunda, 1969) and the *Handbook for English Teachers in Secondary Schools* (Eng. Lang. Panel, 1969).[3]

The third element in the students' work in language at the Colleges of National Education is a programme of development and improvement in the student's own ability to use both Swahili and English. This covers the four basic language skills with some special emphasis, and some limitations. For both languages reading is strongly emphasised. Specific attempts are made to improve the students' ability to read for information, for pleasure and with critical awareness. The materials on which they work are newspapers, magazines, government and official publications, booklets like the TANU Youth League's 'Leadership', or President Nyerere's 'Education for Self Reliance', 'Freedom and Unity and 'Freedom and Socialism', besides longer books and selected articles and passages from a variety of authors. Exercises in intensive and extensive reading and a course of work designed to increase reading speed are included in both English and Swahili.

In speaking, clarity, coherence and a widely acceptable standard of pronunciation is emphasised. In English discrimination between the segments /ɔ/ and /ɔ:/, /u/ and /u:/, /i/ and /i:/, /æ/ and /e/, /ɔ/ and /a:/, /t/ and /θ/, /s/ and /θ/, /s/ and /z/, and /l/ and /r/ is especially stressed, and so too is rhythmic patterning which is structurally significant, as in that which distinguishes "transport" (noun) from "transport" (verb), or "chrome welding-rod" from "chrome-welding rod". Intonations which the students are likely to have to teach in the schools to which they go, are also assiduously practised, so they can, hopefully, provide reasonable models for their pupils to imitate. The patterns to which greatest attention is usually given are the falling pattern on 'Wh-' questions, statements and so on, and the rising pattern for 'Yes/No' questions. Choral speaking as well as individual work is regarded as normal. In one or two colleges where the facilities exist there is work done using language laboratory equipment mainly to further foster fluency and accuracy. Students in every college ought to be familiar with the sound of their own voices on tape. A truly native accent (either British or American, in spite of the sense of "Received Pronunciation" as described by Daniel Jones in *The Pronunciation of English* lurking somewhere in the background) is not the aim of the spoken English course, but the students must be able to speak a variety of English which will be readily understood internationally. They are encouraged to use straightforward direct forms of expression and to reply to questions clearly and without undue hesitation or preamble.

In Swahili the standard of pronunciation aimed at is described in *Kiswahili Vyuoni* and is similar to that of Tucker and Ashton's 'Swahili phonetics' (1942). This is basically a coastal variety of Swahili with a certain number of up-country modifications and is in a very real sense the "speech of educated Tanzanian speakers". However, most students at Colleges of National Education have little difficulty in approximating to the standard and the emphasis in the spoken Swahili course is on ensuring that students can talk in a variety of modes for a variety of purposes. They must be able to speak fluently and clearly in the classroom when they are expounding or explaining material to their pupils. They should be able to give public speeches for a variety of occasions. They are trained in the art of storytelling and, for both English and Swahili, they are expected to be able to read aloud intelligibly and audibly to large as well as small groups of people. They are given special practice in this last rather special skill.

The listening skills as such do not appear to be mentioned in the programmes issued by the Colleges, but undoubtedly students are given considerable practice in this since they listen to lectures the substance of which they are expected to reproduce later in both English and Swahili. They are given instructions, often of a fairly complex kind, in both languages, and they need to be able to follow these instructions correctly if they are to derive full benefit from their course of training so that the motivation for listening and understanding is high.

The writing skill is also given some prominence, especially in Swahili. Students are expected here too to be able to write in a variety of different styles suited to a variety of different purposes. They should be able to write letters, telegrams and notices, to make summaries and take notes, to build up a logical argument, describe a scene, a sequence of events or a process in both languages. In Swahili they should also be able to write verse, tell a story or write a thoughtful and elevating piece for the edification of their fellow citizens. One of the major activities in the Swahili writing course especially, though it has formed part of the English course in some colleges too, has been the writing of suitable supplementary reading material for both children and adults who are newly literate. Many of the booklets produced for this by students at the colleges are of high quality and one hopes that they will soon be published and thus made widely available. Much of the technical literature relating to creative writing and book production of this kind is still wholly in English, but in this field too the publication of *Kiswahili Vyuoni* has made an important initial contribution.

The fourth category of work in the students' programme of language study is what might be termed the "literary" one. In Swahili it is apparently this that is referred to in the *Programme for Grade 'A' Teacher Education*, when it speaks of "showing the students the beauty of the language in forms of writing which express typical African feelings and ideas." (Min. of Nat. Educ, 1969b). Some idea of the type and range of writing that is studied may be gathered from chapter 11, Appendix A. In English the literary element creeps in only incidentally, but not unimportantly, through the extensive reading programme mentioned above. In this students are encouraged to read a minimum of one book every two weeks. Small-group discussions may be held after one or two students have read the same book, and all students are expected to complete a report on each book they read, a report which is controlled by a fairly comprehensive and detailed questionnaire in many colleges. At least half of these English books should be by African authors. Books in the Heinemann African Writers Series are very popular, books like Ngugi's *A Grain of Wheat*, Ekwensi's *Burning Grass*, Achebe's *Things fall Apart* and of course Camara Laye's *African Child*. Books by non-African writers which have been found successful in the past include the works of Pearl S. Buck, things like *The Pavilion of Women* or *The Good Earth*, Steinbeck's *The Pearl*, Alan Paton's *Cry the Beloved Country*, Hemingway's *The Old Man and the Sea*, and Orwell's *Animal Farm*. The range of choice exercised by the students is enormous and for many of them many of the titles listed in the supplement to the *Handbook for English Teachers in*

Secondary Schools (Eng. Lang. Panel, 1969) are unfamiliar and can be readily used.

This then is the programme of language work in Colleges of National Education. As may be seen, it is interesting, intensive and based on sound linguistic and educational principles. It is obvious that it is likely to play an important part in welding the children of Tanzania into a united and self-reliant people and the Ministry of National Education has some cause for satisfaction here.

2.0 The University of Dar es Salaam

2.1 Background

To understand the present position with regard to language study in the University of Dar es Salaam it is necessary to go back a little and provide a certain historical perspective. Language study began seriously in the University College, Dar es Salaam, in 1964, when the Department of Language and Linguistics was set up under Professor W. H. Whiteley. Prior to and including the academic year 1968/69 the Department only offered English and French as degree subjects for a B.A. in English and Linguistics and a B.A. in French and Linguistics. In July 1968 an optional paper in Swahili Literature was introduced. That first ever course in Swahili Literature produced a collection of essays in literary criticism which are being edited by Farouk Topan and which are to be published under the title *Uchambuzi wa Maandishi ya Kiswahili* (1971, 1978). Previously, Swahili was not formally studied except, occasionally, as a "language of examples", in linguistic lectures. In the following year 1969/70, Swahili came more fully into its own as part of a degree programme leading to a B.A. in Swahili and Linguistics within the Department of Language and Linguistics. That year also saw the first postgraduate B. Phil. in Swahili and Linguistics.

In the academic year 1970/71 the University College Dar es Salaam was reorganized as the University of Dar es Salaam and at the same time a new structure within the Faculty of Arts and Social Sciences (which would have emerged even if the status of the College had not been changed) was brought into being. The departments within the Faculty of Arts and Social Sciences which now contribute to language study and appreciation in any form, are the Department of Linguistics and Foreign Languages – essentially the old Department of Language and Linguistics, dealing with Linguistics, English and French – the Department of Swahili and the Department of Literature – both newly created – and the Department of Theatre Arts, which had been in operation since the academic year 1967/68.

2.2 Student Courses

The extent to which students who take courses in these departments are involved differs according to the type of course in which they are enrolled. The structure of both the B.A. and B.Sc. degrees in the University is 3-2-2, i.e. three subjects in the first year, followed by a continued study of two of these three subjects in the second and third years. Each subject is studied by following 4 courses in that subject in each year. Students at the University of Dar es Salaam are divided into three "streams". The first is an Economics based stream and students in this stream may optionally take a language as one of the four courses in each of their three years of study. The second is a Social Sciences based stream whose students may likewise optionally study a language as one of their four courses. If students in this stream are categorised as Foreign Language Specialists they are required to select their four courses from Literature, Swahili Literature, Theatre Arts, Linguistics and English, Linguistics and French, Swahili, and various Anthropological and Political fields in various prescribed combinations, which ensure some knowledge of language and some knowledge of literature. The third stream is Education based, and virtually the whole of their course of study is pedagogically oriented; they are only permitted to follow two courses in their major teaching field, and two in the minor field over the three year period. Among the specified fields (besides mathematics, the physical sciences, history, and so on) are French, English, Literature, Swahili, and Theatre Arts.

2.3 *Department of Swahili*

Students in the Department of Swahili follow courses in General Linguistics, General Phonetics, Swahili Phonetics and Phonology, Swahili Grammar, Varieties and Uses of Swahili, and Swahili Literature. Among the books prescribed in previous years for the study of Swahili Literature are the following:

M. S. Abdullah:	*Mzimu wa Watu wa Kale*
A. M. Abdala:	*Utenzi wa Maisha ya Nabii-Adamu na Hawaa*
K. Amin Abedi:	*Sheria za Kutunga Mashairi na Diwani ya Amin*
E. Hussein:	*Wakati Ukuta*
F. Katalambulla:	*Simu ya Kifo*
Henry Kuria:	*Nakupenda Lakini*
M. Mnyampala:	*Diwani ya Mnyampala*
Shabaan Robert:	*Adili na Nduguze*
Shabaan Robert:	*Wasifu wa siti binti Said*
Shabaan Robert:	*Maisha Yangu na Baada ya Miaka Hamsini*

It is interesting to compare this with the lists of books suggested for use at Form IV and Form VI in the secondary school (see chapter 12).

The main purpose for teaching Swahili at the University is obviously to help to develop the language so that it may fulfill its role as the national language. The study of Swahili as an academic subject in its own right needs no further justification but Swahili was academically respectable long before the needs of a growing nationhood became important, and courses in the language have been offered at foreign universities (notably at the School of Oriental & African Studies of the University of London) for at least 50 years. The main overriding purpose mentioned above has a number of secondary consequences. One of them is that it is necessary to provide adequately equipped and trained Swahili teachers to the secondary schools. The Department of Swahili hopes to play its part in equipping teachers with the knowledge of and about the language which they will need. The Department and Institute of Education will complement this with knowledge of appropriate methodologies and teaching skills. Another is that in order that advanced academic studies of Swahili should go forward a certain number of the most promising students of the department should go on to postgraduate higher degree work. There are two obstacles to this at the moment. One is that the Departments of Linguistics and Swahili are not staffed so that they can deal satisfactorily with higher degree students: they are geared to undergraduate levels of work only, so far. Another is that the very rigid manpower planning controls make it extremely difficult for a promising student to be diverted from his allotted destination in a secondary school. Rigidity of this kind could be harmful to the long term development of academic Swahili studies. It is encouraging to note that some flexibility has been permitted recently to allow students to take advantage of the scholarships awarded by the Survey of Language Use and Language Teaching for the specific purpose of fostering language study at the higher levels.

It may have been noted that there has been no mention of any direct teaching of any language in what has been said so far. French is indeed the only language directly taught from scratch and details of this are given below. What teaching of English as a language takes place is at an advanced level, and this also is discussed later in section 2.4 below. There is no formal study of Swahili. Anyone wishing to learn Swahili from the beginning has to enrol at the University's Adult Education Centre where a wide range of courses is offered. However, the Institute of Education does possess a set of Swahili tapes based on the United States Foreign Service Institute materials and it is possible for members of the staff of the University to make use of these in the Institute's language laboratory.

2.4 *Department of Linguistics and Foreign Languages: English*

From the very foundation of the Faculty of Arts and Social Sciences, it was decided not to follow the traditional British approach of teaching language only as a minor part of a literature course but to establish two separate departments, one responsible for literature in general and one responsible for languages and linguistics. Both departments started teaching in July 1964.

The Department of Language and Linguistics started by teaching English to a few students undergoing a specialised course of training in Linguistics. By the beginning of the 1968/69 academic year, however, the Department and the Ministry of National Education had come to agree that the main aim of the subject "English and Linguistics" should be to produce large numbers of teachers for secondary schools, an area in which there was a serious shortfall on target figures. Thus, whereas in 1968, 1969 and 1970 the numbers of students graduating in English were 4, 9 and 15 respectively, in 1971 there will be a graduation class of 47.

The general philosophy of the teaching of English at the University College also had to change. Instead of the subject being regarded as a specialisation in its own right, it had to be considered as being taught with the explicit and practical aim of enabling a teacher of English to teach better in the classroom. This is not to say that the English courses became confused with the language methodology course in the Department of Education: they were complementary, not tautologous. The English lecturers were trying to equip the student with the solid material of the language itself, whereas the methodology lecturer was explaining how this material could be presented in the classroom situation. The English staff therefore regarded their task as that of equipping the teacher with a wide practical and theoretical knowledge of the language. Practical knowledge is required because the teacher must in no way fall short of the standards he expects from his pupils; he is their model and he must command the language confidently and well. And theoretical knowledge is required because in his selection and preparation of material for presentation to his pupils a language teacher must have a sound theory which enables him to select and prepare in a coherent and consistent manner. The methodology lecturer, of course, made clear that the theory of English presented in the English courses was for the teacher and was not to be regurgitated for pupils in the classroom.

In the student's first year, emphasis was placed on the practical aspects of the courses. In their weekly hour of "Introductory Linguistics", they were presented with general topics in the "Theory of Language" and simple introductions to "Phonetics" "Phonology" "Grammar" "Lexis" "Semantics" and "Sociolinguistics". They also had four hours of English in the classroom and as many hours in the language laboratory as were necessary. The four hours of English in the classroom were divided into two hours of "Spoken English" and two hours of "Written English". In all the English classes, the Department insisted that the maximum number of students be 25; with such limited time for language work, the courses would otherwise have been very unproductive. The "Spoken English" course aimed to equip the student with speech which made him "comfortably intelligible" and the ability to comprehend native English speakers in various registers. Little is known about what exactly constitutes intelligibility, so on practical grounds the students were presented with R.P. as their model both for listening and speaking. They were also trained in the use of Gimson's phonemic script, which at this stage was used merely as a teaching device. The "Written English" course started with eight classes in Efficient Reading and then dealt with selected systems of English, the aim being to ensure, first, that the students had a good productive command of the system and, second, that they were able to express its structure in simple terms of classification. The students experienced difficulty with the simple structure classes, and it was decided to lay less emphasis on this aspect in the following year.

In their second and third years, the students continued with "General Linguistics" but in a more rigorous and detailed manner. Their English courses also became more rigorous. They received lectures in "Hallidayan Phonology" "Systemic Grammar and Lexis" "Stylistics" and simple "Transformational-Generative Theory". The reason for presenting undergraduates with more than one model of the language which they were studying was that it was felt that a fully equipped teacher should be able to understand the literature of his subject in whatever theoretical terms it was presented; a teacher of English should therefore have a grasp of both the Structural and the Transformational-Generative models. However, the Department found that within the English course this aim was too burdensome to be achieved by undergraduates. So in 1970/71, the knowledge will be supplied in one of those two models by the English staff in fully rigorous detail and in the other by lecturers in the "General Linguistics" course. It is then hoped that the student will graduate with a full and coherent capability in one model of English so that he may approach his teaching problems clearly and systematically, and a knowledge of other theories so that he may follow modern developments wherever they may occur. This discussion of the theoretical side of the students' final years must not be read as indicating that the productive aspects were forgotten. On the contrary, each lecture in the theory of English was followed up by small group-work classes in which the students performed practical exercises in that area of the language dealt with by the lecture. The "Stylistics" course was also conducted in this way, which was possible because the course dealt with the most common registers, not esoteric literary ones.

It was considered by the staff of the Department of Language and Linguistics (as it then was known) that the University College in Tanzania was able to justify its existence only in so far as it fulfilled goals laid down by the Government; the Ministry of National Education asked for teachers of English and the courses outlined above were designed to produce them. But those who planned and taught them were constantly searching for improvement, which is why this sketch is confined to only one year. Modified national goals would produce a modified syllabus.

2.5 *Department of Linguistics and Foreign Languages: French*

The official reason given for teaching French at the University, as at the Secondary level, is that it is necessary as a tool for Pan–Africanism. The details of just what this implies do not as yet seem to have been worked out and some discussion of this will be found in chapter 12 above. The main role of the University at the moment then, is to train teachers who will in future ensure the possibility of adequate communication between anglo- and francophone Africa through their pupils, and secondarily to produce a small number of non-teachers who will form a corps of French speakers in universities, para-statal organizations, the nationalised industries and organizations, and so on. At present the intake of students to the Department of Linguistics in French is around 20 a year (15 of them following Education based courses and 5 of them non-education based courses). With the projected figures for teachers of French being what they are (see chapter 12, section 3) it seems likely that the Department, with the intake for the year 1970, will have slightly overproduced the teachers of French required in the secondary schools. This means that the Department will have to re-define its role. First of all the output of non-teachers will have to be properly considered. How many non-teacher speakers of French is the nation really going to need? The answer to this question will clearly require careful study and may be very difficult to arrive at since it will depend on political and administrative factors like the extent of Tanzania's commitment to African unity, the kinds of bilateral agreement made with francophone countries, and the organisational levels at which contact takes place. Furthermore, what kind of skills in the language the non-teachers should be taught must also be considered. Should they be skilled translators, either of written materials or the spoken word, simultaneously? Should they be able to read with facility but not necessarily to speak the language well? Decisions about matters such as these can also only be made sensibly on the basis of adequately researched information.

Secondly the role of the department as it concerns teachers of French will have to be considered. Three years is certainly not enough in itself, once and for all, to produce satisfactory teachers of French. Extensive, continuous refreshment and enrichment of the teachers' own knowledge of French is essential if the quality of French teaching in schools is to be satisfactory. If the number of French teachers is slightly in excess of what is actually required in schools, then refresher courses could be mounted as a continuously ongoing activity of the department with teachers released from the schools on a rotating basis for say one term at a time.

Up till now students studying French at the University have followed the following course:

First Year: The CREDIF Audio-Visual Course – 10 hours each week of classes
General Phonetics – 1 hour each week
Introductory Linguistics – 1 hour each week (12 hrs.)

Second Year: Language Laboratory work – 3 hours each week using mainly materials devised by the staff of the department
Tutorials/conversation groups/formal classes – 1 hour each week
The Linguistics of French – phonology, grammar, lexis – 3 hours each week
Methodology of the Teaching of French – 1 hour each week in the Department of Education – for Education based students (8 hrs.)

Between the second and third year, during the long vacation, students spend 2 to 3 months in the Malagasy Republic where they follow a fairly traditional French *cours pour étrangers*. This is felt by the staff of the department to be an extremely valuable part of the course; indeed, a period of residence in a French-speaking country is felt to be essential.

Third Year: Formal classes – 4 hours each week, for composition, comprehension, grammar review, and study of 4 set texts written by African authors for "language only" study
Linguistics of French – 1 hour each week

> General Linguistics – 1 hour each week
> Language Laboratory work – 2 hours each week, some of this is auditory comprehension work, some is of the more usual structural kind. (8 hrs.)

Because of the trip to Malagasy, Education based students are unable to participate in and teach French during the normal teaching practice exercise with all the other students since this takes place during the long vacation too. They therefore do two to three weeks of teaching practice in September of their third year (the academic year runs from July to March). The students cannot, of course, teach French during the first teaching practice between the first and second years, since their knowledge of the language at that stage is far too elementary. This minute amount of teaching practice is clearly totally unsatisfactory and students with so little practical experience of teaching French in the classroom can scarcely be said to be adequately trained. There are apparently complex administrative difficulties in the way of providing more teaching practice for French teacher students. This is another factor which makes the provision of refresher courses for teachers important.

However, taking the course overall, the graduates that it produces are remarkably competent, and the University has some cause for satisfaction that such good results can be produced in three years. It is with great hopes for the future that the Department looks forward to the first intake of students who have passed a Higher School Certificate level examination. With students of this calibre even greater things can be expected.

2.6 *Department of Education*

The Department of Education is one of the most important departments in the Faculty of Arts and Social Sciences at the University. It is responsible for the Education component in the degrees of all students who are in the Education based stream. These have amounted to almost 200 students each year up till now (1970). In the past the majority of these students have come from the Faculty of Arts and Social Sciences but now the numbers coming from the Faculty of Science are just as great. Education is taken by all these students as one of the three subjects in the first year. It is not taken as a major subject in the second and third year but is included in one fifth of the time allotted to the two academic subjects. Thus one third of the first year and one fifth of the second and third years are given to the study of education. In addition students have two six-week periods of teaching practice in the two vacations between their first and second, and their second and third years. In the first year the education course concentrates on a detailed study of the educational system of Tanzania. This entails a discussion of education in a socialist society and its relationship to the economic, political and social development of the country. In addition there are lectures on child development and educational psychology and a critical review of the theory and practice of teaching. In the second year there is a concentration on the study of methods of teaching two academic subjects, and it is here that the methodologies of teaching English, French and Swahili are dealt with. In the third year there are courses in the "Sociology and Philosophy of Education" and in "Curriculum Development".

Those teaching the language methodology courses at the University of Dar es Salaam share a number of basic problems – indeed, these appear to be problems which concern all trainers of language teachers everywhere. One question for example which has exercised them for a long time is the question of how theory and practice are to be interrelated. The solution arrived at in Dar es Salaam (partly dictated by the overall structure of the course and the place that teaching practice has in it) is that there should be a very brief theoretical introduction (2 lectures) and that all the subsequent specific and practical work should be constantly used to illustrate, demonstrate and test the theory. Students are encouraged to make theoretical generalisations on the basis of their specific activities. They should as far as possible be derived from practical experience. To be useful it is something that should be felt in the bones, hence the necessity for it to be founded on practice. It is intended that the course should take place as close to classroom situations as possible. Close co-operation with schools in Dar es Salaam itself is stressed, with frequent demonstration lessons and a certain amount of single lesson teaching practice on a weekly basis. As far as possible part of the normal routine of Block Teaching Practice observation is the holding of seminars where what has been observed can be discussed and commented on by a supervisor with a group of students. The difficulties of ensuring the greatest possible amount of supervision for students engaged in practical work, which is essential if the proper integration between theory and practice is to take place, are formidable indeed. With secondary schools very widely dispersed across the country and communications between them often slow and difficult, if not prohibitively expensive, the frequency with which students may be visited often falls short of what might be desired. Even when students are visited the supervisor may not necessarily be a specialist in the methodology of the subject he observes the student teaching.

Another of the universal problems of language teacher education is that of the extent to which methodology can be regarded as a "content" subject. In Dar es Salaam it is felt that language methodology is very much a "skill" subject: a matter of what you do rather than of what you know. The skills being taught are therefore felt to be most effectively tested by the students' teaching practice and no formal written examination, linked, for example, with an examination in Psychology, Sociology or Philosophy, should be held. Nor should the assessment of practical teaching contribute towards the class of degree awarded but merely form part of the endorsement on the degree certificate.

A third fundamental difficulty in such teacher training is the degree of specificity which can be included. In Dar es Salaam this difficulty is greatly reduced. The precise situations and conditions under which trainees are going to teach are known and it is therefore possible to look at specific levels, textbooks, techniques, patterns of administration, indeed the whole of the carefully spelled out syllabuses (see chapters 11 and 12), and to ensure that students are familiar with the range of procedures most likely to be effective in the current educational climate. For example the technique described in John Munby's *Read and Think* (1968) wherein small group discussion is used for teaching reading comprehension with multiple choice questions has been very effectively taught to students who use the technique with great effect in almost all schools. Here is a specific instance where the basic political values of African socialism (the sharing of resources and the giving of help to the weak by the strong) have been interestingly incorporated into a teaching technique which has a thoroughly sound base in educational theory and which has been repeatedly proven in circumstances totally different from those of Tanzania, as well as in Tanzania itself, to be an extremely effective device.

Thus instruction in language teaching methodology at the University is practical, down to earth, and realistic, yet forward looking and based on sound theoretical principles.

2.7 *Institute of Education*

The Institute of Education of the University of Dar es Salaam was established under the relevant Act of Parliament in order to serve national education by associating the academic study of education at the University with the practicalities of running schools, providing teacher education at Colleges of National Education, and developing policies with the Ministry of National Education. It does this by providing a centre for curriculum studies and work on curriculum development; by promoting and co-ordinating the provision of conferences, seminars, workshops and in-service courses for teachers and tutors; by promoting and conducting educational research, especially research leading to the preparation and publication of educational materials; by collecting and disseminating information on methods, content, and technological developments in education; by contributing professional expertise on matters directly relating to standards of competence in teaching qualifications to the University of Colleges of National Education and by acting as a centre for discussion and activity for all those concerned with education in Tanzania.

The physical manifestation of the Institute is the Institute of Education building on the campus. Its seminar rooms, language laboratory, science laboratories, audio-visual room, workshop and information room are easily the most heavily used rooms on the campus, busy from early morning until far into the night and all through vacations too. It is here that workshops, in-service training, conferences and all the other activities of the Institute take place.

Of particular interest is the work done by the Language Panels in developing curricula for Tanzania. Some details of the syllabuses and schemes worked out by the English and Swahili panels have already been given in chapter 12. The panels include teachers, staff from Colleges of National Education, the Ministry of Education, University Faculties and the Institute of Education itself. The planning and organisational details worked out by the Panels often result in workshops for the actual production of materials or seminars to ensure distribution of information.

For example, a great deal of material for the Secondary School English Controlled Composition Scheme set out in the *Handbook for English Teachers* (Eng. Lang. Panel, 1969) was produced at workshops sponsored by the Institute. Teachers came together, were briefed on the principles to be followed in divising materials and then co-operatively produced them. The scheme involves 39 separate stages, and materials were written for each stage with a specified linguistic content, a particular type of control built in and a characteristically Tanzanian context and philosophy. The co-operative effort meant that a substantial volume of material was produced, tried out at first instance, revised and made available to coordinators in various areas as sample materials on the basis of which more purpose-written texts and exercises could be produced. To observe the rapid development of these materials both in terms of quality and quantity was very exciting indeed.

Similar workshops have been run for developing Swahili teaching materials including graded readers, comprehension materials, and initial literacy materials.

The Institute is also responsible for substantial educational research. Individual projects of various kinds have produced a series of occasional papers published by the Institute and some work submitted for Higher Degrees at Universities outside Tanzania.

Group research is pursued mainly as "Combined Research Projects" in which students of the Colleges of National Education and their tutors co-operate with staff from the Institute in searching for a solution to some pertinent educational problem or in accumulating relevant data. Two of the major topics dealt with so far are *Absenteeism in Primary Schools in Tanzania* and *The relative academic performance of boys and girls in Standards III and V*. In 1970 the Combined Research Project was set up in conjunction with the Survey of Language Use and Language Teaching in Tanzania. The topic to be investigated covered the relationship between the general language ability of pupils taken as a combined score of tests of English and Swahili and various aspects of their parents' extent of use and ability to use Swahili, English and their vernacular. Although the Combined Research Projects are essentially training exercises in the methods and procedures of educational research, the care in choice of topics and the orthodoxy of the methods employed should produce findings of value to Tanzania.

All of the above gives a picture of vitality, enthusiasm, common sense and sound scholarship striving to serve the fulfilment of the aims of National Education in Tanzania, and it is particularly in the field of language that these qualities are most apparent.

2.8 *The Department of Theatre Arts*
One of the most exciting aspects of the work of the University of Dar es Salaam related to language is the work being done in the Theatre Arts Department. The Department mounts a full scale course leading to a first degree in Theatre Arts, and has a number of students working for higher degrees as well. It is however in the deliberate efforts made to link the

work in the department with the deepest cultural heritage of the people that the originality and strength of what is being done lies. All members of the department, students, as well as tutors belong to the University Theatre Ensemble and in the course of the years 1967 to 1970 were responsible for the following productions:

W. Soyinka: *The Trials of Brother Jero* and *The Swamp Dwellers*;
Athol Fugard: *The Blood Knot*;
Ebrahim Hussein: *Kinjeketile* and *The Trojan Women*;
Rebeka Njau: *The Scar*,
– dance drama created by the staff and students;
G. Z. Kaduma: *Pepo*;
E. N. Hussein: *Ngoma na Violin*,
– a musical based on the story of the Prodigal Son;
B. L. Leshoi: *Mwana Mpotevu*, and *The Vulture*
– again a group creation by students and staff – "... a fantasy and parable for our time".

The excitement that is aroused in looking at this work comes from the way in which cultural and linguistic barriers are crossed and recrossed sometimes within a single production. Some of the productions were in English, some in Swahili. Some reflect the conflicts of a bilingual bi-cultural situation, as in *Ngoma na Violin* whose very title tells a story. It is clear that a truly national theatre is developing of a highly experimental kind. Indeed as the result of a series of Seminars entitled Towards a Truly African Theatre held in August 1969 the Experimental Theatre Group was founded which has set out to be a bold, initiating, revolutionary theatre of the people, experimenting with Swahili plays and poems in schools and among adult groups, experimenting also in using local materials in set design, costumes, make-up and publicity. The experimental theatre aims to uphold the dignity of the traditional theatre forms of Tanzania such as the dance and yet to foster their development and growth as the nation grows.

The involvement of the department with the work of the National Service Folklore Teams, with providing the facilities to train the team of dancers which represented Tanzania at *Expo '70* in Osaka in Japan, with providing a programme for the Saba Saba Celebration, with decorating the walls around the Village Museum on the Bagamoya Road near Dar es Salaam, using splendid mural paintings, all of this shows how wide the scope and how far-sighted the vision of the members of the Department are. There can be little doubt but that if the ferment of activity which is now going on continues, the Department cannot fail to make a very significant contribution to the cultural growth of Tanzania.

3.0 *The Institute of Swahili Research*

In 1964 when the Institute of Swahili Research was incorporated into the University College, Dar es Salaam, the wheel of history had made a complete revolution and returned to where it had started in 1930. It is significant that the Institute should have been placed under the umbrella of the highest seat of learning in the country, for the seeds of the Institute were sown in a concern for education and it is education which today is perhaps the most powerful instrument for the development of national consciousness and pride. In particular it was the search for a suitable language of instruction that resulted in the setting up of the Inter-Territorial Language (Swahili) Committee following the 1925 Education Conference convened by the then Governor of Tanganyika. Nothing could have been more apt than making Swahili that language, for it has since developed into a splendid vehicle for the expression of national independence and identity in terms of history, culture and society.

3.1 *Background*

The Inter-Territorial Language Committee first met on the 1st of January 1930. The need for a suitable vernacular to be used for imparting elementary education to the local population was very evident even to those early colonial administrators, and Swahili was naturally selected by virtue of its wide predominance over large areas of Eastern and Equatorial Africa. The Committee's terms of reference were to promote the standardization and development of the Swahili language in particular:

(i) to standardise the grammar and orthography of the Swahili language;
(ii) to write a new standard dictionary;
(iii) to scrutinise the books in use in schools to ensure that they conformed to set standards;
(iv) to scrutinise material written in Swahili which aimed at publication – especially material intended for use in schools;
(v) to advise upon Swahili language and literature, and
(vi) to translate materials into Swahili for use in schools and for the edification and entertainment of the wider public.

A *Bulletin* was issued, free of charge, containing a variety of material on Swahili and official news related to the work of the Committee.

The most notable achievement of the Inter-Territorial Language (Swahili) Committee was the publication of the "Standard" dictionary prepared by the late Frederick Johnson, who set out initially to revise Madan's dictionary, but ended up re-writing it. On its appearance in 1939, Johnson's dictionary was readily acknowledged as representing a great stride forward in Swahili lexicography, but with the pace of development and change in Swahili accelerating since the days of the fight for independence in Tanzania there can be little doubt that Johnson's dictionary is now no longer wholly adequate. Hence, the current venture of the Institute of Swahili Research into the compilation of a new set of dictionaries to serve the present needs of the language.

On the 1st of January 1948, with the advent of the East African High Commission, the Committee passed under its jurisdiction. At about the same time the East African Literature Bureau was established, and the future policy of the Committee needed reconsideration. The East African Literature Bureau was to take on those functions of the Inter-Territorial

Language (Swahili) Committee relating to the production and publication of books (what might be termed its 'literary' functions) and the Inter-Territorial Language Committee became a separate, primarily linguistic unit, recognised as the major authority on matters of Swahili orthography and research related to the language, that is to say: it took on academic status.

There was indeed a growing concern with research – research into indigenous Swahili literature with the concomitant concern for the collection of manuscripts and records of the oral tradition, along with research into Swahili dialects and regional varieties of the language. As results were made available a constant revision of books and dictionaries was to be undertaken. The Committee did perhaps leave the centre of the stage and move somewhat into the wings while the East African Literature Bureau became better known, but this did not mean that it had lost its importance, rather it meant that a depth of enrichment was added to the language which was just about to emerge as such a powerful means of uniting a people in a common objective.

In 1951 the East African Institute of Social Research at Makerere College, Kampala, planned to undertake research into linguistics, and it was deemed practicable that the Committee should be attached to the Institute. This was effected as from the 1st of September 1952 and Professor W. Whiteley was appointed Senior Fellow in Linguistics within the Institute as well as becoming the Secretary of the Inter-Territorial Language Committee. The Committee's main activities at this time were the scrutiny and correction of manuscripts with a view to authorising publication and the issuing of the Bulletin as a forum for discussion on linguistic matters connected with Swahili. However, it was decided that from now onwards the scrutiny of manuscripts, other than of school textbooks was to be renounced and that the issue of the Bulletin was to be regularised, even if this entailed charging a subscription. Research was to be centred on the study of Swahili dialects and a survey of current Swahili as used in the Swahili press.

Dialect studies were undertaken and published in a special series or in the Committee's *Journal*, which replaced the *Bulletin*. The *Journal* in contrast to the *Bulletin* allowed a wider scope of interest in that it now carried articles of a purely academic kind as well as articles of a more general sort. A series of historical supplements was also initiated. In 1954 the Committee became known as the East African Swahili Committee, and the Journal changed its name to *Swahili* in 1959 when Mr. J. W. T. Allen took over from Dr. Whiteley (now *Kiswahili*). An Historical Sub-Committee whose job was primarily to collect manuscripts of historical interest, was also set up to preserve important documents before they perished.

In 1961 a Senior Research Fellow was appointed in the person of Dr. Jan Knappert who saw the removal of the Committee to Mombasa and thence to Dar es Salaam in 1964, where it was transformed into one of the Research Institutes of the University College, Dar es Salaam. The cycle had been completed.

East Africa became independent and Swahili had already been adopted as Tanzania's national language. The Institute between 1961 and 1964 shifted its focus away from education to standardisation, away from pure linguistic research towards literary and historical studies and towards the collection, contextualisation and cataloguing of new words. In 1965, Mr. Allen, on a Rockefeller Grant, undertook a major project of transcribing, translating, editing and publishing manuscripts which produced the *Utenzi* series. As a result of his work along with that of Dr. Knappert, Miss Margaret Bryan and Sheikh Mbarak Ali Hinawy, the Institute now boasts the largest collection of Swahili/Arabic manuscripts in the world.

The rate of development of Swahili gained momentum and acute need began to be felt for a new dictionary to meet the needs of the expanding language. Thus in 1965, with the help of a Gulbenkian Grant, it was possible to appoint Mr. J. A. Tejani as Research Fellow in Lexicography in the Institute with the task of preparing a new dictionary. The ground work for this is now complete and what remains to be done is to process and publish this long awaited fruit of the Institute's labours.

3.2 *The Present Situation*

In February 1969, Mr. George Mhina was appointed as the Acting Director of the Institute, a post which faces an important challenge in the light of the aspirations of the people of Tanzania. That the challenge has been accepted may be seen in the tasks that the Institute has set itself in a variety of fields.

The primary function of the Institute of Swahili Research of the University of Dar es Salaam is to develop and promote the use of Swahili at all levels in Tanzania, in East Africa and in the wider world. In so doing the Institute hopes to fulfil its role within the academic community of the University as well as in the broader context of the Nation's aspirations; but to fulfil this role and thus justify its existence the Institute requires wider recognition and support of as many kinds as possible so that it may attain its objectives of serving the people.

In lexicography the main task at hand is the preparation for publication of the new series of dictionaries, the Swahili–Swahili, Swahili–English, and English–Swahili volumes. There is also the preparation of specialised dictionaries for primary and secondary schools, and of word lists for technical subjects to be undertaken.

There is an immense amount of work to be done in the processing of the 800 odd Swahili and Arabic manuscripts and of the tape recordings of materials in the Swahili oral tradition which are lying in the safe custody of the Manuscript Collection of the Library of the University of Dar es Salaam. It is hoped to extract the most valuable materials for transliteration, (from Arabic to standard Swahili orthography where necessary) translation, editing and eventually publication. The Institute also has the responsibility of adding to this collection and has therefore appealed to all those who may have manuscripts lying in chests in their homes to share this treasure with their fellow citizens, even if it is only by allowing the manuscript to be photocopied so that an authentic version can be preserved. An appeal has also been made for traditional Swahili songs and stories to be recorded in some way, in writing if not on tape, so that this wealth of the cultural heritage may not be lost as the older generation who are familiar with it die.

Then, there is the journal *Kiswahili* which helps to keep the world informed of the Institute's activities and which by publishing articles of academic or technical linguistic interest as well as articles of a more general kind related to Swahili studies contributes to the furtherance of the language in all its aspects.

The Institute also intends initiating a literary magazine to encourage Swahili writing in poetry or in prose of material dealing with any aspect of life. This magazine is envisaged as a medium of expression for the best in East African thought and style and in this way will help Swahili to expand and become firmly and widely established as an important language of the written word.

One of the ways of stimulating the flow of literature in a developing language would seem to be to prime the pump with a large number of works on different subjects in a variety of styles which might encourage potential writers to put pen to paper. The Institute wishes to play its part here by translating into Swahili a variety of works from other languages, not only to stimulate further writing but also to help to disseminate knowledge and provide entertainment, for some books are meant to be studied while others are to be enjoyed.

The Institute, of course, does not work alone. In all its activities it is fortunate to have the support derived from its links with the Department of Swahili in the Faculty of Arts and Social Sciences of the University; with the Institute of Education, especially with the Swahili language panels and the Swahili tutors there; with the Ministry of National Education, whose Cultural Section, Promoter of Kiswahili and Central Co-ordinator for Swahili have all been extremely helpful; with UKUTA, a private association of people particularly interested in the promotion of Swahili poetry; and most importantly perhaps, with the National Swahili Council. The National Swahili Council was established by Act of Parliament in July 1967 with the special duty of promoting the Swahili language, and so it is in this respect the highest Swahili body in the country.

This then is the Institute of Swahili Research. It celebrates some 40 years in spirit though only six in body. As it moves ahead it keeps only one overriding objective in view: service to the people – a service of research and production.

NOTES

[1] The section on Colleges of National Education was written by C. P. Hill as were sections 2.0 to 2.3 and 2.6 to 2.8; The section (2.4) on English was by J. S. W. Whitley; section 2.5 by D. Constable and that on the Institute of Swahili Research by G. Mhina.

[2] Bibliographical details for publications referred to in this chapter will be found at the end of this Part.

[3] Once again, the basic textbooks on both Swahili and English structure are at the moment available only in English and from British or American publishers. Among the most popular books suggested as suitable sources of information are Ashton's *Swahili Grammar*, Stigand's *Grammar of Dialectal Changes in the Swahili Language*, W. S. Allen's *Living English Speech* and *Living English Structure* and, of course, the *Standard Swahili Dictionaries* and the Oxford University Press's *Advanced Learner's Dictionary* (Hornby et al.)

14 SOME DEVELOPMENTS IN LANGUAGE AND EDUCATION IN TANZANIA SINCE 1969

C. P. Hill

1.0 *Introduction*
It will be quite clear to the reader of the chapters in this volume which relate to language in education that they were written in 1969 and, therefore, much of their interest is as historical documentation reflecting attitudes and states of affairs which were current at that time. Since 1969 a great many developments have taken place both in the educational system and in Tanzanian society as a whole, and it would be wise to look at some of these before embarking on any attempt to describe changes in the specific situations.

1.1 *1969-79 Ujamaa*
Among the most important of the social-cultural changes, which have taken place, must be counted the enormous increase in the population of Tanzania which has been revealed by the latest census, preliminary figures for which were published in January, 1979 (*Daily News*, January 9, 1979). In 1969 the population of Tanzania was just over 12.2 millions. The figures for the present census indicate that the population is something over 17.5 millions. The consequences of this are that some 70% of the population are under 20 years of age and the number of children to be educated has, of course, increased enormously. Thus the sheer scale of the task of providing education for these children has increased out of all recognition. Some of the other changes in the social structure of Tanzania had their origins in the period before 1969, in particular in the series of policy documents which were published by Oxford University Press under the title *Ujamaa: Essays on Socialism* (Nyerere, 1968a). These essays written by Julius Nyerere include the well known 'Ujamaa: the basis of African Socialism', the 'Arusha Declaration' and 'Education for Self-reliance'. The Ujamaa concept, the idea of co-operative endeavour within a community which might lead to a higher standard of living, has been very well described in the Commonwealth Institute paper *Ujamaa in Tanzania* (Commonwealth Inst., 1978). In 1969 Presidential Circular No. 1, *Ujamaa Vijijini* (Un. Rep. of Tanzania, 1969b) was published and this laid down the guidelines for a process of villagisation. In October 1973, the TANU Conference called for complete villagisation by the end of 1976. By that date only 2 million out of 14 million peasants had joined Ujamaa villages and the early impetus and enthusiasm for the adoption of an Ujamaa way of life was flagging. Plans for water development and in particular for the spread of education and health services, were seriously hindered by the continued scattered nature of the rural population. A

campaign to bring all the scattered peasantry into the villages was carried out by party leaders and government officials, on a grand scale throughout the country. By the early part of 1977 the number of villages had risen from 5,628 in March 1973, to nearly 8,000, with an average population of 1,625, and nearly 13 million people out of an estimated total population of 15 million were living in villages. Such an enormous social upheaval was not without its difficulties. In many districts the selection and preparation of the sites, transport and transitional assistance into the new villages as well as the pre-move discussion and explanation were well done and the transition was smooth. In other cases none of these things were properly handled and the President's and the Party's call was interpreted as an order to complete villagisation at whatever cost and by whatever means. There were rumours of people being moved by force and of the burning of homesteads. But there is no doubt that the vast bulk of the people moved on their own with only persuasion and a little help from TANU and the administration.

In 1975 a new Villages and Ujamaa Villages Act was passed, which laid down that any area in mainland Tanzania could be registered as a village if there were a minimum of 250 households within the area and if the area could be suitably defined. Under the new Act any registered village was deemed to be a Co-operative Society "for all intents and purposes". The benefits of co-operation thus accrued to the entire village community, who paid no taxes or dues under the provisions of the Act. The Act further prescribed that as soon as possible after registration, a Village Council would receive a certificate of incorporation as a body corporate, with the power to own property, to enter into legal contracts, and to incur legal liabilities. The Village Council was to be elected by an assembly of all members of the village community aged 18 or more. The statutory functions of the Village Council are to do what is needed for the economic and social development of the village. For example, if a school is to be built this is done by the Village Council and not by the Government. The Council is to control the school, the dispensary, the shop and any other common facilities and can make bye-laws. Further stages in the development of the structure of Ujamaa villages were to follow after initial registration. It was hoped that the introduction of low technology implements such as the ox plough, would lead to larger areas being brought under cultivation, and that this mechanisation could best be done by running the plough across the individual plots and cultivating them as though they were a single field. At harvest time the villagers would take the produce from their own piece of land. A further stage would be reached as soon as the villagers realised that it was just as easy, or easier, to divide up the harvest later too. A further important factor in the development of Ujamaa villages was the setting up, in 1973, of a body known as the Small Industries Development Organisation (SIDO). This organisation operates through setting up model projects and proto-types to stimulate interest and for demonstration. Training is offered in such areas as sheet-metal work, woodwork, blacksmithing, bamboo craft and hand loom weaving. The intention is to reproduce, as far as possible, an actual situation in a village and instruction is closely linked with production and includes such managerial skills as marketing.

1.2 *Universal Primary Education*

This massive move towards villagisation and improved economic conditions has had important consequences in education, for example, a village education centre is frequently built to serve as a primary school and at the same time to provide a meeting place for adult educational activities. In November 1974, the now well known Directive 'The Implementation of Education for Self-reliance', was promulgated by the National Executive Committee of TANU at Musoma and is known generally as the 'Musoma Resolution' (TANU, 1974, also Mmari, 1976A). One of the most important provisions of the resolution was that universal primary education should be aimed for by November 1977. The achievement of this target from government resources would have been entirely out of the question but the demand was clearly very great, and how committed the people of the villages were to achieving universal primary education may be estimated from the increase in the number of children entering primary school during the relevant period. In November 1973 at the time of the Musoma Resolution, 226,071 pupils entered standard one, that is to say little more than 50% of the age group. In November 1975, the entry had gone up to 506,497 and by January 1978, had risen to 898,439 (Un. Rep. of Tanzania, 1978, the Budget Speech). To accommodate this increase something in the region of 15,000 new classrooms needed to be built and as the majority of these classrooms must have been in rural areas, they represent a notable achievement for the spirit of Ujamaa.

1.3 *De-Centralisation*

There are one or two other important developments particularly relevant to the field of education. In 1971/2 the process of de-centralisation of government to the regions began. This meant that the heads of the technical services including education, in the regions, were made answerable to the head of the regional government. The role of the ministries in the capital would be to prepare the policies and priorities and to provide advice where required. A major part of the budget was de-centralised as well. And subsequently Dodoma was designated as the future capital, emphasising the shift of power away from Dar es Salaam on the coast to a site in the centre of Tanzania, in closer touch with the rural population. In 1971, TANU had issued its so called "Guidelines" (*mwongozo*) (TANU, 1971) stating that, if development is to benefit the people, the people must participate in considering, setting out and implementing their development plans. Any action that gives the people more control of their own affairs, is an action for development, even if it does not offer them better health or more bread. It is probably in response to this de-centralisation policy and the democratisation of the development process, that the increase in primary schools must be partly attributed. The control of technical and secondary education has, however, on the whole, remained with the Ministry in Dar es Salaam. There have been some notable exceptions to this, particularly in the Kilimanjaro and Pare regions, where a substantial number of private or unassisted secondary schools have grown up. This phenomenon would appear to be fairly clear evidence that, where there is the economic base, the demand for education continues to grow even at the secondary level and to some extent the de-centralisation of government must make this kind of development possible.

1.4 *Examinations and Evaluations*

Another significant development in the period since 1969, is the setting up of the Tanzania Examinations Council. This followed almost inevitably from the principles set out in 'Education for Self-reliance', 'The Arusha Declaration' and other similar documents emanating from TANU (see Nyerere, 1968a). Clearly the use of an external examining body like the Cambridge Syndicate, was unacceptable and had to be regarded as a vestigial aspect of colonial dominance implying competitive values quite at variance with the spirit of Ujamaa. The National Examinations Council took over the setting and marking of Form IV and Form VI examinations papers, but these school final examinations ceased to be the only means by which selection would be made for further education. A set of guidelines for what are termed "new methods of evaluating a student's progress" were issued by the Ministry of National Education in September 1971. Under these guidelines the methods of evaluating a student's progress would be categorised under three headings (Min. of Nat. Educ., 1971b, see Muze, 1975: 36):

(1) Evaluating a student's daily progress in class through exercises and tests;
(2) Evaluating a student's progress by means of national examinations;
(3) Evaluating a student's daily progress through observing his behavioural attitude and his devotion to duty.

Each of these would carry one third of the total value of any assessment made so that good performance in the national examinations ceased to be the sole criterion for achieving success. This method of evaluating a student's progress is now used not only in secondary schools but also in Colleges of National Education for assessing the progress of teachers in training. The Musoma Resolution of 1974 also had consequences for the assessment of student progress. In particular the principle that university education was adult education was firmly established and it was made clear that formal school education will normally end at the secondary level for those students who reach that level, that is, it must be regarded as entire in itself. Thereafter, all students go either into direct employment or into training for employment. Eligibility for higher education is to be based on one year's compulsory fulltime national service and a minimum of two years' satisfactory work experience, during which time they must have earned recommendations from both their employers and from local Party branches that they are in every way fully suitable to be granted the privilege of admission to higher education (Un. Rep. of Tanzania, 1975a).

The consequences of this for university admissions have been that only in exceptional circumstances are students now admitted directly from secondary schools. The majority of students are mature age entrants who fulfil these requirements.

1.5 MTUU Project

One other occurrence of some significance was the inauguration of MTUU (Mpango wa Tanzania/UNICEF/UNESCO – known in English as "The Tanzania/UNICEF/UNESCO Primary Education Reform Project"). This project was launched at a meeting held at Bagamoyo where Regional Education officers, the principals of Grade A Colleges of National Education and officials of the Ministry of National Education gathered.

The objectives of the project were stated to be:

(1) to develop further the Tanzanian concept of education based on the Arusha Declaration and on the best customs and traditions of Tanzania;
(2) to reform the primary education system by placing emphasis on such knowledge and skills as may be useful in the development of a higher and happier standard of living in rural and urban communities through self-reliance and self-discipline;
(3) to establish and consolidate literacy through the acquisition of basic skills and develop independent, critical and imaginative thinking as a preparation for useful citizenship in village, town and nation;
(4) to further develop the personality of the individual through the fullest use of the natural gifts of intellect, manual and artistic skills and promote as far as possible communication and exchange of ideas between the children themselves. (Auger and Haule, 1977)

These objectives were specified further to relate to:

(a) the reorienting and retraining of the teaching force and of the educational administration in the light of Education for Self-Reliance, assuming that the newly re-written syllabuses published in 1969, which were to form the basis of the retraining exercise, did in fact relate to that ideal. The major instrument of this retraining and reorientation was to be the Itinerant Tutor Educator (ITE). The task of these ITEs was to:

   (i) organise reorientation courses for teachers;
   (ii) visit and advise teachers in selected "Practice Teaching Schools" and those who have attended reorientation courses;
   (iii) disseminate innovations in knowledge and skills among the teachers;
   (iv) participate in the teaching of the pre-service courses in Colleges of National Education (CNEs), but with a reduced teaching load to allow them to carry out their other duties;
   (v) organise 8-week residential courses in CNEs;
   (vi) bring to the attention of the Ministry successes and problems in implementing the project;
   (vii) recommend to the Ministry better ways of implementation;
   (viii) in workshops, seminars and conferences co-ordinate the feedback from the schools;
   (ix) incorporate the feedback into the curriculum;
   (x) define teaching objectives and review implementation of the project; and

DEVELOPMENTS IN LANGUAGE AND EDUCATION

(xi) update their own knowledge and skills in such areas as curriculum development, research and evaluation.

The first 30 ITEs were selected at that Bagamoyo meeting, and it is quite clear that a great deal of the responsibility for the success of the project lay on their shoulders, but there have been problems, particularly with staff continuity. By October 1976, only 9 of the original 30 were still in their posts, though the total number had grown to 39, 3 for each of the Grade A CNEs in the country, each of which had been designated a Project Teacher College. UNICEF/UNESCO support for the work of the ITEs included the provision of Landrovers, VW Combis and Suzuki motor-cycles so that they could get about to do their job. It would seem that they have in fact been able to do it with some success, with some 12,804 teachers having attended courses, the advisory and support activities being properly carried out, and some work on feedback and review being done. (See Auger and Haule, 1977: chap. VI)

(b) provision for furthering Child Development Studies in Tanzania (See Auger and Haule, 1977: chap. XIX). Here it would seem a beginning has been made but little that is novel or uniquely Tanzanian has emerged so far.

(c) provision for experimentation in running Community Schools. The most notable and pioneering work here was done at the school in Kwamsisi Ujamaa village near Korogwe CNE, which was responsible for this aspect of the project. Here the difficulties and the likely lines of success appear to have been defined, and on the basis of the initial experiment a number of other Community Schools are reported to have been set up. Clearly there is a need for the relationship between such schools and the Folk Development Colleges, which seem to be the concern of those working in Adult Education (see section 9.1 below), to be clarified. (See Auger and Haule, 1977: chap. XVIII)

(d) actual curriculum development. For example, Mwajombe and Haule report (Auger and Haule, 1977: chap. I) that a seminar was held at Same in 1975 to revise the Primary Swahili Syllabus, but the value of this exercise seems to have been very questionable. It appears that most of the work involved simply restructuring the syllabus in terms of behavioural objectives rather than in terms of content, linguistic structure and lexis; however, no copy of the revised syllabus has been obtainable so the actual form cannot be judged. This kind of reform of a syllabus does not get down to the fundamentals of why and how the material should be taught, and is not based on sensible answers to questions like those asked by Trappes–Lomax (1978) – see section 3.5 below. It could be said to be re-forming the curriculum, but it is not reforming it, or developing it.

(e) provision of the Print-Pak printing unit to assist with book production for the primary school. The unit was established in August 1974, and by June 1976 had produced some 90 titles (10,214, 250 copies computed to 8vo/64 page units). The unit is apparently not yet functioning at its full capacity, but when it is recognised that these 90 titles represent virtually the whole of the requirement of textbooks for the primary schools, in all subjects, for all years, besides the massive requirements of the Universal Primary Education (UPE) teacher training exercise (see section 3.7 below) then the value of this unit to Tanzania is very clear.

(f) the usual UNESCO/UNICEF evaluation unit. This unit appears to have produced a series of achievement tests for Swahili, mathematics, English, science, history and geography, but how useful or valid these are is unknown. It has not been possible to obtain copies of them. That it was responsible for substantial training of Tanzanians in evaluation techniques seems undeniable, and that it has enabled some record of the work of MTUU as a whole to be kept is also true, but the force of its impact seems to this observer to be disappointing, at least as it is reflected in the account of its work. (Auger and Haule, 1977: chap. XX).

The finance for this very large scale operation has come mainly from the Tanzanian government whose initial investment in 1970 amounted to 685,000 Tanzanian shillings, as against UNESCO's 1,512,000 sh., but by 1976 the Tanzanian share of the cost had risen to 28,267,360 sh. as against UNESCO's 2,563,125 sh. This was indeed an exercise in self-reliance. The bulk of the staff has also been Tanzanian, only eight expatriates being involved, and it is evident that MTUU is nationally accepted and respected to the point where "MTUU" has become part of the national vocabulary.

It is against the background of changes such as those which have been described in the sections above that it is necessary to turn to consider what has happened in the teaching of languages and the ways in which language is used in the educational system in Tanzania.

2.0 *Swahili in the Primary School*

It is quite clear that the implementation of Universal Primary Education (UPE) and the philosophy which is encapsulated in the slogan "Work is Education" have produced some alteration in the primary school syllabus as a whole. Within the bounds of Swahili teaching itself, however, there seems to be little change, beyond what might have been anticipated from the situation in 1969. Mbunda describes the situation in chapter 11 as being one in which, in some classes, Swahili, the medium of instruction and the vehicle through which reading and writing are learned, is the mother tongue of a small group of children. A second and much larger group uses Swahili as a lingua franca. This is particularly true of children living in townships or other urban or semi-urban areas, where the mixture of people of different ethnic backgrounds is high. There is a third group of children, and that is those for whom Swahili is, to all intents and purposes, a foreign language. They are the children who live in remote rural areas with little contact with members of other ethnic groups. It is difficult to tell whether the villagisation programme has reduced the number of such children or not. The likelihood is that groups of people coming to live together in villages who originally spoke the same language will continue to do so. However, there can be no doubt that the increase in adult literacy, which is achieved through the medium of Swahili, and the success of the adult education programmes, which were largely radio-based, those like *Chakula ni Uhai* 'Food is Health', must create a linguistic environment such that the children come into contact with a great deal more Swahili than might have been the case when they were living in remote and isolated homesteads with wholly illiterate parents. So Mbunda's analysis probably remains correct but the number of children in the second group is probably very much greater than it was and for those children in the third group for whom Swahili is still very largely a foreign language the amount of contact which they have with Swahili is very greatly increased.

The *Mutasari ya Kiswahili*, the Swahili Syllabus (Min. of Nat. Educ., 1976d) remains much the same, it has been revised and in particular some attention has been given to the fact that Kiswahili is a foreign language for some children, so that it spells out in some detail just what is to be taught both in the structural and lexical terms. For example, for standards I and II, about sixteen structures are listed, with about 675 words; for standards III and IV there are an additional eleven structures and about a further 1,030 words, additional words. For standards V, VI and VII, fifteen structures are specified and about another 1,025 words. The time allocation for Swahili, including the teaching of reading and writing, remains the same as in 1969. The primary school Swahili text books have been fully revised as was projected in 1969/70. They are now published as *Tujifunze Lugha Yetu* (Min. of Nat. Educ., 1970–77). There are books 1 to 9, together with teachers' books and wall charts and they are published by the Ministry of National Education through the Print-Pak unit. The books are written at each level in three sections. One is called *Lugha*, the second one *Kuandika* and the third *Kusoma*, that is to say, 'language', 'writing' and 'reading'. In use this tripartite division has been found to be inconvenient and there are a number of additional revisions which the teachers and those responsible for the development of these materials feel need to be made. The length of some of the units needs to be adjusted. In some cases units need to be made shorter, in other cases they need to be made longer. Similarly, the difficulty levels need to be adjusted to some extent as well. Again, some units in some parts of the sequence are felt to be too difficult, others are felt to be too easy. So some re-sequencing and re-writing may be necessary here. The content of these books, however, is very firmly directed towards inculcating the principles of Education for Self-reliance and of African Socialism. One of the interesting features of the syllabus in Swahili in 1969 was the emphasis placed upon supplementary or additional reading at each of the levels. The books prescribed for this supplementary reading were fairly limited in number, and it was hoped to produce many more such books. There have been efforts to produce additional supplementary readers, particularly in the teacher training colleges, and in the University in the Department of Swahili and at the Institute of Swahili Research. These supplementary readers are based very largely on traditional tales and accounts of the history and customs of the various peoples of Tanzania. Many of these were collected in the vernacular and have been translated into Swahili, but there appear to be problems in having these manuscripts prepared for printing, and in actually getting them printed and distributed to the schools. There appears to be quite a substantial stock of manuscripts of booklets of this kind which are available for publication if the resources can be found to get them into print. At the moment teachers use what books they can get. The general feeling is that the quantity falls far short of what is desirable or what was set out in the syllabus.

As far as using Swahili as the medium of instruction for primary schools is concerned, this has of course gone from strength to strength. Most of the textbooks required for subjects other than reading and writing and basic Swahili language have been produced, but teachers do complain of shortages or difficulties in obtaining copies of books, particularly in the science, history and geography area. However, there is no doubt that the use of Swahili as a medium is now quite unquestioned, and fully implemented. There is perhaps one further comment which needs to be made about the state of education in Tanzanian primary schools, and that is that it appears very surprising that in a society committed to Education for Self-reliance, that is to say, a system of education which should promote self-discipline and self-control among its pupils, that the forms of control exercised within the schools, are still very rigid and the extent of the use of corporal punishment is a matter which ought to be of some concern to the Tanzanian leadership. Since, if the medium of socialisation which is used in the schools is physical violence, then the likelihood of the use of violence and force in the society at large must increase. William Chamungwana's paper, 'Socialization Problems in Tanzania; an Appraisal of Education for Self-reliance as a Strategy for a Cultural Transformation' (1975) is a significant document in discussing this matter. Similarly, T. J. Manase's paper 'An Insight into Disciplinary Problems in Schools in Tanzania' (1978) discusses similar problems as they relate to the secondary school but the basic principle that discipline, particularly for a self-reliant society, ought to come from the pupils themselves, rather than be imposed upon them by an authority figure, like a teacher, would seem difficult to controvert.

3.0 *English in the Primary School*

3.1 *Changing Role of English*

Before entering into a discussion in detail of the kind of thing that is going on in the primary school, it is probably wise to raise some general points. In June 1978 a high level Colloquium on English language teaching, was held in Dar es Salaam (Ayaz 1978). At that Colloquium the Commissioner for National Education, Mr. Michael Muze, said "the main justification for the teaching of English in Tanzania today, seems to be that of teaching it for practical use in the day to day life of the ordinary Tanzanians who form the majority of the population. It would be doubtful whether primary education has achieved its aim if a young farmer with his primary education failed to understand whether or not his imported article was poisonous, fragile, inflammable or how to handle it through straightforward simple instructions in English" (Ayaz, 1978:20). The acting Director of teacher education Mr. J. S. Meena, suggested that in addition the objectives of teaching English in Tanzania were to provide the community with a second language for learning and acquiring new knowledge, and for promoting international understanding and co-operation (Ayaz, 1978:5). In other words, the aims and functions of teaching English in Tanzania have changed very little. However, at that same colloquium it appeared from many of the comments made by the

DEVELOPMENTS IN LANGUAGE AND EDUCATION

participants, that there was a great concern with "declining standards". H. R. H. Trappes-Lomax (1978) writing about his impressions of the colloquium has summarised very clearly some of the suggestions made as to why standards might be declining:

(1) Absence of opportunity and incentive to use English, particularly in the primary school, associated with the fact that English is no longer a medium of instruction at any level of primary education.
(2) The diminishing functions and declining prestige of English in Tanzania.
(3) The absence of clear official guide lines on what the present functions of English in Tanzania are or should be, or on the value of the language in the development of the Nation.
(4) Uncertainty among teachers as to the nature of their role in teaching English and in creating favourable conditions for its successful use.
(5) Lack of specialist English teachers at primary level.
(6) Generally low qualifications of many primary school teachers; a problem which is likely to be aggravated by the current intensive drive towards universal primary education.[1]
(7) Lack of commitment to the teaching of English in the schools. So that, that subject does not always receive its due share of time and attention in the school curriculum.
(8) Shortcomings of the existing course books at primary level. A lack of any course book at secondary level and a general shortage of good supplementary materials, such as readers.
(9) Uncertainty on the part of parents as to the benefit to be gained by their children from the effort of learning English.
(10) An absence of effective motivation in school pupils to learn the language well (1978: 3).

To this might perhaps be added:

(11) Many of the present generation of teachers in primary schools have not themselves been taught by native speakers or indeed had very much contact with native speakers whereas in the period up to 1969, the majority of primary school teachers would have been taught either directly by native speakers themselves, at least during their teacher training period, or have certainly had much more contact with native speakers than the present generation.

3.2 *Attitudes to English*

Much more important however, and indeed fundamental to all of these is the profound change in attitude to English. Once again Trappes-Lomax has set this out clearly:

> The positive values attached to English as "the language associated with upward social mobility" of access to higher education and the World of International culture has been largely lost and has been replaced with negative values as the language of former colonial

domination as a language to be spoken out of necessity for some rather than out of choice. In the process of change of values and exploitation of values, the rise of Swahili it appears, has to a small extent, resulted from, and to large extent, resulted in the decline of English both in its symbolic and instrumental aspects. To use English unnecessarily is said by some to be *Kasumba*, indicative of a non-Tanzanian mentality, yet the use of English in certain settings, principally in education remains a necessity. How are these two realities to be reconciled? (1978:4)

Informally there was certainly very strong and clear evidence of this change in attitude which is described by Trappes–Lomax. The language of staff rooms in teacher's colleges, the language of ordinary interchange between colleagues in university departments, the language of exposition at institutions like the Institute of Adult Education is always Swahili. There is a very strong tendency to use the Swahili names for institutions like the Institute of Swahili Research, the Institute of Education, the Institute of Adult Education. Names which have resulted in the coining of the neologism *Taasisi* for Institute.

3.3 *The Purpose of Teaching English*

It is also clear that there have been changes in the functions of English in Tanzania. Trappes–Lomax again points out what has been pointed out many times before, that there are now, as previously, four principle functions that English serves in Tanzania. It is a language of international communication, a language of commerce, an official administrative language and a language of education. In all of these functions, it is clear that there has been some reduction in English use. English is much less in evidence in the literature of commerce, in advertising material, warnings, instructions on products and so on than it was in 1969. Advertisements on hoardings which used to say "Drink Coca Cola" now say *Kyunwa Koka Kola*. It is also clear that in such places as post offices, banks, in hotels and shops, the use of Swahili is very much greater than it was ten years ago. In the official administrative field, it is also very clear to someone returning after ten years, that the extent to which Swahili is used is very much greater. Government circulars, instructions, the ordinary passes issued to visitors to Government buildings, all of these are in Swahili. And the ordinary language of interchange between colleagues in the corridors and indeed in matters requiring official discussion is now almost entirely Swahili. There is no doubt that in this function in particular, the need for English is likely to decline even further. With regard to the educational functions of English, the position seems to be fairly well defined, certainly in the long term: it is that English will be retained as the language of higher education for some time.

But the position of English in the secondary school remains much more ambiguous. In 1969 the Ministry of National Education sent a circular to all headmasters and headmistresses for all secondary schools in Tanzania, which discussed the possibility of introducing Swahili as the medium of instruction in secondary schools in at least some subjects. The Ministry circular suggested that political education could be taught in Swahili in 1969/70. Domestic science in 1970, history, geography, biology, agriculture and mathematics in 1971. In the time that has elapsed since the circular was issued, only political education has been taught in Swahili entirely. However, there are rumours that substantial work had already been done on the preparation of books and materials on all the subjects in the secondary school, particularly for history and geography.

That is now almost ten years ago and the situation remains as it was then, that English is the official medium of instruction for all subjects in the secondary school except Swahili and politics and that English is the language of the Form IV 'O' level examinations, with the same exceptions. There is evidently a substantial amount of unofficial use of Swahili as a medium, particularly in the teaching of the science subjects and mathematics (Mlama and Matteru, 1978). However, there is a general feeling that the move to the use of Swahili as the principal, if the not the sole, medium of instruction in secondary schools from Forms I to IV is likely to take place in the not too distant future and that this will eventually extend to Forms V and VI and perhaps even to the University, in the long term. The use of English in its international function is certainly enhanced by present circumstances, rather than diminished. For it is seen not merely as a language for formal international relations but as the nation's window on the world, a way of acquiring knowledge from the outside world as well as for educating the outside world about Tanzania.

In the light of these changes in attitude and in function, it is not surprising that there should be some ambiguity about the aims and purposes for which English is being taught. It seems self evident that if there is to be clear thinking on the methods and the materials to be used for teaching English, then it is extremely important to be clear about general aims and objectives. To quote Trappes–Lomax once again:

> Once we know why then we can start to consider how better. The relationship between the aims of teaching a language and the functions fulfilled by that language within a speech community is not a straight forward or simple one, in which functions exactly determine aims. Account must be taken of first who in social terms the learners are, and the likely future roles they will fulfil in which a knowledge of the language will be needed. And secondly what is educationally feasible in terms of availability of time, materials, teachers and the will to learn. (1978: 7)

Trappes–Lomax illustrates the kind of picture which might emerge by constructing a grid (1978: 8) in which the principal functions fulfilled by English in Tanzania intersect with the four main language skills. Each cell of the grid may then be marked with a plus to indicate a definite need, a minus to indicate a definite lack of need, and a question mark to indicate a possible need. Table 14:1 represents the outcome of one such exercise. The values in the cells are, of course, tentative, and have been modified from those suggested by Trappes–Lomax on the basis of contacts with educators in Tanzania during a recent, very brief visit. Since Tanzania's

Table 14:1 Uses of English in Tanzania

	International	Official	Commercial	Educational
Conversation[2]	–	–	?	?
Listening[2]	?	–	–	?
Reading	?	–	+	+
Writing	–	–	–	+

policy of Education for Self-Reliance (see Nyerere, 1968a) has as one of its fundamental principles that education for the primary school child should be self contained and should not be conceived of merely as the basis for the secondary education that most children will not proceed to, a particular problem is raised for the teaching of English at primary level. The question is, if the needs of secondary education are left entirely out of account, what are the reasons for teaching English in the primary school? The grid (table 14:1) represents one kind of answer. There are obviously very few opportunities for most primary leavers to be involved in personal international communication, but there may be opportunities for using the receptive skills in listening to English language broadcasts and reading overseas English language publications. There seem to be almost no circumstances in which primary leavers in Tanzania would positively require to use English for any official purpose,' unless they became teachers. All documents related to the Unified Teaching Service terms and condition of service, bonding agreements, etc. are still in English (Inst. of Adult Educ., 1976b). In commerce and industry the principal needs that can be realistically included would appear to be the reading of instructions, labels and directions and perhaps some slight conversational English, for example, in the tourist industry or perhaps in negotiating a purchase.

It is in education that the strongest claim for the teaching of English in primary school can be made. English provides access to further learning and with the spread of ideas relating to adult education and *éducation permanente* the likelihood that many Tanzanians will take advantage of such opportunities as may be provided by programmes resulting from such notions, is extremely high. Already some 70,000 Tanzanians are engaged in private study through the correspondence courses of the Institute of Adult Education and the most popular of the evening classes run by the Institute in Dar es Salaam is English, with over 200 students enrolled at the elementary first level course. The principal need would seem to be for the skills relating to the written medium, in particular for skill in reading. Some element of conversational skill may very well be useful for discussion and it is likely that a primary leaver will also need some skill in listening, particularly if the further education programme, which he undertakes, includes an element of radio listening. The skill in writing may also be needed for note taking and essay writing, but the student may, if necessary, or if he prefers, turn to Swahili for communication with himself, his teachers, or his peers. But a course book or a volume from the public library will not translate itself, so that reading seems to be the

DEVELOPMENTS IN LANGUAGE AND EDUCATION

irreducible necessity. Some such analysis is in fact implicit in the aims for teaching English in Tanzanian primary schools as stated in the official teacher education syllabus (Min. of Nat. Educ. 1976c:116). These aims are:

(a) To give primary school leavers permanent reading knowledge of English so that they can have access to ideas and information available in English and useful to Tanzania, or so that they can continue with their education through the use of English as a medium of learning.
(b) To develop through learning English language skills, the pupils' education for self-reliance, politically, technically, socially and culturally.

3.4 *The Level at which English Teaching should Begin*

The details of how these aims may be achieved in terms of the development of suitable materials and teacher education still remain to be worked out.

There are two other factors which affect the teaching of English in the primary school. The first of these concerns at what stage in the primary school curriculum English teaching should begin. Again Trappes–Lomax has analysed the important factors very clearly, suggesting that there are two assumptions which are firmly entrenched about when language learning should start. These may be encapsulated in two slogans. The first is "longer means better" and the other that is "earlier means better". He correctly points out that in fact neither of these assumptions is based on very much more than myth. It is clear that account must be taken not only of the extent of the course, but also of its intensity and, one might add, of the quality of the teaching which goes into it. At present English in the primary school in Tanzania is taught over a period of 20 terms. From the second term of Standard I to the end of Standard VII. If we assume an average of 4 periods a week over that time, we may estimate that each child attends about a thousand lessons. This is equivalent to a hundred days devoted exclusively to the learning of English. Are these hundred days well spent? If we may judge by the widespread comments on declining standards, they represent at present a less than satisfactory investment. This being so it is probably well worth considering whether a reduced but more selective investment, for example a reduction in the extent of the period of learning from 20 terms to 12, thus beginning instruction in the first term of Standard IV partially compensated for by a slight increase in intensity, might not result in an actual improvement in performance. It is certainly tempting to suppose that long and perhaps as viewed by the pupils, sometimes desultory language courses might, after a period of years, begin to prove, if not counter-productive, at least not convincingly productive. At this point the slogan "earlier means better" may be brought in to counter the suggestion that English learning should begin later. There is, however, very little evidence to support the conclusion that earlier means better, indeed such findings as there are from educational research seem to go in the opposite direction. Practical considerations within the Tanzanian context, might have the following advantages:

(1) A later start for English language teaching will enable English to be taught by the more skilled of the present English teachers, particularly those with some degree of specialist training.
(2) It would reduce the problems faced by the Colleges of National Education in training for English teaching large numbers of students whose command of the language is often far from satisfactory.
(3) It would permit a concentration on materials development and supply, on a narrower front, with the possible result of increase in both quality and quantity.
(4) It would allow children in their early primary years to devote all their language learning capacity to the essential task of mastering Swahili and the equally vital task of acquiring literacy in that language.

3.5 *Standard of English Required*

Another factor which needs to be considered is "how good" the English of learners is at the end of the course. Many people have expressed concern about the prevalence of non-standard forms in the English of their students and the difficulty of eradicating these. The "common errors" of Tanzanian English are well documented: for example the reduction of the vowels in 'hot', 'heart', 'hurt' and 'hat' to a single open central vowel as in 'haat'. Or the persistent double subject with relatives as in 'The man who he came last night is my uncle' or in idiomatic expressions like 'this food it is somehow tasteless'. These variants are not random eccentricities of individuals who have not mastered the language properly but are consistent characteristics shared by people who *have* mastered the language properly in Tanzania. Since the available models for language learners at the primary level are all Tanzanians and since few primary leavers have any opportunity to use their English skills in communication with native speakers, and since a number of the usages are well established, and it is certain that many of them are reinforced by first language interference, the effort involved in trying to remove them is very considerable. So, in terms of effective use of resources, it might seem better not to attempt to eradicate such widespread local usages. This is not to suggest that local forms should be taught but merely that they should not be deliberately untaught. They should simply be accepted. Trappes–Lomax reports a number of suggestions made at the colloquium for the improving of the teaching of English in Tanzania:

(1) Clear aims should be established for the teaching of English, especially in the primary school and clear guidelines should be provided for schools and colleges on the role of English in Tanzania's development and in particular on its value in education.
(2) The methods used in teaching English and the course books and materials

provided should be suited to the aims set forth. The apparent need to emphasise the skill of reading at least calls in question the emphasis on the spoken language and the appropriateness of an audio-lingual approach.
(3) There is an urgent need for research in all aspects of language teaching and learning in Tanzania and some of the questions that such research might tackle would be:
What functions are fulfilled at present by English in Tanzania and how do they appear to be changing?
Who uses English in these various functions and what are the attitudes of the people to the teaching and use of the language?
What are the implications for language planning and language pedagogy of the shift away from English as the sole medium, to the use of English as a subsidiary medium of education at the post primary level?
How should the reading and writing skills required by primary leavers be more precisely specified?
What generally, are the needs of language learners at different educational levels?
What language functions must they be competent in?
What concepts must they be able to express?
What lexis and grammar should be taught as appropriate realisations of these functional and semantic categories?
What English is acceptable in Tanzania?
Is there a Tanzanian English?
What model of English are language learners exposed to, i.e. what English do the teachers have?
What is the impact of this model on the language learning behaviour of the pupil?
What methods are best suited at the primary level to a situation in which the main need is for skill in the written medium.
What is the role of the spoken language in achieving facility in reading and writing?
How, in short, do Tanzanian children learn a foreign language?
(4) New materials are needed: a course book for secondary schools, supplementary readers for primary schools and if there is a change in the point at which English is begun in the primary school, then a very radical revision of the primary school course book, if not a complete re-writing of it.
(5) The much needed secondary English course book should, as was done with *English for Tanzanian Schools*, (Min. of Nat. Educ., 1969–73) be developed within Tanzania according to the Tanzanian philosophy of education.
(6) Teachers or tutors should be released from their duties for the purpose of working on the needed materials. Account would need to be taken of the useful work done by some college students in producing reading materials and procedures should be devised for encouraging this work and for editing and producing it.
(7) Certain problems faced by tutors in the colleges of national education, such as the brevity of courses and unpredictable interruptions to the normal routine, should be tackled so as to enable the colleges to fulfil their functions more efficiently. Study, it was said, is also work.
(8) Renewed consideration should be given to the level at which English is introduced in the primary schools.
(9) Consideration should also be given to the possibility of training specialist

English language teachers who would concentrate on English language teaching in schools.
(10) Since the present Grade A English Syllabus is unrealistically full in relation to the time available to teach it, (it was originally designed to take two years but since the Grade A course has been contracted to one year the time scale is now inappropriate) an attempt should be made to identify its more, and its less, essential components. Alternatively the syllabus might be completely re-written.
(11) Opportunities for the use of English by learners should be created through, for instance, the production of specialised radio programmes, or perhaps an E.L.T. column in the Daily News (1978: 21-2, 26-7).

3.6 *Alternative Policies for the Future*

Trappes–Lomax concludes his argument by pointing out that there are two broadly different types of policy with regard to language teaching in developing countries. The first which may be called the minimalist policy proceeds from the identification of the essential irreducible functions that cannot be fulfilled without recourse to the language in question. The nature of the competence called for and the categories of people who need it are established and a programme is devised for teaching of this precise competence to these precise people in the most efficient and economical manner. The recent rapid development in the theory and practice of E.S.P. (English for specific purposes) is in part a response to language learning requirements of this sort.

The second type of policy which may be called maximalist is based on the assumption, first that there is no member of the national speech community for whom some knowledge of the language will be entirely useless. And second that the more extensively it is taught in the schools the higher the overall level of competence in the language will be. Such a policy aims at the teaching of the language to all school pupils. Tanzania is clearly at a point where it may have to decide between one or other of these two policies. The first policy is likely to be most effective where English is being learned as a foreign language. The second policy is likely to be more effective where English fulfills some essential communicative function within the life of the community (1978: 23-4). The situation in Tanzania appears to be that there are conflicting forces at work. On the one hand there are forces which wish to promote Swahili as the national language, pushing English into the position of the foreign language, and on the other there are forces which derive from the long use of English in Tanzania, the wealth of technical, legal, historical and literary material in English in Tanzania. In particular there is the fact that English is the language of much African literature and thought. So there is a conflict of interests. It would seem, however, that at the moment there is a renewed determination to make a maximalist policy work. The Ministry of National Education has called for a greater commitment to the teaching of English. The primary course books are in the process of substantial revision. English language teaching experts from Britain are posted in many of the Colleges of National Education, some of which have been designated as specialist colleges for the teaching of English, and the

DEVELOPMENTS IN LANGUAGE AND EDUCATION 379

Institute of Education is making determined efforts to make the work of the teachers more effective. What the outcome of this may be remains to be seen, but it would seem clear that at least two kinds of experience would need to be taken into account. First the kind of experience that may be exemplified by the teaching of Gaelic in Ireland and secondly the kind of experience that may be exemplified by the teaching of English in Scandanavian Countries (1978:25).

3.7 *Comparison between 1969 and 1979*

Against this background let us now turn to see precisely what has happened in the teaching of English in the primary school since 1969. Brown's section in chapter 11 describes the situation at that time. It is clear that many of the features of the situation, as he described it, are still relevant, but that some of the factors described above in 14:1.0–1.2 have clear consequences. For example, the sheer scale of the UPE (Universal Primary Education) teacher training operation and the form of training which this implies must mean that the fourth assumption which Brown makes about the teachers, which is that the form of training they have received will have prepared them to teach effectively only by following a detailed programme which is fully explicit, is perhaps slightly less certain than it was. The UPE teacher training programme involves distance teaching by correspondence over three years. In the first two years UPE trainees will study Pedagogy, Swahili Methods and Mathematics Methods. In the third year the trainees will study English Language Stage 1, which is planned to raise their level of English to that of Secondary Form II. The methodology of English teaching is to be taught formally during tutorials. These tutorials are given by ward education tutors, but their frequency and duration does not seem to have been spelt out.[3] In addition the trainees are required to follow radio programmes with radio lessons in Pedagogy, Swahili and Mathematics (Inst. of Adult Educ., 1976a, b & c). The most important part of their training seems to be a kind of apprenticeship where the UPE trainee is attached to a practising teacher and learns from him (Ayaz, 1978:23–4). In this situation clearly it is unlikely that the quality of English teaching by UPE teachers will be very much greater than that of the minimally trained Grade C teachers to whom they may well be attached. Those who are fortunate enough to be attached to Grade A teachers may do slightly better, particularly if the Grade A teacher is one of those who has had some specialist training in one of the newly designated English Specialist Teacher Training Colleges of Education.

The number of periods allocated to English in the primary school remains much the same as it was in the past. In Standards I and II there are five periods each week of thirty minutes each. In Standards III and V there are between six and eight periods of forty minutes, in comparison with the designated seven periods of 1969/70. In Standards VI and VII there are between seven and eight periods of forty minutes as against the seven periods of forty five minutes suggested in 1970. The books used in teaching primary school English in stages 1 and 2 are as described by

Brown. Stage 3 consists of a collection of pamphlet readers together with a teacher's book and books for stages 4 and 5 consist of a pupil's book together with a teacher's book. Stages 6 and 7 are as described by Brown and remain slightly anomalous in that they were created from collections of stories written by Grade A teachers in training, and adapted by P. S. Tregido to fit a language progression he had devised. Brown indicates that they have been heavily criticised for inappropriateness of content, but that objection seems to have faded somewhat with time. The primary school syllabus says that 50 titles of small reader pamphlets should be available in each standard from standard 4 to 7, but many of these have not yet been produced. Some schools have and use the Oxford Supplementary readers stages 1 to 4, but in general the objective of emphasising the reading skill seems to be out of reach of most primary school teachers. The vocabulary grading for these books is of some interest. Stage 1 aims at a vocabulary of 110 words, stage 2 at a vocabulary of 300 words, stage 3 at 550, stage 4 at 1,000. Stage 5 at 1,500 and stages 6 and 7 require a vocabulary of 2,000 words. The primary school syllabus (Min. of Nat. Educ. 1976d), lists the vocabulary and the structures which are to be taught at each level. The basic methodology for the course as a whole remains as Brown described it. Each lesson was to have had a section of Revision, one on Presentation, one of Group Imitation, one of Group Demonstration, and one of Group Practice. There has been a very slight modification of this in that the Group Demonstration phase is usually omitted. The oral work is emphasised very strongly all the way through: a trend which seems to run curiously counter to the main objective of ensuring that the Tanzanian primary school leaver, should be able to read English fluently and easily.

4.0 Swahili Teaching in Secondary Schools

4.1 Growth of Schools

One of the principal planks in the policy of education in Tanzania is that of providing secondary education only to meet national manpower requirements. Each secondary school is supposed to have its own bias. It may be agricultural, technical, domestic science or commercial. The intention is that in this diversified secondary programme, the work of the school should be directly linked with concrete economic projects from which the schools are expected to realise at least 25% of their maintenance costs. This follows from the philosophy of Education for Self-reliance and Education is Work (TANU, 1970). The consequences of limiting the provision of secondary education to the needs of national manpower is that the number of state schools has increased only very slightly over the ten year period. In 1969 there were 83 state schools, and the number of private or unaided secondary schools was 28 giving a total of 111 secondary schools. In 1978 there were 85 state schools, with a total of 62 private or unaided schools, a total of 147 schools. The significant increase here in the number of private schools is particularly apparent in certain parts of Tanzania notably in Kilimanjaro (Manase, 1978)[4]. Manase gives an interesting account of this phenomenon, pointing out

DEVELOPMENTS IN LANGUAGE AND EDUCATION

that the increasing pressures on secondary education arise from the increasing number of pupils entering primary school and that in particular where parents have not been fully socialised or have not fully understood the philosophy behind the Musoma directive the desire on their part to ensure that their children get secondary education would be very high. They are, therefore, prepared to spend time and money and to use whatever resources may be available to them to achieve this for their children since they see secondary education as a means of advancement for their children. It is likely that additional pressures may come from the increasing number of graduates who have entered Tanzanian society. The University and associated institutions of higher education have been producing somewhere in the region of a 1,000 graduates a year. Over a ten year period this means that there are some 10,000 graduates likely to be looking for secondary places for their children having enjoyed it themselves, they will seek the same privilege for their children. In 1977, there were just over 9,000 places available for secondary school entrants. So already, even if each graduate only has one child, there would appear to be quite severe pressures on demand for secondary places.

4.2 *Status of Swahili*

The consequences of relatively little growth in secondary capacity has, however, had favourable results for the teaching of Swahili. Firstly the problem of finding suitable staff which was regarded as fairly acute in 1970 has now been somewhat eased. The output of trained graduates from the University has ensured that every secondary school has a properly qualified Swahili teacher, indeed more than one in many instances. The status of Swahili as a subject is much higher now too. Its position as the national language has become very clearly defined and the fall in the prestige of English with its overtones of colonialist oppression has also meant that the status of Swahili has improved. Some teachers now decline to teach Swahili, because they say their own Swahili is not good enough or they do not have the necessary technical knowledge to be able to do it well, so that the Swahili specialist teacher enjoys the respect and approbation of his colleagues. Swahili is no longer timetabled in awkward hours with double periods on Friday afternoons, and irritations of that kind. Refresher courses of various kinds take place from time to time, first of all under the auspices of the Swahili Language Association, and secondly under the direction of the Swahili zonal co-ordinators who hold seminars according to need. They may ask for help from the Institute of Education and a report on the seminars which are held is then forwarded to the National Co-ordinator.

4.3 *Examinations and the Syllabus*

The form of examination by which Swahili is examined has also been substantially improved. There is now an examination at Form VI level, an 'A' level examination, though the pattern of this examination seems to be very structure oriented and rather rigid and traditional and does not seem to conform to the pattern which was suggested by Mbunda in Chapter 12 of this volume. Swahili, like English, has a scheme of continuous assessment (Sango, 1976). This scheme of continuous assessment is used by some teachers as a scheme of work or a detailed syllabus and it is very easy for it to be used this way since it sets out week by week what topics should be covered and what form of exercise or test should be set on each piece of work. Continuous assessment of subjects in secondary schools is of course a requirement for the selection procedure for further education as set out by the Musoma Directive and described in the introductory part of this chapter. The syllabus for Swahili (Min. of Nat. Educ., 1976) has been revised and updated, following on from work in 1969, with the publication of *Kiswahili katika Sekondari* (Mbunda, 1969). The new syllabus includes some specification of the syntactic and morphological structures which are to be focused on, particularly in the early forms of the secondary school. This follows on from the part of the primary school syllabus which recognises that Swahili is a foreign language or at least a second language for a good many of the pupils who study it. The new syllabus also includes a specification of the kind of literary study in Swahili which pupils might engage in. Literature in Tanzanian secondary schools is to be studied not as Literature in Swahili or as Literature in English but as a subject area in its own right, integrated between the two languages. Thus the pattern as set out in Vella (1973) shows Literature 1, *Fasihi* which involves using two of the four Swahili periods in Forms I and II for all students; Literature 2, *Fasihi*, two of the four Swahili periods in Forms III and IV for all students; Literature 3, two periods of the six English periods in Forms III and IV again for all students; Literature 4, four periods in Forms III and IV for those arts students in schools who offer literature at 'O' level; Literature 5, 'A' level literature in schools, which is offered as one of the arts combinations; and Literature 6, *Fasihi*, a component of 'A' level Swahili. Details of what books might be used for the teaching of literature 1, 2, and 6 are not given in Sister Vella's article but one must suppose that they are of the kind outlined in Mbunda's description of the proposed 'A' level examination requirements in chapter 12.

4.4 *Supply of Texts*

However, the principal difficulty which Mbunda saw appears to persist, that is to say, the scarcity of suitable books. Strong efforts are being made to remedy this. For example, the manuscript of the Swahili grammar book, *Sarufi Maumlo* (Morphology) written in Swahili for use in secondary schools, which has been long in preparation, is now at the final editing stage, in the Institute of Swahili Research. It will be followed by *Sarufi Miunda* (Syntax) in about two years' time. Both the Department of Swahili and the Institute of Swahili Research have accumulated manuscripts of collections of folk or traditional tales, many of these originally told in some vernacular local language and translated into Swahili (Sango, 1973). These manuscripts are ready for editing and printing, but there appears to be a shortage of suitable people to do this kind of work. Mbunda also suggested that competitions might be held to encourage the production of works of literary merit and indeed since 1969 a number of such competitions have indeed been held and the works produced by the winners have been published by Tanzania Publishing House. The authors have been given copyright and presumably are drawing royalties for the work that they did. The course book for secondary schools has not yet materialised but once again there appear to be moves afoot to try and get this published. The Ministry of National Education is to establish a school equipment development unit (Ayaz, 1978:11). The Swahili–Swahili dictionary is still needed very badly in secondary schools, but is said to be at page-proof stage at the Institute of Swahili Research. The new Swahili–English, English–Swahili dictionaries are still under preparation.

4.5 *Future Developments*

As for the use of Swahili as a medium of instruction, it would now seem to be more feasible than ever before. Virtually all the staff in secondary schools are Swahili speaking. There are very few expatriates and there seems to be a substantial body of opinion that favours the changeover.

Bhaiji (1976) attempted to discover what the attitudes of pupils and teachers and secondary and primary schools might be towards the change over to Swahili as the medium of instruction. He found that overall both in primary and secondary schools pupils did not want Swahili introduced as a medium of instruction. Teachers in secondary schools did favour the changeover to Swahili as the medium of instruction but teachers in primary schools felt that Swahili should not be introduced at the secondary level. In his final conclusion he is of the opinion that Swahili should be adopted as the medium of instruction in secondary schools. He also suggests that the implementation of this should be done in a phased manner, that is to say, the priority of teaching in Swahili should go to history, geography, commerce, domestic science, maths and sciences in that order. That pressure for the changeover is mounting, of that there can be no doubt (see also Mlama & Matteru, 1978), but it is extremely important that a proper investment of resources in terms of manpower and money should be put into the implementation of the policy when it takes place, otherwise, the results may be very serious for the future of Tanzanian education. As with the teaching of Swahili and English at primary level, there appears to be no complacency about the teaching of Swahili at the secondary level, and energetic efforts are being made to improve the quality of Swahili teaching there still further.

5.0 *English in Tanzanian Secondary Schools*

5.1 *The Syllabus*

The teaching of English now follows the syllabus laid down by the Ministry of National Education (1976:27ff). The syllabus is set out in seven parts. Part 1 deals with aims and objectives and says: "During their study of English, students should grow to appreciate the cultural and political values of Tanzania and to develop socialist attitudes. As their linguistic ability in English grows, they should be able to express these values and attitudes in both national and international situations. English is a tool for world communication for sharing the socialist experience and for personal development". These aims and objectives are to be realised through a programme involving the teaching of structures, which is set out in Part 2, under some 22 principle headings, such as sentence usage, the use of the articles, the use of past tenses, use of countable and uncountable nouns, the use of present tenses and so on. Part 3 describes the reading programme which should be both extensive and intensive and also involve some research reading. The extensive reading programme was originally known as literature 3 (see Vella, 1973 and Mcha, 1978). Language 3, as this part of the course is now known, is organised thematically, treating areas such as "Tradition and the Family", "Conflict", "Building the Future", "Protest", "Self-awareness and Personality". Pupils are expected to choose 4 of these themes and to familiarise themselves very thoroughly with at least three titles from the set of readings suggested for each theme. The Heinemann African Writers' Series features prominently and the various sections include such titles as *No Longer at Ease* (Achebe, 1960) or *A Grain of Wheat* (Ngugi, 1967).

Part 4 of the syllabus deals with the writing programme and suggests that skills related to personal correspondence, business letter writing, summary writing, writing to give factual information or exposition, writing in order to convince (argument), writing about literature and creative writing should be included. The writing of structurally related exercises is also catered for and the writing necessary for the completion of projects which relates to part 6 is also included. The oral-aural part of the programme, part 5, relates to the listening comprehension of news broadcasts, and public speeches and radio feature programmes, on the receptive side. On the productive side, pupils are expected to be able to participate in ordinary dialogues and everyday conversation, telephone conversations, the taking of messages, participation in debates and discussions and so on. Part 6 which relates to project work, is an attempt to include work done for the "school and community" (Nyerere, 1968:71) in the English language syllabus, it involves such activities as the writing of booklets and reports, to be used in the class library, on such topics as geography, biography, travel, economics or history. It should also include the collection of local stories for class publication. Project work might also involve the doing of research, using newspapers, magazines, field trips, interviews with various people in the community in order to accumulate information which might be of use to the community. Part 7 deals with particular problems in the learning of English and consists very largely of a specification of miscellaneous structural and spelling problems of the kind discussed by Trappes–Lomax above and treated in some detail in Ayaz (1978). Accompanying this syllabus is the *Handbook for Teachers of English* (Eng. Lang. Panel, 1973). This is a completely different book from the *Handbook for English Teachers* (Eng. Lang. Panel, 1969) which is mentioned in the section on English in the secondary schools in Chapter 12 above.

The 1973 *Handbook for Teachers of English*, follows the layout of the

DEVELOPMENTS IN LANGUAGE AND EDUCATION

syllabus very closely.[5] It has 7 sections dealing with the same areas as the 7 parts of the syllabus from the Ministry of National Education. Some details of how the various parts of the teaching programme are to be carried out are given, with a good deal of exemplification and a substantial amount of sample materials of one kind or another, incorporated into the actual handbook, in contrast to the 1969 handbook, where the sample materials were generated in workshops and published separately in mimeo. The handbook is used in the basic training of graduates at the University of Dar es Salaam, and it clearly provides substantial help and support for them. In addition to the handbook, however, the Institute of Education has published a series of background notes, discussion materials and exercises to be done on the required reading for language 3. This series is known as the *Looking Together Series* (see Nikundiwe, 1975 & 1977 for a full list), the most informative of this series is probably *Looking Together at Language 3* by Y. Y. Mcha (1978) but it includes other titles like *Looking Together at the Short Story "A Walk In The Night"* by Alex La Guma or *Looking Together At the Poem "My Newest Bride"* by Y. S. Chemba. What other textbooks are used in the schools at the moment apart from those prescribed for language 3, is a little difficult to determine. From such evidence as is available, as for example in Mziray (1975) and from Ayaz (1978), it would appear that many of the books listed in Chapter 12 (n. 4) are still being used. These would include titles like W. S. Allen's *Living English Structure* (1974) and J. A. Bright's *Patterns and Skills* (1965), Mackin's *A Course of English Study* (1968) and Pit Corder's *An Intermediate Practice Book* (1960).

Literature 4 is the most purely literary part of the secondary school course. This part of the course also is organised on the basis of the genre: drama, short stories and novels, biographies and essays, and songs and poems. Pupils are required to read a minimum of four readings from each list suggested under each genre. Literature 4 also has a very strong African writing orientation and there is some overlap between readings for Literature 4 and Language 3, so that the supporting materials produced in the "Looking Together" series is useful for both. Literature 5 is the course offered at 'A' level. This, like Language 3, is structured on a thematic base. The themes suggested are such as "The Response of the Oppressed" and "The Alienated Man". For each theme there is a central list of readings from which students read a minimum of four titles and a supplementary list from which the students should read as many as they possibly can. Each list consists of some eight to ten titles. Pupils are expected to show familiarity with at least four different genres in these themes. A special feature of the 'A' level literature course which is now offered in 7 schools is the Annual Student Workshop on Literature where 'A' level pupils come together to discuss what they have been reading, to write reviews, and in fact to create works of literature, poems and plays and short stories (see Nyagwaswa, 1976 and Mvungi, 1976).

The scheme of examination for English as for all other subjects in the secondary school has been somewhat modified. The National Examination at the end of Form IV now carries only 50% of the total marks for student evaluation. The continuous assessment scheme involving the assessment of exercises and various kinds of work both written and oral, done during the course of the year, together with the project work, accounts for the further 50% and of course the matter of character and behaviour is also taken into account here. A very detailed continuous assessment scheme has been produced by the Institute of Education (Inst. of Educ., 1976). This is in fact virtually a scheme of work and is used by many teachers in this way. It spells out roughly the number of periods which should be devoted to each topic, the number of exercises and tests which should be carried out and the kinds of project that ought to be engaged in. The scheme covers work in English language under all five of the relevant headings of the language teaching syllabus and also work in literature. There seems to be some doubt about how realistic the targets set in these schemes and syllabuses really are (Msuya, 1977) but that a great deal of effort is being put into trying to ensure that standards of English teaching are well maintained is very obvious.

5.2 *Staffing*

The position with regard to the staffing of English Departments appears to be much more stable than it was in the period immediately after 1969. Since 1972 there have been relatively few expatriates in the teaching force in Tanzania. Virtually all the English teachers are University of Dar es Salaam graduates and Tanzanians. In 1975 Mziray reported a shortage of teachers of literature but in the period since then it would appear that some efforts have been made to remedy this. There seems to be some anxiety about the quality of the teachers of English with suggestions that a number of them are themselves so poor at English that they are unable to teach it satisfactorily (Mlama & Matteru, 1978) and there also seems to be some doubt about their understanding of the principles and methods which they should be employing in teaching, but here too it is apparent that the most strenuous efforts are being made to improve things. There appears to have been only a little inservice training of English teachers, mainly in the form of seminars or workshops, but there is to be a major in-service refresher course for teachers of English at the University in Dar es Salaam in June and July in 1979.

5.3 *Problems*

The position of English as a medium of instruction in the secondary schools has already been discussed above (section 3.3). It is fairly clear that in the forseeable future English will cease to be widely used as the medium of instruction and many of the efforts which have been made and indeed are still being made, for example in the continued use in some quarters of *Learning through Language* (Isaac S, 1960) will cease to be necessary. When the time comes that the decision is made that Swahili should take over as the medium of instruction in secondary schools it is likely that a good many problems which currently beset the use of English as the medium will be eased. Until that time pupils and teachers struggle along as best they can using a good deal of Swahili for the purposes of

DEVELOPMENTS IN LANGUAGE AND EDUCATION 387

explanation in all sorts of subjects. The extent to which this occurs is very fully documented in *Haja ya Kutumia Kiswahili Kufundishia katika Elimu ya Juu* (Mlama & Matteru, 1978). This is the report of a research project carried out on behalf of the National Swahili Council in some 16 secondary schools and some 9 primary schools in different parts of Tanzania. The evidence seems incontrovertible that it certainly is a struggle for pupils to use English as the medium of instruction, even at the Form IV level, and it appears to be equally as great a struggle for the primary school teachers to use English for the very elementary purposes for which they require it in the primary school. One of the astonishing things is perhaps that pupils still do appear to be learning some English and to be able to use it in part at least of their education.

6.0 *The Teaching of French in Secondary Schools*

The ordinary and advanced level courses in French now appear to be very well established. The new syllabus for French in secondary schools (Min. of Nat. Educ., 1976a) sets out the objectives which fundamentally are little different from those of 1969. French is intended to further African unity, it is also suggested that it is used "as a discipline for the cognitive development of an individual" (p. 52). Furthermore, pupils should be able to listen to French radio broadcasts from nearby francophone African countries and to read books in French. The syllabus sets out the programme in some detail. There is to be no reading or writing of French in Form I; a hard line audio-lingual approach is advocated. Form II introduces reading, both intensive and extensive, and there is some introduction to writing. Form III develops this programme further with the addition of simple letter writing to friends and relatives. Form IV carries this still further with the writing of letters to the press. In Forms V and VI, however, there will be a change, in the fact that Form IV leavers have been trained to be only "potential French speakers", who can be oriented to any further training and whose French can and should be reactivated according to the needs of the nation at one time or another, while Form VI leavers should be really operational (Min. of Nat. Educ., 1976a: 82). The intention is that Form VI leavers should have control of 3,000 words of *Le Français Fondamental*. The syllabus includes a detailed specification of the structures and usages to be taught, listed form by form.

The materials to be used in teaching this include a specially written *Texte de Français* with a *Livre du Professeur* (French Panel, 1977a & b). Forms II, III and IV will continue to use *Pierre et Seydou* (BELC, 1964–72) along with Hugonnet et al (*Exercices structuraux du 1er et 2ème degrés*, Paris: CEDAMEL) and the *Textes de Français en Tanzanie*, Dossier 1, Form III and Form IV (French Panel, 1975a & b) (see Pochard, 1973). For the extensive reading programme the Didier *Mieux Vivre* Series is recommended along with the Oxford *Easy French Readers* and the *French Readers for West Africa*, also published by Oxford University Press (Constable, 1968). In Forms V and VI *Pierre et Seydou* level 3 (BELC, 1964–72) is recommended along with *Grammaire Français des Lycées* and *Styles and Registers in Contemporary French* (Ager

1970) and various other documents including of course the Larousse Dictionary.

The output of French graduates from the University of Dar es Salaam, which amounts to about 8 per annum, is keeping schools well supplied, and with the Form VI programme now fully operational, it is hoped that standards can be raised even higher than they have been. There is as yet no surplus of French graduates as foreseen and feared by Constable (chapter 12 above).

7.0 *Language in Colleges of National Education*

There appears to have been very little change in the official programme concerning the use and teaching of languages in the Colleges of Education since 1969. *The Programme for Grade A Teacher Education* (Min. of Nat. Educ., 1969b) is still the basis, but the length of the course has been cut to one year from the original two years plus two years probationary supervised teaching. The broad outlines of the Swahili teaching programme, remain much the same *Kiswahili Vyuoni* (Mbunda, 1970) is still used though it requires revision, there is now an increased emphasis on the collecting of traditional stories and folk tales for use first of all in adult literacy programmes and for providing reading material at the early reading stages for adults, as well as for use as supplementary readers in the primary school. For English there has been published *A Teacher Education English Handbook and Syllabi* (Nyagwaswa et al., 1976) which covers the work of both grades A and C. This handbook spells out in great detail what the content of the courses should be, what materials are to be used and what the components of the course are. These are:

(1) Methodology
(2) An aural-oral programme
(3) A structure programme
(4) A vocabulary programme
(5) A reading programme
(6) A writing programme
and (7) How it is all to be evaluated.

There is very heavy emphasis on training the teachers to have enough English to be able to teach *English for Tanzanian Schools* (Min. of Nat. Educ., 1969-73) and the methodology part of the programme emphasises how they should actually use the books. One of the basic reference texts is *An In-service Course for Primary School Teachers* (Chandley, 1967). Another is *A Handbook for Tutors of English in Grade A Colleges of National Education* (Min. of Nat. Educ., 1971).

The *Handbook Syllabi* (Nyagwaswa, et al, 1976) contains model lesson plans and a great many useful hints, and guidelines in some detail, but in this document too, there is much preoccupation with "common errors", and there is clearly a very great deal of concern about the general level of English, not only of the pupils in the schools, but also of the trainees themselves. It must be remembered that many of these are themselves primary school graduates with only seven years of schooling behind them. The aural-oral part of the course seems to focus fairly narrowly on phonetics rather than on communicative intelligibility. In the light of Trappes–Lomax's arguments above, it seems unprofitable to be devoting a great deal of time and attention to distinguishing between 'hat', 'hurt', 'hot' and 'hut', as is suggested in this syllabus, whereas the rather cursory mention of rising and falling intonation (p. 120) leaves out of account one of the most important areas of communicative effectiveness in English. The structure and vocabulary components of the programme also exemplify very fully the preoccupation with "mistakes". The reading programme seems to be somewhat ambitious, given the very short timescale, but it is perhaps the proper emphasis since it is only through reading that trainees can be exposed to substantial amounts of English text. The writing programme also seems to be slightly unrealistic, certainly as far as Grade A teachers are concerned, it is difficult to see in what circumstances they might have to write expository and argumentative prose in English and even more difficult to envisage how they might be expected to involve themselves in creative writing in any real sense, though the objective in the syllabus is that the students should produce an extensive reader for use at the Standard VI or VII level. The Grade C writing programme appears to be much more realistic and suited to the level of the students.

The whole of the work of the teacher training programme is to be evaluated on the by now familiar pattern, in part by continuous assessment with the marking of course work as it is done, in part by internal terminal examinations, the format of which is laid down in the handbook (Nyagwaswa et al., 1976), and in part by the final teacher's Certificate Examination set centrally by the National Examinations Council. The form of this examination is also exemplified in Nyagwaswa (see also McCormick, 1976). A further development is that some Colleges of National Education have been designated English teaching specialist Colleges, for example, Marangu CNE in Kilimanjaro region, and Changombe College of National Education in Dar es Salaam and some of these may be running Diploma level courses (ex form VI plus two years of working experience and National Service is required for entry). The Diploma Courses in general involve specialising in some option. Those who have chosen English as their option are required to spend fifteen hours per week on English as well as studying the other subjects which are offered at the Colleges of National Education, for example, Political Education and General Educational Theory, as well as participating in the general life of the College, including such central activities as self-reliance projects. The Diploma course is aimed primarily at teachers who will teach in secondary schools, but some of these teachers may also, of course, find themselves in Colleges of National Education, particularly if their work experience has already been in education. In either event, familiarity with the *Handbook for Teachers of English* (Eng. Lang. Panel, 1973) and the *Syllabus for Secondary Schools* (Min. of Nat. Educ., 1976a) and the *Primary School Syllabus* (Min. of Nat. Educ., 1976d) will be required. The *Primary School Syllabus* may seem an odd inclusion but it is quite clear that any teacher who is going to teach at the secondary level, ought to be familiar with what happens at the primary level.

The syllabus for the English Diploma specialisation was drafted by the Dar es Salaam College of National Education (Min. of Nat. Educ., 1976b) and modifications with slightly different emphasis have been proposed by the Marangu College of National Education (1978). Both programmes distinguish between language skills, that is to say, the trainee's own, and professional skills or methodology. Both have programmes for the improvement of the trainee's performance and understanding of the speaking of English, the use of its structures and vocabulary, and both include programmes for literature, but the Dar es Salaam syllabus emphasises this very much more than the Marangu one. The Dar es Salaam syllabus mentions planning and organisation as units in the professional course, Marangu does not. The Marangu syllabus mentions intensive reading, library organisation and teaching practice as important elements in the programme, Dar es Salaam does not. Marangu also spells out the scheme of assessment for trainees, this involves a pattern of formal papers on the option subject, English in this case, Education, and Political Education. A scheme of continuous assessment in all of the above together with cultural studies and projects which have to be carried out. The assessment may also involve assignments and term exams. In addition to the marks derived from the formal papers which account for 50% and the continuous assessment which accounts for 50%, grade letters will be awarded for teaching practice, as a teaching practice assessment and also for a character assessment which will be based on the trainees attitudes and his contribution to self-reliance activities and so on. An additional inducement to Diploma students would appear to be the possibility of proceeding to University after the mandatory two years' work experience. The discrepancies between the two syllabuses would seem to indicate that some reconciliation of the programmes outlined in them is needed in order to achieve a well balanced and uniform pattern of training for English Diploma students. It is understood this is already in hand.

The most important single development in teacher education in Tanzania has probably arisen from the need to meet the demand for teachers for universal primary education. Responsibility for training the estimated 45,000 new teachers needed over the three year period from 1974 to 1977 has fallen largely on the correspondence department of the Institute of Adult Education, and some details of this programme have been given above, (section 3.7).

8.0 *Language at the University of Dar es Salaam*

One of the biggest changes to have taken place since 1969 at the University of Dar es Salaam, is in the pattern of admission to the University. Following the Musoma Resolution of 1974 (Mmari, 1976c) Government staff Circular Number 4 of 1975 (U. Rep. of Tanzania, 1975:2) stated:

Eligibility for higher education must be based on:

(a) One year's compulsory full time National Service

(b) A minimum of two years' satisfactory work experience, during which candidates have earned recommendations from both their employers and local party branches, that they are in every way fully suitable to be granted the privilege of admission to higher education.

The circular emphasises the need for economy in implementing the Musoma Resolution. To this end the circular directs that all students will be on leave without pay, will be sponsored by Government, and, upon completion of their studies, will be bonded for five years. They will receive a higher education allowance of 400 shillings per month, will have all course fees paid by Government Ministries, will have free board and lodging, will receive a maintenance grant of seven hundred and fifty shillings a month if not in residence, along with a number of other related matters. The main change from previous practice was the virtual abolition of salaries and the substitution of the 400 shillings monthly allowance. Thus, instead of the students coming straight from school, they are more likely to be more mature and their selection involves a complicated points system to take account of such professional training as they may have had and also clearance from both the applicant's employer and the *Chama cha Mapinduzi* (Party of the Revolution).[6] The new arrangements do not seem to have had any serious deleterious effect on the quality of intake. A second minor change which is a rather interesting indicator of the growth in status and importance of Swahili in the University, is that all non-academic administration in the University is now conducted in Swahili.

8.1 *Swahili*

The departments in the University which are concerned with language and language teaching remain much as in 1969, with a Department of Linguistics and Foreign Languages, which includes English and French, a department of Swahili, a Department of Literature and a Department of Education. The pattern of courses and options remains broadly similar too. It would seem that the Department of Swahili has moved forward rapidly since its inception. Swahili has been a medium of instruction in the department since 1973. The setting up of examinations in Swahili at form IV, and also at form VI, under the aegis of the National Examinations Council, examinations which have been specially designed for Swahili native speakers, and are not, as under the Cambridge Examinations Syndicate, aimed at foreign language speakers (including translation both into Swahili from English, and from English into Swahili) has led to a marked rise in the calibre of students choosing to study Swahili. The prestige of the national language is at work here too. The whole programme for Swahili is currently under review, but it includes courses in Bantu linguistics, in Swahili phonology using Mganga (1979), Swahili syntax and morphology using the traditional Ashton (1944) and Broomfield (1933) and similar texts, and a course in Swahili usage, using Maw (1969). There is a special course in advanced Swahili usage, run specially for Ghanaian students who have been studying Swahili for two years, when they arrive. There has been an M.A. programme since 1977 with an impressive and extremely interesting list of dissertation titles now coming out of the department, and in addition there has been a steady, but small number of students registered for doctorates each year. Clearly the level of staffing has risen quickly to make this very pleasing state of affairs possible.

One of the assignments that first year students are set involves the collection of oral literature, a traditional story or folk tale, a poem or a song, to be written down in Swahili with a view to publication within the next two or three years. Several manuscripts are already to hand. In the third year, students are encouraged to try to write something original of substantial length with a view to commercial publication with royalties to the author in the normal way. The East African Literature Bureau, Tanzania Publishing House, and Longman's Tanzania have declared an interest in anything recommended by the Department of Swahili or by the Institute of Swahili Research. The Department also publishes regularly, *Kioo cha Lugha*. This is an annual periodical of some 100 pages which includes original articles, stories and poems, substantial pieces on Swahili linguistics, and also a series of major book reviews. All of this shows clearly that the Department is flourishing vigorously and that state of affairs must be regarded as highly satisfactory. In the Institute of Swahili Research, work on the Dictionary-making projects goes on, as reported in section 4 above. There is, in addition, a proposal that a Swahili–Arabic Dictionary should be produced and preliminary work on that has started. Work on the production of specialist vocabulary lists continues, and some of these have been published in *Kiswahili*.[7] Others are published separately by the Institute of Swahili Research (e.g. Prins, 1970).

The journal *Kiswahili* continues to come out more or less regularly; the perennial difficulties with printing persist. In addition the literary periodical *Mulika* is published irregularly. There have been 11 issues since 1971. This contains lively and original material which may be regarded as authentically Tanzanian. Among the other publications of the Institute of Swahili Research of interest are further titles in the *Utenzi* series (e.g. Said, 1974) and the series of 8 or more research reports on the oral literature of various districts in Tanzania (Sengo, 1973 and Kiango, 1976), besides those dealing with work on the dialects of Swahili and the collections of *Mashairi ya Mwamko wa Siasa* (political poetry) (Ngole & Sengo, 1965). The Institute is also involved in straight linguistic research on Swahili syntax and in some socio-linguistic research: in particular the use of Swahili in the Law Courts. The University of Dar es Salaam has also been approached by both Ghana and Nigeria to provide staff to teach Swahili as a foreign language, for example, at the University of Port Harcourt, and the Institute of Swahili Research is acting as agent in this matter.

At this point it is probably suitable to mention the continued and flourishing existence of UKUTA which is said to have published a number of 64 page booklets of poetry. Most importantly also, the work of the National Swahili Council continues. The Council remains the principal

DEVELOPMENTS IN LANGUAGE AND EDUCATION 393

policy-making body for Swahili in Tanzania. There are some 40 members from the 20 mainland regions and 5 from Zanzibar, who meet periodically. The executive authority however, is in the hands of a small committee of six who commission research. For example that of Mlama and Matteru (1978) is a very telling documentation of the low levels of performance in English in schools in contrast to the levels of performance in Swahili and argues very strongly for the use of Swahili as the medium of instruction in secondary schools. The executive committee can also, of course, take swift action when it is needed to foster the development of the national language.

8.2 *English and French*

The pattern of courses in the Department of Linguistics and Foreign Languages remains much as in 1969/70. A full review of the curriculum in the Department is currently being undertaken but full-blown courses in general linguistics covering aspects of the theory of phonology, syntax and semantics are offered with introductions to the structuralist, systemic and generative transformational schools. There is some treatment of generative phonology. In addition there are courses in applied linguistics covering topics in socio- and psycho- linguistics and language teaching, and courses in English Language and French Language where topics in the lexical, grammatical and phonological patterning of these languages are dealt with along with some Stylistics and Usage. There seems to be a general feeling that Swahili studies have benefited somewhat at the expense of English language. The absence of an English language paper at Form VI has meant that relatively few students choose English language as a specialism at the University of Dar es Salaam. However, there is apparently a proposal to introduce such a paper in 1980 and this should ensure serious study of the language in Forms V & VI and hopefully bring more recruits to English specialisation. In 1977/78 there was a total of 129 undergraduate students registered in the Department, 72 for English, 57 for French. And of these only 12 were majoring in English (second and third year) and 35 were majoring in French. There appears to be no danger of any surplus of French graduates as yet. There is apparently a great demand for bilingual secretaries in the parastatal organisations and in various commercial concerns. The French graduates are about half teachers and half non-teachers. The non-teachers are combining political science or international relations with their French and so might be regarded as potential foreign office staff. It also appears that at all sorts of official levels there is an increase in the contacts sought with francophone Africa and the need for French graduates keeps being urged upon the University and the Department of Linguistics and Foreign Languages. Four interesting developments are apparent in the work of the Department. First, students who study French used to go to Madagascar for part of their studies. However, since 1972, they have been going to Besançon in France, mainly to permit the teaching practice of the education students to be fitted in appropriately. But with the changes currently being proposed for the curriculum in the Department, it is hoped that they may be able to go to Madagascar again. Secondly, the French Department has been offering a special service course in French for Engineers which has been well received, with some 11 takers in 1977/78. Thirdly the Linguistics and Foreign Languages Department is about to open a Communications Skills Unit which will research the communication needs of University of Dar es Salaam students and provide service instruction for selected students who may need help with communication skills. Perhaps this service may be necessary for all students but it will be first available only to selected students. Fourthly, since 1977 the Department has been running an MA in linguistics in co-operation with the Swahili Department. One student each year has taken the MA with a specialisation in English; in 1978 two students specialised in French and over the period six students have specialised in Swahili. The programme offers:

(a) a core course in phonetics, phonology, morphophonology, theories of syntax and semantics, applied linguistics for teachers and comparative and historical linguistics of Africa for other students.
(b) optional courses – each student must take two of these – in socio- and psycho- linguistics, applied linguistics, analytic or comparative or historical studies of an African language, advanced study of aspects of English, French and Swahili language-including translation and
(c) an independent study resulting in the preparation of a short research paper.

Once again the sense of dynamic enthusiasm that emanates from the Department is very encouraging and it is easy to anticipate great things.

8.3 *Department of Education*

Numbers in the Department of Education at the University of Dar es Salaam remain high, as might be expected with the continuing need for secondary school teachers. In 1977/78, there were some 99 students registered in the faculty who were also in the Faculty of Science and some 96 who were also registered in the Faculty of Arts and Social Sciences. In addition, there is a substantial number from the Faculty of Agriculture. This reflects the need to provide specialist teachers for the secondary schools with particular biases, in particular those with an agricultural bias. The basic programme of the Department remains largely unchanged. Block teaching practice in the first year is spread all over Tanzania. In the second year it is now restricted to four regions, the Coast Region, Dar es Salaam region, Morogoro region and Zanzibar and subject specialists are grouped together to facilitate supervision. Some weekly teaching practice in Dar es Salaam still goes on too. Some undergraduates are now taking specialisms in teacher education and adult education as well as in secondary school education, since some of them are being posted directly to Colleges of National Education, or are to be involved in adult education work. It is hoped soon to appoint a Fellow in Special Education, that is to say, education of the blind and other handicapped children, and thus round out the work of the Department more fully.

DEVELOPMENTS IN LANGUAGE AND EDUCATION 395

Since 1974 in this Department too, there has been an MA Programme with a maximum enrolment envisaged of 15. In 1979 there were 12 students actually enrolled. Evidence of the kind of work this programme is stimulating, is to be found in the series of publications produced by the Department as *Papers in Education and Development* (Mmari, 1975, 1976a, 1976b, 1977 and 1978) and jointly with the Institute of Education *Studies in Tanzanian Education* numbers 1 to 6 (Nyerere, 1970; Auger, 1970 and see UISO 1977) and also in the dissertations submitted in partial fulfilment of the requirements for the award of degrees. Once again, there is a great feeling of vitality about the whole Department.

8.4 *Institute of Education*

The Institute of Education has been disestablished from the University and re-established as a parastatal organisation under the Ministry of National Education. A new site has been acquired off campus on the Bagamoyo Road, Mmari (1975) discusses the proposals and the reasons for their being made. The Institute of Education has always held a rather ambiguous position in the education system of Tanzania. Involved with the Ministry of Education as host to the subject panels, yet independent; seeing educational research as one of its most important responsibilities, and so partly in competition with the Department of Education, especially since the Department has begun to encourage research for higher degree work. It is particularly in its role as an agency for curriculum development that there have been difficulties, particularly in determining policy. With the favour of the Ministry of National Education growing cold in 1972 the staff of the Institute fell to only four but almost immediately thereafter growing warm again in 1973, the staff rose to an all-time high of twenty five. It is in this role that the Institute is likely to survive, but far from being the high level co-ordinating and policy making Institution that it was originally conceived as, it will function virtually as a curriculum development unit, whose work will be to implement the curricular policies drawn up in the Ministry of National Education. That it is likely to be highly effective in its new role, there can be little doubt. The impressive flood of publications pouring from it is fully documented in Margaret Nikundiwe's Bibliographies (1975 & 1977) and it will not have passed unremarked that many of the references cited in this chapter have been published by the Institute of Education. This then is a very rough outline of the current situation in higher education in Tanzania at the present time, as they have appeared to one hurried observer.

9.0 *Adult Education*

In 1969 adult education in Tanzania appeared relatively unimportant yet the seeds of the very dramatic developments which have taken place in this field, since then, had clearly been planted. The Institute of Adult Education had been established as one of the Institutes of the University of Dar es Salaam and was offering instructional and training courses in the main centres of population, on the pattern which is common in The United Kingdom. Its correspondence department had also begun work, but on a relatively modest scale. The five year Work Oriented Literacy Project Pilot Scheme (Viscusi, 1971) was just off the ground. The agreement relative to this having been signed in September 1967 and the project inaugurated in January 1968. The first year was devoted to recruiting staff and ordering equipment. The second year was devoted to experimentation, material development and preparation and teacher training as was also the third year. But this was still a small scale project and still operated as a pilot project (UNDP, 1967). Many other Government Agencies were involved in adult education in a less selfconscious way, for example, through agricultural extension work, health information propaganda and so on. Kivukoni College was running its regular three and six month residential Adult Leadership Training courses, with its special focus on the social sciences. The political education department of TANU was running a variety of conferences, seminars, workshops and in-service courses for teachers as it did for other categories of leaders. The purpose of these was to impart to teachers the spirit of *Ujamaa* Socialism and to assist them in the preparation of their own courses and activities in this field. The Moshi Co-operative College had been established in 1963 as a training institution for staff of the Co-operative movement and in 1968 it had moved to its own campus about a mile from Moshi Town centre. The College had its own Correspondence Institute offering courses in elementary bookkeeping, basic economics and the management of co-operative societies. Residential courses run at the College included those in Management and Accountancy and in Co-operative Retail and Wholesale Management.

The Institute of Adult Education is now established as a body corporate governed by its own Council and separate from the University and has grown considerably. It would seem to have roughly five sections:

(a) The mass media department which is responsible for mass radio campaigns, many of which have been linked to adult literacy activities of one kind or another (see below). The mass radio campaigns involve 12-week series of broadcasts aimed at organised radio listening groups which have trained leaders. In addition to the broadcasts, there are book materials and press releases and so on as well. The 1969 campaign was called *Kuponga ni Kuchagua*. In 1970 it was *Uchaguzi ni Wako*. In 1971 the campaign was called *Wakati wa Furaha* .The 1973 campaign was *Mtu ni Afya* and in 1975 the programme was *Chakula ni Uhai*. There were some 100,000 participants in the 1975 campaign. The campaigns in 1969, 1970 and 1971 were mainly political in orientation, encouraging people to vote and to participate in political activity. The 1973 and 1975 campaigns were aimed at improving health and nutrition.
(b) The diploma department. This is concerned with all aspects of training for present and prospective teachers and organisers in adult education and it includes a full time one year residential diploma course.
(c) The National Correspondence Institute. This runs correspondence courses in national policies, book keeping, accountancy, management and administration, law and teacher in-service courses aimed mainly at those teachers who have been recruited in order to fulfil the demand for teachers for universal primary education (section 1.2). The UPE training programme extends over

three years, and details of this have already been given above (sections 1.5, 3.7). The National Correspondence Institute is also responsible for assisting new literates with further study (Erdos, 1975).
(d) The Institute of Adult Education is also responsible for carrying out research in areas of National Adult Education priorities. This is largely a matter of evaluation studies, but the series Studies in Adult Education (VISO, 1977: 12–16) covers a wide range of topics in adult education.
(e) The Institute also operates regional centres at Dar es Salaam, Moshi, Mwanza, Mbeya, Songea, and also in Lindi, Tanga, Singida, Sumbawanga and Kigoma. These centres run evening classes for the most part, though some full time courses as well, of various kinds. First of all there are what might be called semi-vocational courses such as personnel management and bookkeeping, storekeeping, marketing, shorthand, and commerce. The Dar es Salaam centre for example offers some 9 different subject areas of this kind. Secondly there are what might be called the secondary school subject classes. These include mathematics to 'O' level, English at levels 1, 2, 3, and 4 and also at 'O' and 'A' level, Swahili for beginners (one class only) and classes to 'O' and 'A' level (the main effort in Swahili teaching for beginners is carried out at the Morogoro College of National Education where the Expatriate Workers' Training Centre exists, and this is a Department of the Institute of Adult Education, the EWTC runs a one month crash course for newcomers to the Country), history, geography, French and political education; of these English is by far the most popular. In Dar es Salaam there are four classes of 52 pupils at each of the four levels. Those who enrol appear to be mainly primary school leavers who are working as clerks or who are Grade C teachers who are studying, evidently with the objective of up-grading themselves. The third group of courses offered are those that might be called self-enrichment courses. These include courses in music, and art, and also in languages like Portuguese, Italian and Arabic. The Italian course is a special crash course being run for future employees of an Italian Company. The French classes are taught with the aid of staff from the Alliance Française and is the usual hard line audio-visual type of course.

9.1 *The Campaign against Illiteracy*

Much of this development originated when in November 1969, the then assistant director of National Education and Adult Education, issued a circular under the title *Mapinduzi ya Elimu ya Watu Wazima* 'The Revolution of Adult Education' (Min. of Nat. Educ., 1969c) which spelt out an extremely ambitious programme of Adult Education in politics, agriculture, domestic economy, health, simple technology and general knowledge, and involved the mobilisation of TANU leaders and Government officers in all Departments, education, agriculture, health, veterinary, development, and land and water resources, besides the National Service units and even the Police, at all levels, regional, district and ward down to the TANU 10-household cell. It was following this that things really began to happen. The aim was to create a unified system of Adult Education which would bring about changes in family income, living patterns, sanitary conditions, nutrition, production and consumption practices, participation in social and community organisations and the acceptance of better agricultural methods, improved agricultural varieties, the use of insecticides, fertilizers and so on, in line with the specific priorities for agricultural development in the different regions and zones of Tanzania.

On December 31st, 1969, New Year's Eve, President Nyerere (1969b) launched the national campaign against illiteracy. A year later he declared that no effort would be spared to eradicate illiteracy completely in six named districts around Lake Victoria by 9th December, 1971 (Nyerere, 1970c), the date on which Tanzania celebrated the tenth anniversary of her Independence. The Institute of Adult Education organised some twenty one-week courses for head teachers of primary schools to introduce them to methods of organising adult literacy programmes and of teaching adults. About 2,000 teachers attended, and the programme went ahead, making use of the materials and procedures developed by the Work Oriented Adult Literacy Pilot Project in the Lake regions. The target was just about achieved. In 1972 the Government of Tanzania decided to launch a National Campaign to eradicate illiteracy by the end of 1975 using the same functional approach which had been used in the pilot project and they asked UNESCO for additional assistance. This was granted in 1973. The success of the campaign may be measured in part by the annual enrolment (NLC, 1978). In 1971 the enrolments were 908,351, in 1972 1,508,204, in 1973 3,338,962, in 1974 3,449,989, in 1975 5,184,982, in 1976 5,255,560, in 1977 5,819,612. In 1977 it was estimated that there were 6,001,266 illiterates in Tanzania. That meant that 97% of identified illiterates, had been enrolled in adult literacy classes.

On 10th August 1977, a series of national literacy tests were carried out throughout the country. It was expected that some 3,545,790 would take the examination. 66% of these in fact presented themselves and of that 66%, 34% achieved levels 3 and 4 in the tests. That is to say, some 806,421 persons. In similar tests in August 1975 1,999,011 persons achieved the levels 3 and 4 which indicate virtually functional literacy. These very large figures show the extent of the success of the campaign, but there appears to be no complacency and efforts are being sustained to ensure that the remaining 3% of known non-literate adults will be enrolled into literacy classes and that those who have achieved partial literacy should achieve fully functional literacy within the next two years. A new set of tests is scheduled for August, 1979 and again in August, 1981. By that time the effect of the present national effort to enrol all school age children into primary schools should prevent the present population of children from becoming illiterate adults and it would seem that Tanzania will have come very close to having eradicated illiteracy.

The evident success of the National Campaign is probably due to two main factors, one is the strong administrative structure which has been set up. There is a pyramid of authorities, 21 regional, 85 district, 500 divisional and about 2,000 ward level adult education co-ordinators. This body of full time workers enabled the Adult Education Division to launch the vast programmes which have been undertaken. The second factor is the mobilisation of public opinion. The main difficulty of any mass literacy programme is in the lack of interest people have in actually becoming literate. In an agricultural society improvement through the acquisition of knowledge comes slowly. But Tanzania has succeeded in putting the full weight of public opinion behind the literacy campaign; learning has become popular. Going to class is accepted and not going is frowned upon. This is due in no small part to the favourable national context. All Tanzanians from ministers and members of parliament to village elders and illiterates attend courses or seminars and perhaps one of the best illustrations of this is the fact that the President is called *Mwalimu* or teacher. A good use of media, especially of the radio, has also contributed substantially and there can be little doubt that the activities of the CCM have also contributed substantially.

The major elements of the campaign were the following:

(1) The forming of adult literacy classes through the efforts of adult education officers and volunteers.
(2) Providing the materials: First there were Work Oriented Literacy primers and teachers books. There were some 11 titles of these, including such things as *Uvuvi Bora wa Samaki* and *Pamba ni Mali* (NLC, 1970a). Each primer being provided at two levels. Other materials included a home economics demonstration book and a teacher's guide to rice growing.
(3) Training: this included training of regional training teams and of the teachers who actually did the work with the classes themselves. The training courses involved some which lasted for one or two days, as for example refresher courses for primary school teachers or training courses for supervisors; others lasted a week, like the refresher course for voluntary teachers; others lasted two weeks, for example the training courses for trainers and there is, of course, a regular four week course for voluntary teachers.
(4) Continuous evaluation: first of all there was evaluation by the Evaluation Unit of the National Literacy Centre in Mwanza (see Min. of Nat. Educ., 1975b, NLC, 1973 and 1978a & b). The evaluation unit is also responsible for the National Literacy Tests. These are organised on four levels. Level 4 indicates a person who continuously uses literacy skills and is able to write and read letters, read a newspaper and do-it-yourself books, keep records, do simple arithmetical problems and keep accounts of income and expenditure. In short a functionally literate person. Level 3 indicates a person who can read a simple text with understanding, write a simple text, add and subtract, multiply two figure numbers and divide by one figure numbers, in short a literate person. Level 2 indicates a person who can recognise words and symbols, write a simple short sentence and add and subtract one figure numbers, in short, a semi-literate person. Level 1 indicates a person who has enrolled and attended two thirds of the sessions in one year of literacy activities.
(5) Radio programmes as support to illiteracy classes (Mbakile, 1975): the radio support programmes which have proved such a significant part of the campaign, were brought into operation in three phases: phase 1 was from January to April 1974, phase 2 from May to December 1974 and phase 3 from May to November 1975. The programmes were of a number of different kinds. First of all there were those which were purely motivational whose intention was to give people an awareness of the nature of literacy programmes and to encourage them to participate (Mbakile, 1975:29). Secondly there were the series of programmes known as *Kisomo kwa Redio*.

These were class support programmes, each of 30 minutes, one per week, with a repeat. Each programme was in seven segments. The first related to agriculture and farm work, the second to home life, the third to reading (it reviewed material available for 1 and 2), the fourth, a literacy slogan, the fifth, feedback, that is to say questions sent in by the listening groups and answered over the radio, the sixth, literacy songs, and the seventh discussion questions, dictated for the leader to write down for subsequent discussion by the class. Phase 1 consisted of 17 of the motivational programmes, phase 2 consisted of 32 programmes in the *Kisomo kwa Redio* series. These were backed up by a series of 35 fifteen minute programmes broadcast twice a week, aimed at the class leaders or adult literacy teachers. This series of programmes was called *Mwalimu wa Walimu*. The intention was to provide support and help for the volunteer teachers who constituted three quarters of the teaching force and had had between 2 and 4 weeks initial training with annual refresher seminars (Mbakile, 1975: 36). In phase 3 the *Kisomo kwa Redio* series was continued with a further 35 programmes. In addition during phase 3 a *Mapishi ya Wiki* item was included, this consisted of the recipe of the week broadcast for the benefit of the housewives in the literacy courses. Handbooks to go with the *Kisomo kwa Redio* (NLC, 1974–75) series and to support the *Mwalimu wa Walimu* series have been published. Programme topic notes from the handbook appear also in one of the national Swahili newspapers. On the Tanzanian commercial radio programmes the *Nyimbo ya Kisomo* appeared, (Literacy Songs). This was an expansion of the segment from the *Kisomo kwa Redio* programme which involved literacy songs which had proved so popular that a full thirty minutes twice a week could be devoted to them.

(6) A variety of competitions: in 1974 there was a National Literacy Song and Poem Competition which produced a good many useful poems but not very many songs; so in 1975 there was a National Literacy Song Performance Competition in which classes from all 20 regions competed with one another for the final trophy. There were also slogan, book writing, and poster competitions. A literacy flag was offered as a trophy and a calendar, a cotton textile print and a cassette of literary songs were all produced as support materials.

As the campaign proceeded the success of these various activities led to work aimed at neo-literates. First of all there were rural libraries. The goal is to establish a working library in each of the wards of the nation. A substantial number of books have been bought and are being distributed. Librarians are being trained district by district but the problems remain formidable: lack of personnel to supervise the libraries, poor transport and shortage of books. It is not easy to find books in the large quantities needed because printings of Swahili books seldom exceed 5,000 copies. Premises in general are no more than a room in a small hut furnished with a table and a small cupboard containing some 100 thin paperbacks, but the care and attention given to these is generally reported to be such that it might make some large sophisticated libraries blush. Books are regularly exchanged between the rural libraries by the librarians, each of whom has been given a bicycle and a special book bag by UNESCO. Many of the libraries which have been established are so well used that many of the paperbacks are falling apart. Provision of books especially suited to the needs of neo-literates remains a major problem. A number of writer's workshops have been set up in order to try and cater for this but there then remain the problems of printing and distributing the manuscripts so produced. An example of a book produced in this fashion is *Kuhifadhi Vizuri Nafaka* (Mradi wa Bwakira Chini, Morogoro, 1977). The work of the Colleges of National Education and of the Institute of Swahili Research and the Department of Swahili at the University in the matter of attempting to supply more books has been mentioned earlier.

Secondly there are the rural newspapers the first of these which is published by the national literacy centre is called *Elimu Haina Mwisho*. This is produced monthly with a print run of something over 45,000 copies but is distributed only in the Lake Regions. It carries news international, national and local, information and instruction, and the contents are mostly development oriented. For example, the back page might carry a description of how to dry beans and the instructions are usually well illustrated. But the layout and type face used seem to make few concessions to neo-literates and the degree of linguistic control would seem to leave much to be desired. Then there are the regional newspapers like *Kilimanjaro Leo* or *Mapinduzi ya Kijamaa* (which is produced by Tanga region). These papers contain local news which is likely to be of interest to the people in the locality covering such things as the size of the coffee harvest and which new roads are to be tarmacadamed, but neither the format nor the language used make any concessions to those who are only newly literate. More interesting perhaps is the insert in *Lengo* called *Nuru*, four pages quite specifically aimed at the newly literate. The content of these is extremely appropriate and in addition the linguistic control seems quite good. However, the layout and design make few concessions. Thirdly there has been the phenomenon of the formation of radio listening groups following on from the radio support programmes which are an essential element of the campaign. In particular there is a series of programmes called *Jiendeleze* and it is here too that the mass radio listening campaigns put out by the Institute of Adult Education as mentioned above come into their own, that is to say, campaigns like 'Mtu ni Afya' and so on. Fourthly it is proposed that a general education course lasting two years should be set up for adult learners (UNESCO, 1976 p. 12 ff.) This should cover the metric system (scale, weights, surfaces and so on, particularly calculating fertilizer and insecticide requirements); simple accounting (farm management, balance sheets, the co-operative and its budget); science and its applications for agriculture (levers and forces, improved implements, soil fertility and plant nutrition, water conservation, erosion and irrigation, first aid and the prevention of diseases); the economy (including the economic geography of Tanzania, cash crops and food crops); industry (imports and exports) and of course, political education (covering the philosophy of TANU, development and socialism, voting procedures and so on). In other words a general fleshing out of the work done in the initial literacy campaign. It is repeatedly emphasised (UNESCO, 1976, Mbakile, 1975, Mbakile & Kashushura, 1977, Grenholm, 1975) that post-literacy activities should grow out of the existing structure: that level 3 and 4 learners should stay together for discussion group and further learning activities. The Work Orientated Literacy Pilot Project had a Rural Construction Unit attached to it and this has continued to work and it is proposed, that particularly in the post literacy period, its activities should be expanded. In addition, there are special projects associated with home economics and agriculture which also come under the aegis of the National Literacy Centre. More important than these perhaps, is the establishment of Folk Development Colleges (UNESCO, 1976:14 ff.). The Folk Development Colleges are inspired by, rather than modelled on, the Scandanavian Folk High Schools. Their aim is to bring education to rural people who are not in school. Since they have a reasonable amount of equipment they can give practical instruction, they can also enable learners to make simple equipment needed to carry out the instructions given. The Colleges can thus complement discussion groups by providing short practical courses. They could also supplement them by giving in one short course, a section of the general syllabus, followed by organised discussion groups. This would help the adult education division to identify quickly any defects in the materials prepared and determine how to improve them. One point of special interest is that it is intended that these Colleges should provide courses for the improvement of rural peoples' command of the Swahili language. A typical College might take 60 students at a time, one or two from each of as many villages as possible, chosen by local adult education committees. They include people of all ages. A student aged 72 has been recorded. Students choose what to study and how long to stay and costs are divided evenly between the College, the village and the Government. The teachers are trained, as many as possible, at the Agricultural Training Centre at Kibaha and courses offered include agricultural production, animal husbandry, home economics, child care, arithmetic, carpentry, masonry and *Ujamaa na Kujitegemea* besides Swahili as mentioned above. The "come back" rate is said to be high.

10.0 *Conclusion*

In this volume on Language in Education in Tanzania there has been an interesting opportunity to look at two points in the development of an African nation in this field.

The sections written in 1969 retain interest as historical documents reflecting the thinking, the philosophy and the preoccupations of that time. The final section written in 1979 attempts to gather together the impressions of one fleeting visitor and to mark how the thinking, the philosophy and the preoccupations have changed and yet remained the same.

The basic structure of the education system as a whole appears to have remained much as it was. There is still formal schooling at primary, secondary and tertiary levels, but the growth of Adult Education has added a whole new dimension to the picture. In a way Adult Education could be thought of as a kind of secondary education, especially when the policy of providing universal primary education has been fully implemented, but this kind of secondary education will not end after six years, but is likely to continue throughout the life time of an individual. The growth in demand for more and yet more learning is perhaps one of the most exciting and encouraging manifestations of the education scene in Tanzania.

The administrative structure of education also appears to have remained very similar (compare Appendices 14: C and D) and it may be that this itself may be a conservative influence preventing radical alterations in the fundamental ethos of the system. Thus the continued exercise of central control even at the regional if not at national level might well be inhibiting the growth of real self-reliance. An educational institution whose members know that the vote for foodstuff will be sufficient to ensure that no one will go hungry must inevitably be less motivated to be self-sufficient than one where that assurance is less certain, and the same would apply to the supply of equipment and materials and personnel. Clearly there is a dilemma here, and how it will come to be resolved will be fascinating to observe.

The scale of educational operations is the aspect of the Tanzanian scene that appears to have changed most dramatically in those ten years. (Compare Appendices 14: A and B). The sheer number of children receiving primary education is truly remarkable and when the growth at that level is set beside the growth in Adult Education, some indication of which is given above, the increase has to be expressed in terms which are difficult to begin to grasp adequately.

The fundamental philosophy underlying the Tanzanian education system does not seem to have changed importantly, but it has developed; the implications have been more fully worked out, the conflicts which it engenders have become more explicit and there remain curious ambiguities, like that relating to the tension between self-reliance and control, between satisfaction with things as they are, traditional values and beliefs, and the demand for a better life, for change and improvement and new values and beliefs. There is for example the tension between the officially promulgated view of education as an instrument of socialist policy, fostering the values of service to the community, cooperative endeavour, and self-reliance, a view which is very widely accepted and on the other hand the view of education held by many parents and indeed even now by many pupils in schools of education as a means by which the peasant farmer may escape from a life of hard manual labour, and enjoy prestige and power within the community.

There is also the ambiguity with regard to language policy in the system which has been discussed at length above, an ambiguity which arises from the conflicting pressures of the need to foster a sense of national unity and pride, and to provide certain kinds of knowledge to every citizen, and the demands of access to the benefits of even low level technology, communication and trade with the rest of the world. All such tensions will have to be resolved somehow and so men of goodwill everywhere watch with admiration the enormous activity, the enormous sense of a deep commitment to do everything possible for the good of the people, by the people.

The three great enemies, poverty, ignorance and disease it would seem are being vigorously attacked, and in spite of the scale of the problem with which the people of Tanzania are faced it would seem there is good cause for hope and optimism for the future.

NOTES

[1] A product indeed of the sheer increase in scale, for example, 40,000 UPE teachers are likely to have to be trained and some detail of the programme for their training appears in section 3.

[2] 'Conversation' naturally involves both speaking and listening as inter-related, not easily distinguishable skills. 'Listening' is a clearly separate skill, exercised for example in listening to radio programmes, lectures, and political harangues.

[3] A booklet on the analysis of methods of teaching has been prepared (Inst. of Adult Ed., 1978a) but interestingly the section on teaching English is written in English. It lists what is to be taught (lexis and structure) in a rather unsophisticated and not very helpful way and has very little real methodology in it and surprisingly few references to *English in Tanzanian Schools* (Min. of Nat. Educ., 1969–73).

[4] In 1969 there were three unaided secondary schools in the Kilimanjaro Region, by 1974 this had risen to nine, and by 1978 to nineteen, with the total number of pupils enrolled in unaided secondary schools in Kilimanjaro alone up to 4,620 (Un. Rep. of Tanzania, 1978).

[5] It seems to be much inferior to that of 1969: much more traditional and involving a much poorer integration of the parts of the course. The very beautifully graded composition scheme, for example, has disappeared.

[6] The new name for the combined TANU and the Afro-Shirazi Party of Zanzibar.

[7] See also chapter 4 in this volume.

APPENDIX 14:A THE EDUCATION PYRAMID 1968

(Educational Statistics from the Min. of Nat. Educ., Dar es Salaam 1969)

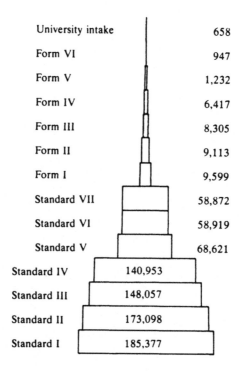

University intake	658
Form VI	947
Form V	1,232
Form IV	6,417
Form III	8,305
Form II	9,113
Form I	9,599
Standard VII	58,872
Standard VI	58,919
Standard V	68,621
Standard IV	140,953
Standard III	148,057
Standard II	173,098
Standard I	185,377

APPENDIX 14:B THE EDUCATION PYRAMID 1978

(Education Statistics, Un. Rep. of Tanzania, Minister of National Education Budget Speech, 1979)

Level	Number
University intake	680
Form VI	2,068
Form V	2,304
Form IV	12,956
Form III	13,584
Form II	14,552
Form I	15,833
Standard VII	181,071
Standard VI	200,008
Standard V	235,065
Standard IV	410,054
Standard III	490,403
Standard II	557,647
Standard I	898,439

APPENDIX 14:C STRUCTURE OF NATIONAL EDUCATIONAL SYSTEM IN TANZANIA – 1968

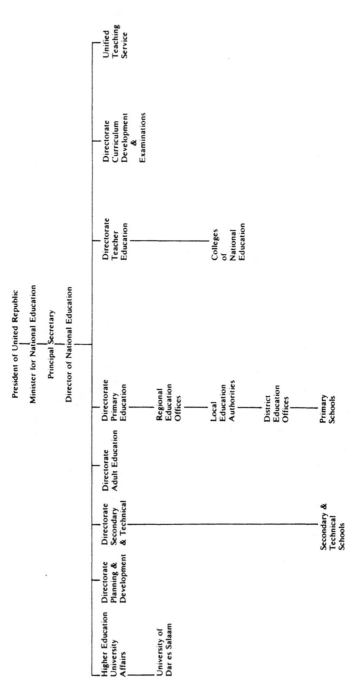

409

APPENDIX 14:D STRUCTURE OF THE NATIONAL EDUCATION SYSTEM IN TANZANIA – 1978

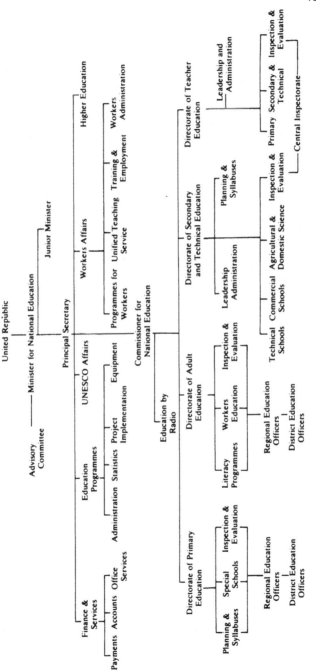

REFERENCES TO PART THREE

Abdala, A. [Mohammedi, A. A.], 1971, *Utenzi wa Maisha ya [Nabii] Adamu na Hawaa*. London etc.: Oxford University Press (OUP).
Abdullah, M. S., 1957, *Mzimu wa Watu wa Kale*. Nairobi: East African Literature Bureau (EALB).
Abedi, K. Amin, 1954, *Sheria za Kutunga Mashairi na Diwani ya Amin*. Nairobi: EALB.
Achebe, C., 1958, *Things Fall Apart*. (African Writers Series) London: Heinemann.
    1960, *No Longer at Ease*. (African Writers Series) London: Heinemann.
Ager, D. E., 1978, *Styles and Register in Contemporary French*. London: Univ. of London Press.
Akilimali, K. H. A., 1963, *Diwani ya Akilimali*. Nairobi: EALB.
Alfa–Lela–Ulela (The 1001 Nights or the Arabian Nights, trans. into Swahili)
Allen, W. S., 1965, *Living English Speech: Stress and Intonation Practice for the Foreign Student*. London: Longman.
    1974, *Living English Structure*. London: Longman.
Ashton, E. O., 1944, *Swahili Grammar*. London: Longman.
Auger, G. A., 1969, *The Difference in Academic Performance between Boys and Girls in Standard III and in Standard VI*. (Report of the Combined Research Project) [mimeo] Dar es Salaam: Inst. of Educ.
    1972, 'Research at the Institute of Education', in Lema (ed.), 1972a.
    1973, *Tanzanian Education since Uhuru: A Bibliography, 1961-71*. Nairobi: East African Academy.
Auger, G. A., Harrit, P. and Myers, R. (eds.), 1970, *Absenteeism in Primary Schools of Tanzania*. (Studies in Tanzania Education, 2) Dar es Salaam: Inst. of Educ. & Univ. Dept. of Educ.
Auger, G. A. and Haule, R. M. (eds.), 1977, *MTUU: Its Role in the Reform of Primary Education in Tanzania, 1968—76*. Vol. I. Dar es Salaam: Min. of Nat. Educ. (see Haule et al., 1978, for Vol. II)
Ayaz, Ifti, 1978, *An English Language Teaching Colloquium: Report and Recommendations*. Dar es Salaam: Inst. of Educ.
    1977, *An Analysis of some Common Errors in English Syntax made by Tanzanian Students*. [mimeo] M. A. dissertation. Univ. of London, Inst. of Educ.
BELC, 1964–72, *Pierre et Seydou: Méthode de français à l'usage des élèves africaines anglophones du second degré*. Livres de l'élève 1–4; livres du maître 1–4; jeau de figurines et tableau de feutre; bandes magnétiques 1–2; filmes fixes 1–2. Paris: Hachette.
Berry, L., 1971, *Tanzania in Maps*. London: Univ. of London Press.
Beti, M., 1957 *Mission to Kala*. (African Writers Series) London: Heinemann.
Bhaiji, A. H., 1976, 'The Medium of Instruction in our Schools: A Study Report', in Mmari (ed.), 1976b.
Biswalo, P. M. (ed.), 1973, *Studies in Curriculum Development, 3*. Dar es Salaam: Inst. of Educ.
Blasio, E. K. T., 1977, *The Concept and Functions of Rural Libraries in Tanzania*. (Paper presented to Tanzania Library Association Seminar on 'Libraries

years after the Arusha Declaration', Dar es Salaam) Mwanza: National Literacy Centre (NLC).
Bolt, R., 1969, *A Man for All Seasons*. London: Heinemann.
Bonnard, H., 1969, *Grammaire françaises des lycées et collèges*. Paris: SUDEL.
Bright, J. A., 1954, *Junior English Composition and Grammar*. Pupil's Book; Teacher's Book. London etc.: Longman.
— 1965, *Patterns and Skills*. Books 1-2. London etc.: Longman.
Broomfield, G. W., 1933, *Sarufi ya Kiswahili*. London.
Brown, W. D., 1971, 'English in Tanzanian Primary Schools', *Bull. of the Lang. Assoc. of Tanzania*, 3.
Brumfit, C. J., 1971, *Report on a Questionnaire on the Teaching of English in Secondary Schools in Tanzania*. [mimeo] Dar es Salaam: Inst. of Educ.
— 1972, 'English Language in the Secondary School', in Lema (ed.), 1972b.
— 1979, *Education, Ideology and Materials Design: A Tanzanian Experience*. (ELT Documents) London: British Council.
Buck, Pearl S., 1931, *The Good Earth*. London: Methuen. (Reprinted, Penguin, 1963)
— 1947, *The Pavilion of Women*. London: Methuen. (Reprinted, Penguin, 1963).
Bulletin of the Language Association of Tanzania [periodical] Dar es Salaam.
Cameron, J. and Dodd, W. A., 1970, *Society, School and Progress in Tanzania*. Oxford: Pergamon Press/OUP.
Chamungwana, W. M., 1975, 'Socialization Problems in Tanzania: An Appraisal of Education for Self-Reliance as a Strategy for Cultural Transformation', in Komba (ed.), 1975.
Chandley, J. (ed.), 1967, *English: An In-Service Course for Primary School Teachers*. Vols 1-2. Dar es Salaam: Inst. of Educ.
Chiraghdin, S. (ed.), 1971, *Matenga wa Mvita*. Nairobi: OUP.
Clark, W. D. and Mackenzie, M. D. M., 1959, *Modern English Practice: Exercises in English for Foreign Students*. London etc.: Longman.
Colonial Office, 1925, *Educational Policy in British Tropical Africa*. (Memorandum from the Advisory Committee on Native Education in the British Tropical African Dependencies to the Secretary of State for the Colonies Cmd. 2374) London: His Majesty's Stationery Office (HMSO).
Commonwealth Institute, 1978, *Ujamaa in Tanzania*. London: Britain-Tanzania Soc./Commonwealth Inst.
Constable, D., 1968, 'French: Materials', *Bull. of the Lang. Assoc. of Tanz.*, 1,2.
Corder, S. P., 1960, *An Intermediate English Practice Book*. London etc: Longman.
CREDIF, 1966, *Voix et Images de France*. Pupil's Book; Teacher's Book; Film strips; Tapes. (The 'CREDIF Audio-Visual Course'.) Paris: Didier.
Daily News, 1976, *Book Publishing Workshop*. (Special supplement, 21 July) Dar es Salaam.
De la Warr Commission, see Sackville, 1937.
Deneve, J. C. (trans.), 1966-72, French Readers for Africa Series, e.g. B. Kimenye, *Moïse et Mildred*, 1972; O. Okojie, *Oziegbe, Docteur*, 1972; J. Fiernes, *Toto, La Petite Girafe*, 1966. London etc.: OUP.
Didier Collection 'Mieux Vivre', e.g. *La vie d'une commune*. Paris: Hatier Internationale.
Dubois, J. and Langane, R., 1971, *Dictionnaire du français contemporain*. Paris: Larousse.
Egero, B. and Henin, R. (eds.), 1973, *The Population of Tanzania: Census Volume 6*. Dar es Salaam: Univ., Bureau of Resources Assessment & Land Use Planning.
Ekwensi, C., 1962, *Burning Grass*. (African Writers Series) London: Heinemann.

Elimu Haina Mwisho (Education has no End) [monthly] Mwanza: NLC.
English Language Panel, 1969, *A Handbook for English Teachers.* Plus Appendices A & B. [mimeo] (Revised ed., 1970) Dar es Salaam: Inst. of Educ.
— 1973, *A Handbook for Teachers of English.* Dar es Salaam: Min. of Nat. Educ.
Erdos, R. F., 1975, 'Correspondence Education in Tanzania', in NAEAT, 1975.
Farsi, S. S., 1958, *Swahili Sayings.* Nairobi: EALB.
— 1966, 'Some Pronunciation Problems of Swahili Speaking Students', *English Language Teaching,* 20, 2.
Fowler, H. W., 1926, *Modern English Usage.* (2nd ed., 1965) London: OUP.
French, F. G., 1956–61, *New Oxford English Course for African Schools.* Books I–VI; Teacher's Books I–VI. London etc.: OUP.
French Panel, 1975, *Textes de français en Tanzanie.* Dossier I. in 2 vols: Form III; Form IV. Dar es Salaam: Inst. of Educ.
— 1977, *Textes de français.* Livre de l'élève; Livre du professeur (both Form I). Dar es Salaam: Inst. of Educ.
Fugard, A., 1966, *The Blood Knot.* Harmondsworth: Penguin.
Gesase, E. S., 1976, 'Struggle over the School in a Tanzanian Village', in Mmari (ed.), 1976a.
Gillette, A. L., 1977, *Beyond the Non-Formal Fashion: Towards Educational Revolution in Tanzania.* Amherst: Univ. of Massachusetts.
Government of Tanganyika, 27, *Education Ordinance (African) No. 1.* Chap. 71 in *Laws of Tanganyika.* Dar es Salaam.
Government, see also United Republic of Tanzania *and* Ministry of National Education.
Grenholm, L. H., 1975, 'The Study Group Approach to Mass Education', in NAAET, 1975.
Haggard, R., 1949, *Mashimo ya Mfalure Selemani* (King Solomon's Mines, trans. F. Johnson) Nairobi etc: Longman.
Hall, Budd, 1976, *Evaluation of a Radio Campaign.* Paris: UNESCO.
Haule, R. M. & Satterthwaite, R. (eds.), 1978, *MTUU: Its Role in the Reform of Primary Education in Tanzania, 1969–76.* Vol. II. Dar es Salaam: Min. of Nat. Educ. (See Auger, 1977, for Vol. I)
Hemingway, E., 1952, *The Old Man and the Sea.* London: Jonathan Cape.
Hill, C. P., 1965, 'Some Problems of the Changeover from English to Swahili as the Medium of Instruction', *English Language Teaching,* 20, 1:49–54.
Hill, L. A., 1964, *An Intermediate Refresher Course.* London etc: OUP.
Hollingsworth, L. W. & Alawi, Yaka, 1944, *Advanced Swahili Exercises.* London: Nelson.
Hornby, A. S., 1954, *A Guide to Patterns and Usage of English.* London: OUP.
Hornby, A. S., Gatenby, E. V. and Wakefield, H., 1948, *The Advanced Learner's Dictionary of Current English.* London: OUP.
Hugonnet, D. Porquier, R. and Zash, G., 1969. *Exersises structuraux du 1er et 2eme degrés.* Paris: SUDEL.
Hussein, E., 1969, *Kinjeketile.* Nairobi etc.: OUP.
— 1971a, *Mashetani.* Nairobi etc.: OUP.
— 1971b, *Wakati Ukuta.* Nairobi East African Publishing House (EAPH).
Institute of Adult Education (Min. of Nat. Educ.), 1974, *Mtu ni Afya: An Evaluation of the 1973 Mass Health Education Campaign in Tanzania.* Dar es Salaam: Planning and Research Dept.
— 1976a, *Jinsi ya Kufundisha Kusoma na Kuandika.* (15 lessons on how to teach reading and writing, for UPE trainee teachers) Dar es Salaam: Nat. Corresp. Inst.
— 1976b, *Malezi ya Taifu.* (8 lessons on pedagogy, for UPE trainee teachers) Dar

es Salaam: Nat. Corresp. Inst.

1976c, *Jinsi ya Kufundisha Hesabu*, (15 lessons on how to teach arithmetic, for UPE trainee teachers) Dar es Salaam: Nat. Corresp. Inst.

1978a, *Kiongozi cha Mratibu–Mkufunzi: Muhtasari ya Shule Msingi: Syansi Kimu, Sayansi, Jiographia, Historia, Kiingereza* (by K. B. Sengo). Dar es Salaam.

1978b, *Adult Education Directory 1978*. Dar es Salaam.

Institute of Education, 1973, *Looking Together at the Short Story 'A Walk in the Night' by Alex La Guma*. Dar es Salaam.

1974, *Looking Together at the Poem 'My Newest Bride' by Y. S. Chemba*. Dar es Salaam.

1976, *Continuous Assessment Scheme for English Language and Literature in English*. Dar es Salaam: Min. of Nat. Educ.

1978, *Some Proposals on the Revision of the Primary School English Syllabus*. Dar es Salaam.

ILO, 1978, *Towards Self Reliance*. (Report of the JSPR Employment Advisory Mission) Geneva: International Labour Office.

Isaacs, R., 1968, *Learning through Language*. Pupil's Books; Teacher's Books. Dar es Salaam: Tanzania Publishing House.

Johnson, F., 1939, *A Standard English–Swahili Dictionary* and *A Standard Swahili–English Dictionary*. London: OUP.

Jones, D., 1909, *The Pronunciation of English*. (Revised and amended, 1958) London: Cambridge Univ. Press.

Jones, T. J., 1925, *Education in East Africa: A Study of East, Central and South Africa*. (By the 2nd African Education commission under the auspices of the Phelps–Stokes Fund, in co-operation with the International Education Board) London: Edinburgh House Press.

Kaduma, H. J., 1976, *Kiingereza katika Shule za Msingi Tanzania Bara*. (English in Primary Schools in Mainland Tanzania) Dar es Salaam: Inst. of Educ.

Kahinga, M. M., 1976, 'Some Reflections on Teacher Education in Tanzania', in Mmari (ed.), 1976b.

Katalambulla, F., 1965, *Simu ya Kifo*. Nairobi: EALB.

Kiango, S. D., 1976, *Taarifu ya Utafiti wa Amali za Fasihi Simulizi Mhofanywa Wilaya Muheza*. Dar es Salaam: Inst. of Swahili Research.

Kijuma, Mohammed (ed.), 1977a *Utenzi wa Fumo Liango*. Dar es Salaam: Inst. of Swahili Research.

1977b, *Utenzi wa Shufaka*. Dar es Salaam: Inst. of Swahili Research.

Kilimanjaro Leo (Kilimanjaro Today) [monthly] Moshi: Regional Office.

Kioo cha Lugha (The Mirror of Language) [occasional] Dar es Salaam: Univ. Dept. of Swahili.

Kilimbila, J. K. (ed.), 1966, *Lila na Fila*. London etc.: Longman.

Kiswahili [twice a year] (Began in 1930 as the *Bulletin*, later the *Journal* of the East African Swahili Committee, then became *Swahili*, then *Kiswahili*) Dar es Salaam: Taasisi cha Kiswahili (Inst. of Swahili Research).

Klaus, A. et al., 1976, *Malezi ya Nyumbani*. Mwanza & Dar es Salaam: NLC/Min. of Nat. Educ.

Komba, P. G. (ed.), 1975, *Studies in Curriculum Development, 5*. Dar es Salaam: Inst. of Educ.

Kuhanga, N., 1978, 'Education and Self-Reliance in Tanzania'. *Development Dialogue*, 2.

Kuria, H., 1957, *Nakupenda Lakini*. Nairobi: EALB.

Laye, Camara, 1954, *The African Child*. (trans. Jane Kirkup, 1955) London: Collins/Fontana.

League of Nations, 1922, *Tanganyika Mandate for East Africa*. Cmd 1974

C.449(1)E M 345(a)1922 VI. London: HMSO.
Lema, A. A. (ed.), 1972a, *Studies in Curriculum Development, 1.* Dar es Salaam: Inst. of Educ.
— (ed.), 1972b, *Studies in Curriculum Development, 2.* Dar es Salaam: Inst. of Educ.
— 1973, 'Education for Self-Reliance: "Old Attitudes Die Hard" ', in Biswalo (ed.), 1973.
Leshoi, B. L., 1969, *Mwana Mpotevu.* (A musical based on the story of the prodigal son) Dar es Salaam.
— 1970, *The Vulture.* Dar es Salaam: Univ. Dept. of Theatre Arts.
Literature Panel, 1971, *Background Notes for Literature in English in Tanzanian Schools.* [mimeo] Dar es Salaam: Inst. of Educ.
Loogman, L., 1950, *Namna ya Kufundisha Kusoma.* London: Nelson.
McCormick, Robert, 1976, *Tanzania: Education for Self-Reliance.* Milton Keynes: Open Univ.
Makin, R., 1960–68, *Exercises in English Patterns and Usage.* Books 1–5; key to Books 1–5. London etc.: OUP.
— 1968–71, *A Higher Course of English Study.* Books 1–2; Tape. London etc.: OUP.
Madan, A. C., 1902, *English–Swahili Dictionary.* Oxford: Clarendon Press.
Maliyamkono, L. et al., 1978, *Health Education for Development: A Case Study of Tanzania.* Palo Alto, Ca.: Educational Communications & Development Inc.
Malya, Simoni, 1978, 'Creating Literacy Surroundings in Tanzania: After Literacy What Next?', *Literacy Discussion* (Tehran Internat. Inst. for Adult Literacy Methods), 8, 4.
Manaze, T. J., 1978, 'The Mushrooming of Unaided Secondary Schools in Tanzania Mainland with Special Reference to Kilimanjaro Region', in Mmari (ed.), 1978.
Manaze, T. J. and Kisanga, E. S., 1978, 'An Insight into Disciplinary Problems in Schools in Tanzania', in Mmari (ed.), 1978.
Manpower Development Ministry, 1975–77, 'Survey of the High and Middle Level Manpower Requirements and Resources 1975–80', in *Annual Manpower Report to the President 1974/75/76* (Appendix 3). Dar es Salaam.
Mapinduzi ya Kijamaa (The African Socialist Revolution)[monthly] Tanga: Regional Office.
Marangu College of National Education, 1978, *A Proposed English Language Diploma Course.* [mimeo] Marangu.
Massachusetts Center for International Education, 1977, *International Education.* Amherst: Univ. of Massachusetts.
Maugier, S. et al., 1964–67, *Le français élémentaire: Méthode progressive de français usuel.* Books 1–2; Teacher's Books 1–2; discs. Paris & London: Hachette.
Maw, Joan, 1969, *Sentences in Swahili.* London: School of Oriental & African Studies.
Mbakile, E. P. R., 1975, *Radio Education Programmes as a Support to Literacy Methods: The Experience of Tanzania.* Mwanza & Dar es Salaam: NLC/Min. of Nat. Educ.
Mbakile, E. P. R. and Kashukura, F. M. K., 1977, *A Report on the Study on the Working of the Rural Newspaper Programme in the Lake Regions.* Mwanza & Dar es Salaam: Min. of Nat. Educ., Evaluation Unit, Literacy Project.
Mbilinyi, M., 1975, 'The Meaning of Education in Rural Tanzania', in Komba (ed.), 1975.
Mbotela, J., 1956, *Uhuru wa Watumwa.* Nairobi: Eagle Press.

Mbunda, F., 1969, *Kiswahili katika Sekondari.* [mimeo] Dar es Salaam: Inst. of Educ.
— (ed.), 1970, *Kiswahili Vyuoni.* Dar es Salaam: Inst. of Educ.
Mcha, Y. Y., 1978, *Looking Together at Language, 3.* (Special Issue of series, see Inst. of Educ.) Dar es Salaam: Inst. of Educ.
Mduma, M., 1976, *Mapishi ya Wiki.* Mwanza & Dar es Salaam: NLC/Min. of Nat. Educ.
Meena, A. S. et al. (eds.), 1974, *Studies in Curriculum Development, 4.* Dar es Salaam: Inst. of Educ.
Mganga, Clement, 1979, *Misingi ya Fonetiki Matamshi.* Dar es Salaam: Longman.
Mgonja, C. Y., 1969, 'Address to the Biennial Conference of TANU', in *Outline of the Second 5-Year Development Plan for the Ministry of National Education.* Dar es Salaam: Min. of Nat. Educ.
Miller, A., 1955, *A View from the Bridge.* New York: Viking Press.
Ministry of National Education, 1969a, *Primary School Syllabus.* Dar es Salaam.
— 1969b, *Programme for Grade A Teacher Education.* Dar es Salaam.
— 1969c, *Mapinduzi ya Elimu ya Watu Wazimia.* (The Revolution in Adult Education) (Circular by Asst Dir. of Nat. Educ.–Adult Educ.) Dar es Salaam.
— 1969d, *Muhtasari ya Kiswahili.* Dar es Salaam: Govt. Publications Agency.
— 1969-73, *English for Tanzanian Schools.* Books I–V; Teacher's Books I–V. Dar es Salaam: Longman. (See also Tregido, 1967-8)
— 1970-77, *Tujifunze Lugha Yetu.* Books 1-9; Teacher's Books 1-7; wall charts. Dar es Salaam. (See also 1974d)
— 1971a, *A Handbook for Tutors of English in Grade A Colleges of National Education.* Dar es Salaam.
— 1971b, *New Methods of Evaluating a Student's Progress.* (Circular letter EDS. Sl./1/409, of 6 Sep. 1971) Dar es Salaam.
— 1974a, *Kufundisha Lugha Yetu.* Teacher's Manual. Dar es Salaam: MTUU/Print Pak.
— 1974b, *Kitabu cha Kusoma.* Pupil's Books 1–4. Dar es Salaam: MTUU/Print-Pak.
— 1974c, *Kufundisha Kiswahili.* Teacher's Manuals 1–4. Dar es Salaam: MTUU/Print-Pak.
— 1974d, *Tujifunze Lugha Yetu.* Teacher's Manuals 4–9. Dar es Salaam: MTUU/PrintPak. (See also 1970-77)
— 1975a, *Tanzania UNDP–UNESCO Functional Literacy Curriculum, Programmes and Materials Development Project.* Report no. 3 (Nov. 1974–Apr. 1975). (UNDP–UNESCO URT/72/025/01/15) Mwanza: NLC.
— 1975b, *Preliminary Investigations of the Formation of Post–Literacy Groups in the Pilot Areas.* (UNDP–UNESCO Projects, see 1975a) Mwanza: NLC, Evaluation Unit.
— 1976a, *Secondary School Syllabi, 1: Kiswahili, English, French.* Dar es Salaam.
— 1976b, *Syllabus for the Diploma English Course (Pre-service).* [mimeo] Dar es Salaam: Inst. of Educ.
— 1976c, *Primary School Syllabi.* Dar es Salaam.
— 1978a, *The Expansion and Consolidation of Plans for the Rural Radio Education Technical Services in Tanzania, 1978–81.* Mwanza: NLC.
— 1978b, *Expansion of the Radio Education Unit of the National Literacy Centre.* (Video Tape Recording). Mwanza: NLC.
Mizambwa, G. L., 1974, 'An Approach towards Evaluating Instruction', in Meena et al., 1974.
Mlama, P. O. & Matteru, M. L., 1978, *Haja ya Kutumia Kiswahili Kufundisha katika Elimu ya Juu.* (The Need to Use Swahili in Teaching in Higher Education)

[mimeo] Dar es Salaam: Baraza la Kiswahili (National Swahili Council).
Mlekwa, V. H., 1975, 'Policy and Practice in Adult Education – A Research Report from Kahama', in Mari (ed.), 1975a.
Mmari, G. R. V. (ed.), 1975a, *Papers in Education and Development, 1.* [mimeo] Dar es Salaam: Univ. Dept. of Educ.

1975b, 'The Changing Role of the Institute of Education', in Komba (ed.), 1975.

(ed.), 1976a, *Papers in Education and Development, 2.* [mimeo] Dar es Salaam: Univ. Dept. of Educ.

(ed.), 1976b, *Papers in Education and Development, 3.* [mimeo] Dar es Salaam: Univ. Dept. of Educ.

1976c, 'Implementation of the Musoma Resolutions: The University of Dar es Salaam Admissions', in Mmari (ed.), 1976b.

(ed.), 1977, *Papers in Education and Development, 4.* [mimeo] Dar es Salaam: Univ. Dept. of Educ.

(ed.), 1978, *Papers in Education and Development, 5.* [mimeo] Dar es Salaam: Univ. Dept. of Educ.
Mnyampala, M., 1967, *Diwani ya Mnyampala*. Nairobi: EALB.
Mohammedi, A. A., 1964, 'Utenzi wa Maisha ya Nabi Adamu na Hawaa', *Swahili*, 34, 1.
Monfries, H., 1972, *Oral Drills in Sentence Patterns for Foreign Students*. 3rd edition. London etc.: Macmillan.
Moshi, E. E., 1974, 'Professional Training of the Primary School Teaching Force', in Meena et al., 1974.
Mradi wa Bwakira Chini, Morogoro, 1977, *Kuhifadhi Vizuri Nafaka*. (Good Crop Storage). Dar es Salaam: Inst. of Adult Educ.
Msuya, P., 1977, 'The Integration of "African Literature" into the English Language Course: The Situation in our Tanzanian Secondary Schools', in Mmari (ed.), 1977.
Muganyizi, L., 1976, 'Implementation and Usefulness of Self-Reliance in Schools: Findings of Research Carried out in Bukoba, May/June 1975', in Mmari (ed.), 1976a.
Mulika (The Light) [occasional] (Begun in 1971) Dar es Salaam: Taasisi cha Kiswahili (Inst. of Swahili Research).
Munby, J., 1968, *Read and Think*. Nairobi: Longman.
Munby, J., Thomas, O. G. & Cooper, M. D., 1966, *Comprehension for School Certificate: Testing and Training with Multiple Choice Questions*. Nairobi: Longman.
Muze, M. S., 1975, 'Evaluating a Student's Progress', in Komba (ed.), 1975.
Mvungi, M., 1976, 'A Report on the Third Annual Student Workshop on Literature', in Mmari (ed.), 1976a.
Mzirai, R. R., 1962, *Maandishi ya Barua Zetu*. (Letter Writing). Nairobi: EALB.
Mziray, S. K. et al., 1975, *Research Findings on the Teaching of Literature in Tanzanian Secondary Schools*. [mimeo] Dar es Salaam: Univ. Dept. of Educ.
NAAET, 1975, *Adult Education and Development in Tanzania*. 2 Vols. Dar es Salaam: National Adult Education Association of Tanzania.
National Examinations Council of Tanzania, 1979, *Regulations 1978/79*. Dar es Salaam: Min. of Nat. Educ.
Ngole, S. Y. A. & Sengo, T. S. Y., 1976, *Mashairi ya Mwamko wa Siasa Nchini Tanzania*. 2 vols: 1900–66; 1967–71. Dar es Salaam: Inst. of Swahili Research.
Ngugi, J., 1967, A Grain of Wheat. (African Writers Series) London: Heinemann.
Nikundiwe, Margaret, 1975, *An Annotated Bibliography of Educational Works Produced by the Institute of Education, Dar es Salaam*. Dar es Salaam: Inst. of Educ.

1977, *An Annotated Bibliography 1975-77*. Dar es Salaam: Inst. of Educ.
Njau, Rebecca, 1970, *The Scar*. Dar es Salaam: Univ. Dept. of Theatre Arts. 1975, *Ripples in the Pool*. Nairobi: Transafrica Publishers.
NLC (National Literacy Centre, Min. of Nat. Educ.), 1970a, *Pamba ni Mali*. (Functional literacy primer) Mwanza.
    1970b, *Uvuvi Bora wa Samaki*. (Functional literacy primer) Mwanza.
    1973, *A Study of the Readability of the Rural Newspaper 'Elimu Haina Mwisho'*. Mwanza: Evaluation Unit.
    1974–75, *Kisomo kwa Redio 1 & 2: Maongozi kwa Mwalimu*. Mwanza.
    1978a, *The National Literacy Campaign – A Summary of Results of National Literacy Tests in the Second Assessment of the Campaign, Aug. 1977*. Mwanza: Evaluation Unit.
    1978b, *Evaluation Report on the Rural Newspaper Programme in the Lake Regions, June 1978*. Mwanza: Evaluation Unit.
    1979a, *Functions and Responsibilities of the National Literacy Centre*. Mwanza.
    1979b, *Jiendeleze I: Maongozi kwa Mwalimu*. (Radio broadcasts, Tue. & Thurs, Jan.–Apr., 1979) Mwanza.
Nwagwu, N. A., 1974, 'Teachers and Curriculum Development', in Meena et al., 1974.
Nyagwaswa, M. P. (ed.), 1976, Special Issue on an 'A' Level Literature Students' Workshop, *Background Notes: A Bulletin for Teaching Literature in Tanzania* (Inst. of Educ.), 10.
Nyagwaswa, M. P., Kaduma, H. K. and Haule, R. M. (eds.), 1976, *A Teacher Education English Handbook and Syllabi*. Dar es Salaam: Min. of Nat. Educ.
Nyerere, President J. K., 1966, Freedom and Unity. London & Dar es Salaam: OUP.
    1967a, *Education for Self-Reliance*. (Reprinted in 1968a)
    1967b, *The Arusha Declaration*. (Reprinted in 1968a)
    1968a, *Ujamaa: Essays on Socialism*. London & Dar es Salaam: OUP.
    1968b, *Freedom and Socialism*. London & Dar es Salaam: OUP.
    1969a, *Nyerere on Socialism*. London & Dar es Salaam: OUP.
    1969b, *1970 Adult Education Year*. (Radio broadcast) (Reprinted in NAAET, 1975)
    1970a, *The Role of the University in Development*. (Studies in Tanzanian Education, 1) Dar es Salaam: Inst. of Educ.
    1970b, Inaugural Speech as Chancellor, in *Inauguration of the University of Dar es Salaam, 23 August, 1970*. Dar es Salaam: University.
    1970c, *Education has No End*. (Radio broadcast) (Reprinted in NAAET, 1975).
    1971, *Tanzania Ten Years after Independence*. (Report to TANU National Conference, 1971) Dar es Salaam: TANU.
    1974, *Speeches during a State Visit to Mauritius, New Zealand, Australia and China, 11–30 March, 1974*. Dar es Salaam: Govt. Info. Services Div.
    1977, *The Arusha Declaration Ten Years After*. Dar es Salaam: Govt. Publications Agency.
Orwell, G., 1945, *Animal Farm*. London: Secker & Warburg. (Reprinted, Penguin, 1965)
Paton, A., 1954, *Cry the Beloved Country*. Harmondsworth: Penguin.
Perren, G., 1956, 'Some Problems of Oral English in East Africa', *English Language Teaching*, 11, 2.
Perrin, P. Y. & Smith, G. H., 1955, *The Perrin-Smith Handbook of Current English*. Chicago: Scott, Foreswan & Co.
Phelps–Stokes Commission, see Jones, 1925.

Pochard, J. C., 1973, 'Guidelines for French Teaching in Secondary Schools Form I to IV', in Biswalo (ed.), 1973.
Pratt, S. A. M. & Bhely-Quenum, D., 1965–68, *New Practical French.* Pupil's Books 1–5; Work Books 1–3; Teacher's Books 1–3; New Key to Books 4–5. London etc.: Longman.
Prins, A. H. J., 1970, *A Swahili Nautical Dictionary.* Dar es Salaam: Inst. of Swahili Research.
Proctor, J. H. (ed.), 1971a, *The Cell System of the Tanganyika African National Union.* Dar es Salaam: Tanzania Publishing House.
— (ed.), 1971b, *Building Ujamaa Villages in Tanzania.* Dar es Salaam: Tanzania Publishing House.
Robert, S., 1949, *Maisha Yangu na Baada ya Miaka Hamsini.* London: Nelson.
— 1951, *Kusadikika.* London: Nelson.
— 1966a, *Adili na Nduguze.* London: Macmillan.
— 1966b, *Pambo la Lugha.* Nairobi: OUP.
— 1967a, *Masomu Yenye Adili.* London: Nelson.
— 1967b, *Wasifu wa Siti Binti Said.* London: Nelson.
— 1968, *Kielezo cha Fasihi.* London: Nelson.
Sackville, Earl H. E. D. B., 1937, *Higher Education in East Africa.* (Report of the De la Warr Commission, Colonial Office no. 142) London: HMSO.
Said, Hemed Abdullah, 1974, *Utenzi wa Kadhi Kassim Bin Jaffar.* Dar es Salaam: Inst. of Swahili Research.
Sawe, J. A., 1967, *Conference on Education for Self-Reliance.* Dar es Salaam: Min. of Nat. Educ.
Schlunk, Martin, 1914, *Die Schulen für Eingeborene in den deutschen Schutzgebeiten.* Hamburg: Friederichsen.
Sengo, T. S. Y., 1973, *Taartifa ya Utafiti was Amali za Fasihi Simulizi Uliofanywa Kisiwani Mafia.* Dar es Salaam: Inst. of Swahili Research.
— (ed.), 1976, *Mwongozo wa Kutathimini wa Kutahini Somo la Kiswahili Sekondari 1–4.* (Guide to Continuous Assessment in Kiswahili in Secondary Schools Forms I–IV) Dar es Salaam: Inst. of Educ.
Shakespeare, W. *Makbeth.* (trans. into Swahili by Mushi, S. S., 1968) Dar es Salaam: Tanzania Publishing House.
— *Juliasi Kaisari.* (trans. into Swahili by Nyerere, J. K., 1969) Dar es Salaam: OUP.
Soyinka, W., 1963, *The Lion and the Jewel.* Nairobi: OUP.
— 1964a, *The Swamp Dwellers.* Nairobi: OUP.
— 1964b, *The Trials of Brother Jero.* Nairobi: OUP.
Steere, E., 1945, *Swahili Exercises.* Nairobi: Sheldon Press.
Steinbeck, J., 1947, *The Pearl.* London: Heinemann.
Stigand, C. H., 1915, *A Grammar of Dialectal Changes in the Swahili Language.* London: OUP.
Swahili, see *Kiswahili.*
Swedish International Development Agency, 1978, *Education Sector Support Annual Joint Review Report 1978/79 and Proposals for 1979/80–1981/82.* Dar es Salaam: Un. Rep. of Tanz./SIDA.
Tanganyika Department of Education, 1959, *Provisional Syllabus of Instruction for Middle Schools.* Dar es Salaam: Government Printer.
TANU (Tanzania African National Union), 1967, *Utaratibu wa Mwongozi ya Chama cha TANU.* (TANU Regulations on Leadership) Dar es Salaam: Govt. Printer.
— 1970, *Elimu ni Kazi.* (Education is Work) Dar es Salaam: Govt. Publications Agency.

DEVELOPMENTS IN LANGUAGE AND EDUCATION 419

1971, *Mwongozo wa TANU 1971.* (TANU Guidelines, 1971) Dar es Salaam: Govt. Publications Agency.

1972, *Decentralization.* Dar es Salaam: Govt. Publications Agency.

1974, 'Directive on the Implementation of "Education for Self-Reliance"', in Mmari (ed.), 1976b.

Tanzania Adult Education Journal. [periodical] (began in 1974) Dar es Salaam: Inst. of Adult Educ.

Taylor, W. E., 1915, 'Introduction' and poetical trans. of poem 'Inkishafi', in Stigand, 1915.

Topan, F., 1971–78, *Uchambuzi wa Maandishi ya Kiswahili.* Books 1–2. Nairobi: OUP.

Trappes–Lomax, H. R. H., 1978, *English Language Teaching in Tanzania: A Colloquium.* (Discussion paper for staff-student seminar, 18 Oct., 1978) [mimeo] Dar es Salaam: Univ. Dept. of Foreign Languages and Linguistics.

Tregido, P. S. (ed.), 1967–68, *English for Tanzanian Schools.* Books VI–VII and Teacher's Books VI–VII. Dar es Salaam: Longman Min. of Nat. Educ. (See also Min. of Nat. Educ., 1969–73)

Trevett, J., 1969, 'Technical English', *Bull. of the Lang. Assoc. of Tanzania*, 2,1:10–12.

Tucker, A. N. & Ashton, E. O., 1942, 'Swahili Phonetics', *African Studies*, 1,2:77–103; 1,3:161–82.

Uiso, G. B. E., 1977, *Publications Catalogue, University of Dar es Salaam.* Dar es Salaam: Univ. Library.

UNDP, 1967, *Plan of Operation for the United Republic of Tanzania Work Oriented Literacy Pilot Project.* Paris: United Nations Development Programme/UNESCO.

UNESCO, 1971, *Teachers and Educational Policy.* (Educational Studies and Documents, 3) Paris: United Nations Educational, Scientific and Cultural Organization (UNESCO).

1976, *United Republic of Tanzania Functional Literacy Curriculum and Materials Development Project: Findings and Recommendations.* (Terminal Report UNDP/URT/72/025:Ser. no. FMR/ED/OPS76/243) Paris: UNESCO.

United Nations Organization, 1946, *Tanganyika Trusteeship Agreement.* (UN Treaty Series p. 91; see Report of UN Trusteeship Mission D 4.3) Geneva.

United Republic of Tanzania (Tanganyika and Zanzibar), 1964, *Tanganyika 5-Year Plan for Economic and Social Development, 1964–69.* 2 vols: General Analysis; The Programmes. Dar es Salaam: Govt. Printer.

1969a, *Tanzania Second 5-Year Plan for Economic and Social Development, 1969–74.* 3 vols: General Analysis; The Programmes; Regional Perspectives. Dar es Salaam: Govt. Printer.

1969b, *Ujamaa Vijijini.* (Presidential circular, 1) Dar es Salaam: Govt. Publications Agency.

1969c, *The Education Act, No. 50 of 1969.* Dar es Salaam: Govt. Printer.

1970, *The University of Dar es Salaam Act, No. 4 of 1970.* Dar es Salaam: Govt. Printer.

1975a, *Staff Circular No. 4 of 1975.* Dar es Salaam: President's Office.

1975b, *The Villages and Ujamaa Villages (Registration, Designation and Administration) Act.* Dar es Salaam: Govt. Publications Agency.

1975c, *The Institute of Education Act, No. 13 of 1975.* Dar es Salaam: Govt. Publications Agency.

1975d, *The Institute of Adult Education Act.* Dar es Salaam: Govt. Publications Agency.

1976, *Budget Speech of the Minister for National Education on the Estimates for the Year 1976/77*. Dar es Salaam.

1978a, *6th IDA Educational Project Proposals*. 2 vols. Dar es Salaam: Min. of Nat. Educ.

1978b, *Budget Speech of the Minister for National Education on the Estimates for the Year 1978/79*. Dar es Salaam: Print Pak/MTUU.

University of Dar es Salaam, 1977, *Report on the Activities for the Year 1975/76*. Dar es Salaam: Univ. Library Technical Services.

Varadi, T. & Athumani, A., 1975, *Vocational Training Needs in Tanzania, 1976–85*. Dar es Salaam: Min. of Labour & Social Welfare.

Vella, Sr. J., 1972, 'Proposed New Directions in Teaching Literature at Secondary School Level', in Lema (ed.), 1972b.

1973, 'Developing a Revised Syllabus in Literature for Tanzanian Secondary Schools', in Biswalo (ed.), 1973.

Viscusi, Margot, 1971, *Literacy for Working: Functional Literacy in Rural Tanzania*. (Educational Studies and Documents, 5) Paris: UNESCO.

Weston, A. B. (ed.), 1968, *Swahili Legal Terms*. Dar es Salaam: Legal Research Centre.

Widstrand, G. Y., 1966, *Radio and Adult Education in Tanzania: Some Considerations*. Dar es Salaam: Inst. of Adult Educ.

Wingfield, R. J., 1967, *Exercises in Situational Composition*. London etc.: Longman.

INDEX

Note: figures in italics refer to the maps and tables; figures followed by n refer to the chapter endnotes

Abdulaziz, M. H. 83, 118, 120, 130n, 140, 144, 162
Abdullah, Ali *xii*
Abedi, Sheikh Amri 156
Abrahams, R. G. 21n
Achebe, Chinua 211, 212–13
Adekunle, M. A. 148
adult education 277, 374, 395–7; literacy programmes 152, 397–402
advertising language use 108
Africanization 115, 117
Aggrey, James 264
agriculture, as school subject 268–9, 272
Akie 68, 73
Allen, John W. T. 157, 164, 358–9
Andersson, Anders 121–2, 133n
Anttilla, R. 3
Apronti, Eric O. 148
Arabic 79, 80, 82, 83, 113, 119, 190, 223, 292
army/police language use 115
Arusha *4*
Arusha Declaration 1967 103, 121, 146–7, 261
Asian language use 109, 111, 135–6n
attitudes to language 121–6, *123*, 133–4n, 160, 371–2
Auger, G. A. 395
Auger, G. A. and Haule, R. M. 366, 367, 368
Augustiny, Julius 6
Ayaz, Ifti 370, 379, 383, 384, 385

Bagamoyo study 200–2
Bantu languages *4*, *15*, 26–67, *30*; genetic classification 18, 36–8 39; grouping by vocabulary 26–52; Guthrie classification *17*, 18; material on 5–6, 7–12, 13–15; spread 19–21; and Swahili 79, 86–7, 140, 292
Bantu Studies 6
Barabaig 12, 72
Barbosa, Duarte 82

Barton, Henry 108
Beidelman, T. O. 22n
Bena 7, *15*, 234
Bender, M. L. 27, 31
Bennett, P. R. 12, 42, 48, 66
Berg, F. J. 83
Berry, L. 3
Besha, R. 91, 96n
Bhaiji, A. H. 383
Bhola, H. S. 152
Blount, Ben *xii*, 16
Blount, Ben and Curley, R. T. 19, 22n
Bobb, Donald 238n
Bondei 12, *15*, 18
Brauner, S. 135n
British administration 140–4, 181–2, 263–70
British linguistic studies 6
Brock, B. 21n
Broome, Max 206
Broomfield, G. W. 79
Brown, David 301–2n, 379–80
Brumfit, Anne *xii*
Brumfit, C. J. 339n, 340n
Bryan, Margaret 4–5, 21n, 23n, 79, 359

Cameron, Sir Donald 142–3, 265
Cameron, J. and Dodd, W. A. 104, 135–6n, 140, 142–3, 281
Castle, E. B. 180, 204n
census information 3–5, *4*
Chaga *xiv*, 3, 7, 12, *15*, 16, 18, 75, 109, 121, 124, 214, 234, 237; group 29, 38, *51*, 52, 56, 62–3
Chaga-Davida group 52, 62–3
Chamungwana, William 370
Changombe Teacher Training College 149
Chittick, N. 81, 83
choice of language 116–19, *123*, *125*, 186–8, 196, *208–9*, 214–20, *215*, *217*, *219*, 230–7, *232*, *234–5*
Christianity 140; mission schools 141–2, 181–2, 262–3, 265
Clarke, P. H. C. 317

clerks' language use 111
Cliffe, Lionel and Saul, J. S. 153
Coast group 45–6
codification, in language planning 163
cognation (vocabulary) 26–7, *32–5*, 37, 39
Cole, J. S. R. and Denison, W. N. 238&*n*
Colleges of National Education 341–6, 354, 355, 365, 376, 388–90
Comparative Bantu (Guthrie) 19, 47
consonantal rules, Nilotic languages 68–72, *71*, 76
Constable, D. 339*n*, 360*n*, 388
Coupez, A. 26
courts *see* legal system
craftsmen's language use 111, 223
Cushitic languages 4, 6

Dadog 68, 71–2, 74
da Gama, Vasco 82
Dahl's Law 12
Dalby, David 19, 21
Dar es Salaam: dialect 144; Itala suburb 176–204; University 5, 149, 151–2, 165, 281–2, 346–56, 390–5
Dawida-Saghala distortion (Taita) 39, 45, 52–3*n*
de Barros, João 80
De Boeck, L.-B. 16
Dempwolff, O. 5
dialect/language distinction 3, 36–8
dialects: continuum 3; mutual support 41; Swahili 41, 84, 85–9, 161, 163–4, 306
diglossic language relationships 162
Digo *15*, 16, 18
dissemination, in language planning 163
Dodds, Tony 106, 128–9*n*
Doe/Kwere-Zigula/Bondei distortion 39–40
Doke, Clement M. 6

East African Examinations Council 312, 317, 324
East African Literature Bureau 164, 357–8, 392
East Nyanza group 29, 42, 54, 58–9
East Ruvu group 29, 46, 56, 64
Eastman, Carol 88
ecology of language 139, 179
economic development 263, 265, 266
education 104, 147–52; curriculum development 280–1, 325–6, 332–3, 395; decentralisation 364–5; English in 141–3, 149, 190–3, 293–301, 370–80, 383–7; examinations, recent developments 365–6; historical background 261–82; Institute of Education 354–5, 395; language units, proposed 335–6; latest developments 274–82, 362–404; position at independence 270; private 380–1, 404*n*; and religion 179–82; Swahili in 104, 112, 140–3, 147–52, 266, 277–8, 283–93, 306–16; teacher education 271–3, 279–80, 283, 312–13, 318–19, 341–6, 352–5, 388–90, 394–5; university education, 272, 281–2, 346–56, 390–5
Education Act 1969 276–7, 280
Education Ordinance 1927 141; 1961 270
Eggert, Johanna 141–2
Ehret, C. 16, 21, 22*n*, 42, 43, 44, 52, 68, 71, 73, 77*n*
elaboration, in language planning 163
English: degree of use 104–8, 186–8, 233, *see also* choice of language; in education 141–3, 149, 190–3, 293–301, 316–29, 342, 348–50, 370–80, 383–7, 393–4; as lingua franca 218; loan-words 92–3; social factors affecting use 190–3; use in Parliament 157; use as referent 161
entertainment/sport language use 107–8
environment, language and 139, 179
Erdos, R. F. 397

farmers' language use 109–10
Ferguson, C. A. 163
Fipa 8, *15*, 18
Fishman, J. A. 146, 163
Fodor, I. 19
Folk Development Colleges 402
Freeman-Grenville, G. S. P. 80, 81, 82, 83, 93*n*, 94*n*
French 223; in education 330–6, 350–2, 387–8, 393–4
functional literacy 152, 204, 277, 398

genetic classification of languages 18, 36–8, 39

geographical distribution of languages 2, 3–5, 16–18; Swahili 80–5
German administration 140, 181, 262–3
German linguistic studies 5–6
Ghai, D. P. 136
Gogo 8, 12, 13, *15*, 121, 234
Gogo-Sangu/Hehe distortion 40
Goldklang, H. A. 87, 91
Goodman, Morris 12, 21*n*
government language use 105, 117, 126, 146, 155
Gray, John 83
Greater Ruvu group 46
Greenberg, J. H. 18–19, 21*n*, 23*n*, 47
groups, language 26–52; disturbances among 38–41, 54–64; internal consistency 29–30, 66–7; strong/weak unity 31–6
Gujrati 109, 111, 113, 121, 216, 220
Gulliver, P. H. 3
Gurnah, A. M. 91
Gusii 5
Guthrie, Malcolm 5, 23*n*, 26, 41, 43, 44, 47, 66, 84, 87, 95*n*, 96*n*, classification system 16, *17*, 18, 28–9, 45
Gweno *15*, 18
Gwere/Soga-Saamia (Luhya) distortion 40

Ha 3, 13, *15*
Habari ya Mwezi 157
Hadimu 85–7
Hadza 12
Hai 3
Hangaza *15*, 16
Harries, Lyndon 6, 84, 133*n*, 157
Haselgrove, J. R. 206
Hatfield, C. R. 130*n*
Haugen, Einar 139, 163
Haya 8, 13, *15*, 121, 214
Hehe 13, *15*, 121, 234
Heine, Bernd *xii*, 3, 5, 18–19, 21, 21*n*, 22*n*, 77*n*, 79, 96*n*
Henrici, A. 19, 27
Hichens, W. 157
higher education, language teaching in 341–60
Hill, C. P. *xiii*, 120*n*, 133*n*, 205*n*, 339*n*, 340*n*, 360*n*
Hinawy, Sheikh M. A. 359
Hindi 121

Hinnebusch, T. J. 44, 79, 93*n*
Hohenberger, J. 23*n*
Holoholo 8
Huntingford, G. W. 23*n*
Hyman, L. M. 95*n*

Ibn Battuta 80, 82, 94*n*
Ikizu 5, *15*, 18
Ikoma 5, 6, *15*
Ilala residents, study of language use 176–200
indigenous culture 145–6, 161, 264, 355–6, 359–60
indirect rule 265
Ingham, K. 82
Ingrams, W. H. 87, 88, 95*n*
Institute of Swahili Research 356–60, 392
Interlacustrine group 43–4
inter-language influences 38–41, 42, 54–64
interpreting 235–7
interrelationships, among languages 198–200
Iraqw 6, 12, *15*, 234
Isaacs, R. 325–7, 334, 386
Isanzu *15*
Isherwood, Mr 142
Islam 80, 82, 83, 140, 183; education 180–1
Issenyi 5
Itandala, Bajuda 77*n*
Itinerant Tutor Educators (ITEs) 366–7

Jacobs, Alan 77*n*
Jita 5, 6, 13, *15*, 18
Johnson, F. 79, 164, 357
Johnston, H. H. 16
Jones, Thomas J. 264

Kabwa 5, *15*, 18
Kachi 109, 111
Kagulu 12, *15*, 16
Kähler-Meyer, Emmi 12
Kami 5, *15*, 16
Kinga 8, *15*
Kaniki, M. H. Y. 145, 153
Karume, A. 105
Kassam, A. O. 135*n*
Kavugha, Douglas 229, 238, 238&*n*
Kavugha, Douglas and Bobb, Donald 127*n*

Kawawa, Mr 146
Kelman, H. C. 159
Kenya dialects 42, 70
Kerege Ujamaa Village study 201-2
Kerewe *15*
Khoisan languages 4, 7
Kibosho 3
Kiha 16
Kilombero group 29, 38, 56, 61
Kimambo, I. N. 81
Kimbu *15*
Kinga *15*
Kiroba 5, *15*, 18
Kiswahili xii, 165, 314, 358, 360, 392
KiUnguja 85, *see also* Unguja
Kloss, H. 163
Knappert, Jan 81, 84-5, 94*n*, 96*n*, 97*n*, 157, 165, 358-9
Köhler, O. 19, 22*n*
Kombo, Sheikh Salim 156
Konde (Ngonde) *15*
Konongo *15*
Kotz, Ernst 6
Krapf, L. 40
Krumm, B. 79
Kuria 5, 6, 12, *15*, 18, 234
Kutu *15*, 16
Kwaya 5, 6, 14, *15*, 18
Kwere *15*

labourers' language use 111, 115
Lacustrine group 38, 41-4, *49*
Ladefoged, P. *et al* 42, 44
Lambert, H. E. 87, 95*n*, 164
Lambya *15*
Langi 12; group 47-8, 56, 61
language, as concept 3
language/dialect distinction 3, 36-8
language planning (LP) 163-70
legal language use 92, 105, 157, 229-38, *239-58*
legal system *229*
Legère, K. 22*n*, 126
Lehmann, Dorothy 15
Lehmann, Winifred P. 3
Leslie, J. A. K. 180, 204*n*
lexical similarity 26
lexicography 164-5, 357, 359
lexicostatistics, value of 38
library services 206
library users' survey 206-24
linguistic structure 16
literacy 108, 115-16, 152, 188, 190, 267, 277, 397-402; factors affecting *195*; and language retention 187
literature, Swahili 84-5, 155, 157-9, 310, 360; *see also* library users' survey
loan-words 26-7, 38-41, 69, 75, 79, 84, 92-3, 153, 169
Lugulu 14, *15*, 16, 186; group 46, 63-4
Luhya group 29, 41-2, 54
Luo *xiv*, 7, 12, 13, *15*, 16, 68, 216
Lyamungo study 202

MTUU Project 366-8
Maasai 7, 12, 13, *15*, 68, 75-6, 234
McCormick, Robert 389
McGivney, James 170*n*
Machame 3, 12
Machinga 4
Madan, Mr 157, 164
Madoshi, F. 87-8
Maji Maji war 1905-7 144
Makonde 8, *15*
Makua 9, *15*
Malila *15*
Malveyev, V. V. and Kubbel, L. E. 94*n*
Mamboleo 157, 267
Mambwe 9
managers' language use 112, 115
Manase, T. J. 370, 380
Manda *15*, 18
Matengo 5, 9, *15*, 18
Mathew, G. 80, 81
Matumbi 5, *15*
Mbakile, E. P. R. 399-400
Mbugu 6, 12 *15*
Mbuguni, L. A. and Ruhumbika, G. 146
Mbugwe *15*
Mbunda, Fulgens 301*n*, 310, 339*n*, 342, 368, 381-2, 388
Mbunga *15*
Mcha, Y. Y. 384, 385
media language use 105-7, 153-5
Meena, J. S. 370
Meinhof, Carl 5; Meinhof's Rule 12
Meru 14, *15*, 109
Meussen, A. E. 12
Mgao 85
Mhaiki, Mr 89
Mhina, George 359, 360*n*
middle schools 267-9
migration 16, 41, 83
Mittelmeyer, J. 122, 124

Mkindi, David 109
Mlama, P. O. and Matteru, M. L. 373, 383, 386, 387, 393
Mlay, Hezekiah 109
Mmari, G. R. V. 390, 395
Mnyampala, Sheikh Mathias 156
Mohamed Ali, Sheikh 92
Molnos, Angela 3
Moshi 12
Mrima 85
Msuya, P. 386
Mtang'ata 85–6
Muhtasari ya Kiswahili 285
multilingualism 108–36, 161–2; and language skills 115–16; in reading 208, 220–4, 222–3; typology 119–26; *see also* choice of language
Munby, John 354
Musoma 3
Musoma Resolution 1974 364, 365, 381, 390–1
Muyaka bin Haji 84
Muze, M. S. 365, 370
Mvita 163
Mvungi, M. 385
Mwangaza 158
Mwera 9, 14, *15*
Mytton, G. L. 128–9n
Mzalendo 158
Mziray, S. K. *et al* 385, 386

Nata 12
National Correspondence Institute 396–7
National Swahili Council 105, 118, 155, 165–9, *167–8*, 360, 392–3
nationalist movements 144
Native Authority schools 142–3
Ndali *15*
Ndamba *15*
Ndendeuli 5
Ndengereko *15*
Ngazija 83–4
Ngindo *15*
Ngoni (Sutu) 9, *15*, 18
Ngulu 12, *15*, 16
Ngurimi 14, *15*, 18
Ngurumo 158
Nikundiwe, Margaret 385, 395
Nilo-Hamitic languages 12, 18–19
Nilotic languages 4, 7, 12, 13, 16, 18–19, *20*, 68–76, *69*, *70*, *73*, *78*; Eastern 68, 74–5; Pre-Southern (PreSN) 68–70; Proto-Southern (ProtoSN) 70–1; Southern 68; Western 68
Nilyamba 12, *15*
non-Bantu languages 4, 15; material on 6–7, 12, 13
North East group 44–8, *50*
North Nyanza group 29, 44, 55, 58
noun formation: Nilotic languages 73–4; Swahili 89–92
Nurse, D. *xii*, 3, 18, 26, 45, 52, 77n
Nurse, D. and Philippson, G. 16
Nyagwaswa, M. P. 385, 388, 389
Nyakyusa 9, *15*, 214, 234
Nyambo (Karagwe) *15*
Nyamwezi 10, *15*, 16, 121
Nyanja 9, *15*
Nyasa (Mpoto) *15*, 18
Nyaturu (Rimi) 10, 12, *15*
Nyerere, President Julius 91, 103–4, 144, 145, 148, 153, 155, 160, 211, 261, 268, 274–5, 282, 295, 333, 344, 362, 365, 384, 395, 398
Nyiha 10, *15*

occupational language use patterns 109–12
Ohly, R. 94n, 95n
Omari, C. K. 97n
Omotik 70–1
Ongamo 7, 68, 75
Ormsby-Gore Commission 264
Osman, Yasin 156

Padgug-Blount, E. 16
Pangwa 5, *15*
Para-Nilotic languages 18
Pare (Chasu) 8, *15*, 114; group 38, 46
Parliament use of Swahili 155–7
Pasua study 202–3
Patel, R. B. 96n
Payton, Walter 83
Pemba 85–6
Perren, G. 337
Phelps-Stokes Commission 142, 264
Philippson, G. 96n
Phillipson, D. W. 19, 21
phonic interference 89
Pimbwe *15*, 18
Pogolu *15*
politics and language use 114–15, 144
Polomé, André R. *xii*, 16

Polomé, Edgar C. *xii*, 87, 88, 93*n*, 96*n*, 97*n*, 114, 118, 120, 170*n*
Polomé, Susan 3, 15
Portuguese settlement 82–3
primary schools 149–51, 266, 267–8, 271, 276, 364; English teaching in 293–301, 370–80; financing of 270, 276; Swahili teaching in 283–93, 368–70
Prins, A. H. J. 21*n*, 204*n*, 392
professionals' language use 111, 216
Proto-Bantu (PB) 26, 44–5, 52*n*

Rangi *15*
Raum, J. 6
reading preferences 207–12, *210*
religious language use 92, 114, 140, 179–82, 188
Resnick, I. N. 104
Reusch, R. 79
Richards, C. 164
Rivers-Smith, Mr 142
Robert, Shabaan 308
Roe, P. J. 319
Rombo 3
Rubin, Joan and Jernudd, Björn 163
Rufiji *15*
Rundi 3, 10
Rungu *15*, 18
Rungwa *15*, 18
Rupper, G. 93
Rupya, Fr John 22*n*
rural/urban language use patterns 112–14, 183
Ruri 5, *15*, 18
Rutara group 29, 43–4, 54, 59–60
Ruthenberg, Hans 110
Rwanda 10–11

Sabaki group 46, 55, 64
Sacleux, C. 84, 88, 94*n*, 95*n*
Safwa 11, *15*, 234
Saghala *15*, 16; group 46
Saguru 16
Said, H. A. 392
Sandawe 7, 12
Sango *15*
Schlunk, Martin 262
Schönenberger, Paul 22*n*
Scotton, C. M. M. 96*n*
secondary schools 151, 267–8, 271–2, 275; English teaching in 316–29, 383–7; French teaching in 330–6, 387–8; Swahili teaching in 306–16, 380–3

Segeju (Daiso) *15*
semantic development, Swahili 89
Sengo, T. S. Y. 382
Seuta group 29, 46–7, 55, 64
sex: and language use 182, 191; and literacy 191–2
Shambala 11, 12, *15*, 18
Shedu Chamungwa, W. M. 130*n*
shopkeepers' language use 111
Shubi *15*, 16
Siha 3
Sillery, A. 6
Simbiti 14, *15*, 18
Sizaki (Shashi) 5, *15*, 18
social variables, and language use 184–6, 188–98, 218
societal changes 103–8, 144–6, 156, 160, 180, 261
Sonjo *15*
South Kalenjin 72–4
Southern Highlands group 29, 38, 56, 61–2
Steere, Edward 157
Struck, B. 79, 133*n*
Suba 5, *15*, 18
Suguti group 29, 42–3, 54, 59
Suguti-Kerewe distortion 39
Sukuma 11, 12, 14, *15*, 16, 121, 214, 234, 292, 296, 343
Sumbwa *15*
Sumbwa-Southern Rutara distortion 40
Sumbwa-Western Highlands distortion 40
Sutton, J. E. G. 21*n*, 23*n*, 81
Swadesh M. 18, 19, 38
Swahili 79–93; and Arabic 79, 292; and Bantu languages 79, 86–7, 140, 292; book supply 310–12, 382–3, 400–1; colloquialisms, coining of 153, 169; degree of use 159, 186–90, *see also* choice of language; derivation and composition 89–92; development 87–93; dialects 41, 84, 85–9, 161, 163–4, 306; in education 104, 112, 140–3, 147–52, 266, 277–8, 283–93, 306–16, 341, 347–8, 368–70, 380–3, 391–3; functional adequacy 163; government promotion 5, 105–8, 114, 117, 126, 146; and Islam 180–1, 188; as lingua franca 81, 82, 117, 139–40, 145, 163; literature 84–5,

155, 157–9, 310, 360; loan-words 92–3, 153, 169; and nationalism 144, 146; origin 79, 180; and political organization 152–3; pronunciation 90; school syllabuses 285–92, 307, 309–10, 314–16, 339n; semantic development 89; social variables affecting use 188–90; spread 80–5, 198–200; standard 163–4; as trading language 183; vocabulary 79, 80–1, 150, 154, 156–7, 161, 165, 169, 171n
Sweta 18
switching language use (code-switching) 109, 112, 162, 237, 256–8

Tanganyika African Association (TAA) 144
Tanganyika African National Union (TANU) 114, 118, 124, 144, 396, 397; and indigenous culture 145–6; and promotion of Swahili 144–6, 152; and *ujamaa* 362
Tanzania Broadcasting Corporation 107
Tanzania Examinations Council 365
Tanzania Today 109
Tato languages 70–2
Taylor, R. W. 157
Taylor, W. E. 157, 163
teachers: language use 112; training 271–3, 279–80, 283, 312–13, 318–19, 341–6, 352–5
technical colleges, language teaching in 336–8
Tejani, J. A. 359
Temu, Canute W. 87, 92, 96n
Ten Raa, Eric 22n
Thagicu group 29, 48, *51*, 52, 56, 62
theatre arts, University department of 355–6
Things Fall Apart (Achebe) 211
Tolmacheva, M. 93n, 94n, 95n
Topan, Farouk 346
trade routes 140, 183
traditional religion, and language use 179–80
Trager, Lillian 91
translation 310
Trappes-Lomax, H. R. H. 367, 371–3, 375, 376–8, 384, 389
Tredigo, P. S. 298, 380
Trevett, J. 338
Tucker, A. N. and Bryan, M. 12, 18, 22n
Tumbatu 85–7
Tumbuka 11–12
Turner, R. L. 94n

UNESCO 152, 398–402
Uganda language groups 42
Uhuru 158
ujamaa 103–4, 110, 153, 261, 274, 291, 341, 362–4
Unguja dialect 86–7, 163–4
urban/rural language use patterns 112–14, 183
Usseri 3
Utendi wa Tambuka 84

Vella, Sr J. 382, 384
vernaculars: features of use 195–8, *196*, 233–4; value of 264; weakening 204; *see also* Bantu languages *and* choice of language *and individual languages by name*
Villages and Ujamaa Villages Act 1975 363
Viscusi, Margot 396
vocabulary: cognation 26–7, *32–5*, *37*, 39; grouping Bantu languages by 26–52; loan-words 26–7, 38–41, 69, 75, 79, 84, 92–3, 153; loss of 38; similarity 26; Swahili 79, 80–1, 150, 154, 156–7, 161, 165, 169, 171n; wordlist 26
vowel systems, Nilotic languages 72, 75, 76
Vumba 85–6
Vunjo 3

Wanji *15*
Weinreich, U. 89
Werner, Alice 6, 157
West Ruvu group 29, 46, 55, 63
West Tanzania group 29, 38, 47–8, 56, 60–1
Western Highlands group 29, 44, 55, 60
Weston, A. B. 92
Westphal, E. O. J. 12, 22n
Whiteley, W. H. 4–5, 13, 22n, 41, 43, 77n, 80, 81, 83, 86, 87, 94n, 95n, 96n, 139, 143, 158, 163–4, 165, 346, 358

Whitley, J. S. W. 360n
Widstrand, C. G. 107, 128n
Willis, Roy G. 21n
Wilson, G. 77n
Wilson, Roger 340n
Woodburn, J. 22n
Wrigley, C. 81
writers, modern 158–9; for textbooks 311

Yao 12, *15*

Zaire language groups 44, 45
Zalamo 12, *15*, 186
Zanaki 5, 6, *15*, 18
Zanzibar dialects 86–7
Zigula 14–15, *15*, 16, 18
Zigulu 12 *see also* Zigula
Zinza 5, *15*